BEHAVIOR THERAPY WITH
CHILDREN AND ADOLESCENTS

D1302846

Behavior Therapy with Children and Adolescents

A CLINICAL APPROACH

Edited by

Michel Hersen
Vincent B. Van Hasselt

A WILEY-INTERSCIENCE PUBLICATION

JOHN WILEY & SONS

New York • Chichester • Brisbane • Toronto • Singapore

Library of Congress Cataloging in Publication Data:

Behavior therapy with children and adolescents.

   (Wiley series on personality processes)
   "A Wiley-Interscience publication."
   Bibliography: p.
   Includes indexes.
   1. Behavior therapy.   2. Child psychotherapy.
3. Adolescent psychotherapy.   I. Hersen, Michel.
II. Van Hasselt, Vincent B.   III. Series.

RJ505.B4B44   1986   618.92'89142   86–11103
ISBN 0–471–82583–2

Printed in the United States of America

10 9 8 7 6 5 4 3 2 1

Contributors

Karen A. Christoff, Ph.D.
Assistant Professor of Psychology
Department of Psychology
University of Mississippi
University, Mississippi

John D. Cone, Ph.D.
Professor of Psychology
Department of Psychology
West Virginia University
Morgantown, West Virginia

Jennifer H. Cousins, Ph.D.
Assistant Professor, Department
   of Medicine
Baylor College of Medicine
Houston, Texas

Lynnda M. Dahlquist, Ph.D.
Assistant Professor of Psychiatry
Department of Psychiatry
Baylor College of Medicine
Houston, Texas

Thomas M. DiLorenzo, Ph.D.
Assistant Professor of Psychology
Department of Psychology
University of Missouri-Columbia
Columbia, Missouri

Pamela G. Dorsett, Ph.D.
Assistant Professor of Psychology
Department of Psychology
Oklahoma State University
Stillwater, Oklahoma

Michael Faulstich, Ph.D.
Assistant Professor of Psychology
Department of Health Care
   Organization and Policy
University of Alabama
Birmingham, Alabama

John P. Foreyt, Ph.D.
Associate Professor, Department
   of Medicine
Baylor College of Medicine
Houston, Texas

Anthony J. Goreczny, M.A.
Graduate Student
Department of Psychology
Louisiana State University
Baton Rouge, Louisiana

Alan M. Gross, Ph.D.
Assistant Professor
Department of Psychology
Emory University
Atlanta, Georgia

Jan S. Handleman, Ed.D.
Educational Director
Douglass Developmental
  Disabilities Center
Rutgers University
New Brunswick, New Jersey

Francis C. Harris, Ph.D.
Assistant Professor of Child
  Psychiatry
Department of Psychiatry
Western Psychiatric Institute and
  Clinic
University of Pittsburgh School of
  Medicine
Pittsburgh, Pennsylvania

Sandra L. Harris, Ph.D.
Professor of Clinical Psychology
Department of Clinical
  Psychology
Rutgers University
Piscataway, New Jersey

Steven A. Hobbs, Ph.D.
Director of Pediatric Psychology
Children's Medical Center
Tulsa, Oklahoma

John J. Horan, Ph.D.
Professor and Director of
  Counseling Psychology
Arizona State University
Tempe, Arizona

Mary Beth Johnston, Ph.D.
Visiting Professor
Department of Psychology
University of Notre Dame
Notre Dame, Indiana

David J. Kolko, Ph.D.
Assistant Professor of Child
  Psychiatry
Department of Psychiatry
Western Psychiatric Institute and
  Clinic
University of Pittsburgh School of
  Medicine
Pittsburgh, Pennsylvania

Ronald A. Mann, Ph.D.
Clinical Psychologist
Private Practice
La Paz Medical Center
Mission Viejo, California

Johnny L. Matson, Ph.D.
Professor of Psychology
Department of Psychology
Louisiana State University
Baton Rouge, Louisiana

Sandra J. McKenzie, M.A.
Graduate Student
Department of Psychology
Louisiana State University
Baton Rouge, Louisiana

Robert J. Myatt, M.A.
Clinical Psychology Student
Department of Psychology
University of Mississippi
University, Mississippi

Vey M. Nordquist, Ph.D.
Professor of Child and Family
  Studies
Department of Child and Family
  Studies
University of Tennessee
Knoxville, Tennessee

Carolyn F. Phelps, M.S.
Graduate Student
Department of Psychology
University of Pittsburgh
Pittsburgh, Pennsylvania

Mark D. Rapport, Ph.D.
Associate Professor of Psychology
Department of Psychology
University of Rhode Island
Kingston, Rhode Island

Edward S. Shapiro, Ph.D.
Assistant Professor of School
  Psychology
School Psychology Program
Lehigh University
Bethlehem, Pennsylvania

Lawrence K. Straus, M.S.
Department of Counseling and
  Educational Psychology
Pennsylvania State University
University Park, Pennsylvania

Cyd C. Strauss, Ph.D.
Instructor in Psychiatry
Department of Psychiatry
Western Psychiatric Institute and
  Clinic
University of Pittsburgh School of
  Medicine
Pittsburgh, Pennsylvania

Joseph M. Strayhorn, Jr., M.D.
Assistant Professor of Child
  Psychiatry
Department of Psychiatry
Western Psychiatric Institute and
  Clinic
University of Pittsburgh School of
  Medicine
Pittsburgh, Pennsylvania

Sandra Twardosz, Ph.D.
Associate Professor of Child and
  Family Studies
Department of Child and Family
  Studies
University of Tennessee
Knoxville, Tennessee

Thomas L. Whitman, Ph.D.
Professor of Psychology
Department of Psychology
University of Notre Dame
Notre Dame, Indiana

Donald A. Williamson, Ph.D.
Associate Professor of Psychology
Department of Psychology
Louisiana State University
Baton Rouge, Louisiana

John T. Wixted, M.A.
Department of Psychology
Emory University
Atlanta, Georgia

David A. Wolfe, Ph.D.
Associate Professor of Psychology
Department of Psychology
University of Western Ontario
London, Canada

Series Preface

This series of books is addressed to behavioral scientists interested in the nature of human personality. Its scope should prove pertinent to personality theorists and researchers as well as to clinicians concerned with applying an understanding of personality processes to the amelioration of emotional difficulties in living. To this end, the series provides a scholarly integration of theoretical formulations, empirical data, and practical recommendations.

Six major aspects of studying and learning about human personality can be designated: personality theory, personality structure and dynamics, personality development, personality assessment, personality change, and personality adjustment. In exploring these aspects of personality, the books in the series discuss a number of distinct but related subject areas: the nature and implications of various theories of personality; personality characteristics that account for consistencies and variations in human behavior; the emergence of personality processes in children and adolescents; the use of interviewing and testing procedures to evaluate individual differences in personality; efforts to modify personality styles through psychotherapy, counseling, behavior, therapy, and other methods of influence; and patterns of abnormal personality functioning that impair individual competence.

Irving B. Weiner

Fairleigh Dickinson University
Rutherford, New Jersey

Preface

When we first developed our outline for *Behavior Therapy with Children and Adolescents: A Clinical Approach,* we recognized that there were a number of books extant that dealt with *some* of the issues we were interested in underscoring. However, on careful examination, it was clear that none of these books in the behavioral child area was comprehensive. Some had a unique theoretical bias; others were basically research oriented; still others primarily had a "how-to" focus. In addition, none specifically differentiated use of behavior therapy with childhood and adolescent disorders. Indeed, in the last few years practitioners of adolescent psychology and psychiatry have developed a unique expertise with the specific age range under their therapeutic aegis. Thus, as in many other areas, the field has become more differentiated, with many of our colleagues specializing in the treatment of certain age groups and particular disorders. As time goes on we see fewer generalists in behavior therapy with children and adolescents.

This book, therefore, is designed to reflect the major changes and trends that have transpired in the field over the last few years. Furthermore, it endeavors to combine research findings and clinical application in readable fashion. The book is organized into three parts. Part One, *General Issues,* consists of chapters that are requisite to understanding the behavioral approach to children and adolescents. In Chapter 1 we outline recent developments and emerging trends that point to the future. In Chapter 2 John D. Cone reviews the application of behavioral assessment, the cornerstone of behavior therapy. Joseph Strayhorn describes in Chapter 3 the importance of medical assessment prior to behavioral intervention. Frequently overlooked by behavior therapists, medical assessment is of paramount clinical importance, inasmuch as behavior therapists need to rule out the possible medical etiology of behavioral problems presented by children and adolescents. In Chapter 4 Sandra Twardosz and Vey M. Nordquist describe the relevance of parent training, particularly when the primary focus of behavioral treatment is a child or adolescent.

The bulk of the book appears in Part Two, *Childhood Disorders and Prob-*

lems, and Part Three, *Adolescent Disorders and Problems.* We might note that there is some inevitable overlap between Parts Two and Three, since some of the problems apply equally to both children and adolescents. However, the somewhat arbitrary division reflects the current status of the art, which undoubtedly will change in the future.

In each of the chapters in Parts Two and Three, our eminent contributors have followed a general outline that includes a description of the disorder or problem, its behavioral assessment, the range of behavioral techniques applied, a general research review, and a case description. Case descriptions are a unique feature of this textbook in that they illustrate the clinician's conceptualization of the problem, assessment, treatment, and follow-up and booster treatment. We contend, and trust that our readers will agree, that inclusion of clinical case material brings to life the descriptive, theoretical, and research material that precedes it.

MICHEL HERSEN
VINCENT B. VAN HASSELT

Pittsburgh, Pennsylvania
October 1986

Acknowledgments

Many people have contributed their time, effort, and thinking to this project. First of all, we thank Herb Reich, our editor at John Wiley & Sons, for his encouragement, excellent advice, and overall support. Next we thank our colleagues in the field who agreed with us as to the timeliness of the project and who were eager to contribute. Without their individual expertise a book of this nature could not be produced. Finally, we are most grateful to our secretaries and research personnel (Jennifer L. Brander, Judith A. Lorenzetty, Louise E. Moore, and Mary H. Newell) for their superb technical assistance.

M. H.
V. B. V.

Contents

PART THREE   ADOLESCENT DISORDERS AND PROBLEMS

BEHAVIOR THERAPY WITH
CHILDREN AND ADOLESCENTS

PART ONE

General Issues

CHAPTER 1

Developments and Emerging Trends

MICHEL HERSEN AND VINCENT B. VAN HASSELT

HISTORICAL ANTECEDENTS

Contemporary behavior therapy with children and adolescents has been in progress for less than three decades and can trace its immediate origins to the application of operant conditioning principles to clinical and educational problems (cf. Baer & Wolf, 1970; Bijou, Peterson, & Ault, 1968; Ferster & DeMyer, 1962; Lovaas, 1967). Proceeding counter to the prevailing theoretical trends of the times, the earlier behavioral efforts were carried out with severely disturbed and handicapped mentally retarded and autistic children, populations that had generally proven resistive to psychoanalytic interventions. These operantly inspired behavior therapists termed their work applied behavior analysis. Following Skinner's (1953) recommendations, they carefully studied the functional relationship between precisely defined treatments and equally precise descriptions of behavioral targets selected for modification in individual clients and patients.

Although rather successful in their interventions with children, applied behavior analysts encountered some initial resistance in publishing their findings. As a consequence, they created their own journal, *Journal of Applied Behavior Analysis*, to disseminate results of intensive analyses of single subjects in children and adults. In the first issue of the journal in 1968, Baer, Wolf, and Risley clearly articulated the directions that the field of behavior analysis should follow. It is noteworthy that in the 1980s many of Baer et al.'s (1968) original recommendations are still being followed in applied behavior analyses with children and adolescents.

Prior to the operant explosion of the 1960s and 1970s, there were scattered reports of a variety of behavioral interventions with children (see Kazdin, 1978). The first, of course, was the establishment of the pioneering Psychological Clinic in 1896 at the University of Pennsylvania by Lightner Witmer. Many of the clients in Witmer's clinic were children who were treated with strategies derived from principles of learning and perception. In that sense

3

Witmer's work may be categorized as a historical antecedent to today's widespread use of behavior therapy with children and adolescents.

The most frequently cited historical antecedent, however, is the work of John B. Watson and his colleagues Rosalie Rayner and Mary Cover Jones. The conditioning and deconditioning of simple fears in young children provided initial evidence that the development and elimination of fears followed the laws of learning (Jones 1924a, 1924b; Watson, 1924; Watson & Rayner, 1920). A second important historical antecedent, a decade and a half later, was Mowrer and Mowrer's (1938) demonstration of the "bell-and-pad" conditioning method of the treatment of nighttime enuresis in children. Interestingly, a variant of this conditioning device is still marketed today by Sears, Roebuck and Company to facilitate treatment of this common but embarrassing disorder. The work by the Mowrers also may be considered a precursor to the numerous behavioral medicine interventions extant in the field of child behavior therapy today.

In most of the earlier behavior therapy applications with children, including those in the late 1950s and early 1960s, precise motoric targets slated for modification were identified. Some sort of contingency arrangement was then established either to increase or decrease the behavior. Such was the approach for behavior therapy in both the clinic and the educational setting. Reports of successful interventions generally detailed the short-term value of treatments, but little attention was devoted to generalization, follow-up, or possible negative concurrent effects (Ollendick & Cerny, 1981). Examined from our retrospective vantage point, many of these treatment applications, albeit effective, appear by today's standards to be rather simplistic and naive. Indeed, there was a certain insularity in the work of the earlier applied behavior analysts, given their overall disregard of developmental factors, cognitive variables contributing to behavioral change, diagnostic considerations, and the possible benefits of the pharmacological approach. But as has been articulated elsewhere (Hersen, 1981),

> "Given the hostile climate in which behavior therapy was born, the somewhat strident "breast-beating" that then took place is understandable today. Were it not for the ultra-assertive voices of yesterday, we would not be here today. However, the exaggerated claims of success, the ease and simplicity with which behavioral therapies were allegedly applied, and the myopia concerning the contribution of other disciplines to mental health still plague us at this time." (p. 18).

Over the course of the last three decades, however, behavior therapy overall, and in particular with children and adolescents, has become more sophisticated. There now is a much greater willingness on the part of behavioral clinicians to maintain an open attitude about the contributions of other *em-*

pirical disciplines. Thus, we now see greater concern with such issues as the importance of formal diagnostic considerations (Kazdin, 1983), the relevance of standard psychological testing (Goldstein, 1979; Nelson, 1980), the role of developmental factors in treatment (Edelbrock, 1984; Harris & Ferrari, 1983, Ollendick & Hersen, 1984), and the complementary treatment effects of pharmacotherapy and behavior therapy (Hersen, 1985). Such broadness of vision, of course, was not possible in the nascent stages of the behavior therapy movement with children and adolescents.

Not only is there enthusiasm about incorporating the empirical findings on assessment and treatment in the overall therapeutic regime, but the range of childhood and adolescent disorders now dealt with has increased considerably. The breadth of approaches carried out and the diversity of child and adolescent populations treated are documented in Table 1.1, where we have listed reviews in the area that have appeared in the 20 volumes of *Progress in Be-*

TABLE 1.1 Reviews of Behavior Therapy with Children and Adolescents

Topic	Reference
Behavior modification with delinquents	Braukmann & Fixsen (1975)
Deceleration of aberrant behavior among retarded individuals	Forehand & Baumeister (1976)
Behavior modification in the classroom	Copeland & Hall (1976)
Behavior modification with learning disabilities and related problems	Lahey (1976)
Parents as behavior therapists	Graziano (1977)
Child noncompliance to parental requests: Behavioral analysis and treatment	Forehand (1977)
Behavioral self-management in children: Concepts, methods, issues, and directions	Karoly (1977)
Assessment and treatment of enuresis and encopresis in children	Doleys (1978)
New directions in behavior modification with children	Craighead & Wilcoxin-Craighead (1978)
Behavioral approaches to fear in dental settings	Melamed (1979)
Fear reduction techniques with children	Ollendick (1979)
Modifying academic performance in the grade school classroom	Klein (1979)
Overcorrection: An examination of its rationale and treatment effectiveness	Marholin, Luiselli, & Townsend (1980)
Behavioral assessment and training of children's social skills	Michelson & Wood (1980)
Behavioral treatment of obesity in children and adolescents	Israel & Stolmaker (1980)
Methodological issues in child behavior therapy	Furman & Drabman (1981)
Modifying children's social withdrawal: Issues in assessment and clinical intervention	Strain & Kerr (1981)

(Continued)

TABLE 1.1 (*Continued*)

Topic	Reference
Assessment of hyperactive children: Psychometric, methodological, and practical considerations	Wallander & Conger (1981)
Self-control procedures with the mentally retarded	Shapiro (1981)
Behavior modification of children's written language	Kerr & Lambert (1983)
Overcorrection	Foxx & Bechtel (1983)
Research on the education of autistic children	Cushing, Adams, & Rincover (1983)
Attention deficit disorder with hyperactivity: Critical treatment parameters and their application in applied outcome research	Rapport (1983)
Behavioral intervention with child abuse and neglect	Gambrill (1983)
Pediatric behavioral medicine: Directions in treatment and prevention	Hobbs, Beck, & Wamsley (1984)
Preventing teenage pregnancy	Schinke (1984)
Behavioral pediatrics: Health education in pediatric primary care	Finney & Christopherson (1984)
Applications of behavioral medicine with children: I. Epidemiology of coronary heart disease.	Cinciripini (1984a)
Applications of behavioral medicine with children: II. Intervention for behavioral risk factors in coronary heart disease	Cinciripini (1984b)
Behavioral medicine with children: Applications in chronic disease	Parker & Cinciripini (1984)
Behavioral assessment and management of pediatric pain	Katz, Varney, & Jay (1984)
Self-reinforcement by children	Blount & Stokes (1984)
Advances in behavioral approaches to adolescent health care	Godley, Lutzker, Lamazor, & Martin (1984)
Progress in parent training	O'Dell (1985)
Childhood and adolescent obesity: Progress in behavioral assessment and treatment	Wells & Copeland (1985)
Behavioral pediatrics: Research treatment, recommendations	Lutzker & Lamazor (1985)
The assessment of anorexia nervosa and bulimia	Chiodo (1985)
Guidelines for the use of contingent electric shock to treat aberrant behavior	Foxx, Plaska, & Bittle (in press)
Behavior therapy for visually handicapped persons	Van Hasselt (in press)

havior Modification in the last decade. Based on our analysis of these reviews, we devote the bulk of the chapter to discussing significant developments and emerging trends in the field of child and adolescent behavior therapy. We do not provide the standard review of the field because this has been done in exemplary fashion by Ollendick and Cerny (1981).

DIAGNOSTIC CONSIDERATIONS

Traditionally, behavior therapists have eschewed the value of formal psychiatric diagnosis and have relied principally on behavioral assessment strategies, selecting specified motoric, cognitive, and physiological targets for modification (see Hersen, 1976, for a historical account of the issues). The many reasons for this extreme position ranged from the political to the empirical. Prior to the advent of the third edition of the *Diagnostic and Statistical Manual* (DSM-III: American Psychiatric Association, 1980), there was little evidence for the reliability and validity of many of the diagnostic categories subsumed under the DSM-I and DSM-II classification systems. Moreover, there appeared to be only a tangential association between the diagnosis made and the treatment eventually applied. Also bolstering this notion was the widespread application of indirect measurement techniques (i.e., the projectives) then used by nonbehavioral psychologists in order to arrive at a diagnostic determination. Thus, for behavior therapists, the clear delineation of targets and strategies in behavioral assessment and treatment initially overshadowed the potential relevance of a more embracing diagnostic scheme.

Cognizant of the numerous deficiencies of DSM-I and DSM-II, the designers of DSM-III made a concerted effort to develop a more reliable and valid classification system that would serve the needs of contemporary mental health workers. Although the new system remains imperfect, its relevance for behavior therapists in general (Hersen & Turner, 1984; Taylor, 1983) and child behavior therapists in particular has been widely acknowledged (Kazdin, 1983). As noted by Hersen and Turner (1984), "The emergence of DSM-III . . . has influenced all clinical practitioners, irrespective of theoretical allegiance, including behavior therapists" (p. 485). Moreover, in contrast to its predecessors (DSM-I and DSM-II), DSM-III has finally accorded significant attention to childhood and adolescent disorders. With respect to this point, Kazdin (1983) astutely argues that "The use of specified diagnostic criteria as well means that the utility of particular diagnostic categories is much more likely to be evaluated empirically now than in previous years. The initial testing might lead to gross alterations in the diagnostic alternatives for children as some disorders are shown only to exist in the minds of diagnosticians and others in the behavior, affect, and cognitions of children" (p. 81).

What, then, are the specific implications for child behavior therapists in establishing psychiatric diagnosis in their clients and patients? The *first*, of course, is that behavior therapy becomes a part of mainstream child psychiatry. As noted by Kazdin (1983), "Failure to recognize or actually use DSM-III may make it difficult to integrate findings from child behavior therapy into clinical work in psychiatry, where the potential impact could and perhaps should be the greatest" (p. 94). There is no reason, however, that psychiatric diagnosis, per se, should supersede the contribution of behavioral assessment.

Rather, the point here is the use of DSM-III will provide the needed common denominator across the varied theoretical positions represented by members of the different mental health professions.

A second major implication of the emerging recognition of DSM-III by child behavior therapists is that the behavioral problems presented by our patients and clients often are quite complex (Hersen, 1981). Exclusive reliance on a narrow-band approach represented by sole reliance on behavioral assessment strategies that only focus on the immediate target(s) for intervention may yield an incomplete evaluation. That is, a narrow-band behavioral assessment approach frequently does not consider: (1) the etiology of the disorder, (2) precipitating stresses, (3) specific onset, (4) chronicity and past episodes, (5) severity, and (6) the complicated interrelationship of targets and symptoms that may be subsumed under a particular diagnostic label (e.g., childhood depression).

The integration and contribution of behavioral assessment procedures within a classificatory system, such as DSM-III, provides the child behavior therapist with some unique opportunities. In addition to potentially providing an empirical basis for the designated categories, it offers an opportunity to test out the relationship between such categories and success in treatment using a variety of clinical applications. Child behavior therapists historically have displayed inventiveness in developing novel treatment strategies, clearly documenting the functional relationship between application and outcome. Now they have renewed opportunity to evaluate the functional relationship but on a much broader scale that may have an impact on child psychiatry in general.

Not only are behavior therapists now concerned with establishing formal diagnoses in their child patients, but they also seem to show an interest in incorporating standard psychological tests (e.g., neuropsychological batteries, intelligence tests) into a comprehensive behavioral assessment (Goldstein, 1979; Horton & Miller, 1985; Nelson, 1980). With regard to neuropsychological evaluation of brain-damaged individuals, Goldstein (1979) points out that such testing is able to identify target behavioral deficits that can then possibly be modified using behavioral treatment strategies. He argues cogently that the neuropsychological evaluation will identify the complex deficit pattern in brain damaged individuals that would receive only superficial evaluation by simply observing behavior in these patients. Thus, a partnership between neuropsychologist and behavior therapist is indicated, with the neuropsychologist providing the targets for modification and the behavior therapist developing specific treatment interventions.

With regard to intelligence tests, Nelson (1980) outlines five specific uses within the context of behavioral assessment: (1) test patterns can provide a framework for identifying particular skills that will be taught or remediated in the educational program, (2) IQ can be employed as a dependent measure in treatment programs, (3) the use of IQ scores can facilitate communication with researchers, clinicians, and educators of differing persuasions, (4) the use of IQ scores can screen children who require academic remediation, and (5) the administration of IQ tests can be used in developing individualized educational plans. With the last, test scores are used prescriptively.

DEVELOPMENTAL FACTORS

Surprising as it may seem, there has been little or no communication between child behavior therapists and developmental psychologists. Only recently have there been calls for integrating findings between the two disciplines. These have appeared in the literature with regard to both behavioral assessment (Edelbrock, 1984) and treatment (Harris & Ferrari, 1983). We fully concur with Harris and Ferrari (1983) that "Developmental psychologists have created a sophisticated methodology for the study of children. By ignoring such advances and pursuing our own efforts, child therapists may be compelled to make mistakes we could have been spared through the exchange of ideas" (pp. 68–69).

Let us consider a number of areas where developmental data would prove invaluable to child behavior therapists. The first, of course, is the child behavior therapist's need for norms and a knowledge of normal variation (see Harris & Ferrari, 1983). If we are committed to accepting Kazdin's (1977) recommendation that the clinical importance of behavior change should be ascertained through the process of social validation, then we need rather precise data in order to target our treatment goals accurately. Otherwise, our systematic attempts (and successes) to increase and decrease target responses are carried out *in vacuo*. The contextual matrix of developmental factors is especially critical in child behavior therapy since the norms for socially appropriate behavior in children and adolescents change rapidly as they mature. This is a factor that has considerably less relevance in behavior therapy for adults, since developmental differences over time vary much more slowly.

Related to the issue of developmental norms are the important sex differences in boys and girls and the varying degrees of maturity attained by the two sexes at given age levels (e.g., toilet training, speech, dating). Again, the question of normalcy and variation is raised with regard to when a clinician should intervene. That is, behaviors (or their absence) in child clients presented for treatment may be age-normal (or high or low but still within normal limits) and *may not* require formal behavioral intervention.

Developmental capacities in children also have a large impact on what we can expect our child clients to do in the therapeutic setting. Given that the behavioral approach to treatment is an active one that involves full participation of the client, it is critical for child behavior therapists to know their clients' intellectual and developmental capabilities at varying age levels. For example, at what age can mental imagery be used as part of a fear-reduction program in children? At what age can we expect a child to use cognitive self-instructional techniques to control behavior (Harris & Ferrari, 1983)? When do we omit parent-directed operant procedures and focus on the child's developing self-control?

Although child behavior therapists have personal norms for arriving at answers to such questions, the lack of developmental guidelines represents a glaring omission. In the future, we foresee considerably more interchange between child behavior therapy and developmental psychology, with theoretical and empirical benefits accruing to both disciplines.

DEPRESSION IN CHILDREN AND ADOLESCENTS

The importance of diagnostic considerations and developmental factors is most clearly seen in the assessment and treatment of depressed children and adolescents. Initially, depression in children was thought to be "masked" by presence of conduct disorders, somatic compliants, and school problems (see Carlson & Cantwell , 1980; Cytryn & McKnew, 1974). Indeed, prior to Rutter and Hersov (1977), child psychiatry textbooks failed to acknowledge the existence of preadolescent depression. This was partly due to the fact that there were no direct methods for assessing depression in such children. However, with the advent of DSM-III and the concurrent development of formal diagnostic interview schedules for children, depression in children and adolescents has become a legitimate area of inquiry for behavioral, pharmacological, and non-behavioral clinicians alike (Kashani, McGee, Clarkson, Anderson, Walton, Williams, Silva, Robins, Cytryn, McKnew, 1983; Kovacs, Feinberg, Crouse-Novak, Paulauskas, Pollock, & Finkelstein, 1984; Puig-Antich & Gittelman, 1982; Reynolds, in press). For example, Kovacs et al. (1984) found that among children who were diagnosed as having a major depression and then recovered, 40% subsequently had a second episode of depression within a two-year period. Thus, not only is the disorder prevalent in children (Kashani et al., 1983: 1.8 to 2.5% in the general population of 9-year-olds) and adolescents, but it tends to recur in a significant proportion of those so diagnosed.

Only recently have behavioral assessors and therapists turned their attention to the assessment and treatment of depression in children and adolescents (e.g., Coats & Reynolds, 1985; Petti, Kovacs, Paulaskas, & Finkelstein, 1982; Reynolds, in press). We believe that behavioral assessors have much to offer in making more precise the diagnostic appraisal of depressed children. Careful behavioral observation of such children undoubtedly will contribute to the precision of the overall diagnostic conclusion now reached on the basis of semistructured and structured interview schedules.

With respect to treatment, there already is some evidence that behavioral approaches, such as cognitive therapy and relaxation training, have some short-term benefits for depressed children and adolescents (Coats & Reynolds, 1985; Petti et al., 1982). We also expect a downward revision of the social skills approach for adults (Hersen, Bellack, Himmelhoch, & Thase, 1984) being applied to adolescent depressives. Thus, in the immediate future, child behavior therapists will be focusing their attention in increasing numbers on the complicated problems of childhood depression.

PEDIATRIC BEHAVIORAL MEDICINE

One of the most exciting developments in child behavior therapy in recent years is the important contribution being made to pediatric behavioral medicine (Cinciripini, 1984b; Finney & Christopherson, 1984; Hobbs, Beck, & Wansley, 1984; Katz et al., 1984; Lutzker & Lamazor, 1985; Melamed, 1979). Schwartz and Weiss (1978) have defined behavioral medicine as the "interdisciplinary field concerned with the development and integration of behavioral and biomedical science knowledge and techniques relevant to health and illness and the application of this knowledge and these techniques to prevention, diagnosis, treatment, and rehabilitation" (p. 250). The range of pediatric medical problems tackled by behavior therapists in the last decade is already impressive and includes treatments for enuresis and encopresis (Doleys, 1978), fear reduction in the dental setting (Melamed, 1979), treatment for obesity in both children and adolescents (Israel & Stolmaker, 1980), health education in pediatric primary care (Finney & Christopherson, 1984), intervention for behavioral risk factors in coronary heart disease (Cinciripini, 1984b), management of pediatric pain (Katz et al., 1984), improved compliance with medical regimes (Epstein, Beck, Figueroa, Farkas, Kazdin, Daneman, & Becker, 1981), and modification of seizure disorder only partially controlled with medication (Zlutnick, Mayville, & Moffat, 1975).

Let us briefly consider for illustrative purposes two important studies in which the contribution of behavioral techniques to pediatric medical problems was clearly documented. The first is the landmark child behavioral medicine intervention reported by Zlutnick et al. (1975) directed to modify seizure disorder by systematically interrupting the preseizure behavioral chain. Although there had been anecdotal reports that seizures could be interrupted before the *seizure* "climax," there were no available empirical data to support this clinical claim. By using a simple interruption procedure for specific behaviors preceding the actual seizure, Zlutnick and his colleagues were able to obtain significant reductions in seizure frequency in four of five children (age range = 4 to 14 years) and reductions in preseizure behavior in three of the five.

For four of the children *interruption* simply consisted of: (1) shouting *no* loudly, and (2) grasping the child by the shoulder and giving him or her one vigorous shake. For the fifth child, a differential-reinforcement procedure was carried out by: (1) placing the child's hand on her side, and (2) giving her primary and secondary reinforcement for hands down. Results of this study "suggest the possibility of promising behavioral interventions for this and other disorders, and highlight the importance of improved communication between the medical and behavioral sciences" (Zlutnick et al., 1975, p. 12).

In the second investigation, behavioral techniques were used to improve adherence to a medical, dietary, and exercise regime in children with insulin-dependent diabetes (Epstein et al., 1981). This is a particularly important demonstration in the child behavioral medicine area, given that the absence of strict adherence to medical regimes in patients with chronic diseases can have life-threatening implications. In the Epstein et al. (1981) study, percentage of negative (i.e., zero) urine concentration tests served as the dependent variable in this multiple baseline analysis across three groups of children suffering from insulin-dependent diabetes. This measure was used since it reflects the excess glucose excreted in the urine, which can be modified with appropriate insulin adjustment, correct diet, and exercise. Behavioral strategies used in the treatment of the 19 families with diabetic children included: (1) instructions in insulin adjustment, (2) decreased intake of simple sugars and saturated fats, and (3) increased exercise. Parents were taught to support improvements in their children's behavior by carrying out a point economy and using contingent praise. Results of this multiple baseline analysis clearly reflect marked improvements in the percentage of negative urines recorded with these children. Most important, improvements were maintained throughout the 10-week follow-up period. Thus, child behavior therapists have in their armanentarium the requisite techniques for improving adherence to overall medical regimes.

Most recently, child behavior therapists have spent time working on inpatient pediatric units, implementing behavioral strategies designed to decrease pain before and after surgery and secondary to aversive medical procedures, such as debridement in burn victims and bone marrow aspirations and chemotherapy in cancer patients (Hickman, Thompson, Feldman, & Varni, 1985). Dependent measures in these investigations typically include crying, verbal pain behaviors, and nonverbal pain behaviors. Behavioral treatment strategies have involved hypnosis, relaxation techniques, filmed modeling, differential reinforcement, emotive imagery, and behavior rehearsal. Hickman et al. (1985) point out that the work in this area is in its beginning stages and that, "pediatric inpatients represent a childhood population where a priority for cognitive-behavioral research efforts must now be directed in order to improve the clinical care of these children" (p. 280).

Commenting on the use of behavioral treatments in chronic illness, Masek, Fentress, and Spirito (1984) note that in "cystic fibrosis, asthma, and some types of childhood cancer, symptoms can arise from the stress in coping with the cardinal manifestations of the illness and the threat to life. In turn, these symptoms (e.g., hyperventilation, gastrointestinal distress, lowered pain tolerance, sleep disturbance, and anxiety) can interfere with medical management and even exacerbate the illness. Behavioral treatment of secondary symptoms is aimed at reducing arousal and developing more effective coping strategies" (p. 561).

It is clear, then, that child behavior therapists working in the medical arena have a considerable opportunity to relieve the tragic suffering of children. This should prove to be a major challenge for them in the latter part of the 1980s and through the 1990s.

PREVENTION

The concept of prevention is hardly a novel one in the field of therapeutics, but it is only in the last few years that child behavior therapists have applied their technical operations in the service of this valuable notion. When referring to prevention, the tripartite model of Caplan (1964) must be considered. In our brief examination of preventative effects by child behavior therapists, we will see whether they have been concerned with *primary*, *secondary*, or *tertiary* prevention. The goal of *primary prevention* is to reduce new cases of a given disorder by teaching individuals to withstand stress and/or to enable them to anticipate how to deal with a variety of problems (e.g., teaching blind children emergency fire safety skills: Jones, Sisson, & Van Hasselt, 1984; or teaching teenage girls refusal skills to prevent unwanted pregnancy: Schinke, 1984). The major goal of *secondary prevention* is to reduce the length of an existing disorder or problem and to prevent its recurrence (e.g., teaching obese preadolescents appropriate nutrition and exercise routines to reduce weight and improve physical fitness: Epstein, Koeske, Zidansek, & Wing, 1983; or teaching abusive parents *appropriate* child management skills to prevent recurrence of abuse: Gambrill, 1983; Kelly, 1983). In *tertiary prevention* the primary objective is to ensure that recovery from a disorder or given problem will proceed smoothly and that the individuals will be reintegrated into their natural settings with a minimum of disruption. Most behavioral treatments, of course, are devoted to that end when remediating childhood psychopathology.

In our examination of prevention in child behavior therapy, we will focus on *primary* and *secondary* prevention, since these involve treatment strategies directed toward decreasing incidence of new cases and overall prevalence in the population. Let us first consider four *primary* prevention approaches used in: (1) teaching emergency fire-safety skills to blind children and adolescents (Jones et al., 1984), (2) preventing cigarette smoking in adolescents (Schinke,

Gilchrist, & Snow, 1985), (3) preventing teenage pregnancy (Schinke, 1984), and (4) preventing antisocial behavior in children (Michelson & Kazdin, 1984).

Primary Prevention

Jones et al. (1984) taught emergency fire-safety skills (e.g., hears fire alarm, slides out of bed and gets into crawl position, crawls to door and checks for hot air, if not hot opens door and crawls to entrance door, crawls to outside door and communicates with roommates, waits in yard) on a group basis to eight blind adolescents from a residential school. Training consisted of instructions, feedback, behavior rehearsal, social and token reinforcement, and behavior and verbal review. Not only did the multiple baseline design across subjects indicate that the eight children learned the components of fire safety skills during training, but unannounced nighttime fire drills showed that generalization occurred in six of the eight blind adolescents. The authors point out that a variety of preventive training efforts (accident prevention, emergency telephone dialing) are also warranted in this vulnerable population of children.

Schinke and his colleagues (Schinke, 1984; Schinke, Gilchrist, & Snow, 1985) have been involved in a number of preventive efforts with adolescents, including the prevention of teenage pregnancy and skills training to prevent cigarette smoking in this age group. In a recent study on smoking prevention, Schinke et al. (1985) contrasted a skills intervention approach to an information approach and a control condition in 689 sixth-grade students (median age = 11.76 years). Skills and information interventions included films about health, peer reports, and homework assignments. In addition, the skills intervention consisted of instruction and practice in how to resist the urge to smoke and how to ward off peer pressures to smoke. Both skills and information approaches involved 10 weekly 1-hour sessions conducted by graduate-student social workers. Results of this study are based on pretest, posttest, and 6-, 12-, and 24-month posttest analyses. Data clearly indicate the statistical superiority of the skills condition over the information condition and controls. That is, skills intervention subjects had significantly lower intentions to smoke and less cigarette use than their counterparts in the other two groups. Therefore, Schinke et al. (1985) rightfully contend that, "Skills interventions for youth at high risk for tobacco use deserve attention" (p. 667).

Teenage pregnancy is a problem of epidemic proportions that, according to Schinke (1984), will affect 780,000 of 2 million girls who will attain the age of 14. The emotional, financial, and social sequelae of such unwanted conceptions are well known and do not warrant repetition here. However, it is important to recognize that "over 300,000 of these pregnancies will be aborted. Most of the babies carried to term will be unwanted, born out of wedlock, and raised by a single mother. Female children in these families will stand a good chance of themselves getting pregnant as teenagers'' (Schinke, 1984, p. 52). Thus, the importance of primary prevention here also has consequences for the succeeding generations.

At this time a number of cognitive-behavioral methods have been used with populations at risk for unwanted pregnancy (see Schinke, 1984, for a review). Results of these efforts generally indicate that participation in prevention sessions (when contrasted to control conditions) yield significantly greater knowledge of human sexuality, better acceptance and use of birth control methods, and better abilities in refusing sexual advances from partners in stressful pressure situations. However, data concerning the long-term benefits of actually preventing unwanted and unplanned pregnancies remain to be adduced in longitudinal studies.

Also in the realm of primary prevention, Michelson and Kazdin (1984) are involved in a massive study of fourth- and fifth-grade elementary school children who have been identified as "at risk" for antisocial behavior and conduct disorders. From an initial pool of 2500 such children, 450 will be selected using the Child Behavior Checklist and the Classroom Adjustment Rating Scale as screening devices. These children will be assigned either to a no-treatment control condition or a combined Interpersonal Cognitive Problem Solving plus Behavioral Social Skills Training Group. The treatment condition involves 60 sessions carried out over the course of two school years. Assessments are to be conducted before, during, and after training, and at 12- and 24-month follow-ups. The preventive value of the program will be assessed through parent and teacher ratings, measures of self-control, sociometrics, psychiatric status, academic performance, interpersonal behavior, legal contacts, substance abuse, and most important, *delinquent behavior*. If successful, this program will have enormous implications for the early detection and prevention of delinquent behavior and could prove to be a landmark investigation.

Secondary Prevention

Secondary prevention strategies have been used with good success by child behavior therapists working with obese children (e.g., Epstein, Koeske, Zidansek, & Wing, 1983) and with remedial efforts in cases of child abuse (e.g., Wolfe, Sandler, & Kaufman, 1981). In both instances, the focus has been on teaching parents new and more effective strategies in dealing with the problems presented by their children. For obese children the addition of a child parenting skills course to the usual weight reduction strategies resulted in significant improvements in maintenance of weight loss at the one-year follow-up (Israel, Stolmaker, & Andrian, 1985). Similarly, Epstein, Koeske, Zindansek, and Wing (1983) found that point economies, based on parent-child contracts, facilitated proper eating, exercise, and weight loss in obese pre-adolescents, whose overweight posed significant cardiovascular risk (Epstein, Wing, Kuller, & Becker, 1983). Thus, for maintaining weight reduction in obese children and adolescents, it appears that parental retraining is a critical therapeutic component.

Nowhere is the attention to parental child-rearing strategies of greater significance than in the case of child abuse. According to Straus, Gelles, and Steinmetz (1979), the violent behavior of parents toward their children results in physical injury to 1.4 to 1.9 million children each year. It is well recognized that physically abused children are often difficult to manage, generally less socially competent, and more prone to evincing depressive symptoms than nonabused children (Kazdin, Moser, Colbus, & Bell, 1985; Wolfe & Mosk, 1983). Also, when they mature, there is evidence of an increased likelihood that they will become abusers themselves as parents (cf. Schinke et al., in press). At this time there are ample studies documenting that "abusers are more likely to report stress-related symptoms, such as depression and health problems, that are linked to the parenting role. Comparative studies of family interactions have also indicated that "abusers display reciprocal patterns of behavior with their children and spouses that are proportonately more coercive and less prosocial than nonabusers" (Wolfe, 1985, p. 462). Therefore, given the interactive nature of the problem, secondary prevention efforts targeting abusive parents, child-rearing skills, and stress levels would appear to be imperative.

An example of such an approach is a study carried out by Wolfe et al. (1981). In a preliminary study, eight families of abused children were assigned to treatment and eight served as controls. Treatment consisted of instruction in human development and child management, problem solving and modeling of appropriate child management techniques, self-control through deep muscle relaxation, and individualized home-based training procedures. Control families received standard services offered to abusive families. Results indicated that treated families improved in parenting skills, as determined through home observation, reports of child-behavior problems, and caseworker reports. Such improvements were not as pronounced in the control families. Moreover, at the one-year follow-up, there were no additional reports of child abuse in the treated group of abusive parents.

As Gambrill (1983) notes, the behavioral approach to child abuse is "promising." She outlines the advantages of its precision, specification of relationships, and careful evaluation. However, she does underscore that there are other behavioral avenues that have not been "systematically pursued," including the social skills training of both parents and abused children. Such efforts of secondary prevention, also recommended at the clinical level by Kelly (1983), need to be evaluated empirically in the next few years by child behavior therapists.

DRUGS AND BEHAVIOR THERAPY

For many years behavior therapists and pharmacotherapists worked in parallel, rarely communicating with one another. Recently, attempts to integrate the two empirically based strategies have been increasing (see Hersen, 1985). These efforts have taken a number of forms: (1) evaluation of pharmacological strategies using behavioral observation techniques, (2) use of drugs to facilitate behavioral treatment (i.e., bringing psychotic symptoms under sufficient control so that the patient can benefit from behavioral intervention), (3) behavioral treatments applied to enhance the effects above and beyond that achieved with drugs, (4) the synergistic effects of drugs and behavior therapy, and (5) the use of behavioral techniques to improve medication compliance. In general, the integrated pharmacological and behavioral approach has been evaluated empirically with single-case experimental designs (Barlow & Hersen, 1984), although crossover designs and group controlled comparisons have been carried out as well (Hersen, 1985).

Child behavior therapists have recently collaborated with their pharmacological colleagues in the treatment of autism (Schroeder, Gaultieri, & Van Bourgondien, 1985), attention deficit and conduct disorders (Pelham & Murphy, 1985), learning disabilities (Gadow, Torgesen, Greenstein, & Schell, 1985), and epilepsy (Spunt, Hermann, & Rousseau, 1985). Although apparently representative of the wave of the future, the research in this area is still in its early stages. As noted by Pelham and Murphy (1985):

"Methodological errors have been pervasive and are the most reasonable explanation for the failure of some studies to find incremental, beneficial effects of combined interventions. Much additional research is needed with careful attention paid to the methodological issues raised herein. In particular, concurrent parametric analyses of the variables that influence psychopharmacological and behavioral interventions and the individual differences that mediate these effects should be conducted. Single-subject methodology appears to be ideally suited both for research and for clinical practice in this area" (p. 138).

To illustrate, let us briefly refer to an example of a single-case study showing how the two approaches complement one another. Williamson, Calpin, DiLorenzo, Garris, and Petti (1981) evaluated the effects of Dexedrine and activity feedback and reinforcement procedures in a 9-year-old hyperactive boy. In a very fine-grained analysis, the investigators documented how Dexedrine improved classroom on-task behavior and gross motor behavior observed in the lunchroom. However, activity level, as measured with a movement monitor placed on the boy's wrist, was unaffected by the drug. In a subsequent phase of the study, when activity feedback and contingent reinforcement for reducing activity level were applied, a marked reduction in activity level was seen. This single-case analysis clearly showed that Dexedrine was effective on "goal-directed behavior," but that the behavioral procedure was more effective on the "remaining excessive activity" (which was very precisely measured).

We should note that the careful evaluation of pharmacological and behavioral strategies over time in extended single-case analyses has proven to be most revealing at times. Although it is gratifying to the clinical researcher to be able to document the complementary action of the two strategies, it is equally important to be able to document when either one or both of the approaches are ineffective (Schroeder et al., 1985). Negative findings here obviously have implications for clinical practice, as they forestall the needless application of particular drugs or behavioral techniques that may not be effective for given symptoms of a disorder (or the disorder in its entirety) (Abikoff & Gittelman, 1985).

BEHAVIORAL ASSESSMENT AND TREATMENT OF THE BLIND

Behavior therapists working in the child area have a long history in developing innovative assessment and treatment strategies for the developmentally and physically disabled (for a review, see Hersen, Van Hasselt, & Matson, 1983). But only in the last few years has the focus been specifically directed to blind children and adolescents (Ammerman, Van Hasselt, & Hersen, 1985; Van Hasselt, 1983, in press). Many of the current efforts have emanated from the laboratories of Van Hasselt and Hersen and their colleagues (e.g., Ammerman, Van Hasselt, & Hersen, 1985; Sisson, Van Hasselt, Hersen, & Strain, 1985; Van Hasselt, Hersen, & Kazdin, 1985; Van Hasselt, Hersen, Kazdin, Simon, & Mastantuono, 1983; Van Hasselt, Hersen, Moore, & Simon, in press; Van Hasselt, Kazdin, Hersen, Simon, & Mastantuono, 1985). Use the single-case experimental designs by these investigators with visually impaired individuals (Van Hasselt & Hersen, 1981) has yielded precision in evaluation and treatment and has overcome the problems of conducting controlled group research with this relatively low-incidence disability. Indeed, single-case research in the field of blindness has proven invaluable, given the difficulty of precise matching that is required in group comparison studies.

Van Hasselt and Hersen's behavioral work with visually impaired children and adolescents has taken a number of directions. First has been the identification of specific social skill deficits in blind adolescents using a behavioral-analytic model of assessment (Van Hasselt et al., 1985). Results of this investigation confirm the widely held notion that many blind people evince difficulties in a variety of social situations.

Second has been the development of social skill strategies (Ammerman et al., 1985) suitable for implementation with this population. Initial results in single-case analyses (Van Hasselt et al., 1983) indicate that instructions, feedback, behavioral rehearsal, modeling, and manual guidance are effective components of social skills in bringing about improvements in targeted behaviors (e.g., posture, gaze, hostile tone, and requests for new behavior). However, much work remains to be done in developing treatment strategies that generalize across social situations. Also, unique behavioral treatments will be required to enable multihandicapped blind individuals, such as the deaf-blind, to acquire the rudiments of appropriate social responding.

Third has been the use of normal peers to increase social behaviors in 9 to 11-year-old blind multihandicapped children (Sisson et al., 1985). Preliminary investigation here shows that increase in play initiations by peers functioned to increase the social behavior of these multihandicapped children. There was also some evidence for generalization and maintenance of gains at follow-up four months later.

Fourth involves a careful evaluation of the interactive patterns of families with blind children (Van Hasselt et al., in press), differentiating them from families with "normal children" and those with children who have another disability (spina bifida). Following the identification of specific problem areas in the families with a blind child, efforts at remediation are being carried out using a variety of behavioral family treatment strategies, such as communications training, contracting, and behavioral rehearsal.

As child behavioral researchers we feel that we have made some initial inroads in the evaluation of the interactive skills of blind children, blind adolescents, and their families. However, we see this as only a beginning, with concerted efforts in other laboratories required to replicate and perhaps expand on our efforts. Moreover, there are many areas in the field of visual impairment in children where the remedial efforts of behavior therapists should prove to be fruitful. In particular, we foresee additional attempts in the future to develop programs for the blind child who also suffers from additional handicaps. To date this is an area of inquiry and remediation that has received scant attention.

COGNITIVE BEHAVIOR THERAPY

Since the 1970s we have witnessed the rapid development of cognitive-behavioral strategies for application to a wide variety of childhood problems. We have already alluded to some of these techniques in previous sections of this chapter when outlining some of the more comprehensive approaches that have been carried out. In considering the genesis of cognitive behavior therapy with children, Meyers and Craighead (1984) argue that,

"Gradually, behavior therapy increased its involvement with less severely disturbed children such as those seen in outpatient clinics and children in nursery schools and day-care centers. This expansion was accompanied by an increased concern with internal thought processes as both *targets* and *mechanisms* of change. In addition, in educational settings there was a shift from an emphasis on the modification of attentive and disruptive motor behaviors to a concern with educational tasks that involve cognitive or thinking skills" (p. 5).

Although a number of diverse cognitive therapy approaches have been developed over the last two decades, these treatments share the theoretical assumption that the client or patient's problems are either due to his or her cognitive activity or maintained by it (cf. Beidel & Turner, 1986). Current strategies in the field of child cognitive behavior therapy have emanated from Bandura's work on modeling (Rosenthal & Bandura, 1978), Meichenbaum's (1977) studies on self-instruction training, Spivack and Shure's (1974) cognitive approach to solving problems, Kanfer's notions on self-control (Kanfer & Karoly, 1972), and the cognitive treatment approaches of Ellis (1962) and Beck (1976).

Beginning efforts at applying cognitive behavioral techniques with children have appeared with learning-disabled pupils, mentally retarded children, psychotic children, agressive and delinquent adolescents, and depressed children and adolescents (see Meyers & Craighead, 1984). Although the cognitive behavioral approach with children and adolescents appears to hold promise, there are insufficient controlled treatment studies extant pitting these strategies against other behavioral strategies (and nonbehavioral strategies as well) to warrant any firm conclusions. Moreover, in light of Beidel and Turner's (1986) recent critique pointing out the absence of empirical evidence documenting the "importance of cognition in influencing emotional behavior, and the relationship of cognitive-behavioral theories to cognitive-behavior therapy," it is clear that much work in this area should be forthcoming in the next decade. Further, it often is unclear how the actual mechanics of treatment differ (if at all) between cognitive-behavioral and more traditional behavioral approaches. Indeed, many of the standard behavioral techniques are incorporated by child cognitive behavior therapists in their overall treatments.

SUMMARY

In this chapter, we have considered some of the developments and emerging trends in the field of child behavior therapy. First, however, we briefly traced the historical antecedents of current practice. Then we looked at diagnostic considerations as related to behavior therapy applications with children and adolescents. It is clear that in this area, as in many other aspects of their work, child behavior therapists have shown a greater openness to the contributions of the other empirical disciplines (e.g., psychiatry, medicine, neuropsychology, developmental psychology, pharmacology). Behavior therapists no longer eschew the value of the diagnostic process when it has an empirical basis. Next, we looked at the emerging discourse between child behavior therapists and developmental psychologists—an important but unfortunately neglected interchange that has critical implications for both disciplines. In a related vein, we then considered the diagnostic and developmental issues related to the diagnosis of depression in children and adolescents, which in recent years has become a diagnostic entity that has received therapeutic attention from a number of our colleagues.

In the following section on pediatric behavioral medicine, we have described what we believe to be some of the most exciting developments in the field of child behavior therapy. The collaboration between child behavior therapists and pediatric physicians has resulted in some impressive programs for alleviating suffering in children and adolescents. This is one area where behavioral expertise should yield further innovation in the future. In the next section, we considered how child behavioral practitioners have applied strategies in the service of primary and secondary prevention in such diverse areas as fire-safety skills, childhood obesity, child abuse, and the prevention of teenage smoking and pregnancy. Finally, we examined some of the recent work carried out in the assessment and treatment of the blind. Although child behavior therapists have a long history in designing innovative techniques in their work with the developmentally and physically disabled, only recently have they targeted the blind and visually impaired, with particular emphasis on their social behavior.

REFERENCES

Abikoff, H., & Gittelman, R. (1985). Hyperactive children treated with stimulants: Is cognitive training a useful adjunct? *Archives of General Psychiatry, 42,* 953–961.

American Psychiatric Association (1980). *Diagnostic and statistical manual of mental disorders* (3rd ed.). Washington, DC: Author.

Ammerman, R. T., Van Hasselt, V. B., & Hersen, M. (1985). Social skills training for visually handicapped children: A treatment manual. *Psychological Documents, 15,* 6 (MS. no. 2684).

Baer, D. M., & Wolf, M. M. (1970). The entry into natural communities of reinforcement. In R. Ulrich, T. Stachnik, & J. Mabry (Eds.), *Control of human behavior: Vol. II* (pp. 319–324). Glenview, IL: Scott, Foresman.

Baer, D. M., Wolf, M. M., & Risley, T. R. (1968). Some current dimensions of applied behavior analysis. *Journal of Applied Behavior Analysis, 1,* 91–97.

Barlow, D. H., & Hersen, M. (1984). *Single case experimental designs: Strategies for studying behavior change* (2nd ed.). New York: Pergamon.

Beck, A. T. (1976). *Cognitive therapy and the emotional disorders.* New York: International Universities Press.

Beidel, D. C., & Turner, S. M. (1986). A critique of the theoretical bases of cognitive-behavior theories and therapy. *Clinical Psychology Review, 6,* 177–197.

Bijou, S. W., Peterson, R. F., & Ault, M. H. (1968). A method of integrate descriptive and experimental field studies at the level of data and empirical concepts. *Journal of Applied Behavior Analysis, 1,* 175–191.

Blount, R. L., & Stokes, T. F. (1984). Self-reinforcement by children. In M. Hersen, R. M. Eisler, & P. M. Miller (Eds.), *Progress in behavior modification* (Vol. 18; pp. 195–225). New York: Academic.

Braukmann, C. J., & Fixsen, D. L. (1975). Behavior modification with delinquents. In M. Hersen, R. M. Eisler, & P. M. Miller (Eds.), *Progress in behavior modification* (Vol. I; pp. 191–231). New York: Academic.

Caplan, G. (1964). *Principles of preventive psychiatry.* New York: Basic.

Carlson, G. A., & Cantwell, D. P. (1980). Unmasking masked depression in children and adolescents. *American Journal of Psychiatry, 137,* 445–449.

Chiodo, J. (1985). The assessment of anorexia nervosa and bulimia. In M. Hersen, R. M. Eisler, & P. M. Miller (Eds), *Progress in behavior modification* (Vol. 19; pp. 255–292). New York: Academic.

Cinciripini, P. M. (1984a). Applications of behavioral medicine with children: I. Epidemiology of coronary heart disease. In M. Hersen, R. M. Eisler, & P. M. Miller (Eds.), *Progress in behavior modification* (Vol. 17; pp. 73–110.) New York: Academic.

Cinciripini, P. M. (1984b). Applications of behavioral medicine with children: II. Intervention for behavioral risk factors in coronary heart disease. In M. Hersen, R. M. Eisler, & P. M. Miller (Eds.), *Progress in behavior modification* (Vol. 17; pp. 111–134). New York: Academic.

Coats, K. I., & Reynolds, W. M. (1985). *A comparison of cognitive-behavioral therapy and relaxation training for the treatment of depression in adolescents.* Unpublished manuscript.

Copeland, R., & Hall, R. V. (1976). Behavior modification in the classroom. In M. Hersen, R. M. Eisler, & P. M. Miller (Eds.), *Progress in behavior modification* (Vol. 3; pp. 45–78). New York: Academic.

Craighead, W. E., & Wilcoxin-Craighead, L. (1978). New directions in behavior modification with children. In M. Hersen, R. M. Eisler, & P. M. Miller (Eds.), *Progress in behavior modification* (Vol. 6; pp. 159–201). New York: Academic.

Cushing, P., Adams, A., & Rincover, A. (1983). Research on the education of autistic children. In M. Hersen, R. M. Eisler, & P. M. Miller (Eds.), *Progress in behavior modification* (Vol. 14; pp. 1–48). New York: Academic.

Doleys, D. M. (1978). Assessment and treatment and enuresis and encopresis in children. In M. Hersen, R. M. Eisler, & P. M. Miller (Eds.), *Progress in behavior modification* (Vol. 6; pp. 85–121). New York: Academic.

Edelbrock, C. Developmental considerations (1984). In T. H. Ollendick & M. Hersen (Eds.), *Child behavioral assessment: Principles and procedures* (pp. 20–37). New York: Pergamon.

Ellis, A. (1962). *Reason and emotion in psychotherapy.* New York: Lyle Stuart.

Epstein, L. H., Beck, S., Figueroa, J., Farkas, G., Kazdin, A. E., Daneman, D., & Becker, D. (1981). The effects of targeting improvements in urine glucose on metabolic control in children with insulin dependent diabetes. *Journal of Applied Behavior Analysis, 14,* 365–375.

Epstein, L. H., Koeske, R., Zidansek, J., & Wing, R. R. (1983). Effects of weight loss on fitness in obese children. *American Journal of Diseases of Children, 137,* 654–657.

Epstein, L. H., Wing, R. R., Kuller, L., & Becker, D. (1983). Parent-child obesity and cardiovascular risk factors. *Preventive Medicine, 12,* 437–446.

Ferster, C. B., & DeMyer, M. K. (1962). A method for the experimental analysis of the behavior of autistic children. *American Journal of Orthopsychiatry, 32,* 89–98.

Finney, J. W., & Christophersen, E. R. (1984). Behavioral pediatrics: Health education in pediatric primary care. In M. Hersen, R. M. Eisler, & P. M. Miller (Eds.), *Progress in behavior modification* (Vol. 16; pp. 185–229). New York: Academic.

Forehand, R. (1977). Child noncompliance to parental requests: Behavioral analysis and treatment. In M. Hersen, R. M. Eisler, & P. M. Miller (Eds.), *Progress in behavior modification* (Vol. 15; pp. 111–147). New York: Academic.

Forehand, R., & Baumeister, A. A. (1976). Deceleration of aberrant behavior among retarded individuals. In M. Hersen, R. M. Eisler, & P. M. Miller (Eds.), *Progress in behavior modification* (Vol. 2; pp. 223–278). New York: Academic.

Foxx, R. M., & Bechtel, D. R. (1983). Overcorrection. In M. Hersen, R. M. Eisler, & R. M. Miller (Eds.), *Progress in behavior modification* (Vol. 13; pp. 227–288). New York: Academic.

Foxx, R. M., Plaska, T. G., & Bittle, R. G. (in press). Guidelines for the use of contingent electric shock to treat aberrant behavior. In M. Hersen, R. M. Eisler, & P. M. Miller (Eds.), *Progress in behavior modification* (Vol. 20). New York: Academic.

Furman, W., & Drabman, R. S. (1981). Methodological issues in child behavior therapy. In M. Hersen, R. M. Eisler, & P. M. Miller (Eds.), *Progress in behavior modification* (Vol. 11; pp. 31–64). New York: Academic.

Gadow, K. D., Torgesen, J. K., Greenstein, J., & Schell, R. (1985). Learning disabilities. In M. Hersen (Ed.), *Pharmacological and behavioral treatment: An integrative approach* (pp. 149–177). New York: Wiley.

Gambrill, E. D. (1983). Behavioral intervention with child abuse and neglect. In M. Hersen, R. M., Eisler, & P. M. Miller (Eds.), *Progress in behavior modification* (Vol. 15: pp. 1–56). New York: Academic.

Goldstein, G. (1979). Methodological and theoretical issues in neuropsychological assessment. *Journal of Behavioral Assessment, 1,* 23–41.

Goodley, M. D., Lutzker, J. R., Lamazor, E. A., & Martin, J. A. (1984). Advances in behavioral approaches to adolescent health care. In M. Hersen, R. M. Eisler,

& P. M. Miller (Eds.), *Progress in behavior modification* (Vol. 18; pp. 227–265). New York: Academic.

Graziano, A. M. (1977). Parents as behavior therapists. In M. Hersen, R. M. Eisler, & P. M. Miller (Eds.), *Progress in behavior modification* (Vol. 4; pp. 251–298). New York: Academic.

Harris, S. L., & Ferrari, M. (1983). Developmental factors in child behavior therapy. *Behavior Therapy*, *14*, 54–72.

Hersen, M. (1981). Complex problems require complex solutions. *Behavior Therapy*, *12*, 15–29.

Hersen, M. (Ed.). (1985). *Pharmacological and behavioral treatment: An integrative approach*. New York: Wiley.

Hersen, M., Bellack, A. S., Himmelhoch, J. M., & Thase, M. E. (1984). Effects of social skill training, amitriptyline, and psychotherapy in unipolar depressed women. *Behavior Therapy*, *15*, 21–40.

Hersen, M., & Turner, S. M. (1984). DSM-III and behavior therapy. In S. M. Turner & M. Hersen (Eds.), *Adult psychopathology and diagnosis* (pp. 485–502). New York: Wiley.

Hersen, M., Van Hasselt, V. B., & Matson, J. L. (Eds.). (1983). *Behavior therapy for the developmentally and physically disabled*. New York: Academic.

Hickman, C. S., Thompson, K. L., Feldman, W. S., & Varni, J. W. (1985). Pediatric medical problems. In M. Hersen (Ed.), *Practice of inpatient behavior therapy* (pp. 267–282). New York: Grune & Stratton.

Hobbs, S. A., Beck, S. J., & Wansley, R. A. (1984). Pediatric behavioral medicine: Directions in treatment and prevention. In M. Hersen, R. M. Eisler, & P. M. Miller (Eds.), *Progress in behavior modification* (Vol. 16; pp. 1–29). New York: Academic.

Horton, A. M., & Miller, W. G. (1985). Neuropsychology and behavior therapy. In M. Hersen, R. M. Eisler, & P. M. Miller (Eds.), *Progress in behavior modification* (Vol. 19; pp. 1–55). New York: Academic.

Israel, A. C., & Stolmaker, L. (1980). Behavioral treatment of obesity in children and adolescents. In M. Hersen, R. M. Eisler, & P. M. Miller (Eds.), *Progress in behavior modification* (Vol. 10; pp. 81–109). New York: Academic.

Israel, A. C., Stolmaker, L., & Adrian, C. A. G. (1985). The effects of training parents in general child management skills on a behavioral weight loss program for children. *Behavior Therapy*, *16*, 169–180.

Jones, M. C. (1924a). The elimination of children's fears. *Journal of Experimental Psychology*, *7*, 382–390.

Jones, M. C. (1924b). A laboratory study of fear: The case of Peter. *Journal of Genetic Psychology*, *31*, 308–315.

Jones, R. T., Sisson, L. A., & Van Hasselt, V. B. (1984). Emergency fire-safety skills for blind children and adolescents: Group training and generalization. *Behavior Modification*, *8*, 267–286.

Kanfer, F. H., & Karoly, P. (1972). Self-control: A behavioristic excursion into the lion's den. *Behavior Therapy*, *3*, 389–416.

Karoly, P. (1977). Behavioral self-management in children: Concepts, methods, issues, and directions. In M. Hersen, R. M. Eisler, & P. M. Miller (Eds.), *Progress in behavior modification* (Vol. 5; pp. 197–262). New York: Academic.

Kashini, J. H., McGee, R. O., Clarkson, S. E., Anderson, J. C., Walton, L. A., Williams, S., Silva, P. A., Robins, A. J., Cytryn, L., & McKnew, D. H. (1983). Depression in a sample of 9-year-old children. *Archives of General Psychiatry, 40*, 1217–1223.

Katz, E. R., Varni, J. W., & Jay, S. M. (1984). Behavioral assessment and management of pediatric pain. In M. Hersen, R. M. Eisler, & P. M. Miller (Eds.), *Progress in behavior modification* (Vol. 18; pp. 163–193). New York: Academic.

Kazdin, A. E. (1977). Assessing the clinical and applied importance of behavior change through social validation. *Behavior Modification, 1*, 427–452.

Kazdin, A. E. (1978). *History of behavior modification.* Baltimore: University Park Press.

Kazdin, A. E. (1983). Psychiatric diagnosis, dimensions of dysfunction, and child behavior therapy. *Behavior Therapy, 14*, 73–99.

Kazdin, A. E., Moser, J., Colbus, D., & Bell, R. (1985). Depressive symptoms among physically abused and psychiatrically disturbed children. *Journal of Abnormal Psychology, 94*, 298–307.

Kelly, J. A. (1983). *Treating Child-abusive families: Intervention based on skills training principles.* New York: Plenum.

Kerr, M. M., & Lambert, D. L. (1983). Behavior modification of children's written language. In M. Hersen, R. M. Eisler, & P. M. Miller (Eds.), *Progress in behavior modification* (Vol.12: pp. 79–108). New York: Academic.

Klein, R. D. (1979). Modifying academic performance in the grade school classroom. In M. Hersen, R. M. Eisler, & P. M. Miller (Eds.), *Progress in behavior modification* (Vol. 8; pp. 293–321). New York: Academic.

Kovacs, M., Feinberg, T. L., Crouse-Novak, M., Paulauskas, S. L., Pollock, M., & Finkelstein, R. (1984). Depressive disorders in childhood: II. A longitudinal study of the risk for a subsequent major depression. *Archives of General Psychiatry, 41*, 643–649.

Lahey, B. B. (1976). Behavior modification with learning disabilities and related problems. In M. Hersen, R. M. Eisler, P. M. Miller (Eds.), *Progress in behavior modification* (Vol. 3; pp. 173–205). New York: Academic.

Lovaas, O. I. (1967). A behavior therapy approach to the treatment of childhood schizophrenia. In J. P. Hill (Ed.), *Minnesota symposium on child psychology.* Minneapolis: University of Minnesota Press.

Lutzker, J. R., & Lamazor, E. A. (1985). Behavioral pediatrics: Research, treatment, recommendations. In M. Hersen, R. M. Eisler, & P. M. Miller (Eds.), *Progress in behavior modification* (Vol. 19; pp. 217–253). New York: Academic.

Marholin, D., Luiselli, J. K., & Townsend, N. M. (1980). Overcorrection: An examination of its rationale and treatment effectiveness. In M. Hersen, R. M. Eisler, & P. M. Miller (Eds.), *Progress in behavior modification* (Vol. 9; pp. 49–80). New York: Academic.

Masek, B. J., Fentress, D. W., & Spirito, A. (1984). Behavioral treatment of symptoms of childhood illness. *Clinical Psychology Review, 4*, 561–570.

Meichenbaum, D. (1977). *Cognitive-behavior modification: An integrative approach.* New York: Plenum.

Melamed, B. G. (1979). Behavioral approaches to fear in dental settings. In M. Hersen, R. M. Eisler, P. M. Miller (Eds.), *Progress in behavior modification* (Vol. 7; pp. 171–203). New York: Academic.

Meyers, A. W., & Craighead, W. E. (Eds.). (1984). *Cognitive behavior therapy with children.* New York: Plenum.

Michelson, L., & Kazdin, A. E. (1984). *Prevention of antisocial behavior in children.* National Institute of Mental Health. Grant (MH 39642).

Michelson, L., & Wood, R. (1980). Behavioral assessment and training of children's social skills. In M. Hersen, R. M. Eisler, & P. M. Miller (Eds.), *Progress in behavior modification* (Vol. 9; pp. 241–292). New York: Academic.

Mowrer, O. H., & Mowrer, W. M. (1938). Enuresis—A method for its study and treatment. *American Journal of Orthopsychiatry, 8*, 436–459.

Nelson, R. O. (1980). The use of intelligence tests within behavioral assessment. *Behavioral Assessment, 2*, 417–423.

O'Dell, S. L. (1985). Progress in parent training. In M. Hersen, R. M. Eisler, & P. M. Miller (Eds.), *Progress in behavior modification* (Vol. 19; pp. 57–108). New York: Academic.

Ollendick, T. H. (1979). Fear reduction techniques with children. In M. Hersen, R. M. Eisler, & P. M. Miller (Eds.), *Progress in behavior modification* (Vol. 8; pp. 126–168). New York: Academic.

Ollendick, T. H., & Cerny, J. A. (1981). *Clinical behavior therapy with children.* New York: Plenum.

Ollendick, T. H., & Hersen M. (1984). An overview of child behavioral assessment. In T. H. Ollendick & M. Hersen (Eds.), *Child behavioral assessment: Principles and procedures.* New York: Pergamon.

Parker, L. H., & Cinciripini, P. M. (1984). Behavioral medicine with children: Applications in chronic disease. In M. Hersen, R. M. Eisler, & P. M. Miller (Eds.), *Progress in behavior modification* (Vol. 7; pp. 135–165). New York: Academic.

Pelham, W. E. & Murphy, H. A. (1985). Attention deficit and conduct disorders. In M. Hersen (Ed.), *Pharmacological and behavioral treatment: An integrative approach.* New York: Wiley.

Petti, T. A., & Kovacs, M., Feinberg, T., Paulauskas, S., & Finkelstein, R. (1982, October). *Cognitive therapy of a 12-year-old boy with atypical depression: A pilot study.* Paper presented at the Annual Meeting of the American Academy of Child Psychiatry. Washington, D.C.

Puig-Antich, J., & Gittelman R. (1982). Depression in childhood and adolescence. In E. S. Paykel (Ed.), *Handbook of affective disorders.* New York: Guilford.

Rapport, M. D. (1983). Attention deficit disorder with hyperactivity: Critical treatment parameters and their application in applied outcome research. In M. Hersen, R. M. Eisler, & P. M. Miller (Eds.), *Progress in behavior modification* (Vol. 14; pp. 219–298). New York: Academic.

Reynolds, W. M. (in press). Depression in childhood and adolescence: Diagnosis, assessment intervention strategies and research. In T. R. Kratochwill (Ed.), *Advances in school psychology* (Vol. 4.) Hillsdale, NJ: Erlbaum.

Rosenthal, T. L., & Bandura, A. (1978). Psychological modeling: Theory and practice. In S. L. Garfield & A. E. Bergin (Eds.), *Handbook of psychotherapy and behavior change* (2nd ed., pp. 621–658). New York: Wiley.

Rutter, M., & Hersov, L. (Eds). (1977). *Child Psychiatry*. London: Blackwell.

Schinke, S. P. (1984). Preventing teenage pregnancy. In M. Hersen, R. M. Eisler, & P. M. Miller (Eds.), *Progress in behavior modification* (Vol. 16; pp. 31–64). New York: Academic.

Schinke, S. P., Gilchrist, L. D., & Snow, W. H. (1985). Skills intervention to prevent cigarette smoking among adolescents. *American Journal of Public Health, 75,* 665–667.

Schinke, S. P., Schilling R. F., Barth, R. P., Gilchrist, L. D., & Maxwell, J. S. (in press). Stress-management intervention to prevent family violence. *Journal of Family Violence.*

Schroeder, S. R., Gualtieri, C. T., & Van Bourgondien, M. E. (1985). Autism. In M. Hersen (Ed.), *Pharmacological and behavioral treatment: An integrative approach.* New York: Wiley.

Schwartz, G., & Weiss, S. (1978). Behavioral medicine revisited: An amended definition. *Journal of Behavioral Medicine, 1,* 249–251.

Shapiro, E. S. (1981). Self-control procedures with the mentally retarded. In M. Hersen, R. M. Eisler, & P. M. Miller (Eds.), *Progress in behavior modification* (Vol. 12; pp. 265–297). New York: Academic.

Sisson, L. A., Van Hasselt, V. B., Hersen, M., & Strain, P. S. (1985). Increasing social skill behaviors in multi-handicapped children through peer intervention. *Behavior Modification, 9,* 293–321.

Skinner, B. F. (1953) *Science and human behavior.* New York: Free Press.

Spivack, G., & Shure, M. B. (1974). *Social adjustment of young children: A cognitive approach to solving real-life problems.* San Francisco: Jossey-Bass.

Spunt, A. L., Hermann, B. P., & Rousseau, A. M. (1985). Epilepsy. In M. Hersen (Ed.), *Pharmacological and behavioral treatment: An integrative approach* (pp. 178–196). New York: Wiley.

Strain, P. S., & Kerr, M. M. (1981). Modifying children's social withdrawal: Issues in assessment and clinical intervention. In M. Hersen, R. M. Eisler, & P. M. Miller (Eds.), *Progress in behavior modification* (Vol. 11; pp. 203–248). New York: Academic.

Straus, M. A., Gelles, R. J., & Steinmetz, S. K. (1979). *Behind closed doors: Violence in the American family.* Garden City, NY: Doubleday.

Taylor, C. B. (1983). DSM-III and behavioral assessment. *Behavioral Assessment, 5,* 5–14.

Van Hasselt, V. B. (1983). Visual impairment. In M. Hersen, V. B. Van Hasselt, & J. L. Matson (Eds.), *Behavior therapy for the developmentally and physically disabled* (pp. 109–189). New York: Academic.

Van Hasselt, V. B. (in press). Behavior therapy for visually handicapped persons. In

M. Hersen, R. M. Eisler, & P. M. Miller (Eds.), *Progress in behavior modification* (Vol. 20). New York: Academic.

Van Hasselt, V. B., & Hersen, M. (1981). Applications of single-case experimental designs to research with the visually impaired. *Journal of Visual Impairment and Blindness, 75*, 359–362.

Van Hasselt, V. B., Hersen, M., & Kazdin, A. E. (1985). Assessment of social skills in visually-handicapped adolescents. *Behaviour Research and Therapy 23*, 53–63.

Van Hasselt, V. B., Hersen M., Kazdin, A. E., Simon, J., & Mastantuono, A. K. (1983). Training blind adolescents in social skills. *Journal of Visual Impairment and Blindness, 77*, 199–203.

Van Hasselt, V. A., Hersen, M., Moore, L. E., & Simon, J. (in press). Assessment and treatment of families with visually handicapped children: A project description *Journal of Visual Impairment and Blindness*.

Van Hasselt, V. B., Kazdin, A. E., Hersen, M., Simon, J., & Mastantuono, A. K. (1985). A behavioral-analytic model for assessing social skills in blind adolescents. *Behaviour Research and Therapy, 23*, 395–405.

Wallander, J. L., & Conger, J. C. (1981). Assessment of hyperactive children: Psychometric, methodological, and practical considerations. In M. Hersen, R. M. Eisler, & P. M. Miller (Eds.), *Progress in behavior modification* (Vol. 11; pp. 249–291). New York: Academic.

Watson, J. B. (1924). *Behaviorism*. Chicago: University of Chicago Press.

Watson, J. B., & Rayner, R. (1920). Conditioned emotional reactions. *Journal of Experimental Psychology, 3*, 1–14.

Wells, K. C., & Copeland, B. (1985). Childhood and adolescent obesity: Progress in behavioral assessment and treatment. In M. Hersen, R. M. Eisler, & P. M. Miller (Eds.), *Progress in behavior modification* (Vol. 19; pp. 145–176). New York: Academic.

Williamson, D. A., Calpin, J. P., DiLorenzo, T. M., Garris, R. P., & Petti, T. A. (1981). Treating hyperactivity with dexedrine and activity feedback. *Behavior Modification, 5*, 399–416.

Wolfe, D. A. (1985). Child abusive parents: An empirical review and analysis. *Psychological Bulletin, 97*, 462–482.

Wolfe, D. A. , & Mosk, M. D. (1983). Behavioral comparisons of children from abusive and distressed families. *Journal of Consulting and Clinical Psychology, 51*, 702–708.

Wolfe, D. A., Sandler, J., & Kaufman, K. (1981). A competency-based parent training program for child abusers. *Journal of Consulting and Clinical Psychology, 49*, 633–640.

Zlutnick, S., Mayville, W. J., & Moffat, S. (1975). Modification of seizure disorders: The interruption of behavioral chains. *Journal of Applied Behavior Analysis, 8*, 1–12.

CHAPTER 2

Behavioral Assessment with Children and Adolescents

JOHN D. CONE

Having lagged behind the development of behavior therapy-modification-analysis for many years, behavioral assessment has recently established itself firmly as a discipline of scientific and practical value. In the middle and late 1970s numerous books on the subject began appearing (e.g., Barlow, 1980; Ciminero, Calhoun, & Adams, 1977; Cone & Hawkins, 1977; Hayes & Nelson, 1986; Haynes, 1978; Hersen & Bellack, 1976, 1981; Keefe, Kopel, & Gordon, 1978; Mash & Terdal, 1976; 1981; Ollendick & Hersen, 1984) and two journals, *Behavioral Assessment* and the *Journal of Behavioral Assessment* (now the *Journal of Psychopathology and Behavioral Assessment*) began publication, helping to establish behavioral assessment as a discipline in its own right. Testimony to the strength and importance of this general approach is the emergence of subdisciplines differentiated along the dimensions of age, e.g., child behavioral assessment (Mash & Terdal, 1981; Ollendick & Hersen, 1984) and adult behavioral assessment (Barlow, 1980); specific populations, such as severely developmentally delayed persons (Powers & Handleman, 1984); and specific settings, e.g., hospitals and clinics (Tryon, 1985).

However, the emergence of a robust and healthy discipline with comparably healthy offspring should not be interpreted to mean that researchers and clinicians agree on a corpus of principles, methods, and procedures of implementation. There is extensive pluralism in the field with respect to each of these variables. Within child behavioral assessment, for example, both operant and cognitive perspectives are strongly represented (Cone & Hoier, 1986; Mash & Terdal, 1981). There is diversity in methods with some researchers and clinicians preferring self-reports (e.g., Deluty, 1979), some relying heavily on parent report (e.g., Achenbach & Edelbrock, 1978), and some relying extensively on direct observation (e.g., Jones, Reid, & Patterson, 1975; Wahler, House, & Stambaugh, 1976).

There also is healthy diversity concerning the value of certain traditional concepts. For example, with regard to psychometric properties of assessment devices, some (Cone, 1977; Johnson & Bolstad, 1973; Mash & Terdal, 1981; Phillips, 1983) argue for their incorporation, while others (Barrett, Johnston, & Pennypacker, 1986; Cone, 1981; Cone & Hoier, 1986) argue for their selective incorporation, at best. The use of traditional diagnostic categories in organizing books on behavioral assessment is also controversial (Mash & Terdal, 1981). Other dimensions along which diversity exists include the value of idiographic versus nomothetic approaches to the development of an assessment science, the subject matter to be studied, whether inductive or deductive strategies should be pursued, and whether the discipline should rely primarily on variability within or between individuals in conducting its research (Cone, 1986).

Such diversity poses a dilemma for authors of child behavioral assessment chapters for books such as this one. Since this is a book about behavioral approaches to children's problems, and since the chapters are organized around traditional diagnostic groupings, one can expect contributors to direct some attention to assessment considerations specific to their problem area. Thus, it would be redundant to do the same in an introductory chapter such as this. Moreover, despite well-articulated arguments for the specificity of assessment techniques to problem areas (e.g., Mash & Terdal, 1981), a counterargument can be made for the *general* applicability of assessment concepts and methods.

For these reasons the present focus will be on the consideration of basic conceptual and methodological issues. The aim will be to provide readers with a verbal repertoire that can be applied consistently across the various diagnostic categories of child and adolescent problems that follow in this book. It is hoped that a consideration of fundamental concepts and organizational schema will also help readers to approach their own research and applied uses of assessment more effectively.

ORGANIZING THE ASSESSMENT PROCESS

Assessment Content

Regardless of problem area, it is helpful to organize the behavior characterizing a problem into different content areas. Within the behavior therapy-modification-analysis literature it is common to consider responses in three categories: cognitive (subjective), motor, and physiological (Hersen & Barlow, 1976; Lang, 1971). Because of research showing the relative independence of these three systems or content areas, it has been contended that comprehensive assessment must target all three (Lang, 1971). That is, one cannot infer that a child's subjective reactions to a given situation will parallel his or her motor or physiological reactions with any consistency.

For example, in assessing a child's fears and anxieties, it is customary to obtain data about subjective reactions to certain situations using self-report measures, such as fear survey schedules (Ollendick, in press; Scherer & Nakamura, 1968). More general self-report measures are also used, such as the Children's Manifest Anxiety Scale (Casteneda, McCandless, & Palermo, 1956). Information about the child's motor behavior or overt behavioral reactions in specific situations is commonly obtained via direct observation using behavioral avoidance tests (BATs). A typical BAT (e.g., Bandura, Grusec, & Menlove, 1967) requires the child to make successively closer approaches to a feared stimulus. The resulting score reflects the degree of proximity achieved. Motor behavior of fearful children has also been assessed using ratings by others (e.g., Melamed & Siegel, 1975; Sarason, Davidson, Lighthall, Waite, & Ruebush, 1960). Information concerning the child's physiological reactions in specific situations would most likely be obtained through direct observation of autonomic nervous system reactivity assisted by appropriate sensors, transducers, and amplifiers. For example, heart rate has been monitored in children who are needle phobic (Shapiro, 1975) or dental phobic (Melamed, Yurcheson, Fleece, Hutcherson, & Hawes, 1978).

Thus, the careful clinician will attend to a broad range of child behavior to clarify the "meaning" of fear or anxiety in a particular situation. It is helpful to attend to behavior in each of the three major content areas. Organizing one's approach to assessment in this way helps assure some degree of comprehensiveness. It should be noted that the empirical basis for considering subjective, motor, and physiological behavior separately has been questioned (Cone, 1979a; Barrios, Hartmann, & Shigetomi, 1981). That is because the lack of correspondence between measures of cognitive, motor, and physiological responding has often confounded content area and method of assessment. Consequently, motor behavior assessed through direct observation has been compared with cognitive behavior assessed via self-report. Since both method and content area have been allowed to vary, failure to find a relationship might be the result of content area differences, method differences, or both.

The Assessment Funnel

Inadequate empirical bases notwithstanding, the child behavioral assessor would still do well to sort potential targets of assessment into three content areas such as these. Once that has been done, the task of narrowing the assessment focus within each area can begin. This should result in the determination of specific pinpoints for intervention. Systematically narrowing the range of content can be conceptualized in terms of a funnel (Cone & Hawkins, 1977; Hawkins, 1979). At the top, or mouth, of the funnel are a broad range of subjective, motor, or physiological responses to be surveyed. Salient classes or groups of responses are selected, and those of less clinical relevance to the particular case are rejected. The process continues until a few behavioral pinpoints remain. By the time the neck of the funnel has been reached, specific intervention targets have been ascertained. When the appropriate intervention tactic has been chosen, its effectiveness is monitored by repeatedly noting changes in the targeted behavior over time. This monitoring process is represented as progress through the neck of the funnel.

Assessment Methods

In the course of moving from the mouth of the funnel to its neck, a variety of different assessment methods will typically be employed. At the outset the clinician will use rather broad-band, low-fidelity approaches, such as interviews and self-reports. These strategies are efficient and inexpensive ways of covering considerable behavioral territory in a short time. When working with children, parents and/or teachers are interviewed as well as the child. After certain problem areas have been identified at this initial survey or screening stage, they are subjected to further analysis and clarification using more focused methods such as ratings by others on checklists or scales. For example, parents of an 8-year old boy recently seen by the author initially complained that he "doesn't take care of himself or his things." Upon elaboration during the initial interview it was determined that taking care of himself and his things meant keeping his hair combed, teeth brushed, and toys in the appropriate storage location when not being used. The parents wanted the child to do these things on his own. However, they were especially upset at his refusal to do them when reminded. Through use of the *Eyberg Child Behavior Inventory* (*ECBI:* Eyberg & Ross, 1978) the assessment focus was further narrowed and it was determined that the parents' major concerns had to do with the boy's complying with their requests. Since there was reasonable agreement between mother's and father's *ECBI*s, both in terms of overall number of problems identified (81%) and the content of specific items, it was possible to shift to a narrower-band, higher-fidelity method of assessment. Direct observation of requests complied with by the child was chosen. First, the author observed each parent in free play and command play interactions (Forehand & McMahon, 1981) with the child. Second, parents collected data on requests complied with each day and brought these to weekly intervention sessions. After baseline rates of compliance were established, intervention was begun. Parents' direct observation of requests that the child complied with each day continued to be used to monitor treatment effectiveness.

Behavioral Assessment Grid

In the discussion thus far, two heretofore separately considered organizational concepts, the Behavioral Assessment Grid (BAG, Cone, 1978) and the funnel analogy (Cone & Hawkins, 1977; Hawkins, 1979), have been suggested. The

BAG is a three-dimensional organizational scheme that crosses content area, method of assessment, and universe of generalizability. The face of the BAG includes three content areas and eight methods of assessment. Methods are divided into indirect and direct categories. The former includes interview, self-report, rating-by-other; the latter includes self-observation, observations by others in analogue situations with role play ("as if") instructions, analogue situations with instructions to behave normally, natural situations with role play instructions, and natural situations with instructions to behave normally. Methods are ordered from top to bottom along a directness (indirect to direct) continuum that parallels the bandwidth fidelity (broad band, low fidelity to narrow band, high fidelity) continuum on the one hand, and the assessment funnel (mouth to neck) on the other. Within the overall process of narrowing the assessment focus, more and more direct methods are employed. At the same time, these approaches become more restricted in focus and produce more veridical assessment information.

By considering the dimensions of content area and assessment method simultaneously, the BAG makes clear the theoretical possibility that each type of content is assessable in at least eight different ways. Of course, subjective or cognitive content is not directly observable by others. Consequently, it cannot be evaluated using rating-by-other and direct observation-by-other methods.

Generalizability of Assessment Methods

As the assessment proceeds through the funnel, not only do classes of assessment methods vary but specific exemplars within classes vary as well. In assessing motor behavior in the presence of feared objects, for example, the clinician might use passive or active forms of behavioral avoidance tests. That is, one might approach stationary children with a snake and observe their reaction. This is a passive form of BAT utilized by Murphy and Bootzin (1973). Alternatively, one might require children to engage in progressively more intimate interaction with snakes, the more active form of BAT (Murphy & Bootzin, 1973). In observing a child's responses to parent requests, the assessor might use Forehand and McMahon's (1981) observational system, Mash, Terdal, and Anderson's (1973) Response Class Matrix, or one of numerous other direct observation systems.

The specific exemplar of each assessment method to be chosen while moving through the funnel will depend on several factors. Among them are ease of use, availability, acceptability to the assessor and client, and reliability and validity of the instrument. With respect to the last, the assessor will want to know whether scores on the device can be generalized in certain ways. That is, are they invariant across different assessors, across time, setting, and so on? For example, consider a direct observation measure of marital interaction that has been shown to produce comparable information from observations conducted in the office and in the home. Clinicians working with marital couples are more likely to select such a measure than one that has not been shown to have acceptable generalizability.

Variation in scores with changes in major aspects of the assessment process is represented by the third dimension of the BAG (i.e., universes of generalizability). It was originally proposed that extant behavioral assessment instruments could be collected and categorized according to content, method, and type of generalizability. Though the inclusion of the third dimension was interpreted by some (e.g., Nelson, Hay, & Hay, 1977) as suggesting that all instruments should possess all forms of generalizability, this was not the intention. By including universe of generalizability in the taxonomy, users could merely be directed toward those devices possessing the types of generalizability required for his or her own particular application.

Thus, the Behavioral Assessment Grid provides a potentially useful tool for clinical assessors. It can clarify and organize the behavior content to be assessed, suggest a sequence of progressively more specific methods to use in reaching intervention targets, and allow data-based choices among assessment instruments when more than one is available for the same purpose.

When the assessment enterprise is conceptualized in this way, it becomes apparent that different methods are needed at different points in the narrowing process. It follows that different specific instruments are also required. Consequently, it is unrealistic to expect a particular strategy (e.g., direct observation, self-report) to serve all required assessment functions. A specific exemplar of a particular method cannot serve all functions either. For example, the *Beck Depression Inventory for Children* (Kovacs, 1978) might serve very well as a relatively broad-band, low-fidelity, indirect instrument for initial mapping of the depressive repertoire. However, it would be unsuited to the task of pinpointing ultimate intervention targets. For that purpose, a system of self-observation or direct observation by others would be more appropriate. Failure to recognize the proper place of specific instruments in the assessment armamentarium can lead to criticizing such devices when they fail to perform a particular function (e.g., Costello, 1981). The fact that they were never intended (or should never have been used) for that purpose is often overlooked. This is due, in part, to the failure to appreciate the multilevel requirements of comprehensive assessment. Also, proponents of new devices often fail to identify clearly the purpose(s) for which they are intended.

When the funnel analogy or general-to-specific narrowing model is appreciated, it becomes apparent that adequate assessment of an individual child or adolescent requires the use of multiple measures. However, a return to the old "battery of tests" strategy with its associated "kitchen sink" flavor is not being recommended. Rather, a careful selection of instruments designed to reflect behavior at general and progressively more specific levels within each of the major content areas is suggested. Ideally, such a collection of instruments would be designed to interface with one another so that information obtained at each level would lead logically to the next. Unfortunately, the present state of assessment technology does not lend itself easily to the production of such integrated systems. This is because indirect methods, such as structured interviews and self-reports, have been produced by one researcher with one view of the phenomenon under study. More direct methods (e.g., role plays in analog settings) have been developed by other investigators with different views of the phenomenon. Aggregating these measures to produce comprehensive, multilevel assessment results in a collection of ill-fitting instruments rather than a smoothly integrated system. Much interpretive effort must be expended by the assessor to move from one level of information to the next with these collections. A good illustration of some of these difficulties is provided in Costello's (1981) discussion of methods for assessing depression.

ASSESSING ADAPTIVE BEHAVIOR USING AN INTEGRATED SYSTEM

The assessment of adaptive behavior in developmentally disabled children provides an arena in which at least some effort has been directed toward producing a multilevel system of integrated procedures. It is not too difficult to imagine the applicability of the general model to other populations and problem areas as well.

The work to be described comes from developing a comprehensive set of procedures leading from initial assessment to the identification of precise intervention targets and specific ways of intervening to teach the targeted behavior. The West Virginia System (Cone, 1982) is a compilation of assessment, intervention, and program monitoring procedures designed to facilitate comprehensive programming for developmentally delayed children. As such, it provides for assessment of adaptive behavior at multiple levels of specificity using methods varying in bandwidth and fidelity.

After initial clinical interviews and broadband assessment to determine program eligibility (i.e., establish a diagnosis of developmental disability), parents or others who know the child well are asked about the presence of an extensive repertoire of adaptive behavior in 20 areas. This interview is structured around the administration of *The Pyramid Scales* (Cone, 1984), a set of 568 specifically worded items covering such categories as auditory, visual, and tactile responsiveness; gross motor and fine motor skills; and behavior related to eating, dressing, language, social interaction, reading, vocational skills, money, and time. A profile of functioning across the 20 areas is produced. Analysis of the profile can lead to the identification of relative strengths and weaknesses, as well as problem areas that can be singled out for further assessment.

The Pyramid Scales are intended to serve the general mapping function necessary in the early stages of any comprehensive assessment process. The task at this stage is to rule in or out certain general areas of functioning important to all healthy individuals. By using a broad-band checklist such as *The Pyramid Scales,* the assessor's attention is directed to each area in turn, with the result that significant information is unlikely to be overlooked. A similar checklist with relatively normal adolescents might include many of the same areas (e.g., social interaction, vocational skills, academic performance, participation in recreation and leisure activities).

Again, the purpose of assessment at this stage is to identify *general areas* of adequate or inadequate functioning. For this purpose it is sufficient to rely on indirect assessment via interview, self-report, or ratings by others. With children it is especially likely that parents will be asked for information in interviews or ratings. When general problem areas are identified through profile analysis, a narrower band, higher fidelity procedure can be used to isolate specific behaviors within the problem area for eventual intervention. In developing and using integrated assessment systems, it is essential that each level of specificity be dealt with by methods designed and related in such a way that information from one level leads logically to the next.

In the West Virginia System, identification of a general problem area is followed by further analysis to narrow the focus within that area. This is initially accomplished by examining the responses to individual items in the scale tapping the problem area. If, for example, gross motor skills have been found to be deficient, the pattern of responses to items on the gross motor scale is examined. Since items are organized in an empirically determined hierarchy from easy to more difficult, it is customary to find a pattern of early passes followed by a mix of passes and failures followed by consistent failures. An example of such a pattern is provided in Figure 2.1. Each of the eight items

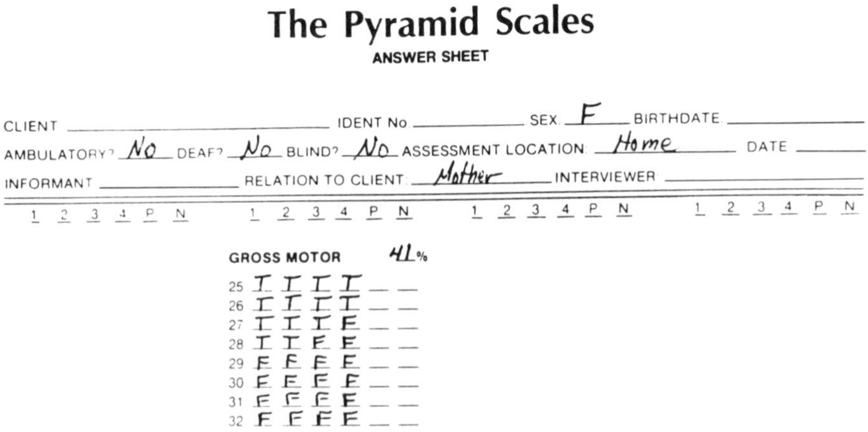

The Pyramid Scales
ANSWER SHEET

CLIENT _____ IDENT No _____ SEX _F_ BIRTHDATE _____

AMBULATORY? _No_ DEAF? _No_ BLIND? _No_ ASSESSMENT LOCATION _Home_ DATE _____

INFORMANT _____ RELATION TO CLIENT _Mother_ INTERVIEWER _____

1 2 3 4 P N	1 2 3 4 P N	1 2 3 4 P N	1 2 3 4 P N

GROSS MOTOR _41_%

25 I I I I _ _
26 I I I I _ _
27 I I I F _ _
28 I I F F _ _
29 F F F F _ _
30 F F F F _ _
31 F F F F _ _
32 F F F F _ _

Figure 2.1. An example of responses to items on the gross motor scale of *The Pyramid Scales.*

(Numbers 25–32) in the gross motor scale has four subitems calling for a response of "true," "false," "physiologically incapable," or "no opportunity to observe." Actual items from the gross motor scale are presented in Figure 2.2. By examining the pattern of responses in Figure 2.1 and referring to item content in Figure 2.2, it can be seen that this particular child turns and rolls

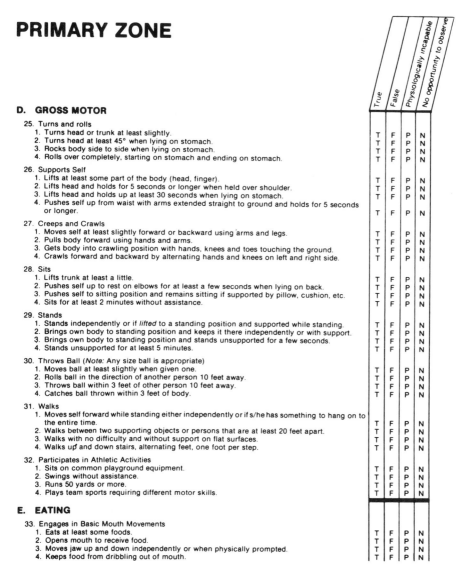

PRIMARY ZONE

D. GROSS MOTOR

	True	False	Physiologically incapable	No opportunity to observe
25. Turns and rolls				
1. Turns head or trunk at least slightly.	T	F	P	N
2. Turns head at least 45° when lying on stomach.	T	F	P	N
3. Rocks body side to side when lying on stomach.	T	F	P	N
4. Rolls over completely, starting on stomach and ending on stomach.	T	F	P	N
26. Supports Self				
1. Lifts at least some part of the body (head, finger).	T	F	P	N
2. Lifts head and holds for 5 seconds or longer when held over shoulder.	T	F	P	N
3. Lifts head and holds up at least 30 seconds when lying on stomach.	T	F	P	N
4. Pushes self up from waist with arms extended straight to ground and holds for 5 seconds or longer.	T	F	P	N
27. Creeps and Crawls				
1. Moves self at least slightly forward or backward using arms and legs.	T	F	P	N
2. Pulls body forward using hands and arms.	T	F	P	N
3. Gets body into crawling position with hands, knees and toes touching the ground.	T	F	P	N
4. Crawls forward and backward by alternating hands and knees on left and right side.	T	F	P	N
28. Sits				
1. Lifts trunk at least a little.	T	F	P	N
2. Pushes self up to rest on elbows for at least a few seconds when lying on back.	T	F	P	N
3. Pushes self to sitting position and remains sitting if supported by pillow, cushion, etc.	T	F	P	N
4. Sits for at least 2 minutes without assistance.	T	F	P	N
29. Stands				
1. Stands independently or if *lifted* to a standing position and supported while standing.	T	F	P	N
2. Brings own body to standing position and keeps it there independently or with support.	T	F	P	N
3. Brings own body to standing position and stands unsupported for a few seconds.	T	F	P	N
4. Stands unsupported for at least 5 minutes.	T	F	P	N
30. Throws Ball (*Note:* Any size ball is appropriate)				
1. Moves ball at least slightly when given one.	T	F	P	N
2. Rolls ball in the direction of another person 10 feet away.	T	F	P	N
3. Throws ball within 3 feet of other person 10 feet away.	T	F	P	N
4. Catches ball thrown within 3 feet of body.	T	F	P	N
31. Walks				
1. Moves self forward while standing either independently or if s/he has something to hang on to the entire time.	T	F	P	N
2. Walks between two supporting objects or persons that are at least 20 feet apart.	T	F	P	N
3. Walks with no difficulty and without support on flat surfaces.	T	F	P	N
4. Walks up and down stairs, alternating feet, one foot per step.	T	F	P	N
32. Participates in Athletic Activities				
1. Sits on common playground equipment.	T	F	P	N
2. Swings without assistance.	T	F	P	N
3. Runs 50 yards or more.	T	F	P	N
4. Plays team sports requiring different motor skills.	T	F	P	N
E. EATING				
33. Engages in Basic Mouth Movements				
1. Eats at least some foods.	T	F	P	N
2. Opens mouth to receive food.	T	F	P	N
3. Moves jaw up and down independently or when physically prompted.	T	F	P	N
4. Keeps food from dribbling out of mouth.	T	F	P	N

Figure 2.2. Items from the gross motor scale of *The Pyramid Scales.*

over completely, has good head control, and crawls forward and backward. Further, the child performs some of the subskills involved in sitting (Item 28, Subitems 1 and 2) but does not yet sit without assistance. It would appear, therefore, that an appropriate starting point for intervention would involve instruction in sitting. Recall, however, that this conclusion is based on indirect assessment using interviews and ratings by others. Before initiating intervention the clinician must be certain that the information provided is accurate. Would a parent's description of individual child behaviors agree with a trained observer's? Considerable research indicates that it would not (e.g., Eyberg & Johnson, 1974; Lapouse & Monk, 1958; Schnelle, 1974; Yarrow, Campbell, & Burton, 1970).

Such lack of agreement between assessment methods is not surprising given the differences in scope and accuracy for the methods individually. It is unrealistic to expect agreement at the level of individual responses between broadband, low-fidelity measures and narrow-band, high-fidelity ones. There is no doubt that agreement could eventually be produced between them if enough time and research energy were to be devoted to the issue. The solution would probably involve making the two methods more alike, such that parents were converted to trained observers, or trained observers of specific behaviors were turned into raters of general behavior classes.

Critics of the lack of correspondence between methods at the level of individual responses fail to appreciate the different purposes served by assessment methods at various points along the directness continuum of the BAG. Broadband, low-fidelity indirect methods serve the all-important mapping function, and do so relatively economically. Narrowband, high-fidelity direct methods serve a pinpointing or targeting function, and do so relatively expensively. Because their purposes are dissimilar, they can be held to different standards of accuracy. For example, it is enough to know that parents' reports of their children's gross motor skills produce *scale* scores that agree with the *scale* scores produced by trained observers who watch the children and score the presence or absence of each behavior in Figure 2.2 (Cone, 1984). That they do not produce *individual item* scores that agree is not surprising and not to be expected. After all, we have not trained them to be skilled observers at that level of precision, nor would we ever undertake the expense of doing so. We need them as general mappers and as informants to provide information cheaply that can funnel us to specific sets of behavior to assess more precisely with direct observation procedures.

Knowing from parent reports that our client child is having problems in the gross motor area and, more specifically, in sitting, allows us to proceed to the next level in our assessment system and probe more specifically. In the West Virginia System, *The Pyramid Scales* are the entry point to an assessment system that includes over 5,000 items. Once an area (e.g., gross motor) and a subarea (e.g., sitting) are identified through interviews and ratings by others, the specific skills within that subarea are assessed through direct observation. Written procedures instruct the assessor in exactly how each of the specific skills is to be observed. The observer starts with the first skill in the particular subarea (e.g., sitting) and assesses each skill in turn, stopping when it becomes clear that the limits of the child's performance have been reached. The last skill demonstrated is identified as the child's present level of functioning (with respect to sitting). The first skill not demonstrated (or failed) becomes the specific intervention pinpoint or target.

Note that through the careful interdigitation of different methods of assessment representing different levels of information specificity, an integrated system of assessment procedures has been developed. While the example provided here deals with adaptive behavior of developmentally disabled children, the model would seem to have general applicability. It certainly works reasonably well for each of the 20 areas of functioning covered by *The Pyramid Scales,* some of which (e.g., social interaction) are remarkably comparable to areas dealt with every day by practicing behavioral clinicians.

The suggestion that we develop integrated systems of carefully interfaced assessment methods is consonant with the notion of higher-order assessment procedures discussed by Paul (1979), Fiske (1979), and others (Mariotto, 1979; Power, 1979; Redfield, 1979). As Fiske (1979) has observed, when working on societal problems, researchers are dealing with behavior people *judge* as good, bad, and so on. Thus, the task is to obtain low-inference, direct observation data in as objective a fashion as possible, without sacrificing the evaluative component. A danger with narrowband, highly objective direct observation assessment is that it can be limited to very specific responses that are devoid of clinical or societal import (Kazdin, 1985). Paul (1979) and his colleagues appear to have achieved the objectivity of the highly specific direct observation approach while preserving the social significance of the assessment process. They have accomplished this largely through construction of higher-order measures consisting of directly observed, discrete responses. Direct observation data are aggregated using "replicate rules" (Mariotto, 1979) or computer summaries. For example, in the *Time Sample Behavioral Checklist* (TSBC: Paul, in press), direct observation counts of individual occurrences of screaming, swearing, verbal intrusion, destroying property, injuring self, and physical intrusion are aggregated by computer summarization into a global index labeled "hostile-belligerence" (Power, 1979). Such higher-order scores have been found to correlate "on absolute levels in the .60's and .70's with standardized ward rating scales" (Power, 1979, p. 206).

It appears that Paul and his colleagues have succeeded in isolating specific client behaviors that control the evaluative behavior of clinical assessors. This is only one step removed from the ultimate aim of the entire assessment process, which is to isolate specific client behaviors controlling the judgments of the client and/or significant others. While it might seem that Paul and his colleagues have produced their higher-order categories strictly on an inductive basis, the molecular responses participating in the computer summaries (of at least the TSBC) were originally derived from existing assessment devices and patient descriptions provided in textbooks and diagnostic manuals in much the same way as items for *The Pyramid Scales* (Cone, 1984) were developed. It would be interesting to trace their ancestry further. The point, however, is that assessment systems show objective, replicable trails between broadband, low-fidelity, socially significant instruments at the mouth of the assessment funnel, and narrowband, high-fidelity instruments at its neck. If they do, there is some likelihood of preserving the societal significance referred to by Fiske (1979) and avoiding the targeting of behaviors for intervention that have little or nothing to do with the client's presenting complaints (Kazdin, 1985).

SELECTING TARGET BEHAVIORS

The development and application of integrated, multilevel assessment systems can facilitate target behavior selection. Examples in the preceding section showed that once areas of general functioning had been identified, the logical progression through a series of narrower-band, higher-fidelity methods could lead to specific intervention pinpoints. Initial determination of the general functioning area was not discussed, however. How does one decide that gross motor skills should be a training priority? How does one establish the relative priority among areas when several seem to require intervention?

One answer to these questions can be found in recent attempts to design interactionist approaches to assessment in psychology generally (e.g., Bem, 1982; Bem & Funder, 1978; Bem & Lord, 1979, Lord,1982). In an early paper, Bem and Funder (1978) reasoned that one of the difficulties in making accurate predictions about behavior from one setting to another is the lack of a common vocabulary for describing persons on the one hand and settings on the other. They suggested that descriptions of settings could be produced in terms of the behavior of idealized performers in the settings; that is, rather than describe the setting in terms of its physical characteristics or in terms of theoretical notions of behavior appropriate in it, observe the behavior of exemplary performers and describe the setting as one in which a person who behaves comparably is likely to be judged effective. The behaviors of exemplary performers in the setting can then be collected into a template against which to match the behavior of clients or other persons whose adjustment in that setting is being predicted.

Behavioral Profiles of Less Restrictive Environments

When judgments of other people are a critical aspect of the definition of a person's adjustment in certain settings (as is true for children and adolescents), those other people can be used to produce templates. Consider the issue of moving persons out of large residential facilities and into smaller living arrangements nearer their home community. Group homes, specialized care homes, and supervised apartments are just some of the examples of community living alternatives that might be used. For the most successful placement of clients, it would be important to select living arrangements where behavioral requirements matched the behavioral repertoire of the client. One way to develop a template or behavioral profile for community living alternatives would be to interview persons staffing them and use that information to construct templates.

In a pilot study investigating the feasibility of such an approach (Cone, Bourland, & Wood-Shuman, 1983), behavioral profiles for 15 group homes in West Virginia were developed using *The Pyramid Scales* (Cone, 1984) and Part II of the *Adaptive Behavior Scale* (Nihara, Foster, Shellhaas, & Leland, 1974). The first measure allowed an estimate of the minimum level of adaptive behavior needed to function effectively in the homes. The second provided an estimate of the maximum maladaptive behavior tolerated. Assessment consisted of interviewing key staff at each home and completing the assessment devices on the basis of their responses to each individual item. Subsequent scoring of answer sheets produced profiles of the minimum adaptive behavior required and the maximum maladaptive behavior tolerated at each home.

As might be expected, behavior profiles varied considerably across the 15 homes surveyed. Figure 2.3 presents profiles of adaptive behavior for the most demanding (Group Home Z) and least demanding (Group Home X) homes in the sample. Figure 2.4 presents profiles of maladaptive behavior for the most tolerant (Group X) and least tolerant (Group Home Y) of the homes.

The behavioral descriptions (or templates) of each of the homes were made available to institutional staff responsible for placement decisions. By comparing client profiles with the group home profiles, the home with the profiles closest to those of the client could be selected. In cases where the client's adaptive behavior in all 20 areas was clearly above the minimum levels required and his or her maladaptive behavior was below the maximum levels tolerated, a "fit" was defined. More commonly, there were a few points of discrepancy. The profiles in Figure 2.5 (on page 44) illustrate such a case. It can be seen that the client's adaptive behavior is clearly above minimum levels in 14 of the 20 areas. However, his dressing, washing-grooming, receptive and expressive language, recreation-leisure, and vocational skills are very close to or below minimum levels. Of these, two areas (dressing and washing-grooming) are clearly discrepant with the group home's requirements. These two areas would thus be targeted for immediate intervention. Specific behaviors requiring change could be determined from an item-by-item comparison and assessment using the direct observation methods of the West Virginia System described earlier.

Producing descriptions of available residential settings in the same termi-

The Pyramid Scales
PROFILE SHEET

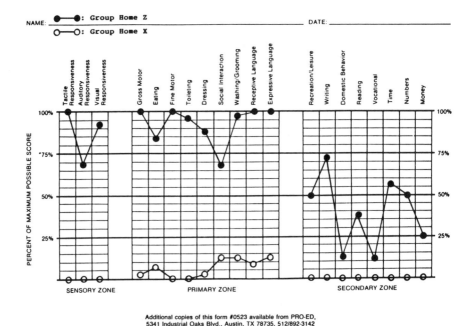

NAME: ●──●: Group Home Z   DATE: _____
      ○──○: Group Home X

Additional copies of this form #0523 available from PRO-ED,
5341 Industrial Oaks Blvd., Austin, TX 78735, 512/892-3142

Figure 2.3. Adaptive behavior profiles for the most demanding (Group Home Z) and least demanding (Group Home X) homes in the sample.

nology used to describe clients permits an interactionist approach to assessment and placement. Moreover, comparisons of client and setting profiles allow an empirical basis for target area selection. Finally, the use of the narrowband, high-fidelity, direct observation methods of the assessment system permits pinpointing specific behavior for immediate intervention.

Template Matching to Assess Social Skills

The general strategy being recommended here is not limited to developmentally disabled persons. This is illustrated in recent work by Hoier (1984) that focused on social skills in third- and fourth-grade elementary schoolchildren. Concerned with the general area of peer relations, Hoier adapted a template matching approach that had been recommended for assessment of adult social skills (Cone, 1979b, 1980). Briefly, Hoier's approach involves the production of templates of behavior of exemplary playmates, a description of the client child, and the selection of target behaviors on the basis of matching or comparing the client's description against the templates.

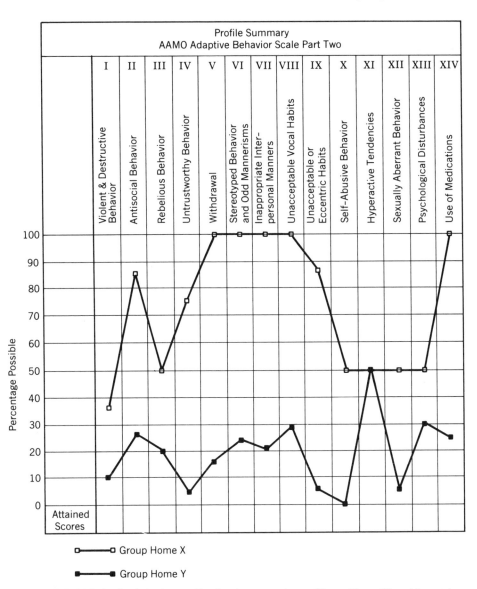

Figure 2.4. Maladaptive behavior profiles for the most tolerant (Group Home X) and least tolerant (Group Home Y) homes in the sample.

Templates are produced by having the client child indicate several peers with whom he or she would like to play. Descriptions by those peers (referred to as desired playmates) of children with whom they actually do play are then obtained. Behaviors used repeatedly by the desired playmates to describe their

The Pyramid Scales
PROFILE SHEET

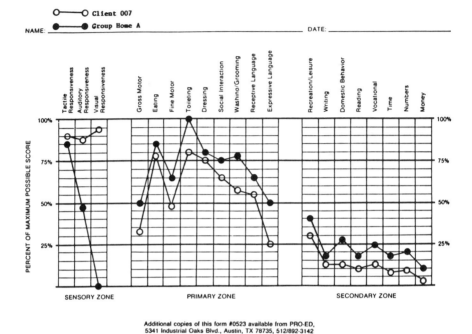

Figure 2.5. Comparison of a client's behavioral repertoire with the adaptive behavior required by the closest fitting group home.

friends are collected into templates. Descriptions of the client child on the same behaviors are compared against the template, and discrepancies become targets for intervention. In an experimental validation of the procedure Hoier (1984) found that when children's template behaviors were increased during intervention, other children interacted with them more than they had during the baseline phase. More complete descriptions of the procedures are provided by Hoier (1984) and Cone and Hoier (1986).

The process of determining relevant intervention pinpoints through template matching procedures is again illustrative of the value of an integrated system of assessment methods. In determining exactly what interpersonal behaviors are important in a given child, an assessment is made of the social context most relevant to that child. This is done using broadband, low-fidelity interview and rating methods in which desired playmates are asked to sort a large number of descriptive statements into "like my friend"–"not like my friend" categories. The "like my friend" descriptions are subsequently sorted into "very much like my friend"–"a little like my friend" categories. The process is continued until a small number of behaviors remains. These behaviors are then operationalized, and a direct observation system is developed for assessing their specific frequencies. Intervention decisions can then be based on these higher-fidelity, direct observation data. In addition, the direct observation system can be used to monitor intervention effectiveness. Hoier (1984) has provided data showing that individual children can produce templates quite reliably. Future work will explore the usefulness of template matching with other types of behavior and compare the relative efficacy of the approach with the more nomothetic strategies typical of child assessment generally.

SUMMARY

Throughout this chapter the focus has been on the *process* of assessment rather than the content of the specific assessment methods and instruments encountered in work with children and adolescents. A general model of assessment with applicability across the broad range of client problems has been described. Details of assessing specific behavioral complaints will be presented in other chapters that focus on particular problem areas.

It has been argued that efficient assessment progresses from general to specific information gathering using a variety of methodologies along the way. Starting with broadband, low-fidelity methods such as interviews and self-reports, the process eventuates in the utilization of narrowband, high-fidelity methods such as direct observation. General areas of behavioral dysfunction are defined by broadband techniques, while specific behaviors to be modified are defined by narrowband techniques.

Given that assessment is a multilevel phenomenon requiring use of different types of methods at each level to produce different types of information, it is important to identify the kind of information needed and to select the method best designed to provide it. It is unlikely that any given instrument will serve effectively at multiple levels. Moreover, it is inappropriate to criticize instruments for failing to do so. At the present time one must identify the type of information required at each level and select the instrument most likely to provide it. This can result in a rather disconnected set of measures that do not lead readily to an organized picture of the person being assessed.

What is needed is the development of assessment *systems* containing a set of carefully interrelated measures. These should range from broadband, low-fidelity methods employed in the early inquiry and general mapping stage to narrowband, high-fidelity methods used to identify specific intervention targets. Information produced at each level of such assessment systems will lead logically to the next. The development of higher-order assessment systems by Paul (1979) and the procedures used to assess adaptive behavior in the West

Virginia System by Cone (1982) are promising examples of what is needed. As the reader explores the problem-specific chapters elsewhere in this book, it might be instructive to apply the concepts described here. In this way perhaps we can depart from the single-purpose, single-methodology bandwagon and begin taking more systematic and comprehensive approaches to the assessment problems confronting us.

REFERENCES

Achenbach, T. M., & Edelbrock, C. S. (1978). The classification of child psychopathology: A review and analysis of empirical efforts. *Psychological Bulletin, 85,* 1275-1301.

Bandura, A., Grusec, E., & Menlove, F. L. (1967). Vicarious extinction of avoidance behavior. *Journal of Personality and Social Psychology, 5,* 16-23.

Barlow, D. H. (1980). *Behavioral assessment of adult disorders.* New York: Guilford.

Barrett, B. H., Johnston, J. M., & Pennypacker, H. S. (1986). Behavior: Its units, dimensions, and measurement. In S. C. Hayes & R. O. Nelson (Eds.), *The conceptual foundations of behavioral assessment.* New York: Guilford.

Barrios, B. A., Hartmann, D. P., & Shigetomi, C. (1981). Fears and anxieties in children. In E. J. Mash & L. G. Terdal (Eds.), *Behavioral assessment of childhood disorders.* New York: Guilford.

Bem, D. J. (1982). Assessing situations by assessing persons. In D. Magnusson (Ed.), *Toward a psychology of situations: An interactional perspective.* Hillsdale, NJ: Erlbaum.

Bem, D. J., & Funder, D. C. (1978). Predicting more of the people more of the time: Assessing the personality of situations. *Psychological Review, 85,* 485-501.

Bem, D. J., & Lord, C. G. (1979). Template matching: A proposal for probing the ecological validity of experimental settings in social psychology. *Journal of Personality and Social Psychology, 37,* 833-846.

Castaneda, A., McCandless, B. R., & Palermo, D. S. (1956). The children's form of the manifest anxiety scale. *Child Development, 27,* 317-326.

Ciminero, A. R., Calhoun, K. S., & Adams, H. E. (Eds.). (1977). *Handbook of behavioral assessment.* New York: Wiley.

Cone, J. D. (1977). The relevance of reliability and validity for behavioral assessment. *Behavior Therapy, 8,* 411-426.

Cone, J. D. (1978). The behavioral assessment grid (BAG): A conceptual framework and a taxonomy. *Behavior Therapy, 9,* 882-888.

Cone, J. D. (1979a). Confounded comparisons in triple response mode assessment research. *Behavioral Assessment, 1,* 85-95.

Cone, J. D. (1979b, March). Inductive behavioral assessment. Paper presented at the meeting of the Southeastern Psychological Association, New Orleans.

Cone, J. D. (1980, November). Template matching procedures for idiographic behavioral assessment. Paper presented in a symposium at the Association for the Advancement of Behavior Therapy meeting, New York.

Cone, J. D. (1981). Psychometric considerations. In M. Hersen and A. S. Bellack (Eds.), *Behavioral assessment: A practical handbook* (2nd ed.). New York: Pergamon.

Cone, J. D. (Ed.). (1982). *The West Virginia System curriculum for moderately, severely, and profoundly handicapped persons* (20 vols.). Unpublished manuscripts, West Virginia University, Morgantown.

Cone, J. D. (1984). *The Pyramid Scales.* Austin, TX: PRO-ED.

Cone, J. D. (1986). Idiographic, nomothetic, and other perspectives in behavioral assessment. In S. C. Hayes & R. O. Nelson (Eds.), *Conceptual foundations of behavioral assessment.* New York: Guilford.

Cone, J. D., Bourland, G., & Wood-Shuman, S. (1983). *Group homes in West Virginia: A descriptive analysis of the entrance requirements of group homes serving developmentally disabled persons.* Unpublished manuscript, West Virginia University, Morgantown.

Cone, J. D., & Hawkins, R. P. (1977). *Behavioral assessment: New directions in clinical psychology.* New York: Brunner/Mazel.

Cone, J. D., & Hoier, T. S. (1986). Assessing children: The radical behavioral perspective. In R. Prinz (Ed.), *Advances in behavioral assessment of children and families* (Vol. 2). New York: JAI.

Costello, C. G. (1981). Childhood depression. In E. J. Mash & L. G. Terdal (Eds.), *Behavioral assessment of childhood disorders.* New York: Guilford.

Deluty, R. H. (1979). Children's Action Tendency Scale: A self-report measure of aggressiveness, assertiveness, and submissiveness in children. *Journal of Consulting and Clinical Psychology, 47,* 1061–1071.

Eyberg, S. M., & Johnson, S. M. (1974). Multiple assessment of behavior modification with families: Effects of contingency contracting and order of treated problems. *Journal of Consulting and Clinical Psychology, 42,* 594–606.

Eyberg, S. M., & Ross, A. W. (1978). Assessment of child behavior problems: The validation of a new inventory. *Journal of Clinical Child Psychology, 16,* 113–116.

Fiske, D. W. (1979). A demonstration of the value of interchangeable observers. *Journal of Behavioral Assessment, 1,* 251–258.

Forehand, R. L., & McMahon, R. J. (1981). *Helping the noncompliant child.* New York: Guilford.

Hawkins, R. P. (1979). The functions of assessment: Implications for selection and development of devices for assessing repertoires in clinical, educational, and other settings. *Journal of Applied Behavior Analysis, 12,* 501–516.

Hayes, S. C., & Nelson, R. O. (Eds.). (1986). *Conceptual foundations of behavioral assessment.* New York: Guilford.

Haynes, S. N. (1978). *Principles of behavioral assessment.* New York: Garden Press.

Hersen, M., & Barlow, D. H. (1976). *Single case experimental designs.* New York: Pergamon.

Hersen, M., & Bellack, A. S. (1976). *Behavioral assessment: A practical handbook.* New York: Pergamon.

Hersen, M., & Bellack, A. S. (1981). *Behavioral assessment: A practical handbook* (2nd ed.). New York: Pergamon.

Hoier, T. S. (1984). *Target selection of social skills for children: An experimental investigation of template matching procedures.* Unpublished doctoral dissertation, West Virginia University, Morgantown.

Johnson, S. M., & Bolstad, O. D. (1973). Methodological issues in naturalistic observation: Some problems and solutions for field research. In L. A. Hamerlynck, L. C. Handy, & E. J. Mash (Eds.), *Behavior change: Methodology, concepts, and practice.* Champaign, IL: Research Press.

Jones, R. R., Reid, J. B., & Patterson, G. R. (1975). Naturalistic observation in clinical assessment. In P. McReynolds (Ed.), *Advances in psychological assessment* (Vol. 3). San Francisco: Jossey-Bass.

Kazdin, A. E. (1985). Selection of target behaviors: The relationship of the treatment focus to clinical dysfunction. *Behavioral Assessment, 7,* 33–47.

Keefe, F. J., Kopel, S. A., & Gordon, S. B. (1978). *A practical guide to behavioral assessment.* New York: Springer.

Kovacs, M. (1978). *Children's Depression Inventory.* Unpublished manuscript, University of Pittsburgh, Pittsburgh.

Lang, P. J. (1971). The application of psychophysiological methods to the study of psychotherapy and behavior modification. In A. E. Bergin and S. L. Garfield (Eds.), *Handbook of psychotherapy and behavior change.* New York: Wiley.

Lapouse, R., & Monk, M. A. (1959). Fears and worries in a representative sample of children. *American Journal of Orthopsychiatry, 29,* 223–248.

Lord, C. G. (1982). Predicting behavioral consistency from an individual's perception of situational similarities. *Journal of Personality and Social Psychology, 6,* 1076–1088.

Mariotto, M. J. (1979). Observational assessment systems for basic and applied research. *Journal of Behavioral Assessment, 1,* 239–250.

Mash, E. J., & Terdal, L. G. (1976). *Behavior therapy assessment: Diagnosis, design, and evaluation.* New York: Springer.

Mash, E. J., & Terdal, L. G. (Eds.). (1981). *Behavioral assessment of childhood disorders.* New York: Guilford.

Mash, E. J., Terdal, L., & Anderson, K. (1973). The response-class matrix: A procedure for recording parent-child interaction. *Journal of Consulting and Clinical Psychology, 40* (1), 163–164.

Melamed, B. G., & Siegal, L. J. (1975). Reduction of anxiety in children facing hospitalization and surgery by use of film modeling. *Journal of Consulting and Clinical Psychology, 43,* 511–521.

Melamed, B. G., Yurcheson, R., Fleece, E. L., Hutcherson, S., & Hawes, R. (1978). Effects of filmed modeling on the reduction of anxiety-related behaviors in individuals varying in level of previous experience in the stress situation. *Journal of Consulting and Clinical Psychology, 46,* 1357–1367.

Murphy, C. M., & Bootzin, R. R. (1973). Active and passive participation in the contact desensitization of snake fear in children. *Behavior Therapy, 4,* 203–211.

Nelson, R. O., Hay, L. R., & Hay, W. M. (1977). Comments on Cone's "The relevance of reliability and validity for behavioral assessment." *Behavior Therapy, 8,* 427–430.

Nihara, K., Foster, R., Shellhaas, M., & Leland, H. (1974). *AAMD Adaptive Behavior Scale.* Washington, DC: American Association on Mental Deficiency.

Ollendick, T. H. (in press). Reliability and validity of the Revised Fear Survey Schedule for Children (FSSC-R). *Behaviour Research and Therapy.*

Ollendick, T. H., & Hersen, M. (Eds.). (1984). *Child behavioral assessment.* New York: Pergamon.

Paul, G. L. (1979). *New assessment systems for residential treatment, management, research, and evaluation: A symposium. Journal of Behavioral Assessment, 1,* 181–184.

Paul, G. L. (Ed.) (in press). *Observational assessment instrumentation for service and research: The Time-Sample Behavioral Checklist—Assessment in residential treatment settings, part 2.* Campaign, IL: Research Press.

Phillips, J. S. (1983). Review of *Behavioral assessment of childhood disorders. Behavioral Assessment, 5,* 177–180.

Power, C. T. (1979). The *Time-Sample Behavioral Checklist:* Observational assessment of patient functioning. *Journal of Behavioral Assessment, 1,* 199–210.

Powers, M. D., & Handleman, J. S. (1984). *Behavioral assessment of severe developmental disabilities.* Rockville, MD: Aspen Systems.

Redfield, J. (1979). *Clinical Frequencies Recording System:* Standardizing staff observations by event recording. *Journal of Behavioral Assessment, 1,* 211–219.

Sarason, S. B., Davidson, K. S., Lighthall, F. F., Waite, R. R., & Ruebush, B. K. (1960). *Anxiety in elementary school children.* New York: Wiley.

Scherer, M. W., & Nakamura, C. Y. (1968). A fear survey schedule for children (FSS-FC): A factor analytic comparison with manifest anxiety (CMAS). *Behaviour Research and Therapy, 6,* 173–182.

Schnelle, J. F. (1974). A brief report on invalidity of parent evaluations of behavior change. *Journal of Applied Behavior Analysis, 1,* 341–343.

Shapiro, A. H. (1975). Behavior of Kibbutz and urban children receiving an injection. *Psychophysiology, 12,* 79–82.

Tryon, W. W. (Ed.). (1985). *Behavioral assessment and behavioral medicine.* New York: Springer.

Wahler, R. G., House, A. E., & Stambaugh, E. E. (1976). *Ecological assessment of child problem behavior.* New York: Pergamon.

Yarrow, M. R., Campbell, J. D., & Burton, R. V. (1970). Recollections of childhood: A study of the retrospective method. *Monographs of the society for research in child development, 35,* Serial No. 138.

CHAPTER 3

Medical Assessment of Children with Behavioral Problems

JOSEPH M. STRAYHORN, JR.

A mental health professional is working with the family of a 7-year-old child who has come to treatment because of disobedience and hostility. A first-rate program of parent training is instituted, and great progress occurs. When the mother complains that the child has become more "irritable" and "cranky" in the last few days, she is helped to tolerate the fact that progress will not take a smooth path upward. Later the mother mentions that the child has begun wetting herself again; the mother has already worked out some plans for using reinforcement contingencies for the enuresis in a logical way, and the therapist helps her refine her plans. In the next visit the mother states that the child willfully persists in drinking large quantities of water, as if to try to make herself wet the bed; the therapist helps her plan ways of helping the child not be so rebellious. The child's behavior only worsens, however, and the mother states that the child is starting to say really crazy things and to have wide emotional swings. The therapist starts to rethink the DSM-III diagnosis, considering borderline personality. The next day the child is admitted to the hospital comatose; the diagnosis is diabetes mellitus, with ketoacidosis.

This tale is a psychotherapist's nightmare. Those of us primarily interested in psychotherapy must have some sort of organized plan to avoid being the protagonist in such nightmares.

Let us experience a couple more horror stories. A child is treated with psychotherapy for 2 years because of worsening peer relationships, poor school performance, and problems paying attention. She is given a trial of methylphenidate as well, and this drug seems to help. She complains of headaches, but these are felt to be side effects of the methylphenidate. It is only when her legs develop weakness and incoordination that she is taken to a neurologist. The diagnosis is a meningioma, a brain tumor that would have been curable with no residual damage if operated on earlier. As it is, the child is likely to sustain permanent brain damage.

A child from a low-income family is seen because of acting-out at home and at school, refusal to cooperate with his teacher, trouble doing his school-work, and frequent crying. His family has undergone a great deal of stress lately, and a therapist begins family therapy aimed at helping the family provide a more secure emotional environment for the child. The family seems to report that things are getting better as this happens, but the mother complains, "He still has his days." After some months the child visits a pediatrician for a routine visit; he is found to be anemic, and further diagnostic tests reveal lead toxicity. The mother says, "Well, yes, come to think of it his stomach had hurt him every once in a while." The mental health professional is told by the pediatrician that the parents have observed the child eating paint chips for several months. If the child's lead toxicity had been treated earlier, the pediatrician says, the rather severe permanent intellectual disablement that the child will probably suffer would have been much less severe.

Such horror stories seem to be rather rare. A pediatric neurology service admitting approximately 550 children a year reported that in one year 12, or about 2%, had initially had their symptoms attributed to psychiatric illness (Rivinus et al., 1975). A mental health professional could probably ignore the possibility of unrecognized medical illness for many consecutive patients without encountering such a case. But the infrequency of these problems makes the situation more difficult rather than easier. Rare events do not cause systems to maintain vigilance the way more common events do. Indeed, to maintain high vigilance by routinely ordering a very expensive set of laboratory tests for each patient would be harmful, not only increasing the cost of mental health care but also setting up powerful barriers to entry into the mental health system.

Thus, the mental health professional must continually seek to tread the border between hypervigilance and hypovigilance with respect to medical problems. This chapter seeks a strategy for treading that line in the most logical manner, despite the fact that the quantitative information necessary to decide most rationally on that strategy is scarce and hard to access.

A thorough discussion of medical assessment in children is not possible here. Indeed, fairly thorough discussions exist—they are known as textbooks of pediatrics. This chapter will limit its goals in several ways. It will single-mindedly devote itself to helping the mental health professional know when to ask for further work-up to detect organic illness that might be masquerading as psychiatric disorder. It will not attempt to discuss the psychiatric consequences of known physical illness, such as brain damage from head injuries or the consequences of Down's syndrome. It will restrict itself primarily to information the professional is able to get from the history, rather than delving into the physical examination or laboratory tests. It will devote itself mainly to those illnesses that are treatable, but will avoid in-depth discussions of how the illnesses should be treated.

I will first present general guidelines on when to suspect medical illness.

Then, after presenting a large table on the differential diagnosis of behavioral symptoms, I will discuss some specific illnesses and the types of histories that should lead one to suspect them. Finally, I will present a checklist of medical history questions to include in the assessment interview, grouped according to illnesses that they sometimes accompany.

GENERAL GUIDELINES ON THE SUSPICION
OF ORGANIC ILLNESS

The rules to be listed here are nowhere close to perfectly reliable. Nevertheless, they provide some help.

The first rule is that the more grossly the patient's functioning is impaired, the more likely there is an organic contribution to that impairment. Unfortunately, however, this rule is of little help when we need it most. Organic illnesses in their early stages, when we most wish to diagnose them, can most closely mimic the milder behavior disturbances.

The second rule is that a loss of previous ability in intellectual functioning or memory should prompt a search for organic illness. The converse is not true, however; intact intellectual functioning by no means rules out all medical illnesses as contributors to psychiatric symptoms.

The third rule is that organic illness should be more strongly suspected when there is less explanation for the symptoms on other grounds. A child who had been doing well prior to an unexplained personality change is a candidate for a medical work-up. However, an imaginative clinician or parent can usually come up with some sort of environmental explanation for the most random symptom; stress and maladaptive learning exposures of some degree occur with almost all children almost all the time.

The fourth rule is that organic explanations for psychiatric disturbance are more likely when the child has physical complaints and symptoms in addition to the psychiatric ones. Again, however, the converse is not always true; some organic illnesses can present first with psychiatric disturbance in the abscence of physical complaints.

The fifth rule is that "ruling out" organic illness is never fully complete. If no organic illness is evident at a certain point in time via certain tests, organic illness may be more detectible at a later point in time or with more thorough tests. Therefore, cases should be followed, and if the clinical response is unsatisfactory, the question of organic illness should be raised repeatedly rather than only once. A corollary of this rule is that hearing that the child has been given a check-up by a pediatrician and that nothing was found does not provide closure on the question of organic illness. Many of the illnesses I will mention are of the sort that one must specifically search for in order to find.

DIFFERENTIAL DIAGNOSIS OF BEHAVIORAL SYMPTOMS

I can assert with confidence that the differential diagnosis of behavioral and mental disturbance is the most difficult and complex in all of medicine; it makes such symptoms as chest pain look like child's play. Many different illnesses can be responsible for behavioral symptoms; let us divide them into groups. We can remember the types of illnesses by the mnemonic *TIN Cev, M.D.* The categories are: toxic, traumatic, infectious, idiopathic, neoplastic, nutritional, collagen vascular and autoimmune, congenital and hereditary, endocrine, vascular, metabolic, multiple causes, and degenerative.

Table 3.1 presents a differential diagnosis arranged according to these categories.

TABLE 3.1   Differential Diagnosis of Organically Caused Behavioral Symptoms In Children and Adolescents

---

Toxic:

Alcohol and other sedatives: Acute alcohol intoxication, intoxication with other sedatives, alcohol withdrawal syndrome, withdrawal syndrome from other sedatives

Over-the-counter drugs: Bromide poisoning, scopolamine poisoning, salicylate poisoning, vitamin A poisoning, vitamin D poisoning, caffeinism

Prescription drugs: Reaction to steroids, isoniazid, digitalis, reserpine, antihistamines, methylphenidate and other stimulants, insulin, propranolol, methyldopa, barbiturates (e.g. phenobarbital), other sedatives, other anticonvulsants, theophylline, lithium, procaine penicillin, narotics, birth control pills, ergotamine, catecholamines

"Recreational" drugs: LSD, phencyclidine, marijuana, mescaline, psilocybin, cocaine, and others

Heavy metals: Lead, mercury, arsenic, calcium, manganese

Fumes and gases: Carbon monoxide, benzene, carbon tetrachloride, gasoline, glue, insecticides, carbon disulfide

Idiosyncratic reactions to foods and food additives, monosodium glutamate syndrome

Traumatic:

Blow to the head resulting in concussion, contusion, laceration, subdural or epidural bleeding, cerebral edema, postconcussive symptoms, punch-drunk syndrome, electircal injury.

Subdural effusion.

Infectious:

Bacterial meningitis, brain abscess, syphillis, viral encephalitis (including, among others, herpes simplex, herpes zoster, rabies, infectious hepatitis, infectious mononucleosis, mumps) tuberculous meningitis, fungal infections (cryptococcosis, coccidiomycosis, histoplasmosis), rickettsial diseases (including Rocky Mountain spotted fever), parasitic illnesses (including trichinosis, echinococciasis, cysticerosis, (or tapeworm, toxoplasmosis), brucellosis, Sydenham's chorea, kuru, Creutzfeldt-Jakob disease, subacute sclerosing panencephalitis

Idiopathic:

Narcolepsy, sleep apnea syndromes, Reye's syndrome

(*Continued*)

TABLE 3.1 (*Continued*)

Neoplastic:

Brain tumors, metastatic tumors, remote effects of other tumors

Nutritional:

Folate deficiency, vitamin B_{12} deficiency, scurvy, protein-calorie malnutrition, thiamin deficiency, pellagra (nicotinic acid deficiency), vitamin A deficiency

Collagen Vascular, Autoimmune, and Allergic:

Systemic lupus erythematosus, periarteritis nodosa, temporal arteritis
Multiple sclerosis
Allergies

Congenital and Hereditary:

Hepatolenticular degeneration (Wilson's disease), Huntington's chorea, tuberous sclerosis, Friedreich's ataxia, muscular dystrophies, neurofibromatosis, galactosemia, Gilles de la Tourette's disease
Aminoacidurias, including phenylketonuria and Hartnup disease
Acute intermittent porphyria, other porphyrias
Central nervous system lipidoses, including Gaucher's disease, Niemann-Pick disease, cerebromacular degeneration
Leukodystrophies, including adrenoleukodystrophy, metachromatic leukodystrophy
Mucopolysaccharidoses, including Hurler's syndrome
Chromosomal abnormalities, including Down's syndrome, fragile X syndrome, Turner's syndrome, Klinefelter's syndrome

Endocrine:

Hyperthyroidism, hypothyroidism, Cushing's syndrome, Addison's disease, pheochromocytoma, hypopituitarism, hyperparathyroidism, hypoparathyroidism, diabetes mellitus, insulinoma, hypoglycemia, carcinoid, inappropriate ADH syndrome

Vascular:

Subdural hematoma, epidural hematoma, subarachnoid hemorrhage, hypertensive encephalopathy, migraine, large unruptured cerebral aneurysms

Metabolic:

Cerebral hypoxia, uremia, hepatic encephalopathy, dehydration, water intoxication, hyponatremia, sodium depletion, potassium depletion, potassium excess, hypercalcemia, hypermagnesemia, hypomagnesemia, alkalosis, acidosis, hypercapnia, hyperthermia

Multiple Causes:

Vision problems, hearing problems
Epilepsy: Petit mal, postconvulsive confusion following grand mal, psychomotor (i.e., complex partial or temporal lobe)
Anemias
Sleep Apneas

SPECIFIC ILLNESSES AND WHEN TO SUSPECT THEM

In the sections that follow it is impossible to cover all the illnesses mentioned in Table 3.1. I will focus on illnesses chosen according to an informal weighting of three variables: (1) how likely the illness is to present with behavioral symptoms, (2) how common the illness is, and (3) how much better is the prognosis when the illness is treated early.

Toxic: Lead Toxicity

Lead toxicity, especially of the milder sorts, is common, is likely to present with behavioral symptoms, and has a much better outcome if treated early; accordingly, it is a problem that behavioral clinicians should be familiar with.

A child with early lead toxicity could have a totally normal physical examination with only such symptoms as increased irritability, decreased appetite, and decreased play activity. Although paint chips from older houses are a well-known source of lead, a history of eating paint chips is not required for a suspicion of lead toxicity. It is a frightening fact that dirt is often found to have high lead concentrations—sometimes approaching half the concentration in paint chips (Graef, 1983; Chisolm, 1983). Rutter (1983) cites five studies to the effect that children's blood lead levels are related to soil concentrations in their neighborhoods; further evidence (Russell Jones, & Stephens, 1983) supports the conclusion that the major source of such lead is that released by the burning of leaded gasoline. Elevated lead levels (over 30 micrograms per deciliter) have been found in 4.5% of preschool children screened in 1980 (Graef, 1983). (This figure is down from 8% in 1975; the decrease is thought to be partly due to a decreased use of lead in gasoline.) Increased exposure to lead, without overt clinical toxicity, has been found to correlate with greater distractibility from schoolwork, less organization, greater impulsivity, reduced ability to follow directions, and lowered overall classroom functioning; this correlation remained after statistical control for age, sex, and more than 30 demographic and socioeconomic variables (Needleman, 1979).

How should the clinician carrying out a behavioral assessment avoid missing lead toxicity? It has been argued that free erythrocyte protoporphyrin levels and/or blood lead levels, both of which are fairly inexpensive blood tests, should routinely be performed on children presenting with behavioral symptoms. Short of that, what factors in the clinical history should increase the clinician's suspicion of lead toxicity?

Children with a history of pica (i.e., the eating of any nonfood substances) are at higher risk, as are children who live in older housing with crumbling paint. (The use of lead additives in residential paint decreased through the 1950s, 1960s, and 1970s; in 1977 the use of lead additives in residential paints was banned in the United States: Chisholm, 1983). Children who are less closely supervised by adults seem to be at higher risk. Reports of exposure to lead in cooking vessels or water pipes, swallowing of lead shot, exposure to the fumes from fires where storage batteries have been burned, and exposure to the dust from sanding the walls of old houses should raise the suspicion of lead toxicity, as should the report that a child gets a lot of dirt on his mouth. Abdominal pain, loss of appetite, vomiting, constipation, and anemia accompany the more severe levels of lead intoxication. One would hope that the toxicity is detected before these occur. More severe toxicity results in confusion, staggering, persistent vomiting, seizures, and coma. By this time the child should be hospitalized, and the illness should be clearly under the bailiwick of a medical specialist.

Toxic: Toxicity from "Recreational" Drugs

In adolescents the toxic effects of alcohol, marijuana, cocaine, hallucinogens, and other drugs constitute probably the most frequent biologic cause of behavioral difficulties. I will not discuss here the individual effects of each drug, but simply note that the key to diagnosis is the history of drug ingestion. This may sometimes be obtained from significant others when it is not obtained from the patient. Another clue that might raise the hypothesis of drug toxicity as a cause of altered behavior is the gradual spontaneous remission of symptoms after several days of hospital admission.

Toxic: Side Effects of Prescribed Drugs

When assessing a child's behavioral problems, it is important to find out if the child is on any medications. A variety of medications sometimes have psychological side effects. I will mention only a few of the most common drug reactions resulting in psychological symptoms.

Theophylline is a drug used in the treatment of asthma. Irritability, insomnia, and tremor have occurred even at therapeutic doses of this drug. The restlessness that can be a side effect of this drug can be mistaken for attention deficit disorder (Weinberger & Hendeles, 1980; Bukowskyj, Nakatsu, & Munt, 1984).

Corticosteroid drugs such as cortisone and prednisone are used in the treatment of asthma, rheumatoid arthritis, inflammatory bowel diseases, and a variety of other illnesses. Emotional lability, depression, mania, and psychosis have been noted with substantial doses of these drugs.

Antihistamine drugs, which are often given for allergies, may produce either excitation or sedation in children. At other times these drugs have been known to cause a decrease in mental alertness, resulting in school difficulties.

Phenobarbital, which is often used to control epileptic seizures, has been found to produce symptoms mimicking attention deficit disorder: trouble concentrating, restlessness, hyperactivity, and reduced impulse control. Experiments with psychometric tests given with and without this drug suggest that it may impair school performance in some children (Stores, 1975).

Phenytoin, another drug for epileptic seizures, also can impair concentration, especially when levels of the drug get too high. The classic picture of toxicity with this drug is staggering, lethargy, slurred speech, and jerky movements of the eyes (Stores, 1975).

Any of the stimulant medications used for attention deficit disorder (i.e., methylphenidate, dextroamphetamine, or pemoline) can produce psychiatric symptoms if the dose becomes too high; symptoms such as agitation, confusion, hallucinations, and highly inappropriate behavior may occur.

When diabetic children who take insulin are found to be confused, "not with it," irritable, irrational, or not their usual selves, one possibility is that the glucose in their bloodstreams may be too low because of too much insulin relative to how much they have eaten. Since the brain requires a constant supply of energy in the form of glucose to function properly, a variety of psychological symptoms can occur even with moderately low blood sugar. If the glucose gets still lower, the child can become unconscious, have his or her brain permanently injured, or die. The other symptoms that go along with low blood glucose are trembling, sweating, pounding of the heart, and a feeling of hunger. If a child with diabetes acts strangely or has any of the other symptoms, low blood glucose should be suspected. When diabetic children say that they feel that their sugar is low, they should be taken seriously. They should immediately be allowed to eat or drink whatever is available with the highest carbohydrate content.

Vitamins A and D, when taken in too large doses, can cause behavioral toxicity. For vitamin A, symptoms of appetite loss and irritability may be accompanied by itching, limited motion of joints, and tender swelling of bones. For vitamin D, symptoms of appetite loss and irritability may be accompanied by constipation, floppy and loose muscle tone, much urination and drinking of liquids, and pallor (Barness, 1983).

Toxic: Idiosyncratic Reactions to Foods or Inhaled Substances

I list this form of problem under "toxic" illnesses rather than under illnesses involving the immune system because there is some question as to whether most "allergic" reactions to foods are truly mediated by the immune system or whether some other mechanism is involved.

In 1954 Speer described "the allergic tension–fatigue syndrome," describing cases in which children presented with some combination of irritability and/or listlessness, sometimes accompanied by aching muscles. These children improved when an offending food substance was removed from their diet or when desensitization to an inhaled allergen was carried out. In some cases the children had relapse of symptoms when they started to eat the food again and remission when the food was again removed from the diet. Many other reports linking allergens to disordered behavior have accumulated (reviewed by Hall, 1976). Apparently, milk, eggs, chocolate, wheat, and corn lead the list of foods that people have concluded to be related to symptoms. Because of methodologic problems, these conclusions must be regarded as tentative.

The problem of behavioral toxicity to food additives was brought to the attention of the lay public by Feingold (1975), who claimed that a high fraction of hyperactive children were experiencing behavioral toxicity from foods and food additives. Feingold's hypothesis was dismissed by most of the scientific community. However, according to my reading of the literature, a modification, not a total rejection, is in order. That is, some (perhaps very few) children experience certain behavioral symptoms (not necessarily those of hyperactivity) reliably in response to certain commonly used food additives. For example, Weiss (1984) tested 22 children who had reportedly benefited from the Feingold diet and found that with two of them, the benefit could be demonstrated by careful placebo-controlled study. For one of these subjects the negative response to the food dyes was so severe that there was essentially no overlap between behavior ratings on placebo days and challenge days.

At this point there is no consensus on an organized strategy for diagnosing behavioral toxicity from foods or inhaled substances. My recommendation is that if a parent or child has noticed a connection between symptoms and ingestion or inhalation of a certain substance, it is worthwhile to attempt a single-case experiment to test the hypothesis. Perhaps in the future it will be possible to recommend a systematic strategy for a trial of "elimination diets" for certain subsets of patients; at this time the yield for such a procedure in proportion to the time and energy it requires appears too small to be generally advisable.

Traumatic: Subdural Effusions

The phrase *subdural effusion* refers to a collection of fluid between the brain and the skull. The subdural space is the space under the dura, which is one of the coverings of the brain. The fluid forms a mass that presses on the brain underneath it; the symptoms depend on what brain regions are affected and how rapidly the fluid collects.

The origin of subdural effusions is bleeding into the subdural space caused by a blow to the head. If the resulting bleeding is very fast, the symptoms are more obviously neurological: the child's head hurts; he or she vomits, might have weakness or numbness on one side of the body, and has other symptoms that effectively route the child to a neurosurgeon. The more slowly progressing situation is called a chronic subdural effusion. The child can get knocked out from a blow on the head and seemingly recover totally from the injury. But sometimes blood has escaped from one of the veins over the brain, and the clot that forms in the subdural space liquifies, after which water is drawn into the space around it to maintain osmotic equilibrium. As a result, the mass pushing on the brain gradually gets bigger. The size of the mass and the intensity of the symptoms can increase over the course of days or sometimes weeks. The first symptoms can be behavioral symptoms of any sort. The history of the blow on the head is the main clue to a chronic subdural; the appearance of headache, vomiting, or neurological symptoms (e.g., weakness, numbness, seizures, clumsiness, staggering, newly occurring visual problems) should raise the suspicion even further.

Infectious: Meningitis

Meningitis, or infection of the coverings of the brain and spinal cord, is often accompanied by infection of the brain tissue itself; if untreated or unsuccessfully treated, it can result in permanent brain damage or death. It is another illness where a high premium should be placed on early diagnosis.

Bacterial meningitis, caused by inflammation of the brain and meninges by bacteria such as meningococcus or pneumococcus or hemophilus, progresses in a matter of hours or days to a problem that is clearly medical. Headache and pain on flexing the neck are early symptoms that tend to route this illness away from the mental health professional. However, in the earliest stages of this illness the child may present as "not himself," "irritable," "out of it," or otherwise changed with respect to psychological state. Fever, feeling "sick," and the beginnings of headache and stiff neck can, if picked up by the astute mental health professional, be the clues for the very early diagnosis of bacterial meningitis. Bacterial meningitis is most common among infants, less common in toddlers and preschool children, and fairly rare among school-aged children or adolescents (Broome & Schlech, 1985). It should be more strongly suspected if the child has recently had an infection of an ear, a sinus, the scalp, the gums, or the blood that could have seeded the infection of the meninges.

Viral infections of the brain and spinal cord can produce symptoms running the full range from a mild sick feeling and altered behavior to the full-blown picture of fever, stiff neck, headache, vomiting, coma, and eventual death. Infection of the brain and meninges with herpes simplex is the most common type of nonepidemic brain infection in the United States (Phillips, 1983); it is now treatable with the drug acyclovir. The history of a herpes infection of the mouth or genitals may be a clue to this illness. Otherwise, the distinction between viral and bacterial meningitis is one made by laboratory methods and is not a distinction the referring mental health professional need be concerned with during the gathering of the history.

The bacilli responsible for tuberculosis, as well as several types of fungi, can cause meningitides that progress much more slowly; in the early stages mental symptoms may appear before any physical signs of meningitis (Lishman, 1978). The psychological symptoms may include lack of interest in playing, having periods of idly staring into space, having abrupt mood changes, declining in school performance, and becoming lethargic and apathetic or irritable. The child may have fever during this stage. Headache and stiff neck may be totally absent. As the disease progresses untreated, more obvious neurologic signs and symptoms appear, but by this time the prognosis is much worse. These sorts of meningitis are much rarer than bacterial and viral meningitides. How can the clinician avoid missing such cases? Tuberculosis is still a problem in the United States, but it is a far worse problem in the "third world" countries. Immigrants and travelers are more deserving of consideration of tuberculosis. The presence of a family member or close acquaintance with known tuberculosis should also increase suspicion. A history of tuberculosis of the lungs or a conversion to a positive tuberculin skin test that was not adequately treated should also raise suspicion of tuberculous meningitis. Children who have been treated for cancer or some other illness with immunosuppressive drugs are more susceptible to infections of all sorts, including fungal and tuberculous meningitis.

Infectious: Rocky Mountain Spotted Fever

Rocky Mountain spotted fever is caused by a microorganism that is bigger than a virus but smaller than a bacterium, and possessing some of the characteristics of each. The infection is introduced into the human body by the bite of an infected tick. (These ticks seem to be most common not in the Rocky Mountains but in the Southeastern United States: North and South Carolina, Virginia, Tennessee, and their neighbors.) After the infection has entered the body, it can incubate to 8 days, after which a progression of symptoms begins; early symptoms may sometimes consist of changed personality, bizarre behavior or restlessness, or other psychological symptoms. Headache, fever, and loss of appetite are also frequent early symptoms. As the disease progresses, more obvious medical symptoms rapidly appear, such as a rash that starts on the ankles and legs, muscle pain, intense "sick feeling," and others. Early treatment is very helpful, because there are antibiotics that can successfully cure this illness if diagnosis is correctly made soon enough.

Infectious: Brain Abscess

An abscess is a collection of pus surrounded by infected tissue. In some children with brain abscesses the disease evolves over a course of several weeks (Till, 1975). Sometimes the first symptom can be irritability. Headache and vomiting can occur, especially if the abscess is big enough or at the right place to cause an obstruction of flow of the cerebrospinal fluid and an increase in the pressure inside the brain. If obvious neurologic signs appear (such as weakness, numbness, trouble with eye movements, trouble with vision, seizures, staggering, newly appearing incoordination, or loss of consciousness) the diagnosis is more readily made. Also, if the child has fever, the diagnostician is clued to search for infections. But all these clues can be absent in the child with a brain abscess. Sometimes the tip-off is the history of an infection elsewhere that could have been spread to the brain: infection of the ear, sinus, scalp, gum, or blood. Children with certain sorts of congenital heart diseases, such as those where blood can go directly from the right side of the heart to the left, are more likely to get brain abscesses (Till, 1975).

Idiopathic: Reye's Syndrome

As the word *idiopathic* implies, the exact cause of Reye's syndrome is unknown. It affects the cells of various organs, especially the liver and the brain. Although it is not a viral infection itself, it tends to develop as the child is recovering from a viral infection. Taking aspirin during that infection seems to increase the risk of Reye's syndrome (Starko, Ray, Dominguez, Stromberg, & Woodall, 1980). It, like bacterial meningitis, Rocky Mountain spotted fever, and several others, is obviously a medical illness once it gets to its full-blown form. In its early stages it has been known to be confused with psychiatric illness. The illness can start out with bizarre behavior, confusion, restlessness, irritability, combativeness, or other behavioral symptoms. More frequently, however, the patient develops severe nausea and vomiting at the beginning of the course. As the disease progresses, the child can become stuporous, have seizures, go into a coma, or die. The disease is usually ended within a matter of a few days, either by recovery or by death. Although there is no specific treatment for it, the control of swelling of the brain and other such parameters accomplished by "supportive measures" in the hospital substantially reduces the chance of dying from Reye's syndrome (Riela & Roach, 1983).

Neoplastic: Brain Tumors

Brain tumors fortunately cannot be said to be common in children; the incidence of nervous system tumors in children under 15 is somewhere in the region of 25 per million children per year (Till, 1975). However, tumors are second only to accidents as a cause of death in children, and nervous system tumors are the second most frequent type of tumors in children (Till, 1975).

The symptoms of brain tumors are determined mainly by where in the brain they are located and how big they have grown. If the tumor produces an obvious neurologic symptom, such as localized weakness, numbness, impaired movement of the eyes, reduced field of vision in one or both eyes, staggering, newly appearing incoordination, or a seizure, it is likely to be discovered quickly. However, more often than not, tumors in children develop in "silent" areas that do not produce localized symptoms quickly. Often symptoms develop slowly, insidiously, and nonspecifically. The child may have irritability, poor concentration, and diminished school achievement. Physical symptoms such as clumsiness of gait and headaches may be the tip-offs that prompt a search for brain tumor. In children, headaches are not nearly so common as they are in adults, and they should be taken seriously when they persist (Till, 1975). As the tumor progresses, the flow of cerebrospinal fluid in the brain may be obstructed and pressure inside the head may increase; vomiting is a prominent symptom of such a condition.

Nutritional: Vitamin Deficiencies

Vitamin deficiencies of several sorts can first present with behavioral symptoms: apathy, restlessness, irritability, poor concentration, fatigue. The vitamin B complex, that is, thiamin, riboflavin, and niacin, is present in the same group of foods, and thus deficiencies in these vitamins tend to occur together. Deficiencies in these vitamins can cause a variety of physical symptoms, such as numbness, dizziness, nausea, fissuring of the angles of the mouth, and soreness of the tongue (Barness, 1983).

Juvenile pernicious anemia is a disease caused by the inability of the child to absorb vitamin B_{12}; it is quite rare.

Deficiencies in the vitamin folic acid have been linked to depression and dementia in adults (Lishman, 1978). The relation to behavioral symptoms in children has been less thoroughly studied. Certain of the anticonvulsant drugs (e.g., phenytoin, phenobarbital) seem to interfere with the absorption of folic acid.

Protein malnutrition, in its early stages, also manifests itself by vague behavioral symptoms: lethargy, apathy, irritability, difficulty concentrating, restlessness.

Perhaps the best clue for malnutrition as a cause of symptoms is some fairly brief questioning about the child's diet. Grossly abnormal diets should point toward further investigation of this possibility.

Hereditary: Wilson's Disease

Wilson's disease is genetic, transmitted by an autosomal recessive gene. Like all other illnesses caused by recessive genes, it is more common in children whose parents are blood relatives of each other. The primary defect is located in the liver, which becomes incapable of properly excreting the copper that is present in small degrees in the normal diet. As copper accumulates in the body, it damages the liver, brain, kidneys, and corneas. In the early stages of the illness, the effects on the brain may mimic psychiatric symptoms; in from 10% to 25% of symptomatic patients, the first clinical manifestation of Wilson's disease is psychiatric (Scheinberg & Sternlieb, 1984). Impaired intellectual performance, irritability, impulsiveness, unexplained personality change, emotional lability, or other nonspecific psychological symptoms may occur. As the disease progresses undiagnosed, slurred speech, tremors, muscle rigidity, involuntary twitches, and/or an immobile open-mouthed grinning facial expression may develop. Psychiatric symptoms may progress to manic or schizophrenic symptoms, neurotic symptoms, or bizarre behavior, sometimes including criminal behavior. Almost every patient with clinically manifest Wilson's disease suffers psychiatric symptoms of some sort (Scheinberg & Sternlieb, 1984). For the school child, school academic performance would be expected to deteriorate over this course. There begin to develop the "Kayser-Fleischer rings" around the outer rim of the corneas: these are grayish, start as an arc, and gradually encircle the cornea. Because psychiatric symptoms can be the only manifestations of this treatable illness in its early stages, at least one major psychiatric center runs a laboratory screening test for Wilson's disease on nearly every inpatient. The reason this is not done more frequently is the rarity of the illness. Its worldwide incidence is estimated at 3 cases per million new patient visits (Scheinberg & Sternlieb, 1984). Scheinberg and Sternlieb recommend ordering the serum ceruloplasmin, which is a laboratory test for Wilson's disease, in psychiatric patients if there is a family history of the disorder, if there is a history of unexplained liver disease, if the psychiatric illness is less responsive to treatment than expected, or if neurologic signs and symptoms supervene. Early treatment with penicillamine, a drug that binds copper, can abort the progression of the damage.

Hereditary: Tourette's Disease

Tourette's disease barely escaped being listed in the "idiopathic" category, since little is known of its causation. However, it does appear to run in families, and most researchers think that it has a genetic contribution (Kidd & Pauls, 1982). It begins in childhood, between the ages of 2 and 15 years. The symptoms are interesting: there are several types of involuntary jerky muscle movements, for example, jerks of the shoulders or the arms, jerks of the neck, or twitches of the face. In addition, there are "vocal tics": involuntary grunts, barks, clicks, snorts, mutterings, or other noises. The most bizarre symptom is known as coprolalia: irresistable utterings of "dirty words." This symptom occurs in a little over half of the children with Tourette's disease (Nuwer, 1982). As may be imagined, the syndrome causes social problems for patients that may be quite severe. The prevalence is about a hundredth to five hundredths of a percent of the population (American Psychiatric Association, 1980). It is somewhat responsive to drug therapy: haloperidol and clonidine are most frequently used.

Endocrine: Hypothyroidism, Hyperthyroidism

If we compare the body to a motor, thyroid hormone seems to turn up the idling speed. Hyperthyroidism results in greater expenditure of energy, increased heart rate, weight loss despite increased eating, quicker muscle stretch reflexes, increased activity level, faster thought processes, diarrhea, feeling too hot in regions where other people are comfortable, and increased sweating. Hypothyroidism results in the opposite: lower expenditure of energy, decreased heart rate, weight gain, slower reflexes, reduced activity level, slowed thought processes, constipation, feeling too cold in temperatures where others feel comfortable, and dryness of the skin.

The increased activity level, reduced ability to concentrate, greater irritability, and greater tendency to cry characteristic of hyperthyroidism may resemble attention deficit disorder. Tip-offs that hyperthyroidism is the culprit may include any of the symptoms or signs listed above. In addition, other symptoms can be clues. A goiter, or swollen thyroid gland (located in the lower part of the front of the neck) was reported present in all of one series of patients with juvenile hyperthyroidism (Fisher, 1978). Other frequently appearing signs and symptoms were prominence or bulging of the eyes, rapid heartbeat, nervousness, increased perspiration, and increased appetite with weight loss. Deteriorated school work, emotional disturbance, breathlessness, and diarrhea were also often present in this series (Fisher, 1978).

The apathy, sluggishness, reduced energy level, poor appetite, deteriorated school performance, and constipation characteristic of hypothyroidism may be confused with a depressive syndrome. Any of the symptoms listed earlier might be the tip-off for hypothyroidism. In addition, the complaint or finding that the child's rate of growth has been slower than expected, the finding of coarse, brittle hair, the presence of a sallow complexion, or the presence of the enlarged thyroid gland (or goiter) characteristic of certain causes of hypothyroidism may also be clues that laboratory investigation is warranted.

These conditions rate high on the treatability scale, high on the scale of possible confusion with psychiatric syndromes, and fairly low on the scale of frequency.

Endocrine: Diabetes

Diabetes is caused by a shortage of insulin, the hormone that causes glucose to be moved from the bloodstream into the muscles and other tissues where it can be used. (Glucose, however, can move into the brain without insulin.)

When there is too little insulin and the muscles cannot get glucose, a variety of metabolic changes ensue, resulting in increasingly higher blood glucose and eventually in a state known as diabetic ketoacidosis. The progression to this state can start with personality change and move to confusion and bizarre behavior to stupor, coma, and to death. In the case mentioned at the beginning of this chapter, the hallmarks of the beginnings of diabetes were described. In children the onset often follows a viral illness. The early symptoms are increased frequency and total volume of urine output, increased drinking of liquids, a tired feeling, and sometimes the beginning again of bedwetting in a child who had previously been dry. Diabetes is a common illness, very treatable, and one that in the early stages can be confused with behavioral problems. As mentioned in an earlier section, once the child is already diagnosed as having diabetes, maladaptive behavior may be the result of either too much or too little insulin, resulting in either too low or too high a blood glucose.

Other Endocrine Illnesses

We should mention other endocrine illnesses that can sometimes be confused with psychiatric illness: Cushing's disease (too much secretion from the adrenal cortex), Addison's disease (too little secretion from the adrenal cortex), pheochromocytoma (too much secretion, at times, of adrenalin or noradrenalin, the hormones secreted by the adrenal medulla), an insulinoma (a tumor of the pancreas that secretes insulin and causes symptoms of low blood glucose), and hypoparathyroidism and hyperparathyroidism (i.e., shortage or excess of a hormone regulating calcium metabolism). These are rare enough that I will not go into the symptoms they produce.

Multiple Causes: Epileptic Seizures, Especially Complex Partial or "Psychomotor"

Epileptic seizures of any sort are caused by repetitive firing of groups of neurons in the brain; in grand mal seizures such activity spreads widely through the brain and results in the classic fits of falling, shaking, tongue-biting, wetting oneself, being unconscious, and being confused after regaining consciousness. These are almost always clearly recognized as medical problems and quickly routed to a neurologist.

Psychomotor epilepsy, which is also referred to as complex partial seizures or temporal lobe seizures, usually involves the repetitive firing of neurons in a restricted portion of the brain, almost always a temporal lobe or both temporal lobes. These discharges occur at unpredictable times and can apparently be activated by emotional stress; this fact makes the differentiation of their effects from purely psychological phenomena often difficult.

The temporal lobes connect extensively with other brain regions and serve a variety of functions; therefore, the discharges from these regions can produce a wide variety of symptoms. The psychological symptoms may include hallucinations of sight, sound, smell, or taste. Feelings of depersonalization or unreality of things around one can be produced; feelings of déja vu (the feeling that the present event has been experienced before) jamaise vu (the feeling that familiar things are new and unfamiliar), states of high emotion for which there is no appropriate cause, and the utterance of commonplace or jumbled phrases can also be phenomena of these seizures. The child may experience vertigo. The child may run to the mother in fear, or may reject the mother during the attack and run to her for consolation afterwards. Sometimes, but not always, amnesia for the events of the attack and the events just before it occurs; sometimes the child is too embarrassed to talk about the events without a great deal of encouragement. Pallor or flushing can occur during the seizures (Brett, 1983).

The movements carried out during a complex partial seizure can vary greatly from case to case. Sometimes there is no movement, but just a blank stare. At other times there is repetitive fumbling with buttons or clothing, rubbing or patting oneself, running, picking up objects and dropping them, smacking lips, chewing, or swallowing. However, more seemingly purposive or antisocial actions have been reported to occur. Throughout such activities the child appears "out of it"; usually he or she is not responsive to conversation except to a limited degree. The particular pattern of activity during the seizure varies less from episode to episode in one child than among a group of children. Therefore, a stereotyped pattern that a given child repeats would raise the suspicion more than would episodes of widely varying strange behavior.

A seizure usually lasts a few seconds, but "complex partial status epilepticus," in which the seizure activity has lasted for hours, has occasionally been reported (Brett, 1983).

The diagnosis of complex partial seizures is usually established by the electroencephalogram (EEG). False negatives exist, though; in other words, a normal EEG does not rule out complex partial seizures. Taking the EEG during sleep, after sleep deprivation, and with nasopharyngeal leads reduces the fraction of false negatives.

The disorder is usually at least somewhat responsive to treatment, either with anticonvulsant drug therapy or with surgery or other treatment of the underlying cerebral disorder.

The other form of seizure that sometimes may be confused with psychological problems is the petit mal seizure. It involves a different pattern of neuronal firing than does the temporal lobe seizure. The petit mal attack is characterized by a blank stare lasting on the order of 10 seconds, accompanied by unawareness and amnesia and sometimes by flickering eyelids or turned-up eyes. Mild shaking of a limb or drooping or sinking in posture can also accompany these seizures. As is apparent from the above description, these sorts of symptoms can also be produced by temporal lobe seizures; in fact, blank staring "absences" are more frequently caused by temporal lobe seizures than by petit mal attacks. The distinction, which is confirmed by EEG, is relevant to drug treatment and prognosis. Petit mal attacks respond to different drugs and tend to go away of their own accord when the child grows up (Brett, 1983).

Multiple Causes: Hearing Problems

Herskowitz and Rosman (1982) report a typical case in which a 5-year-old child presented with "hyperactivity and inattention." His mother complained that the child could "tune her out," and that the child got along poorly with other children. It turned out that this child had a 30 to 40 decibel hearing deficit in both ears, apparently due to collections of fluid in the middle ears. When these were treated, the child's behavioral symptoms improved to the extent that drug treatment for attention deficit problems was not necessary.

Undetected hearing loss can be the cause of a variety of problems with speech and language, with schoolwork, or with relations with people. These problems can in turn create a variety of secondary effects, from fights, disobedience, and other conduct problems to somatic complaints or social withdrawal.

The approach to detecting hearing loss might include questioning parents regarding risk factors, such as a history of many ear infections; maternal history of rubella or cytomegalovirus, or exposure to these during pregnancy; treatment of the child with aminoglycoside antibiotics such as streptomycin, kanamycin, or gentamycin; or family history of deafness or hearing loss. Problems with articulation in the speech of young children should also raise the question of hearing deficit. However, the easiest approach to this problem is a quick gross test of the child's hearing. The examiner asks the child if he has had any trouble hearing what people say. Then the examiner explains that he will briefly test the child's hearing, and asks the child to repeat the words that the examiner says. The examiner covers his mouth with his hand (to preclude lip-reading) and softly whispers familiar words such as *school bus* and *baseball*. If the child can repeat these words, hearing problems as a cause of psychiatric difficulties are essentially ruled out.

Multiple Causes: Vision Problems

Anything that interferes with a child's performance in school can contribute to behavioral problems. Some school-aged children who are handicapped by uncorrected poor vision essentially diagnose themselves by complaining that they cannot see the chalkboard or make out the letters in books. The mental health professional can perhaps pick up some children with visual difficulties simply by asking them if they ever have trouble seeing and recognizing the letters on the chalkboard or in books. Charts are available at low expense for the professional who would like to include vision screening in the assessment.

Multiple Causes: Anemias

Anemia is a shortage of the red blood cells, whose job it is to carry oxygen to the tissues. The anemic child may be irritable, fatigue easily, suffer a decrement in school performance, and have difficulty concentrating. The most prevalent cause of anemia in children is iron deficiency. Iron deficiency apparently may have an effect on behavior over and above that of the anemia it causes (Pearson, 1983). Pallor of the skin is one of the tip-offs for anemia; a history of a diet poor in iron is another clue.

Multiple Causes: Sleep Apnea Syndromes

In sleep apnea syndromes, the patient periodically stops breathing during sleep, for one of two reasons: either the brain does not send signals to the breathing muscles (central apnea) or there is an obstruction produced by closure of the throat that blocks breathing (obstructive apnea). People with sleep apneas do not sleep well, as might be imagined. Sometimes partially or fully waking up is the body's mechanism for restarting of breathing. As a result, the patient may complain of excessive sleepiness in the daytime or troubled sleeping. In addition, personality change or deterioration in intellectual functioning may be noted (Strohl, Sullivan, & Saunders, 1984). Snoring may be noted in patients with obstructive apneas. Diagnosis is made by the patient's sleeping in a sleep laboratory where his respiration can be continuously monitored throughout the night. Research on these syndromes is at too early a stage to tell how frequently they cause behavioral difficulties in children.

SUMMARY

The medical differential diagnosis of altered behavior or mental function is more complex and difficult than that of any other symptom. The clinician's plight is made even more difficult by the fact that so many of the diseases that cause altered mental status are so rare that to test for them routinely with definitive laboratory studies would result in a very low yield and a waste of much time and money. The best way to avoid missing medical illness without wasting large amounts of money on tests is to be familiar with the signs and symptoms of the illnesses most commonly implicated and to elicit such information in the interview. If such information leads to suspicion, referral for further work-up can take place. In general, the clinician should most highly suspect medical illness when there is a change in personality without some compelling explanation for it, or when the child has specific physical symptoms or simply seems to feel "sick." The specific questions that would make us suspect one of the more common illnesses are listed in Table 3.2. The clinician can without a great expenditure of time include these in the interview and thus be more likely to recognize one of these diseases when it occurs.

TABLE 3.2   Questions to Ask in Screening for Medical Illness

General:

Recent change in personality without other explanation?
Physical complaints?

Lead toxicity:

Does the child tend to eat or put in his or her mouth things that are not food?
Does the child get a lot of dust or dirt on his mouth?
Is the child not closely supervised by adults?
Does the child spend time in an old house, with crumbling paint?
Has the child been exposed to sanding of paint in an old house, fumes from fires burning storage batteries, game killed by lead shot, or other source of lead?
Abdominal pain, loss of appetite, vomiting, constipation, or anemia?

Toxicity from "Recreational" Drugs:

History of ingestion of such drugs?
Spontaneous recovery after drugs become unavailable?

Toxicity from prescribed or over-the-counter drugs:

Is the child taking theophylline, corticosteroids, antihistamines, phenobarbital, phenytoin, other anticonvulsants, methylphenidate, dextroamphetamine, pemoline, insulin, or vitamin A or D?
Do the symptoms have any temporal relationship to the starting or increase of such drugs?

Idiosyncratic Reactions to Foods or Inhalants:

Is there worsening of symptoms after exposure to a particular food or inhaled substance?

Subdural Effusion:

Recent head trauma?
Headache, vomiting, or neurological symptoms?
Behavioral symptoms developing over a course of days or a couple of weeks?

Acute Meningitis (Bacterial or Viral):

Fever? Feeling "sick?" Headache? Stiff neck? History of infection in ear, sinus, scalp, gum, mouth, herpes lesions in genitalia?
Behavioral symptoms developing over a course of hours or a couple of days?

(Continued)

TABLE 3.2 (*Continued*)

Tuberculous or Fungal Meningitis:

Fever?
History of exposure to someone with the illness? Travel to place where illness is endemic?
Conversion of TB skin test?
Treatment with immunosuppressive drugs?
Behavioral symptoms developing over a course of weeks or months?

Rocky Moutain Spotted Fever:

In Southeastern United States?
History of tick bite?
Headache, fever, loss of appetite?
Rash?
Behavioral symptoms developing over a course of hours or days?

Brain Abscess:

History of infection of scalp, ear, gum, or sinus?
Congenital heart disease?
Behavioral symptoms developing over a course of hours, days, or weeks?

Reye's Syndrome:

Recent viral infection?
Recent taking of aspirin?
Nausea or vomiting?
Behavioral symptoms developing over a course of hours or a couple of days?

Brain Tumor:

Clumsiness?
Headaches?
Nausea or vomiting?
Neurological symptoms (i.e., localized weakness, numbness, impaired visual field, trouble moving eyes, seizure, staggering)?
Behavioral symptoms developing over a course of weeks or months?

Vitamin Deficiency or Protein Malnutrition:

Grossly abnormal diet?

Wilson's Disease:

Family history of Wilson's disease?
Are parents blood relatives?
Slurred speech?
Tremors?
Muscle rigidity?
Twitches?
Immobility of face?
Rings around edge of corneas?

TABLE 3.2 *(Continued)*

History of unexplained liver disease?
Behavioral symptoms developing over a course of months?

Tourette's Disease:

Multiple motor tics?
Vocal tics?

Hyperthyroidism:

Rapid heart rate?
Increased food intake, producing less than expected or no weight gain?
Increased activity level?
Faster thought processes?
Goiter?
Diarrhea?
Heat intolerance?
Increased sweating?
Prominence or bulging of eyes?
Behavioral symptoms developing over a course of weeks or months?

Hypothyroidism:

Slowed heart rate?
Decreased food intake, producing less than expected or no weight loss?
Decreased activity level?
Slowed thought processes?
Constipation?
Cold intolerance?
Dry skin?
Coarse, brittle hair?
Sallow complexion?
Goiter?
Behavioral symptoms developing over a course of weeks or months?

Diabetes:

Increased drinking of liquids?
Increased urination?
Fatigue?
Bedwetting?
Recent viral illness?
Behavioral symptoms developing over the course of hours or a few days?

Psychomotor Seizures:

Hallucinations?
Depersonalization?
Déja vu? Jamais vu?
Inappropriately intense emotion?
Blank stare during the episode?

(Continued)

TABLE 3.2   (*Continued*)

Psychomotor Seizures (*cont.*):
Stereotyped movements during episode?
Pallor or flushing during the episode?
Nonresponsiveness to conversation during episode?
Amnesia for events of the episode, after it is over?
Symptoms occuring in episodes lasting seconds to minutes?

Petit Mal Seizures:

Blank stare during the episode?
Loss of postural tone during episode?
Episodes lasting approximately 10 seconds?

Hearing Problems:

Can the child not repeat words whispered by the examiner?
Does the child complain of not being able to hear?

Vision Problems:

Can the child complain of trouble seeing?
Does the child fail the gross or quantitative tests of vision given by the examiner?

Anemias:

Pallor of the skin?
History of a diet poor in iron (for example, one composed primarily of milk)?
Behavioral symptoms developing over a course from days to months?

Sleep Apneas:

Excessive daytime sleepiness?
Difficulty maintaining sleep?
Snoring?

REFERENCES

American Psychiatric Association. (1980). *Diagnostic and statistical manual of mental disorders* (3rd ed.). Washington, DC: Author.

Barness, L. A. (1983). Nutrition and nutritional disorders. In R. E. Behrman, V. C. Vaughan, & W. E. Nelson (Eds.), *Nelson textbook of pediatrics* (12th ed.). Philadelphia: Saunders.

Brett, E. M. (1983). Epilepsy and convulsions. In E. M. Brett (Ed.), *Paediatric neurology.* New York: Churchill Livingstone.

Broome, C. V., & Schlech, W. F. (1985). Recent developments in the epidemiology of bacterial meningitis. In M. A. Sande, A. L. Smith, & R. K. Root (Eds.), *Bacterial meningitis.* New York: Churchill Livingstone.

Bukowskyj, M., Nakatsu, K., & Munt, P. W. (1984). Theophylline reassessed. *Annals of Internal Medicine, 101,* 63–73.

Chisholm, J. J. (1983). Increased lead absorption and lead poisoning. In R. E. Behrman, V. C. Vaughan, & W. E. Nelson (Eds.), *Nelson textbook of pediatrics* (12th ed.). Philadelphia: Saunders.

Feingold, B. F. (1975). *Why your child is hyperactive.* New York: Random House.

Fisher, D. A. (1978). Pediatric aspects (of hyperthyroidism). In S. C. Werner & S. H. Ingbar (Eds.), *The thyroid: A fundamental and clinical text* (4th ed.). New York: Harper & Row.

Graef, J. W. (1983). Environmental toxins. In M. D. Levine, W. B. Carey, A. C. Crocker, & R. T. Gross (Eds.), *Developmental-behavioral pediatrics.* Philadelphia: Saunders.

Hall, K. (1976). Allergy of the nervous system: A review. *Annals of Allergy, 36,* 49–64.

Herskowitz, J., & Rosman, N. P. (1982). *Pediatrics, neurology, and psychiatry—Common ground.* New York: Macmillan.

Kidd, K. K., & Pauls, D. L. (1982). Genetic hypotheses for Tourette syndrome. In A. J. Friedhoff & T. N. Chase (Eds.), *Advances in Neurology: Vol. 35. Gilles de la Tourette syndrome.* New York: Raven.

Lishman, W. A. (1978). *Organic psychiatry: The psychological consequences of cerebral disorder.* Oxford: Blackwell Scientific Publications.

Needleman, H. L., Gunnoe, C., Leviton, A., Reed, R., Peresie, H., Maher, C., & Barnett, P. (1979). Psychological performance of children with elevated lead levels. *New England Journal of Medicine, 300,* 689–694.

Nuwer, M. R. (1982). Coprolalia as an organic symptom. In A. J. Friedhoff & T. N. Chase (Eds.) *Vol. 35. Advances in Neurology: Gilles de la Tourette Syndrome.* New York: Raven.

Pearson, H. A. (1983). Diseases of the blood. In R. E. Behrman, V. C. Vaughan, & W. E. Nelson (Eds.), *Nelson textbook of pediatrics* (12th ed.). Philadelphia: Saunders.

Phillips, C. F. (1983). Herpes simplex. In R. E. Behrman, V. C. Vaughan, & W. E. Nelson (Eds.), *Nelson textbook of pediatrics* (12th ed.). Philadelphia: Saunders.

Riela, A. R., & Roach, E. S. (1983). Reye's syndrome: Twenty years in perspective. *North Carolina Medical Journal, 44,* 351–355.

Rivinus, T. M., Jamison, D. L., & Graham, P. J. (1975). Childhood organic neurological disease presenting as psychiatric disorder. *Archives of Disease in Childhood, 50,* 115–119.

Russell Jones, R., & Stephens, R. (1983). The contribution of lead in petrol to human lead intake. In M. Rutter & R. Russell Jones (Eds.), *Lead versus health.* New York: Wiley.

Rutter, M. Low Level lead exposure: Sources, effects and implications. In M. Rutter & R. Russell Jones (Eds.), *Lead versus health.* New York: Wiley.

Scheinberg, I. H., & Sternlieb, I. (1984). Wilson's disease. In (Vol. 23) *Major problems in internal medicine* Philadelphia: Saunders.

Speer, F. (1954). The allergic tension-fatigue syndrome. *Pediatric Clinics of North America,* 1029–1037.

Starko, K. M., Ray, C. G., Dominguez, L. B., Stromberg, W. L., & Woodall, D. F. (1980). Reye's syndrome and salicylate use. *Pediatrics, 66,* 859–864.

Stores, G. (1975). Behavioural effects of anti-epileptic drugs. *Developmental Medicine and Child Neurology, 17,* 647–658.

Strohl, K. P., Sullivan, C. E., & Saunders, N. A. (1984). Sleep apnea syndromes. In N. A. Saunders & C. E. Sullivan (Eds.), *Sleep and breathing.* New York: Dekker.

Till, K. (1975) *Paediatric neurosurgery for paediatricians and neurosurgeons.* Oxford: Blackwell Scientific Publications.

Weinberger, M., & Hendeles, L. (1980). Pharmacologic management. In C. W. Bierman & D. A. Pearlman (Eds.), *Allergic diseases of infancy, childhood, and adolescence.* Philadelphia: Saunders.

Weiss, B. (1984). Food additive safety evaluation: The link to behavioral disorders in children. In B. B. Lahey & A. E. Kazdin (Eds.), *Advances in clinical child psychology* (Vol. 7). New York: Plenum.

CHAPTER 4

Parent Training

SANDRA TWARDOSZ AND VEY M. NORDQUIST

Behavioral parent training involves helping parents change some aspect of their relationship with their child. Generally, this has been accomplished by teaching parents to rearrange the antecedents and consequences for their children's behavior through contingency management, or to negotiate such changes through contingency contracting. In addition, parents have been instructed in operant training procedures which they then use to teach their handicapped children basic self-care, social, and communication skills. A wide range of child behavior disorders and problems have responded favorably to this approach.

However, as research and program development have continued, it has become clear that some families do not benefit from parent training despite the sophisticated technology. Some drop out of treatment or are unable to learn the skills. Others are resistant to change or do not use their skills after completing the program. Still others participate reluctantly because they are required to do so by a social service agency, and an unknown number never seek treatment. The failures in parent training have been discussed and studied in terms of variables such as marital conflict, single parenting, social isolation, depression, the severity of the problem, household disorganization, and temperamental characteristics of the child. It is now generally agreed that parent training for many families involves much more than simply teaching parenting skills, and that a greater understanding of both successes and failures results from considering the functioning of individual family members, the family unit, and the impact of the surrounding environment. Parent trainers have responded to these additional challenges by modifying their programs and adding treatment components to help ameliorate factors that interfere with participation in training and maintenance of treatment gains.

The authors express their appreciation to Gordon Burghardt and Richard Saudargas for helpful comments and suggestions.

The behavioral parent training literature is enormous, complex, and of wide interest, judging from the number of recent books, chapters, and discussion articles that have appeared (e.g., Altman & Mira, 1983; Baker, 1984; Dangel & Polster, 1984; Gordon & Davidson, 1981; Graziano, 1977; Moreland, Schwebel, Beck, & Wells, 1982; O'Dell, 1985; Ross, 1981; Sanders, 1984; Sanders & James, 1983; Wells & Forehand, 1981; Wilson, Franks, Brownell, & Kendall, 1984). The topics these authors address include the history of the field, comparison to other approaches to child problems and disorders, issues in the investigation and programming of maintenance and generalization, and the search for predictors of success and failure in parent training.

Rather than provide an exhaustive review and critique of the parent training literature, which would mandate cursory attention to any particular program or issue, we have elected to focus more intensively on four major topics. The programs and research described for each topic are representative of the characteristics of others in the field, or represent relatively new areas of investigation. Unfortunately, we will be unable to describe many well-developed and important parent training programs (e.g., Czyzewski, Christian, & Norris, 1984; Patterson, Chamberlain, & Reid, 1982).

In this chapter we first describe the skills parents are taught, including contingency management and operant training procedures, contingency contracting, conflict resolution skills training, parent-child interaction, and household organization. The last two areas are relatively recent developments. A brief section on parent training modalities (i.e., didactic instruction, modeling, individual and group training) is followed by a description of some of the approaches parent trainers have used to individualize treatment to match the needs of clients. These modifications have been made to ameliorate personal and family problems that interfere with treatment outcome. The final section addresses the issue of the relationship between therapist and client, an area that is poorly understood and just beginning to be explored.

PARENT TRAINING CURRICULUM

Parents have been taught to modify a wide range of child behavior problems and to teach basic skills to handicapped children. In general, contingency management procedures have been used extensively with younger children who have behavior problems, while contingency contracting and conflict resolution skills training have been used more often with older children and adolescents. In addition, because some parents are deficient in basic skills, such as home safety and maintaining a daily schedule, parent training methods are beginning to be applied to teaching household organization. Other types of parent-child interaction, such as play and the expression of affection, have recently become a focus of training as parent trainers have become interested in aspects of parenting other than contingency management.

Contingency Management and Operant Training Procedures

Although the majority of contingency management studies and programs have been designed for children who are noncompliant (oppositional) or antisocial and aggressive, the procedures have also been demonstrated effective for numerous other childhood problems. Some recent studies have focused on the parents' role in the treatment of obesity (e.g., Israel, Stolmaker, & Andrian, 1985), adherence to medical procedures (e.g., Carney, Schechter, & Davis, 1983), and stuttering (Budd & Madison, 1983). The possibility of involving parents in their children's social skills training has also been discussed (Budd, in press).

Gordon and Davidson (1981) summarized the basic content of contingency management parent training programs. The program developed and evaluated by Forehand and his colleagues and described in a detailed manual for parent trainers (Forehand & McMahon, 1981) exemplifies this content. The program is designed for parents of 3- to 8-year-old noncompliant children who have been referred by professionals (i.e., pediatricians, ministers, mental health workers). It is designed to change the pattern of parent-child interaction rather than discrete behaviors such as refusing to go to bed or failing to complete chores. The participation of both parents is encouraged but not required so that mothers usually complete the program. Most families are lower-middle class, although a wide range of socioeconomic status is represented.

The initial assessment consists of a parent interview, a brief child interview, and the completion of questionnaires by parents concerning their perceptions of child adjustment, perceptions of personal adjustment and marital satisfaction, and knowledge of social learning principles. The parent is asked to record problem behavior in the home, and direct observations are conducted both in the clinic and at home. Observers record the parent behaviors of rewards, attends, questions, commands, warnings, and time-out, and the child behaviors of compliance, noncompliance, and other deviant behavior. Observational data may not show that the child is noncompliant, indicating that perhaps the parents' expectations rather than the child's behavior should be changed. Referrals to physicians and other professionals can be made if they appear warranted.

After the initial assessment the therapist provides a conceptualization of the problem in terms of parent-child interaction and a rationale for the treatment program. The child, who has been asked to play alone, is either praised by the therapist for compliance or ignored for noncompliance, thus demonstrating these skills for the parent.

Treatment is conducted in a clinic playroom during twice weekly sessions. During Phase 1 (Child's Game), the parent is taught to use differential attention in a series of steps (i.e., attending to and describing appropriate behavior; eliminating commands, questions, and criticisms; using praise and affectionate physical contact for appropriate behavior; and ignoring inappropriate behavior). During Phase 2, (Parents' Game), the parent is taught to give commands appropriately, to reward the child for compliance, to use a warning if compliance is not initiated within 5 seconds and to use a brief time-out if compliance is not initiated within 5 seconds of the warning. The child is placed in a chair in a corner of the room for 3 minutes and must be quiet and still for the last 15 seconds. The parent then repeats the command.

Each treatment session is 60 to 90 minutes long and includes a period during which the parent and child interact to demonstrate the skill being taught and data are collected; discussion with the parent about the use of the skill at home and during the observation period; modeling by the therapist; role-play with the therapist acting the part of the child; explanation and role-play of procedures to the child; a practice period during which the parent receives instructions and feedback via a bug-in-the-ear; practice without feedback; and assignment of homework. Parents must meet a performance criterion before moving to the next training step. Home observations are conducted immediately after training and at follow-up, and parents provide feedback on their satisfaction with the program.

Forehand and his colleagues conducted numerous investigations concerning parameters of the program: initial treatment outcome; generalization across settings, time, siblings, and behavior; and social validity. These studies support the effectiveness of the program, not only in terms of changes in maternal and child behavior, but in maternal perceptions of their children. However, it was also found that some parents dropped out, and some did not maintain the skills because of personal distress. Summaries of this research are found in Forehand and McMahon (1981) and McMahon and Forehand (1984).

Parents of handicapped children generally require training in both contingency management and operant training procedures because they frequently must teach basic self-care, communication, and play skills to children who do not respond to typical child-rearing practices. Thus, we will describe a program developed by Baker and his colleagues (Baker & Heifetz, 1976; Heifetz, 1977) for parents of moderately to severely retarded children between 3 and 13 years of age. The program consists of an initial assessment session, ten 2-hour training sessions, a postassessment session, and several follow-up sessions. Training is conducted in groups of 8 to 10 families. The child is present only during one session midway through training and the two assessment sessions.

During assessment sessions data are gathered through a structured parent interview, parent completion of paper-and-pencil measures on their children's skills and their own knowledge of behavioral principles and techniques, and videotapes of parent-child interaction. After the initial assessment, four training sessions are devoted to self-help skills and operant training procedures, including setting behavioral objectives; task analysis; using prompting, fading, and backward chaining; and learning how to select and dispense rewards. During the fifth session, parents work directly with their children and receive feedback from trainers and other parents. Modeling is used to illustrate techniques when necessary. Sessions six, seven, and eight are devoted to contingency management procedures, such as differential attention and time-out, and parents also are shown how to toilet-train their children if it is warranted. The last two training sessions provide instruction in communication and play. Formal, discrete-trial training is emphasized initially to establish new skills. Later, parents are encouraged to teach informally during daily household routines to promote generalization.

Before each training session parents are required to read relevant material in *Steps to Independence,* a series of eight training manuals. (Baker, Brightman, Heifetz, & Murphy, 1976, 1977, 1978, 1980). Didactic presentations make up only a small portion of the program, which consists primarily of demonstrations, role-playing, videotapes, and discussions with and between parents concerning the program and their performance. Parents conduct approximately 10 minutes of formal teaching at home each day. The program concludes with a posttraining assessment of the parents' teaching skills, which is conducted in the same manner as the pretraining assessment, and several follow-up meetings.

A number of program evaluation studies have been summarized by Baker and Clark (1983). The results indicated that most parents who began the program completed it despite the fact that many came from low-income backgrounds and had limited educations. Parents who completed training possessed a greater knowledge of learning principles and teaching strategies and were more proficient teachers than those assigned to a delayed-training control group. Moreover, children's self-help skills and problem behaviors improved substantially after training. However, no observations were obtained in the homes.

Follow-up data collected through structured interviews and questionnaires revealed that families varied greatly in their performance after training, with a substantial number reporting that they did not apply the program's formal procedures. Families who experienced severe and multiple stresses (i.e., death of a loved one, illness, or marital problems) were less likely to follow through after training, especially if they had to reserve a special time for this purpose.

A program developed for parents of autistic children (Koegel, Schreibman, Johnson, O'Neill, & Dunlap, 1984; Schreibman, Koegel, Mills, & Burke, 1984) is noteworthy, not only because of its effects on children's behavior but also because the investigators have assessed its effects on other aspects of family functioning. The program teaches parents to use instructions, prompts, consequences, shaping, and chaining in the clinic. Training methods include reading manuals, watching and discussing a videotape, and receiving feedback from a therapist while working on target behaviors with one's child. After parents have reached criterion in the clinic, training shifts to the home for the programming of generalization.

When comparing clinic treatment of children to parent training, the investigators found that trained parents reported spending more time teaching, using their skills in interactions with their children at home, and spending less time in custodial activities than parents of children in the clinic treatment group. Furthermore, parents who received parent training increased dramatically the amount of time spent in leisure activities (i.e., visits from friends, family outdoor recreation, and quiet time alone).

The programs described above illustrate several features of current approaches to parent training. The sophistication of the technology for changing child behavior and the range of available methods for communicating that information is impressive. Furthermore, both the immediate and longer-term outcomes of training are measured with a variety of behavioral assessment methods. These focus not only on changes in maternal and child behavior but on parents' perceptions of their children and, most recently, on changes in other aspects of family functioning. Finally, it is clear that parent training is not effective for some families.

Contingency Contracting

A contingency contract is a written agreement between parents and child in which troublesome aspects of their relationship are specified in terms of behaviors and consequences (Gambrill, 1977). It is a formal means of stating explicitly *who* does *what* to *whom* and *when,* so that parents and child give and receive more positive reinforcement and engage in fewer aversive interactions. One critical aspect of contigency contracting is reciprocity. Reciprocity implies that each family member has rights as well as obligations, and that things that members value and include in their social interchanges must be exchanged on an equal and fair basis (Stuart, 1971). To accomplish this objective, contracts must be negotiated, usually with the help of a therapist. Contingency contracting requires the active involvement of all family members in the negotiation process and necessitates verbal and conceptual skills that usually are beyond the ability of young children. For this reason, nearly all of the literature on contingency contracting involves families of older children and adolescents (Lutzker, 1980).

A contingency contract is often used when communication between the parents and adolescent has broken down. Consequently, conflict resolution skills training usually accompanies the use of contracts and may be more important for seriously troubled families than the actual reinforcement contingencies (Weathers & Liberman 1978). Conflict resolution skills training is discussed in the next section.

Although contingency contracting appears to have face validity and early reports of its success offered hope for troubled families (Cantrill, Cantrill, Huddleston, & Woolridge, 1969; Tharp & Wetzel, 1969), its effectiveness has not been well supported by recent research (see Lutzker, 1980; Weathers & Liberman, 1978; Wells & Forehand, 1981). The best results have occurred when one behavior problem, such as academic performance, was the focus of intervention.

For example, Blechman, Kotanchik, and Taylor (1981) identified 35 high-risk children in the second through fifth grades who were consistently not performing up to their abilities in math and reading. Children were assigned randomly to either an experimental ($n = 20$) or control ($n = 15$) group. In addition, 33 low-risk children were placed in a stable comparison group. Family involvement treatment was conducted in a clinic where parent and child played the Solutions board game. The game guided them through writing a contingency contract and making decisions about rewards the child would receive when the teacher sent home a "good news" note, which indicated that the child had performed at or above baseline means for math and/or reading. A project director maintained weekly telephone contacts with the family. Results showed that children in the experimental group performed more consistently and with greater accuracy on academic measures, rated themselves as better students, and narrowed the gap between themselves and low-risk children more than children in the control group.

In a replication and extension of this study, Blechman, Taylor, and Schrader (1981) demonstrated that contingency contracting rather than the "good news" note alone was a critical component of the family involvement treatment package. It not only produced improvements in the consistency and accuracy of high-risk children that resembled the performance of low-risk children, but it also was the only condition (compared to home note and control conditions) that produced generalized effects during probe days when no notes were earned. Thus, contingency contracting may be very effective when applied to single, discrete, and easily monitored behaviors, and when parents still have control over a child's reinforcers.

Contingency contracts are more likely to fail when families of adolescents have multiple problems and parents no longer control significant reinforcers. For example, Weathers and Liberman (1975) treated six families of delinquent adolescents with contingency contracting and conflict resolution skills training. Sixteen families who originally consented to treatment but dropped out after the first session served as a no-treatment control group. All 22 adolescents had been adjudicated to the program by juvenile court authorities. Of four target behaviors (school attendance, completion of chores, verbal abusiveness, and curfew compliance), only verbal abusiveness improved during treatment. Parent reports and unannounced telephone calls by the investigators indicated that adolescents in both groups broke curfews as often during intervention as during baseline. Behavior checklist data and school grades recorded before treatment and three months after treatment failed to show any differences between the contracting and control groups. Weathers and Liberman concluded that contingency contracting is not likely to work with highly deviant and disorganized families that are plagued by divorce, crime, and drug abuse, and whose members are incapable of learning communication and negotiation skills. Perhaps with multiply distressed families that have a long history of serious conflicts, it may be necessary to relinquish contingency contracting in favor of an intervention that encompasses the entire living environment (Lutzker, 1980).

Conflict Resolution Skills Training

Families of delinquent adolescents have poorer communication skills than families of normal adolescents (Prinz, Rosenblum & O'Leary, 1978), suggesting that the disruptive behavior of adolescents may be, in part, an inappropriate reaction to ineffective communication. One approach to this problem is to teach adolescents and parents to resolve their conflicts using more appropriate and effective communication skills (Wells & Forehand, 1981). What follows is a sample of some of the methods that have been used to teach conflict resolution skills. More detailed reviews are available in Wells and Forehand (1981), Lutzker (1980), and Moreland et al. (1982).

Martin (1975) and Martin and Twentyman (1976) trained parents to express their feelings directly and briefly and to listen carefully to their adolescents. They also taught them to make reflective comments and to reach agreements before terminating discussions. Training consisted of listening to an audiotaped model and then practicing, initially with a therapist and then with their child. Once the parent and child had acquired the requisite skills, they were shown how to generate several solutions to their own problems and then choose one that was most acceptable. When these procedures were applied to 28 families of conduct problem adolescents, parent-recorded descriptions of problem situations and the average parent-estimated weekly rate of conflict were significantly lower than in a control group of 15 families assigned to a waiting list. Moreover, these effects were maintained over a six-month follow-up period.

Blechman and her colleagues developed the Family Contract Game, a very different approach to reducing family conflict and strengthening problem-solving skills. The parent and child select problems that must be solved and potential rewards that each will receive when resolution of a problem is reached. Problems and rewards are selected from a card sort. After selections are made, they are entered into the game's problem card deck and reward card deck. Then parent and child begin playing. Depending on which of 14 board squares are selected, they receive written instructions in the use of specific problem-solving skills. The game is played until the parent and child are able to write a contract that specifies the behaviors they have agreed to use to resolve a particular problem. The game usually takes about 15 minutes to play. Blechman and her colleagues (Blechman, Olsen, & Hellman, 1976; Blechman, Olsen, Schornagel, Halsdorf, & Turner, 1976) found that children between the ages of 8 and 15 and their mothers, who were experiencing conflicts, produced more problem-solving behaviors during treatment in a clinic than they did during baseline. Unfortunately, when the game was not played, problem-solving behaviors declined significantly but were still substantially higher in some cases than they had been prior to treatment. Contracts carried out at home significantly reduced parent-child conflicts, suggesting that participants generalized problem-solving skills.

Rather than using a "therapeutic" approach to training, Kifer, Lewis, Green, and Phillips (1974) took an "educational" approach. They used a task analysis method to separate negotiating skills into distinct components and then used instructions, practice, and feedback to train two mother-daughter pairs and one father-son pair (in which the youths had juvenile court contacts) to negotiate. The age range of the adolescents was 13 to 17 years. Observations of conflict situations were made in the homes one week before training, during classroom training sessions (where the pairs received instruction, practice, and feedback), and finally in the home after training where the pairs attempted to use their skills to resolve family conflicts. The classroom sessions included role-playing hypothetical conflict situations, discussing, and practicing conflict resolution using Roosa's (1973) situations-options-consequences simulation model of negotiation. The results indicated that all three pairs negotiated more often during training and posttraining simulation sessions than during a pretraining session. Most important, all three parent-youth pairs used negotiation skills in their homes after training. However, as Lutzker (1980) noted, these results could have been due to a reactivity effect produced by a tape recorder that was placed in the homes to record verbal exchanges.

Although contingency contracting and conflict resolution skills training have been discussed separately, in practice they are often combined. Some investigators believe that contracts alone are not likely to resolve disputes between parents and adolescents, especially in cases where the conflicts are severe and have a long history (Weathers & Liberman, 1975). A thoughtful approach to the problem of disruptive parent-adolescent relationships, therefore, should consist of assessment and treatment of each conflict area presented by individual families (Wells & Forehand, 1981).

Parent-Child Interaction

Most behavioral parent training has been focused on contingency management and operant training procedures, with relatively little attention given to other areas of the parent-child relationship. Lutzker, McGimsey, McRae, and Campbell (1983) posed the question of whether good parents do more than praise appropriate behavior, use time-out for inappropriate behavior, and give clear, concise commands, and concluded that most behavior therapists would probably reply that good parents should also be loving, supportive, creative, involved, and consistent. Mash and Terdal (1981) noted the prevalence of observational systems for categorizing parental directives and child compliance compared to those available for describing parents' and children's affectional behaviors. They stated that this both follows from and contributes to a view of childhood disturbance centering around command-compliance sequences. They did not deny the validity and utility of such hypotheses but believed that the types of measurement systems used may favor some assessment outcomes over others.

A focus on contingency management and operant training procedures seems clearly necessary for many of the child and family problems parent trainers encounter. It is probably virtually impossible to teach the nuances of creative play or affectionate expression to parents and children whose primary form of interaction is coercive and who may not even like each other. It would be inappropriate to do so when the parent-child relationship is already loving and supportive but when parents need skills to deal with discrete childhood problems or to teach their handicapped child. Nevertheless, the assessment, teaching, and modification of parent-child interaction is extremely important for a number of reasons.

First, it is crucial to determine the effects of current parent training approaches on broader areas of family functioning, such as whether or not family members feel and act more affectionately toward each other, particularly when family interaction has been primarily negative and focused on the problem behavior of a specific child. If the parent-child relationship had deteriorated before parents sought treatment, or if a positive relationship had never existed between them, then parent training focused on play, affection, and sensitivity to others' behavior could be offered. Similarly, if one aspect of the problem was the inappropriate display of affection or excessive dependency, than it would be important to determine if this had been modified.

Second, little information exists on the changes in reinforcement value of parents and children that may occur as a result of parent training. Wahler (1969) demonstrated that use of a contingency management program for noncompliance with two families resulted not only in increased compliance but also in an increase in the reinforcement value of the parents' praise, as measured by a marble drop task, and an increase in children's approaches to their parents. Parents also reported that they enjoyed their children more. The relationship between contingency management programs for noncompliance and enhanced reinforcement value of adults has been evaluated in only two other studies (Nordquist & McEvoy, 1983; Wahler & Nordquist, 1973). Only one of the four adults was a parent; three were teachers. In every case noncompliant children spontaneously imitated and interacted more frequently with these adults during intervention than during baseline. Additional research with parents would have important clinical implications because parent trainers frequently report that parental attention may not be reinforcing at the beginning of treatment (e.g., Forehand & McMahon, 1981). Failure to obtain an increase in reinforcement value could be associated with poor maintenance of treatment effects.

An emphasis on positive parent-child interaction is implicit in behavioral parent training. Most programs (e.g., Forehand & McMahon, 1981; Miller, 1975) begin by teaching parents to discriminate appropriate behavior and provide positive social attention for it before teaching the use of punishment procedures. However, in most studies, positive social attention was reported as a single behavioral category, so the specific behaviors that parents used more frequently are not known. Furthermore, there is some evidence that gains in this area do not generalize or maintain as well as other skills. For example, Sanders and Dadds (1982) reported that a reduction in parental aversive instructions and aversive social attention generalized to nontraining settings after contingency management and planned activities training, but that praise and nonaversive social attention did not generalize. Similarly, Baum and Forehand (1981) reported that parents' decrease of inappropriate commands maintained during an extended follow-up after training in contingency management, while a significant reduction in rewards and contingent attention occurred. However, such a decrease may have resulted from program instructions to reduce reinforcement as the child's deviant behaviors decreased.

Several investigators have taught parents to interact in emotionally positive ways with their children. Wolfe, St. Lawrence, Graves, Brehony, Bradlyn, and Kelly (1982) provided bug-in-the-ear training to a child-abusive mother during compliance and cooperative tasks in a clinic. Training focused first on reducing hostile physical and verbal behavior (e.g., pushing, grabbing, threatening, insulting) by providing instructions on the use of ignoring and brief time-out in a chair for misbehavior. Training was then begun to increase positive verbal and physical behavior (e.g., praise, hugging, patting) contingent on appropriate child behavior. A multiple baseline design across behaviors was used. Homework assignments were provided, and observations were periodically conducted in the home during similar tasks. In the clinic positive verbal and physical behavior increased concurrent with the reduction in hostile verbal and physical behavior that occurred during the first phase of training, and it continued to increase during the second phase. Positive verbal behavior maintained better than positive physical behavior while training was faded and during follow-up, and hostile behavior remained near zero. Similar results occurred at home.

Lutzker, Megson, Webb, and Dachman (1985) taught adult-child interaction skills to the mothers of two families reported for child abuse. Training was conducted in the home in the context of structured play situations via discussion, modeling, role-play, and feedback. The behaviors measured included affectionate physical contact, simple and complex verbal statements, appropriate commands, congruence between verbal and physical behavior, and praise. Mothers were taught to increase or decrease only the behaviors that did not meet criteria established by expert judges. The judges had viewed pretraining and posttraining videotapes of professionals who received similar training in a simulated playroom with preschool children. Both adults increased the percentage of behaviors performed at criterion only after training began and maintained their behavior during follow-up. Unfortunately, data were not presented concerning which behaviors were trained in each family and which met criterion.

Finally, Webster-Stratton (1981b) developed a unique videotape modeling program to illustrate concepts such as nurturance, sensitivity, authoritative style, individual differences in children, and behavior management skills. Vignettes of interaction between parents and children were developed to illustrate effective play techniques, setting limits, handling misbehavior, and communication and feelings. For example, the videotape on play shows parent models following the child's lead rather than competing, and participating in role-play and fantasy rather than being rigid, controlling, and concrete. Parents are asked to practice these techniques for 15 minutes each day at home.

Webster-Stratton (1981a, 1982b, 1982a) evaluated the effectiveness of the videotapes and group discussion with 35 volunteer middle-class mothers of preschool-aged children. Although these children did not exhibit serious behavior problems, they were significantly above the norms reported for the Eyberg Child Behavior Inventory (Eyberg & Ross, 1978), a parent report measure. The first two studies reported the effects of the program on mothers and children respectively. Behavior observations were obtained from videotapes of mother-child interaction in the clinic playroom. Experimental group mothers, who had attended four weekly 2-hour sessions, showed decreases in lead taking, nonacceptance, and dominance and an increase in positive affect; they reported fewer and less intense behavior problems than the control group. Their children showed a decrease in negative affect and submissive behaviors and an increase in positive affect. These effects were replicated subsequently with the control group. In a 1-year follow-up (Webster-Stratton, 1982a), in which virtually all of the mothers who had completed training participated, it was found that almost all gains had been maintained or improved except that the positive affect of both mothers and children had decreased and mothers reported feeling less confident of their parenting skills. However, positive affect was higher than during baseline and fell within the range of a normative sample. The author acknowledged that the absence of a control group at the 1-year follow-up must be considered when evaluating these results. Observations were not conducted in the homes.

The paucity of data available on the types and frequencies of interaction that occur in both clinic and nonclinic families makes it difficult to judge whether decreases in positive social or affectionate behavior that occur after treatment are cause for concern. Thus, it would be helpful if parent trainers used observation systems that focused on a variety of behaviors in addition to those designed specifically to measure the effectiveness of their programs. Several measurement systems would be appropriate. For example, Twardosz, Schwartz, Fox, and Cunningham (1979) developed and socially validated a system to measure affectionate behavior. The Interpersonal Behavior Construct Scale (Kogan & Gordon, 1975) consists of 23 categories of behaviors that are summed to form the five main dimensions of positive affect, negative affect, nonacceptance, dominance, and submissiveness. Use of such measures may provide information that would help indicate a family's progress in training, the necessity for additional training, and the probability of maintenance and generalization.

Household Organization

Parents who lack basic skills in household organization require training either because the children experience neglect or because disorganized household routines interfere with the implementation or effectiveness of contingency management procedures. Lutzker and his colleagues conducted several studies with parents who were referred to Project 12-Ways. This program provides a variety of services to abuse and neglect families in an effort to combat the varied environmental factors associated with these problems (e.g., Lutzker, 1984). For example, Tertinger, Greene, and Lutzker (1984) developed the Home Accident Prevention Inventory to measure fire, electrical, suffocation, firearms, and poison hazards. Intervention consisted of instructions, demonstrations, and feedback to six families in a multiple baseline design across hazardous categories. All families showed a reduction in hazards that was maintained over a 7-month period. However, because of the amount of time and effort required by the parent counselors, Barone, Greene, and Lutzker (1986) substituted an audio-slide show and review manual during home visits for the live instructions and demonstrations. This approach proved effective with the three families who participated.

Deficits in household organization skills are important not only because of direct effects on children, but because they may interfere with participation in parent training programs and the implementation or effectiveness of contingency management procedures. Doherty (1975), who worked with parents of acting-out adolescent boys who spent most of the week in residential treatment, found that training in contingency management was inadequate for some families because of chaotic household routines. One mother, for example, could not find time to do the reading required by the program until the child care workers had shown her how to prepare meals and how to manage the morning routine so that the children arrived at school on time.

Sanders and Dadds (1982) illustrated a possible relationship between the success of parent training in child management (CMT) and the provision of planned activities (PAT) for preschool-aged children. They taught five families to use child management (including prompts, praise, response cost, and time-out) in a multiple baseline design, but only one child's deviant behavior decreased despite the fact that parents used the procedures accurately (assessed by direct observation) in both training and generalization settings (i.e., shopping trips, visitors in the home, meals). After the authors taught the parents to discuss rules in advance and provide something for the children to do while the parents were occupied, the deviant behavior of three additional children decreased. Although the separate contribution of the planned activities cannot be assessed because the contingency management procedures continued during PAT and had been implemented first for all families, this study suggests that organizational conditions may either support or hinder the operation of procedures learned in parent training programs.

In a subsequent study (Sanders & Christensen, 1985), a group of 10 parents of noncompliant children received CMT alone while another group of 10 received both CMT and PAT. The addition of PAT did not produce results superior to CMT alone. The authors argued that CMT may have produced ceiling effects, and that PAT may be more appropriate when parents fail to generalize their skills, when the child is more difficult in some settings than in others, or when the parents engage in more coercive behavior in some settings than others. Because PAT teaches parents educational and relational skills, it may ultimately be more acceptable than an exclusive focus on child management.

Because little research has been conducted on this topic with families in their homes, specific conclusions cannot be drawn concerning the effect of various household organization strategies on parents' implementation and maintenance of contingency management procedures. However, a large number of studies conducted in caregiving environments (e.g., daycare centers, institutions for the retarded, homes for the elderly, schools) collectively demonstrate the effects of specific ways of organizing the physical, social, and programmatic environment (see Twardosz, 1984). For example, the provision of appropriate materials and planned activities was found to increase social interaction among children in an after-school recreation program (Quilitch & Risley, 1973), to decrease self-stimulation and self-injury with profoundly retarded children (Favell, McGimsey, & Schell, 1982; Horner, 1980), and to decrease aggression on an elementary school playground (Murphy, Hutchinson, & Bailey, 1983). Studies conducted in nursing homes, a residential facility for the retarded, and a psychiatric treatment facility for adolescents indicated that serving food family-style increased social interaction, improved eating behavior, and increased time spent at meals (Doke, Feaster, & Predmore, 1977; Melin & Gotestam, 1981; VanBiervliet, Spangler, & Marshall, 1981). There is also empirical support for the beneficial effects of predictable activity and staff schedules (Durand, 1983; Frederiksen & Frederiksen, 1977) and for assigning responsibilities by functional areas rather than by specific children (LeLaurin & Risley, 1972).

Such information may provide ideas for research and application to parent training. For example, the members of some families may have learned to spend as much time as possible away from each other in order to avoid being targets of verbal attacks and coercive interaction. They may even arrange not to eat meals together regularly. Such families might benefit from the implementation of family-style dining, where preparation and clean-up tasks are shared; people sit down together; and food is placed in serving bowls, requested, and passed around the table. These activities could provide a context for pleasant interaction, which family members might resume as parents learn effective contingency management procedures. Alternatively, family members may need to be taught to interact pleasantly if such behavior is not in their repertoires. Family-style dining could also set the occasion for teaching handicapped children table manners and the functional use of language through incidental teaching (e.g., Hart & Risley, 1978).

Another problem that prevents the consistent use of contingency management procedures, and that might even be contributing to the need for those procedures, is the absence of a predictable daily family schedule. For example, a program in which a child earns privileges, such as shopping trips, by improving in academic work is badly hampered if parents cannot find time to monitor school performance or deliver reinforcers. The parent or parents may have changing work schedules that cannot be modified, or both parents may voluntarily spend most of their day working and meeting social responsibilities while leaving their children in the care of numerous and rapidly changing babysitters. Some parents may prefer to operate on an unpredictable schedule rather than feel that their freedom is being curtailed. Such families may benefit from participation in planning sessions where activities that are known in advance are scheduled, responsibilities for household routines and the implementation of contingency management procedures are assumed, and leisure activities are planned.

Persuading parents to implement household organization procedures will probably not be any easier than motivating them to use contingency management procedures. However, for those who do use them, the probability of maintenance and generalization of skills learned during parent training may increase because the environment would be contributing to that goal.

PARENT TRAINING MODALITIES

A variety of methods have been used, either individually or in combination, to teach parents contingency management and operant training procedures, contingency contracting, conflict resolution skills, parent-child interaction, and household organization. The methods include oral and written instructions, live and videotape modeling, and direct prompting, shaping, and feedback by the trainer. Parents have been trained individually or in groups, and some or all of the training has occurred in either the clinic or the home. Examples of the use of these methods appear throughout the chapter.

A detailed review of the literature pertaining to these methods is beyond the scope of this chapter. However, three recent reviews (Altman & Mira, 1983; Gordon & Davidson, 1981; O'Dell, 1985) provide such information. Altman and Mira specifically address the topic of training parents of handicapped children. The following conclusions were drawn from O'Dell (1985):

1. Some empirical support for the effectiveness of each of the methods mentioned above, used either singly or in combination, can be mustered. However, it is clear that the effectiveness of a method often depends upon the type of problem and the characteristics of the family. For example, written instructions can be effective only if parents have the vocabulary to understand them; some skills may not even be able to be conveyed verbally.

2. Studies in which different methods were used to convey the same information have indicated that, while some methods have sometimes produced better results than others, different training methods do not account for a large portion of the variance in parent training outcome. Such studies also do not provide information concerning which methods are most effective for particular problems and parent characteristics.

3. Modeling appears to be a particularly effective training method. However, specific information regarding variables that may contribute to its effectiveness, such as similarity of the model to the parent, is not available.

4. Training parents in groups has been found to be as effective and more cost-effective than training them individually. However, specific rea-

sons for its effectiveness are not known. In addition, group vs. individual training was sometimes confounded with other aspects of training such as content and length.

5. Little information is available concerning the relative effectiveness of conducting training in the clinic, home, or a combination of both. However, both methods have been shown to be effective in some situations.

Clearly, no definitive conclusions can be drawn concerning the relative efficacy of particular training methods. The situation becomes even more complex when parent trainers must choose methods or modify an existing program based on their assessment of the problems and characteristics of an individual family. Group comparison studies provide one source of information, but it is difficult to generalize group results to individual cases. Also, in a number of these studies, parents were volunteers, or their children did not exhibit serious behavior problems, or parents were recruited to help develop child management materials and were tested with child confederates who were trained to misbehave in specific ways (e.g., Christensen, Johnson, Phillips, & Glasgow, 1980; O'Dell et al., 1982; O'Dell, Mahoney, Horton, & Turner, 1979). Although these research methods may increase the probability that differences among the groups will be found, applicability of the results to the treatment of parents who are required by a social service agency to participate, or who have serious and longstanding problems with their child, or who are under a great deal of stress is unknown. In the following section the tailoring of parent training to the needs of individual families, or to groups of families who share common characteristics, is discussed.

MODIFICATIONS FOR INDIVIDUAL FAMILIES

Some parent trainers design programs that are specifically tailored to the problems and characteristics of individual families (e.g., Pinkston, 1984). Others have developed programs with standardized content and format for types of child and family problems (e.g., Baker & Heifetz, 1976; Forehand & McMahon, 1981). Although behavioral parent training has been criticized for running the risk of fitting parents to training techniques (Gordon & Davidson, 1981), it is clear that modifications and additions are frequently made in response to parent and child reactions to the intervention and family characteristics and circumstances. Two methods of accomplishing this are to modify the curriculum and/or training modalities of the program itself, and to add components to reduce the impact of factors interfering with progress in treatment or to increase the probability of maintenance and generalization.

Modifications in Training Programs

Several investigators have discussed the manner in which they vary their standardized programs in response to clients' reactions and characteristics. Forehand and McMahon (1981) elaborated on a number of commonly occurring situations. For example, older children may respond to their parents' frequent attention during the clinic training sessions by commenting that their parents are behaving peculiarly. The amount of attention can then be decreased. Parents who praise with flat affect may need modeling in more appropriate and varied affect after they have learned to attend to their children's appropriate behavior. Parents of extremely deviant children may first need to be taught the use of time-out and then taught to attend to and reward behavior.

Wolfe and Manion (1984) described modifications in their uniform skills approach to training parents in child-abusive families. Because the mothers typically cope with problems by avoiding them and are reluctant to interact with their children, the parent initially assumes a passive role while the therapist interacts with the child. The parent is integrated into the interaction gradually. Either modeling or a more didactic approach can be used, depending on parents' level of functioning. The authors also noted that an interesting training format seems much more effective in keeping parents in the program than extrinsic reinforcers and that parents particularly enjoy videotaped feedback. Like Forehand and McMahon (1981), the authors indicated that punishment procedures may need to be introduced before contingent positive attention. However, because of the potential for misuse, this is done infrequently. Stress reduction and relaxation techniques may be used to help parents cope with their children's reaction to punishment.

For some parents the opportunity to participate in training for as long as it takes to acquire the skills may be beneficial. Embry (1984) reported the results of a contingency management program in which parents with varying levels of stress participated. Stress factors included being an abusive parent, having a handicapped child, experiencing marital problems, and having less than a high school education. Severely stressed families were those in which two or more factors were identified. All parents reached the criterion of exhibiting improvements over a 3-week period, but varied in length of time required to complete the program. Families with few or no stress factors learned the skills within 3 months while severely stressed families generally required 9 months. Similarly, Budd and Greenspan (1984) found that retarded parents required more intensive, directive, and longer programs than nonhandicapped parents and that favorable outcomes were fewer.

Adjunctive Treatments

Parent trainers recognized quite early that parent training procedures alone were frequently insufficient to produce change, and that change was often resisted or interfered with by a variety of factors. Tharp and Wetzel (1969) discussed difficulties in working with the parents of the predelinquents in their residential treatment program and noted resistances such as family discord, an insistence that all children be treated alike, the need for a scapegoat, a preference for aversive control, and the desire not to see a child improve. The latter point also was mentioned by Gordon and Davidson (1981), who indicated that parents may enter treatment with the hidden agenda of demonstrating that change is not possible so that the child must be removed from the home. Recently, investigators have found that factors such as maternal depression, marital problems, being a single parent, socioeconomic disadvantage, and social isolation are related to poor outcomes in parent training programs (e.g., Forehand, Furey, & McMahon, 1984; Griest & Forehand, 1982; Webster-Stratton, 1985).

Miller (1975) described three types of counseling that are incorporated within his contingency management parent-training program to combat interfering problems. Brief counseling is appropriate, for example, for the overwhelmed parent who is having difficulty incorporating intervention procedures into the daily schedule, or whose child exhibits extreme disruptive behavior just when the intervention is producing behavior change. Intensive time-limited counseling is initiated to help insure that parents resume and complete the program; it deals with problems such as inconsistency in implementing the procedures and parents' negative attitudes toward their children and marriage. Concomitant counseling is required when the child's problems are too intense or well-established to respond to parent training and require in-patient treatment, or when the primary focus of treatment should be not the child's behavior but the behavior of the parents, who may require marital or other types of counseling.

In more recent studies contingency management training has been offered to families in conjunction with training directed toward other personal and family problems. Work with abusive families, for example, has been based on the assumption that more than the child's behavior can precipitate abuse. Scott, Baer, Christoff, and Kelly (1984) analyzed the antecedents to an abusive mother's violent episodes and then applied training in assertiveness/anger control, child management, and problem solving in a multiple-baseline design. The effectiveness of the intervention was demonstrated using a variety of knowledge, self-monitoring, and direct observation measures. Fifteen months following treatment the child welfare agency reported that the child was no longer at risk. Similarly, Campbell, O'Brien, Bickett, and Lutzker (1983) implemented treatment for migraine headaches, child management, and marital counseling to a low-income family who had been referred to the protective service agency after the mother expressed the desire to kill her daughter. Improvements occurred in all areas and the case was terminated.

Wahler and his colleagues (e.g., Wahler & Dumas, 1984; Wahler & Dumas, (1983) have developed an adjunctive treatment procedure called mand review specifically for mothers who can be labeled "insular" based on their frequent negative (coercive) contacts with relatives and helping agency personnel and few positive contacts with friends. These mothers typically demonstrate poor outcomes at follow-up compared to noninsular mothers and are more likely to describe their children's behaviors in a blame-oriented and global manner, indicating that they are unable to attend to and discriminate what their children are doing even after training (Wahler & Afton, 1980). These inaccurate global reports are believed to be controlled not only by the children's behavior but also by the nature of the mothers' interactions with other people in their environment. Furthermore, coercive interactions with others such as boyfriends, relatives, and helping agencies may function as setting events for coercive episodes with their children (i.e., after experiencing a coercive interaction, these mothers are more likely to treat their children aversively, thus prompting them to behave aversively in turn).

The goal of mand review is for the mother to understand that her child is only one element of a coercive environment and that her global summary reports (i.e., "I always bend over backwards" or "I am just a dishrag") actually summarize the way in which she interacts with a variety of people. The trainer encourages her both to provide specific examples for the global reports and to match specific interactions with a global statement. Thus, she may become a more reliable observer of her encounters with others, a prerequisite for the use of contingency management procedures.

There is some evidence that mothers maintain parent training gains while participating in the mand review process. However, the authors indicated that the results thus far are only suggestive and that the effective elements of the process have not been isolated. Further analyses are ongoing.

The previous studies illustrate the manner in which adjunctive treatments can be combined with parent training in an effort to improve outcome. However, these studies do not provide empirical demonstrations that the addition of such components improves progress in parent training. An exception is a study by Griest et al. (1982) in which a group of eight mothers of noncompliant children completed parent training alone while a group of nine mothers completed parent training plus parent enhancement therapy. The parent enhancement therapy comprised presentation of developmental norms to change unrealistic expectations for children's behavior, spouse communication and marital problem-solving skills, modification of depression and anxiety by cognitive restructuring, and increasing positive and decreasing negative community contacts (Forehand et al. 1984). Didactic presentation, modeling, role-playing, and homework assignments were used as training methods, and components of parent enhancement were presented intermittently with the standard parent training program. The results indicated that both groups improved relative to the no-treatment control group. However, the group that received parent enhancement therapy was better able to maintain these gains at the 2-month follow-up. The authors indicated that the parents who participated were not selected because they exhibited difficulties in the areas addressed by the additional training, so it is difficult to generalize the results to families who are experiencing severe difficulties in one or more of these areas.

The programs and studies described have been focused on parents of behavior-problem children. However, similar issues arise for families of severely developmentally disabled children. Harris (1984) discussed the fact that some families are able to adapt to their autistic child after training in behavior modification despite experiencing periodic sadness and frustration about the child's handicap. Other parents cannot follow through with procedures, sometimes because the child is unresponsive, but in other cases because they cannot organize themselves. Such problems may be expressed through passive resistance to the therapist's suggestions, disengagement of family members from the treatment process, and a reluctance to do the required work. Although many of the obstacles are similar to those encountered when working with behavior problems (i.e., depression, anger, marital instability, and unavailability of resources), others are specific to autism. Adjunctive treatments must therefore be administered with an appreciation for the incredible child-care demands made by an autistic child coupled with the knowledge that the child will never behave in a developmentally normative manner regardless of what the parents do. For example, training couples in problem-solving and communication skills would need to include topics such as negotiating responsibilities for child care and planning for the child's future. Parents and siblings may need to learn to negotiate private time together, focused on activities important to the siblings.

Varying standardized programs to match clients' responses and including adjunctive treatments appear to be promising strategies for combating factors that pose serious threats to the successful outcome of parent training. They also illustrate the range of clinical as well as parent training skills that must be accessible for some families.

THE THERAPIST–CLIENT RELATIONSHIP

The process of producing change in parent behavior occurs within the context of a developing relationship between parent and therapist. At present, this aspect of the process is poorly understood. Parent trainers sometimes provide informal guidelines for building rapport or providing direction, but little empirical information exists to support specific recommendations.

For example, Tharp and Wetzel (1969), who trained parents of the delinquents in their residential program, emphasized that the therapist must become reinforcing to parents, should avoid arguing with them, and should contact them only frequently enough to maintain desirable behavior. Gordon and Davidson (1981) also discussed the importance of social reinforcement, as well as support, warmth, and encouragement, and indicated that appropriate self-disclosure can increase perceived similarity of therapist and parent. They argued that, in addition to training in parent training techniques, therapists should also be trained in self-confidence, energy, warmth, and the ability to create positive expectations.

Schopler, Mesibov, Shigley, and Bashford (1984) have resisted pressures to develop a parent-training package for educating autistic children because they want the roles of parent and therapist to evolve through discussion of the problem. They believe that parents and therapists who respect one another can assume a variety of roles and shift among them depending on the situation. For example, parents can function as both trainee and trainer and provide as well as receive support from the therapist. This type of arrangement appears ideal for highly motivated parents.

Wahler and Dumas (1984) discussed the importance of establishing a friendship relationship with multiply coerced mothers when using the mand review procedure. The absence of friends (i.e., people who listen, ask for clarification, and occasionally provide opinions rather than criticize, demand, or instruct the mother to behave differently) is one of the deficits in the lives of these mothers. It is important for the therapist not to resemble these other individuals who attempt to change behavior through coercion.

Parent trainers have become increasingly aware of relationship variables in recent research. Griest et al. (1982), in their study comparing the relative effectiveness of parent training alone and parent training in conjunction with parent enhancement therapy, controlled for nonspecific treatment variables by rating the three primary therapists on believability, unconditional positive regard, empathy, and genuineness. Ratings did not differ between the groups, thus eliminating these therapist behaviors as confounding variables.

Alexander, Barton, Shiavo, and Parsons (1976) investigated therapist characteristics that would be associated with good or poor outcomes in training of delinquent families. Twenty-one families were randomly assigned to 21 therapists who ranged from graduate students with little prior therapy experience to PhDs with extensive experience. Few of the therapists, however, had prior experience with this specific intervention, which involved modifying family communication patterns in a clinical setting, and all participated in a 10-week training program. Therapist and family behaviors were measured by direct observation. Results showed that both structuring skills (directiveness and self-confidence) and relationship skills (affect-behavior integration, humor, and warmth) contributed independently to outcome variance (i.e., remaining in versus dropping out of therapy, recidivism within 15 months, and an increase in the ratio of supportive to defensive communication during treatment sessions). The authors suggested that both structuring and relationship skills may be crucial determinants of therapy outcome, although causal statements cannot be made about their contribution.

In response to the inconsistent results produced by parent training programs, Patterson and his colleagues (Patterson, in press) have begun an intensive study of clinical skills. They argue that standardized, time-limited intervention provided by students who have received short-term training may not be sufficient to produce change in noncooperative families, particularly those with older, extremely deviant children. In addition to a parent training technology, therapists must know how to reduce parental resistance and should have a support group of other therapists so that difficult cases do not succeed in extinguishing and punishing their efforts. On the assumption that noncooperation results from interactions between therapist and client as well as client characteristics, these investigators are studying interaction sequences to determine what therapist behaviors seem to increase parental noncooperation within sessions. It appears that confronting and teaching prompt parental noncooperation (i.e., not attending, introducing other topics, challenging the therapist). They hypothesize that supporting the client through warmth, humor, understanding, and encouragement; acknowledging clients' remarks; reframing the objectives for treatment so that parents can cooperate; and persistence in teaching can eventually reduce noncooperation.

Both discussion and research on the therapist-client relationship in parent training are sparse, and conclusions are limited to associations between therapist behavior and outcome. Global concepts such as warmth and genuineness are typically not defined. The manner in which one would use this information with individual parents is left to the sensitivity and creativity of the therapist.

A consistent theme emerges, however; it is that, in addition to instructing parents in behavioral technology, therapists should be warm, empathetic, supportive, encouraging, and humorous. Such behavior would undoubtedly benefit the change process for many people. However, as Turkat and Brantley (1981) argued, standard warmth and empathy may not be appropriate for every client, and the therapist-client relationship should depend on a behavioral formulation of the case. They gave an example of a client whose problem was fear of criticism. The therapist was at first very accepting and became progressively more critical to parallel the treatment of gradual exposure to criticism.

As research proceeds in this area it is likely that some therapist behaviors will be shown to be generally more effective than others in establishing and maintaining a productive relationship with parents. However, such behaviors will undoubtedly need to be modified in response to client reactions. For example, some parents may prefer a cool, distant therapist who simply instructs them in the use of behavioral procedures. Other parents may find praise threatening or punishing (DeVoge & Beck, 1978). Still others may demand a friendlier or more dependent relationship than would be appropriate or beneficial.

SUMMARY

In the preceding sections we have tried to convey several main ideas. First, a well-developed technology for helping parents to change their children's behavior by changing their own behavior exists and is constantly being improved. In addition, parent training methods are now being used to teach aspects of parent-child interaction that go beyond contingency management, such as play and the expression of affection. Second, some parents do not benefit from current parent training approaches, due to such factors as personal and family distress and the severity of the problem. Current efforts are being focused on how to modify programs and what types of adjunctive treatments will effectively address factors that interfere with participation in parent training and maintenance of skills. Third, parent trainers are becoming more interested in the possibility that specific therapist behaviors and the therapist-client relationship will prove to be important variables in producing favorable outcomes.

It has become increasingly clear that parent trainers must not only be skilled in conveying behavioral technology to parents who are willing and able to learn but must also be skilled in working with, or have access to services for, families whose problems extend far beyond child behavior problems. Thus, matching clients to appropriate treatments is a major issue. For example, Blechman (1981) discussed the possibility of comprehensive behavioral intervention that would serve a heterogeneous population and be composed of replicable decision rules. She presented a strategy for matching client families with available treatments based on factors such as whether or not the child was uncontrollable, whether basic life maintenance problems were unresolved, and whether the family wanted to change its style of interaction. The further development and testing of such strategies would perhaps help make the delivery of parent training and related treatments more effective and efficient.

REFERENCES

Alexander, J. F., Barton, C., Schiavo, R. S., & Parsons, B. V. (1976). Systems-behavioral intervention with families of delinquents: Therapist characteristics, family behavior, and outcome. *Journal of Consulting and Clinical Psychology, 44,* 656–664.

Altman, K., & Mira, M. (1983). Training parents of developmentally disabled children. In J. L. Matson & F. Andrasik (Eds.), *Treatment issues and innovations in mental retardation* (pp. 303–371). New York: Plenum.

Baker, B. L. (1984). Intervention with families with young, severely handicapped children. In J. Blacher (Ed.), *Severely handicapped young children and their families: Research in review* (pp. 319–375). Orlando, FL: Academic.

Baker, B. L., Brightman, A. J., Heifetz, L. J., & Murphy, D. M. (1976, 1977, 1978, 1980). *Steps to independence series.* Champaign, IL: Research Press.

Baker, B. L., & Clark, D. B. (1983). The family setting: Enhancing the retarded child's development through parent training. In K. T. Kernan, M. J. Begab, & R. B. Edgerton (Eds.), *Settings and the behavior and study of retarded persons* (pp. 297–309). Baltimore: University Park Press.

Baker, B. L., & Heifetz, L. J. (1976). The READ Project: Teaching manuals for parents of retarded children. In T. D. Tjossem (Ed.), *Intervention strategies for high risk infants and young children* (pp. 351–369). Baltimore: University Park Press.

Barone, V. J., Greene, B. F., & Lutzker, J. R. (1986). Home safety with families being treated for child abuse and neglect. *Behavior Modification 10,* 93–114.

Baum, C. G., & Forehand, R. (1981). Long term follow-up assessment of parent training by use of multiple outcome measures. *Behavior Therapy, 12,* 643–652.

Blechman, E. A. (1981). Toward comprehensive behavioral family intervention: An algorithm for matching families and interventions. *Behavior Modification, 5,* 221–236.

Blechman, E. A., Kotanchik, N. L., & Taylor, C. J. (1981). Families and schools together: Early behavioral intervention with high-risk students. *Behavior Therapy, 12,* 308–319.

Blechman, E. A., Olsen, D. H. L., & Hellman, I. D. (1976). Stimulus control over problem-solving behavior: The family contract game. *Behavior Therapy, 7,* 686–692.

Blechman, E. A., Olsen, D. H. L., Schornagel, C. Y., Halsdorf, M., & Turner, A. J. (1976). The family contract game: Technique and case study. *Journal of Consulting and Clinical Psychology, 44,* 449–455.

Blechman, E. A., Taylor, C. J., & Schrader, S. M. (1981). Family problem-solving versus home notes as early intervention with high-risk children. *Journal of Consulting and Clinical Psychology, 49,* 919–926.

Budd, K. S. (in press). Parents as mediators in social skills training of children. In L. L'Abate & M. Milan (Eds.), *A handbook of social skills training and research.* New York: Wiley.

Budd, K. S., & Greenspan, S. (1984). Mentally retarded mothers. In E. A. Blechman (Ed.), *Behavior modification with women* (pp. 477–506). New York: Guilford.

Budd, K. S., & Madison, L. S. (1983, August). *Parent training: An integral component in the treatment of stuttering.* Paper presented at the meeting of the American Psychological Association, Anaheim, CA.

Campbell, R. V., O'Brien, S., Bickett, A. D., & Lutzker, J. R. (1983). In-home parent training, treatment of migraine headaches, and marital counseling as an ecobehavioral approach to prevent child abuse. *Journal of Behavior Therapy and Experimental Psychiatry, 14,* 147–154.

Cantrill, H., Cantrill, C., Huddleston, B., & Woolridge, R. (1969). Contingency contracting with school problems. *Journal of Applied Behavior Analysis, 2,* 215–220.

Carney, R. M., Schechter, K., & Davis, T. (1983). Improving adherence to blood glucose testing in insulin-dependent diabetic children. *Behavior Therapy, 14,* 247–254.

Christensen, A., Johnson, S. M., Phillips, S., & Glasgow, R. E. (1980). Cost-effectiveness in behavioral family therapy. *Behavior Therapy, 11,* 208–226.

Czyzewski, M. J., Christian, W. P., & Norris, M. B. (1984). Preparing the family for client transition: Outreach parent training. In W. P. Christian, G. T. Hannah, & T. J. Glahn (Eds.), *Programming effective human services: Strategies for institutional change and client transition* (pp. 177–202). New York: Plenum.

Dangel, R. F., & Polster, R. A. (1984). *Parent training: Foundations of research and practice.* New York: Guilford.

DeVoge, J. T., & Beck, S. (1978). The therapist-client relationship in behavior therapy. In M. Hersen, R. M. Eisler, & P. M. Miller (Eds.), *Progress in behavior modification* (Vol. 6, pp. 203–248). New York: Academic.

Doherty, G. (1975). Basic life skills and parent effectiveness training with the mothers of acting-out adolescents. *Journal of Clinical Child Psychology, 4,* 3–6.

Doke, L. A., Feaster, C. A., & Predmore, D. L. (1977). Managing the "eat-and-run" behavior of adolescents via family-style dining. *Behavior Modification, 1,* 73–92.

Durand, V. M. (1983). Behavioral ecology of a staff incentive program: Effects on absenteeism and resident disruptive behavior. *Behavior Modification, 7,* 165–181.

Embry, L. H. (1984). What to do? Matching client characteristics and intervention techniques through a prescriptive taxonomic key. In R. F. Dangel & R. A. Polster (Eds.), *Parent training: Foundations of research and practice* (pp. 443–473). New York: Guilford.

Eyberg, S. M., & Ross, A. W. (1978). Assessment of child behavior problems: The validation of a new inventory. *Journal of Clinical Psychology, 16,* 113–116.

Favell, J. E., McGimsey, J. F., & Schell, R. M. (1982). Treatment of self-injury by providing alternate sensory activities. *Analysis and Intervention in Developmental Disabilities, 2,* 83–104.

Forehand, R., Furey, W. M., & McMahon, R. J. (1984). The role of maternal distress in a parent training program to modify child non-compliance. *Behavioural Psychotherapy, 12,* 93–108.

Forehand, R. L., & McMahon, R. J. (1981). *Helping the noncompliant child: A clinician's guide to parent training.* New York: Guilford.

Frederiksen, L. W., & Frederiksen, C. B. (1977). Experimental evaluation of classroom environments: Scheduling planned activities. *American Journal of Mental Deficiency, 81,* 421–427.

Gambrill, E. D. (1977). *Behavior modification: Handbook of assessment, intervention, and evaluation.* San Francisco: Jossey-Bass.

Gordon, S. B., & Davidson, N. (1981). Behavioral parent training. In A. S. Gurman & D. P. Kniskern (Eds.), *Handbook of family therapy* (pp. 517–555). New York: Brunner/Mazel.

Graziano, A. M. (1977). Parents as behavior therapists. In M. Hersen, R. M. Eisler, & P. M. Miller (Eds.), *Progress in behavior modification* (Vol. 4, pp. 251–298). New York: Academic.

Griest, D. L., & Forehand, R. (1982). How can I get any parent training done with all these other problems going on? The role of family variables in child behavior therapy. *Child and Family Behavior Therapy, 4,* 73–80.

Griest, D. L., Forehand, R., Rogers, T., Breiner, J., Furey, W., & Williams, C. A. (1982). Effects of parent enhancement therapy in the treatment outcome and generalization of a parent training program. *Behaviour Research and Therapy, 20,* 429–436.

Harris, S. L. (1984). Intervention planning for the family of the autistic child: A multilevel assessment of the family system. *Journal of Marital and Family Therapy, 10,* 157–166.

Hart, B., & Risley, T. R. (1978). Promoting productive language through incidental teaching. *Education and Urban Society, 4,* 407–429.

Heifetz, L. J. (1977). Behavioral training for parents of retarded children: Alternative formats based on instructional manuals. *American Journal of Mental Deficiency, 82,* 194–203.

Horner, R. D. (1980). The effects of an environmental "enrichment" program on the behavior of institutionalized profoundly retarded children. *Journal of Applied Behavior Analysis, 13,* 473–491.

Israel, A. C., Stolmaker, L., & Andrian, C. A. G. (1985). The effects of training parents in general child management skills on a behavioral weight loss program for children. *Behavior Therapy, 16,* 169–180.

Kifer, R., Lewis, M., Green, D., & Phillips, E. (1974). Training predelinquent youths and their families to negotiate conflict situations. *Journal of Applied Behavior Analysis, 7,* 357–364.

Koegel, R. L., Schreibman, L., Johnson, J., O'Neill, R. E., & Dunlap, G. (1984). Collateral effects of parent training on families with autistic children. In R. F. Dangel & R. A. Polster (Eds.), *Parent training: Foundations of research and practice* (pp. 358–378). New York: Guilford.

Kogan, K. L., & Gordon, B. M. (1975). A mother-instruction program: Documenting change in mother-child interactions. *Child Psychiatry and Human Development, 5,* 189–200.

LeLaurin, K., & Risley, T. R. (1972). The organization of day care environments: "Zone" versus "man-to-man" staff assignments. *Journal of Applied Behavior Analysis, 5,* 225–232.

Lutzker, J. R. (1980). Deviant family systems. In B. B. Lahey & A. E. Kazdin (Eds.). *Advances in clinical child psychology* (Vol. 3, pp. 97–148). New York: Plenum.

Lutzker, J. R. (1984). Project 12-Ways: Treating child abuse and neglect from an ecobehavioral perspective. In R. F. Dangel & R. A. Polster (Eds.), *Parent training: Foundations of research and practice* (pp. 260–297.) New York: Guilford.

Lutzker, J. R., McGimsey, J. F., McRae, S., & Campbell, R. V. (1983). Behavioral parent training: There's so much more to do. *the Behavior Therapist, 6,* 110–112.

Lutzker, J. R., Megson, D. A., Webb, M. E., & Dachman, R. S. (1985). Validating and training adult-child interaction skills to professionals and to parents indicated for child abuse and neglect. *Child and Adolescent Psychotherapy, 2,* 91–104.

Martin, B. (1975). Brief family intervention: Effectiveness and the importance of including the father. Unpublished manuscript, University of North Carolina, Chapel Hill.

Martin, B., & Twentyman, C. (1976). Teaching conflict resolution skills to parents and children. In E. J. Mash, L. C. Handy, & L. A. Hamerlynck (Eds.), *Behavior modification approaches to parenting* (pp. 141–151). New York: Brunner/Mazel.

Mash, E. J., & Terdal, L. G. (1981). Behavioral assessment of childhood disturbance. In E. J. Mash & L. G. Terdal (Eds.), *Behavioral assessment of childhood disorders* (pp. 3–76). New York: Guilford.

McMahon, R. J., & Forehand, R. (1984). Parent training for the noncompliant child: Treatment outcome, generalization, and adjunctive therapy procedures. In R. F. Dangel & R. A. Polster (Eds.), *Parent training: Foundations of research and practice* (pp. 298–328). New York: Guilford.

Melin, L., & Gotestam, K. G. (1981). The effects of rearranging ward routines on communication and eating behavior of psychogeriatric patients. *Journal of Applied Behavior Analysis, 14,* 47–51.

Miller, W. H. (1975). *Systematic parent training: Procedures, cases, and issues.* Champaign, IL: Research Press.

Moreland, J. R., Schwebel, S. B., Beck, S., & Wells, R. (1982). Parents as therapists: A review of the behavior therapy parent training literature—1975 to 1981. *Behavior Modification, 2,* 250–276.

Murphy, H. A., Hutchinson, J. M., & Bailey, J. S. (1983). Behavioral school psychology goes outdoors: The effects of organized games on playground aggression. *Journal of Applied Behavior Analysis, 16,* 29–35.

Nordquist, V. M., & McEvoy, M. A. (1983). Punishment as a factor in early childhood imitation. *Analysis and Intervention in Developmental Disabilities, 3,* 339–357.

O'Dell, S. L. (1985). Progress in parent training. In M. Hersen, R. M. Eisler, & P. M. Miller (Eds.), *Progress in behavior modification* (Vol. 19, pp. 57–108). New York: Academic.

O'Dell, S. L., Mahoney, N. D., Horton, W. G., & Turner, P. E. (1979). Media-assisted parent training: Alternative models. *Behavior Therapy, 10,* 103–110.

O'Dell, S. L., O'Quin, J. A., Alford, B. A., O'Briant, A. L., Bradlyn, A. S., & Giebenhain, J. E. (1982). Predicting the acquisition of parenting skills via four training methods. *Behavior Therapy, 13,* 194–208.

Patterson, G. R. (in press). Beyond technology: The next stage in the development of parent training. In L. L'Abate (Ed.), *Handbook of family psychology and psychotherapy.* New York: Dow Jones–Irwin.

Patterson, G. R., Chamberlain, P., & Reid, J. B. (1982). A comparative evaluation of a parent-training program. *Behavior Therapy, 13,* 638–650.

Pinkston, E. M. (1984). Individualized behavioral intervention for home and school. In R. F. Dangel & R. A. Polster (Eds.), *Parent training: Foundations of research and practice* (pp. 202–238). New York: Guilford.

Prinz, R. J., Rosenblum, R. S., & O'Leary, K. D. (1978). Affective communication differences between distressed and nondistressed mother-adolescent dyads. *Journal of Abnormal Child Psychology, 6,* 373–383.

Quilitch, H. R., & Risley, T. R. (1973). The effects of play materials on social play. *Journal of Applied Behavior Analysis, 6,* 573–578.

Roosa, J. B. (1973, August). *SOCS: Situations, options, consequences, and simulation: A technique for teaching social interaction.* Paper presented at the American Psychological Association, Montreal.

Ross, A. O. (1981). *Child behavior therapy: Principles, procedures, and empirical basis.* New York: Wiley.

Sanders, M. R. (1984). Clinical strategies for enhancing generalization in behavioral parent training: An overview. *Behaviour Change, 1,* 25–35.

Sanders, M. R., & Christensen, A. P. (1985). A comparison of the effects of child management and planned activities training in five parenting environments. *Journal of Abnormal Child Psychology, 13,* 101–117.

Sanders, M. R., & Dadds, M. R. (1982). The effects of planned activities and child management procedures in parent training: An analysis of setting generality. *Behavior Therapy, 13,* 452–461.

Sanders, M. R., & James, J. E. (1983). The modification of parent behavior: A review of generalization and maintenance. *Behavior Modification, 7,* 3–27.

Schopler, E., Mesibov, G. B., Shigley, R. H., & Bashford, A. (1984). Helping autistic children through their parents: The TEACCH model. In E. Schopler & G. B. Mesibov (Eds.), *The effects of autism on the family* (pp. 65–81). New York: Plenum.

Schreibman, L., Koegel, R. L., Mills, D. L., & Burke, J. C. (1984). Training parent-child interactions. In E. Schopler & G. B. Mesibov (Eds.), *The effects of autism on the family* (pp. 187–205). New York: Plenum.

Scott, W. O., Baer, G., Christoff, K. A., & Kelly, J. A. (1984). The use of skills training procedures in the treatment of a child-abusive parent. *Journal of Behavior Therapy and Experimental Psychiatry, 15,* 329–336.

Stuart, R. B. (1971). Behavioral contracting with families of delinquents. *Journal of Behavior Therapy and Experimental Psychiatry, 2,* 1–11.

Tertinger, D. A., Greene, B. F., & Lutzker, J. R. (1984). Home safety: Development and validation of one component of an ecobehavioral treatment program for abused and neglected children. *Journal of Applied Behavior Analysis, 17,* 159–174.

Tharp, R. G., & Wetzel, R. J. (1969). *Behavior modification in the natural environment.* New York: Academic.

Turkat, I. D., & Brantley, P. J. (1981). On the therapeutic relationship in behavior therapy. *the Behavior Therapist, 4,* 16–17.

Twardosz, S. (1984). Environmental organization: The physical, social, and programatic context of behavior. In M. Hersen, R. M. Eisler, & P. M. Miller (Eds.), *Progress in behavior modification* (Vol. 18, pp. 123–161). New York: Academic.

Twardosz, S., Schwartz, S., Fox, J., & Cunningham, J. L. (1979). Development and evaluation of a system to measure affectionate behavior. *Behavioral Assessment, 1,* 177–190.

Van Biervliet, A., Spangler, P. F., & Marshall, A. M. (1981). An ecobehavioral examination of a simple strategy for increasing mealtime language in residential facilities. *Journal of Applied Behavior Analysis, 14,* 295–305.

Wahler, R. G. (1969). Oppositional children: A quest for parental reinforcement control. *Journal of Applied Behavior Analysis, 2,* 159–170.

Wahler, R. G., & Afton, A. D. (1980). Attentional processes in insular and noninsular mothers. *Child Behavior Therapy, 1980, 2,* 25–41.

Wahler, R. G., & Dumas, J. E. (1983, June). *Stimulus class determinants of mother-child coercive interchanges in multidistressed families: Assessment and intervention.* Paper presented at the Vermont Conference on the Primary Prevention of Psychopathology, Bolton Valley, VT.

Wahler, R. G., & Dumas, J. E. (1984). Changing the observational coding styles of insular and noninsular mothers: A step toward maintenance of parent training effects. In R. F. Dangel & R. A Polster (Eds.), *Parent training: Foundations of research and practice* (pp. 379–416). New York: Guilford.

Wahler, R. G., & Nordquist, V. M. (1973). Adult discipline as a factor in childhood imitation. *Journal of Abnormal Child Psychology, 1,* 40–56.

Weathers, L. R., & Liberman, R. P. (1975). Contingency contracting with families of delinquent adolescents. *Behavior Therapy, 6,* 356–366.

Weathers, L. R., & Liberman, R. P. (1978). Modification of family behavior. In D. Marholin (Ed.), *Child behavior therapy* (pp. 150–186). New York: Gardner Press.

Webster-Stratton, C. (1981a). Modification of mothers' behaviors and attitudes through a videotape modeling group discussion program. *Behavior Therapy, 12,* 634–642.

Webster-Stratton, C. (1981b). Videotape modeling: A method of parent education. *Journal of Clinical Child Psychology, 10,* 93–98.

Webster-Stratton, C. (1982a). The long-term effects of a videotape modeling parent-training program: Comparison of immediate and 1-year follow-up results. *Behavior Therapy, 13,* 702–714.

Webster-Stratton, C. (1982b). Teaching mothers through videotape modeling to change their children's behavior. *Journal of Pediatric Psychology, 7,* 279–294.

Webster-Stratton, C. (1985). Predictors of treatment outcome in parent training for conduct-disordered children. *Behavior Therapy, 16,* 223–243.

Wells, K. C., & Forehand, R. (1981). Childhood behavior problems in the home. In S. M. Turner, K. S. Calhoun, & H. E. Adams (Eds.), *Handbook of clinical behavior therapy* (pp. 527–567). New York: Wiley.

Wilson, G. T., Franks, C. M., Brownell, K. D., & Kendall, P. C. (1984). *Annual review of behavior therapy: Theory and practice* (Vol. 9). New York: Guilford.

Wolfe, D. A., & Manion, I. G. (1984). Impediments to child abuse prevention: Issues and directions. *Advances in Behaviour Research and Therapy, 6,* 47–62.

Wolfe, D. A., St. Lawrence, J., Graves, K., Brehony, K., Bradlyn, D., & Kelly, J. A. (1982). Intensive behavioral parent training for a child abusive mother. *Behavior Therapy, 13,* 438–451.

PART TWO

Childhood Disorders and Problems

CHAPTER 5

Anxiety

CYD C. STRAUSS

Fear and anxiety in children are often viewed as common and transient, and consequently, they have frequently been overlooked by behavior therapists and researchers (Graziano, DeGiovanni, & Garcia, 1979). However, anxiety in childhood can be intense, distressing, and persistent, thus requiring the attention of professionals.

The symptoms associated with anxiety in children resemble those found in adults, including overt behavioral avoidance, covert feelings of distress and irrational thoughts, and physiological manifestations (Gittelman, 1985; Graziano et al., 1979). When one or more of these three response systems is excessive, persistent, and maladaptive, it is generally agreed that a phobia or anxiety disorder is present and worthy of intervention (Miller, Barrett, & Hampe, 1974). For example, Marks (1969) has distinguished a phobia from a normal fear by defining a phobia as a fear that "is out of proportion to demands of the situation, cannot be explained or reasoned away, is beyond voluntary control, and leads to avoidance of the feared situation" (p. 3). Graziano et al. (1979) have similarly but alternatively defined anxiety as clinically meaningful when its intensity or duration is greater than found in most children. It is important that normal fears be differentiated from phobias or anxiety disorders for purposes of treatment, so that treatment can be efficiently provided to anxious children needing professional services and unnecessary intervention can be avoided in children with normal and rational fears.

A tentative classification of childhood anxiety disorders is provided in the third edition of the *Diagnostic and Statistical Manual of Mental Disorders* (DSM-III: American Psychiatric Association, 1980). Clinicians' observations have primarily provided the impetus for the subcategories of anxiety disorders with an onset in childhood, which include separation anxiety, avoidant, and

---

The author would like to express appreciation to Susan Glor-Scheib, Cindy Lease, and Mary Lou Borgen for their assistance in the preparation of this chapter.

overanxious disorders. In addition, children can be diagnosed with simple phobia or social phobia, which are among the adult diagnoses in the DSM-III classification scheme. Children less commonly exhibit other adult anxiety diagnoses: panic disorder, agoraphobia, and obsessive-compulsive disorder. At this point, these diagnoses are provisional since their reliability and validity have not yet been supported by empirical investigations.

Separation anxiety disorder consists of extreme distress on separation from a major attachment figure, excessive worrying about potential dangers that threaten the child or major attachment figures, and an intense need to be near family members. These features are considered to be pathological when they limit the child's activities, such as school attendance or play outside the home or neighborhood, or cause the child great discomfort.

Avoidant disorder is a persistent and excessive shyness with nonfamilial persons. This shyness interferes with the child's peer relationships. For shyness to be considered pathological in children, it needs to be consistent over time and present in numerous social settings (Gittelman, 1985). Children with this disorder are rarely referred to outpatient clinics for treatment, although extreme social withdrawal has been identified in school populations of children (O'Connor, 1969).

Overanxious disorder refers to fearfulness or excessive worry that is not specific to a particular object or situation. Children with this disorder often show an overconcern with their performance in a variety of areas, a heightened need for reassurance from teachers or parents, perfectionism, and feelings of self-consciousness and embarrassment when they are the center of attention in groups. They worry about future and past events, such as test performance, the possibility of bodily injury, and peer perceptions of them. Overanxious children often are tense and have difficulty relaxing.

Simple phobias are irrational fears of unthreatening situations or objects that interfere with the child's adjustment. As noted previously, the duration and intensity of the child's fearfulness, as well as level of personal distress, often are taken into account in distinguishing a phobia from a normal fear. Common phobias present in childhood include excessive fears of animals, snakes, and the dark.

Although the prevalence of common fears in children has been studied fairly extensively, investigations of the rate of clinically meaningful anxiety disorders in children are more rare. Estimates of the prevalence of excessive fears or anxieties have ranged from 1.7% in a study assessing the rate of school phobia in a school population (Kennedy, 1965) to 16% in a study of 5 to 8-year-old children based on teacher reports (Werry & Quay, 1971). More typically, the prevalence of intense fears is found to be about 7 or 8 % (Agras, Sylvester, & Oliveau, 1969; Earls, 1980; Graziano & DeGiovanni, 1979).

Several factors have been shown to be related to the presence of anxiety in children, including gender, age, socioeconomic status, and other problem behaviors. A fairly consistent finding across studies is that girls tend to display anxiety more commonly than do boys (e.g., Croake & Knox, 1973; Lapouse & Monk, 1959). However, it is unclear whether the higher number of fears reported by girls actually reflects a greater incidence of fearfulness in girls or a greater willingness by girls to admit to having fears (Graziano et al., 1979). Some studies have also found the content of fears to differ for boys and girls (e.g., Tennes & Lampl, 1964).

Graziano et al. (1979) noted that in general the number of fears reported as well as the percentage of youngsters reporting one or more fears seems to decline from young childhood to adolescence. Some studies have demonstrated an increase in the number of reported fears between the ages of 9 and 11 (e.g., MacFarlane, Allen, & Honzik 1954), with a peak occurring at age 11 (e.g., Chazan, 1962). However, not all studies have obtained significant correlations between number of fears and age (e.g., Croake & Knox, 1973; Lapouse & Monk, 1959). Not surprisingly, the type of fears displayed in children seem to vary with age (e.g., Jersild & Holmes, 1935). For example, Graziano et al. (1979) found in their review of the literature that there seems to be an age-related decrease in reported fears of animals, the dark, and imaginary creatures and an age-related increase in school and social anxieties.

Some studies report a higher number of fears in low socioeconomic status (SES) children (e.g., Croake & Knox, 1973; Lapouse & Monk, 1959), although other investigations do not find a differential rate of fears among different SES groups (e.g., Richman, Stevenson, & Graham, 1982). Differences in SES have been reported in some clinical populations of anxious versus nonanxious children (Gittelman-Klein & Klein, 1973), with anxious children coming from higher SES groups. However, this finding does not necessarily imply that anxiety is more prevalent among children in high SES groups, since these differences may result merely from a differential referral rate. Further, these differences in SES among clinic populations have not been found consistently (Berney, Kolvin, Bhate, Garside, Jeans, Kay, & Scarth, 1981).

Some preliminary findings suggest that anxious children also display other problem behaviors. School-phobic children have been reported to exhibit negative self-perceptions (Nichols & Berg, 1970), immaturity, and dependency on their mothers (Berg & McGuire, 1971), and passive and inhibited behavior (Hersov, 1960). As Gittelman (1985) pointed out, however, these data must be interpreted cautiously since these studies typically assessed small clinic samples of inpatient children that may not be comparable to samples of children who are not hospitalized.

Data regarding the developmental course of anxiety in children are sparse and inconsistent. Several studies suggest that fears in children are generally short-lived (e.g., MacFarlane et al., 1954; Marks, 1969). In particular, Agras, Chapin, and Oliveau (1972) reported that 100% of untreated phobic children improved over a 5-year period. On the other hand, there are preliminary data that some fears are more persistent than others. Agras et al. (1972) indicated that more specific and focused fears were associated with better long-term outcome. Follow-up data for school-phobic children have suggested that this form of anxiety is related to later problems in adjustment (Coolidge, Brodie, & Feeney, 1964; Waldron, 1976). These inconsistencies in findings indicate that different prognoses may be associated with distinct types of anxiety and with varying levels of severity of fearfulness.

ASSESSMENT

The modes of assessing the motor, physiological, and cognitive aspects of anxiety in children and adolescents have included structured clinical interviews with children and parents, self-report questionnaires, direct observations, parent and teacher ratings, and physiological techniques. Most research and clinical experience to date suggests that a multimethod assessment approach should be taken in assessing a child's need for treatment.

Structured Clinical Interviews

Several structured clinical interviews have been devised recently to determine the presence and severity of psychopathology in children. These include the Diagnostic Interview Schedule for Children (DISC: Costello, Edelbrock, Kalas, Dulcan & Klaric, 1984), the Diagnostic Interview for Children and Adolescents (DICA: Herjanic & Reich, 1982), the Schedule for Affective Disorders and Schizophrenia for School-Age Children (KIDDIE-SADS: Puig-Antich, Orvaschel, Tabrizi, & Chambers, 1978), and the Interview Schedule for Children (ISC: Kovacs, 1983). Each of these involves interviewing children and their parents individually with a standard set of questions covering all symptoms of psychopathology in children. Portions of each of these interview formats assess anxiety disorders.

The reliability and validity of anxiety diagnoses using these instruments have not yet been clearly established. Preliminary studies have found acceptable interrater reliability of separation anxiety, overanxious, and simple phobic symptoms using the DISC (Edelbrock, Costello, Dulcan, Kalas, & Conover, 1985) and the ISC (Kovacs, 1983). However, poor concordance between parent and child reports of anxiety symptoms have typically been found (Edelbrock, Costello, Dulcan, Kalas, & Conover, in press; Herjanic & Reich, 1982; Kovacs, 1983), with children tending to report more anxiety features than parents. That finding may merely reflect the fact that children's parents are not as aware of their internal emotional states as the children themselves are. The validity of these interviews has only begun to be examined, although one preliminary investigation suggests that this approch shows promise in assessing anxiety in children (Costello et al., 1984).

Self-Report Measures

Children's reports have been viewed as critical in assessment of anxiety or fearfulness. Despite their wide acceptance and use, self-report measures have several features that limit the conclusions that can be derived from them. These include the child's potential unwillingness or inability to reveal negative characteristics (Glennon & Weisz, 1978), the small number of empirical studies researching psychometric properties of many scales (Barrios, Hartmann, & Shigetomi, 1981), and the fact that the items included in most measures do not identify the specific situations that induce anxiety (Barrios et al., 1981). Several self-report questionnaires have been developed to identify anxious children and to measure the effectiveness of interventions. The Children's Manifest Anxiety Scale–Revised (RCMAS: Reynolds & Richmond, 1978) is one of the more widely employed instruments. This 37-item scale has been shown to have construct (Reynolds & Richmond, 1978), concurrent (Reynolds, 1980) content (Reynolds & Richmond, 1978), and predictive (Reynolds, 1981) validity. In addition, national normative and reliability data have been obtained for the RCMAS (Reynolds & Paget, 1982). Three factors have emerged for the measure: physiological, worry/oversensitivity, and concentration factors.

A second self-report questionnaire, derived from the Wolpe-Lang Scale for adults, is the Fear Survey Schedule for Children (Scherer & Nakamura, 1968). Children rate their degree of fearfulness on a 5-point scale for each of the 80 items, which represent specific objects or situations. A factor analysis yielded the following factors for this measure: fear of failure/criticism, major fears (e.g., fire, sight of blood), minor fears, (e.g., travel), medical fears, fear of death, fear of the dark, home-school fears, and miscellaneous fears. Investigations of the psychometric properties of this measure have been limited to reports of high internal consistency and a moderate relationship with another self-report measure of anxiety (Scherer & Nakamura, 1968). Subsequently, Ollendick (1983) provided data supporting the internal consistency, test-retest reliability, and the convergent and discriminative validity of a slightly modified version of the Fear Survey Schedule for Children (FSSC-R).

The State-Trait Inventory for Children (STAIC: Speilberger, 1973) is a third frequently employed self-report measure. The inventory is comprised of two 20-item scales, which attempt to measure separately anxiety that varies across situations and anxiety that is stable across time and situations. However, studies generally have failed to support the validity of the state-trait distinction (Johnson & Melamed, 1979). High split-half and moderate test-retest reliabilities have been reported for both scales of the STAIC (Morris & Kratochwill, 1983).

Direct Observations

The most commonly used direct observation procedure for assessing anxiety in children is the Behavioral Avoidance Test (BAT: Lang & Lazovik, 1963). This observational approach involves instructing the child to enter a room in which the feared object is placed and to approach and touch or pick up the object. The child's latency to respond, distance traveled toward the object, and time spent handling the feared object are recorded. This procedure has been used to assess children's fears of dogs (Bandura, Grusec, & Menlove, 1967), darkness (Kelley, 1976), physical examinations (Freeman, Roy, & Hemmick, 1976), water (Lewis, 1974), and snakes (Kornhaber & Schroeder, 1975). Despite the fairly extensive use of the BAT in examining children's fearful reactions, several features of this approach currently limit its usefulness (Barrios et al., 1981). As noted by Barrios et al. (1981), the BAT has not been standardized in terms of types of instructions provided and number of tasks presented. Kelley (1976) has shown that variations in instructions and demand characteristics can significantly influence children's approach responses. Also, the BAT is somewhat restricted in its application, in that it cannot be implemented to assess certain fears such as separation anxiety, test anxiety, and overanxious features. In addition, the reliability and validity of the BAT as an assessment device for children have not been studied sufficiently.

Observer rating scales have also begun to be implemented to observe overt anxious mannerisms and behaviors in children. Several rating scales have been developed to observe anxiety in particular situations or settings, such as reactions to surgery (Melamed & Siegel, 1975), dental treatment (Melamed, Yurcheson, Fleece, Hutcherson, & Hawes, 1978), public speaking (Paul, 1966), peer interactions (O'Connor, 1969), and hospitalization (Vernon, Foley, & Schulman, 1967). The actual behaviors vary depending on the context in which the child is observed, but include crying, stuttering, trembling hands, physical or verbal complaints, clinging, and quivering voice. Generally, reliability and validity data regarding these coding systems are quite promising, although investigations of psychometric properties have been few in number. A comprehensive and detailed observational coding system for preschool children that can be used to assess anxiety in multiple settings has been developed by Glennon and Weisz (1978).

Parent and Teacher Ratings

Parent and teacher ratings and checklists have figured less prominently in evaluating anxiety than in other childhood psychopathology. Despite their infrequent use, numerous behavior rating scales are available that contain an anxiety or withdrawal dimension, including the Conners' Teacher Rating Scale (Conners, 1969), the Child Behavior Checklist (Achenbach & Edelbrock, 1983), and the Revised Behavior Problem Checklist (Quay & Peterson, 1983). The validity and reliability of these indices of anxiety have been supported (Quay, 1979).

Several rating scales have been developed specifically for parents or teachers to provide evaluations of children's anxiety or fearfulness. The Louisville Fear Survey Schedule (Miller, Barrett, Hampe, & Noble, 1972) can be completed by parents or teachers as well as by the children themselves. This measure assesses three factors: fear of physical injury, of natural events, and of psychic stress. Parents have also been asked to rate their children's anxiety levels following hospitalization on the Posthospital Behavior Questionnaire (Vernon, Schulman, & Foley, 1966) relative to behavior displayed prior to hospitalization. Doris, McIntyre, Kelsey, and Lehman (1971) presented two questionnaires, the Parent Anxiety Rating Scale and the Teacher's Separation Anxiety Scale, which contain questions concerning the child's general anxiety and anxiety related to separating from parents.

Physiological Measures

A virtually unexplored area in the behavioral assessment of anxiety disorders in children is physiological measurement. Assessment of heart rate and electrodermal responses has been utilized most frequently with children. Physiological responses associated with anxiety can be monitored prior to and concurrently with the presentation of anxiety-provoking stimuli in vivo, through imagery, via audiotapes or films, or pictorially (Barrios et al., 1981).

The value of this approach has been supported by a few studies demonstrating that heart rate and electrodermal changes can be reliably measured and are correlated with presentation of fearful stimuli in children (Melamed et al., 1978; Shapiro, 1975; Stricker & Howitt, 1965). However, numerous studies have failed to find significant correlations between physiological states and other indices of anxiety, such as self-reports of fearfulness (Darley & Katz, 1973; Kutina & Fischer, 1977; Sternbach, 1962). Advantages of this assessment modality include the fact that physiological responses are not under the voluntary control of participants for the most part and therefore are less susceptible to subject bias and that measurement of physiological responses can be done reliably (Bellack & Lombardo, 1984). Another disadvantage of physiological assessment is the expense of equipment and level of expertise required for measurement (Bellack & Lombardo, 1984).

RANGE OF BEHAVIORAL TECHNIQUES APPLIED

The primary methods for reducing anxiety and fearfulness in children include systematic desensitization, operant procedures, and modeling. Cognitive approaches have only recently been applied to decrease anxiety in children. Implosion and flooding are less widely used techniques with children due to ethical issues associated with arousing extremely high levels of anxiety in young children and to the lack of research supporting their use in children (Graziano et al., 1979).

Systematic Desensitization

Systematic desensitization (Wolpe, 1958) is the most widely used approach in treating anxiety in children (Ollendick & Cerny, 1981). The procedure consists of gradually exposing the child to the fear-evoking situation while the child engages in an activity incompatible with fear. The child and parents assist in the development of an anxiety hierarchy by listing stimuli or situations ranked in order from least to most anxiety provoking. The child is typically trained in deep-muscle relaxation as an anxiety-inhibiting response, although other responses such as eating or assertiveness have also been suggested (Wolpe, 1958).

Special relaxation training scripts for children that employ fantasy, simple language, and special wording have been prepared, to enhance children's understanding and interest (Koeppen, 1974; Ollendick, 1979; Ollendick & Cerny, 1981). Ollendick and Cerny (1981) recommend 15- to 20-minute sessions held twice weekly for teaching relaxation to children. Following development of the hierarchy and mastery of relaxation techniques, children are instructed to relax while hierarchy items are presented. Systematic desensitization can take place *in vivo* or through imagery, so that the child employs anxiety-inhibiting techniques either in real situations or while imagining progressively more fearful situations.

Systematic desensitization has been used to treat fears of school (Lazarus & Abramovitz, 1962), loud noises (Tasto, 1969; Wish, Hasazi, & Jurgela, 1973), water (Bentler, 1962; Ultee, Griffioen, & Schellekens, 1982), separation (Miller, 1972), dogs (Kissell, 1972), physical examination (Freeman et al., 1976), gaining weight (Ollendick, 1979), the dark (Kelley, 1976; Sheslow, Bondy, & Nelson, 1983), test-taking (Barabasz, 1973; Mann & Rosenthal, 1969), and multiple objects (Van Hasselt, Hersen, Bellack, Rosenbloom, & Lamparski, 1979), as well as other fears.

Flooding and Implosion

Flooding and implosive procedures involve presentation of the feared stimuli for an extended period at intense levels, either *in vivo* or imaginally. Rather than providing the child with an anxiety-inhibiting response to reduce fearfulness, as in systematic desensitization, the child is required to remain in the situation until the anxiety response is extinguished. Although implosive therapy and flooding are similar techniques, implosion is restricted to the imaginal presentation of anxiety-provoking stimuli, so that both psychodynamic themes of conflict (e.g., rejection, guilt, expression of fear of aggression) and descriptions of the phobic stimuli can be presented (Stampfl & Levis, 1967). In flooding, the child is typically exposed to the actual fear-eliciting stimuli rather than visually imagining the phobic object.

These approaches have only rarely been employed in clinical practice due to the controversial nature of exposing children to situations that arouse high anxiety. However, Kennedy (1965) has incorporated aspects of flooding into his treatment program for school phobia. Kennedy (1965) successfully treated 50 cases of school phobia by having parents use whatever tactics were necessary to force school attendance, in addition to other treatment components. Flooding has also been implemented to overcome a fear of loud noises (Yule, Sacks, & Hersov, 1974), dogs (Sreenivasan, Manocha, & Jain, 1979), and bodily injury (Ollendick & Gruen, 1972).

Operant Approaches

The goal of operant approaches is to strengthen approach behaviors and to reduce fear responses. Various operant procedures have been employed effectively, including positive reinforcement, shaping, stimulus fading, extinction, or some combination of these approaches. Positive reinforcement involves providing praise or a tangible reward for an approach behavior to increase the frequency of that behavior. Positive reinforcement has been used in conjunction with other contingency management procedures to eliminate school phobia (Ayllon, Smith, & Rogers, 1970), nocturnal anxiety (Kellerman, 1980), social withdrawal (Strain & Timm, 1974), toilet phobia (Luiselli, 1977), separation anxiety (Patterson, 1965), and other fearful behaviors.

Shaping is used when the targeted approach behavior is likely to be unresponsive to positive consequences because it is either too difficult or complex for the child to perform. A shaping procedure involves providing praise or material rewards following successive approximations to the desired behavior. For example, a child who is fearful of riding in cars may first be rewarded for sitting in a stationary car for a short time and then for longer times; for remaining in the car while the ignition is on, for taking brief rides, and finally for taking long rides. In this way, the time the child is in contact with the feared stimulus is gradually lengthened and reinforced. Shaping has been found helpful in alleviating separation anxiety (Neisworth, Madle, & Goeke, 1975) and fear of riding in a school bus (Luiselli, 1978).

Extinction involves the removal of reinforcing consequences for avoidance responses. Through careful assessment the therapist identifies and controls these reinforcing consequences. Parental attention can often contribute to the continuation of avoidance behaviors, so that asking parents to ignore fearfulness can sometimes lead to discontinuation of the child's anxious behavior. Most typically, extinction is used in combination with positive reinforcement for nonfearful behavior.

An anxiety-reduction procedure called reinforced practice has been developed by Leitenberg and Callahan (1973). It combines a number of successful operant components. Children's avoidance responses are treated by reinforcing graduated approach responses to the feared stimulus. The components of reinforced practice are: (1) repeated and graduated *in vivo* practice in approaching the phobic stimuli, (2) social reinforcement for small improvements, (3) trial-by-trial feedback on performance, and (4) the therapist's communication to the child of expectations of gradual success.

Modeling

Modeling (Bandura, 1969) has been applied to the treatment of childhood anxiety or fears by having children observe child or adult models approach the feared object or engage in the anxiety-producing behavior. The modeling procedure is believed to teach the child new approach behaviors or to extinguish anxious responses by having the child witness other people's behavior, the affective reactions of the model, and consequences for the approach behavior (Bandura, 1968, 1969). Several types of modeling have been distinguished, including symbolic, live (or vicarious), and participant modeling.

In symbolic modeling the child observes a child or adult model approach the feared situation or object on videotape or film. One advantage of this approach is that the therapist has greater control over the behavior of the model and the phobic object. Symbolic modeling also permits repeated presentations of the gradual approach sequence (Ross, 1981). In live modeling, children watch a "live" model interact with the feared object or engage in the feared behavior, without the child's actually participating in the activity associated with the phobic object. In participant modeling the child actively makes approach responses after observing a model (Rosenthal & Bandura, 1978). Children first observe a model approach the feared object in a graded sequence with gentle prompting and praise. Finally, the child performs the approach responses unassisted.

Modeling has been used to reduce common childhood fears, such as fear of water (Lewis, 1974), dogs (Bandura et al., 1967), snakes (Ritter, 1968), and heights (Ritter, 1969). In addition, observational learning has been employed in the treatment of children displaying intense, situation-specific fears, such as fears experienced in anticipation of surgery (Melamed & Siegel, 1975) or anxiety associated with dental procedures (Melamed, Weinstein, Hawes, & Katin-Borland, 1975). Modeling has also been used effectively to increase the rate of peer interactions of socially withdrawn children (O'Connor, 1969).

Cognitive Procedures

Three cognitive strategies have recently been applied to the treatment of childhood anxiety: (1) directly training the child to recite statements of self-competence, (2) stress inoculation training, and (3) covert modeling. The first approach, which involves directly teaching children to rehearse statements emphasizing the child's competence in handling feared situations, has been employed by Kanfer, Karoly, and Newman (1975). They had children recite coping verbalizations (e.g., "I am a brave boy/girl") or statements focusing on the pleasant qualities of the situation (e.g., "The dark is a fun place to be") to overcome their fear of the dark.

Nelson (1981) employed a "stress inoculation technique" (Meichenbaum, 1975; Meichenbaum & Turk, 1976) to reduce a child's dental phobia. The child learned to rehearse coping self-statements to lessen anxiety associated with three aspects of the dental visit: (1) preparing for dental visits (e.g., "worrying won't help anything"), (2) confronting and handling stress or pain ("remember what the dentist said and it will be over a lot quicker"); and (3) coping with feelings of being overwhelmed by stress or pain at critical moments (e.g., "distract yourself by counting to 20 quickly"). The child was also taught to use positive self-statements following successful use of cognitive strategies (e.g., "I did it").

Chertock and Bornstein (1979) employed a covert modeling approach to reduce dental fears. Children were first asked to visualize a hierarchy of increasingly anxiety-provoking scenes related to dental visits. Scenes were described by the therapist while children were told to close their eyes and relax. Children were then instructed to imagine a model or multiple models coping with dental situations, without the children ever actually observing live or filmed models.

TREATMENT OUTCOME

Systematic Desensitization

A number of studies have examined the usefulness of systematic desensitization in the treatment of fears or anxiety in children. There have been a number of case reports of clinically referred children with phobias who were successfully treated using this procedure (e.g., Chapel, 1967; MacDonald, 1975), although many of these were uncontrolled or confounded studies (Hatzenbuehler & Schroeder, 1978). However, several case studies that employ adequate treatment designs have demonstrated the successful application of this technique with phobic children. For example, Van Hasselt et al. (1979) successfully treated an 11-year-old multiphobic child using systematic desensitization.

Analogue studies that evaluate the effectiveness of this treatment approach with nonclinic children who show only mild fearfulness are also available. In his review of these studies, Ollendick (1979) found that three of the four studies presented in the literature report positive outcomes with desensitization treatment (Barabasz, 1973; Kondas, 1967; Mann & Rosenthal, 1969). One recent analogue study compared the effectiveness of imaginal versus *in vivo* desensitization in treatment of 5- to 10-year-old children with a fear of water (Ultee et al., 1982). The findings suggested that the *in vivo* desensitization procedure was more effective than either imaginal desensitization or no treatment. As Wells and Vitulano (1984) point out, however, these data are somewhat limited due to the short duration of treatment (i.e., four sessions), use of nonclinical children, and failure to train children in relaxation or other anxiety-antagonistic procedures.

Miller et al. (1972) provide a group outcome study, with clinically phobic children, comparing imaginal desensitization, psychotherapy, and no treatment. Both treatments produced significantly greater improvement in parent report measures than no treatment, with no differences found between the two treatment approaches, although clinicians' evaluations showed no effects of treatment. The 6- to 10-year-old children showed significant improvements on clinicians' ratings compared to untreated children, regardless of type of treatment; however, no differences were obtained between treated and untreated groups of 11- to 15-year-old children. When outcome was assessed using parent reports, both younger and older groups again showed significant responsiveness to both treatments, relative to no treatment.

Flooding and Implosion

Evaluation of the use of flooding or implosion in the treatment of fearful children has been limited primarily to case reports. Although case studies can be valuable to identify potentially useful techniques, they do not provide the methodological rigor necessary to assess the effectiveness of treatment procedures adequately. Nonetheless, several case studies have reported positive findings employing these forced exposure techniques (Kennedy, 1965; Ollendick & Gruen, 1972; Yule et al., 1974).

For example, Sreenivasan et al. (1979) successfully treated an 11-year-old girl with a severe dog phobia using a flooding technique after desensitization had failed. The child was required to remain in a room with a live dog for a total of six sessions lasting about an hour each. Long-term elimination of the child's fear of dogs was reported. The paucity of controlled studies examining these approaches combined with the ethical concerns associated with forced exposure techniques (Barrios et al., 1981) suggest that flooding and implosion may most appropriately be used only when other interventions have failed (Carlson, Figueroa, & Lahey, 1985).

Operant Approaches

Numerous case studies are available that support the use of operant strategies with fearful children. For example, social and material rewards have been utilized successfully to treat school phobia (Ayllon et al., 1970; Neisworth et al., 1975). Controlled single-case studies have also been reported using operant procedures to produce positive outcomes in fearful children (Allen, Hart, Buell, Harris, & Wolf, 1964; Walker & Hops, 1973). In particular, social withdrawal or avoidant behavior has been reduced by rewarding increased rates of peer interactions or social approaches (e.g., Allen et al., 1964).

On the other hand, controlled group-comparison studies investigating the utility of operant techniques have only rarely been reported. Leitenberg and Callahan (1973) evaluated the efficacy of reinforced practice in reducing fear of the dark in a small group of preschool children compared to a no-treatment control group. They found that treated children were able to remain in the dark significantly longer than untreated children. These results may not be applicable to clinically anxious children, however, since the children were recruited for treatment. In a second group-comparison study, Obler and Terwilliger (1970) examined the effectiveness of a treatment package incorporating contingent rewards in a sample of 30 emotionally disturbed, neurologically impaired children who were phobic of riding on a public bus or of dogs. Children rewarded for successful approaches to the feared stimulus were compared to untreated controls. Parents of treated children reported less fearful behavior than parents of children who received no intervention. The absence of objective outcome measures and inability to discern the active treatment component(s) limit the conclusions to be drawn regarding the usefulness of operant approaches in this study (Begelman & Hersen, 1971).

Overall, the systematic empirical evaluation of an operant approach in the clinical treatment of anxious children has been fairly meager. In particular, controlled investigations of operant techniques applied to clinic children with anxiety disorders are absent.

Modeling

The existing research literature on the clinical efficacy of modeling for the treatment of childhood anxiety disorders is extensive but weak. Numerous analogue studies have been conducted of nonclinic children with relatively mild specific fears (reviewed by Ollendick, 1979), but there are no controlled studies using clinic children with phobias. Moreover, no studies have been conducted of the appropriateness of modeling for other types of anxiety disorders, such as separation anxiety or overanxious disorders.

Ollendick (1979) reviewed 11 analogue studies of children with fears of animals, water, and heights. These studies rather consistently showed that each of several different versions of modeling was superior to no treatment in reducing these fears. However, these studies indicate that the particular type of modeling procedure used influences the outcome of treatment. Participant modeling has frequently been found to be superior to modeling alone (Ollendick, 1979). Similarly, exposure to models who interact fearlessly with the stimulus has sometimes but not always been found to be less effective than fearful models who "cope" with their fears (Ginther & Roberts, 1983).

Although no controlled studies of modeling have been conducted using children with clinically significant anxiety disorders, another type of applied usefulness of modeling procedures has been clearly demonstrated by Melamed and others (Johnson & Melamed, 1979; Klingman, Melamed, Cuthbert, & Hermecz, 1984; Melamed et al., 1978). These studies have shown that exposure to coping models reduces children's fears of medical and dental procedures.

Cognitive Procedures

A few studies of the effectiveness of cognitive approaches in treating fearful children have provided tentative evidence supporting its use (Ross, 1981; Graziano et al., 1979). The most extensively examined cognitive approach involves training children to rehearse coping self-statements emphasizing self-competence of positive aspects of the feared situation in a nonclinic group of 5- and 6-year-old children with a fear of the dark. In perhaps the most well-controlled study employing a verbally mediated, self-control approach, Graziano and Mooney (1980) obtained positive outcomes with 6- to 12-year-old children with severe fears of going to bed alone in the dark. Unfortunately, the cognitive procedure was combined with muscle relaxation, the imagining of a pleasant scene, and a token-reward system for implementation of the self-control technique, thus making it difficult to assess the contribution of the cognitive component (Ross, 1981). Nevertheless, children who recited brave self-statements were found to show reductions in their fears relative to an untreated control group at 2-, 6-, and 12-month follow-up assessments (Graziano & Mooney, 1980), as well as at a 2 ½- to 3-year follow-up evaluation (Graziano & Mooney, 1982). In a comparative treatment study, Peterson and Shigetomi (1981) showed that similar cognitive strategies combined with filmed modeling were more effective than either intervention used alone in treating children anticipating surgery and hospitalization.

In contrast to these studies supporting the use of training children to employ coping self-statements, two studies found no evidence for the effectiveness of a verbal coping strategy in treating fearful or anxious children (Fox & Houston, 1981; Sheslow et al., 1983). Possible aspects of these latter studies that may have contributed to the negative findings obtained included: use of children too young to employ cognitive strategies (Sheslow et al., 1983); using an anxiety-provoking situation requiring task performance rather than passive endurance as in previous studies (Fox & Houston, 1981); and employing self-statements negating unpleasant aspects of the situation instead of emphasizing positive features, as had previously been done. Overall, these studies suggest that this cognitive approach shows promise in treating childhood fears, although further study is clearly needed.

CASE DESCRIPTION

Martin was a 10-year-old male who was referred for treatment at the suggestion of his school psychologist. The primary referral complaint was Martin's chronic refusal to attend school, which had resulted in his receiving a homebound tutoring program rather than attending his local elementary school. Martin was an only child and resided at home with both natural parents.

PRESENTING COMPLAINTS

Martin's school refusal began in the third grade, at which time he began to go through periods when he would not go to school. On some occasions Martin stayed at home; at other times he went to school for a short period and then ran away during the school day. Frequently, when he ran away, he walked the five miles from school to the family's home. During the 4 months preceding referral for treatment, Martin completely refused to attend school. The parents reported that the child locked himself in the bathroom and threw temper tantrums in order to prevent his parents from forcing him to go to school. He also frequently complained of stomach aches and headaches in apparent efforts to avoid school attendance.

Because the parents were unable to get Martin to attend school at all, he began a homebound tutoring program twice weekly for two hours. However, Martin subsequently became resistant to working with the tutor and was falling considerably behind in his school work.

CONCEPTUALIZATION

The parents noted that the onset of each episode of Martin's refusal to attend school followed an extended period during which he had remained at home due to illness, school holidays, or vacations. Observations by the therapist in the boy's home revealed that the consequences of Martin's refusal to go to school were quite positive. The mother, apparently having given up hope of getting her son to school, permitted him to sleep beyond the time necessary for him to awaken to go to school. During the day, Martin watched television, went outside to play with much younger children who did not attend school, or engaged in other enjoyable activities at home with his mother. It was clearly a pleasant alternative to school attendance.

It appeared that Martin's school refusal first started and was being maintained by the comfortable routine he enjoyed at home with his mother and in the neighborhood. There were no negative consequences for the child's school absences and, in fact, he was able to avoid school work almost completely.

In addition, it was noteworthy that Martin always remained close to his home and mother when he was not in school. It was also learned that when he was separated from his parents, Martin became anxious and worried about his own and his parents' welfare. Thus, it seemed that Martin's refusal to go to school was associated with a fear of being separated from his mother rather than a fear of some aspect of the school environment.

Based on this conceptualization, it was decided to change the contingencies at home so that school attendance would be followed by positive consequences and refusal to attend school would no longer be rewarding or would even be mildly unpleasant. Since it was believed that most rewards that the parents could offer would be insufficiently powerful to encourage voluntary school attendance, a shaping procedure was implemented in which the child's gradual separation from his mother and attendance at school was systematically reinforced.

ASSESSMENT

Initial clinical interviews were conducted with parents and child separately to determine the nature and history of school refusal, antecedents and consequences of failure to attend school, previous interventions, and family members' perceptions of possible causal and contributory factors related to the problem. In addition, a structured clinical interview, the ISC (Kovacs, 1983), was administered, first to the parents and then to Martin, to assess the presence of an anxiety disorder. Both the parents' and the child's responses suggested that Martin met diagnostic criteria for separation anxiety disorder, according to the DSM-III (American Psychiatric Association, 1980). The following DSM-III criteria were confirmed: (1) unrealistic worry about possible harm befalling the parents when separated from them; (2) persistent refusal to go to school in order to stay with his mother; (3) complaints of physical symptoms on school days; and (4) signs of excessive distress on separation, or when anticipating separation, from the mother. As noted previously, these responses suggested that a fear of separation from his mother, rather than anxiety associated with school, was contributing to the child's ongoing school refusal.

Home observations were done to assess consequences of school refusal further. Martin and his parents completed a fear and avoidance hierarchy and participated in a behavioral avoidance test in order to assess levels of anxiety experienced as he approached school and separated from his mother. These latter two measures were also completed during and following treatment to evaluate the child's progress throughout treatment and to assess clinical outcome.

The parents helped to devise a graded hierarchy that contained 10 items that caused Martin increasing levels of discomfort or anxiety. All items were related to separation from his mother and school attendance. Each situation was rated using a 10-point scale by the child to indicate the degree of anxiety anticipated in response to each item. The following hierarchical items and ratings were obtained prior to intervention:

Items	Ratings (1 = relaxed or no anxiety; 10 = extremely nervous)
1. Awakening at 7 a.m. and getting ready for school.	2
2. Being driven to school by mother.	4
3. Going to school on the bus.	6
4. Standing outside of the school with mother.	6
5. Standing outside of the school alone.	8
6. Entering the school.	9
7. Going into the classroom and sitting down.	10
8. Sitting in class for 5 minutes.	10
9. Remaining in class until lunch.	10
10. Remaining in class all day.	10

A behavioral approach test consisted of a subset of the items from the fear and avoidance hierarchy. The child's behavior was observed during each situation, and ratings of anxiety were provided by the child at various times during the assessment. The results of the behavioral avoidance test are presented below.

The teacher was asked to complete the Teacher Version of the Child Behavior Checklist (Achenbach & Edelbrock, 1983) in order to obtain her appraisal of the child's classroom behavior. The teacher's responses indicated that Martin displayed anxiety, social withdrawal, and obsessive-compulsive be-

	Completed		
Item	Yes	No	Rating
1. Awakening and getting ready for school.	×		3
2. Driving to school with mother.	×		5
3. Standing outside the school.	×		6
4. Entering the school.			
5. Going into the classroom and sitting down.		×	—
		×	—

havior in the classroom. An interview with the teacher and principal was also conducted to evaluate specific behaviors related to school refusal and to assess how school personnel had previously handled the child's behavior. It was learned that Martin had received considerable attention as a result of refusal to remain in the classroom. Attention took the form of the teachers and principal having frequent discussions with Martin regarding reasons for his behavior, their acceptance and tolerance of his behavior, and so on. The interview with the principal and teacher was also used to determine their willingness to participate in the planned intervention and to elicit their cooperation. The principal and teacher agreed to implement the portion of the treatment program that would take place in the school. Finally, potentially rewarding activities or objects were also assessed to determine items that could be used to reinforce approximations to school behavior. The child and parents together developed a list of rewards, including a G.I. Joe, toy army artillary, play handcuffs, money, candy, and other items.

TREATMENT

Initially, forced exposure or flooding was selected as a treatment approach, since it has repeatedly been found to be effective with other children with school refusal similar to Martin's (Kennedy, 1965). The parents stated that they were prepared to insist that Martin attend school. Due to the father's unavailability in the mornings prior to school, the help of a male family friend was solicited in case the child would not comply with the mother. It was explained to Martin that in order for him to overcome his separation anxiety and avoidance of school, it would be necessary for him initially to experience fear and discomfort in the situation that he had been avoiding. He was told that through repeated and prolonged exposure to being in school and separated from his mother, his anxiety would eventually subside. Both Martin and his parents consented to this approach.

On the first day of the flooding procedure, the child cried, screamed, and refused to attend school. He subsequently locked himself in the bathroom. The mother and family friend gently coaxed Martin to come out of the bathroom. However, the mother was strongly opposed to using physical force to get Martin to school, despite her verbal agreement to do so prior to treatment. Similarly ineffective attempts were made to encourage Martin to attend school on the following school days. Martin remained at home and his mother required that he remain in his room throughout the school day.

An alternative shaping procedure was then selected, in which the child would be rewarded for successive approximations to school attendance. During the next three weeks, Martin was reinforced for confronting increasingly difficult situations, some of which were selected from his fear and avoidance hierarchy.

As with the forced exposure procedure, the contingencies at home and at school needed to be altered. Both parents were advised to ignore Martin's crying, arguments, and somatic complaints and to attend to and praise enthusiastically compliance with school attendance and the treatment program. Although the mother initially had difficulty overlooking the child's protests, she gradually became comfortable with this approach as she was able to see its effectiveness with Martin. The therapist's support and daily phone contact with the mother was critical at this particular point in treatment.

In addition to the parental attention and praise that were provided contingent on approach behavior, a chart was prominently placed in the home for Martin and a sticker was put on the chart at the end of each day during which Martin successively and voluntarily completed a step in the graduated exposure program. In addition, Martin also received an item from his list of rewards (e.g., money, small toy) that was developed prior to treatment. A bonus treat or special weekend activity was offered for perfect compliance during the week (i.e., if Martin received five stickers during the week). If Martin was resistant by crying or screaming and had to be coerced to comply with his mother, then he did not earn a sticker but received a small reward of candy since it was felt that there should be some positive feedback for attending school, even though it was not done voluntarily. In efforts to enhance the value of the rewards, placement of the sticker on the chart and giving Martin his prize were accompanied by verbal praise and occurred when both the mother and father were home.

School personnel were also asked to modify their responses to Martin's requests to leave the classroom or crying that took place in class. Rather than talking with Martin or sending him to the principal's office at these times, it was requested that he be required to remain in the classroom when he got to that stage in the hierarchy and that his inappropriate behavior be ignored. His teacher and principal were concerned that the child's behavior might disrupt the class and were somewhat reluctant to agree to this tactic. However, they agreed to cooperate once they understood the rationale behind this approach and realized that it was the only way to overcome the child's school refusal.

The graduated stages in the hierarchy were developed and fully agreed to by the entire family. Some of the items were based on the fear and avoidance hierarchy devised during assessment. The steps are presented below.

1. Getting dressed to go to school
2. Driving with mother to school
3. Entering the front door of the school with mother
4. Walking to classroom with mother
5. Attending class for 15 minutes with mother sitting in the back of the class
6. Attending class for 30 minutes with mother in the classroom
7. Attending class for one hour with mother in the classroom
8. Attending class for one hour while mother waits outside classroom
9. Attending class for one hour while mother voluntarily works in the school
10. Attending a half-day of school (until lunch) while mother voluntarily works in the school
11. Attending a whole day of school while mother voluntarily works in the school
12. Attending a whole day of school

The shaping procedure consisted of Martin's receiving rewards and positive feedback following successful completion of increasingly more difficult items. It was decided prior to initiation of the procedure for Martin to remain at each step for two days before progressing to the next step. If Martin showed a great deal of discomfort, then he was to return to the previous step and an intermediate step was to be added to facilitate succession to the next item. If it was apparent that Martin was ready to advance to the next step prior to two days, the parents would move on.

Martin successfully progressed through the graded hierarchy without noticeable difficulty at any particular stage. It was necessary to remain at steps 1 through 4, 6, and 9 for only one day each. All other items required two days before Martin verbally agreed to move to the next step. The mother encountered no resistance at any point and so Martin earned stickers daily for 18 consecutive school days. The treatment program required 16 days before Martin attended a full day of school completely unaccompanied by his mother. The rewards were gradually discontinued once Martin had attended school voluntarily for four consecutive days. Then Martin received rewards on Mondays, Wednesdays, and Fridays for school attendance. The reward contingency was gradually discontinued over an additional 2-week period until it no longer was necessary to provide prizes to maintain the child's regular school attendance.

FOLLOW-UP

The parents were asked to contact the therapist if problems with school refusal reemerged. When the parents had not contacted the therapist 1 month following termination of therapy, the therapist called the parents to assess the child's continued ability to attend school. The parents and child reported no problems with the child's attendance. A 6-month follow-up contact with the family similarly revealed that Martin continued to attend school regularly and voluntarily. The follow-up assessment included administration of the fear and avoidance hierarchy and the behavioral avoidance test that had also been completed prior to initiation of treatment. The child provided ratings on the fear and avoidance hierarchy indicating that no anxiety was being experienced associated with any of the items. Similarly, Martin was observed to awaken for school, travel to school on the school bus, and attend school without difficulty, and he reported no anxiety during the observations.

SUMMARY

Children are considered to have anxiety disorders when they manifest fears, anxiety, avoidance behaviors, related irrational thoughts, and autonomic arousal that are more intense or enduring than found in most children. Because of the multiple manifestations of these disorders, they are best assessed using multimethod approaches that combine information from child self-reports, observations and ratings made by adults, and in some instances, measures of physiological arousal. A tentative classification system of childhood anxiety disorders has been provided in DSM-III, but these diagnostic subtypes are based primarily on clinical impressions and are yet to be fully substantiated by research.

A considerable corpus of research now suggests that a variety of behavior therapy techniques are effective in the treatment of anxiety disorders of children and adolescents. Numerous studies point to the effectiveness of systematic desensitization, the use of operant procedures to promote exposure to the feared stimulus and reduce avoidance responses, modeling, and several cognitive procedures. In addition, implosion and flooding appear to be effective based on limited studies, but serious ethical questions limit their applicability to children.

Although the treatment outcome research generally supports the use of these techniques, there are serious shortcomings in our current data base. In particular, most studies have focused on nonclinical populations with specific fears. It is not clear that these findings are applicable to children with clinical phobias and especially unclear that these studies can be considered relevant to other forms of anxiety disorders, such as overanxious and separation anxiety disorders.

REFERENCES

Achenbach, T. M., & Edelbrock, C. (1983). *Manual for the Child Behavior Checklist and Revised Child Behavior Profile*. Burlington, VT: Department of Psychiatry, University of Vermont.

Agras, W. S., Chapin, H. H., & Oliveau, D. C. (1972). The natural history of phobia. *Archives of General Psychiatry*, *26*, 315–317.

Agras, W. S., Sylvester, D., & Oliveau, D. (1969). The epidemiology of common fears and phobia. *Comprehensive Psychiatry*, *10*, 151–156.

Allen, K. E., Hart, B., Buell, J. S., Harris, T. R., & Wolf, M. M. (1964). Effects of social reinforcement on isolate behavior of a nursery school child. *Child Development*, *35*, 511–518.

American Psychiatric Association. (1980). *Diagnostic and statistical manual of mental disorders* (3rd ed.). Washington, DC: Author.

Ayllon, T., Smith, D., & Rogers, M. (1970). Behavioral management of school phobia. *Journal of Behavior Therapy and Experimental Psychiatry*, *1*, 125–138.

Bandura, A. (1968). A social learning interpretation of psychological dysfunctions. In P. London & D. Rosenhan (Eds.), *Foundation of abnormal psychology*. New York: Holt, Rinehart & Winston.

Bandura, A. (1969). *Principles of behavior modification*. New York: Holt, Rinehart & Winston.

Bandura, A., Grusec, J., & Menlove, F. (1967). Vicarious extinction of avoidance behavior. *Journal of Personality and Social Psychology*, *5*, 16–23.

Barabasz, A. (1973). Group desensitization of test anxiety in elementary schools. *Journal of Psychology*, *83*, 295–301.

Barrios, B. A., Hartmann, D. P., & Shigetomi, C. (1981). Fears and anxieties in children. In E. J. Mash & L. G. Terdal (Eds.), *Behavioral assessments of childhood disorders*. New York: Guilford.

Begelman, D. A., & Hersen, M. (1971). Critique of Obler and Terwilliger's "Systematic desensitization with neurologically impaired children with phobic disorders." *Journal of Consulting and Clinical Psychology*, *37*, 10–13.

Bellack, A. S., & Lombardo, T. W. (1984). Measurement of anxiety. In S. M. Turner (Ed.), *Behavioral theories and treatment of anxiety* (pp. 51–89). New York: Plenum.

Bentler, P. M. (1962). An infant's phobia treated with reciprocal inhibition therapy. *Journal of Child Psychology and Psychiatry*, *3*, 185–189.

Berg, I., & McGuire, R. (1971). Are school phobic adolescents overdependent? *British Journal of Psychiatry*, *119*, 167–168.

Berney, T., Kolvin, I., Bhate, S. R., Garside, R. F., Jeans, J., Kay, B., & Scarth, L. (1981). School phobia: A therapeutic trial with clomipramine and short-term outcome. *British Journal of Psychiatry, 138,* 110–118.

Carlson, C. L., Figueroa, R. G., & Lahey, B. B. (1985). Behavior therapy for childhood anxiety disorders. In R. Gittleman (Ed.), *Anxiety disorders of childhood.* New York: Plenum.

Chapel, J. C. (1967). Treatment of a case of school phobia by reciprocal inhibition. *Canadian Psychiatric Association Journal, 12,* 25–28.

Chazan, M. (1962). School phobia. *British Journal of Educational Psychology, 32,* 209–217.

Chertok, S. L., & Bornstein, P. H. (1979). Covert modeling treatment of children's dental fears. *Child Behavior Therapy, 1,* 249–255.

Conners, C. K. (1969). A teacher rating scale for use in drug studies with children. *American Journal of Psychiatry, 126,* 884–888.

Coolidge, J., Brodie, R., & Feeney, B. (1964). A ten-year follow-up study of 66 school-phobic children. *American Journal of Orthopsychiatry, 34,* 675–684.

Costello, A. J., Edelbrock, D., Kalas, R., Dulcan, M. K., & Klaric, S. H. (1984). *Development and testing of the NIMH Diagnostic Interview Schedule for Children (DISC) in a clinic population: Final report.* Rockville, MD: Center for Epidemiological Studies, NIMH.

Croake, J. W., & Knox, F. H. (1973). The changing nature of children's fears. *Child Study Journal, 3,* 91–105.

Darley, S., & Katz, I. (1973). Heart rate changes in children as a function of test versus game instructions and test anxiety. *Child Development, 44,* 784–789.

Doris, J., McIntyre, J. R. Kelsey, C., & Lehman, E. (1971). Separation anxiety in nursery school children. *Proceedings of the 79th Annual Convention of the American Psychological Association, 79,* 145–146.

Earls, F. (1980). Prevalence of behavior problems in 3-year-old children: A cross-national replication. *Archives of General Psychiatry, 37,* 1153–1157.

Edelbrock, C., Costello, A. J., Dulcan, M. K., Kalas, R., & Conover, N. C. (1985). Age differences in the reliability of the psychiatric interview of the child. *Child Development, 56,* 265–275.

Edelbrock, C., Costello, A. J., Dulcan, M. K., Kalas, R., & Conover, N. C. (in press). Parent-child agreement on child psychiatric symptoms assessed via structured interview. *Journal of Child Psychology and Psychiatry.*

Fox, J. E., & Houston, B. K. (1981). Efficacy of self-instructional training for reducing children's anxiety in an evaluative situation. *Behaviour Research and Therapy, 19,* 509–515.

Freeman, B. J., Roy, R. R., & Hemmick, S. (1976). Extinction of a phobia of physical examination in a 7-year-old mentally retarded boy: A case study. *Behaviour Research and Therapy, 14,* 63–64.

Ginther, L. J., & Roberts, M. C. (1983). A test of mastery versus coping modeling in the reduction of children's dental fears. *Child and Family Behavior Therapy, 4,* 41–51.

Gittelman-Klein, R., & Klein, D. (1973). School phobia: Diagnostic considerations in the light of imipramine effects. *Journal of Nervous and Mental Disease, 156,* 199–215.

Gittelman, R. (1985). Anxiety disorders in children. In B. B. Lahey & A. E. Kazdin (Eds.), *Advances in clinical child psychology* (Vol. 9). New York: Plenum.

Glennon, B., & Weisz, J. R. (1978). An observational approach to the assessment of anxiety in young children. *Journal of Consulting and Clinical Psychology, 46,* 1246–1257.

Graziano, A., & DeGiovanni, I. S. (1979). The clinical significance of childhood phobias: A note on the proportion of child-clinical referrals for the treatment of children's fears. *Behaviour Research and Therapy, 17,* 161–162.

Graziano, A., DeGiovanni, I. S., & Garcia, K. (1979). Behavioral treatment of children's fears: A review. *Psychological Bulletin, 86,* 804–830.

Graziano, A., & Mooney, K. (1980). Family self-control instruction for children's nighttime fear reduction. *Journal of Consulting and Clinical Psychology, 48,* 206–213.

Graziano, A., & Mooney, K. (1982). Behavioral treatment of "nightfears" in children: Maintenance of improvement at 2½–3-year follow-up. *Journal of Consulting and Clinical Psychology, 50,* 598–599.

Hatzenbuehler, L., & Schroeder, H. (1978). Desensitization procedures in the treatment of childhood disorders. *Psychological Bulletin, 85,* 831–844.

Herjanic, B., & Reich, W. (1982). Development of a structured psychiatric interview for children: Agreement between child and parent on individual symptoms. *Journal of Abnormal Child Psychology, 10,* 307–324.

Hersov, L. A. (1960). Persistent non-attendance at school. *Child Psychology and Psychiatry, 1,* 130–136.

Jersild, A. T., & Holmes, F. B. (1935). Methods of overcoming children's fears. *Journal of Psychology, 1,* 75–104.

Johnson, S. B., & Melamed, B. G. (1979). Assessment and treatment of children's fears. In B. B. Lahey & A. E. Kazdin (Eds.), *Advances in clinical child psychology* (Vol. 2, pp. 111–134). New York: Plenum.

Kanfer, F., Karoly, P., & Newman, A. (1975). Reduction of children's fears of the dark by competence-related and situational threat-related verbal cues. *Journal of Consulting and Clinical Psychology, 43,* 251–258.

Kellerman, J. (1980). Rapid treatment of nocturnal anxiety in children. *Journal of Behavior Therapy and Experimental Psychiatry, 11,* 9–11.

Kelley, C. K. (1976). Play desensitization of fear of darkness in preschool children. *Behaviour Research and Therapy, 14,* 79–81.

Kennedy, W. (1965). School phobia: Rapid treatment of 50 cases. *Journal of Abnormal Psychology, 79,* 285–289.

Kissell, S. (1972). Systematic desensitization therapy with children: A case study and some suggested modifications. *Professional Psychology, 3,* 164–168.

Klingman, A., Melamed, B. G., Cuthbert, M. I., & Hermecz, D. A. (1984). Effects of participant modeling on information acquisition and skill utilization. *Journal of Consulting and Clinical Psychology, 52,* 414–422.

Koeppen, A. S. (1974). Relaxation training for children. *Elementary School Guidance and Counseling*, *9*, 521–528.

Kondas, O. (1967). Reduction of examination anxiety and "stage fright" by group desensitization and relaxation. *Behaviour Research and Therapy*, *5*, 275–281.

Kornhaber, R., & Schroeder, H. (1975). Importance of model similarity on extinction of avoidance behavior in children. *Journal of Consulting and Clinical Psychology*, *43*, 601–607.

Kovacs, M. (1983). *The Interview Schedule for Children (ISC): Interrater and parent-child agreement*. Unpublished manuscript, University of Pittsburgh.

Kutina, J., & Fischer, J. (1977). Anxiety, heart rate and their interrelation with mental stress in school children. *Activitas Nervos Superior*, *19*, 89–95.

Lang, P. J., & Lazovik, A. D. (1963). Experimental desensitization of a phobia. *Journal of Abnormal and Social Psychology*, *66*, 519–525.

Lapouse, R., & Monk, M. A. (1959). Fears and worries in a representative sample of children. *American Journal of Orthopsychiatry*, *29*, 803–818.

Lazarus, A. A., & Abramovitz, A. (1962). The use of "emotive imagery" in the treatment of children's phobias. *Journal of Mental Science*, *108*, 191–195.

Leitenberg, H., & Callahan, E. (1973). Reinforced practice and reduction of different kinds of fears in adults and children. *Behaviour Research and Therapy*, *11*, 19–30.

Lewis, S. (1974). A comparison of behavior therapy techniques in the reduction of fearful avoidance behavior. *Behavior Therapy*, *5*, 648–655.

Luiselli, J. K. (1977). Case report: An attendant-administered contingency management program for the treatment of toileting phobia. *Journal of Mental Deficiency Research*, *21*, 283–288.

Luiselli, J. K. (1978). Treatment of an autistic child's fear of riding a school bus through exposure and reinforcement. *Journal of Behavior Therapy and Experimental Psychiatry*, *9*, 169–172.

MacDonald, M. L. (1975). Multiple impact behavior therapy in a child's dog phobia. *Journal of Behavior Therapy and Experimental Psychiatry*, *6*, 317–322.

MacFarlane, J. W., Allen, L., & Honzik, M. P. (1954). *A developmental study of the behavior problems of normal children between twenty-one months and fourteen years*. Berkeley: University of California Press.

Mann, J., & Rosenthal, T. L. (1969). Vicarious and direct counterconditioning of test anxiety through individual and group desensitization. *Behaviour Research and Therapy*, *7*, 359–367.

Marks, I. M. (1969). *Fears and phobias*. New York: Academic.

Meichenbaum, D. (1975). A self-instructional approach to stress management: A proposal for stress innoculation training. In C. D. Spielberger & I. Sarason (Eds.), *Stress and anxiety* (Vol. 2). New York: Wiley.

Meichenbaum, D., & Turk, D. (1976). The cognitive-behavioral management of anxiety, anger, and pain. In P. O. Davidson (Ed.), *The behavioral management of anxiety, depression and pain*. New York: Brunner/Mazel.

Melamed, B. G., & Siegel, L. J. (1975). Reduction of anxiety in children facing hospitalization and surgery by use of filmed modeling. *Journal of Consulting and Clinical Psychology*, *43*, 511–521.

Melamed, B., Weinstein, D., Hawes, R., & Katin-Borland, M. (1975). Reduction of fear related dental management problems using filmed modeling. *Journal of the American Dental Association, 90,* 822–826.

Melamed, B. G., Yurcheson, R., Fleece, E. L., Hutcherson, S., & Hawes, R. (1978). Effects of film modeling on the reduction of anxiety-related behaviors in individuals varying in levels of previous experience in the stress situation. *Journal of Consulting and Clinical Psychology, 46,* 1357–1367.

Miller, L. C. (1972). School Behavior Check List: An inventory of deviant behavior for elementary school children. *Journal of Consulting and Clinical Psychology, 1,* 134–144.

Miller, L. C., Barrett, C. L., & Hampe, E. (1974). Phobias of childhood in a pre-scientific era. In A. Davids (Ed.), *Child personality and psychopathology: Current topics.* New York: Wiley.

Miller, L. C., Barrett, C. L., Hampe, E., & Noble, H. (1972). Comparison of reciprocal inhibition, psychotherapy, and waiting list control for phobic children. *Journal of Abnormal Psychology 79,* 269–279.

Morris, R. J., & Kratochwill, T. R. (1983). *Treating children's fears and phobias.* New York: Pergamon Press.

Neisworth, J. T., Madle, R. A., & Goeke, K. E. (1975). Errorless elimination of separation anxiety: A case study. *Journal of Behavioral Therapy and Experimental Psychiatry, 6,* 79–82.

Nelson, W. M., III (1981). A cognitive-behavioral treatment for disproportionate dental anxiety and pain: A case study. *Journal of Clinical Child Psychology, 10,* 79–82.

Nichols, K., & Berg, I. (1970). School phobia and self-evaluation. *Journal of Child Psychology and Psychiatry, 11,* 133–141.

Obler, M., & Terwilliger, R. F. (1970). Pilot study on the effectiveness of systematic desensitization with neurologically impaired children with phobic disorders. *Journal of Consulting and Clinical Psychology, 34,* 314–318.

O'Connor, R. D. (1969). Modification of social withdrawal through symbolic modeling. *Journal of Applied Behavior Analysis, 2,* 15–22.

Ollendick, T. H. (1979). Fear reduction techniques with children. In M. Hersen, R. Eisler, & P. Miller (Eds.), *Progress in behavior modification* (Vol. 8, pp. 127–168). New York: Academic.

Ollendick, T. H. (1983). Reliability and validity of the Revised Fear Surgery Schedule for Children (FSSC-R). *Behaviour Research and Therapy, 21,* 685–692.

Ollendick, T. H., & Cerny, J. A. (1981). *Clinical behavior therapy with children.* New York: Plenum.

Ollendick, T. H., & Gruen, G. E. (1972). Treatment of bodily injury phobia with implosive therapy. *Journal of Consulting and Clinical Psychology, 38,* 389–393.

Patterson, G. R. (1965). A learning theory approach to the treatment of the school phobic child. In L. P. Ullmann & L. Krasner (Eds.), *Case studies in behavior modification.* New York: Holt, Rinehart & Winston.

Peterson, L., & Shigetomi, C. (1981). The use of coping techniques in minimizing anxiety in hospitalized children. *Behavior Therapy, 12,* 1–14.

Paul, G. L. (1966). *Insight vs. desensitization in psychotherapy*. Stanford, CA: Stanford University Press.

Puig-Antich, J., Oravaschel, H., Tabrizi, R. N., & Chambers, W. J. (1978). *Schedule for affective disorders and schizophrenia for school-age children*. New York: New York State Psychiatric Institute.

Quay, H. C. (1979). Classification. In H. C. Quay & J. S. Werry (Eds.), *Psychopathological disorders of childhood* (2nd ed.). New York: Wiley.

Quay, H. C., & Peterson, D. R. (1983). *Interim manual for the Revised Behavior Problem Checklist*. Coral Gables, FL: University of Miami.

Reynolds, C. R. (1980). Concurrent validity of What I Think and Feel: The Revised Children's Manifest Anxiety Scale. *Journal of Consulting and Clinical Psychology, 48*, 774–775.

Reynolds, C. R. (1981). Long-term stability of scores on the Revised Children's Anxiety Scale. *Perceptual and Motor Skills, 53*, 702.

Reynolds, C. R., & Paget, K. D. (1982). *National normative and reliability data for the Revised Children's Manifest Anxiety Scale*. Paper presented at the annual meeting of the National Association of School Psychologists, Toronto.

Reynolds, C. R., & Richmond, B. O. (1978). What I think and feel: A revised measure of children's manifest anxiety. *Journal of Abnormal Child Psychology, 6*, 271–280.

Richman, N., Stevenson, J., & Graham, P. (1982). Prevalence of behaviour problems in 3-year-old children: An epidemiological study in a London borough. *Journal of Child Psychology and Psychiatry, 16*, 272–287.

Ritter, B. (1968). The group desensitization of children's snake phobias using vicarious and contact desensitization procedures. *Behaviour Research and Therapy, 6*, 1–6.

Ritter, B. (1969). Treatment of acrophobia with contact desensitization. *Behaviour Research and Therapy, 7*, 41–45.

Rosenthal, T. L., & Bandura A. (1978). Psychological modeling: Theory and practice. In S. L. Garfield & A. E. Bergin (Eds.), *Handbook of psychotherapy and behavior change* (2nd ed., pp. 621–658). New York: Wiley.

Ross, A. O. (1981). *Child behavior therapy: Principles, procedures, and empirical basis* (pp. 251–289). New York: John Wiley.

Scherer, M. W., & Nakamura, C. Y. (1968). A fear survey schedule for children (FSS-FC): A factor analytic comparison with manifest anxiety (CMAS). *Behaviour Research and Therapy, 6*, 173–182.

Shapiro, A. H. (1975). Behavior of kibbutz and urban children receiving an injection. *Psychophysiology, 12*, 79–82.

Sheslow, D. V., Bondy, A. S., & Nelson, R. O. (1983). A comparison of graduated exposure, verbal coping skills, and their combination in the treatment of children's fear of the dark. *Child and Family Behavior Therapy, 4*, 33–45.

Speilberger, C. (1973). *Manual for the State-Trait Inventory for Children*. Palo Alto, CA: Consulting Psychologists Press.

Sreenivasan, V., Manocha, S. N., & Jain, V. K. (1979). Treatment of severe dog phobia in childhood by flooding: A case report. *Journal of Child Psychology and Psychiatry, 20*, 255–256.

Stampfl, T., & Levis, D. (1967). Essentials of implosive therapy: A learning theory-based psychodynamic behavioral therapy. *Journal of Abnormal Psychology*, *72*, 496–503.

Sternbach, R. (1962). Assessing differential autonomic patterns in emotions. *Journal of Psychosomatic Research*, *6*, 87.

Strain, P. S., & Timm, M. A. (1974). An experimental analysis of social interaction between a behaviorally disordered preschool child and her classroom peers. *Journal of Applied Behavior Analysis*, *7*, 583–590.

Stricker, G., & Howitt, J. (1965). Physiological recording during simulated dental appointments. *New York State Dental Journal*, *31*, 204–213.

Tasto, D. (1969). Systematic desensitization, muscle relaxation and visual imagery in the counter-conditioning of a 4-year-old phobic child. *Behaviour Research and Therapy*, *7*, 409–411.

Tennes, K. H., & Lampl, E. E. (1964). Stranger and separation anxiety in infancy. *Journal of Nervous and Mental Disease*, *139*, 247–254.

Ultee, C. A., Griffioen, D., & Schellekens, J. (1982). The reduction of anxiety in children: A comparison of the effects of 'systematic desensitization in vitro' and 'systematic desensitization in vivo.' *Behaviour Research and Therapy*, *20*, 61–67.

Van Hasselt, V. B., Hersen, M., Bellack, A. S., Rosenbloom, N. D., & Lamparski, D. (1979). Tripartite assessment of the effects of systematic desensitization in a multi-phobic child: An experimental analysis. *Journal of Behavior Therapy and Experimental Psychiatry*, *10*, 51–55.

Vernon, D., Foley, J. L., & Schulman, J. L. (1967). Effect of mother-child separation and birth order on young children's responses to two potentially stressful experiences. *Journal of Personality and Social Psychology*, *5*, 162–174.

Vernon, D., Schulman, J. L., & Foley, J. M. (1966). Changes in children's behavior after hospitalization. *American Journal of the Diseases of Children*, *3*, 581–593.

Waldron, S. (1976). The significance of childhood neurosis for adult mental health: A follow-up study. *American Journal of Psychiatry*, *133*, 532–538.

Walker, H. M., & Hops, H. (1973). Group and individual reinforcement contingencies in the modification of social withdrawal. In L. A. Hamerlynck, L. Handy, & E. Mash (Eds.), *Behavior change: Methodology, concepts and practice*. Champaign, IL: Research Press.

Wells, K. C., & Vitulano, L. A. (1984). Anxiety disorders in childhood. In S. M. Turner (Ed.), *Behavioral theories and treatment of anxiety* (pp. 413–433). New York: Plenum.

Werry, J. S., & Quay, H. C. (1971). The prevalence of behavior symptoms in younger elementary school children. *American Journal of Orthopsychiatry*, *41*, 136–143.

Wish, P., Hasazi, J., & Jurgela, A. (1973). Automated direct deconditioning of a childhood phobia. *Journal of Behavior Therapy and Experimental Psychiatry*, *4*, 279–283.

Wolpe, J. (1958). *Psychotherapy by reciprocal inhibition*. Stanford, CA: Stanford University Press.

Yule, W., Sacks, B., & Hersov, L. (1974). Successful flooding treatment of a noise in an 11-year-old. *Journal of Behavior Therapy and Experimental Psychiatry*, *5*, 209–211.

CHAPTER 6

Depression

DAVID J. KOLKO

The study and treatment of adults presenting with depressive symptomatology have advanced our understanding of major affective disorders over the past decade. For example, research has fostered the development of more suitable diagnostic and assessment tools, description of the associated clinical picture in diverse populations, documentation of family and genetic correlates, and evaluation of both pharmacologic and psychosocial treatment approaches (see Rehm & Kaslow, 1984). Less progress, however, has been made in critically examining the concept of depression in children and adolescents. This discrepancy in interest and involvement assumes significant proportions in light of the apparent seriousness and prevalence of depressive symptomatology and the relationship between depression and other adjustment disturbances (Carlson, 1983; Poznanski, 1983). Current knowledge about depression in childhood has been disseminated in several reviews (Cantwell, 1983; Kaslow & Rehm, 1983; Petti, 1984; Puig-Antich & Gittelman, 1982; Reynolds, 1984). These sources provide important background information as well as an overview of the available evidence regarding models, diagnosis, assessment, and treatment of depressive symptoms. This chapter will focus on recent advancements in the area that draw on previous research findings in an attempt to broaden the psychosocial perspective taken in conceptualizing and remediating childhood depression.

OVERVIEW AND CURRENT STATUS

Conceptualization

The investigation of depression in childhood has, to some extent, been hindered by difficulties in the articulation of legitimate diagnostic criteria for this age group. Over the years diagnostic criteria for depression have been both

The author acknowledges the collaboration of Judith A. Dygdon, PhD, who served as the therapist in the case presented in this chapter.

vague and quite controversial. Currently, the criteria invoked from the third edition of the *Diagnostic and Statistical Manual of Mental Disorders* (DSM-III; American Psychiatric Association, 1980) to classify major depressive episodes in adults are likewise applied to similar episodes in children and adolescents. Second, confusion often surrounds the use of the term *depression*, which can refer to an individual symptom, a syndrome describing a clinical picture, or a full disorder having a set of delineated characteristics, typical correlates, and course. Although the characteristics of depressed patients can generally be differentiated from those of patients with other disorders, there may be some overlap in clinical picture (Cantwell, 1983).

There has been considerable debate as to whether the clinical picture of depression in childhood can be identified and, if so, whether it is comparable to that seen in adults. As noted by some authors (Cantwell, 1983; Puig-Antich & Gittelman, 1982; Kaslow & Rehm, 1983), several alternative views have suggested that clinical depression in children does not exist, is highlighted by different attributes (e.g., irritability, somatic complaints), or is masked by other symptoms (e.g., conduct disorder, hyperactivity). The view that depressed children display a disorder analogous to that experienced by depressed adults appears to have earned considerable support (Carlson & Cantwell, 1980; Kashani, Husain, Shekim, Hodges, Cytryn, & McKnew, 1981; Cytryn, McKnew, & Bunney, 1980; Puig-Antich, Blau, Marx, Greenhill, & Chambers, 1978). For example, Puig-Antich et al. (1978) identified 13 prepubertal children who met formal adult diagnostic criteria for major depressive disorder. Using related sets of criteria, Cytryn et al. (1980) also found that children diagnosed with depression exhibited symptoms similar to those in depressed adults. Nevertheless, children suffering from depressive disorders have exhibited a diverse range of symptoms (Costello, 1981; Poznanski, 1982).

Diagnostic Criteria

Support for the position that childhood depression constitutes a formal descriptive category has been buttressed by advances in diagnostic theory of affective disorders in adults (Spitzer & Williams, 1980). Thus, it is not surprising that adult criteria for depression have been applied to the diagnosis of depression in children. The earliest operational criteria for adults were originally developed by Feighner (Feighner, Robins, Guze, Woodruff, Winokur, & Munoz, 1972) and later expanded into the Research Diagnostic Criteria (RDC: Spitzer, Endicott, & Robins, 1972). The primary diagnostic features of childhood depression were described by Ling, Oftedal, and Weinberg (1970) and later modified by Weinberg, Rutman, Sullivan, Penic, and Dietz (1973). The criteria, known as the Weinberg criteria, required: (1) both dysphoric mood and self-deprecatory ideation, (2) at least two related symptoms such as aggression, sleep disturbance, change in school performance, or somatic complaints, (3) a duration of at least 1 month, and (4) a change in a child's usual behavior. Investigators have demonstrated that the diagnosis of depression based on these criteria can be made with good reliability (Cytryn & McKnew, 1972; Kovacs & Beck, 1977). Others have employed unmodified RDC criteria (Strober, Green, & Carlson, 1981a) and the more recent DSM-III criteria (Cytryn et al., 1980; Kashani, Barbero, & Bolander, 1981) with similar outcomes.

Three recent studies support the diagnostic reliability of the syndrome of childhood depression. Carlson and Cantwell (1982) found that 28 (27%) of 102 psychiatrically disturbed children were diagnosed as having affective disorders using DSM-III criteria. Children meeting DSM and Weinberg criteria for depression were significantly more depressed on the Children's Depression Inventory than those meeting only the Weinberg criteria. Lobovits and Handal (1985) also obtained evidence for the validity of DSM-III criteria and other depression rating scales. While supporting use of diagnostic criteria for childhood depression, both studies highlight the discrepancy between the Weinberg criteria and more rigorous DSM-III criteria. A related study found that 9 of 33 (27%) hospitalized adolescents met RDC criteria for major depressive disorder (Robbins, Alessi, Cook, Poznanski, & Yanchyshyn, 1982). As noted by the authors, the findings primarily reflect symptoms of an affective nature and may be more legitimately employed to assess the severity rather than diagnosis of depression. Nevertheless, the evidence overall suggests the utility of using such operational criteria for the diagnosis of major depression in children and adolescents(Apter & Tyano, 1984; Puig-Antich, 1982).

Epidemiology

With increased credibility in the reliability of the diagnosis of depression, estimates of the prevalence and incidence of depression in children have been derived among psychiatric clinic populations. The rates of affective disorders have varied, including 1% (Poznanski & Zrull, 1970), 23% (Pearce, 1977), 27% (Carlson & Cantwell, 1982; Robins et al., 1982), 34% (Lobovits & Handal, 1985); 59% (Petti, 1978), and 60% (Murray, 1970). The rates for children seen in other specialty clinics have been less discrepant, with reported rates of 35% (Gittelman-Klein & Klein, 1971), 40% (Ling et al., 1970), and 58% (Weinberg et al., 1973). The presence of depressive disorders is, understandably, lower in the general child population as recruited from family practice clinics or medical centers (1.9%; Kashani & Simonds, 1979) and a pediatric ward (7%; Kashani, Barbero, & Bolander, 1981). In a nonclinic community study, Lefkowitz and Tesiny (1980) evaluated 3020, 9- ,10-, and 11-year old children and obtained a 5.2% overall prevalence rate.

Two recent studies investigated prevalence rates in high school adolescents (Kaplan, Hong, & Weinhold, 1984; Reynolds, 1983). Reynolds' (1983) survey of 2800 students revealed an estimate of 18% using criteria for moderate and severe depression (see Beck, 1967). Kaplan et al. (1984) administered the Beck Depression Inventory (BDI: Beck, Ward, Mendleson, Mock, & Erbaugh, 1961) to 385 junior and seniors and found that five (1.3%) were severely, 28 (7.3%) were moderately, and 52 (13.5%) were mildly depressed. An overall prevalence rate of 8.6% was found using a cut-off score of 16. The wide variation in prevalence rate is to be expected given several methodological differences across studies, including different subject samples and characteristics, informants, assessment instruments, and diagnostic criteria (see Lobovits & Handal, 1985).

ASSESSMENT

Methods for the assessment of childhood depression have generally reflected the trends towards collecting detailed psychiatric information from a variety of sources (see Carlson & Cantwell, 1979; Rutter, Tizard, & Whitmore, 1970). With the need to develop specific measures in the case of children, investigators have recently evaluated several procedures designed to assess the clinical syndrome and symptom clusters of depression, or the severity (i.e., depth or level) of individual depressive phenomenon (see Kazdin, 1981; Kazdin & Petti, 1982; Kaslow & Rehm, 1983). The former strategy primarily entails diagnostic classification using categories delineated on the basis of meeting formerly stated inclusion criteria. The Weinberg and RDC criteria in previous years, and DSM-III criteria now, were developed for this purpose. Essentially, the practitioner determines the presence of specific diagnostic criteria through interviews conducted with the child and the parents, evaluating the degree to which depressive symptomatology endorsed. A few notable psychiatric interviews will be described followed by a brief review of alternative assessment measures.

Interviews

Several interview procedures have been devised to assess the syndrome and correlates of depression in children. The most salient interview is the Schedule for Affective Disorders and Schizophrenia for School-Aged Children (KIDDIE-SADS), developed using unmodified RDC criteria for children (see Puig-Antich, Chambers, & Tabrizi, 1983). The KIDDIE-SADS is a semistructured interview for children and adolescents that yields DSM-III diagnoses for numerous categories. Ratings for each item are made following separate interviews with the parents and the child. Parents provide essential information about observable behaviors (e.g., affective expression), onset, and severity of each symptom, while children contribute general details regarding current functioning, emotional status, and subjective phenomena (e.g., emotional and cognitive experiences). Empirical studies suggest the diagnostic reliability of this instrument in assessing childhood depression (Orvaschel, Puig-Antich, Chambers, Tabrizi, & Johnson, 1982). Further considerations in using the KIDDIE-SADS can be found in Puig-Antich and Gittelman (1982).

Other interviews providing diagnostic information include the Diagnostic Interview for Children and Adolescents (DICA: Herjanic, 1980), the Interview Schedule for Children (ISC: Kovacs, 1978), and the Child Assessment Schedule (CAS: Hodges, Kline, Stearn, Cytryn, & McKnew, 1982). Critical examination of these instruments for the assessment of depression must be deferred until sufficient empirical data are availiable.

Clinician Rating Scales

Two other interview measures specifically designed to evaluate the severity of depression are the Bellevue Index of Depression (BID: Petti, 1978) and Children's Depression Rating Scale (CDRS: Poznanski, Cook, & Carroll, 1979). The BID, a semistructured interview for children or parents, is an extension of the Weinberg (1973) criteria for depression, which consists of 40 items covering 10 symptom categories (e.g., dysphoric mood, anhedonia). Items are rated for absence or degree of severity (0–3). Petti (1978) originally reported high correlations between BID scores and criterion ratings of depression. Subsequent studies using a modified version of the BID (consisting of 26 items rated for severity and duration) obtained significant interrater reliabilities (Petti, 1984), 6-week test-retest reliabilities, and correlations with the Children's Depression inventory (Kazdin, French, Unis, & Esveldt-Dawson, 1983). Kazdin, Esveldt-Dawson, Unis, and Rancurello (1983) found that children diagnosed as depressed received higher scores on the BID than those without this diagnosis.

The CDRS was modified from the Hamilton Depression Rating Scale for use with 6 to 12-year-old children (Poznanski et al., 1979). Each of its 15 items is assessed on a graduated scale of symptom severity, with operational criteria for each level and scores ranging from 15 to 61. The CDRS possesses good reliability (Poznanski et al., 1979) and has been found to correlate with global depression ratings (Poznanski, Carroll, Banegas, Cook, & Grossman, 1982; Poznanski, Cook, Carroll, & Corzo, 1983). Similar findings were obtained for a recent version of the CDRS (CDRS-R), which includes 17 items rated on a 1 to 7 point scale reflecting four categories of symptoms (e.g., mood, subjective behavior) (Poznanski, Grossman, Buchsbaum, Banegas, Freeman, & Gibbons, 1984). Children who received the clinical diagnosis of depression had higher scores than those who received nondepressed psychiatric diagnoses.

A related interview measure that yields individual ratings is the Children's Affective Rating Scale (CARS: Cytryn & McKnew, 1974; McKnew & Cytryn, 1979; McKnew, Cytryn, Efferin, Gershon, & Bunney, 1979). Cytryn and McKnew (1974) outlined three manifestations of themes of the depressive process in childhood: fantasy (e.g., mistreatment, suicide) verbal expression (e.g., worthlessness, hopelessness), and mood and behavior (e.g., sadness, limited responsiveness). In the CARS, each of these subscales is evaluated on a 10-point scale following a brief inteview. McKnew and Cytryn (1979) reported high interrater reliabilities for all four subscales, while McKnew et al. (1979) reported good interrater reliabilities and significant correlations with global depression ratings and clinical diagnoses using Weinberg (1973) criteria. A potential obstacle to good reliability and validity is the use of 10-point items that do not include adequate subcategory definitions.

Self-Report Measures

Alternative assessment techniques to comprehensive and focused interviews include several self-report inventories, rating scales, and specific measures designed to evaluate the severity of depression. Perhaps the most commonly documented self-report measure is the Children's Depression Inventory (CDI: Kovacs & Beck, 1977; Kovacs, 1980/1981), derived from the adult BDI. The CDI consists of 27 items comprising three response choices (0, 1, 2) that sample a variety of symptoms (e.g., sadness, anhedonia, sleep disturbance) during the past 2 weeks. Initial psychometric studies of the CDI found that it possessed adequate test-retest reliability, internal consistency, and criterion validity (Kovacs, 1980/1981; Kovacs, 1983).

Recent large-scale studies have more fully examined the CDI's psychometric properties. Basic information has been disseminated about sex and grade norms (Finch, Saylor, & Edwards, 1985) and administration format (Saylor, Finch, Baskin, Saylor, Darnell, & Furey, 1984). Using factor analysis, Hodges Siegel, Mullins, and Griffin (1983) obtained evidence for four factors in an outpatient sample (i.e., cognitive, motivational, poor social integration, somatic) and two factors in a nonclinic sample (i.e., general, noncompliance). A related study reported a four-factor structure, adequate internal reliability, and significant differences between depressed and nondepressed children on all 27 items (Helsel & Matson, 1984). Studies with psychiatric inpatients and their parents have likewise reported good test-retest reliabilities and higher scores for children receiving DSM-III diagnoses (Esveldt-Dawson, Unis, & Rancurello, 1983; Kazdin, French, Unis, & Esveldt-Dawson, 1983).

Saylor, Finch, Spirito, and Bennett (1984) obtained adequate 1-week test-retest reliabilities, split-half reliabilities, and alpha coefficients with normal and emotionally distressed children. Although CDI scores differentiated the two groups, no significant difference in CDI scores were found between children who did and did not receive DSM-III diagnoses of depression. Further, CDI scores were not significantly associated with ratings of depressive symptoms or a peer nomination of depression, but were related to negative self-concept, anxiety, external locus of control, and depressive attributional style.

The authors suggested that while CDI scores may correspond with child reports of depressive phenomena, the construct being measured "is not necessarily a unique syndrome and not necessarily 'depression' as defined by DSM-III" (p. 965). Others have also noted its modest reliability (Carlson & Cantwell, 1979).

The concurrent validity of the CDI has also been documented in a recent study by Strauss, Forehand, Frame, and Smith (1984) of children with either extremely high (≥ 11) or low (< 5) CDI scores. The study employed a broad range of self, peer, and teacher report measures. Children with high CDI scores: (1) viewed themselves as higher in anxiety and lower in self-concept and assertion, (2) were reported as doing worse in school by teachers, and as less smart by peers, (3) were less popular and preferred as friends, and (4) were viewed as more withdrawn. Such findings lend support to the validity of the CDI while suggesting the comparability between the clinical pictures of nonclinical depressed children and those of depressed adults and children seen in clinics.

Two recent self-report measures deserve mention. The Children's Depression Scale (CDS: Lang & Tisher, 1978) consists of 66 items: 48 depressive and 18 positive items. There are five separate depression subscales (e.g., effective response, social problems) and one positive scale (pleasure), with 9 depression and 10 positive items not associated with any scale. The measure is completed by placing a small card printed with each item into one of five boxes, each with a slit on top. The response choices range from "very wrong" to "very right." Preliminary data collected on a group of school-refusing children and regular school attenders, as well as their mothers and fathers, indicated that higher scores were obtained for school-refusers and their parents (Lang & Tisher, 1978). A number of technical developments have been reported by Tisher and Lang (1983). One of the many benefits to this scale is the opportunity to compare child and parental responses on a variety of important subscales; another is its novel response choice format.

A second new self-report measure is the Child Depression Scale for use with children (ages 8 to 13) in regular schools (Reynolds, 1980, cited in Reynolds, 1984). The Child Depression Scale consists of 30 items reflecting depressive symptomatology whose severity is evaluated on 4-point scales from "never" to "all the time." Preliminary studies suggest that the scale has high internal consistency and is significantly associated with both CDI scores and teacher ratings of depression (Bartell & Reynolds, 1983; Reynolds, Anderson, & Bartell, in press).

To assess depression in adolescents, investigators have examined the utility of the BDI, given its documented application with adults. The BDI consists of 21 items, each rated on four levels of severity. Strober, Green, and Carlson (1981b) administered the BDI to 78 psychiatric inpatients, 20 of whom received diagnoses of major depression, and reported good internal consistency,

5-day test-retest reliability, and item-remainder correlations. BDI scores correlated significantly with global clinical ratings of depression and differentiated depressed from nondepressed patients. Working with normal adolescents, Teri (1982) also obtained high internal consistency and a four-factor structure similar to that found with adults. Sixty-eight percent of adolescents reported no minimal or mild depression, while 5% reported severe depression. An alternative measure originally designed for adolescents called the Reynolds' Adolescent Depression Scale (RADS) has also been described (Reynolds, 1981). Studies suggest that the RADS possesses high internal consistency and 6-week test-retest reliability, and is significantly correlated with the BDI, Zung Self-Rating Depression Scale, and Hamilton Depression Rating Scale (see Reynolds, 1984).

Parent Rating Measures

A few parent rating measures of depression have been reported. The Child Behavior Checklist (CBCL: Achenbach & Edelbrock, 1983) has been used to collect epidemiological data on the prevalence of various psychiatric disorders and includes a scale that evaluates depressive symptomatology. Although the utility of this instrument has been documented in several studies, its specific utility in discriminating depressed from nondepressed children has not been well documented. The previously described CDI and BID have also been employed as parent rating measures (Kazdin, Esveldt-Dawson, Unis, Rancurello, 1983; Kazdin, French, Unis, & Esveldt-Dawson, 1983). The former found that mother's and father's ratings of their children using both measures were significantly related and that measures of the severity of depression completed by either source discriminated those children diagnosed as depressed. However, child and parent ratings of the same measure were only minimally correlated, with children rendering lower ratings than their parents.

Peer Rating Scales

Drawing on the advantages of peer ratings of various childhood behaviors, Lefkowitz and Tesiny (1980) examined the use of a Peer Nomination Inventory for Depression. The PNID consists of 20 items comprising 14 overt aspects of depression, 4 that define happiness, and 2 that describe popularity. The sample consisted of 450 boys and 492 girls from fourth- and fifth-grade classrooms. Children in small groups nominated one or more children for each item in the PNID. The PNID was found to be internally consistent, to possess high test-retest reliability after 2 months for both depression and happiness, and to correlate with modified CDI scores, Zung Self Ratings of Depression, and teacher-rated depression, among other construct validity measures (e.g., popularity, self-esteem, locus of control). Four factors were obtained: loneliness, inadequacy, dejection, and happiness. However, no diagnostic comparison of depressive disorder was made. Nevertheless, this list of various symptoms provides a description of observable behaviors that may be accurately evaluated by significant others.

Teacher Measures

A novel approach to examining teacher-based impressions involved the use of teacher-nominated students exhibiting specific behavioral characteristics viewed as integral to the syndrome of depression. Seagull and Weinshank (1984) noted that children whose reading skills failed to improve after tutoring tended to show five behavioral characteristics: (1) flat affect, (2) passive response to praise/blame, (3) motor lethargy, (4) unpredictable classroom performance, and (5) a pattern of failing to bring work to class. The characteristics were then arranged in two categories (1–3, 4–5) and used to construct two groups of 16 children, one nominated for both categories and the other nominated for neither category. Results indicated that the group nominated for both categories was lower on achievement and extroversion and higher in anxiety and general disability. Although no differences were found on the behavior problem scales of the CBCL, the nominated group received lower ratings on the social competence, social activities, and school competence scales. Behavioral measures rated following individual interviews revealed that the nominated students smiled and laughed less, were less animated vocally and more lethargic, and were more flat and sad in facial expression. Nominated students were also more often tardy or absent. No differences were found in terms of self concept, locus of control, or family and personal variables (e.g., divorce, family history of affective illness). These initial findings suggest that certain overt behaviors may be associated with characteristics commonly found in depressed children. However, the study would have been enhanced had independent measures of depression and formal DSM-III diagnoses been used.

Behavioral Assessment

Evaluation of the relationship between specific overt behaviors and childhood depression has only recently been described in an attempt to facilitate clinical recognition and validation of this disorder (Kazdin, Esveldt-Dawson, Sherick, & Colbus, 1985; Kazdin, Sherick, Esveldt-Dawson, & Rancurello, 1985). Kazdin, Esveldt-Dawson, Sherick, & Colbus (1985) found that depressed children exhibited less social activity and affective expressions during a free-play period than nondepressed children. The observational measures were associated with parent-reported, but not child-reported, depression instruments. Measures of nonverbal behavior (e.g., facial expressiveness, body movements, gestures, tearfulness) obtained during a brief interview were found to correlate with standardized inventories of depression (Kazdin, Sherick, Esveldt-Dawson, & Rancurello, 1985). However, most nonverbal behaviors did not correlate with these inventories, nor did any behavior correlate with psychiatric diagnosis of depression. While such findings may have clear diagnostic and treatment implications, studies using nonhospitalized samples, more diverse nonverbal behaviors, and alternative assessment contexts are clearly needed before conclusions can be made about the validity of behavioral observations.

TREATMENT APPROACHES: THEORY AND THERAPY

The evidence considered in the previous section highlights the broad clinical picture of the syndrome of depression in childhood. Not surprisingly, the many facets to depression and perspectives from which it is discussed (Kashani, Husain, Shekim, Hodges, Cytryn, & McKnew, 1981; Petti, 1984) have generated alternative therapeutic approaches. Such approaches attempt to highlight what are believed to be critical components or factors from different domains that significantly contribute to the emergence and maintenance of the child's dysfunction. These approaches have generally followed application to adult patients and have only recently been invoked in the case of children.

Learned Helplessness and Attribution Retaining

Theory

The learned helplessness model originally posited a relationship between uncontrolled environmental events and such reactions as impaired motivation, cognition, and adaptive behavior (Seligman, 1974; Miller & Seligman, 1975). A reformulation of this approach has narrowed its focus to the development of faulty attributions about one's expectation of control and efficacy (Abramson, Seligman, & Teasdale, 1978). The parameters affecting the nature of this attribution have been stated along three dimensions: internal versus external source of control, stable versus unstable perception of the duration of control, and global versus specific expectation of the impact or implication of an event. Depressed persons are believed to make more internal-stable-global attributions for failure and more external-unstable-specific attributions for success than nondepressed persons. The model further suggests that (1) internal attributions are associated with depressive reactions characterized by loss of self-esteem, (2) stable attributions are associated with long-lasting depression, and (3) global attributions are associated with pervasive depression. Experimental work with adults has supported this causal attribution model (Golin, Sweeney, & Schaffer, 1981; Harvey, 1981; Miller & Norman, 1981; Peterson, Semmel, von Baeyer, Abramson, Metalsky, & Seligman, 1982; Seligman, Abramson, Semmel, & von Baeyer, 1979).

Experimental evidence with children has lent some support for the relationship between attributional style and helplessness on academic and performance tasks. Studies by Dweck and her colleagues have shown that "helpless" children who are less likely to persist in the face of failure more often attributed the experience to limited personal ability rather than limited effort (Dweck & Reppucci, 1973), and then experienced negative emotional reactions (Diener & Dweck, 1978, 1979). In contrast, they were less likely to attribute mastery to ability and were more pessimistic about the outcome of future performances. Similar findings in terms of children's social performance were obtained by Goetz and Dweck (1980). Schwartz, Freedman, Lindsay, and Narrol (1982) found that depressed school children were slower on a performance task, made more errors, and performed less efficiently or adaptively than nondepressed school children. Such findings were interpreted as support for differences in the "conceptual tempo" of depressed children.

Other studies directly evaluating children's attributional styles are consistent with these findings. Kaslow, Tannenbaum, Abramson, Peterson, and Seligman (1983) administered two problem-solving tasks (20 five-letter anagrams, 10 trials of the Block Design Subtest of the Wechsler Intelligence Scale for Children–Revised; WISC-R) to 40 elementary schoolchildren who initially completed the CDI. Results indicated that higher CDI scores were associated with slower performances when completing the Block Design subtest and solving the anagrams. No relationship was found between CDI scores and verbal intelligence. In an extension of this work, 108 elementary school children also completed the CDI and the Children's Attributional Style Questionnaire (KASTAN), among other measures (Kaslow, Rehm, & Siegel, 1984). Depressed children made more internal-stable-global attributions for failure and more external-unstable-specific attributions for success than nondepressed children. CDI scores were negatively correlated with performance on the Block Design, Coding, and Digit Span subtests, but not the vocabulary subtest of the WISC-R. A related study found a similar relationship between attributional style and depression, in addition to showing that negative attributional style predicted the emergence of depressive symptoms 6 months later (Seligman, Peterson, Kaslow, Tannenbaum, Alloy, & Abramson, 1984).

Therapy

Therapeutic strategies for the remediation of depression that derive from this approach have been proposed, though few actual applications have been conducted (Beach, Abramson, & Levine, 1981). Seligman (1981) has suggested the following four treatment components: (1) environmental enrichment to change the likelihood of desired and unwanted outcomes; (2) personal control training to heighten expectations of control; (3) resignation training to make highly preferred unobtainable outcomes less preferred; and (4) attribution training designed to encourage external, unstable, and specific attributions in place of unrealistic attributions of failure, and to develop internal, stable, and global attributions to replace unrealistic attributions for success. Some of the methods used to reverse depressive affect and performance deficits with adults have included the use of successful experiences with solvable discrimination problems (Klein & Seligman, 1976), mood elevation using the repetition of positive self-statements (Raps, Reinhard, & Seligman, 1980), and internal attributions of success (Miller & Norman, 1981).

Attributional retraining in children has been described by Dweck (1977) based on her early experimental work (Dweck & Reppucci, 1973). Dweck (1975) reported that helpless children tended to attribute failure to their limited competence or to certain external causes. Thus, such children failed to persist in their efforts to solve problems. To remediate this motivational deficit, 12 children were exposed to one of two training procedures: success-only training (success experiences) and attribution retraining in which failure was attributed to insufficient effort. The six children exposed to the former program continued to experience performance deficits on problem-solving tasks, while those six children exposed to the latter program maintained or improved their performance. Those in the reattribution group exhibited competent performance, especially following failure, which was suggested by the authors as evidence that poor performance became a prompt to produce more effort. General cognitive measures, however, failed to show significant improvement following training. Yet, anecdotal reports noted that children in the reattribution group appeared to exhibit greater effort and to approach failure in a different way following training. Despite the many findings in support of this general conceptual model, Dweck's work represents the only empirical examination of a treatment approach for children based on its major components. It remains to be documented whether previously mentioned antihelplessness strategies used with adults bear fruitful application to children.

Cognitive Distortion and Cognitive Therapy

Theory

The cognitive approach to depression as advanced by Beck and his colleagues (Beck, 1967; 1976; Beck, Rush, Shaw, & Emery, 1979; Rush & Giles, 1981) suggests that individuals respond to situational stressors with certain dysfunctional beliefs consisting of negative ideas about the self, world, and future (i.e., cognitive triad). Further, they postulate a systematic processing distortion (the depressogenic or negative cognitive schema) by which new information is interpreted in a negative manner. Such childhood events as unexpected losses or reversals in relationships are examples of conditions that may precipitate depressive schemata. Given this mechanism, individuals are prone to making systematic logical or cognitive errors so that information that is consistent with their depressive schema is accepted while discordant information is rejected. These errors are often described as automatic thoughts and include, but are not limited to, dichotomous thinking, selective abstraction, overt generalization, and catastrophizing. Thus, depressed individuals may believe that (1) they are personally inadequate; (2) their experiences are generally negative, and (3) their present misfortunes will persist in time. The consequence of this interpretive evaluation may be dysphoria or sadness. Much empirical evidence has accumulated bearing on the conceptual integrity of Beck's (1976) theory (Lewinsohn & Hoberman, 1982, Rush & Giles, 1981; Young & Beck, 1981). Although mixed support has been obtained for certain theoretical predictions, there is evidence to suggest that depressed persons exhibit selective recall of negative events (DeMonbreun & Craighead, 1977), negative expectancies (Lewinsohn, Larson, & Munoz, 1978), cognitive distortions (Krantz & Hammen, 1979; Lewinsohn, Larson, & Munoz, 1982; Norman, Miller, & Klee, 1983), and limited problem-solving (Heppner, Baumgardner, & Jackson, 1985).

Given developmental differences in cognitive and verbal ability between children and adults, the application of a cognitive approach to childhood depression has only recently been examined. Emery, Bedrosian, and Garber (1983) provide a comprehensive discussion of the role of cognitive deficits ("thinking errors") in children and advocate the viability of the cognitive model. It is suggested that children have the cognitive capabilities to experience depressive reactions and misinterpret or distort their experiences. Further, children are able to experience the affective component of depression (i.e., anger, guilt, self-depreciation), particularly as it relates to self-esteem.

Claims as to the feasibility of this approach with children and adolescents have generally preceded empirical examination. In one of the few studies evaluating negative cognitive processes associated with depression in children, Hammen and Zupan (1984) evaluated the relevance of self-schemas to information processing (recall) and the relationship between negative self-schemas and depression. An incidental memory recall task was employed using words coded under self-reference, semantic, or structural instructions. It was found that recall under the self-reference instructions was highest. Children with positive self-views recalled more positive and fewer negative attributes, as would be expected. However, depressed children failed to recall significantly more negative self-descriptive attributes.

Studies evaluating other cognitive symptomatology have yielded more support. A study of schoolchildren described earlier (Kaslow et al., 1984) reported a significant negative relationship between self-esteem as measured by the Coopersmith Self-Esteem Inventory (CSEI) and depth of depression as measured by the CDI. The depressed children had more expectancies of failure, fewer expectancies of success, and more stringent standards for doing poorly. They also evaluated their performance more negatively. Using hospitalized children, Kazdin, French, Unis, Esveldt-Dawson, and Sharick (1983) obtained significant correlations between hopelessness about the future as measured by the Hopelessness Scale for Children and several measures of depression (CDI, BID, CSEI). However, depressed children were not significantly more hopeless than nondepressed children. Such findings highlight the similarity between depression and certain cognitive symptoms evidenced by both adult and child depressives (Friedman, Hurt, Clarkin, Corn, & Aronoff, 1983).

A final cognitive characteristic of depression evaluated in children has been problem-solving ability. Doerfler, Mullins, Griffin, Siegel, and Richards (1984) conducted a series of studies using the Means-Ends Problem-Solving Scale (MEPS: Platt and Spivack, 1975) with elementary and high school children. Study 1 using elementary children found a relationship between depression and the number of irrelevant means given on the social MEPS, but not with the number of means on the social or emotional MEPS, or the number of alternatives on the Optional Thinking Test. Study 2 found no significant relationship between depression and problem-solving with junior high and high school students. Study 3 found similar findings using depressed and nondepressed adults. A related study with children likewise reported no relationship between problem-solving and depression (Mullins, Siegel, & Hodges, 1985). Although such findings suggest that depressed persons may possess adequate problem-solving skills, they do not examine deficits due to motivational problems that would impede problem-solving functioning.

Therapy

Treatment from a cognitive perspective for adults has been extensively described and evaluated (Beck et al., 1979, Coleman & Beck, 1981; Hollon, 1984; Rehm & Kaslow, 1984; Rush & Giles, 1981). In general, treatment is described as a process of collaborative empiricism in which continuous feedback is given and specific techniques are implemented to enable the patient to identify, confront, and replace maladaptive and distorted thinking patterns. Major cognitive techniques include eliciting automatic dysfunctional thoughts using self-recordings, testing the validity of automatic thoughts by initiating experiments and generating alternative solutions to problems, and analyzing the validity of maladaptive assumptions to determine their advantages and disadvantages (Young & Beck, 1981). Several behavioral techniques have also been employed, such as activity scheduling, graded tasks and homework assignments, cognitive rehearsal, role-playing, and diversion techniques. Recent reviews highlight the clinical utility of this approach with adults (Hollon, 1984).

Only a few investigators have described the application of cognitive therapy to depressive symptoms in children or adolescents. Emery et al. (1983) provide the only account of specific techniques recommended for use with both children and adolescents. Not surprisingly, standard techniques for adults must be modified for younger patients. For example, self-monitoring of mood, activity, and success experiences may be compared with similar ratings obtained by parents for validation purposes. In terms of behavioral techniques, children may be encouraged to plan and then participate in various scheduled activities. Contingent reinforcement is a complementary procedure used to maximize exposure to such events. To facilitate performance of daily tasks, graded task assignments are often made. Cognitive techniques designed to evaluate the presence of the child's thoughts involve the verbalization of self-statements ("think aloud" procedure) and recording of specific thoughts at scheduled times. To modify such thoughts, Emery et al. (1983) recommend the use of self-statement modification and coping self-statements to assist in developing a cognitive repertoire for challenging their beliefs.

A large-scale group treatment study conducted in the schools compared a cognitive structuring program based on Beck's (1976) principles with a social problem-solving role-playing group and an attention-placebo and classroom control group (Butler, Miezitis, Friedman, & Cole, 1980). The two treatments were administered during ten 1-hour sessions. The sample consisted of 56 fifth- and sixth-grade children who met criteria on a self-report depression battery and who were referred by their teachers. The cognitive restructuring program involved teaching children how to recognize automatic thoughts and substitute more adaptive ones for them, while the role-playing program involved behavioral rehearsal of responses to problematic interpersonal situations and problem solving. The assessment measures in the battery consisted of: (1) an abbreviated Piers-Harris Children's Self-concept Scale (PHCSC), (2) CDI, (3) Moyal-Miezitis Stimulus Appraisal Questionnaire (MMSAQ), and (4) Nowicki-Strickland Locus of Control Scale for Children (NSLCS).

Pre–post analyses showed significant reductions in CDI scores and PHCSC scores for the two treatment groups, with change also noted on the CDI for the control group. In addition, only the role-playing group showed an overall significant reduction in scores on the MMSAQ and NSLCS. In terms of individual improvement, a total of 9, 4, 3, and 2 students were reported to have been improved academically and emotionally by their teachers in the role-playing, cognitive restructuring, attention-placebo, and control groups, respectively. It was also noted that depression scores had shown comparable patterns of improvement among children in all four groups. In explaining the apparent superiority of the role-playing group, Butler et al. (1980) suggested that thematic enactment may have been more relevant to and preferred by children of this age than verbalization and introspection as required in the cognitive restructuring group. The addition of explicit severity selection criteria, comparison groups, and multiple outcome measures are clear methodological advances. Nevertheless, concerns must be raised about the integrity of the independent variables, clinical significance of the impact of treatment, and generalization and maintenance of therapeutic gains.

A cognitive-behavioral program for school students, also drawing on the work of Beck (1976), as well as Lewinsohn (1974) and Rehm (1977), was recently compared with a progressive muscle relaxation program and a waiting-list control group (Coates & Reynolds, 1983). Thirty moderately and severely depressed adolescent students were randomly assigned to each group. The treatment programs were structured, emphasized self-monitoring and homework, and were conducted by an experienced school psychologist during ten, 1-hour sessions. Pre–post analyses revealed a significant reduction in BDI scores for both treatment groups with no change reported for the control group. Further reductions in scores were evident at 1-month follow-up for the cognitive-behavioral group and, to a lesser extent, the relaxation group. Such encouraging outcomes provide preliminary evidence for the potential therapeutic impact of a cognitive approach. This approach may be enhanced by drawing on the work of Shure and Spivack (Shure & Spivack, 1982; Spivack, Platt & Shure, 1976) to develop generalized cognitive problem-solving skills (see Meyers & Craighead, 1984; Pellegrini & Urbain, 1985), affective understanding and expressiveness (see Durlak & Jason, 1984), and interpersonal awareness (Drinkmeyer, 1970).

Social Skills Deficits and Training

Theory

Social skill approaches to depression have their origins in early claims that depression may be precipitated by a reduction in positive reinforcement, a situation that may be contributed to by insufficient interpersonal or social skills designed to elicit positive consequences (Ferster, 1973; McLean, Ogston, & Grauer, 1973). Such difficulties may dispose the depressed individual to experience an inability to control the interpersonal environment and corresponding emotional reactions of anger or dysphoria (Lewinsohn & Arconad, 1981). Indeed, several studies have contrasted depressed and nondepressed persons on several measures of skill, sociability, assertion, and interactiveness, among other verbal and motoric measures (Lewinsohn, Weinstein, & Alper, 1970; Libet & Lewinsohn, 1973; Linden, Hantzinger, & Hoffman, 1983; Sanchez & Lewinsohn, 1980; Youngren & Lewinsohn, 1980).

Studies have also documented social and interpersonal difficulties with depressed children (Petti, 1983). For example, Helsel and Matson (1984) found that a factor labeled appropriate social skills of the Matson Evaluation of Social Skills with Youngsters (MESSY) was negatively correlated with severity of depression on the CDI. Lefkowitz and Tesiny (1980) found that teacher-rated social behavior and two peer nomination popularity items were significantly correlated with PNID scores of normal children, although ratings of passivity were not. Peer unpopularity has also been found to correlate with CDI scores of unselected regular school children (Jacobsen, Lahey, & Strauss, 1983). In addition to being unpopular, children with high CDI scores were less preferred and were more often perceived as socially withdrawn, unathletic, and unattractive (Strauss et al., 1984). Studies of unpopular isolated children suggest that they have a less optimistic prognosis than those children not so described and also engage in fewer skillful behaviors (Gottman, Gonso, & Rasmussen, 1975). Further, children who reported having a close ("chum") relationship scored significantly higher on the Piers-Harris Children's Self-Concept Scale than those without this relationship (Mannarino, 1978). In a study described previously, Seagull and Weinshank (1984) found that children perceived as exhibiting the characteristics of depression were rated lower in level of prosocial behavior and extroversion and higher in social withdrawal, and actually engaged in fewer socially skillful behaviors on interview than those not so nominated. Similar deficits in social relationships and communication were reported with children meeting criteria for major depression (Kazdin, Esveldt-Dawson, Sherick, & Colbus, 1985; Kazdin, Sherick, Esveldt-Dawson, & Rancurello, 1985; Puig-Antich, Lukens, Davies, Goetz, Brennan-Quattrock, & Todak, 1985a, 1985b).

The significance of social withdrawal as a component in childhood depression has also been examined with other measures. Winder and Wiggins (1964) obtained evidence for a primary factor involving social withdrawal using a peer nomination inventory. In an examination of developmental trends, one study using the BID found greater difficulties with social withdrawal in older than younger adolescents (Kaplan et al., 1984). However, a BID factor entitled "social withdrawal" failed to distinguish between children with depression and those with conduct disorder (Feinstein, Blouin, Egan, & Connors, 1984), while no differences were found on the CBCL social competence factors in one study of depressed and nondepressed schoolchildren (Kaslow et al., 1984).

Therapy

Although early application of social skills approaches with adults was occasionally reported, large-scale applications with various patient populations have only recently been described (see Rehm & Kaslow, 1984; Lewinsohn & Hoberman, 1982; McLean, 1981). Perhaps the most significant systematic extension of social skills training is found in the work of Bellack and Hersen (Bellack, Hersen, & Himmelhoch, 1981, 1983; Hersen, Bellack, Himmelhoch, & Thase, 1984). These studies documented the relative superiority of social skills training plus placebo over other treatments (e.g., amitriptyline, social skills training plus amitriptyline, psychotherapy plus placebo) in terms of completion rate and clinical improvement (Bellack et al., 1981). The social skills training groups also performed better on almost all role-play measures of inter-personal skill (Bellack et al., 1983), although all four treatments were equivalent on measures of depression and neurotic symptoms at 6-month fol-low-up (Hersen et al., 1984).

The social skills approach has been widely applied to remediate such social adjustment and peer relationship difficulties in children as withdrawal, iso-lation, and skill deficiencies (Hops, 1983; French & Tyne, 1982; Kendall & Morrison, 1984). Programs have attempted to promote skill acquisition in or-der to expand the child's repertoire, enhance weak or limited behaviors, and replace dysfunctional or inhibiting behaviors with more adaptive skills (Ladd, 1984) with different populations (Berler, Gross, & Drabman, 1982; Bierman & Furman, 1984; Bornstein, Bellack, & Hersen, 1977; Kolko, Dorsett, & Milan, 1981; Van Hasselt, Griest, Kazdin, Esveldt-Dawson, & Unis, 1984).

In the case of depressed children, comprehensive or multimodal programs that include a skills training component have been described by Petti and Wells (1980) and Petti, Bornstein, Delameter, and Connors (1980). Petti and Wells (1980) provided training in the use of conflict-resolution/problem-solving skills to a $12\frac{1}{2}$-year-old hospitalized boy. Anecdotal reports suggested improvements in handling problematic situations which were rated to have been maintained at 6- and 14-month follow-up. Working with a $10\frac{1}{2}$-year-old hospitalized girl, Petti et al. (1980) offered social skills training following a series of alternative treatments (pharmacotherapy, individual psychotherapy, family work). Train-ing consisted of nine sessions of instructions, modeling, rehearsal, and feed-back and was implemented sequentially across four target behaviors (eye con-tact, smiles, duration of speech, requests for new behavior). Dramatic improvements were observed for all four behaviors on role-play scenes used throughout training. A 6-week follow-up revealed moderate maintenance us-ing the same scenes and mixed evidence for generalization to novel scenes. However, it is not possible to assess the respective impact of the alternative treatment components or the perceived effect of skills training on depressive symptoms or social adjustment in these two programs.

Calpin and Kornblith (1977) and Calpin and Cinciripini (1978) evaluated the effects of social skills training with hospitalized depressed children using a multiple baseline design. Calpin and Kornblith (1977) treated four boys with severe aggressive behavior who met RDC criteria for depression. The target behaviors were requests for new behaviors, affect statements, and overall so-cial skills. Training consisted of instructions regarding desired behaviors, modeling, behavioral rehearsal, and videotape feedback. Using the Behavioral Assertiveness Test for Children (Bornstein et al., 1977), improvements of all three targeted behaviors were documented for all four patients. One- and three-month follow-up assessment revealed maintenance of therapeutic gains for three of the boys. However, no specific measures of depression were reported.

Calpin and Cinciripini (1978) treated two children (one boy, one girl) with significant peer relationship difficulties. There were five target behaviors for the boy (ratio of eye contact to speech duration, frequency of praise statements, affective expression, requests for new behaviors, overall social skills) and four for the girl (ratio of eye contact to speech duration, frequency of noncompliance to unreasonable requests, affective expression, overall social skills). Training (instructions, modeling, and videotape feedback) resulted in significant improvements in terms of eye contact and noncompliance for the girl on training and generalization scenes, and on all target behavior for the boy except affect statements, which showed moderate change. One- and three-month follow-up for the boy indicated maintenance of all gains, excluding affective statements. The authors reported that the boy's suicidal ideation had subsided, although he remained oppositional and affectively labile. Unfortunately, the girl's treatment program was discontinued prematurely by her mother.

A similar but more comprehensive program for a 10-year-old hospitalized boy was reported by Frame, Matson, Sonis, Fialkov, and Kazdin (1982). Referral reasons included suicidal ideation and gestures, temper tantrums, and declining school performance. Standardized assessments confirmed a diagnosis of depression, while preliminary observations revealed a variety of interpersonal skill deficiencies. Four specific target behaviors were evaluated on 12 role-play scenarios (inappropriate body position, lack of eye contact, poor speech quality, bland affect). Treatment was sequentially introduced for each behavior in accord with a multiple-baseline design and consisted of instructions, modeling, role-playing, and feedback. The program resulted in dramatic reductions in the occurrence of all target behaviors; reductions were generally maintained at 3-month follow-up. The authors acknowledge, justifiably, that the impact of this program on salient aspects of the clinical picture of depression (e.g., vegetative symptoms) cannot be directly evaluated. Repeated assessment with the standardized measures used to establish the diagnosis would have been helpful in this regard.

Working with three male adolescents diagnosed with schizoaffective disorder, Schloss, Schloss, and Harris (1984) implemented an interpersonal skills training (modeling, rehearsal, feedback) and contingency management program (snacks and socials) during group sessions. Each participant had multiple opportunities to observe and practice the following five targeted skills: greeting an adult who enters the room, saying goodbye, saying hello on entering a room, saying goodbye on leaving, and maintaining a conversation following a greeting. Using a multiple-baseline design, dramatic improvements were observed for the first three behaviors on introduction of treatment in the training setting. Considerable change in the last two behaviors occurred prior to treatment, suggesting response generalization. In examining the percentage of responses exhibited in the natural environment, the first two behaviors showed improvements after treatment, whereas the last three behaviors actually obtained posttreatment levels before treatment was initiated. A 9-month follow-up for two patients showed continued improvement in offering greetings and maintaining conversations, but there was no maintenance for the other two behaviors. The third student was discharged before follow-up due to improved social functioning. Generalized improvements in related behaviors (e.g., attention, academics, social greetings) were reported by different staff members. Nevertheless, the use of more complex social behaviors might have facilitated the achievement of greater therapeutic gains. Further, the study neglected to assess depressive symptoms.

Self-Control

Theory

Although not as well represented in the children's literature, the self-control model holds that individuals who experience depression exhibit deficiencies in specific skills or processes, such as self-monitoring, self-evaluation, and self-reinforcement (Rehm, 1977, 1981). As summarized by Rehm (1981), two major deficits are expected in each process. Briefly, they include selective attention to negative events and immediate consequences, the setting of stringent performance criteria and commission of self-attributional errors, and the administration of insufficient rewards or excessive punishment. It is argued that the specific clinical picture in a given case is influenced by the nature of the impairments observed in these self-management processes.

Self-control deficits have likewise been reported for children. The study of elementary schoolchildren by Kaslow et al. (1984) found that depressed children set more stringent standards for poor scores on performance tasks, were more likely to recommend the use of punishment than reward, evaluated their performance more negatively, and reported lower self-esteem. Reduced self-concept has also been reported for other depressed schoolchildren (Strauss et al., 1984), but not for a different sample (Seagull & Weinshank, 1984).

Therapy

Treatment from this perspective has been described in several outcome studies with adults (see Rehm, 1981; Rehm & Kaslow, 1984). The basic procedures involve training in the following activities: monitoring positive events and self-statements, engaging in those behaviors and thoughts associated with positive affect, emphasizing long-term positive consequences and development of achievable goals, making more legitimate attributions, and providing more frequent self-reinforcement. The evidence suggests that self-control therapy results in reduced levels of depression compared to no-contact control, non-specific group therapy, cognitive therapy, or assertion skills training (Rehm & Kaslow, 1984).

Treatment programs for children have emphasized various aspects of self-management. One of the initial steps in the self-control process is self-monitoring, that is, paying careful attention to one's specific behaviors by recording specific acts or outcomes following a careful self-assessment. Self-monitoring has been used successfully in educational applications to enhance attention and productivity (Graziano & Mooney, 1983; Hallahan, Lloyd, Kauffman, & Loper, 1983). Likewise, self-evaluation and self-reinforcement have been closely tied to the development of self-control programs for children. (Blount & Stokes, 1984; Graziano & Mooney, 1983).

Evolving from these steps, procedures designed to enhance self-control have emphasized both cognitive and behavioral self-regulative skills, particularly noteworthy in the treatment of children exhibiting hyperactivity and impulsivity (Kendall, 1981). The major therapeutic objective has been to teach the child to engage in a cognitive evaluation of all response alternatives as a means of determining whether to express or inhibit a given behavior. Training often involves instruction in the use of step-by-step self-verbalizations to mediate one's activity, modeling their use in practical situations, and contingent consequation in accord with the child's selected behavior. By internalizing these statements or instructions, the child may employ them when solving specific problems. Several outcome investigations have suggested the effectiveness of such self-instructional procedures to promote generalization of improvements to the classroom (Kendall & Wilcox, 1980; Kendall & Zupan, 1981), facilitate exposure to previously avoided fearful stimuli (see Morris & Kratochwill, 1983), inhibit aggression (see Kazdin & Frame, 1983), and remediate academic underachievement (Hallahan et al., 1983).

This emerging technology may have applicability to depression in children, especially in light of recent therapeutic guidelines (Meichenbaum, Bream, & Cohen, 1985). Steps for the application of certain self-management principles in the control of affective reactions have recently been articulated (Klinger, 1982), which might be best applied upon considering the developmental and environmental context that shapes the emergence of self-regulatory behaviors in children (Harter, 1982), and salient training and clinical considerations (Copeland, 1982). Pertinent assessment tasks, games, and specific recommendations for evaluating self-management in children can be found in Kendall and Williams (1982). Finally, the development of Rational-Emotive Therapy (RET) principles and procedures for children may also have implications for the conceptualization and treatment of depression (Bernard & Joyce, 1984). These and other encouraging advances may prompt systematic investigation of the self-control approach to depression in children.

Contingency Management

Theory

The use of operant principles to alter depressive symptomatology was initially advocated in early conceptualizations highlighting the role of activity level reductions due to insufficient positive reinforcement (Ferster, 1973; Lewinsohn, 1974). Thus, the social environment has been modified to facilitate increases in activity and to stimulate the individual's behavioral repertoire. These changes are believed to generate improvements in corresponding depressive symptoms, including dysphoric mood and hopelessness. Indeed, descriptive studies with adults indicated that depressed persons reported experiencing few pleasant activities and that a significant association exists between mood and the number and kind of pleasant activities engaged in by the person (Lewinsohn & Hoberman, 1982). Although a reduction in activity level, especially in terms of pleasant events, is reported in clinical reports with children (e.g., Poznanski, 1982; Petti, 1984), empirical documentation of the magnitude of this phenomenon has not been provided.

Therapy

In an attempt to arrange explicit contingencies designed to increase positive activity, token economy programs have been used to increase self-care, social, and affective behaviors in adult patients (Lewinsohn, 1975). Programs designed to increase activity level have also reported an increase in engagement in positive activities and a reduction in depression, although minimal changes in either of these measures have also been reported (see Rehm & Kaslow, 1984). An activity increase group has been found superior to self-monitoring, expectancy control, and attention control (Turner, Ward, & Turner, 1979).

Only one study has empirically evaluated the use of operant reinforcement procedures with children. Molick and Pinkston (1982) described the application of four reinforcement procedures with a 15-year-old female high school student who exhibited such behavioral deficits as reduced speech and social interaction, psychomotor retardation, and academic underachievement. In the first intervention, contingent teacher comments, praise, and eye contact were found to increase the girl's appropriate responses (from 41% to 92%). The second intervention employed similar components (e.g., instructions, cues, praise) to increase her social interactions. To modify a variety of other responses (e.g., peer interaction, academic responses, grooming), behavior exchanges that provided access to different reinforcers (e.g., music, money, hospital pass) were devised. The results indicated that all of the criteria for earning these reinforcers were reached. A final intervention in which she was trained to say "thank you" to adults resulted in more positive verbalizations from staff. To the author's credit, objective data and controlled designs were employed to assess outcome. However, it is not clear whether this child actually met diagnostic criteria for depression and which concomitant symptoms (e.g., dysphoria) were modified by intervention. There is clear need for more careful examination of contingency management programs with depressed children.

CASE PRESENTATION

BACKGROUND

The case to be described here involves a 12.8-year-old girl, named E., who was hospitalized on a children's psychiatric unit. The primary reasons for referral were severe school refusal, increasing depression, withdrawal at home and school, and sleep disturbance. The parents reported that E.'s current difficulties were first noticed approximately 13 months prior to admission following the mother's hospitalization for pneumonia. Although E. was attending a regular sixth grade, she began to refuse to attend school and to withdraw from various activities. She would frequently complain about stomach pains before school, offering them as legitimate explanations for her inability to attend school. E.'s social and interpersonal behavior also deteriorated at this time, as she showed increased preference to remain close to her mother and made frequent requests for assistance with her responsibilities. E. became extremely quiet, appeared sad and unhappy, and withdrew from social activities with others both at home and in school. Reduced self-esteem was also noted. These symptoms were then closely followed by complaints of sleep problems, notably insomnia and sleep continuity disturbance. Concomitantly, her school performance began to decline from a previous record of earning mostly A's and B's.

Approximately 3 months before admission, the family initiated outpatient treatment for E.'s school refusal and depressive symptomatology. A psychiatrist worked with the parents around the issue of limit setting to facilitate E.'s return to school. However, numerous struggles occurred in the service of taking her to school so that the parents soon discontinued any such efforts. E. was seen concurrently by a psychologist who tried to discuss her current behavioral difficulties, but she declined any invitation to discuss these concerns and often avoided even entering the room.

In terms of developmental and family history, E. was an unplanned pregnancy following an initial miscarriage, the adoption of a son, and birth of a sister. The pregnancy and E.'s early life were described as uncomplicated and generally happy. She also reached developmental milestones late, required extra assistance with tasks, was quite reserved and uncommunicative, and experienced speech articulation problems. Parents tended to "baby" the child since she was seen as "slow." E. was similarly described as developmentally immature by her teachers, although her attendance and academic performance were consistently good ever since she repeated the first grade. E.'s adopted brother, age 23, attended a local college and lived at home. Her sister, age 16, also lived at home and attended high school. E.'s mother had trained to become a registered nurse; her father held a PhD in chemistry and had a managerial position in a research department of a large company. There were no significant problems reported for the other children, with the exception of some difficulty in establishing independence by the brother. The mother had described experiencing a significant depression after each of her pregnancies and following her father's death one year previously, a loss that was reported to have been a very painful one to E. and her mother. The father reported no particular difficulties and was considered a stable and dependable person. Family history was significant for heart disease, migraine headaches, high blood pressure, and arteriosclerosis.

On preadmission intake, a mental status indicated that E. presented herself as a quiet, uncommunicative, and resistant girl who employed only a few basic social skills. She rarely made eye contact, spoke in an inaudible tone of voice, used few words, infrequently initiated a conversation, and was unable to report anything positive about herself. She admitted to feeling depressed and denied any positive attributes, giving few details regarding her experiences. She also acknowledged sleep difficulties. E. denied any anxiety or panic attacks. She denied suicidal or homicidal ideation, intent, or plan, gave no evidence for perceptual or thought disturbance, and was oriented.

Following admission, E. continued to look quite unhappy but claimed that any perceived dysphoria was due to her dislike of the hospital. She denied being bothered by any specific problems except stomach aches and was most persistent about obtaining immediate discharge, frequently claiming that hospitalization was not needed. Observations by unit staff during the first 2 weeks underscored her reluctance to interact with staff and peers, and the near lack of rudimentary social skills during conversation (e.g., poor eye contact, low voice volume, bland facial expression, infrequent initiations). Affect was also blunted. Separation from parents after visits was usually followed by periods of tearfulness and isolation. No problems occurred in terms of school refusal, sleep disturbance, or appetite.

PSYCHIATRIC EVALUATION

Standardized psychiatric and psychological assessments were conducted during the first two weeks of hospitalization. Major areas of concern reported on the Child Behavior Checklist (CBCL) were somatic complaints, depressed/withdrawn, and anxious/obsessive. On the KIDDIE-SADS diagnostic interview, the parents identified depressive symptoms as major concerns, including sadness, isolation, disinterest in formerly enjoyed activities, reduced self-image, somatic complaints, low energy level and reduced concentration, and chronic deteriorating sleep difficulties. Based on the mother's completion of the CDI,

E.'s score was above average for a general child population. The mother's BID highlighted moderate dysphoria of average duration. E.'s self-report measures indicated low severity and duration of depression, average hopelessness, and below average self-esteem. It was felt that E.'s low scores highlighted her denial of problems and desire to return home promptly. In terms of psycho-educational assessment, her academic achievement scores were all above grade level (9.5 math, 8.2 reading). On the WISC-R, her verbal, performance, and full-score IQ scores were 107, 105, and 106, respectively. She attended and performed in the unit school classroom regularly and with no difficulty. DSM-III diagnoses based on this information were major depressive episode, separation anxiety disorder, and developmental articulation disorder.

The admission assessment findings suggested the need for treatment of three significant problems: school refusal, depression, and social/interpersonal deficiencies. To target her school refusal, a program was implemented in which E. was required to attend class on a daily basis and was consequated accordingly. She earned points from attendance, participation, and completion of other expectations through a comprehensive unit-wide token economy. School refusal and noncompliance were consequated with token losses and brief periods of time-out from positive reinforcement. This program resulted in consistent attendance and high levels of accurate performance on academic tasks.

BEHAVIORAL ASSESSMENT

For treatment of her prominent depressive symptoms, an imipramine trial was initially recommended. However, information from her community school and other informants suggested that depressive symptoms were secondary to severe social interaction difficulties experienced in different situations. Therefore, a social-cognitive skills training program was administered to address both of these problems concurrently. Several outcome evaluation measures were employed. Behavioral role-play scenarios were developed to assess the performance of socially skillful behaviors. E.'s primary staff nurse and therapist jointly developed eight different scenarios designed to tap her specific interpersonal difficulties. The role-plays were administered in 11 individual sessions conducted in a private videotaping studio off the unit. Each role-play consisted of a narration of the situation and a prompt either for the confederate or E. to initiate. In general, each role-play contained two confederate responses, the second of which was unstandardized and thus could vary as a function of E's initial response. A sample role-play is described below:

NARRATION: You are sitting in the cafeteria eating lunch. A girl from the unit carrying her tray comes over to your table and sits across from you. Seeing that no else is close by, she says to you:

CONFEDERATE: Hi, Margarite: How's your lunch?. . . .

[Second confederate response]

Preliminary observations indicated several social skills deficits for assessment. These target behaviors were described along 3-point, ordinal and nominal, behaviorally referenced scales, and are shown in Table 6.1. The behaviors reflected nonverbal (gaze, facial expression, body posture), paralinguistic (voice volume/inflection), and verbal (speech content) categories. The behaviors were evaluated independently by two research assistants once the entire program was completed. The interrater reliabilities in terms of exact percentage agreement for each behavior were as follows: Gaze, 100%; facial expression, 88%; body posture, 82%; voice volume, 86%; and speech content, 82%.

The remaining measures examined social and interpersonal functioning on the children's unit. *In vivo* behavioral observations of social interactions with staff or peers were collected during baseline and after training by an independent observer using a 10-second partial-interval recording procedure. The 30-minute observation periods were conducted during classroom free-play and at lunchtime. Peer sociometric ratings were obtained from all children on the unit. The children nominated five peers whom they liked a lot, ignored, and disliked, and then rated how much they liked to play with each other child on the unit (1 = don't like to at all; 3 = like to a little; 5 = like to a lot). These ratings were obtained during baseline and following treatment. Staff ratings were also collected to assess weekly changes in three global interpersonal attributes: sociability—responding to initiations or initiating interactions in a

TABLE 6.1   Target Behaviors and Behavioral Definitions

Gaze

2 = Maintains gaze in direction of speaker; breaks in eye contact only fleeting (less than 3 seconds)

1 = Brief, occasional glances at speaker; covers eyes only briefly

0 = No gaze or covers eyes with hands; fleeting eye contacts of 1 second or less

Facial Expression

2 = Very expressive, appropriate use of smile head pulled in toward body and held rigidly

Voice Volume

2 = Appropriate expression, clear diction; easy to understand; appropriate expression

1 = Some difficulty in understanding all spoken words

0 = Much difficulty in understanding spoken words; mumbling or whispering

Speech Content

2 = Complete sentences, use of descriptive phrases revealing personal thoughts and feelings, or requesting information

1 = Brief affirmations or responses to questions with minimal elaboration; two-word phrases

0 = Single-word or extremely vague/irrelevant responses, or no response

friendly/pleasant manner; skillfulness—use of social skills in an adaptive, expressive, and flexible manner; and composure—showing confidence and poise during conversation. Staff ratings were also used to assess daily changes in four specific social-emotional behaviors: expressed ideas clearly, initiated positive interactions, participated in group activities, shared with others, and was cheerful/happy. The weekly ratings were stated along 5-point scales (1 = poor/none; 5 = excellent/very much), and the daily ratings were stated along 4-point scales (1 = not true; 4 = completely or always true).

To examine any long-term impact on social adjustment and depression, E. and her mother completed again many of the self-report measures completed on admission (baseline) at a one-year follow-up (follow-up). Specifically, E. completed the CDI, BID, CSEI, Hopelessness Scale for Children, and MESSY. Her mother completed the CDI, BID, BDI, MESSY, and CBCL. Weinberg criteria were derived based on each respondent's BID scores.

TREATMENT

The training program consisted of three components. The first component involved social skills training, which consisted of instruction, modeling of appropriate and inappropriate behaviors, role-playing or rehearsal, coaching, video and corrective feedback, and final role-playing (Berler et al., 1982; Kolko et al., 1981). This sequence of training steps was employed twice for each role-play scenario in each session. E.'s therapist served as the role-play confederate, while the unit psychologist narrated and reviewed the role-plays. For each performance, improvements were praised before deficiencies or weaknesses were described. The second component was concurrent training in general problem-solving skills as well as in self-evaluation and self-reinforcement. E. was encouraged to invoke certain cues or questions (e.g., What do I want to accomplish? What do I want to do first? How do I do this now?) that would prompt the correct use of her individual skills in different situations. In addition, she was required to evaluate the adequacy of each role-play performance and to determine whether she had improved on each skill. To provide back-up support for this self-critique, a third component was included in the form of a contingency whereby points were earned for both improvements in performance and accurate judgments of the adequacy of her role-plays. After each role-play, E.'s judgment was compared with that of the two therapists, and a point was earned for each agreement. Points could be exchanged for a social reinforcer (e.g., 1:1 with staff member and peer).

The immediate impact of this intervention was first observed in the form of increased affective expression and social responsiveness on the unit. Staff reported that she would exhibit more smiling and less debate about the need for hospitalization. E. began to assert herself more nonverbally as well as vocally. Occasional attempts to have her speak up in class were met with considerable success. Although she continued to remain occasionally withdrawn, she did engage in more interactions with staff members. There was a gradual increase in her participation in activities and a brightening in her mood. Further, she made periodic efforts at initiating conversations, primarily at times when she had a request. In general, E. became more reciprocal in her interactions with both staff and peers, while still initiating few conversations.

The results of the behavioral role-play assessment are found in Figure 6.1. E.'s performance of the five target behaviors was quite variable. In contrast to her admission behavior, she exhibited moderate gaze and good voice volume during baseline. However, she showed deficits during baseline on the other three behaviors, which remained at low levels. Training was initially introduced to all three nonverbal behaviors with variable results. She showed reasonable improvement in gaze and body posture, with only slight improvement in facial expression. Training was then introduced to voice volume and speech content, which showed steady and significant improvement across sessions. By the end of training, near 100% levels of performance were exhibited for all behaviors except facial expression. The percent of time spent engaging in *in vivo* interaction with staff and peers during baseline and after training was also examined. In the classroom, E. showed a significant change in the amount

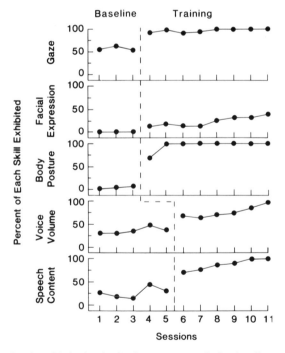

Figure 6.1. Results of behavioral role-play assessment during baseline and training.

of interaction with staff (2% vs. 29%) but less change with peers (3% vs. 11%). In the lunchroom, E. exhibited greater change in interactions with peers (2% vs. 14%) than with staff (11% vs. 22%). It was frequently noted that E. might respond to a peer's initiation but would not maintain the interaction for long.

In terms of peer sociometric ratings, the number of nominations during baseline and following training showed a slight increase for being liked (1 vs. 3), no ratings for being disliked, and a slight increase in being ignored (1 vs. 2). The rating of how much peers liked to play with E. showed a slight increase after treatment (3.17 vs. 3.93). The different staff global attribute ratings are presented in Table 6.2. A significant increase was reported for perceived likeability, while a modest increase was reported regarding E.'s social skillfulness and composure. Table 6.2 also shows the average daily social-emotional behavior ratings rendered by staff. Considerable improvement was documented in all five behaviors, especially for sharing with others and initiating interactions.

At discharge, E. was described as more interactive and assertive, with greater facility at using socially appropriate verbal and nonverbal skills during conversation. Although still affectively restricted, she was less dysphoric and more animated. Her depressive episode was believed to be resolved. Approximately one year after hospitalization, E. and her mother completed several follow-up questionnaires. Table 6.3 presents the results of this assessment and the results obtained at admission (baseline) for comparison purposes. On measures of depression (CDI, BID, Weinberg criteria), E. continued to endorse few symptoms as she did on admission, including few feelings of hopelessness. She did receive a more positive score on the SEI, although this change was only a modest one. On the MESSY, E. reported engaging in slightly fewer positive social skills and negative social behaviors at follow-up. The mother's

TABLE 6.2 Staff Ratings of Global Attributes and Social-Emotional Behaviors

Measure	Baseline	Posttraining
Weekly Global Attributes		
Sociability	2.4	3.5
Skillfulness	2.0	2.7
Composure	3.0	3.7
Daily Social-Emotional Behaviors		
Expressed ideas clearly	1.6	2.5
Initiated positive interactions	1.2	2.2
Participated in group activities	2.3	2.6
Shared with others	0.8	2.2
Was cheerful/happy	1.2	2.3

TABLE 6.3   Child Self-Report and Parent-Report Assessment Questionnaires

Measure	Baseline	Follow-Up
Child		
Children's Depression Inventory	2	1
Bellevue Index of Depression		
Severity	36	33
Duration	10	6
Total	46	39
Weinberg Criteria	3	2
Coopersmith Self-Esteem Inventory	45	52
Hopelessness Scale for Children	3	2
Matson Evaluation of Social Skills of Youngsters		
Positive	164	139
Negative	50	45
Total	114	94
Parent		
Children's Depression Inventory	19	12
Bellevue Index of Depression		
Severity	83	53
Duration	21	35
Total	104	88
Weinberg Criteria	10	3
Beck Depression Inventory	8	2
Matson Evaluation of Social Skills of Youngsters		
Positive	81	151
Negative	53	75
Total	28	76
Child Behavior Checklist		
Anxious-Obsessive	59	49
Somatic Complaints	60	54
Schizoid	55	51
Depressed-Withdrawn	59	53
Immature-Hyperactive	55	53
Delinquent	43	37
Aggressive	43	37
Cruel	47	45

self-report measures provide somewhat more evidence for the benefit of treatment as her completion of the CDI revealed a moderate reduction in depressive symptoms, which was likewise reflected in lower severity and duration scores on the BID. Consequently, she endorsed fewer of the Weinberg criteria for depression. The mother's own BDI was likewise lower at follow-up. On the Messy, mother assigned E. higher positive behavior and negative behavior scores, resulting in a higher total score than on admission. Improvement was also reported on certain scales of the CBCL, with greatest change found in the somatic complaints and anxious-obsessive scales.

RECOMMENDATIONS AND FUTURE DIRECTIONS

The studies reviewed in this chapter have begun to elucidate the clinical manifestations of depression in children and adolescents, as well as their evaluation and remediation. Promising assessment instruments that possess adequate psychometric properties have been described, and progress has been made in understanding the relationship among multiple sources and measures. This development may contribute to a more refined approach to identifying and evaluating the various aspects of this syndrome while highlighting salient targets for treatment (Saylor, Finch, Spirito, & Bennet, 1984). Continued examination of the comparability, specificity, content, and factor structure of recent assessment measures is necessary to encourage more critical and selective application. Recent reviews of self-report measures of depression for adults underscore a number of pertinent psychometric and practical considerations (Boyle, 1985).

Although statements regarding the etiology of depression in childhood are premature, there is growing appreciation for the need to separately examine the multiple correlates of depression and their formulation as a syndrome composed of a cluster of symptoms. Both psychological and general psychiatric approaches have advocated for more comprehensive perspectives in terms of the domains or variables selected for assessment and treatment (Cantwell, 1983; Petti, 1983). This shift in orientation includes paying more attention to current knowledge regarding the psychobiology of major depression in childhood (Puig-Antich, 1984). Given the emerging similarity in the clinical pictures of childhood and adult depression, studies have more carefully examined social and affective covariates (Strauss et al., 1984), cognitive correlates (Kaslow et al., 1984), and behavioral characteristics (Kazdin, Esveldt-Dawson, Sherick, & Colbus, 1985; Kazdin, Sherick, Esveldt-Dawson, & Rancurello, 1985). Two commonly associated characteristics of depression, suicide and parasuicide, have actually emerged as significant behavioral problems in their own right (Brent, Perper, & Kolko, 1985; Cantwell, 1983; Carlson, 1983; Linehan, 1981).

Among the many clinical assessment issues to be addressed are questions regarding gender differences in the manifestation of depression, the relationship between parent and child measures, differences between clinical depression and "normal" sadness or dysphoria, situational determinants of depressive reactions, differences in selection criteria, and natural history (see Cantwell, 1983). For example, recent longitudinal studies have delineated the course of depression, and the processes and factors associated with poor prognosis or recovery (Kovacs, Feinberg, Crouse-Novak, Paulauskas, & Finkelstein, 1984; Kovacs, Feinberg, Crouse-Novak, Paulauskas, Pollock, & Finkelstein, 1984). Other studies have identified specific subtypes or subgroups of depression (Dosen, 1984; Freeman, Poznanski, Grossman, Buchsbaum, & Banegas, 1985). Information regarding the aforementioned issues may help to clarify the clinical picture of depression and assess the reasons why many children continue to experience depressive symptoms even after several years (Eastgate & Gilmour, 1984).

An understanding of potential antecedants and consequences, such as parental psychopathology and family functioning, has also been promoted. Recent evidence suggests that children of depressed parents are more at risk for several categories of behavioral and emotional difficulties (Cytryn, McKnew, Zahn-Waxler, Radke-Yarrow, Gaensbauer, Harmon, & Lamour, 1984; Billings & Moos, 1983; Hirsch, Moos, & Reischl, 1985; Beardslee, Bemporad, Keller, & Klerman, 1983; Weissman, Prusoff, Gammon, Merikangas, Leckman, & Kidd, 1984). Moreover, parents of depressed children have received higher ratings of various oppressive behaviors (e.g., control of life goals, suppression of self-expression) during family decision making than parents of overanxious children (Amanat & Butler, 1984). Other studies have documented deficiencies in child-rearing practices of parents (Davenport, Zahn-Waxler, Adland, & Mayfield, 1984) and peer interaction difficulties of children (Zahn-Waxler, McKnew, Cummings, Davenport, & Radke-Yarrow, 1984) in families having one partner with manic-depressive illness. Assessment of the specific role of parent psychopathology (e.g., depression) and parenting practices in the origins of depression, and their potential impact on treatment outcome is clearly warranted.

Expansion of the situational context in which depressive disorders are studied has occasionally generated greater attention to the child's psychosocial adjustment. Recent empirical findings highlight impairment in verbal and affective communication with parents and siblings as well as social relationship deficits in prepubertal depressives as compared to nondepressed neurotics (Puig-Antich et al., 1985a) which are only partially improved following sustained recovery from an affective episode (Puig-Antich et al., 1985b). Such findings argue strongly for more critical evaluation of psychological and behavioral functioning following treatment and the development of adjunctive psychotherapeutic interventions. Most of the programs reviewed here have neglected to evaluate significant aspects of psychosocial adjustment (e.g., peer relationships, school functioning) and the depressive syndrome (e.g., vegetative symptoms). Such information would shed light on the "side-effects" associated with psychological interventions for depression. Thus, much more information is needed to assess treatment outcome, generalization, and maintenance adequately across a wide range of valid measures. This broadened assessment focus should be paralleled by more concern for clinical impact (vs. statistical significance) and for evaluation of long-term follow-up.

In terms of treatment considerations, one of the more significant developments is the emergence of programs designed to remediate specific deficits or modify the child's cognitive-behavioral repertoire. Drawing on different conceptual models from the adult literature, interventions have included attribution retraining (Dweck, 1975), cognitive restructuring (Butler et al., 1980), social skills training (Frame et al., 1982; Schloss et al., 1984), and contingency management (Molick & Pinkston, 1982), among other components. Clinical recommendations have been made to foster rational selections of treatment strategies (Kaslow & Rehm, 1983; Reynolds, 1984; Schloss, 1983). The promise of these interdependent approaches may be realized by paying greater attention to various programmatic and clinical considerations, such as the age and sex of the child, characteristics and involvement of parents and siblings in the treatment process, and both the format and multidimensionality of treatment. The emergence of a developmental perspective regarding the conceptualization (Kaslow et al., 1984) and treatment (Emery et al., 1983) of depression in children should also facilitate the design of more specialized and individualized interventions. Likewise, therapeutic benefit may be enhanced by teaching both specific (i.e., molecular) and general (i.e., molar) target behaviors or skills. Perhaps training in higher-order or complex social and cognitive skills may be associated with more dramatic and long-lasting therapeutic effects.

Continued refinement of the aforementioned theoretical models should promote greater application of different procedures with children. For example, preliminary studies are needed to examine the clinical utility and comparative effectiveness of the helplessness, cognitive, self-control, and contingency management approaches. Such efforts might borrow from alternative programs previously employed with nondepressed problem children, such as interpersonal problem-solving training (Shure & Spivack, 1982), affective education (Elias & Maher, 1983), cognitive-behavioral modification of social interactions (Kendall & Morrison, 1984), and social support interventions (Felner, Ginter, & Primavera, 1982). The effectiveness of parent training and family involvement should also be investigated. Of course, regardless of the specific program under examination, adequate attention must be paid to methodological concerns, such as the use of controlled experimental designs, objective and psychometrically valid assessment instruments, repeated measures analyses, and checks on treatment integrity. A final consideration deals with the integration of psychosocial and pharmacological interventions. Increasing evidence attests to the clinical utility of antidepressant medications such as imipramine with prepubertal depressed children on behavioral and self-report measures (Petti, 1983; Rancurello, 1985). Subsequent studies should examine each form of intervention alone and in combination, as both have been advocated in the context of multimodal programs with adults (Klerman & Schechter, 1982) and children (Cantwell, 1983; Puig-Antich et al., 1985b).

SUMMARY

In summary, psychosocial assessment and treatment procedures have emerged as continued investigation of the syndrome of depression in children and adolescents have been pursued. With the development of a greater variety of evaluation instruments and therapeutic techniques has come increased recognition of the scope of treatment and the need for more careful empirical scrutiny of the use and utility of this clinical armamentarium. While expanding the repertoire of the behavioral clinician, these tools must be more critically applied to determine the types of depressive phenomena and child populations with which they work best. As additional efforts are made to revise and expand these psychosocial approaches, there will be a better understanding of the clinical complexities, causes, and consequences of depression and, ultimately, the most judicious methods by which they may be alleviated.

REFERENCES

Abramson, L. Y., Seligman, M. E. P., & Teasdale, J. D. (1978). Learned helplessness in humans: Critique and reformulation. *Journal of Abnormal Psychology*, *87*, 49–74.

Achenbach, T. M., & Edelbrock, C. (1983). *Manual for the Child Behavior Checklist and Revised Child Behavior Checklist*. Vermont: Queen City Printers.

Amanat, E. & Butler, C. (1984). Oppressive behaviors in the families of depressed children. *Family Therapy*, *11*, 65–77.

American Psychiatric Association (1980). *Diagnostic and statistical manual of mental disorders (3rd. ed.)*. Washington, DC: Author.

Apter, A., & Tyano, S. (1984). Childhood depression: A review. *Israeli Journal of Psychiatry and Related Sciences*, *21*, 117–126.

Bartell, N., & Reynolds, W. M. (1983). *Depression and self-esteem in academically gifted and nongifted children: A comparison study*. Manuscript submitted for publication.

Beach, S. R. H., Abramson, L. Y., & Levine, F. M. (1981). Attributional reformulation of learned helplessness and depression: Therapeutic implications. In J. F. Clarkin & H. I. Glazer (Eds.), *Depression: Behavioral and directive intervention strategies* (pp. 131–165). New York: Garland.

Beardslee, W. R., Bemporad, J., Keller, M. B., & Klerman, G. L. (1983). Children of parents with major affective disorder: A review. *American Journal of Psychiatry*, *140*, 825–832.

Beck, A. T. (1967). *Depression: Causes and treatment*. Philadelphia: University of Pennsylvania Press.

Beck, A. T. (1976). *Cognitive therapy and the emotional disorders*. New York: International Universities Press.

Beck, A. T., Rush, A. G., Shaw, B. F., & Emery, G. (1979). *Cognitive therapy for depression*. New York: Guilford.

Beck, A. T., Ward, C. H., Mendelson, M., Mock, J., & Erbaugh, J. (1961). An inventory for measuring depression. *Archives of General Psychiatry, 4,* 561-571.

Bellack, A. S., Hersen, M., & Himmelhoch, J. M. (1981). Social skills training compared with pharmacotherapy and psychotherapy in the treatment of unipolar depression. *American Journal of Psychiatry, 138,* 1562-1567.

Bellack, A. S., Hersen, M., & Himmelhoch, J. M. (1983). A comparison of social skills training, pharmacotherapy, and psycotherapy for depression. *Behaviour Research and Therapy, 21,* 101-107.

Berler, E. S., Gross, A. M., & Drabman, R. S. (1982). Social skills training with children: Proceed with caution. *Journal of Applied Behavior Analysis, 15,* 41-53.

Bernard, M. E., & Joyce, M. R. (1984). *Rational-emotive therapy with children and adolescents: Theory, treatment strategies, preventive methods.* New York: Wiley.

Bierman, K. L., & Furman, W. (1984). The effects of social skills training and peer involvement on the social adjustment of preadolescents. *Child Development, 55,* 151-162.

Billings, A. G., & Moos, R. H. (1983). Comparisons of children of depressed and nondepressed parents. A social-environmental perspective. *Journal of Abnormal Child Psychology, 11,* 463-486.

Blount, R. L., & Stokes, T. F. (1984). Self-reinforcement by children. In M. Hersen, R. M. Eisler, & P. M. Miller (Eds.), *Progress in behavior modification* (Vol. 18, pp. 195-225). New York: Academic.

Bornstein, M., Bellack, A. S., & Hersen, M. (1977). Social-skills training for unassertive children. *Journal of Applied Behavior Analysis, 10,* 183-195.

Boyle, G. J. (1985). Self-report measures of depression: Some psychometric considerations. *British Journal of Clinical Psychology, 24,* 45-59.

Brent, D. A., Perper, J., & Kolko, D. J. (1985). *The epidemiology of suicidal behavior in Western Pennsylvania.* Project funded by the Health Research Service Foundation, Pittsburgh.

Butler, L. F., Miezitis, S., Friedman, R. J., & Cole, E. (1980). The effect of two school-based intervention programs on depressive symptoms in preadolescent children. *American Educational Research Journal, 17,* 111-119.

Calpin, J. P. & Cinciripini, P. M. (1978, May). *A multiple baseline analysis of social skills training in children.* Paper presented at the Midwestern Association for Behavior Analysis, Chicago.

Calpin, J. P., & Kornblith, S. J. (1977, November). *Training of aggressive children in conflict resolution skills.* Paper presented at the meeting of the Association of Advancement for Behavior Therapy, Chicago.

Cantwell, D. P. (1983). Childhood depression: A review of current research. In B. B. Lahey & A. E. Kazdin (Eds.), *Advances in clinical child psychology* (Vol. 5, pp. 39-93). New York: Plenum.

Carlson, G. A. (1983). Depression and suicidal behavior in children and adolescents. In D. P. Cantwell & G. A. Carlson (Eds), *Affective disorders in childhood and adolescence: An update* (p. 335-352). New York: Spectrum Publications.

Carlson, G. A., & Cantwell, D. P. (1979). A survey of depressive symptoms in child and adolescent psychiatric population. *Journal of the American Academy of Child Psychiatry, 18,* 587–599.

Carlson, G. A., & Cantwell, D. P. (1980). A survey of depressive symptoms and disorder in a child psychiatric population. *Journal of Child Psychology and Psychiatry, 21,* 19–25.

Carlson, G. A. & Cantwell, D. P. (1982). Diagnosis of childhood depression: A comparison of the Weinberg and DSM-III criteria. *Journal of the American Academy of Child Psychiatry, 21,* 247–250.

Coates, K. I., & Reynolds, W. M. (1983). *A comparison of cognitive-behavioral and relaxation therapies for depression with adolescents.* Manuscript submitted for publication.

Coleman, R. E., & Beck, A. T. (1981). Cognitive therapy for depression. In J. F. Clarkin & H. I. Glazer (Eds.), *Depression: Behavioral and directive intervention strategies* (pp. 111–130). New York: Garland.

Copeland, A. P. (1982). Individual difference factors in children's self-management: Toward individualized treatments. In. P. Karloy & F. H. Kanfer (Eds.), *Self-management and behavior change: From theory to practice* (pp. 209–239). New York: Pergamon.

Costello, C. G. (1981). Childhood depression. In E. J. Mash & L. G. Terdal (Eds.), *Behavioral assessment of childhood disorders* (pp. 305–346). New York: Guilford.

Cytryn, L., & McKnew, D. H., Jr. (1972). Proposed classification of childhood depression. *American Journal of Psychiatry, 129,* 149–155.

Cytryn, L., & McKnew, D. H. (1974). Factors influencing the changing clinical expression of the depressive process in children. *American Journal of Psychiatry, 131,* 879–881.

Cytryn, L., McKnew, D. H., & Bunney, W. E. (1980). Diagnosis of depression in children: A reassessment. *American Journal of Psychiatry, 137,* 22–25.

Cytryn, L., McKnew, D. H., Zahn-Waxler, C., Radke-Yarrow, M., Gaensbauer, T. J., Harmon, R. J., & Lamour, M. (1984). A developmental view of affective disturbances in the children of affectively ill parents. *American Journal of Psychiatry, 141,* 219–222.

Davenport, Y. B., Zahn-Waxler, C., Adland, M. L., Mayfield, A. (1984). Early child-rearing practices in families with manic-depressive parent. *American Journal of Psychiatry. 141,* 230–235.

DeMonbreun, B. G., & Craighead, W. E. (1977). Distortion of perception and recall of positive and neutral feedback in depression. *Cognitive Therapy and Research, 1,* 311–329.

Diener, C. I., & Dweck, C. S. (1978). An analysis of learned helplessness: Continuous changes in performance, strategy, & achieving cognitions following failure. *Journal of Personality and Social Psychology, 36,* 451–462.

Diener, C. I., & Dweck, C. S. (1979). *An analysis of learned helplessness: (II) The processing of success.* Unpublished manuscript, University of Illinois.

Dinkmeyer, D. (1970). *Developing understanding of self and others.* Circle Pines, MN: American Guidance Service.

Doerfler, L. A., Mullins, L. L., Griffin, N. J., Siegel, L. J., & Richards, C. S. (1984). Problem-solving deficits in depressed children, adolescents, and adults. *Cognitive Therapy and Research, 8*, 489–500.

Dosen, A. (1984). Depressive conditions in mentally handicapped children. *Acta Paedopsychiatrica, 50*, 29–40.

Durlak, J. A., & Jason, L. A. (1984). Preventive programs for school-aged children and adolescents. In M. C. Roberts & L. Peterson (Eds.), *Prevention of problems in childhood* (pp. 103–132). New York: John Wiley.

Dweck, C. S. (1975). The role of expectations and attributions in the alleviation of learned helplessness. *Journal of Personality and Social Psychology, 31*, 674–685.

Dweck, C. S. (1977). Learned helplessness and negative evaluation. In E. R. Keislar (Ed.), *The educator: Evaluation and motivation, 14*, 44–49.

Dweck, C. S., & Reppucci, N. D. (1973). Learned helplessness and reinforcement responsibility in children. *Journal of Personality and Social Psychology, 25*, 109–116.

Eastgate, J., & Gilmour, L. (1984). Long-term outcome of depressed children: A follow-up study. *Developmental Medicine and Child Neurology, 26*, 68–72.

Elias, M. J., & Maher, C. A. (1983). Social and affective development of children: A programmatic perspective. *Exceptional Children, 49*, 339–346.

Emery, G., Bedrosian, R., & Garber, J. (1983). Cognitive therapy with depressed children and adolescents. In D. P. Cantwell & G. A. Carlson (Eds.), *Affective disorders in childhood and adolescence* (pp. 445–471). New York: Spectrum.

Feighner, J. P., Robins, E., Guze, S. B., Woodruff, R. A., Winokur, G., & Munoz, R. (1972). Diagnostic criteria for use in psychiatric research. *Archives of General Psychiatry, 26*, 57–63.

Feinstein, C., Blouin, A. G., Egan, J., & Connors, C. K. (1984). Depressive symptomatology in a child psychiatric outpatient population: Correlations with diagnosis. *Comprehensive Psychiatry, 25*, 379–391.

Felner, R. D., Ginter, M. & Primavera, J. (1982). Primary prevention during school transitions: Social support and environmental structure. *American Journal of Community Psychology, 10*(3), 277–289.

Ferster, C. B. (1973). A functional analysis of depression. *American Psychologist, 28*, 857–870.

Finch, A. J., Saylor, C. F., & Edwards, G. L. (1985). Children's Depression Inventory: Sex and grade norms for normal children. *Journal of Consulting and Clinical Psychology, 53*, 424–425.

Frame, C., Matson, J. L., Sonis, W. A., Fialkov, M. J., & Kazdin, A. E. (1982). Behavioral treatment of depression in a prepubertal child. *Journal of Behavior Therapy and Experimental Psychiatry, 3*, 239–243.

Freeman, L. N., Poznanski, E. O., Grossman, J. A., Buchsbaum, Y. Y., & Banegas, M. E. (1985). Psychotic and depressed children: A new entity. *Journal of the American Academy of Child Psychiatry, 24*(1), 95–102.

French, D. C., & Tyne, T. F. (1982). The identification and treatment of children with peer-relationship difficulties. In J. P. Curran & P. M. Monti (Eds.), *Social skills training: A practical handbook for assessment and treatment* (pp. 280–308). New York: Guilford.

Friedman, R. C., Hurt, S. W., Clarkin, J. F., Corn, R., & Aronoff, M. S. (1983). Symptoms of depression among adolescents and young adults. *Journal of Affective Disorders, 5,* 37–43.

Gittelman-Klein, R., & Klein, D. F. (1971). Controlled imipramine treatment of school phobia. *Archives of General Psychiatry, 25,* 204–207.

Goetz, T. E., & Dweck, C. S. (1980). Learned helplessness in social situations. *Journal of Personality and Social Psychology, 39,* 246–255.

Golin, S., Sweeney, P. D., & Shaeffer, D. E. (1981). The casuality of causal attributions in depression: A cross-lagged panel correlational analysis. *Journal of Abnormal Psychology, 90,* 14–22.

Gottman, J., Gonso, J., & Rasmussen, B. (1975). Social interaction, social competence, and friendship in children. *Child Development, 46,* 709–718.

Graziano, A. M., & Mooney, K. C. (1983). *Children and behavior therapy.* New York: Aldine.

Hallahan, D. P., Lloyd, J. W., Kaufmann, J. M., & Loper, A. B. (1983). Academic problems. In R. J. Morris & T. R. Kratochwill (Eds.), *The practice of child therapy* (pp. 113–141). New York: Pergamon.

Hammen, C. & Zupan, B. A. (1984). Self-schemas, depression, and the processing of personal information in children. *Journal of Experimental Child Psychology, 37,* 598–608.

Harter, S. (1982). A developmental perspective on some parameters of self-regulation in children. In. P. Karloy & F. H. Kanfer (Eds.), *Self-management and behavior change: From theory to practice* (pp. 165–204). New York: Pergamon.

Harvey, D. M. (1981). Depression and attributional style: Interpretations of important personal events. *Journal of Abnormal Psychology, 90,* 134–142.

Helsel, W. J., & Matson, J. L. (1984). The assessment of depression in children: The internal structure of the Children's Depression Inventory (CDI). *Behaviour Research and Therapy, 22,* 289–298.

Heppner, P. P., Baumgardner, A., & Jackson, J. (1985). Problem-solving self appraisal, depression, and attributional style: Are they related? *Cognitive Therapy and Research, 9,* 105–113.

Herjanic, B. (1980). *Washington University Diagnostic Interview for Children and Adolescents (DICA).* Washington University School of Medicine, St. Louis, MO.

Hersen, M., Bellack, A. S., Himmelhoch, J. M., & Thase, M. E. (1984). Effects of social skill training, amitriptyline and psychotherapy in unipolar depressed women. *Behavior Therapy, 15,* 21–40.

Hirsch, B. J., Moos, R. H., & Reischl, T. M. (1985). Psychosocial adjustment of adolescent children of a depressed, arthritic, or normal parent. *Journal of Abnormal Psychology, 94*(2), 154–164.

Hodges, K., Kline, J., Stern, L., Cytryn, L., & McKnew, D. (1982). The development of a child assessment interview for research and clinical use. *Journal of Abnormal Child Psychology, 10,* 173–189.

Hodges, K. K., Siegel, L. J., Mullins, L., & Griffin, N. (1983). Factor analysis of the Children's Depression Inventory. *Psychological Reports*, *53*, 759-763.

Hollon, S. D. (1984). Cognitive therapy for depression: Translating research into practice. *The Behavior Therapist*, *7*, 125-127.

Hops, H. (1983). Children's social competence and skill: Current research practices and future directions. *Behavior Therapy*, *14*, 3-18.

Jacobsen, R. H., Lahey, B. B., & Strauss, C. C. (1983). Correlates of depressed mood in normal children. *Journal of Abnormal Child Psychology*, *11*, 29-40.

Kaplan, S. L., Hong, G. K., & Weinhold, C. (1984). Epidemiology of depressive symptomatology in adolescents. *Journal of the American Academy of Child Psychiatry*, *23*, 91-98.

Kashani, J., & Simonds, J. F. (1979). The incidence of depression in children. *American Journal of Psychiatry*, *136*, 1203-1205.

Kashani, J. H., Barbero, G. J., & Bolander, F. D. (1981). Depression in hospitalized pediatric patients. *Journal of the American Academy of Child Psychiatry*, *20*, 123-134.

Kashani, J. H., Husain, A., Shekim, W. O., Hodges, K. K., Cytryn, L., & McKnew, D. H. (1981). Current perspectives on childhood depression: An overview. *American Journal of Psychiatry*, *138*(2), 143-153.

Kaslow, N. J., & Rehm, L. P. (1983). Childhood depression. In R. J. Morris & T. R. Kratochwill (Eds.), *The practice of child therapy: A textbook of methods* (pp. 27-51). New York: Pergamon.

Kaslow, N. J., Rehm, L. P., & Siegel, A. W. (1984). Social-cognitive correlates of depression in children. *Journal of Abnormal Child Psychology*, *12*, 605-620.

Kaslow, N. J., Tannenbaum, R. L., Abramson, L. Y., Peterson, C., & Seligman, M. E. P. (1983). Problem solving deficits and depressive symptoms among children. *Journal of Abnormal Child Psychology*, *11*, 497-502.

Kazdin, A. E. (1981). Assessment techniques for childhood depression: A critical appraisal. *Journal of the American Academy of Child-Psychiatry*, *20*, 358-375.

Kazdin, A. E., Esveldt-Dawson, K., Sherick, R. B., & Colbus, D. (1985). Assessment of overt behavior and childhood depression among psychiatrically disturbed children. *Journal of Consulting and Clinical Psychology*, *53*, 201-210.

Kazdin, A. E., Esveldt-Dawson, K., Unis, A. S., & Rancurello, M. D. (1983). Child and parent evaluations of depression and aggression in psychiatric inpatient children. *Journal of Abnormal Child Psychology*, *11*, 401-413.

Kazdin, A. E., & Frame, C. (1983). Aggressive behavior and conduct disorder. In R. J. Morris & T. R. Kratochwill (Eds.), *The practice of child therapy* (pp. 167-192). New York: Pergamon.

Kazdin, A. E., French, N. H., Unis, A. S., & Esveldt-Dawson, K. (1983). Assessment of childhood depression: Correspondence of child and parent ratings. *Journal of the American Academy of Child Psychiatry*, *22*, 157-164.

Kazdin, A. E., French, N. H., Unis, A. S., Esveldt-Dawson, K., & Sherick, R. B. (1983). Hopelessness, depression and suicidal intent among psychiatrically disturbed inpatient children. *Journal of Consulting and Clinical Psychology*, *51*, 504-510.

Kazdin, A. E., & Petti, T. (1982). Self-report and interview measures of childhood and adolescent depression. *Journal of Child Psychology and Psychiatry*, *23*, 437–457.

Kazdin, A. E., Sherick, R. B., Esveldt-Dawson, K., & Rancurello, M. D. (1985). Nonverbal behavior and childhood depression. *Journal of the American Academy of Child Psychiatry*, *24*, 303–309.

Kendall, P. (1981). Cognitive-behavioral interventions with children. In B. Lahey & A. E. Kazdin (Eds.), *Advances in clinical child psychology* (Vol. 4, pp. 53–90). New York: Plenum.

Kendall, P. C., & Morrison, P. (1984). Integrating cognitive and behavioral procedures for the treatment of socially isolated children. In A. W. Meyers & W. E. Craighead (Eds.), *Cognitive behavior therapy with children* (pp. 261–288). New York: Plenum

Kendall, P., & Wilcox, L. E. (1980). A cognitive-behavioral treatment for impulsivity: Concrete versus conceptual training with non-self-controlled problem children. *Journal of Consulting and Clinical Psychology*, *48*, 80–91.

Kendall, P. C., & Williams, C. L. (1982). Assessing the cognitive and behavioral components of children's self-management. In P. Karoly & F. H. Kanfer (Eds.), *Self-management and behavior change: From theory to practice* (pp. 240–284). New York: Pergamon.

Kendall, P., & Zupan, B. A. (1981). Individual versus group application of cognitive-behavioral self-control procedures with children. *Behavior Therapy*, *12*, 344–359.

Klein, D. C., & Seligman, M. E. P. (1976). Reversal of performance deficits in learned helplessness and depression. *Journal of Abnormal Psychology*, *85*, 11–26.

Klerman, G. L., & Schechter, G. (1982). Drugs and psychotherapy. In E. S. Paykel (Ed.), *Handbook of affective disorders* (pp. 329–337). New York: Guilford.

Klinger, E. (1982). On self-management of mood, affect, and attention. In P. Karoly & F. H. Kanfer (Eds.), *Self-management and behavior change: From theory to practice* (pp. 129–164). New York: Pergamon.

Kolko, D. J., Dorsett, P. G., & Milan, M. A. (1981). A total-assessment approach to the evaluation of social skills training: The effectiveness of an anger control program for adolescent psychiatric patients. *Behavioral Assessment*, *3*, 383–402.

Kovacs, M. (1978). *Interview Schedule for Children (ISC) (10th rev.)*. University of Pittsburgh School of Medicine, Pittsburgh.

Kovacs, M. (1980/1981). Rating scales to assess depression in school-aged children. *Acta Paedopsychiatrica*, *46*, 305–315.

Kovacs, M. (1983). Definition and assessment of childhood depressions. In D. F. Picks & B. S. Dohrenivend (Eds.), *Origins of psychopathology: Problems in research and public policy* (pp. 109–127). New York: Cambridge University Press.

Kovacs, M., & Beck, A. T. (1977). An empirical-clinical approach toward a definition of childhood depression. In J. G. Schulterbrandt & A. Raskin (Eds.), *Depression in childhood: Diagnosis, treatment and conceptual models* (pp. 1–25). Raven Press.

Kovacs, M., Feinberg, T. L., Crouse-Novak, M. A., Paulauskas, S. L., & Finkelstein, R. (1984). Depressive disorders in childhood: I. A longitudinal prospective study of characteristics and recovery. *Archives of General Psychiatry*, *41*, 229–237.

Kovacs, M., Feinberg, T. L., Crouse-Novak, M., Paulauskas, S. L., Pollock, M., & Finkelstein, R. (1984). Depressive disorders in childhood: II. A longitudinal study of the risk for a subsequent major depression. *Archives of General Psychiatry, 41*, 643-649.

Krantz, S., & Hammen, C. L. (1979). Assessment of cognitive bias in depression. *Journal of Abnormal Psychology, 88*, 611-619.

Ladd, G. W. (1984). Social skill training with children: Issues in research and practice. *Clinical Psychology Review, 4*, 317-337.

Lang, M., & Tisher, M. (1978). *Children's Depression Scale*. Victoria, Australia: Australian Council for Educational Research.

Lefkowitz, N. N., & Tesiny, E. P. (1980). Assessment of childhood depression. *Journal of Consulting and Clinical Psychology, 48*, 43-50.

Lewinsohn, P. M. (1974). A behavioral approach to depression. In R. M. Friedman and M. M. Katz (Eds.), *The psychology of depression: Contemporary theory and research*. New York: Wiley.

Lewinsohn, P. M. (1975). The behavioral study and treatment of depression. In M. Hersen, R. M. Eisler & P. M. Miller (Eds.), *Progress in behavior modification (Vol. 1)*, New York: Academic.

Lewinsohn, P. M., & Arconad, M. (1981). Behavioral treatment of depression: A social learning approach. In J. F. Clarkin & H. I. Glazer (Eds.), *Depression: Behavioral and directive intervention strategies* (pp. 33-67). New York: Garland.

Lewinsohn, P. M., & Hoberman, H. M. (1982). Depression. In A. S. Bellack, M. Hersen, & A. E. Kazdin (Eds.), *International handbook of behavior modification and therapy* (pp. 173-207). New York: Plenum.

Lewinsohn, P. M., Larson, D. W., & Munoz, R. F. (1978, November). *The measurement of expectancies and other cognitions in depressed individuals*. Paper presented at the Annual Meeting of the Association for Advancement of Behavior Therapy, Chicago.

Lewinsohn, P. M., Larson, D. W., & Munoz, R. F. (1982). The measurement of expectancies and other cognitions in depressed individuals. *Cognitive Therapy and Research, 6*, 437-466.

Lewinsohn, P. M., Weinstein, M. S., & Alper, T. (1970). A behavioral approach to the group treatment of depressed persons: Methodological contribution. *Journal of Clinical Psychology, 26*, 525-532.

Libet, J., & Lewinsohn, P. M. (1973). The concept of social skills with special reference to the behavior of depressed persons. *Journal of Consulting and Clinical Psychology, 40*, 304-312.

Linden, M., Hautzinger, M. & Hoffman, N. (1983). Discriminant analysis of depressive interactions. *Behavior Modification, 7*, 403-422.

Linehan, M. M. (1981). A social-behavioral analysis of suicide and parasuicide: Implications for clinical assessment and treatment. In J. F. Clarkin & H. I. Glazer, (Eds.), *Depression: Behavioral and directive intervention strategies* (pp. 229-294). New York: Garland.

Ling, W., Oftedal, G., & Weinberg, W. (1970). Depressive illness in childhood presenting as severe headache. *American Journal of Diseases in Children, 120*, 122–124.

Lobovits, D. A., & Handal, P. J. (1985). Childhood depression: Prevalence using DSM-III criteria and validity of parent and child depression scales. *Journal of Pediatric Psychology, 10*, 45–54.

Mannarino, A. (1978). Friendship patterns and self-concept development in preadolescent males. *Journal of Genetic Psychology, 133*, 105–110.

McKnew, D. H. & Cytryn, L. (1979). Urinary metabolites in chronically depressed children. *American Academy of Child Psychiatry, 18*, 608–615.

McKnew, D. H., Cytryn, L., Efron, A. M., Gershon, E. S. & Bunney, E. (1979). Offspring of patients with affective disorders. *British Journal of Psychiatry, 134*, 148–152.

McLean, P. (1981). Remediation of skills and performance deficits in depression. Clinical steps and research findings. In J. F. Clarkin & H. I. Glazer (Eds.), *Depression: Behavioral and directive intervention strategies* (pp. 179–204). New York: Garland.

McLean, P. D., Ogston, K., & Grauer, L. (1973). A behavioral approach to the treatment of depression. *Journal of Behavior Therapy and Experimental Psychiatry, 4*, 323–330.

Meichenbaum, D. H., Bream, L. A., & Cohen, J. S. (1985). A cognitive-behavioral perspective on child psychopathology: Implications for assessment and training. In R. J. McMahon & R. D. Peters (Eds.), *Childhood disorders: Behavioral-developmental approaches* (pp. 36–52). New York: Brunner/Mazel Publishers.

Meyers, A. W., & Craighead, W. E. (Eds.), (1984). *Cognitive behavior therapy with children*. New York: Plenum.

Miller I. W. & Norman, W. H. (1981). Effects of attributions for success on the alleviation of learned helplessness and depression. *Journal of Abnormal Psychology, 90*, 113–124.

Miller, W. R., & Seligman, M. E. P. (1975). Depression and learned helplessness in man. *Journal of Abnormal Psychology, 84*, 228–238.

Molick, R., & Pinkston, E. M. (1982). Using behavioral analyses to develop adaptive social behavior in a depressed adolescent girl. In E. M. Pinkston, J. L. Levitt, G. R. Green, N. L. Linsk, & T. L. Rzepnicki (Eds.), *Effective social work practice* (pp. 364–375). San Francisco: Jossey-Bass.

Morris, R. J., & Kratochwill, T. R. (1983). Childhood fears and phobias. in R. J. Morris & T. R. Kratochwill (Eds.), *The practice of child therapy* (pp. 53–85). New York: Pergamon.

Mullins, L. L., Siegel, L. J., & Hodges, K. (1985). Cognitive problem-solving and life event correlates of depressive symptoms in children. *Journal of Abnormal Child Psychology, 13*, 305–314.

Murray, P. A. (1970). The clinical picture of depression in school children. *Journal of the Irish Medical Association, 63*, 53–56.

Norman, W. H., Miller, I. W., & Klee, S. H. (1983). Assessment of cognitive distortion in a clinically depressed population. *Cognitive Therapy and Research, 7*, 133–140.

Orvaschel, H., Puig-Antich, J., Chambers, W., Tabrizi, M. A., & Johnson, R. (1982). Retrospective assessment of prepubertal major depression with the Kiddie-SADS-E. *Journal of the American Academy of Child Psychiatry, 21,* 392–397.

Pearce, J. (1977). Depressive disorder in childhood. *Journal of Child Psychology and Psychiatry, 18,* 79–82.

Pellegrini, D. S., & Urbain, E. S. (1985). An evaluation of interpersonal cognitive problem solving training with children. *Journal of Child Psychology and Psychiatry, 26,* 17–41.

Peterson, C., Semmel, A., von Baeyer, C., Abramson, L. Y., Metalsky, G. I., & Seligman, M. E. P. (1982). The Attributional Style Questionnaire. *Cognitive Therapy and Research, 6,* 287–300.

Petti, T. A. (1978). Depression in hospitalized child psychiatry patients: Approaches to measuring depression. *Journal of the American Academy of Child Psychiatry, 17,* 49–59.

Petti, T. A. (1983). Active treatment of childhood depression. In J. F. Clarkin & H. I. Glazer (Eds.), *Depression: Behavioral and directive intervention strategies* (pp. 311–343). New York: Garland.

Petti, T. A. (1984). Depression and withdrawal in children. The T. H. Ollendick and M. Hersen (Eds.), *Handbook of child psychopathology* (pp. 293–321). New York: Plenum.

Petti, T. A., Bornstein, M., Delameter, A., & Conners, C. K. (1980). Evaluation and multimodal treatment of a depressed prepubertal girl. *Journal of the American Academy of Child Psychiatry, 19,* 690–702.

Petti, T. A., & Wells, K. (1980). Crisis treatment of a preadolescent who accidentally killed his twin. *American Journal of Psychotherapy, 34,* 434–443.

Platt, J. J., & Spivack, G. (1975). *Manual for the Means-Ends Problem-Solving Procedure (MEPS).* Philadelphia: Hahnemann Medical College & Hospital, Department of Mental Health Sciences.

Poznanski, E. O. (1982). The clinical phenomenology of childhood depression. *American Journal of Orthopsychiatry, 52,* 308–313.

Poznanski, E. O. (1983). Controversy and conflicts in childhood depression. In T. A. Petti (Ed.), *Childhood depression* (pp. 3–10). New York: Haworth Press.

Poznanski, E. O., Carroll, B. J., Banegas, M. C., Cook, S. C., & Grossman, J. A. (1982). The dexamethasone suppression test in prepubertal depressed children. *American Journal of Psychiatry, 139,* 321–324.

Poznanski, E. O., Cook, S. C., & Carroll, B. J. (1979). A depression rating scale for children. *Pediatrics, 64,* 442–450.

Poznanski, E. O., Cook, S. C., Carroll, B. J., & Corzo, H. (1983). Use of the Children's Depression Rating Scale in an inpatient psychiatric population. *Journal of Clinical Psychiatry, 44,* 200–203.

Poznanski, E. O., Grossman, J. A., Buchsbaum, Y., Banegas, M., Freeman, L., & Gibbons, R. (1984). Preliminary studies of the reliability of the Children's Depression Rating Scale. *Journal of the American Academy of Child Psychaitry, 23,* 191–197.

Poznanski, E. O. & Zrull, J. P. (1970). Childhood depression: Clinical characteristics of overtly depressed children. *Archives of General Psychiatry, 23,* 8–15.

Puig-Antich, J. (1982). The use of RDC criteria for major depressive disorder in children and adolescents. *Journal of the American Academy of Child Psychiatry, 21,* 291–293.

Puig-Antich, J. (1984). Psychobiology in prepubertal major depression. In E. B. Weller & R. A. Weller (Eds.), *Current perspectives on major depressive disorders in children.* Washington, DC: American Psychiatric Association. (pp. 78–90).

Puig-Antich, J., Blau, S., Marx, N., Greenhill, L. L. & Chambers, W. (1978). Prepubertal major depressive disorder. *Journal of the American Academy of Child Psychiatry, 17,* 695–707.

Puig-Antich, J., Chambers, W. J., & Tabrizi, M. A. (1983). The clinical assessment of current depressive episodes in children and adolescents: Interviews with parents and children. In D. P. Cantwell & G. A. Carlson (Eds)., *Affective disorders in childhood and adolescence: An update* (pp. 157–180). New York: Spectrum.

Puig-Antich, J., & Gittelman, R. (1982). Depression in childhood and adolescence. In E. S. Paykel (Ed.), *Handbook of affective disorders* (pp. 379–392). New York: Guilford.

Puig-Antich, J., Lukens, E., Davies, M., Goetz, D., Brennan-Quattrock, J., & Todak, G. (1985a). Psychosocial functioning in prepubertal major depressive disorders: I. Interpersonal relationships during the depressive episode. *Archives of General Psychiatry, 42,* 500–507.

Puig-Antich, J., Lukens, E., Davies, M., Goetz, D., Brennan-Quattrock, J., & Todak, G. (1985b). Psychosocial functioning in prepubertal major depressive disorders: II. Interpersonal relationships after sustained recovery from affective episode. *Archives of General Psychiatry, 24,* 511–517.

Rancurello, M. D. (1985). Clinical applications of antidepressant drugs in childhood behavioral and emotional disorders. *Psychiatric Annals, 15,* 88–100.

Raps, C. S., Reinhard, K. E., & Seligman, M. E. P. (1980). Reversal of cognitive and affective deficits associated with depression and learned helplessness by mood elevation in patients. *Journal of Abnormal Psychology, 89,* 342–349.

Rehm, L. P. (1977). A self-control model of depression. *Behavior Therapy, 8,* 787–804.

Rehm, L. P. (1981). A self-control therapy program for treatment of depression, In J. F. Clarkin & H. I. Glazer (Eds.), *Depression: Behavioral and directive intervention strategies* (pp. 68–110). New York: Garland Publishing.

Rehm, L. P. & Kaslow, N. J. (1984). Behavioral approaches to depression: Research results and clinical recommendations. In C. M. Franks (Ed.), *New developments in behavior therapy: From research to clinical application* (pp. 155–229). New York: Haworth Press.

Reynolds, W. M. (1981). *Development and validation of a scale to measure depression in adolescents.* Unpublished manuscript.

Reynolds, W. M. (1983, March). *Depression in adolescents: Measurement, epidemiology, and correlates.* Paper presented at annual meeting of the National Association of School Psychologists, Detroit.

Reynolds, W. M. (1984). Depression in children and adolescents: Phenomenology, evaluation and treatment. *School Psychology Review, 13*, 171-182.

Reynolds, W. M., Anderson, G., & Bartell, N. (in press). Measuring depression in children: A tripartite assessment approach. *Journal of Abnormal Child Psychology.*

Robbins, D. R., Alessi, N. E., Cook, S. C., Poznanski, E. O., & Yanchyshyn, G. W. (1982). The use of the Research Diagnostic Criteria (RDC) for depression in adolescent psychiatric inpatients. *Journal of the American Academy of Child Psychiatry, 21*, 251-255.

Rush, A. J., & Giles, D. E. (1981). Cognitive therapy: Theory and research. In A. J. Rush (Ed.), *Short-term psychotherapies for depression: Behavioral, interpersonal, cognitive, and psychodynamic approaches* (pp. 143-181). New York: Guilford.

Rutter, M., Tizard, J., & Whitmore, K. (Eds.), (1970). *Education, health and behavior.* New York: John Wiley.

Sanchez, V., & Lewinsohn, P. M. (1980). Assertive behavior and depression. *Journal of Consulting and Clinical Psychology, 48*, 119-120.

Saylor, C. F., Finch, A. J., Jr., Baskin, C. H., Saylor, C. B., Darnell, G., & Furey, W. (1984). Children's Depression Inventory: Investigation of procedures and correlates. *Journal of the American Academy of Child Psychiatry, 23*, 626-628.

Saylor, C. F., Finch, A. J., Spirito, A., & Bennett, B. (1984). The Children's Depression Inventory: A systematic evaluation of psychometric properties. *Journal of Consulting and Clinical Psychology, 52*, 955-967.

Schloss, P. J. (1983). Classroom-based intervention for students exhibiting depressive reactions. *Behavioral Disorders, 8*, 231-236.

Schloss, P. J., Schloss, C. N., & Harris, L. (1984). A multiple baseline analysis of an interpersonal skills training program for depressed youth. *Behavioral Disorders, 9*, 182-188.

Schwartz, M., Friedman, R., Lindsay, P., & Narrol, H. (1982). The relationship between conceptual tempo and depression in children. *Journal of Consulting and Clinical Psychology, 50*, 488-490.

Seagull, E. A. W., & Weinshank, A. B. (1984). Childhood depression in a selected group of low-achieving seventh-graders. *Journal of Clinical Child Psychology, 13*, 134-140.

Seligman, M. E. P. (1974). Depression and learned helplessness. In R. J. Friedman & M. M. Katz (Eds.), *The psychology of depression: Contemporary theory and research* (pp. 83-125). New York: Wiley.

Seligman, M. E. P. (1981). A learned helplessness point of view. In L. P. Rhem (Ed.), *Behavior therapy for depression* (pp. 123-141). New York: Academic Press.

Seligman, M. E. P., Abramson, L. Y., Semmel, A. & von Baeyer, C. (1979). Depressive attributional style. *Journal of Abnormal Psychology, 88*, 242-247.

Seligman, M. E. P., Peterson, C., Kaslow, N. J., Tanenbaum, R. L., Alloy, L. B., & Abramson, L. Y. (1984). Attributional style and depressive symptoms among children. *Journal of Abnormal Psychology, 93*, 235-238.

Shure, M. B., & Spivak, G. (1982). Interpersonal problem-solving in young children:

A cognitive approach to prevention. *American Journal of Community Psychology*, *10*, 341–356.

Spitzer, R. L., Endicott, J., & Robins, E. (1972). Research Diagnostic Criteria. Rationale and reliability. *Archives of General Psychiatry*, *35*, 773–782.

Spitzer, R. L., & Williams, J. B. (1980). Classification of mental disorders and DSM-III. In H. Kaplan, A. Freedman, & B. Sadock (Eds.), *Comprehensive textbook of psychiatry* (Vol. 1, 3rd ed., pp. 1035–1072). Baltimore: Williams & Wilkens.

Spivack, G., Platt, J. J., & Shure, M. B. (1976): *The problem-solving approach to adjustment: A guide to research and intervention.* San Fransisco: Jossey-Bass.

Strauss, C. C., Forehand, R., Frame, C., & Smith, K. (1984). Characteristics of children with extreme scores on the Children's Depression Inventory. *Journal of Clinical Child Psychology*, *13*, 227–231.

Strober, M., Green, J., & Carlson, G. (1981a). Phenomenology and subtypes of major depressive disorders in adolescents. *Journal of Affective Disorders*, *3*, 281–290.

Strober, M., Green, J., & Carlson, G. (1981b). Utility of the Beck Depression Inventory with psychiatrically hospitalized adolescents. *Journal of Consulting and Clinical Psychology*, *49*, 482–483.

Teri, L. (1982). The use of the Beck Depression Inventory with adolescents. *Journal of Abnormal Child Psychology*, *10*, 277–284.

Tisher, M., & Lang, M. (1983). The Children's Depression Scale: Review and further developments. In D. P. Cantwell and G. A. Carlson (Eds.), *Affective disorders in childhood and adolescence* (pp. 181–203). New York: Spectrum.

Turner, R. W., Ward, M. F., & Turner, J. D. (1979). Behavioral treatment for depression: An evaluation of therapeutic components. *Journal of Clinical Psychology*, *55*, 166–175.

Van Hasselt, V. B., Griest, D. L., Kazdin, A. E., Esveldt-Dawson, K., & Unis, A. S. (1984). Poor peer interactions and social isolation: A case report of successful in vivo social skills training on a child psychiatric inpatient unit. *Journal of Behavior Therapy and Experimental Psychiatry*, *15*, 271–276.

Weinberg, W. A., Rutman, J., Sullivan, L., Penick, E. C. & Dietz, S. G. (1973). Depression in children referred to an educational diagnostic center: Diagnosis and treatment. *The Journal of Pediatrics*, *83*, 1065–1072.

Weissman, M. M., Prusoff, B. A., Gammon, G. D., Merikangas, K. R., Leckman, J. F., & Kidd, K. K. (1984). Psychopathology in the children (ages 6–18) of depressed and normal parents. *Journal of the American Academy of Child Psychiatry*, *23*(1), 78–84.

Winder, C. L. & Wiggins, J. S. (1964). Social reputation and social behavior: A further validation of the peer nomination inventory. *Journal of Abnormal and Social Psychology*, *68*, 681–684.

Young, J. E., & Beck, A. T. (1981). Cognitive therapy: Clinical applications. In A. J. Rush (Eds.), *Short-term psychotherapies for depression: Behavioral, interpersonal, cognitive, and psychodynamic approaches* (pp. 182–214). New York: Guilford Press.

Youngren, M. A., & Lewinsohn, P. M. (1980). The functional relationship between depression and problematic interpersonal behavior. *Journal of Abnormal Psychology*, *89*, 333–341.

Zahn-Waxler, C., McKnew, D. H., Cummings, E. M., Davenport, Y. B., Radke-Yarrow, M. (1984). Problem behaviors and peer interactions of young children with a manic-depressive parent. *American Journal of Psychiatry*, *141*, 236–240.

CHAPTER 7

Mental Retardation

THOMAS L. WHITMAN AND MARY BETH JOHNSTON

Dramatic changes in conceptualizations and treatment approaches have revolutionized the field of mental retardation during the last few decades. Changes have occurred in our understanding of what mental retardation is, of how mental retardation differs from other learning disorders and mental illness, and of its many causes. These changes have resulted from both basic and applied research examining the cognitive and learning processes of mentally retarded and intellectually average children. Not surprisingly, this research has also precipitated the development of sophisticated strategies for assessing and treating mentally retarded children and adolescents, strategies that are predominantly behavioral in orientation. In the sections below, we will define mental retardation, survey a variety of behavioral approaches to assessment and treatment of mentally retarded children and adolescents, and present a representative case illustrating how behavioral clinicians utilize behavioral strategies in assessment and in treatment design and implementation.

MENTAL RETARDATION: DESCRIPTION AND DEFINITION

The AAMD Definition

The most widely cited and influential definition of mental retardation is that presented by the American Association on Mental Deficiency (AAMD) (Grossman, 1983). According to this definition, mental retardation refers to "significantly subaverage general intellectual functioning existing concurrently with deficits in adaptive behavior and manifested during the developmental period" (Grossman, 1983, p. 1). This definition has several components. First, subaverage intellectual functioning involves performance two or more standard deviations below the mean on an individually administered general intelligence test. Within the subaverage range, four levels of retardation are defined—mild, moderate, severe, and profound—corresponding to successive standard deviations below the mean. Second, deficits in adaptive behavior are defined in terms of the degree to which individuals fail to meet age and cultural standards of personal independence and social responsibility. While expectations concerning adaptive behavior vary for different ages and levels of mental retardation, deficits in adaptive behavior are generally reflected in the following areas: sensorimotor development, communication skills, socialization, academic skills, reasoning and judgment, and vocational skills. Although intellectual deficiencies are essential for the diagnosis of a child as mentally retarded, it is adaptive behavior deficits that dictate his or her need for "special" training and the type of training needed. Finally, the developmental period is considered the period between birth and the 18th birthday (Grossman, 1983).

Mentally retarded children are often viewed as comprising two distinct but overlapping populations (Zigler, 1967). Members of one group typically show evidence of central nervous system pathology, often have "associated handicaps and stigmata," usually have IQs in the moderately retarded range or below, and are diagnosed as mentally retarded at birth or in early childhood (Grossman, 1983). In contrast, members of the other group manifest no signs of neurological dysfunction or other readily detectable physical or clinical signs of mental retardation, have IQ's in the mildly retarded range, and, often, are members of the lowest socioeconomic groups. Whereas these children frequently share many characteristics with learning disabled children, they have a lower measured intelligence and are often psychosocially disadvantaged.

Behavioral Definitions

Behavioral definitions of mental retardation are similar to the 1983 AAMD definition (Bijou, 1966; Whitman, Scibak, & Reed, 1983). Whitman et al. (1983) view a retarded child as a child with one or more response deficiencies that, at least in part, are produced and/or maintained by the environment. These investigators do not relate the response deficiencies to any general hypothetical cause or internal organic or intellectual deficit. Whereas they do not deny that such a deficit may be present, they point out that speculation about possible internal deficits does little to facilitate our understanding of retardation. Moreover, they suggest that to the extent that the retarded child's response deficiencies are a function of his or her social and physical environment, these deficiencies can be modified through the systematic rearrangement of environmental stimuli. Finally, Whitman et al. (1983) stress that retarded children differ considerably in the number, type, and extent of their response deficiencies and point out a continuum of retardation ranging from children who have extensive response deficiencies to those who are deficient only in academic, social, or vocational situations.

Educational Perspectives

While there has been considerable refinement in our conceptualizations about the nature of mental retardation, questions persist about the extent to which mental retardation is modifiable. As pointed out previously, as the severity of mental retardation increases, organic rather than social-environmental factors are seen as instrumental in producing behavioral deficiencies. In turn, there is a corresponding increase in skepticism concerning the effectiveness of habilitation programs. Definitions of mental retardation used by educators suggest that mildly and, to a lesser extent, moderately retarded children are capable of achieving some degree of independence in the community. On the other hand, they characterize severely retarded children as capable of learning only very basic self-help, academic, social, and vocational skills. Finally, they view profoundly retarded children as unable to acquire sufficient skills to care for even their basic needs.

With the advent of behavioral treatment of mentally retarded children and adolescents, there has been increasing optimism about the remediation of the skills deficits of more severely retarded children. In the most recent AAMD definition of mental retardation, no prognostic statements are made about chronicity and irreversibility. This position is in distinct contrast to earlier positions on mental retardation, which asserted that it is constitutional in origin and essentially incurable (Doll, 1941). With the successful introduction of behavior modification programs into "special" education settings, there is growing recognition that the learning potential of mentally retarded children and adolescents is greater than previously thought.

BEHAVIORAL ASSESSMENT OF MENTALLY RETARDED CHILDREN AND ADOLESCENTS

Assessment of mentally retarded children and adolescents serves many purposes. First, assessment is required for the diagnosis of mental retardation and for the classification of children as mildly, moderately, severely, or profoundly retarded. Second, assessment is needed to identify the presence of psychological disorders existing concurrently with mental retardation, and which require treatment for successful remediation of deficits specifically related to mental retardation (Matson & Barrett, 1982, Matson & Frame, 1983). Third, assessment is required to identify behavioral deficits and excesses and variables that control their occurrence (Nelson & Hayes, 1979). Fourth, assessment is needed to identify children's strengths and resources so that these can be utilized in treatment. Finally, assessment is needed to evaluate the ongoing and long-range effectiveness of treatment (Kazdin & Straw, 1976; Ross, 1980; Shapiro & Barrett, 1983). In the following pages, a comprehensive plan for behavioral assessment of mentally retarded children is presented. For more extensive reviews, readers are referred to Reschley (1982) for information about diagnostic and classification issues, to Matson and Barrett (1982) and Matson and Frame (1983) for information about psychopathology in mentally retarded persons, and to Bates and Hansen (1983) and Poling and Parker (1983) for information about techniques used to monitor treatment effectiveness.

Behavioral assessment of mentally retarded children parallels that of similarly aged intellectually average children with other disabilities. It utilizes multiple methods (interviews, checklists, standardized tests, observation) and multiple informants (mentally retarded children and their parents, teachers, and/or other caretakers) to assess children's overt behaviors, cognitions, affect, and somatic and physiological states within the range of situations (family, school, neighborhood, formal and informal peer groups) children encounter daily. The content of behavioral assessment is influenced by developmental considerations. Generally, self-help, social, and academic skills are evaluated, depending on the children's age, level of retardation, personal needs, and social context (Mash & Terdal, 1981; Shapiro & Barrett, 1983).

Behavioral assessment can be conceptualized as involving three stages: problem identification, problem analysis and treatment design, and treatment evaluation. These are discussed below.

Problem Identification

In the problem identification stage, multiple methods, including interviews and assessment of a child's cognitive, academic, and adaptive skills are used to identify problem behaviors, conditions that precipitate and/or maintain them, and resources likely to facilitate treatment.

Interviews

Despite numerous and well-documented problems (Ciminero & Drabman, 1977; Haynes & Jensen, 1979; Kratochwill, 1982), most clinicians believe that interviews play an important part in behavioral assessment (Haynes & Jensen, 1979; Linehan, 1977). They are convenient and flexible; they provide information about emotional disturbances and interpersonal skills that might be missed through other methods; they allow the assessor to gather information from persons with limited ability to provide information by other means. Interviews with parents, the mentally retarded child, and teachers provide an opportunity to establish the rapport needed to secure information useful for treatment planning, facilitate collaboration in treatment planning, enhance compliance to treatment, and increase expectations for successful outcome.

Because mental retardation is a developmental disorder, a major function of the parent interview is to secure a developmental history. Information about the parent's age at pregnancy, the number of pregnancies and births before and after the birth of the mentally retarded child, the child's weight at birth, his or her Apgar score, childhood illnesses and traumas, the accomplishment of developmental milestones, and the academic and vocational success of his or her siblings provide a background for understanding current functioning and allows the assessor to make inferences about the contribution of organic and environmental factors in etiology and current functioning (Beck, 1983).

In the parent interview, cognitive variables, such as the parents' understanding of their child's mental retardation, his/her etiology and prognosis, and their attitudes and expectations about future performance, are assessed. Because parents of developmentally delayed children experience significantly more emotional upheaval than do parents of nonhandicapped children (Friedrich & Friedrich, 1981), the presence of psychopathology within the family is evaluated. In addition, other stresses faced by parents, such as financial difficulties, the presence of another handicapped individual in the home, and/or marital difficulties, are assessed. Finally, parents' knowledge of and skill at using community resources are evaluated.

Besides gathering a developmental history and assessing the family's overall functioning, the parent interview is used to identify behavioral deficits, behavioral excesses, problems in environmental stimulus control, and inappropriate contingency management (Kanfer & Grimm, 1977; Shapiro & Barrett, 1983). The interviewer seeks information about the frequency, duration, and severity of problem behaviors and about the settings in which they occur. He or she inquires about events that occur before and after problem behaviors and about methods parents have used to handle the problem in the past. Barkley (1981) suggests an interview format for obtaining this information that is a useful guide for assessors. Finally, the interviewer inquires about potential reinforcers that may be incorporated into treatment.

Interviewing the mentally retarded child, while infrequently done (Shapiro & Barrett, 1983), is an important way of obtaining information about the child's awareness of his or her problem behavior and his or her understanding of its cause, about the child's language skills, social skills, affective functioning and temperament, and about potential reinforcers for use in treatment. Since mentally retarded children are likely to be apprehensive in unfamiliar situations and to have poor comprehension, poor retention, and short attention spans, special interview skills are needed. First, explaining the purpose and structure of the interview may allay unnecessary anxiety. Second, smiles, praise, tangible reinforcement, and/or gentle physical contact may improve rapport. Third, breaks and changes of topic may be used to accommodate the child's attention span. Finally, as Sigelman and his colleagues have pointed out (Sigelman, Budd, Spanhel, & Schroenrock, 1981; Sigelman, Schroenrock, Spanhel, Thomas, Winer, Budd, & Martin, 1981), since some mentally retarded persons have a tendency to respond affirmatively to questions, regardless of their content, it is important to rephrase important questions so that they require both affirmative and negative responses.

Because problems with academic achievement and often with classroom behavior typify mentally retarded children, an interview with the child's teacher is an important part of the problem identification stage. The teacher can provide information about the child's academic, self-management, and social skills, the nature and extent of the child's problem behavior in school, the settings in which it occurs most frequently, previous attempts to modify it, and plans for the future. Care should be taken to gather highly specific accounts of the child's interactions with the teacher and with peers (Barkley, 1981).

As an initial assessment strategy, interviews have several advantages, notably convenience, flexibility, and the fact that the unstructured format provides an opportunity to form a working relationship with the mentally retarded child and his or her family. Unfortunately, the limitations of the interview are considerable due to the suspect validity and reliability of self-report data collected from mentally retarded individuals (Sigelman, Budd, Spankel, & Schroenrock, 1981; Sigelman, Schroenrock, Spankel, Thomas, Winer, Budd, & Martin, 1981) and from parents (Beck, 1983; Ciminero & Drabman, 1977, Evans & Nelson, 1977). Consequently, interviews should always be used in conjunction with other methods of assessment.

Standardized Intelligence and Achievement Tests

Standardized tests may be conceptualized as structured interviews/observations designed to assess a child's accumulated knowledge, information processing skills, self-management skills, and motivation, factors that have predictive validity concerning success in school (Shapiro & Barrett, 1983).

The Stanford-Binet (Terman & Merrill, 1973), now being revised, is the intelligence test most widely used with mentally retarded children because it assesses children as young as 2 years old, it derives relatively low levels of ability, and its format is appealing to mentally retarded children (Robinson & Robinson, 1976). The Wechsler Preschool and Primary Scale of Intelligence (WPPSI: Wechsler, 1967), also undergoing revision, and the Wechsler Intelligence Scale for Children–Revised (WISC-R: Wechsler, 1974) are the most popular alternatives to the Stanford-Binet. The WISC-R, which covers the age range 6 through 18, is used for the identification of mental retardation in school settings. Whereas its usefulness is limited since it is not normed for children under 6 and it does not accurately reflect IQ scores below the mildly retarded range, due to the extensive research on it, Kaufman (1979) argues that it gives the fairest assessment of children labeled mentally retarded due to psychosocial disadvantage. The System of Multicultural Pluralistic Assessment (SOMPA: Mercer & Lewis, 1977), a battery of measures incorporating medical, social, and pluralistic information, is recommended for use with minority children. The Kaufman Assessment Battery for Children (K-ABC: Kaufman & Kaufman, 1983) measures mental processing (sequential processing and simultaneous processing) and achievement in children ages 2 through 12. The K-ABC has several characteristics that recommend its use with mentally retarded children: its theoretical base, its appeal to young children, the 1980 census-based standardization sample, the availability of sociocultural norms, and the availability of a nonverbal scale to assess mental processing in hearing impaired and language deficient children (Kaufman, Kamphaus, & Kaufman, 1985). For a review of methods of assessing intelligence with mentally retarded children, see Barrett and Breuning (1983).

IQ tests have been severely criticized. In the past, they have been viewed as immutable reflections of the construct of intelligence. They yield "labels" that can become reified, allowing for harmful underestimations of what a child can achieve as a result of concentrated and thorough training. If used "intelligently" as vehicles for gaining information about children's strengths and weaknesses (Kaufman, 1979), however, they yield information useful for classification, placement, and treatment design.

Achievement tests are commonly used adjuncts to intelligence tests. The Wide Range Achievement Test–Revised (WRAT-R: Jastak & Wilkinson, 1984), the Kaufman Test of Educational Achievement (K-TEA: Kaufman & Kaufman, 1985), the Woodcock-Johnson Psychoeducational Battery (Woodcock & Johnson, 1978), and the Peabody Individual Achievement Test (PIAT: Dunn & Markwardt, 1970), currently being restandardized, are achievement tests routinely used to assess the academic skills of school-age childen and are adequate for screening purposes with mildly retarded children. They assess current skill in such areas as spelling, math, and reading. Once general areas of weakness are identified, additional assessment, preferably based on a task analysis of the skills determined to be deficit, is required.

Adaptive Behavior Scales

Behavioral checklists are widely used in the behavioral assessment of children (Kratochwill, 1982). According to Morrow & Coulter (1978), the AAMD Adaptive Behavior Scale–School Version (Lambert, Windmiller, Cole, & Figuerra, 1981), the Adaptive Behavior Inventory for Children (Mercer & Lewis, 1977), and the AAMD Adaptive Behavior Scale–Clinical version (Nihira, Foster, Shellhaas, & Leland, 1974) are frequently used methods of assessing the adaptive behavior of mentally retarded children. The Vineland Adaptive Behavior Scales (VABS: Sparrow, Balla, & Cicchetti, 1984), a revision of the original Vineland Social Maturity Scale (Doll, 1935, 1965), assesses the personal and social sufficiency of individuals from birth to adulthood. Like other adaptive behavior measures, the VABS require a respondent—a parent, teacher, or primary caretaker—who is familiar with the child's behavior. Three versions are available: an Interview Edition, Survey Form; an Interview Edition, Expanded Form; and a Classroom Edition. Each version measures adaptive behavior in four domains: communication, daily living skills, social skills, and motor skills. Interview editions also assess maladaptive behaviors, such as sleep disturbance, temper tantrums, poor eye contact, self-injurious behaviors, etc. The reader is referred to reviews by Reschley (1982), Meyers, Nirhira, and Zetlin (1979), Shapiro and Barrett (1983) and Wallander, Hubert, and Schroeder (1983) for information about available instruments for assessing adaptive behavior.

While adaptive behavior scales involve rating behavior retrospectively (Cone, 1977) and do not provide information sufficiently specific to design effective interventions, they do have a number of advantages (Ciminero & Drabman, 1977). They are economical in cost, effort, and therapist time. They provide a comprehensive view of a child's repertoire of adaptive and maladaptive behavior, including some behavior that might be missed with other assessment procedures, and facilitate the selection of behaviors for more close scrutiny during the problem analysis and treatment design stage. Data obtained are usually relatively easy to quantify and thus are useful in classification decisions. Finally, they frequently serve as useful pretreatment and posttreatment measures.

At the close of the problem identification stage, assessors have a number of hypotheses about the mentally retarded child's problem behavior and personal resources and about his or her parents' and/or teachers' ability to collaborate in treatment. In addition, assessors have frequently noted potential problems in areas best dealt with by other professionals—pediatricians, developmental neurologists, speech and language therapists, occupational therapists, physical therapists, and/or child psychiatrists. Referral is often made to these professionals at this time so that information from their evaluations can be utilized during the problem analysis and treatment design stage.

Problem Analysis and Treatment Design

After the problem identification stage has been completed, the mentally retarded child (depending on his or her age and level of retardation), his or her parents and teachers, and the assessor establish goals for treatment and a treatment plan. Since mentally retarded children often have skills deficits in a number of areas, guidelines are needed to determine what behaviors to address first. Such factors as the extent to which particular behaviors are troublesome to the child and/or others (Beck, 1983), the extent to which several people have concurred that a problem exists (Sulzer-Azaroff & Mayer, 1977), and the extent to which the behavior disrupts the acquisition of important skills (Bates & Hanson, 1983) are considered in determining treatment goals. In addition, Kazdin (1977) recommends social comparison (i.e., the extent to which a child's behavior differs from that of intellectually average children) and subjective evaluation (i.e., the extent to which the child's behavior is judged problematic by "experts" in mental retardation or significant others in the child's life) (Kazdin & Matson, 1981) as methods for determining foci for treatment.

The problem analysis and treatment design stage involves (1) collecting specific data regarding behaviors targeted for change, their frequency and duration, and their antecedents and consequences, in order to perform a functional analysis (Kazdin & Straw, 1976), (2) gathering baseline data in the treatment setting and in settings in which generalization is desired, and sometimes (3) evaluating which of a variety of available interventions is best suited to the mentally retarded child and/or his or her parents and teachers. Three assessment procedures are commonly used during the problem analysis and treatment design stage: self-monitoring, analogue assessment, and naturalistic observation.

Self-Monitoring

Self-monitoring requires an individual to gather data on his or her own behavior at the time of its occurrence (Cone, 1977). Many different methods have been used for self-monitoring, including checklists, counters, and diaries. Self-monitoring can be used to assess any behavior amenable to direct observation (e.g., math performance, time on task). Despite potential problems with accuracy and reactivity (McFall, 1977), self-monitoring has a number of advantages. It is inexpensive and provides information about behaviors that occur when observers are not available and about covert events. Also, in combination with other assessment methods, it can help verify the existence of a problem (Kratochwill, 1982).

Data suggest that, with training, mentally retarded children can accurately record their own behavior (Litrownik & Freitas, 1980; Litrownik, Freitas, & Franzini, 1978). To enhance the accuracy of mentally retarded children's self-monitoring, it is recommended that their accuracy be monitored, that they be alerted to the fact that their accuracy is being monitored, and that they be periodically reinforced for accurate recording (McFall, 1977).

Analogue Assessment

Analogue assessment requires that children respond to stimuli that simulate those found in the natural environment (Kratochwill, 1982). Role-playing is one form of analogue assessment that can be used with mentally retarded children. For instance, as part of an assessment of a mentally retarded adolescents' social skills, he or she may be asked to role-play asking someone for a date, accepting or refusing a request for a date, or expressing preferences about social activities. Further, the adolescent may be asked to role-play self-statements prior to or following these behaviors. Or, as part of the assessment of parents' skill at engaging in positive interaction with or eliciting compliance from their mentally retarded child, parents and child may be observed while making puzzles or putting away toys. Barkley (1981) recommends this procedure for assessing compliance/parenting skills with hyperactive children and their mothers.

Analogue methods make several contributions. They are flexible. By minimizing the impact of extraneous variables sometimes present in the natural environment, they permit opportunities for increased experimental control. They allow assessment of behaviors that are impossible to monitor in naturalistic settings. They provide the opportunity to "pilot test" complex or costly interventions to determine their effectiveness before implementing them in other settings. Disadvantages of analogue assessment include the potential lack of a close match between the analogue and natural environments and the inability of analogue methods to secure information regarding antecedents and consequences related to the target behavior.

Naturalistic Observation

Naturalistic observation involves observation of a specific behavior or class of behaviors and the events that occur before and after in the environment in which the behavior typically occurs. A three-column sheet, labeled antecedents (A), behaviors (B), and consequences (C), is often used. Antecedents include interpersonal variables (e.g., teacher-provided reinforcers), setting variables (e.g., noise level), and structural variables (e.g., schedule of activities, exposure to nonhandicapped models). Consequences influence the rate of occurrence of the behaviors they follow and serve as discriminitive stimuli for subsequent behaviors. Through ABC analysis, the functional relationships between antecedents, behaviors and consequences are examined. By collecting ABC data for several days and in several settings, assessors can have increased confidence that problem behaviors have been well defined and that the relationships between antecedents and consequences have been accurately evaluated. This information results in more efficient and effective intervention designs (Bates & Hanson, 1983). Naturalistic observation is also used to secure. information about the frequency and duration of target behaviors prior to treatment, information that is particularly useful for treatment evaluation. This approach can be carried out at home, at school, or in other relevant environments. Independent trained observers are preferred; however, parents, teachers, program staff, and volunteers can be trained and generally provide adequate data for treatment design.

Naturalistic observation is not without limitations (Ciminero & Drabman, 1977; Haynes, 1978). The presence of an observer may alter the child's behavior such that it is no longer typical. Having parents or teacher confirm the representativeness of the behavior observed can remedy this problem to some extent. Observing during informal activities or in settings in which visitors are common are other ways of minimizing reactivity (Arrington, 1943). Low-frequency or highly variable behaviors (e.g., breaking windows) may not occur during observation periods. Normative data are not available to aid in objective assessment of behavioral excesses or deficits (Shapiro & Barrett, 1983). Personnel, equipment (taperecorders, ear jacks, observation sheets), and training observers to the desired level of reliability are costly. Failure to address these limitations may decrease accuracy in the data as well as the value of information for treatment planning.

Besides utilizing self-monitoring, analogue assessment, and naturalistic observation to secure data needed for problem analysis, treatment design involves decisions about what behaviors to target, who the change agent will be, the setting in which treatment will be delivererd, and the means to program generalization (Borkowski & Cavanaugh, 1979; Stokes & Baer, 1977).

Treatment Evaluation

Once the treatment is designed, it is implemented and its impact is observed. If the intervention results in behavior change in the direction specified by the goals, the treatment plan is considered effective and is continued until the desired behavior change has been accomplished. If treatment does not result in the desired behavior change, the original data are reevaluated and another plan is developed and implemented.

Both single-subject and group designs are useful for investigating the efficacy of intervention efforts (Hersen & Barlow, 1976; Poling & Parker, 1983; Shapiro & Barrett, 1983). Further, direct observation by trained observers is the most desirable method for ongoing assessment of treatment. However, because of problems noted above, self-monitoring, observation by parents and teachers, and rating scales can also be used. Treatment can also be evaluated through the use of social comparison and subjective evaluation (Bates & Hanson, 1983; Kazdin, 1977). By showing that treatment resulted in performance that makes the mentally retarded child's behavior more like that of nonhandicapped children and/or more acceptable to others, the social significance of the behavior change is established. In addition, treatment evaluation can include measures of "consumer satisfaction" with the treatment process and outcome (Kazdin, 1977).

Finally, a comprehensive assessment is not complete until the target behaviors are observed under generalization (including follow-up) conditions. This requires observation of behavior in a variety of settings and at different times. Assessment of generalization is required to determine that the training's effectiveness is not limited to the setting in which it was delivered to the person who served as change agent, or to the tasks specifically involved in training. It is also needed to identify unanticipated, unacceptable consequences of treatment (negative side effects) (Willems, 1974; Voeltz & Evans, 1982).

BEHAVIORAL PROCEDURES UTILIZED WITH MENTALLY RETARDED CHILDREN AND ADOLESCENTS

Since the 1960s when behavioral programs were first implemented with mentally retarded children, there have been several changes in the children treated, the skills taught, and the treatment techniques employed. Whereas earlier programs focused mostly on teaching self-help and social skills and on modifying a variety of inappropriate behaviors of severely and profoundly retarded children, recent programs have also focused on teaching academic and community-living skills to children of all levels of retardation. Within each of these areas there has been a shift in treatment goals from very basic and simple skills to more advanced and refined ones. As program goals have changed, treatment procedures have included not only procedures conceptually rooted in an operant model, but also procedures derived from the cognitive-behavioral paradigm. In the following sections, behavior modification procedures utilized with mentally retarded children and adolescents are reviewed. These procedures are employed in complex training programs aimed at teaching a number of skills. Next, research evaluating these training programs is presented.

Reinforcement

Reinforcement refers to the process by which the future probability of a response is increased through the arrangement of a stimulus event following the response. The ultimate test of whether a stimulus serves as a reinforcing event is whether it increases behavior.

Behavior modifiers use numerous theoretical and practical methods to select potential reinforcers: (a) making a "best guess" based on information gathered from the child, significant others, or one's intuition, and then observing if it works; (b) using stimuli such as food (primary reinforcers) that are drive-reducing or stimuli that have become conditioned reinforcers through association with primary reinforcers (drive reduction theory; see Hull, 1943; Miller & Dollard, 1941); (c) employing stimuli that excite the senses because of their novelty and/or complexity (sensory stimulation hypothesis; see Bandura, 1969); (d) using higher-probability responses (Premack, 1959); and (e) using responses to which the individual has been denied his or her usual access (response deprivation hypothesis; see Konarski, Johnson, Crowell, & Whitman, 1981).

Several other factors should be taken into account when choosing a reinforcer. Optimally, a reinforcer should be easy to administer, change behavior rapidly, and be inexpensive. To maximize reinforcer effectiveness, a reinforcer should be applied only when the target behavior occurs. In educational programs, the rule of thumb is to reinforce frequently, to change from a continuous to an intermittent schedule once the target behavior is occurring regularly, and to gradually reduce the amount of a primary reinforcer (e.g., food) given on any particular occasion. Praise is associated with tangible reinforcers and eventually serves as the only reinforcer employed.

When a response occurs regularly in the presence of only specific antecedent stimuli, the behavior is considered under stimulus control. Stimulus control can be achieved by consistently reinforcing a behavior when it occurs in the presence of a particular stimulus and withholding reinforcement in the presence of other stimuli. Conceptually, this process, which is called differential reinforcement, results in a discrimination being formed. Instructional and imitation training are two common discrimination training procedures used with mentally retarded children. In instructional training, a verbal cue is presented, (e.g., "stand up") and the child is reinforced only for a particular response to the cue (e.g., standing up). In imitation training, the cue presented is visual rather than verbal. Typically, discrimination training is terminated when the child reliably makes the appropriate response in the presence of the verbal or visual cue.

Behavior Induction Procedures

For reinforcement to be utilized, the target behavior must be within the child's repertoire. When the target behavior does not naturally occur or occurs infrequently, a variety of prompting procedures are employed to induce it: verbal instructions, modeling, and physical guidance. Typically, instructing or verbally prompting a child to emit a particular response is tried initially. An alternative method for prompting involves modeling the desired behavior and then reinforcing the child's imitations. When modeling procedures are used, the trainer prefaces a demonstration of the behavior by the instruction, "Do this." If neither verbal nor visual prompts are effective in inducing the behavior, physical guidance is employed. Verbal instructions, modeling, and physical guidance serve as types of stimulus prompts that precede or accompany the target behavior. In each of these procedures, prompts are faded gradually; that is, instructions are abbreviated, visual cues attenuated, and physical guidance withdrawn.

A fourth procedure, shaping, employs a special type of reinforcement procedure. Shaping involves differentially reinforcing successively closer approximations to the target behavior. Reinforcement is initially administered for a single response, then for two responses emitted in proper sequence, and so on until only successful performance of the complex behavior is reinforced.

Behavior Reduction Procedures

Many mentally retarded children and adolescents, particularly those who are severely and profoundly retarded, display a variety of maladaptive responses (e.g., aggression and stereotypy). A wide variety of procedures have been developed to decrease these behaviors. These include extinction, differential reinforcement, and punishment procedures.

During extinction, the process by which behavior is developed and maintained through positive reinforcement is reversed by withholding reinforcement. In order to apply an extinction procedure successfully, the reinforcers maintaining a response must be identified and controlled. Frequently, an extinction program is combined with positive reinforcement to promote desirable, adaptive behavior. This joint procedure is called differential reinforcement. The focus of a differential reinforcement procedure can be to increase a desirable behavior, decrease an undesirable behavior, or both.

In addition to extinction and differential reinforcement, punishment techniques are used to decelerate inappropriate behavior. Punishment can refer to either the withdrawal or presentation of a stimulus following a response; in both cases the result is a decrease in the frequency of the response.

Two procedures that bear some similarity to extinction techniques and to each other have been used in punishment programs with mentally retarded children. These are response cost and time-out from positive reinforcement, commonly referred to as time-out. Response cost involves the loss of a specific positive reinforcer that a child currently has in his or her possession. Time-out involves the loss of an opportunity to receive positive reinforcers for a certain period of time.

In contrast to time-out and response cost, some punishment procedures involve the administration of aversive stimuli. A variety of aversive stimuli have been utilized including shock, squirting lemon juice into a child's mouth, placing aromatic ammonia under a child's nose, spanking, and verbal reprimands. Several punishment procedures are difficult to categorize because they appear to be a hybrid of time-out, response cost, and/or aversive-stimulus application procedures. Overcorrection, a prominent example of this type of strategy, involves an array of procedures that require an offender to restore an environment disturbed by his or her deviant behavior not only to its original state but to an improved state, and/or to practice more appropriate modes of responding within the environment in which the misbehavior occurred. These two techniques have been referred to, respectively, as restitutional and positive-practice overcorrection (Foxx & Azrin, 1972, 1973).

Cognitive-Behavioral Procedures

Whereas proponents of various cognitive-behavior modification approaches differ in the methods they employ, they generally agree that human beings develop adaptive behavior through cognitive processes. Further, there is consensus that the task of the educator is to assess a child's maladaptive cognitive processes and to arrange learning experiences that will alter these processes and their behavioral correlates (Mahoney & Arnkoff, 1978). Cognitive-behavioral procedures used with mentally retarded children have been classified into five categories: self-regulation, problem-solving, cognitive strategy training, correspondence training, and self-instructional training (Whitman, Burgio & Johnston, 1984). The emphasis in self-regulation programs is on developing self-monitoring, standard setting, self-evaluation, and self-reinforcement skills (see Litrownik & Steinfeld, 1982). Problem-solving approaches help children generate a variety of potentially effective solutions to a problem situation, recognize the best solution, and implement that solution (see Ross & Ross, 1973). Similarly, cognitive strategy training teaches children to generate verbal responses that will function as mediators in a problem-solving situation and, more generally, to become aware of their own thought processes (Brown & French, 1979). While types of correspondence training programs differ, their emphasis has been on establishing antecedent verbal control of motor behavior by reinforcing children for doing what they say they will do (Whitman, Scibak, Butler, Richter, & Johnson, 1982). Finally, self-instructional training also involves using a child's verbal behavior to guide his or her nonverbal behavior (Whitman & Johnston, 1983).

REVIEW OF RESEARCH ON TREATMENT STRATEGIES USED WITH MENTALLY RETARDED CHILDREN AND ADOLESCENTS

One of the hallmarks of the behavioral approach is its use of empirical methods to evaluate treatment effectiveness. As part of the treatment design stage, the clinician reviews available research to identify "tried and true" methods of intervention. He or she develops an intervention based on a review of existing literature and the "goodness of fit" between that literature and the needs/resources of the mentally retarded child or adolescent and his or her family, school, and/or community. A review of recent research regarding treatment programs aimed at teaching self-help, social, and academic skills and at decreasing maladaptive behaviors is presented below. The section concludes with a discussion of parent and paraprofessional staff training efforts.

Self-Help Skills

As noted above, early behavioral programs implemented with mentally retarded children focused on self-help skills. In 1963 Ellis provided an operant analysis of toileting that was operationalized and evaluated by several investigators (Baumeister & Klosowski, 1965; Giles & Wolf, 1966). Many of these studies, which employed procedures only approximating those suggested by Ellis, were methodologically flawed and frequently unsuccessful. Subsequent research on toilet training was characterized by both methodological and technological improvements. Several programs incorporated electronic devices as part of the treatment program. One electronic device, a buzzer alarm for detecting inappropriate eliminations, was activated by moisture and permitted immediate intervention by the trainer (Azrin, Bugle, & O'Brien, 1971; Van Wagenen & Murdock, 1966). A mechanical apparatus was also designed to deliver reinforcers automatically and contingently for appropriate elimination (Passman, 1975). A number of studies utilized prompting and reinforcement techniques to shape independent toileting (i.e., walking to the toilet, removing and replacing appropriate clothes). These investigators employed either a forward-moving procedure (Van Wagenen, Meyerson, Kerr, & Mahoney, 1969; Mahoney, Van Wagenen, & Meyerson, 1971) or a program developed by Azrin and Foxx (Azrin & Foxx, 1971; Azrin, Bugle, & O'Brien, 1971) that focused on reinforcement of appropriate eliminations in the toilet and on the use of overcorrection for inappropriate eliminations. Azrin, Sneed, and Foxx (1973) used similar techniques as part of a rapid method for decreasing bedwetting.

Behavioral research on self-feeding has focused on teaching skills ranging from use of a spoon to elaborate dining skills (Matson, Ollendick & Adkins, 1980; Richman, Sonderby, & Kahn, 1980; Wilson, Reid, Phillips, & Brugio, 1984), and on deceleration of inappropriate mealtime behaviors, such as food spilling, food refusal, throwing and stealing food (Martin, McDonald, & Omichinski, 1971; Riordan, Iwata, Finney, Wohl, & Stanley, 1984; Stimbert, Minor, & McCoy, 1977). Typically, faded guidance or a combination of faded guidance and behavior shaping (either forward or backward) was employed in the acquisition studies. To increase number of learning opportunities, Azrin and Armstrong (1973) instituted a short, intensive mini-meal procedure in which each meal was divided into three smaller meals. Programs involving deceleration of inappropriate behavior frequently used either time-out, restitution, and/or positive practice procedures (Stimbert, Minor, & McCoy, 1977).

Few empirical studies are available in which dressing and dental hygiene have been taught. Those studies that have been conducted have typically used one or more of the following procedures: task analysis, verbal instructions, modeling, fading, and positive reinforcement (Colwell, Richards, McCarver, & Ellis, 1973; Horner & Kielitz, 1975; Jarman, Iwata, & Lorentzson, 1983).

Social Skills

With the growing emphasis on normalization and community involvement, behavioral theorists and practitioners have given greater attention to communication and community living skills. Receptive and expressive language deficiencies are quite common among mentally retarded children. Researchers studying the expressive language of mentally retarded children have focused on developing both speech and nonvocal communication. Early studies examined methods of improving language skills, including use of plural morphemes (Sailor, 1971), use of past tense (Schumaker & Sherman, 1970), use of comparative and superlative noun suffixes (Baer & Guess, 1973), sentence generation (Stremel, 1972), question asking (Twardosz & Baer, 1973), and question answering (Garcia, 1974). Recent investigators have targeted verbal requests (Bray, Biasini, & Thrasher, 1983), word labeling (Fabry, Mayhew, & Hanson, 1984), object and picture labeling (Handleman, Powers, & Harris, 1984), conversational responses (Leifer & Lewis, 1984), generative yes/no responses (Neef, Walters, & Egel, 1984), and preposition use (McGee, Krantz & McClannahan, 1985).

While researchers have been actively involved in developing and evaluating expressive language programs, less attention has been directed to receptive language programs. Generally, training of receptive language has emphasized verbal control of motor behavior. For example, Whitman, Zakara, and Chardos (1971) used physical guidance, fading, and positive reinforcement to increase severely retarded children's compliance to trained and untrained instructions. In a series of subsequent studies, Striefel and his colleagues tested the effects of generalized instruction-following behavior. They determined that generalized compliance could be facilitated through the systematic training of noun-verb combinations in a stepwise fashion (Striefel & Wetherby, 1973; Striefel, Bryan, & Atkins, 1974; Striefel, Wetherby, & Karlan, 1976). Other studies have developed an array of procedures for improving prepositional responding (Egel, Shafer, & Neef, 1984) and instruction-following behavior (Lancioni, Smeets, & Oliva, 1984; McLivane, Bass, O'Brien, Gerovac, & Stoddard, 1984).

Because some mentally retarded children are unable to acquire vocal speech, investigators have taught them to communicate through nonvocal means. In a series of excellent studies, Reid and his associates used verbal instructions, modeling, manual guidance, verbal reinforcement, and feedback to teach profoundly retarded adolescents to respond to pictures with manual signs and to use and maintain signing in a natural environment (Faw, Reid, Schepis, Fitzgerald, & Welty, 1981). In a subsequent incidental teaching program (Schepis, Reid, Fitzgerald, Faw, van den Pol, & Welty, 1982), manual signing was increased in a natural environment through a training program involving rearrangement of the physical environment and staff training and minitraining sessions. The development, maintenance, and generalization of signing have also been examined (Bonta & Walters, 1983; Bucher, 1983; Dukes & Michaelsen, 1983; Dukes & Morsink, 1984; Fitzgerald, Reid, Schepis, Faw, Welty, & Pyfer, 1984). Researchers have also demonstrated the efficacy of nonvocal communication programs employing the use of Bliss symbols (Elder & Bergman, 1978; Song, 1979). In this type of program, the child learns to communicate by pointing to a symbol displayed along with the corresponding word on a communication board.

Besides communication skills, behavior therapists have focused on teaching social skills necessary for adapting to complex community environments. Some investigators emphasized training of rudimentary social skills, such as ball rolling (Whitman, Mercurio, & Caponigri, 1970) and pushing a swing (Paloritzian, Haspazi, Streifel, & Edgar, 1971). Others have taught interpersonal language skills within a game context (Whitman, Burish, & Collins, 1972), peer interaction (Odom, Hoyson, Jamieson, & Strain, 1985; Shafer, Egel, & Neef, 1984; Twardosz, Nordquist, Simon, & Botkin, 1983), and complex game behavior (Marchant & Wehman, 1979). Still others have focused on teaching conversation skills in analogue situations (Matson, Kazdin & Esveldt-Dawson, 1980; Meredith, Saxon, Doleys, & Kyzer, 1980) and on developing dance skills (Lagomarcino, Reid, Ivancic, & Faw, 1984). While training strategies have varied, they typically have consisted of instructions, modeling, physical guidance, and/or reinforcement.

Although there are many behaviors important to community living, particular emphasis has been placed on teaching telephone usage and money management to mentally retarded children and adolescents. Telephoning skills have been targeted because of their importance in obtaining assistance in emergency situations and in contacting others quickly and efficiently. Leff (1974, 1975) paired colors with numbers to assist dialing. In a methodologically rigorous study, Risley and Cuvo (1980) employed an elaborate task analysis to teach emergency telephone usage in a sheltered workshop. Although these researchers employed the procedure with adults, it could be readily applied to children and adolescents.

Knowledge of money management has been stressed in a number of studies. Research has involved teaching basic discriminations and concepts needed in handling money. For example, Wunderlich (1972) taught mildly retarded children to discriminate among five coins and to choose an equivalent coin or coins from a collection of coins. Cuvo and his associates trained mentally retarded adolescents to choose different combinations of coins that were equivalent in sum (Trace, Cuvo, & Criswell, 1977), to discriminate coins, to count by ones and fives, to sum coin values (Lowe & Cuvo, 1976), and to make change (Cuvo, Veitch, Trace, & Konke, 1978).

Finally, programs have been designed to teach personal and home living skills (Schalock, Gadwood, & Perry, 1984), a complex photocoping skill (Wacker & Berg, 1984), job-related social skills (Whang, Fawcett, & Mathews, 1984), classroom interaction skills (Strain, 1983), time-telling and promptness (Smeets, Lancioni, & Van Lieshout, 1985), and shopping skills (Aeschleman, & Schladenhauffen, 1984). For a description of other social skills training programs the reader is referred to a special issue of *Applied Research in Mental Retardation* (1983 Vol. *4*, Number 4).

Academic Skills

A number of studies have attempted to develop academic skills in classroom settings. This literature has investigated the relationship between attentional behaviors and the acquisition and performance of specific academic skills. Attention has been defined in terms of eye contact (Foxx, 1977), posture (Whitman, Scibak, Butler, Richter, & Johnson, 1982), and on-task behavior (Bornstein & Quevillon, 1976; Burgio, Whitman, & Johnson, 1980). Burgio et al. (1980) used a self-instructional package to develop on-task behavior in mildly retarded children in an academic situation. Although improvement in on-task behavior was marked, consistent positive changes in academic performance were not exhibited. Using correspondence training, Whitman et al. (1982) produced direct increases in attentional responses in five or six students. Moreover, in contrast to the findings of Burgio et al. (1980), general gains in quantity and accuracy of classroom work were observed. Attentional skills were also modified through correspondence training in a listening development program described by Keogh, Burgio, Whitman, and Johnson (1983). Although no definitive research has been conducted in this area, existing data suggest that increases in academic performance achieved by programs aimed at improving attention occur only when the academic skills are already firmly entrenched in the student's repertoire. For a description of other self-management programs employed in classroom settings, the reader is referred to studies by Anderson-Inman, Paine, and Deutchman (1984), Baer, Fowler, and Carden-Smith (1984), Shapiro, Browder, and D'Huyvetters (1984), and Litronik, White, McInnis, and Licht (1984).

Attempts to improve academic skills directly have generally worked with reading, writing, and math. Dorry and Zeaman (1975) examined three paired-associates methods for teaching decoding of a simple reading vocabulary to moderately and severely retarded children. They found the most effective method to be one in which a word was presented along with a pictorial representation of that word followed by fading of the picture. Lally (1981) described an innovative computer-assisted instruction program for improving handwriting skills; the value of this program, however, needs to be empirically demonstrated. Guided by response deprivation theory, Konarski, Crowell, and Duggan (1981) used math as a reinforcer for teaching writing skills. In a series of studies, the effectiveness of self-instructional programs for teaching math concepts has been supported (Grimm, Bijou, & Parsons, 1973; Johnston, Whitman, & Johnson, 1980; Leon & Pepe, 1978; Whitman & Johnston, 1983).

Inappropriate Behavior

Besides evaluating programs for increasing self-help, social, and academic skills, investigators have given considerable attention to examining procedures for reducing stereotypies (e.g., body rocking), self-injurious behaviors, aggression, and a number of other inappropriate behaviors. Operant theory has had considerable impact on the selection of treatment strategies in this area. Differential reinforcement programs have been employed to reduce the frequency of stereotypies (Eason, White, & Newsom, 1982; Flavell, 1973; Mulick, Hoyt,

Rojahn, & Schroeder, 1978; Repp, Deitz, & Deitz, 1976). Other methods, such as removal of positive reinforcement and response cost, have also been successfully employed (Laws, Brown, Epstein, & Hocking, 1971; Murphy, Nunes, & Hutchings-Ruprecht, 1977). Rincover (1975) has suggested that the sensory stimulation provided by stereotypic behavior may constitute the critical controlling reinforcer. Findings from this research (Rincover, 1975; Rincover, Cook, Peoples, & Packard, 1979) as well as from other investigators (Favell, McGimsey, & Schell, 1981) suggest that developing adaptive behaviors that provide the same sensory stimulation as the stereotypy assists in suppressing stereotyped behavior. Finally, punishment in the form of shock, verbal reprimand, and overcorrection has been applied to reduce stereotypies (Bailey, Pokrzywinski, & Bryant, 1983; Corte, Wolf, & Locke, 1971; Friman, Cook, & Finney, 1984; Mayhew & Harris, 1978).

Treatment strategies similar to those employed in stereotypy reduction programs have been evaluated for decreasing self-injurious and aggressive behaviors. For a critical discussion of the many and diverse behavior therapy programs for controlling these and other inappropriate behaviors (e.g., vomiting, rumination, pica, coprophagy), the reader is referred to Berkson (1983), LaGrow and Repp (1984), O'Brien (1981), Repp and Buille (1981), Schroeder, Schroeder, Rojahn, and Mulick (1981), Whitman, Scibak, and Reid (1983), and to a special issue of *Analysis and Intervention in Developmental Disabilities* (1983, Volume 2, Number 1).

Parent and Paraprofessional Staff Training

Parents of mentally retarded children are increasingly becoming involved in the treatment of their children. Berkowitz and Graziano (1972) recommended involving parents in treatment because parents have moral, ethical, and legal responsibility for their children, have the greatest contact with and impact on their children, and are typically willing to assist in remedial and/or preventative programs. An especially compelling reason for involving parents in treatment is that, because of the long-term and persistent nature of the problems associated with mental retardation, great consistency of treatment is required. This is more likely to occur when parents serve as the primary teachers of their children. With consistent and effective treatment, greater maintenance and generalization of program effects are likely. Berkowitz and Graziano (1972) urged behavior therapists not to deliver treatment directly but rather, through training programs, to assist parents in providing training for their children.

Parents of mentally retarded children have assumed active, varied, and complex roles in the training of their children (Altman & Mira, 1983). They have dealt with a range of problem behaviors, some of which are similar to problems encountered with intellectually average children: noncompliance and tantrums (Terdal & Buell, 1969), problems with social interaction (Mash & Terdal, 1973), high activity rates (Frazier & Schneider, 1975), and destructive or aggressive behavior (Christophersen & Sykes, 1979). Parents of mentally retarded children have taught their children a variety of skills, including motor skills (Watson & Bassinger, 1974) and self-help skills (Longin, Cone, & Longin, 1975; Miller, Patton, & Henton, 1971). In addition, they have shaped eye contact (Watson & Bassinger, 1974) and decreased self-injurious (Altman, Haavik, & Cook, 1978; Harris & Romanzyk, 1976), self-stimulatory, and stereotypic behaviors (Cook, Altman, Shaw, & Blaylock, 1978). Finally, with the growing emphasis on parents' functioning as decision makers and advocates for their children, they have been involved in the design, implementation, and evaluation of training programs for their children (Hayden, 1976; Ora & Reisinger, 1971).

In addition to greater involvement of parents in the training of mentally retarded children and adolescents, paraprofessional staff have increasingly become involved in the training of these children. Within residential institutions where severely and profoundly mentally retarded children and adolescents are cared for and/or trained, the persons who most often provide direct care are the paraprofessional staff. In fact, paraprofessional staff, who constitute the largest segment of the direct care personnel in these facilities, spend more time working directly with residents than does any other group. While these caregivers typically do not have education beyond high school and often begin their jobs without formal experience, they are in the best position to deliver behavior therapy programs. Consequently, it is not surprising that recent efforts have been addressed to the training of these caregivers.

As a consequence of this emphasis on training parents and paraprofessional staff, considerable research has emerged evaluating an array of procedures for training these individuals. The technology bears many similarities to the technology used in teaching retarded children; verbal instruction, modeling, behavioral rehearsal, feedback and/or reinforcement are frequently employed training procedures. For a thorough discussion and evaluation of this technology, the reader is referred to Altman and Mira (1983), Tymchuk, 1983, and Reid and Whitman (1983).

Having considered the nature of mental retardation and having surveyed various assessment and treatment procedures used with mentally retarded children and adolescents, a representative case is presented to illustrate how behavioral clinicians apply assessment and treatment strategies in the service of mentally retarded children and their families.

CASE PRESENTATION

Timmy P. was a 5-year, 5-month-old boy who was referred for treatment by Ms. M., program director of Timmy's preschool, a preschool for developmentally delayed children. Ms. M. referred Timmy because of deficits in academic skills and behavior problems at home and at school.

The assessment process began with interviews with Timmy's mother and teacher and with standardized psychoeducational testing. These procedures were designed to (a) establish rapport, (b) outline the general nature of Timmy's problems, (c) obtain a broad picture of his history, family functioning, school functioning, and strengths and weaknesses, and (d) develop preliminary hypotheses concerning factors precipitating and/or maintaining his behavior problems against the backdrop of his overall life situation.

Ms. P., Timmy's mother, provided information about his developmental history, current family situation, and problem behavior at home. Ms. P., Timmy, and his brother, Todd, age 3, lived in a small apartment in a midsize midwestern community. Ms. P. had been divorced from her husband for almost two years. Timmy had no regular contact with his father. A high school dropout, Ms. P. had been laid off from her last job in a factory 8 months prior to the interview. Ms. P. talked freely about her history of relationship and job problems and her difficulty managing her children. Although she appeared distracted, exhibited some depression, and seemed without significant social supports, she did seem concerned about Timmy, motivated to help, and willing to improve her parenting skills.

Ms. P. described her pregnancy and Timmy's birth as normal, except that she was under stress during this period because of serious marital conflict. Timmy walked and was toilet trained at the appropriate times. From the beginning, however, he had difficulty with speech. He was slow to develop speech and when he did, his speech was often unintelligible. Timmy's speech problems alerted his pediatrician to refer Ms. P. to Timmy's preschool.

In response to questions regarding her current concerns about Timmy, Ms. P. spoke of Timmy's increasing defiance and his refusal to do anything she asked. He would not get dressed for school without a struggle, refused to put away his toys when asked to do so, and would not go to bed without a fuss. He became angry whenever she asked anything of him and was beginning to "sass" her and to have temper tantrums. In addition, Timmy would "bully" Todd by taking toys from him, slapping him, and making him cry. When asked how frequently these problems occurred, Ms. P. said, "All the time." When asked how she responded to them, Ms. P. said, "Sometimes I yell, sometimes I spank him, and sometimes I give up." According to Ms. P., Timmy's behavior did not change no matter what type of discipline she used.

Ms. P. served as informant for the VABS (Sparrow, Balla, & Cicchetti, 1984). Timmy achieved an Adaptive Behavior Composite standard score of 59 $+/-$ 5 at the 95% confidence level placing him "low" in comparison to same age children in the standardization sample. Ms. P's answers to the VABS presented a picture of Timmy as a child who had considerable communication difficulties, lacked the skills needed to relate effectively with other children, and exhibited a significant number of maladaptive behaviors, including impulsivity, defiance, stubborness, teasing, and bullying.

When Timmy's teacher was interviewed, he identified several problems of a mild to moderate level of severity: poor attention, impulsivity, noncompliance to classroom rules, social isolation, and general failure to achieve in the classroom. No systematic attempts had been made to modify these behaviors at school. The teacher attributed Timmy's problems to an unstable home environment.

An extensive psychoeducational assessment was completed, providing an opportunity for an informal interview/behavioral observation of Timmy. Timmy's attention span was short and it was necessary to extend the assessment over two sessions. He listened to the directions and appeared to try hard. Initially, his articulation problems made him difficult to understand. On a number of occasions, Timmy was asked to repeat answers; typically, he did this with few overt signs of frustration. Timmy's frequent eye contact with the examiner and his frequent smiles suggested that he was more intent on gaining the examiner's approval than on succeeding on the tasks prescribed. Timmy's problem-solving style was somewhat impulsive; he did not appear to utilize self-control strategies to accomplish the tasks. He made errors frequently, often due to his responding without thinking or evaluating all of the alternatives.

On the K-ABC (Kaufman & Kaufman, 1983), Timmy earned a standard score of 64 +/− 9 in sequential processing and of 66 +/− 10 in simultaneous processing. Timmy's intellectual functioning was best summarized by his Mental Processing Composite of 65 +/− 8. In addition, he attained an achievement standard score of 59 +/− 7. On the Peabody Picture Vocabulary Test-Revised (Dunn & Dunn, 1981), Timmy achieved an age equivalent score of 4–0, indicating an extremely low to moderately low performance in receptive vocabulary. Timmy's score on the Developmental Test of Visual Motor Integration (Beery & Buktenica, 1967) also indicated below-average performance in visual-motor integration and fine motor skills. The results of the latter two tests were consistent with the overall findings of the K-ABC. Thus, psychoeducational assessment found Timmy significantly deficient in mental processing, achievement, basic language skills, and visual-motor integration and fine motor skills.

Ms. P., Ms. M., and Timmy's teacher attended a meeting at which the results of the problem identification stage were presented. After agreeing that further evaluation by a speech and language pathologist and an occupational therapist be completed and that their recommendations be implemented, the group defined three potential areas for further assessment and eventual treatment: compliance at home and school, "bullying" at home, and self-control skills at school.

It was decided that analogue assessment and naturalistic observation would be used to gather more information on target behaviors. First, the examiner observed Timmy and Ms. P. through a one-way mirror. Ms. P. was asked to interact with Timmy for 15 minutes. For the first 5 minutes, the two engaged in unstructured play. Then Ms. P. was instructed to ask Timmy (a) to play with certain toys, (b) to play by himself while she wrote a letter, and (c) to put the toys in the toy box. During this time the therapist observed and coded the mother-child interaction. Ms. P. was then given several data collection sheets and asked to record the frequency of two behaviors, noncompliance and "bullying," on 4 consecutive days. Ms. P. was asked to record when and where these behaviors occurred and to describe briefly how she had handled each incident. Ms. P. was also asked to record Todd's instances of noncompliance.

At school Timmy was observed by the examiner and two trained volunteers on 4 consecutive days in his classroom, at lunch, and with the speech therapist and the occupational therapist. This observation indicated that Timmy exhibited a range of 6 to 11 incidents of noncompliance over the 4 days. For instance, despite prompts by his teacher that he do so, on 2 of the 4 days, Timmy refused to finish his lunch. Four times he was slow to comply with his teacher's request that he join his classmates for a group activity. During speech therapy, he appeared to deliberately respond incorrectly to his therapist's questions. Only during his occupational therapy evaluation did Timmy comply in every instance. The therapist utilized positive reinforcement at a higher rate than any of the other professionals with whom Timmy was observed to interact. In his classroom, Timmy was frequently inattentive and off-task during both group instruction and during his independent work. Moreover, closer analysis of his strategies during independent work revealed that he could not say what he had been asked to do or how to do it. Timmy did not get as much attention from his teacher as did other members of his class. What attention he did receive was almost all negative. He was scolded from 3 to 7 times per day; only occasionally did he receive positive attention from his teacher (once on 3 out of 4 days). It was observed that on entry into the classroom, Timmy routinely followed the preestablished procedure of hanging up his coat, putting his lunch on the table, and placing his notebook on the teacher's desk. Though Timmy's compliance to this procedure appeared to be somewhat unusual for his classroom (three of the other four children needed to be reminded to do these things), he was not reinforced for this behavior.

During the first day of observation, one of the observers noted that Timmy infrequently interacted with his peers. Thereafter, in addition to data on classroom compliance and self-control skills, Timmy's interaction with teachers and peers was systematically observed. This observation indicated that Timmy did, in fact, interact infrequently with his peers. In the presence of other children he watched what they did but did not participate. During classroom lessons Timmy was considerably slower than his peers in responding to questions and in offering to recite. During unstructured play, Timmy spent the majority of the time by himself.

On the basis of analogue and naturalistic observations, it was clear that Timmy frequently exhibited problems with noncompliance; it appeared that his noncompliance was a function of infrequent positive reinforcement for appropriate behavior and inconsistent consequating of negative behaviors. In addition, it appeared that Timmy's inattentive and off-task behavior was a function of his not knowing what he was to do or how to do it. Finally, it became apparent that Timmy interacted less frequently with teachers and peers than his peers did.

After collaborating with Ms. P., Ms. M., and Timmy's teacher, treatment was designed to include (a) parenting training to assist Ms. P. in managing Timmy's noncompliance and "bullying" at home, (b) self-control training to assist Timmy in improving his academic achievement, and (c) social skills training to help Timmy increase his social interaction with teachers and peers in school.

Despite some initial reluctance, Ms. P. agreed to participate in a parent training program with three other parents of mentally retarded children. The program provided (a) didactic instruction about mental retardation, its nature, causes, and prognosis, (b) information about community agencies and support groups providing service to handicapped children and their families, and (c) training in behavioral techniques for child management. Initially, methods of increasing positive interaction between Timmy and Ms. P. (tracking, use of positive reinforcement contingent on desirable behavior, increased verbal interaction) were the foci of attention. Modeling, role playing, and behavior rehearsal were employed to teach these skills. Because Ms. P. had difficulty acquiring these skills, it was suggested that she observe a classroom teacher particularly skilled at verbal interaction with children. Eventually, Ms. P. interacted with children under this teacher's supervision and received feedback on her performance. Once every 4 weeks, Timmy accompanied Ms. P. to the parenting class and Ms. P. had the opportunity to use her skills with Timmy as the other parents and the trainer observed. Other weeks, she observed other parents interacting with their children and gave them feedback on their performance.

The parents took turns discussing their problems with their children, developing strategies and skills to handle the problems and developing plans to evaluate the effectiveness of the strategies. Initially, Ms. P. decided to modify Timmy's noncompliance at bedtime. The group helped Ms. P. with general skills related to achieving compliance. Specifically, she was taught to establish eye contact, speak assertively, and use unambiguous language to express her wishes. She was warned not to repeat or withdraw commands. She decided on a stable bedtime and devised an evening ritual that included one TV program, one story, and reminders that bedtime was approaching. She used verbal praise and a star chart to reinforce Timmy's compliance with the new routine and a Saturday treat to reinforce compliance 3, then 4, and, finally, 5 times per week. Within a month, Ms. P. noted a significant decrease in problems at bedtime. Ms. P. then worked on compliance with "picking up toys" with similar success.

Despite his increasing compliance, Timmy continued to bully Todd. With the help of the group, Ms. P. devised a behavioral program to deal with this problem. First, Ms. P. spent 15 minutes each day playing with Timmy and Todd. She demonstrated playing with dolls, taking turns, and sharing; she praised the boys when they used these skills. Second, whenever Timmy took a toy from Todd or hurt Todd, she explained that his behavior was unacceptable and told him to go to a "time-out" chair. Initially, Timmy resisted this procedure and on one occasion had a full-blown temper tantrum. Despite this setback, Ms. P. continued the procedure. She told Timmy that when he hurt Todd, he would have to go to the time out chair for 5 minutes and that if he did not go to the chair when told to do so, she would take him to the chair and his 5 minutes would begin only after he began to sit quietly. After about four very unpleasant incidents, Timmy learned that if he complied with the command, "Go to the chair," his punishment would be shorter. Eventually, Timmy would go to chair without complaint. Ms. P. praised Timmy for whatever appropriate behavior he demonstrated immediately after leaving the chair. Eventually, Ms. P. used the time-out procedure for other instances of misbehavior, such as "sassing" and playing with food. She began to use similar procedures with Todd.

Parent training continued for 20 sessions. Every 3 weeks, Ms. P. recorded noncompliance (of both Timmy and Todd) and bullying on data collection sheets. These data revealed a gradual decrease to an acceptable level of noncompliance and bullying at the end of 18 weeks; they also revealed decreases in noncompliance in Todd. Although no direct attempt to increase Timmy's compliance at school was made, the observers monitored his compliance in school every 3 weeks. These data indicated a significant reduction in noncompliance.

When parent training was completed, several additional individual sessions were scheduled for Ms. P. These occurred biweekly for 2 months and then on an "as needed" basis. Ms. P. decided to participate in an Allenon group (her former husband was an alcoholic) and in a vocational rehabitation program.

A cognitive-behavioral intervention modeled after those of Meichenbaum and Goodman (1971) and Kendall and Braswell (1985) was employed to help Timmy develop age-appropriate self-control skills. Initially, while playing games, Timmy was taught to ask himself a series of questions—What am I supposed to do? How do I do it? How am I doing? and How did I do?—in order to develop skill at problem definition, generating alternatives and selecting the best one, self-monitoring, and self-reinforcement and/or coping strategies. Modeling, prompting, and reinforcement were used in teaching Timmy to use the questions. Later Timmy was taught to apply these questions while completing classroom tasks and in social situations. He was encouraged to present the teacher with examples of how he had used the questions in the classroom, at recess, at lunch, and at home. He was reinforced each time he used the questions as well as for improved attention to task and academic performance. Further, Timmy was encouraged to ask the teacher and/or his mother whenever he did not know the answer to one of the questions.

A multicomponent program was introduced to improve Timmy's social interaction with teachers and peers. First, Timmy's teachers used social praise when Timmy was in a group setting (whether he actively participated or not). They did not attend to Timmy when he engaged in solitary behavior while group activities were available. Initially, Timmy was reinforced for joining a group with prompting; later, prompts were faded and reinforcement was contingent on his joining a group without prompting. Second, Timmy was given a token whenever he answered a question or demonstrated a skill within a group setting when prompted to do so. Eventually, prompting was faded and reinforcement was contingent on his participation without prompting. Tokens could be exchanged for small prizes or extra time in the gym. Finally, Timmy was reinforced (e.g., social praise, placing his name on the "Excellent Students" list) for initiating classroom activities or games.

To further improve Timmy's social skills with peers, he was paired with a socially skilled peer for a 10 week program of social skills training. The two boys role-played social skills in a game context. Initially, Timmy and his peer played games together with a trainer who provided prompts and reinforcement for socially skilled behavior (e.g., taking turns, sharing, taking a chance when not sure). Then the boys engaged in problem solving around hypothetical situations (e.g., "There's a new boy at school. What can you do to help him be happy?"). Eventually, each boy took a turn picking a card that required a role-play of a frequently occurring social situation (e.g., "Pretend it's recess time and ask a friend to play catch," or "You like Johnny very much. Without talking, show Johnny that you like him.")

As noted above, observers continued to monitor Timmy's classroom behavior every 3 weeks throughout treatment. Besides a decrease in noncompliant behavior to a level similar to that of his classmates and improved attention to his independent work, Timmy evidenced a significant increase in interaction with teachers. Timmy participated in group activities frequently. At the end of training, although Timmy's interaction with peers had increased and become more skillful, it was still less frequent and somewhat less skilled than that of his peers. Ms. P., Ms. M., and Timmy's teacher decided to continue to monitor the frequency and quality of his interactions with peers. They hypothesized that with continued speech and occupational therapy, opportunities for group interaction, and prompting and reinforcement of peer interactions, his skills would continue to improve.

Eight months after formal treatment ended, Timmy began first grade in a local public school. Although he continued to need special services for his speech difficulties, Timmy was able to meet the academic and social demands of a mainstreamed classroom. Ms. P. reported occasional problems with noncompliance and bullying. However, she did not regard these as more frequent or more intense than same-aged peers. Timmy's first-grade teacher reported no significant social or behavioral problems, and this was verified by classroom observation. Finally, although he still needed special services in reading and math, Timmy's attention and self-control skills resembled those of his peers.

SUMMARY

Behavior therapy programs for mentally retarded children and adolescents have expanded at a phenomenal rate within the last few decades. This expansion is seen in the dramatic increases in empirical research in this area (see Whitman, Scibak, & Reid, 1983), the emergence of new journals devoted either exclusively or in large part to presenting this research (e.g., *Analysis and Intervention in Development Disabilities*, *Applied Research in Mental Retardation*), and the publication of numerous texts devoted to describing and evaluating behavioral approaches to educating mentally retarded children (see Matson & McCartney's *Handbook of Behavior Modification with the Mentally Retarded*, 1981). Whereas early programs concentrated on treatment of severely and profoundly retarded children, programs for mildly and moderately retarded children have increasingly become available.

In this chapter, assessment of mentally retarded children and adolescents was conceptualized as paralleling that of similarly aged intellectually average children. We presented and illustrated the use of multiple methods and informants in multiple situations to assess children's covert and overt behaviors. Assessment was viewed as encompassing three stages: problem identification, problem analysis and treatment design, and treatment evaluation, with specific methods of assessment uniquely suited to each of these stages.

In addition, the range of behavioral procedures employed in treating mentally retarded children and adolescents was described and research evaluating treatment programs aimed at improving retarded children's self-help, social, and academic skills and at decreasing self-stimulatory and self-injurious behaviors was reviewed. Further, arguments and the research supporting involvement of parents and paraprofessional staff in treatment design, implementation, and evaluation were discussed. Finally, a case study illustrating how behavioral clinicians employ behavioral strategies in assessment and treatment was presented. Although the behavioral approach currently offers no miracle cure for mental retardation, there is increasing optimism concerning the usefulenss of this approach for more effectively treating this disorder.

REFERENCES

Aeschleman, S. R., & Schladenhauffen, J. (1984). Acquisition, generalization and maintenance of grocery shopping skills by severely mentally retarded adolescents. *Applied Research in Mental Retardation, 5,* 245–258.

Altman, K. & Mira, M. (1983). Training parents of developmentally delayed children. In J. Matson & F. Andrasik (Eds.). *Treatment issues and innovations in mental retardation.* New York: Plenum.

Altman, K., Haavik, S., & Cook, J. W. (1978). Punishment of self-injurious behaviour in natural settings using contingent aromatic amonia. *Behaviour Research and Therapy, 16,* 85–96.

Anderson-Inman, L., Paine, S. C., & Deutchman, L. (1984). Neatness counts: Effects of direct instruction and self-monitoring on the transfer of neat-paper skills to nontraining settings. *Analysis and Intervention in Developmental Disabilities, 4,* 137–155.

Arrington, F. (1943). Time sampling in studies of social behavior: A critical review of techniques and results with research suggestions. *Psychological Bulletin, 40,* 81–124.

Azrin, N. H., & Armstrong, P. M. (1973). The "mini-meal": A method for teaching eating skills to the profoundly retarded. *Mental Retardation, 11,* 9–13.

Azrin, N. H., Bugle, C., & O'Brien, F. (1971). Behavioral engineering: Two apparatuses for toilet training retarded children. *Journal of Applied Behavior Analysis, 4,* 249–253.

Azrin, N. H., & Foxx, R. (1971). A rapid method of toilet training the institutionalized retarded. *Journal of Applied Behavior Analysis, 4,* 89–99.

Azrin, N. H., Sneed, J. J., & Foxx, R. M. (1973). Dry bed: A rapid method eliminating bed-wetting (enuresis) of the retarded. *Behaviour Research and Therapy, 11,* 427–434.

Baer, M., Fowler, S. A., & Carden-Smith, L. (1984). Using reinforcement and independent-grading to promote and maintain task accuracy in a mainstreamed class. Analysis and Intervention in Developmental Disabilities, 4, 157–169.

Baer, D. M., & Guess, D. (1973). Teaching productive noun suffixes to severely retarded children. *American Journal of Mental Deficiency, 77,* 498–505.

Bailey, S. L., Pokrzywinski, J., & Bryant, L. E. (1983). Using water mist to reduce self-injurious and stereotypic behavior. *Applied Research in Mental Retardation, 4,* 229–241.

Bandura, A. (1969). *Principles of behavior modification.* New York: Holt, Rinehart & Winston.

Barkley, R. A. (1981). Hyperactivity. In E. J. Mash & L. G. Terdal (Eds.), *Behavioral assessment of childhood disorders.* New York: Guilford.

Barrett, R. P., & Breuning, S. E. (1983). Assessing intelligence. In J. L. Matson & S. E. Breuning (Eds.), *Assessing the mentally retarded.* New York: Grune & Stratton.

Bates, P. E., & Hanson, H. B. (1983). Behavioral assessment. In J. L. Matson &

S. E. Breuning (Eds.), *Assessing the mentally retarded*. New York: Grune & Stratton.

Baumeister, A., & Klosowski, R. (1965). An attempt to group toilet train severely retarded patients. *Mental Retardation, 3*, 24–26.

Beck, S. (1983). Overview of methods. In J. L. Matson & S. E. Breuning (Eds.), *Assessing the mentally retarded*. New York: Grune & Stratton.

Beery, K. E., & Buktenica, N. A. (1967). *Developmental test of visual-motor integration*. Chicago: Follett.

Berkowitz, B. & Graziano, A. (1972). Training parents as behavior therapists: A review. *Behavior Research and Therapy, 10*, 297–317.

Berkson, G. (1983). Repetitive stereotyped behaviors. *American Journal of Mental Deficiency, 8*, 239–246.

Bijou, S. W. (1966). A functional analysis of retarded development. In N. R. Ellis (Ed.), *Research in mental retardation*. New York: Academic.

Bonta, J., & Walters, R. G. (1983). Use of manual signs by developmentally disordered speech-deficient children in delayed auditory-to-picture matching-to-sample. *Analysis and Intervention in Developmental Disabilities, 3*, 295–309.

Borkowski, J. G., & Cavanaugh, J. (1979). Maintenance and generalization of skills and strategies by the retarded. In N. Ellis (Ed.), *Handbook of mental deficiency: Psychological theory and research* (2nd ed.) Hillsdale, NJ: Erlbaum.

Bornstein, P. H., & Quevillon, R. P. (1976). The effects of a self-instructional package on overactive preschool boys. *Journal of Applied Behavior Analysis, 9*, 179–188.

Bray, N. W., Biasini, F. J., & Thrasher, K. A. (1983). The effect of communicative demands on request-making in the moderately and severely mentally retarded. *Applied Research in Mental Retardation, 4*, 13–27.

Brown, A., & French, L. (1979). The zone of potential development: Implications for intelligence testing in the year 2000. *Intelligence, 3*, 253–271.

Bucher, B. (1983). Effects of sign-language training on untrained sign use for single and multiple signing. *Analysis and Intervention in Developmental Disabilities, 3*, 261–277.

Burgio, L. W., Whitman, T., & Johnson, M. R. (1980). A self-instructional package for increasing attending behavior in educably mentally retarded children. *Journal of Applied Behavior Analysis, 13*, 433–459.

Christophersen, E. R., & Sykes, B. W. (1979). An intensive, home-based family training program for developmentally delayed children. In L. A. Hammerlynck, (Ed.), *Behavioral systems for the developmentally disabled: Vol. I. School and family environments*. New York: Brunner/Mazel.

Ciminero, A. R., & Drabman, R. A. (1977). Current developments in the behavioral assessment of children. In B. B. Lahey & A. E. Kazdin (Eds.), *Advances in clinical child psychology* (Vol. 1). New York: Plenum.

Colwell, C. N., Richards, E., McCarver, R. B., & Ellis, N. R. (1973). Evaluation of self-help habit training of the profoundly retarded. *Mental Retardation, 11*, 14–18.

Cone, J. D. (1977). The relevance of reliability for behavioral assessment. *Behavior Therapy, 8*, 411–426.

Cook, J. W., Altman, K., Shaw, J., & Blaylock, M. (1978). Case histories and shorter communications: Use of contingent lemon juice to eliminate public masturbation by a severely retarded boy. *Behaviour Research and Therapy, 16,* 131–134.

Corte, H. E., Wolf, M. M., & Locke, B. J. (1971). A comparison of procedures for eliminating self-injurious behavior of retarded adolescents. *Journal of Applied Behavior Analysis, 4,* 201–213.

Cuvo, A. J., Veitch, V. C., Trace, M. W., & Konke, J. L. (1978). Teaching change computation to the mentally retarded. *Behavior Modification, 2,* 531–548.

Doll, E. A. (1935). A genetic scale of social maturity. *American Journal of Orthopsychiatry, 5,* 180–188.

Doll, E. A. (1941). The essentials of an inclusive concept of mental deficiency. *American Journal of Mental Deficiency, 46,* 214–219.

Doll, E. A. (1965). *Vineland Social Maturity Scale.* Circle Pines, MN: American Guidance Service.

Dorry, G. W., & Zeaman, D. (1975). The use of a fading technique in paired-associate teaching of a reading vocabulary with retardates. *Mental Retardation, 11,* 3–6.

Duker, P. C., & Michaelsen, H. M. (1983). Cross-setting generalization of manual signs to verbal instructions with severely retarded children. *Applied Research in Mental Retardation, 4,* 29–40.

Duker, P. C., & Morsink, H. (1984). Acquisition and cross-setting generalization of manual signs with severely retarded individuals. *Journal of Applied Behavior Analysis, 17,* 93–103.

Dunn, L. M., & Dunn, S. (1981). *Peabody Picture Vocabulary Test–Revised.* Circle Pines, MN: American Guidance Service.

Dunn, L. M., & Markwardt, F. C. (1970). *Peabody Individual Achievement Test.* Circle Pines, MN: American Guidance Service.

Eason, L. J., White, M. J., & Newsom, C. (1982). Generalized reduction of self-stimulatory behavior: An effect of teaching appropriate play to autistic children. *Analysis and Intervention in Developmental Disabilities, 2,* 157–169.

Egel, A. L., Shafer, M. S., & Neef, N. A. (1984). Receptive acquisition and generalization of prepositional responding in autistic children: A comparison of two procedures. *Analysis and Intervention in Developmental Disabilities, 4,* 285–298.

Elder, P. S., & Bergman, J. S. (1978). Visual symbol communication instruction with nonverbal, multiply-handicapped individuals. *Mental Retardation, 16,* 107–112.

Ellis, N. R. (1963). Toilet training the severely defective patient. An S-R reinforcement analysis. *American Journal of Mental Deficiency, 68,* 98–103.

Evans, I. M., & Nelson, R. O. (1977). Assessment of child behavior problems. In A. R. Ciminero, K. S. Calhoun, & H. E. Adams (Eds.). *Handbook of behavioral assessment.* New York: Wiley.

Fabry, B. D., Mayhew, G. L., & Hanson, A. (1984). Incidental teaching of mentally retarded students within a token system. *American Journal of Mental Deficiency, 89,* 29–36.

Favell, J. E. (1973). Reduction of stereotypes by reinforcement of toy play. *Mental Retardation, 11,* 21–23.

Favell, J. E., McGimsey, J. F., & Schell, R. M. (1981). *Ecological analysis and intervention with four cases of self-injury*. Paper presented at the Fourteenth Annual Gatlinburg Conference on Research in Mental Retardation and Developmental Disabilities, Gatlinburg, TN.

Faw, G. D., Reid, D. H., Schepis, M. J., Fitzgerald, J. R., & Welty, P. A. (1981). Involving institutional staff in the development and maintenance of sign language skills with profoundly retarded persons. *Journal of Applied Behavior Analysis*, *14*, 411–423.

Fitzgerald, J. R., Reid, D. H., Schepis, M. M., Faw, G. D., Welty, P. A., & Pyfer, L. M. (1984). A rapid training procedure for teaching manual sign language skills to multidisciplinary institutional staff. *Applied Research in Mental Retardation*, *5*, 451–469.

Foxx, R. M. (1977). Attention training: The use of overcorrection avoidance to increase the eye contact of autistic and retarded children. *Journal of Applied Behavior Analysis*, *10*, 489–499.

Foxx, R. M., & Azrin, H. H. (1972). Restitution: A method of eliminating aggressive-disruptive behavior of mentally retarded and brain-damaged patients. *Behaviour Research and Therapy*, *10*, 15–27.

Foxx, R. M., & Azrin, H. H. (1973). *Toilet training the retarded*. Champaign, IL.: Research Press.

Frazier, J. R., & Schneider, H. (1975). Parental management of inappropriate hyperactivity in a young retarded child. *Journal of Behavior Therapy and Experimental Psychiatry*, *6*, 246–247.

Friedrich, W. N., & Freidrich, W. L. (1981). Psychological aspects of parents of handicapped and nonhandicapped children. *American Journal of Mental Deficiency*, *85*, 551–553.

Friman, P. C., Cook, J. W., & Finney, J. W. (1984). Effects of punishment procedures on the self-stimulatory behavior of an autistic child. *Analysis and Intervention in Developmental Disabilities*, *4*, 39–46.

Garcia, E. (1974). The training and generalization of a conversational speech form in nonverbal retardates. *Journal of Applied Behavior Analysis*, *7*, 137–149.

Giles, D. K., & Wolf, M. M. (1966). Toilet training institutionalized, severe retardates by application of operant behavior modification techniques. *American Journal of Mental Deficiency*, *70*, 766–780.

Grimm, J., Bijou, S., & Parsons, J. (1973). A problem-solving model for teaching remedial arithmetic to handicapped young children. *Journal of Abnormal Child Psychology*, *7*, 26–39.

Grossman, H. J. (Ed.). (1983). *Classification in mental retardation*. Washington, D.C.: American Association on Mental Deficiency.

Handleman, J. S., Powers, M. D., & Harris, S. L. (1984). Teaching of labels: An analysis of concrete and pictorial representations. *American Journal of Mental Deficiency*, *88*, 625–629.

Harris, S. L., & Romanczyk, R. G. (1976). Treating self-injurious behavior of a retarded child by overcorrection. *Behavior Therapy*, *7*, 235–239.

Hayden, A. H. (1976). A center-based parent-training model. In D. L. Lillie, P. L. Trohanis, & K. W. Goin (Eds.), *Teaching parents to teach*, New York: Walker.

Haynes, S. M. (1978). *Principles of behavioral assessment*. New York: Gardner.

Haynes, S. M., & Jensen, B. H. (1979). The interview as a behavioral assessment instrument. *Behavioral Assessment*, *1*, 97–106.

Hersen, M., & Barlow, D. H. (1976). *Single case experimental designs: Strategies for studying behavior change*. New York: Pergamon.

Horner, R. D., & Keilitz, I. (1975). Training mentally retarded adolescents to brush their teeth. *Journal of Applied Behavior Analysis*, *8*, 301–309.

Hull, C. L. (1943). *Principles of behavior*. New York: Appleton-Century-Crofts.

Jarman, P. H., Iwata, B. A., & Lorentzson, A. M. (1983). Development of morning self-care routines in multiply handicapped persons. *Applied Research in Mental Retardation*, *4*, 113–122.

Jastak, J. F., & Wilkinson, F. (1984). *The Wide-Range Achievement Test: Manual of instructions*. Wilmington, DE: Jastak Association.

Johnston, M. B., Whitman, T. L., & Johnson, M. (1980). Teaching addition and subtraction to mentally retarded children: A self-instructional program. *Journal for Applied Research in Mental Retardation*, *1*, 141–160.

Kanfer, K. H., & Grimm, L. G. (1977). Behavioral analysis: Selecting target behaviors in the interview. *Behavior Modification*, *1*, 7–28.

Kaufman, A. S. (1979). *Intelligent testing with the WISC-R*. New York: Wiley.

Kaufman, A. S., Kamphaus, R. W., & Kaufman, N. L. (1985). The Kaufman Assessment Battery for Children (K-ABC). In C. S. Newmark (Ed.), *Major psychological assessment instruments*. Newton, MA: Allyn & Bacon.

Kaufman, A. S., & Kaufman, N. L. (1983). *Kaufman Assessment Battery for Children*. Circle Pines, MN: American Guidance Service.

Kaufman, A. S., & Kaufman, N. L. (1985). *Kaufman Test of Educational Achievement*. Circle Pines, MN: American Guidance Service.

Kazdin, A. E. (1977). Assessing the clinical or applied significance of behavior change through social validation. *Behavior Modification*, *1*, 427–452.

Kazdin, A. E., & Matson, J. L. (1981). Social validation in mental retardation. *Applied Research in Mental Retardation*, *2*, 39–53.

Kazdin, A. E., & Straw, M. L. (1976). Assessment of behavior of the mentally retarded. In M. Hersen & A. S. Bellack (Eds.), *Behavioral assessment: A practical handbook*. New York: Pergamon.

Kendall, P. C. & Braswell, L. (1985). *Cognitive-behavioral therapy for impulsive children*. New York: Guilford.

Keogh, D. A., Burgio, L., Whitman, T. L., & Johnson, M. R. (1983). Development of listening skills in retarded children: A correspondence training program. *Child and Family Behavior Therapy*, *5*, 51–71.

Konarski, E. A., Crowell, C. R., & Duggan, L. M. (1981). *Application of the response deprivation hypothesis to improve the handwriting of EMR students*. Paper presented at the Fourteenth Annual Gatlinburg Conference on Research in Mental Retardation and Developmental Disabilities, Gatlinburg, TN.

Konarski, E., Johnson, M., Crowell, C., & Whitman, T. (1981). An alternative approach to reinforcement for applied researchers: Response deprivation. *Behavior Therapy, 12,* 653–666.

Kratochwill, T. R. (1982). Advances in behavioral assessment. In C. R. Reynolds & T. B. Gutkin (Eds.), *The handbook of school psychology.* New York: Wiley.

Lagomarcino, A., Reid, D. H., Ivancic, M. T., & Faw, G. D. (1984). Leisure-dance instruction for severely and profoundly retarded persons: Teaching an intermediate community-living skill. *Journal of Applied Behavior Analysis, 17,* 71–84.

LaGrow, S. J., & Repp, A. C. (1984). Stereotypic responding: A review of intervention research. *American Journal of Mental Deficiency, 88,* 595–609.

Lally, M. (1981). *Computer-assisted handwriting instruction for intellectually handicapped children.* Paper presented at the Fourteenth Annual Gatlinburg Conference on Research in Mental Retardation and Development Disabilities, Gatlinburg, TN.

Lambert, N., Windmiller, M., Cole, L., & Figuerra, R. (1981). *AAMD adaptive behavior scale: Public school version.* Monterey, CA: Publishers Test Service.

Lancioni, G. E., Smeets, P. M., Oliva, D. S. (1984). Teaching severely handicapped adolescents to follow instructions conveyed by means of three-dimensional stimulus configurations. *Applied Research in Mental Retardation, 5,* 107–123.

Laws, D. R., Brown, R. A., Epstein, J., & Hocking, N. (1971). Reduction of inappropriate social behavior in disturbed children by an untrained paraprofessional therapist. *Behavior Therapy, 2,* 519–533.

Leff, R. B. (1974). Teaching the TMR to dial the telephone. *Mental Retardation, 12,* 12–13.

Leff, R. B. (1975). Teaching TMR children and adults to dial the telephone. *Mental Retardation, 13,* 9–12.

Leifer, J. S., & Lewis, M. (1984). Acquisition of conversational response skills by young Down syndrome and nonretarded young children. *American Journal of Mental Deficiency, 88,* 610–618.

Leon, H. A., & Pepe, H. (1978). *Self-instructional training: Cognitive behavior modification as a resource strategy.* Unpublished manuscript, Illinois State University, Normal.

Linehan, M. M. (1977). Issues in behavioral interviewing. In J. D. Cone & R. P. Hawkins (Eds.), *Behavioral assessment: New directions in clinical psychology.* New York: Bruner/Mazel.

Litrownik, J. A. & Freitas, J. L. (1980). Self-monitoring in moderately retarded adolescents: Reactivity and accuracy as a function of valence. *Behavior Therapy, 11,* 245–255.

Litrownik, A. J., Freitas, J. L., & Franzini, L. (1978). Self-regulation in retarded persons: Assessment and training of self-monitoring skills. *American Journal of Mental Deficiency, 82,* 499–506.

Litrownik, A. J., & Steinfeld, B. I. (1982). Developing self-regulation in retarded children. In P. Karoly & J. J. Steffen (Eds.), *Improving children's competence: Advances in child behavioral analysis and therapy* (Vol. 1). Lexington, MA: Heath.

Litrownik, A. J., White, K., McInnis, E. T., & Licht, B. G. (1984). A process for designing self-management programs for the developmentally disabled. *Analysis and Intervention in Development Disabilities, 4*, 189–197.

Longin, N. S., Cone, J. D., & Longin, H. E. (1975). Training behavior modifiers: Parents' behavioral and attitudinal changes following general and specific training. *Mental Retardation, 13*, 42.

Lowe, M. L., & Cuvo, A. J. (1976). Teaching coin summation to the mentally retarded. *Journal of Applied Behavior Analysis, 9*, 483–489.

Mahoney, K., Van Wagener, R. K., & Meyerson, L. (1971). Toilet training of normal and retarded children *Journal of Applied Behavior Analysis, 4*, 173–181.

Mahoney, M. J. & Arnkoff, D. C. (1978). Cognitive and self-control therapies. In S. L. Garfield & A. E. Bergin (Eds.). *Handbook of psychotherapy and behavior change: An empirical analysis* (2nd ed). New York: Wiley.

Marchant, J., & Wehman, P. (1979). Teaching table games to severely retarded children. *Mental Retardation, 17*, 150–152.

Martin, G. L., McDonald, S., & Omichinski, M. (1971). An operant analysis of response interactions during meals with severely retarded girls. *American Journal of Mental Deficiency, 76*, 68–75.

Mash, E. J., & Terdal, L. G. (1973). Modification of mother-child interactions: Playing with children. *Mental Retardation, 11*, 44–49.

Mash, E. J., & Terdal, L. G. (Eds.). (1981). *Behavioral assessment of childhood disorders.* New York: Guilford

Matson, J. L., & Barrett, R. P. (Eds.), (1982). *Psychopathology in the mentally retarded.* New York: Grune & Stratton.

Matson, J. L., & Frame, C. (1983). Psychopathology. In J. L. Matson & S. E. Bruning (Eds). *Assessing the mentally retarded.* New York: Grune & Stratton.

Matson, J. L., Kazdin, A. E., & Esveldt-Dawson, K. (1980). Training interpersonal skills among mentally retarded and socially dysfunctional children. *Behavior Research and Therapy, 18*, 419–427.

Matson, J. L., & McCartney, J. R. (1981). Handbook of behavior modification with the mentally retarded. New York: Plenum.

Matson, J. L., Ollendick, T. A., & Adkins, J. (1980). A comprehensive dining program for mentally retarded adults. *Behavior Research and Therapy, 18*, 107–112.

Mayhew, G. L., & Harris, F. C. (1978). Some negative side effects of a punishment procedure for stereotyped behavior. *Journal of Behavior Therapy and Experimental Psychiatry, 9*, 245–251.

McFall, R. M. (1977). Analogue methods in behavioral assessment: Issues and prospects. In J. D. Cone & R. P. Hawkins (Eds.), *Behavioral assessment: New directions in clinical psychology.* New York: Brunner/Mazel.

McGee, G. G., Krantz, P. J., & McClannahan, L. E. S. (1985). The facilitative effects of incidental teaching on preposition use by autistic children. *Journal of Applied Behavior Analysis, 18*, 17–31.

McIlvane, W. J., Bass, R. W., O'Brien, J. M., Gerovac, B. J., & Stoddard, L. T. (1984). Spoken and signed naming of foods after receptive exclusion training in severe retardation. *Applied Research in Mental Retardation, 5*, 1–27.

Meichenbaum, D., & Goodman, J. (1971). Training impulsive children to talk to themselves: A means of self-control. *Journal of Abnormal Psychology, 77*, 115–126.

Mercer, J. R., & Lewis, J. F. (1977). *System of Multicultural Pluralistic Assessment: SOMPA*. New York: Psychological Corporation.

Meredith, R., Saxon, S., Doleys, D. M., & Kyzer, B. (1980). Social skills training with mildly retarded young adults. *Journal of Clinical Psychology. 36*, 1000–1009.

Meyers, C. E., Nihira, K., & Zetlin, A. (1979). The measurement of adaptive behavior. In N. R. Ellis (Eds.), *Handbook of mental deficiency: Psychological theory and research* (2nd ed.). Hillside, NJ: Erlbaum.

Miller, N. E., & Dollard, J. (1941). *Social learning and imitation*. New Haven: Yale University Press.

Miller, H. R., Patton, M. E., & Henton, K. R. (1971). Behavior modification in a profoundly retarded child: A case report. *Behavior Therapy, 2*, 375–385.

Morrow, H. W., & Coulter, W. A. (1978). A survey of state policies regarding adaptive behavior. In W. A. Coulter & H. W. Morrow (Eds.), *Adaptive behavior: Concepts and measurement*. New York: Grune & Stratton.

Mulick, J. A., Hoyt, P., Rojahn, J., & Schroeder, S. R. (1978). Reduction of a "nervous habit" in a profoundly retarded youth by increasing toy play. *Journal of Behavior Therapy and Experimental Psychiatry, 9*, 381–385.

Murphy, R. J., Nunes, D. L., & Hutchings-Ruprecht, M. (1977). Reduction of stereotyped behavior in profoundly retarded individuals. *American Journal of Mental Deficiency, 82*, 238–245.

Neef, N. A., Walters, J., & Egel, A. L. (1984). Establishing generative yes/no responses in developmentally disabled children. *Journal of Applied Behavior Analysis, 17*, 453–460.

Nelson, R. O., & Hayes, S. C. (1979). Some current dimensions of behavioral assessment. *Behavioral Assessment, 1*, 1–16.

Nihira, K., Foster, R., Shellhaas, N., & Leland, H. (1974). *AAMD Adaptive Behavior Scale, manual*. Washington, D.C.: American Association on Mental Deficiency.

O'Brien, F. (1981). Treating self-stimulatory behavior. In J. Matson & J. McCartney (Eds.), *Handbook of behavior modification with the mentally retarded*. New York: Plenum.

Odom, S. L., Hoyson, M., Jamieson, B., & Strain, P. S. (1985). Increasing handicapped preschoolers' peer social interactions: Cross-setting and component analysis. *Journal of Applied Behavior Analysis, 18*, 3–16.

Ora, J. P., & Reisinger, J. J. (1971). *Preschool intervention: A behavior service delivery system*. Paper presented at the meeting of the American Psychological Association, Washington, DC.

Paloritzian, R., Haspazi, J., Streifel, J., & Edgar, C. (1971). Promotion of positive social interaction in severely retarded young children. *American Journal of Mental Deficiency, 75*, 519–524.

Passman, P. H. (1975). An automatic device for toilet-training. *Behavior Research and Therapy, 13*, 215–220.

Poling, A. D., & Parker, C. (1983). Empirical strategies. In J. L. Matson & S. E. Bruening (Eds.), *Assessing the mentally retarded*. New York: Grune & Stratton.

Premack, D. (1959). Toward empirical behavior laws: Positive reinforcement. *Psychological Review, 66*, 219–233.

Reid, D., & Whitman, T. (1983). Behavioral staff management in institutions: A critical review of effectiveness and acceptability.

Repp, A., & Buille, A. (1981). Reducing aggressive behavior. In J. Matson & J. McCartney (Eds.), *Handbook of behavior modificaton with the mentally retarded.* New York: Plenum.

Repp, A. C., Deitz, S. M., & Deitz, D. E. D. (1976). Reducing inappropriate behavior in classrooms and in individual sessions through DRO schedules of reinforcement. *Mental Retardation, 14*, 11–15.

Reschley, D. J. (1982). Assessing mild mental retardation: The influence of adaptive behavior, sociocultural status, and prospects for nonbiased assessment. In C. R. Reynolds & T. B. Gutkin (Eds.), *The handbook of school psychology.* New York: Wiley.

Richman, J. S., Sonderby, T., & Kahn, J. (1980). Prerequisite vs. in vivo acquisition of self-feeding skill. *Behavior Research and Therapy, 18*, 327–332.

Rincover, A. (1975). Sensory extinction: A procedure for eliminating self-stimulatory behavior in psychotic children. *Journal of Applied Behavior Analysis, 8*, 235–246.

Rincover, A., Cook, R., Peoples, A., & Packard, D. (1979). Sensory extinction and sensory reinforcement principles for programming multiple adaptive behavior change. *Journal of Applied Behavior Analysis, 12*, 221–233.

Riordan, M. M., Iwata, B. A., Finney, J. W., Wohl, M. K., & Stanley, A. E. (1984). Behavioral assessment and treatment of chronic food refusal in handicapped children. *Journal of Applied Behavior Analysis, 17*, 327–341.

Risley, T. R., & Cuvo, A. (1980). Training mentally retarded adults to make emergency telephone calls. *Behavior Modification, 4*, 513–526.

Robinson, N. M., & Robinson, H. G. (1976). *The mentally retarded child.* New York: McGraw-Hill.

Ross, A. O. (1980). *Psychological disorders of children: A behavioral approach to theory, research and therapy.* New York: McGraw-Hill.

Ross, D. M., & Ross, S. A. (1973). Cognitive training for the EMR child: Situational problem solving and planning. *American Journal of Mental Deficiency, 78,* 20–26.

Sailor, W. S. (1971). Reinforcement and generalization of productive plural allomorphs in two retarded children. *Journal of Applied Behavior Analysis, 4*, 305–310.

Schalock, R. L., Gadwood, L. S., & Perry, P. B. (1984). Effects of different training environments on the acquisition of community living skills. *Applied Research in Mental Retardation, 5*, 425–438.

Schepis, M. M., Reid, D. H., Fitzgerald, J. R., Faw, G. D., van den Pol, R. A., & Welty, P. A. S. (1982). An incidental teaching program for increasing manual signing by autistic and profoundly retarded youth. *Journal of Applied Behavior Analysis, 15*, 363–379.

Schroeder, S., Schroeder, C., Rojahn, J., & Mulick, J. (1981). Self-injurious behavior: An analysis of behavior management techniques. In J. Matson & J. McCartney

(Eds.), *Handbook of behavior modification with the mentally retarded*. New York: Plenum.

Schumaker, J., & Sherman, J. A. (1970). Training generative verb usage by imitation and reinforcement procedures. *Journal of Applied Behavior Analysis, 3*, 273-287.

Shafer, M. A., Egel, A. L., & Neef, N. A. (1984). Training mildly handicapped peers to facilitate changes in the social interaction skills of autistic children. *Journal of Applied Behavior Analysis, 17*, 461-476.

Shapiro, E. S., & Barrett, R. P. (1983). Behavioral assessment of the mentally retarded. In J. L. Matson & F. Andraskik (Eds.), *Treatment issues and innovations in mental retardation*. New York: Plenum.

Shapiro, E. S., Browder, D. M., & D'Huyvetters, K. K. (1984). Increasing academic productivity of severely multi-handicapped children with self-management: Idiosyncratic effects. *Analysis and Intervention in Developmental Disabilities, 4*, 171-188.

Sigelman, C. K., Budd, E. C., Spanhel, C. L., & Schroenrock, C. J. (1981). When in doubt, say yes: Acquiescence in interviews with mentally retarded persons. *Mental Retardation, 2*, 53-58.

Sigelman, C. K., Schroenrock, C. J., Spanhel, C. L., Thomas, S. G., Winer, J. L., Budd, E. C., & Martin, P. W. (1981). Surveying mentally retarded persons: Responsiveness and response validity in three samples. *American Journal of Mental Deficiency, 84*, 479-486.

Smeets, P. M., Lancioni, G. E., & Van Lieshout, R. W., (1985). Teaching mentally retarded children to use an experimental device for telling time and meeting appointments. *Applied Research in Mental Retardation, 65*, 51-70.

Song, A. Y. (1979). Acquisition and use of Bliss symbols by severely mentally retarded adolescents. *Mental Retardation, 17*, 253-255.

Sparrow, S., Balla, D. A., & Cicchetti, D. V. (1984). *Vineland Adaptive Behavior Scales*. Circle Pines, MN: American Guidance Service.

Stimbert, V. E., Minor, J. W., & McCoy, J. F. (1977). Intensive feeding training with retarded children. *Behavior Modification, 1*, 517-529.

Stokes, T., & Baer, D. (1977). An implicit technology of generalization. *Journal of Applied Behavior Analysis, 10*, 394-367.

Strain, P. S. (1983). Generalization of autistic children's social behavior change: Effects of developmentally integrated and segregated settings. *Analysis and Intervention in Developmental Disabilities, 3*, 23-34.

Stremel, K. (1972). Language training: A program for retarded children. *Mental Retardation, 10*, 47-49.

Striefel, S., Bryan, K. S., & Atkins, D. A. (1974). Transfer of stimulus control from motor to verbal stimuli. *Journal of Applied Behavior Analysis, 7*, 123-135.

Striefel, S., & Wetherby, B. (1973). Instruction following behavior of a retarded child and its controlling sitmuli. *Journal of Applied Behavior Analysis, 6*, 663-670.

Striefel, S., Wetherby, B., & Karlan, G. R. (1976). Establishing generalized verb-noun instruction following skills in retarded children. *Journal of Experimental Child Psychology, 22*, 247-260.

Sulzer-Azaroff, B., & Mayer, G. R. (1977). *Applying behavior analysis procedures with children and youth*. New York: Holt, Rinehart & Winston.

Terdal, L., & Buell, J. (1969). Parent education in managing retarded children with behavior deficits and inappropriate behaviors. *Mental Retardation, 7*, 10–13.

Terman, L. M., & Merrill, M. A. (1973). *The Stanford-Binet intelligence scale* (3rd ed.). Boston: Houghton Mifflin.

Trace, M. W., Cuvo, A. J., & Criswell, J. L. (1977). Teaching coin equivalance to the mentally retarded. *Journal of Applied Behavior Analysis, 10*, 85–92.

Twardosz, S., & Baer, D. M. (1973). Training two severely retarded adolescents to ask questions. *Journal of Applied Behavior Analysis, 6*, 655–661.

Twardosz, S., Nordquist, V. M., Simon, R., & Botkin, D. (1983). The effect of group affection activities on the interaction of social isolate children. *Analysis and Intervention in Developmental Disabilities, 3*, 311–338.

Tymchuk, A. J. (1983). Interventions with parents of the mentally retarded. In J. L. Matson & J. A. Mulick (Eds.), *Handbook of mental retardation*, New York: Pergamon.

Van Wagenen, R. K., & Murdock, E. E. (1966). A transistorized signal-package for toilet-training of infants. *Journal of Experimental Child Psychiatry, 3*, 312–314.

Van Wagenen, R. K., Meyerson, L., Kerr, N. J., & Mahoney, K. (1969). Field trials of a new procedure for toilet training. *Journal of Experimental Child Psychiatry, 8*, 147–159.

Voeltz, L., & Evans, I. (1982). The assessment of behavioral interrelationships in child behavior therapy. *Behavioral Assessment, 4*, 131–165.

Wacker, D. P. & Berg, W. K. (1984). Use of peer instruction to train a complex photocopying task to moderately and severely retarded adolescents. *Analysis and Intervention in Developmental Disabilities, 4*, 219–234.

Wallander, J. L., Hubert, N. C., & Schroeder, C. S. (1983). Self-care skills. In J. L. Matson & S. E. Breuning (Eds.), Assessing the mentally retarded. New York: Grune & Stratton.

Watson, L. S., & Bassinger, J. F. (1974). Parent training technology: A potential service delivery system. *Mental Retardation, 12*, 3–10.

Wechsler, D. (1967). *Manual for the Wechsler Preschool and Primary Scale of Intelligence*. New York: Psychological Corporation.

Wechsler, D. (1974). *The Wechsler Intelligence Scale for Children–Revised*. New York: Psychological Corporation.

Whang, P. L., Fawcett, S. B., & Mathews, R. M. (1984). Teaching job-related social skills to learning disabled adolescents. *Analysis and Intervention in Developmental Disabilities, 4*, 29–38.

Whitman, T. L., & Johnston, M. B. (1983). Teaching addition and subtraction with regrouping to educable mentally retarded children: A group self-instructional program. *Behavior Therapy, 14*, 127–143.

Whitman, T. L., Burgio, L., & Johnston, M. B. (1984). Cognitive-behavioral interventions with mentally retarded children. In A. W. Meyers & W. E. Craighead, *Cognitive behavior therapy with children*. New York: Plenum.

Whitman, T. L., Burish, T., & Collins, L. (1972). Development of interpersonal language in two moderately retarded children. *Mental Retardation, 10,* 41–45.

Whitman, T. L., Mercurio, J. R., & Caponigri, V. (1970). Development of social responses in two severely retarded children. *Journal of Applied Behavior Analysis, 3,* 133–138.

Whitman, T. L., Scibak, J., & Reid, D. H. (1983). *Behavior modification with the severely and profoundly retarded: Treatment and research*. New York: Academic.

Whitman, T. L., Scibak, J., Butler, K., Richter, O., & Johnson, M. (1982). Improving classroom behavior in mentally retarded children through correspondence training. *Journal of Applied Behavior Analysis, 15,* 545–564.

Whitman, T. L., Zakaras, M., & Chardos, S. (1971). Effects of reinforcement and guidance procedures on instruction following behavior of severely retarded children. *Journal of Applied Behavior Analysis, 4,* 283–290.

Willems, E. P. (1974). Behavioral technology and behavior ecology. *Journal of Applied Behavior Analysis, 7,* 151–165.

Wilson, P. G., Reid, D. H., Phillips, J. F., & Burgio, L. D. (1984). Normalization of institutional mealtimes for profoundly retarded persons: Effects and noneffects of teaching family-style dining. *Journal of Applied Behavior Analysis, 17,* 189–201.

Woodcock, R. W., & Johnson, M. B. (1978). *Woodcock-Johnson Psycho-Educational Battery*. D.L.M. Teaching Resources, Allen, TX.

Wunderlich, R. A. (1972). Programmed instruction: Teaching coinage to retarded children. *Mental Retardation, 10,* 21–23.

Zigler, E. (1967). Familial mental retardation: A continuing dilemma. *Science, 155,* 292–298.

CHAPTER 8

Autism

SANDRA L. HARRIS AND JAN S. HANDLEMAN

Autism is a rare disorder, occurring at a rate of only 2 to 4 per 10,000 people (American Psychiatric Association, 1980). It is a pervasive, severely handicapping condition that begins in the child's earliest months and typically lasts a lifetime. The unmanageable and often bewildering behaviors of the autistic child can create a chaotic family environment; identification and assessment are thus essential not only for the proper care of the child but also for the welfare of the entire family. In the pages that follow we will address problems of differential diagnosis, behavioral assessment, treatment, and current research. A case description will summarize many of the issues covered in the chapter.

DIFFERENTIAL DIAGNOSIS

Two major, overlapping diagnostic schema for the identification of autism are in common use at this time: that of the third edition of the *Diagnostic and Statistical Manual of Mental Disorders (DSM-III*; American Psychiatric Association, 1980), and that of the National Society for Children and Adults with Autism (NSAC; 1978).

According to *DSM-III* (American Psychiatric Association, 1980), the essential criteria for the diagnosis of infantile autism are (a) onset of symptoms before 30 months of age; (b) a pervasive lack of response to other people; (c) gross deficits in the development of language; (d) in children who do speak peculiar language, with oddities such as echolalia and reversal of pronouns; and (e) bizarre responses to the environment, such as resistance to change or a fascination with animate or inanimate objects. These symptoms must be found in the absence of indications of thought disorder such as hallucinations or delusions.

The NSAC (National Society for Autistic Children, 1978) definition of autism emphasizes (a) onset before 30 months of age; (b) disturbances in the developmental rate or sequence, such as normal development in some areas and delay in others; (c) abnormal responses to sensory stimuli; (d) disturbances in the development of speech, language, and cognitive skills; and (e) abnormalities in relationships to people, events, and objects.

Schopler and Sloan (1983) indicate that the NSAC definition encompasses a larger group of children than that of *DSM-III*, since the NSAC drafters were attempting not only to clarify the identification of autism, but also to increase the availability of appropriate resources for children with autistic behaviors. Thus, while the narrower DSM-III definition may have more value for some research and for greater precision in communication, the broader NSAC definition may be more useful in providing help for many children whose behavior resembles those of the child with infantile autism.

In distinguishing autism from other disorders with overlapping symptoms, one must be sensitive to several issues. One is that as the autistic child grows older, the intensity of the symptoms may be dampened; thus, greater expertise and a more careful developmental history is needed to recognize the presence of the disorder. DeMyer (1979) notes that the early onset of symptoms in autism is insidious, occurring from late in the first year through the second, tending to grow worse in the preschool years, then improving at about 4 years of age. It must be emphasized that "improvement" is relative, and that a decrease in severity nonetheless leaves these youngsters pervasively handicapped, often mute, self-stimulating, terrified of change, and profoundly withdrawn from others.

Ornitz, Guthrie, and Farley (1977) report that many young autistic children are thought to be mentally retarded or neurologically impaired before they are identified as autistic. These authors indicate that in half the cases they studied, parents were concerned about their child's development by the time he or she was 14 months old, yet the median age for correct diagnosis was 46 months. In light of the importance of early intervention, such delays are unfortunate.

Childhood-onset pervasive development disorder, a condition that might be confused with autism, differs significantly in that the onset of symptoms is after 30 months but before 12 years (American Psychiatric Association, 1980). Although this distinction may sound clear-cut, it is often difficult, when relying on retrospective report, to determine when a child's symptoms began. The diagnostic distinction is probably less important for treatment purposes than for some research.

Infantile autism must also be distinguished from schizophrenia in childhood. In childhood schizophrenia the onset of symptoms is typically later than in autism and over time will come to include clear indications of thought disorder, such as hallucinations and delusions (Eggers, 1978).

The majority of autistic children test in the mentally retarded range on standardized measures of intelligence. According to *DSM-III* (American Psychiatric Association, 1980), 40% of children with infantile autism have IQs below

50 and only 30% have IQs of 70 or better. Hence, one must take care to distinguish mental retardation from infantile autism.

Although some mentally retarded children will exhibit autistic behaviors, including social withdrawal and severe language deficits, it is usually possible to discriminate the retarded youngster from the autistic since mentally retarded children do not typically show the full syndrome of autism. Ando and Yoshimura (1979) note that the autistic child's social withdrawal changes relatively little with time, whereas the retarded child becomes less withdrawn through intervention or the passage of time. Likewise, language in autistic children is likely to be impaired to a greater degree than one would expect on the basis of IQ, whereas there is usually a closer link between IQ and language in retarded children (e.g., Spreat, Roszkowski, Isett, & Alderfer, 1980).

BEHAVIORAL ASSESSMENT

Vital as the process of accurate diagnosis may be in the treatment of an autistic child, a thorough on-going behavioral assessment is nonetheless of far greater importance for generating a detailed treatment plan. The label of infantile autism carries with it few if any specific implications for treatment, and we must therefore examine in detail the symptoms of autism as they are manifested in the child to be treated.

As Newsom and Rincover (1981) note, behavioral assessment is a vital component of the decision-making process in placement and intervention for children with autism. However, some of the questions posed for a placement decision are different from those for intervention. For example, in deciding whether a child should remain at home or be placed in a residential setting, enter one of several classrooms, or be assigned to different living arrangements such as a foster home, group home, or residential school, we need to consider his or her current level of functioning, specific managment problems posed, and the nature of the resources available in each setting. Placement decisions call for an evaluation of the child's disruptive behaviors; special physical needs posed by handicaps, such as visual or auditory impairment; communication skills, age, and size. In addition, we would want to evaluate the skills and expertise of the placement's staff in providing special care for unusual problems such as self-injury or aggression, and the availability of specialized training programs such as prevocational or vocational workshops.

In conducting a behavioral assessment prior to intervention with a specific target behavior, we define precisely the behavioral excesses and deficits shown by the child. This requires a detailed behavioral definition of the target activity, the conditions under which the target behavior occurs, the priority ranking of this behavior for intervention, and an assessment of the resources available to facilitate the intervention.

Fortunately, a significant body of research addresses the assessment of many of the most frequent or troublesome behaviors of the child with autism, including self-injury (Carr, 1977), language deficits (Harris, 1975; Lovaas, 1977, 1981), aggressive behavior (Favell, 1983), self-help skills (Lovaas, 1981), and educational needs (Koegel, Rincover, & Egel, 1982). A general summary of behavioral assessment for the severely developmentally disabled has been provided by Powers and Handelman (1984). We will therefore focus on one major area of assessment to give a general sense of how these problems are approached.

Language Deficits

Language assessment begins with an evaluation of the skills and deficits of the individual child. It incorporates procedures that speech and hearing specialists, psychologists, and educators have used over the years. We ask basic questions, such as, what is the child's language level in relation to his or her intellectual performance? Typically in autism, the area of speech and language is significantly more impaired than other areas of cognitive functioning. We also wish to determine whether the child's hearing is adequate to acquire speech without special amplification (Handleman, Arnold, Veniar, Kristoff, & Harris, 1982).

Once we have assessed the child's general level of language functioning, we look in detail at precisely what kinds of vocalizations are present, under what conditions, and with what apparent intent on the part of the child. Does this child make any sounds? Will he or she imitate sounds or words on request? Is echolalia present? Does the child use gestures to communicate? What is the present level of receptive language functioning? Will the child follow simple commands? Identify objects? Solve complex problems? The child's nonverbal imitation skills are also evaluated, since if a child is unable to imitate nonverbal behaviors or control the movements of his or her mouth, speech may be a remote goal.

The research of Howlin and her colleagues (e.g., Howlin, 1981a, 1981b) suggests that if a child has little comprehension of speech, makes no spontaneous vocalizations, and shows severely retarded social and play skills, he or she is unlikely to make major gains in speech through operant techniques. The work of this group of British researchers indicates that behavioral techniques are more effective for motivating children to use existing speech skills than for creating new linguistic forms. Such findings suggest that in assessing the mute child, the use of manual signs should be considered as an alternative to speech (Carr, 1982).

In addition to assessing the child's linguistic skills, the teaching skills of classroom teachers and/or parents should be assessed to ensure that they are able to use appropriate training techniques. In order to be an effective lan-

guage trainer, the parent or teacher must be well versed in behavior modification techniques. It is also important to assess the interaction between the
teacher and child to ensure that the child is attending to the trainer, that
the trainer is matching the complexity of his or her speech to the needs of the
child, and that attempts at communication on the part of the child are being
reinforced by the trainer. The environment should be structured in such a fashion as to demand the use of the child's available language (Sosne, Handleman,
& Harris, 1979).

In doing a behavioral assessment the clinician must also be sensitive to
whether parents (or others) are emotionally ready to assume the responsibilities of teaching. Here, one must directly address the impact the child is having
upon the family, the resources available in the nuclear and extended family,
and the functioning of the marital unit, siblings, and family as a whole. Indications of distress among family members or the family as a unit should be
addressed to ensure the long-term, sustained efforts of the family on behalf
of the autistic child and the well-being of the family unit (Harris, 1983).

RANGE OF BEHAVIORAL TECHNIQUES APPLIED

Treating the autistic child and his or her family demands a knowledge of a
broad range of behavioral interventions. Although work with the child focuses
primarily on creative application of traditional operant procedures, interventions with parents and siblings extend to the full range of cognitive-behavioral
methods.

Teaching New Skills

Much of our clinical effort is devoted to teaching the autistic child new skills.
These children tend to be so indifferent to their external environment and so
unresponsive to natural reinforcers that their rate of observational learning
prior to treatment is low. Thus, we must begin by identifying events that are
reinforcing to the child and use these to shape simple attending and imitative
behaviors that will ensure that the child is focused on the teacher.

For many children food is an effective early reinforcer; for others anti-
gravity play, music, vibration, or an opportunity to play with a favorite object
may be effective (Ferrari & Harris, 1981). Some children may respond only to
the negative reinforcement of being released briefly from the learning setting.
For less impaired children and for children later in treatment, social reinforcers, tokens, and other symbolic forms of reward are possible. Whenever we
use primary reinforcers such as food, we take great care to link these consistently with praise and physical affection in order to establish these events as
secondary reinforcers.

Because most autistic children are mentally retarded, it is important to address ourselves with great care to the challenge of breaking skills into their component parts. Thus, we rely heavily on shaping, fading, and chaining to teach new behaviors. For example, in teaching speech we initially reinforce any sound emitted by the child, gradually shape those sounds towards the target behavior by selective reinforcement, provide manual and visual prompts as needed, and fade these prompts over time. Small units of sound are taught and then combined to form words (Harris, 1975; Lovaas, 1981). Such teaching is slow, effortful for both the child and adult, but in many cases ultimately yields functional speech; for higher-functioning autistic children the units of material can be larger and the degree of prompting less.

After the child has mastered basic attending skills, such as eye contact and quiet sitting, and has demonstrated some capacity to imitate the behaviors of an adult model on request, it can be useful to introduce training in observational learning to heighten the likelihood that the youngster will benefit from the experiences of other children and adults. It is essential in working with the autistic child to recognize that these youngsters have difficulty generalizing newly learned skills to novel stimuli, people, or places. Hence, considerable effort should be devoted to teaching material in multiple settings, with various teachers, and with a variety of instances of the stimulus object (Handleman, 1979; Handleman & Harris, 1980). McGee, Krantz, Mason, and McClannahan (1983) describe the use of incidental-teaching procedures to facilitate the generalized use of skills by autistic youngsters.

The importance of ensuring generalization to the natural environment and maintenance of change over time led to extensive involvement of parents in the treatment of their autistic children (Lovaas, Koegel, Simmons, & Long, 1973). We have discussed elsewhere the techniques involved in training parents to work with their children and the kinds of interventions necessary to enhance the functioning of the family of a child with autism (Harris, 1983, 1984).

Suppressing Unwanted Behaviors

The self-injury, self-stimulation, tantrums, aggression, and other behavior management problems exhibited by autistic children require that the clinician be able to use punishment procedures. Although use of differential reinforcement of other behavior, teaching incompatible responses, and ignoring will decrease many behavior problems, others persist in spite of a highly structured and richly rewarding teaching setting. In instances when behavior problems intrude on learning, punishment procedures may free the child to enter more fully into the learning situation.

The broad gamut of aversive procedures has been applied to the behavior problems of autistic children (Harris & Ersner-Hershfield, 1978). Time-out and extinction procedures can be useful in some instances of tantrum behavior, noncompliance, or mild aggression (Foxx & Shapiro, 1978). However, in using these procedures the clinician should be aware that for some autistic children being ignored is an opportunity to engage in rewarding self-stimulation or be released from the demands of learning. In addition, being placed in isolation involves some risk for children who engage in self-injury. Thus, the application of ignoring procedures must be done judiciously and with a careful eye on the data to ensure that a reinforcing context has not inadvertently been created.

The development of overcorrection procedures (Foxx & Azrin, 1972) has made a significant contribution to the treatment of autistic children. Our own experience has been that these procedures are helpful in the treatment of many problem behaviors, including self-injury (Harris & Romanczyk, 1976) and self-stimulation (Harris & Wolchik, 1979). Used creatively, developed overcorrection procedures can teach the child an adaptive new skill while serving to suppress unwanted behavior (Hinerman, Jenson, Walker, & Petersen, 1982).

Other punishment procedures that have been used with developmentally disabled children include a water mist (Dorsey, Iwata, Ong, & McSween, 1980), facial screening (McGonigle, Duncan, Cordisco, & Barrett, 1982), aversive tasting substances (Friman, Cook, & Finney, 1984), and restraint (Singh & Bakker, 1984). Although electric shock has been used for the treatment of self-injury, it must be regarded as a potentially dangerous procedure that requires considerable clinical skill and should be used only when the less drastic alternatives have failed (Harris & Ersner-Hershfield, 1978). Court consent may be required for the use of electric shock.

RESEARCH REVIEW

Because it is impossible to summarize all the research in the field of autism in a few pages, we have selected a few areas that we regard as especially creative or promising to give the reader a sense of the work being done. An examination of the past few years of the *Journal of Autism and Developmental Disorders* is a good way for the interested person to gain a more comprehensive sense of the state of the art in autism research.

Creative Alternatives to Punishment

An important development in recent years has been the search for nonaversive techniques to suppress unwanted behaviors. As professionals in the field began to recognize the problems inherent in obtaining generalized suppression with aversive techniques and noted that more skilled clinicians seemed to need fewer aversive procedures than less skilled clinicians, the search grew for methods that could be widely used and would be at least as effective as the older, more unpleasant procedures.

An example of the development of such a creative approach in the suppression of self-stimulation, inappropriate verbalizations, and aggression has been the use of vigorous physical exercise. Watters and Watters (1980) noted that levels of self-stimulation by autistic boys in language training sessions were lower when the boys had a period of 8 to 10 minutes of jogging prior to language class than when they had watched television or done regular academic work. It should be noted that this exercise was noncontingent; that is, it occurred independent of any disruptive behavior on the part of the child.

Other, more recent examinations of noncontingent physical exercise have suggested that jogging not only decreases self-stimulation but also increases appropriate responding as well (Kern, Koegel, Dyer, Blew, & Fenton, 1982). This same group of researchers notes that mild exercise in the form of playing ball has little or no influence on self-stimulation, while vigorous jogging serves to reduce the frequency of these stereotypic behaviors (Kern, Koegel, & Dunlap, 1984).

Examining contingent exercise as a consequence for inappropriate verbal or aggressive responses, Luce, Delquadri, and Hall (1980) found that requiring two boys with autistic-like behaviors to engage in brief exercise reduced the frequency of the target behaviors.

In our own center we compared the benefits of contingent versus noncontingent jogging on the out-of-seat behavior of an autistic boy and found that noncontingent jogging had little beneficial effect, while contingent jogging led to a marked reduction in inappropriate behavior (Gordon, Handleman, & Harris, 1984).

These studies suggest that physical exercise, a desirable activity in promoting good health, can also suppress unwanted, maladaptive behaviors of autistic children. It is not yet clear what differential impact contingent and noncontingent exercise have on various target behaviors or with different children.

Other creative approaches to work with autistic children have included adult imitation of the child's actions to increase the child's gaze behavior (Tiegerman & Primavera, 1984), the systematic use of peer modeling to increase learning (Charlop, Schreibman, & Tryon, 1983), the masking of sensory feedback to reduce self-stimulation (Aiken & Salzberg, 1984), and an emphasis on teaching skills within the natural environment (McGee, Krantz, & McClannahan, 1984).

Organic Etiology

Substantial effort is being devoted to examining organic factors in the etiology of autism. Thus, the entire June 1982 issue of the *Journal of Autism and Developmental Disorders* was devoted to review of current work in the area.

It appears likely that the causes of autism will ultimately be traced to biological factors. Based on the work to date it is probably appropriate to speak of autisms in the plural since we are finding a number of different factors that seem to contribute to the development of autistic behavior. Thus, a variety of co-occuring disorders have been identified, including chromosomal or genetic defects such as fragile X syndrome (Gillberg, 1983; Meryash, Szymanski, & Gerald, 1982), infectious diseases such as rubella syndrome (Chess, 1977), viral infection (Markowitz, 1983; Stubbs, 1978), and physical trauma (Weir & Salisbury, 1980), all of which may be accompanied by autistic behaviors.

CASE STUDY

OVERVIEW

The following case report describes the diagnosis, placement, and treatment of a preschool-aged autistic child. The intricacies of admissions are discussd as well as the design of a transition process from a highly specialized behavioral program to a less structured community placement. Descriptions of curriculum development, parent training, and follow-up efforts are provided.

BACKGROUND INFORMATION

Mr. and Mrs. Howard initially contacted the Douglass Developmental Disabilities Center because of concern about their daughter's lack of responsiveness, avoidance of eye-contact, and preference to be left alone. These concerns had prompted them to consult with a pediatric neurologist a few months earlier, and that physician indicated that Carla presented symptoms consistent with the diagnosis of infantile autism according to *DSM-III* (American Psychiatric Association, 1980). The neurologist suggested that the parents enroll Carla in a program for autistic children as soon as possible.

At the time of our evaluation, Carla was $2\frac{1}{2}$ years old. She was the third of four children, had a 6-month-old brother, and 6- and 9-year-old sisters. Mr. and Mrs. Howard were both high school graduates, and the family resided in a small town bordering a large metropolitan area.

Carla's developmental history was given by her parents during the intake session. Her mother reported some spotting during the first 3 months of a relatively uneventful full-term pregnancy. Labor lasted for 4 hours, and Carla was born weighing 7 pounds, 4 ounces. Her Apgar scores were 9 and 10, respectively.

Developmental milestones during Carla's first year were reported by her parents as being within normal limits. Carla ate and slept well and began walking at 12 months. Although she said her first words when about a year old, her parents indicated that Carla stopped speaking at 14 months and had only recently resumed using a few single-syllable words. The parents stressed their concern for Carla's lack of interpersonal responsiveness and language development. They discussed how Carla would sometimes rock and described frequent episodes of body twirling.

Our admissions report indicated that Carla was an alert, well-coordinated youngster who exhibited a number of autistic behaviors. Her language development was sharply delayed, her response to other people quite limited, and she had great difficulty tolerating environmental changes. We were impressed during the intake by the parents' ability to understand and apply the concepts taught in a behavioral parenting group that had brought Carla some clear benefits. As a result of their efforts, she was reported as being more responsive and affectionate, engaging in more verbal play than before such programming. These changes were viewed as documentation of Carla's ability to prosper in a correct educational setting and made more compelling the urgency of her early school placement. Carla's admission to our center was strongly recommended, and it was suggested that she appeared to be one of those youngsters for whom early intervention could make a significant difference.

Carla's placement at the Douglass Developmental Disabilities Center necessitated active and aggressive advocacy on the part of her parents to convince their local school district to fund her placement. At the time of admission, preschool education was not a state mandate but only an option for individual boards of education. Thanks to her parents' advocacy skills, Carla was officially enrolled in our program that summer.

TREATMENT

Treatment initially included the parents' participation in a parent training program. The training program consisted of 6 weekly training seminars, led by the center's professional staff, that focused on behavior modification and speech and language development. Each session included a brief lecture on a specific topic followed by demonstrations, modeling of procedures, and feedback on parent performance. Topics covered included data collection, reinforcement, punishment, shaping, chaining and fading, and generalization and maintenance. In addition to the weekly meetings, Carla's parents received a home visit once every 2 weeks to focus on application of techniques.

When Carla was admitted to the center, she was placed in an entry-level classroom with three other children. The entry-level curriculum was highly structured and intensive and focused on establishing basic instructional control. A one-to-one tutorial relationship was available on a daily basis to implement programs designed to increase attending, general compliance, and the rudiments of communication. Attention was also placed on eliminating those behaviors that competed with learning. Figure 8.1 presents those programs that were selected as priorities for Carla.

Our efforts during the first few weeks of school focused on establishing basic instructional control. As Figure 8.1 indicates, Carla mastered sitting, eye contact, and following direction programs by mid-November, and she was beginning to make progress in the areas of basic communication and academic readiness. Programming in speech and language development included syntactic and semantic elements and rapidly progressed to focus on spontaneous use of language. Initial attention to preacademic skills of shape, number, and letter identification was expanded to basic reading, math, and writing activities.

Carla's rate of skill acquisition showed consistent progress. An example of her skill mastery is depicted in Figure 8.2. During the initial days of programming in picture discrimination, Carla performed below 15% correct. During the second, third, and fourth weeks of instruction, performance steadily approached the mastery criterion of 85% correct over two consecutive 20-trial sessions. This pattern of acquisition was noted across many areas of programming.

Social skills training initially focused on compliance training and was ex-

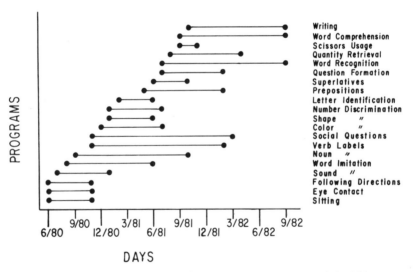

Figure 8.1. Progression of behavioral programming for an autistic child.

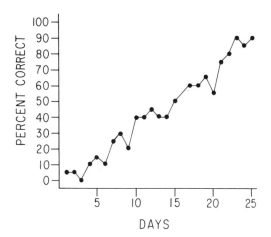

Figure 8.2. Acquisition of picture discriminations by an autistic child.

panded to include independent play and work, group instruction, and eventually, appropriate social interaction with adults and children. By January of her first year, Carla was consistently complying with complex commands, and behavior management concerns focused only on decreasing out-of-seat behavior. Although Carla's independent abilities grew, she demonstrated some difficulty with sharing teacher attention during small-group instruction. Redirecting programming to the specific skills of turn taking and quiet waiting helped to improve her group abilities.

Programming in social interaction included many components. Our instructional effort was first directed toward appropriate interactions with adults and then with children in the form of cooperative play and verbal responsiveness. Unfortunately, Carla's social development was limited by the lack of response of the other children in her class, and as a result a decision was made to have her attend the university's daycare center for normal preschoolers one morning a week. When the assistant who accompanied Carla to the daycare center faded her involvement, participation increased to two mornings a week. Within one semester, Carla was actively participating in informal and formal activities at the daycare center.

In addition to our classroom work with Carla, our instructional efforts were maximized by continued family involvement. Every 6 weeks there were at least two face-to-face contacts between Carla's family and the staff of the school. One meeting took place in the school at a parents' night, where there was opportunity to review school programming and meet with Carla's teacher. The second meeting occurred in the home where attention was placed on active home programming in areas supportive of school efforts and those appropriate to the home environment such as self-care and daily living. Carla's parents actively supported home programming efforts.

Carla's progress and responsiveness during her first 18 months in the program prompted a decision to consider a program transition for the 1982–1983 school year. Initially, Carla's teacher surveyed public and private programs and identified a private school for neurologically impaired/communication handicapped children that seemed appropriate. A team consisting of members of our staff, school district professionals, and Carla's parents conducted a series of visits to the potential program and ultimately agreed to pursue a fall placement. The initial visits, combined with visits to our program by the staff of the new school, resulted in a transition needs assessment that guided our programming for the remaining months. Increased attention was focused on helping Carla acheive greater independence and more group participation. The appropriateness of the program selected was confirmed by the success of a 3-day trial placement during late spring.

FOLLOW-UP

Formal follow-up of Carla's progress was conducted for a 2-year period after her discharge from the Developmental Disabilities Center. A phone contact with Carla's teacher during late fall of the first year indicated that Carla was adjusting well to the new class and was responsive to instructional efforts. Carla's former teacher visited the program the following spring. During the half-day visit, Carla was observed in group and independent activities and was reported to be making good progress in language, social, and cognitive areas. When a second follow-up visit was conducted the following winter, marked improvement was noted in Carla's language ability, particularly with regard to increased spontaneous expression. Progress in academic areas was also reported as continuing, and social interactions with other children and adults were described as improving in both frequency and quality.

COMMENT

The success of treatment during the years outlined by this case report was probably due to several factors, including the importance of early diagnosis and intervention as well as the effects of active and systematic programming. The parents' role as advocates clearly facilitated the placement process, and their role as teachers maximized educational efforts. Carla's early and consistent responsiveness to the intensified program was also a key variable for the successful transition to the community placement.

SUMMARY

Infantile autism is a rare, pervasively handicapping condition that begins early in life and typically has a severe impact through the life span. Accurate diagnosis requires considerable skill and becomes more complex as the child matures since the symptoms become somewhat muted with increasing age. The clinician must take care to distinguish autism from schizophrenia, mental retardation, and childhood-onset pervasive developmental disorder.

Systematic behavioral assessment of the child with autism is essential for treatment planning and placement decisions. Behavioral intervention with these youngsters has focused primarily on the creative application of operant techniques, including the use of a "discrete trial format" for the presentation of material, and careful use of shaping procedures to build new skills. Punishment procedures may be necessary to eliminate disruptive behaviors that threaten the child's welfare.

Innovative research in the area of infantile autism has emphasized nonaversive alternatives to traditional punishment procedures and creative methods of enhancing generalization of newly learned skills. Considerable research effort is also being devoted to indentifying the biological factors that cause various forms of autism.

REFERENCES

Aiken, J. M., & Salzberg, C. L. (1984). The effects of a sensory extinction procedure of sterotypic sounds of two autistic children. *Journal of Autism and Developmental Disorders*, *14*, 291–299.

American Psychiatric Association (1980). *Diagnostic and statistical manual of mental disorders (3rd ed.)*. Washington, DC: Author.

Ando, H., & Yoshimura, I. (1979). Effects of age on communication skill levels and prevalence of maladaptive behaviors in autistic and mentally retarded children. *Journal of Autism and Developmental Disorders*, *9*, 83–93.

Carr, E. G. (1977). The motivation of self-injurious behavior: A review of some hypotheses. *Psychological Bulletin*, *84*, 800–816.

Carr, E. G. (1982). Sign language. In R. L. Koegel, A. Rincover, & A. L. Egel (Eds.), *Educating and understanding autistic children* (pp. 142–157). San Diego, CA: College-Hill.

Charlop, M. H., Schreibman, L., & Tryon, A. S. (1983). Learning through observation: The effects of peer modeling on acquisition and generalization in autistic children. *Journal of Abnormal Child Psychology*, *11*, 355–366.

Chess, S. (1977). Follow-up report on autism in congenital rubella. *Journal of Autism and Childhood Schizophrenia*, *7*, 69–81.

DeMyer, M. K. (1979). *Parents and children in autism.* New York: Wiley.

Dorsey, M. F., Iwata, B. A., Ong, P., & McSween, T. E. (1980). Treatment of self-injurious behavior using a water mist: Initial response suppression and generalization. *Journal of Applied Behavior Analysis, 13,* 343-353.

Eggers, C. (1978). Course and prognosis of childhood schizophrenia. *Journal of Autism and Childhood Schizophrenia, 8,* 21-36.

Favell, J. E. (1983). The management of aggressive behavior. In E. Schopler & G. Mesibov (Eds.) *Autism in adolescents and adults* (pp. 187-222). New York: Plenum.

Ferrari, M., & Harris, S. L. (1981). The limits and motivating potential of sensory stimuli as reinforcers for autistic children. *Journal of Applied Behavior Analysis, 14,* 339-343.

Foxx, R. M., & Azrin, N. H. (1972). Restitution: A method of eliminating aggressive-disruptive behavior of retarded and brain damaged patients. *Behaviour Research and Therapy, 10,* 15-27.

Foxx, R. M., & Shapiro, S. T. (1978). The timeout ribbon: A nonexclusionary timeout procedure. *Journal of Applied Behavior Analysis, 11,* 125-136.

Friman, P. C., Cook, J. W., & Finney, J. W. (1984). Effects of punishment procedures on the self-stimulatory behavior of an autistic child. *Analysis and Intervention in Developmental Disabilities, 4,* 39-46.

Gillberg, C. (1983). Identical triplets with infantile autism and the fragile-X syndrome. *British Journal of Psychiatry, 143,* 256-260.

Gordon, R., Handleman, J. S., & Harris, S. L. (1984, May). *The effects of contingent vs. non-contingent running on the out-of-seat behavior of an autistic boy.* Paper presented at the meeting of the Association for Behavior Analysis, Nashville, TN.

Handleman, J. S. (1979). Generalization by autistic-type children of verbal responses across settings. *Journal of Applied Behavior Analysis, 12,* 273-282.

Handleman, J. S., Arnold, M., Veniar, F. A., Kristoff, B., & Harris, S. L. (1982). Assessment and remediation of hearing loss in an autistic youngster. *Hearing Instruments, 33,* 10-11.

Handleman, J. S., & Harris, S. L. (1980). Generalization from school to home with autistic children. *Journal of Autism and Developmental Disorders, 10,* 323-333.

Harris, S. L. (1975). Teaching language to nonverbal children—with emphasis on problems of generalization. *Psychological Bulletin, 82,* 564-580.

Harris, S. L. (1983). *Families of the developmentally disabled: A guide to behavioral intervention.* Elmsford, NY: Pergamon.

Harris, S. L. (1984). The family of the autistic child: A behavioral-systems view. *Clinical Psychology Review, 4,* 227-239.

Harris, S. L., & Ersner-Hershfield, R. (1978). The behavioral suppression of seriously disruptive behavior in psychotic and retarded patients: A review of punishment and its alternatives. *Psychological Bulletin, 85,* 1352-1375.

Harris, S. L., & Romanczyk, R. G. (1976). Treating self-injurious behavior of a retarded child by overcorrection. *Behavior Therapy, 7,* 235-239.

Harris, S. L., & Wolchik, S. A. (1979). Suppression of self-stimulation: Three alternative strategies. *Journal of Applied Behavior Analysis, 12,* 185–198.

Hinerman, P. S., Jenson, W. R., Walker, G. R., & Petersen, P. B. (1982). Positive practice overcorrection combined with additional procedures to teach signed words to an autistic child. *Journal of Autism and Developmental Disorders, 12,* 253–263.

Howlin, P. A. (1981a). The effectiveness of operant language training with autistic children. *Journal of Autism and Developmental Disorders, 11,* 89–105.

Howlin, P. A. (1981b). The results of a home-based language training programme with autistic children. *British Journal of Disorders of Communication, 16,* 73–88.

Kern, L., Koegel, R. L., & Dunlap, G. (1984). The influence of vigorous versus mild exercise on autistic stereotyped behaviors. *Journal of Autism and Developmental Disorders, 14,* 57–67.

Kern, L., Koegel, R. L., Dyer, K., Blew, P. A., & Fenton, L. R. (1982). The effects of physical exercise on self-stimulation and appropriate responding in autistic children. *Journal of Autism and Developmental Disorders, 12,* 399–419.

Koegel, R. L., Rincover, A., & Egel, A. L. (1982). *Educating and understanding autistic children.* San Diego, CA: College-Hill.

Lovaas, O. I. (1977). *The autistic child.* New York: Irvington.

Lovaas, O. I. (1981). *Teaching developmentally disabled children: The me book.* Baltimore, MD: University Park Press.

Lovaas, O. I., Koegel, R., Simmons, J. Q., & Long, J. S. (1973). Some generalization and follow-up measures on autistic children in behavior therapy. *Journal of Applied Behavior Analysis, 6,* 131–165.

Luce, S. C., Delquadri, J., & Hall, R. V. (1980). Contingent exercise: A mild but powerful procedure for suppressing inappropriate verbal and aggressive behavior. *Journal of Applied Behavior Analysis, 13,* 583–594.

Markowitz, P. I. (1983). Autism in a child with congenital cytomegalovirus infection. *Journal of Autism and Developmental Disorders, 13,* 249–253.

McGee, G. G., Krantz, P. J., Mason, D., & McClannahan, L. E. (1983). A modified incidental-teaching procedure for autistic youth: Acquisition and generalization of receptive object labels. *Journal of Applied Behavior Analysis, 16,* 329–338.

McGee, G. G., Krantz, P. J., & McClannahan, L. E. (1984). Conversational skills for autistic adolescents: Teaching effectiveness in naturalistic game settings. *Journal of Autism and Developmental Disorders, 14,* 319–330.

McGonigle, J. J., Duncan, D., Cordisco, L., & Barrett, R. P. (1982). Visual screening: An alternative method for reducing sterotyped behaviors. *Journal of Applied Behavior Analysis, 15,* 461–467.

Meryash, D. L., Szymanski, L. S., & Gerald, P. S. (1982). Infantile autism associated with the fragile-X syndrome. *Journal of Autism and Developmental Disorders, 12,* 295-301.

National Society for Autistic Children. (1978). National Society for Autistic Children definition of the syndrome of autism. *Journal of Autism and Childhood Schizophrenia, 8,* 162–167.

Newsom, C., & Rincover, A. (1981). Autism. In E. J. Mash & L. G. Terdal (Eds.), *Behavioral assessment of childhood disorders* (pp. 397–439). New York: Guilford.

Ornitz, E. M., Guthrie, D., & Farley, A. H. (1977). The early development of autistic children. *Journal of Autism and Childhood Schizophrenia, 7*, 207–229.

Powers, M. D., & Handleman, J. S. (1984). *Behavioral assessment of severe developmental disabilities*. Rockville, MD: Aspen.

Schopler E., & Sloan, J. L. (1983). Recent developments in the diagnosis and assessment of autism. In S. Ray, M. J. O'Neill, & N. T. Morris (Eds.). *Low incidence children: A guide to psychoeducational assessment* (pp. 8–65). Nachitoches, LA: Steven Ray.

Singh, N. N., & Bakker, L. W. (1984). Suppression of pica by overcorrection and physical restraint: A comparative analysis. *Journal of Autism and Developmental Disorders, 14*, 331–341.

Sosne, J. B., Handleman, J. S., & Harris, S. L. (1979). Teaching spontaneous-functional speech to autistic-type children. *Mental Retardation, 17*, 241–245.

Spreat, S., Roszkowski, M., Isett, R., & Alderfer, R. (1980). Emotional disturbance in mental retardation: An investigation of differential diagnosis. *Journal of Autism and Developmental Disorders, 10*, 361–367.

Stubbs, E. G. (1978). Autistic symptoms in a child with congenital cytomegalovirus infection. *Journal of Autism and Childhood Schizophrenia, 8*, 37–43.

Tiegerman, E., & Primavera, L. H. (1984). Imitating the autistic child: Facilitating communicative gaze behavior. *Journal of Autism and Developmental Disorders, 14*, 27–38.

Watters, R. G., & Watters, W. E. (1980). Decreasing self-stimulatory behavior with physical exercise in a group of autistic boys. *Journal of Autism and Developmental Disorders, 10*, 379–387.

Weir, K., & Salisbury, D. M. (1980). Acute onset of autistic features following brain damage in a ten-year-old. *Journal of Autism and Developmental Disorders, 10*, 185–191.

CHAPTER 9

Tic Disorders

STEVEN A. HOBBS, PAMELA G. DORSETT, AND LYNNDA M. DAHLQUIST

Tics are defined as involuntary, stereotyped, rapid, and purposeless motor movements that involve the muscles of the face, torso, or extremities (American Psychiatric Association, 1980). Several muscle groups may be involved either simultaneously or sequentially, and vocalizations may occur in some types of tics.

Three major types of tics are distinguished in the third edition of the *Diagnostic and Statistical Manual of Mental Disorders (DSM-III:* American Psychiatric Association, 1980), primarily on the basis of the number and duration of movements, although variations in intensity over time and age of onset also are considered. The first of these, transient tic disorder, has its onset during childhood or early adolescence. Diagnosis of transient tic disorder requires that the tic be exhibited for at least 1 month but no longer than 1 year. In contrast, chronic motor tic disorder involves three or fewer muscle groups at a given time and a duration of at least 1 year. Onset may occur in childhood or after 40 years of age. Unlike transient tic disorder, chronic motor tics do not vary in intensity for periods of weeks to months.

The third major movement disorder is Gilles de la Tourette's syndrome or Tourette's disorder. Multiple muscle groups are affected for a period in excess of 1 year. The disorder appears between the ages of 2 and 15 years, though typically before age 13. The mean age of onset has been reported as 7 or 8 years (Shapiro, Shapiro, & Wayne, 1972). Most frequently, the initial symptom is an eye-blink tic. Both the intensity and the topography of the tics may vary over time, and some movements may "blend" into others. For example, a grunt or bark may develop into a word or words over time. The disorder is progressive; in 25% of the cases, subsequent tics become more complex and

The authors wish to acknowledge the contributions of F. Danny Armstrong and Karen M. Gil to the clinical case material presented and the contribution of Melanie Jenkins to the preparation of this manuscript.

appear to involve voluntary movements such as kicking, jumping, or touching ones self or others (Bruun, 1984). Although the presence of multiple vocal tics such as grunts, hisses, or barking sounds is included in the DSM-III diagnostic criteria, Shapiro and Shapiro (1982) question the appropriateness of requiring occurrence of phonic tics for the diagnosis of Tourette's disorder. Coprolalia (i.e., vocalization of obscenities) may appear late in the pattern of behaviors, typically during puberty and adolescence (Lucas, 1970; Shapiro, Shapiro, Bruun, & Sweet, 1978).

As milder cases of the disorder are diagnosed, recent figures indicate that coprolalia may occur in only 33% of Tourette's cases as compared to earlier estimates of 60% (Shapiro & Shapiro, 1982). Other behaviors indicative of Tourette's disorder include copropraxia (obscene gestures), echolalia (repetition of others' verbalizations), echopraxia (repetition of others' gestures), and palilalia (repetition of one's own verbalizations) (Bauer & Shea, 1984). As is the case with the transient and chronic motor tics, such behaviors can be controlled by the individual for periods of minutes to hours.

The incidence of transient tic disorder of childhood has been estimated at 12 to 24% of the population (Shapiro et al., 1978), whereas incidence of both Tourette's disorder and chronic motor tic disorder has been estimated at 1.6% of the population (Baron, Shapiro, Shapiro, & Rainer, 1981). Tic disorders and Tourette's disorder occur about three times more frequently in males than in females (Bakwin & Bakwin, 1972; Corbett, Matthews, Connell, & Shapiro, 1969). A recent review by Bauer and Shea (1984) indicates that familial incidence of tic disorders, including Tourette's syndrome, ranges from 10% (Corbett et al., 1969) to 40% (Shapiro & Shapiro, 1982).

DIFFERENTIAL DIAGNOSIS

The higher prevalence rates of tics in families with Tourette's disorder has led some investigators to postulate that all three types of tics represent points on a continuum of severity rather than distinct conditions (Bruun, 1984; Golden, 1982). Other factors include similarity in age at onset, similarity in the nature of individual tics, and the generally positive response of tics to treatment with haloperidol and their adverse response to stimulant medications (Golden, 1982).

Whether or not differentiation among the three types of tics results in differential treatment remains controversial. However, many professionals would agree that tics, including Tourette's disorder, should be distinguished from other types of movement disorders. As noted by King and Ollendick (1984), Tourette's disorder in particular may be misdiagnosed, thus resulting in undesirable consequences, such as inappropriate treatment and/or the development of problems (e.g., anxiety, depression) related to the embarrassing nature of the tics (Shapiro et al., 1978). Difficulties of diagnosis are illustrated by a study (Golden, 1977) reporting that only 1 of 15 individuals with Tourette's disorder had been accurately diagnosed. Ten of the patients were judged instead as having nervous habits or exhibiting attention-getting behaviors.

Yates (1970) has recommended evaluation of several features of motor disturbances, including voluntary versus involuntary control of the movement, presence versus absence of muscle atrophy, occurrence or nonoccurrence of pain associated with movement, and presence versus absence of the movement during sleep. This latter feature may be questionable in light of recent evidence that suggests that some individuals with Tourette's disorder do exhibit the tics during sleep (Glaze, Jankovic, & Frost, 1982).

Medical problems that may be confused with tics include various types of choreas, dystonias, tremors (particularly in association with Wilson's disease), and myoclonus. Golden (1982) has described several movement disorders of childhood. Because movement disorders may be indicative of a neurodegenerative condition, proper diagnosis made early in the course of the illness is critical. For example, in the case of Wilson's disease, a disorder that affects copper metabolism, early diagnosis and treatment can prevent the neurologic deterioration that otherwise results (Valente & Valente, 1983).

It also may be useful to differentiate tics from other types of stereotyped movements (e.g., rocking, headweaving, finger-gazing) that may frequently occur in mentally retarded, autistic, and schizophrenic individuals. These movements are distinguished from tics primarily on the basis of their voluntary nature and the fact that such movements do not cause subjective distress on the part of the client.

ETIOLOGY

Several theoretical explanations for tics have been proposed. Psychoanalytic theorists postulate the operation of various underlying processes or mechanisms to account for the occurrence of tics. Ferenczi (1921) wrote that the motor disturbances were the result of fixated libido on that part of the body associated with some traumatic experience. Later, Fenichel (1945) proposed that conversion was the mechanism underlying Tourette's syndrome, and Mahler and Luke (1946) maintained that tensions produced by conflicts related to sexual or aggressive impulses were released through the tics. Difficulties during the anal stage of psychosexual development have also been implicated in the appearance of the motor disturbances (Morphew & Sim, 1969).

Two major theories emphasizing learning processes have been proposed to account for the development of tics. The first, posited by Yates (1958), has as its basis Hullian learning theory (Hull, 1943). According to this model, tics are drive-reducing conditioned avoidance responses originating from some traumatic experience. The behavior is assumed to acquire habit strength because its performance results in anxiety reduction. Hence, the tics are more likely to occur in anxiety-provoking situations because relief follows their occurrence (St. James-Roberts & Powell, 1979).

The second explanation is based on an operant model (Skinner, 1938) that views tics as learned behaviors maintained by consequences. Tics may begin as normal movements but eventually change topographically and increase in frequency (Azrin & Nunn, 1973; Yates, 1970). The movements may be more likely to occur under particular stimulus conditions and reinforcement may be external or perhaps internal (e.g. proprioceptive feedback) (Yates, 1970). Sanders (1973) has suggested that imitation may play a role in the acquisition of tics.

Medical explanations for tics have focused on Tourette's disorder and include two major areas: genetics and neurochemistry. Shapiro and Shapiro (1982) note a higher concordance rate of Tourette syndrome in identical versus fraternal twins, and that females more frequently transmit the disorder than males. This occurs despite the higher incidence of the disorder among males. These authors conclude that "genetic factors are strongly suggested by the frequency of tics and TS (Tourette Syndrome) in families of patients with TS," (p. 385). Baker, Platt, and Fine (1983) maintain, however, that reports of familial incidence have not constituted "attempts to systematically investigate possible hereditary factors" and that "occasional family concurrence of tics, in itself, does not demonstrate genetic transmission" (p. 163). Bruun (1984) suggests that factors unrelated to genetics, such as its appearance following encephalitis or treatment with stimulants and neuroleptics, are implicated in Tourette's disorder.

Neurotransmitters and enzymes have been the major focus of neurochemical studies (Shapiro & Shapiro, 1982). According to Cohen, Detlor, Shaywitz, and Leckman (1982), the attenuation of Tourette's disorder with haloperidol and its exacerbation or precipitation by stimulants constitute the strongest case for a neurochemical dysfunction in Tourette's. Because haloperidol is a dopamine blocker, it has been hypothesized that the disorder is related to overproduction of dopamine, perhaps in the corpus striatum. Dopamine seems to be the primary neurotransmitter in the corpus striatum, which is connected with extrapyramidal systems and implicated in other movement disorders (Baker et al., 1983). However, given the research to date, a causal role cannot yet be assigned to neurochemical imbalance in the development of Tourette's.

BEHAVIORAL ASSESSMENT

The strategies most often employed in behavioral assessment of tic disorders are the interview, direct observation, and self-report or self-monitoring procedures.

Interviewing

Several functions of the initial interview (Haynes & Jensen, 1979; Mash & Terdal, 1981) have particular relevance for the assessment of children's tics. These include obtaining information about: (1) the parents' and child's perceptions and descriptions of the problem and goals; (2) possible setting and maintaining conditions for the behavior; (3) the history of the problem and previous interventions; (4) the child's developmental history and relevant family background information; and (5) the parents' motivation to participate actively in the child's treatment (since parents may be called on to record data as well as apply treatment procedures). The interview also gives the therapist an opportunity to directly observe the child and family interactions as well as the child's movements.

Age and conditions of onset, changes in topography or intensity of tics over time, duration of the problem, number of movements involved, and control (at least temporarily) over the movements are important factors to consider in evaluating the severity and chronicity of the tic disorder as well as in guiding the therapist in making referral decisions. A general recommendation is that the child be evaluated by a physician in order to rule out movement disorders associated with medical conditions including neurological disease.

Preliminary information about environmental conditions under which tics are more or less frequent or severe is important. With such information direct observations of the disorder may be more efficiently arranged. Preliminary information may also suggest possible precipitating, exacerbating, or maintaining variables for manipulation.

Direct Observation

The interview alone is unlikely to provide sufficient information to formulate a complete, descriptive definition of the target behavior or to identify conditions associated with higher and lower probabilities of its occurrence. Direct observation may be necessary for defining target behaviors, for selecting an appropriate recording procedure, and for assessing the current level and changes in tics as a function of intervention.

Response definitions may be difficult to formulate, especially when multiple tics are present. Extended observations may be necessary to get a complete picture of the range and characteristics of a client's tics (Thomas, Abrams, & Johnson, 1971). For example, Finney, Rapoff, Hall, and Christophersen (1983) carefully studied videotapes of clients to arrive at complete definitions.

In addition to observing the complexity of the movements, a number of investigators have noted changes in topography and/or intensity of tics after treatment has been applied (Billings, 1978; Friedman, 1980; Lahey, McNees, & McNees, 1973; Nicassio, Liberman, Patterson, Ramirez, & Sanders, 1972;

Sand & Carlson, 1973; Thomas et al., 1971; Varni, Boyd, & Cataldo, 1978). Definitions and/or recording procedures need to take into account dimensions in addition to rate. Varni et al. (1978), for example, changed definitions to include less severe responses as treatment continued.

The recording technique most often employed in research in the area has been frequency per unit of time or rate, typically recorded by means of wrist counters or by tallies on index cards. Observation periods ranging from 5 to 15 minutes in duration have been conducted 1 to 3 times daily. Partial interval recording has been used to score videotape observations (Finney et al., 1983) as well as *in vivo* observations (Thomas et al., 1971), although in the latter case the authors noted that no more than one tic could be reliably recorded at a time.

Selection of an appropriate recording procedure depends on several factors, including number of different movements being recorded, current rate and complexity of the tic, conditions under which the responses will be recorded, and skills (and perhaps motivation) of the observer. Mostofsky (1981) has suggested that tic behaviors may occur at too high a rate for accurate manual recording. In addition, measures of behavior should be obtained from several sources, and exclusive reliance on self-report data should be avoided if possible (Mostofsky, 1981). The importance of assessing several dimensions of tics, such as severity, topography, duration, and pattern, also has been emphasized. Videotaping has been recommended as a means to track changes in parameters in addition to frequency (Mostofsky, 1981; Sand & Carlson, 1973), and researchers have been encouraged to develop some measure of intensity (Billings, 1978). To date, however, investigators have not quantified and recorded tic intensity/severity.

In addition to response definition and recording strategy, one must also consider who will record direct observations. In the studies reviewed, such observations have been conducted by trained observers in the clinic (Billings, 1978; Doleys & Kurtz, 1974; Hollandsworth & Bausinger, 1978; Sand & Carlson, 1973; Surwillo, Shafii, & Barrett, 1978; Varni et al., 1978) and in more "natural" settings (Finney et al., 1983; Thomas et al., 1971), or they have been conducted by parents (Friedman, 1980; Sand & Carlson, 1973; Schulman, 1974; Surwillo et al., 1978; Varni et al., 1978) and teachers (Lahey et al., 1973; Poth & Barnett, 1983).

Clinic observations have been employed most frequently as a primary measure of tics. Most often, 5 to 10 minute observation periods have been conducted during weekly therapy sessions (Billings, 1978; Doleys & Kurtz, 1974; Hollandsworth & Bausinger, 1978; Sand & Carlson, 1973; Varni et al., 1978). Trained observers also have recorded data in more natural settings. For example, Finney et al. (1983) videotaped two child ticquers in their homes and scored tics from the tapes. Thomas et al. (1971) recorded tics as well as major activities of an 18-year old male in a residential treatment setting. The client was observed for 15-minute periods as he engaged in daily activities and for 10-minute periods in several real-life situations arranged by the therapist (e.g., going to the supermarket or church). These observations provided information about overall response to treatment as well as differences in rate of tics as a function of various stimulus conditions.

Obtaining measures in the natural environment is particularly important given the fact that tics can be controlled by the subject for periods of time. If recording is done unobtrusively in the natural environment, reactivity may be less of a problem than it would be in a clinic setting. Furthermore, observations made in the clinic may not produce data representative of the pattern of behavior observed in less contrived settings. Finally, problematic situations can be assessed in the natural environment, whereas such conditions perhaps can merely be simulated in the clinic. Investigators can observe the client engaged in a variety of tasks to ascertain those activities associated with varying frequencies of the behavior (Doleys & Kurtz, 1974).

Studies that have included observations conducted by significant others in the natural environment have rarely reported reliability measures. In some reports, however, systematic assessment of reliability has included comparisons of data recorded independently by both parents in the home (Finney et al., 1983), by a teacher and observer in the classroom (Lahey et al., 1973), or by a parent and observer in a clinic setting (Varni et al., 1978).

Several methods are suggested for assessing the reliability of data obtained in home and/or school settings. In either setting the therapist might arrange periodic assessment by an independent observer. Alternatively, if both parents or two adults reside in the home, each could independently record the behavior(s). These adults would initially be trained by the therapist (Ollendick, 1981), and periodic recalibration could be accomplished in the clinic with videotapes. When it is possible for a teacher to record occurrences of tics during specific periods at school, a second observer might be brought in for reliability checks (e.g., a parent or assistant).

Self-Report

Self-report data have been obtained in most tic studies (Azrin & Nunn, 1973; Azrin, Nunn, & Frantz, 1980; Billings, 1978; Hollandsworth & Bausinger, 1978; Ollendick, 1981; Sand & Carlson, 1973; Thomas et al., 1971; Varni et al., 1978), with self-monitoring frequently being the primary or exclusive component of the treatment package. Frequency counts, recorded via wrist counters, have been collected either continuously or during designated periods. With one exception (Ollendick, 1981), researchers have not systematically assessed the reliability of self-report data. Ollendick successfully employed self-monitoring with two boys, ages 9 and 11 years, to obtain reliable self-report data at school and at home. However, self-monitoring may not be feasible for all children. Accurate self-monitoring also may require initial rates of behavior low enough so that recording does not disrupt daily activities (Billings, 1978). Ollendick and Cerny (1981) note that some children may be poor candidates for accurate self-monitoring due to problems such as noncompliance, oppositional behavior, or inadequate motivation. However, when given specific training to record their behaviors accurately, many children can successfully use self-monitoring.

RANGE OF BEHAVIORAL TECHNIQUES APPLIED

Massed Practice

Massed practice (sometimes referred to as negative practice) is a paradoxical technique that involves voluntary practice of the tic. Consistent with Yates's (1958) formulation of tics as drive-reducing conditioned avoidance responses, massed practice is conducted in such a manner as to associate drive reduction (and thereby reinforcement) with nonperformance of the tic. This is accomplished by amassing a large number of trials in which the client voluntarily practices the tic over a brief time period. As a result of the effort involved in rapid practice, the patient will become fatigued and will be unable to perform the tic for a period of time. It is at this point that drive reduction and reinforcement for nonperformance of the tic occur.

Introduced as a therapeutic technique by Dunlap (1932), massed practice has been used primarily with adults to reduce or eliminate a variety of tics including eye blinking (Costello, 1963; Yates, 1958), head-jerking (Agras & Marshal, 1965; Turner, Hersen, & Alford, 1974), facial grimaces (Chapel, 1970; Rafi, 1962), and verbal tics demonstrated in Tourette's disorder (Clark, 1966). In clinical practice with children and adolescents, several daily periods of massed practice of from 30 seconds (Azrin, Nunn, & Frantz, 1980) to 5 minutes (Feldman & Werry, 1966; Sand & Carlson, 1973) are commonly interspersed with brief rest intervals. Results with children and adolescents generally have ranged from slight reductions (Sand & Carlson, 1973) in tics to reductions of approximately one-third to one-half in select cases (Azrin et al., 1980; Lahey et al., 1973).

Self-Monitoring

In addition to its use as an assessment method, self-monitoring has produced therapeutic effects in several investigations of tic disorders. In applications with tics, self-recording each occurrence may increase client awareness of tic responses, allow the client (and therapist) to identify antecedents and consequences of the target behavior, and produce client self-evaluation and/or self-administered consequences that alter the frequency of the target behavior.

In the course of assessing multiple tics (neck jerking, barking, and hissing-like sounds) of an 18-year-old with Tourette's disorder, Thomas et al. (1971) observed that self-monitoring resulted in lower rates of vocal tics than did other observation procedures. During successive applications of self-monitoring, tic frequencies were reduced to near zero, first for the bark-like response, then for the neck tic, and finally for the remaining tic-like vocalizations. Similar results have been reported in the case of a 9-year-old boy whose eye-blink and facial tics were eliminated with self-monitoring (Ollendick, 1981). Substantial, although less dramatic, reductions also have been achieved for tics involving head-jerking and barking in a child with Tourette's disorder (Hutzell, Platzek, & Logue, 1974) and for eye blinking and nasal sounds exhibited by an adolescent girl (Billings, 1978).

Incompatible Response Training

Several investigators have reported treatment programs designed to teach behaviors regarded as incompatible with tic responses. Incompatible responses such as appropriate verbalizations or conversational behaviors have been selected in cases of verbal tics, and relaxation often has been selected in cases of motor tics. Such competing responses have been modeled and rehearsed in clinic settings and their use then reinforced by the therapist as well as by parents, teachers, and/or other significant persons in the natural environment.

For example, Doleys and Kurtz (1974) reported increasing social behaviors such as eye contact, greeting people, and initiating conversations in an adolescent with Tourette's disorder. Friedman (1980) successfully taught an 11-year-old girl with Tourette's to substitute "clean" words for obscenities. Training in relaxation as a means of controlling motor responding also decreased facial, shoulder, and neck tics. When combined with token reinforcement for its use, relaxation has been shown to reduce tic-like episodes consisting of palsy-like hand movements and tensing of the upper body and arms in a 3-year-old boy (Poth & Barnett, 1983).

Presentation/Removal of Positive Reinforcement

In several studies tics have been modified using procedures in which reinforcing events were either administered contingent on low rates of the target behavior, withdrawn by ignoring the occurrence of tic responses, or removed by means of time-out procedures made contingent on tic responses. Shulman (1974) reduced tic responses by training the mother of a 9-year-old to effectively ignore her son's facial, arm, leg, and torso spasms, as well as grunts and shouts. Varni et al. (1978) combined a time-out procedure (placing the child in a barren room for 5 minutes contingent on occurrences of tics) with social, token, and activity reinforcers for low (or zero) rates of targeted tic responses. Decreases in facial grimacing, vocal tics, and several untreated tics were observed in the client, a 7-year-old hyperactive boy. In the classroom treatment of a 10-year-old boy, Lahey et al. (1973) also reported reductions in an obscene verbal tic with the use of time-out. In contrast, few studies have reported the effective use of other forms of punishment in the treatment of tics in children or adolescents (Stevens & Blachley, 1966).

Habit Reversal Treatment

A package of behavioral techniques described as habit reversal treatment was developed by Azrin and Nunn (1973) to deal specifically with tics and other nervous habits. In general, the rationale underlying use of habit reversal procedures is that behaviors such as tics consist of relatively normal responses that have increased to such a high frequency as to become somewhat automatic.

Intervention consists of training clients to become aware of each occurrence of a tic response by having them describe the details of the movement while reenacting the tic in a mirror. They also self-monitor each occurrence of the tic and review situations in which the tic frequently occurs as well as details regarding inconvenience and embarrassment that result from the tic. Clients are taught to perform a relatively inconspicuous competing response at the first sign of a tic or following its occurrence. For example, a competing response for head-jerking consists of isometric contraction of the neck by pulling the chin in and down (Azrin & Nunn, 1973). A competing response for eye-blinking might involve opening the eyes very widely, blinking deliberately for several seconds, and periodically shifting gaze (Finney et al., 1983).

In addition to these treatment elements, environmental support is solicited from family and friends in the form of social reinforcement and periodic reminders encouraging continued practice of the competing response. Thus, the habit reversal package incorporates many of the techniques (e.g., self-monitoring, training of incompatible responses, positive reinforcement) employed by other investigators in the treatment of tic disorders.

The habit reversal approach has been successfully used in the treatment of an 11-year-old boy demonstrating eye and facial twitching (Ollendick 1981) as well as in two boys, 11 and 13 years of age, who exhibited head, eye, and facial tics (Finney et al., 1983). In group investigations Azrin and his colleagues reported the effectiveness of habit reversal with 4 ticquers who were among 12 clients demonstrating nervous habits (Azrin & Nunn, 1973) and with a group of 10 ticquers of whom an unspecified number were children and adolescents (Azrin, Nunn, & Frantz, 1980). Results of these investigations generally have demonstrated reductions in target responses of at least 90% and in many cases to near-zero levels.

RESEARCH REVIEW

In examining the research on behavioral interventions with tic disorders, several aspects of treatment studies need to be evaluated. These include adequacy of research designs employed, assessment of covariation in treated and untreated tic responses, outcomes of intervention programs in producing socially valid changes in behavior, and duration of reported follow-up assessments.

Experimental Designs

Examination of the experimental designs employed in interventions with child and adolescent tic disorders reveals that the overwhelming majority have involved treatment of a single subject. Of these single-case studies, approximately one-half are found to be lacking in experimental control procedures sufficient to document that the specific treatment procedure effected change in tic responses. Most common among this group of studies has been the use of A-B designs.

Of those single-case studies demonstrating adequate controls, investigators typically have employed multiple baseline designs. Studies involving self-monitoring have been among the better-controlled investigations in this group, with some form of multiple baseline design across responses being most common (Billings, 1978; Hutzell et al., 1974; Varni et al., 1978).

Investigations that have examined the effects of treatment with multiple cases of tic disorders possess two common features: clients who exhibit transient or chronic tics and a treatment program involving habit reversal (Azrin & Nunn, 1973; Azrin et al., 1980; Finney et al., 1983; Ollendick, 1981). In contrast, single-subject interventions have included cases of Tourette's disorder and examined a wider range of treatment methods.

Studies that have assessed the effects of interventions for tic disorders by means of group designs (Azrin & Nunn, 1973; Azrin et al., 1980) also have several limitations. First, rather than presenting data on clients with tic disorders either individually or separately from data on individuals with other disorders, investigators have combined results from tic disorders with those for other nervous habits (Azrin & Nunn, 1973: Azrin et al., 1980). Second, the exact numbers of clients with tic disorders have not been indicated in these studies, although Azrin et al. (1980) report that four ticquers were included in their earlier investigation. Finally, neither study employed direct observation procedures, quantitative assessments of the reliability of self-report data, or standard control groups.

Response Covariation

A consideration relevant to the evaluation of treatment outcome as well as the assessment of tic disorders is the phenomenon of response covariation. In persons in whom several tics have been measured concurrently and treated sequentially, investigators have noted changes in untreated tics. Moreover, researchers also have reported alterations in the intensity and/or topography of those tics that have been treated. Thomas et al. (1971) found that topographically dissimilar responses emerged after the presenting tic was eliminated. For example, a "bark" was eliminated and a "hiss" subsequently began to occur. The authors suggested that all of these vocal responses may constitute an operant class.

Very similar explanations have been posited by investigators who have reported alterations in the rates of untreated tics. Nicassio et al. (1972) and Varni et al. (1978) noted that reductions in untreated tics occurred when the intervention was applied to one tic. In contrast, Finney et al. (1983) found that multiple tics decreased only when treatment was applied to each; furthermore, one untreated behavior actually increased in frequency as two other tics were reduced. Nicassio et al. (1972) suggest that tics are arranged into a "behavioral complex" whereby change in one component affects other components in the same or opposite directions. Finney et al. (1983) elaborated on this hypothesis by proposing that the complex or functional response class be composed of either positively co-occurring or negatively co-occurring responses. When responses in the class are positively co-occurring, change in the direction of one tic is accompanied by a change in the same direction by another tic. For example, untreated behaviors decrease concomitantly with one or more treated tics. If the response class consists of negatively co-occurring behaviors, they may be arranged hierarchically such that reduction of one member results in an increase in the next response in the hierarchy. Varni et al. (1978) suggest the development of procedures for systematically identifying "functional response classes and possible key or controlling behaviors in those functional response classes on an *a priori* basis (p. 357)."

The issue of covariation of tic responses is particularly important when evaluating the internal validity of treatment approaches. Use of single-subject research designs involving a multiple baseline across behaviors may not be advisable given that tics often are interdependent. Rather, use of nested designs (e.g., multiple baseline across behaviors nested within a multiple baseline across participants) and multiple baseline designs across participants or settings may be preferred. Use of such designs with concurrent monitoring of several tics would allow for evaluation of treatment effects as well as for assessment and potential identification of "key or controlling behaviors" (Varni et al., 1978).

Social Validation

Although a number of treatment studies demonstrate change in tic responses, it is unclear from most investigations what impact such changes have on the overall functioning of the client. Finney et al. (1983) note that the unusual appearance and social embarrassment caused by tics are frequently cited reasons for seeking treatment for these disorders. Consequently, using a social validation framework (Kazdin, 1977; Wolf, 1978), Finney et al. (1983) collected pre-treatment and posttreatment ratings of the degree to which persons in the natural environment viewed two clients as demonstrating distracting head and face movements or as demonstrating a need for treatment.

If improvements in rate of tics resulting from treatment are to be viewed as socially meaningful, changes in the manner in which the client is perceived by other persons in the environment should accompany decreases in rate. Global judgments of this type also may take into account meaningful changes in dimensions such as intensity, duration, topography, and pattern of tics that are not measured directly.

In addition, successful methods of intervention have commonly required the client to engage in physically competing responses that may also be somewhat distracting to observers in the natural environment. Therefore, it would be useful to evaluate the distracting nature of these movements from observers' perspectives. In this manner the social validity of overall improvements in motor behavior of the client can be documented.

Follow-up Assessment

A review of behavioral intervention studies with childhood and adolescent tic disorders indicates that only approximately one-third of these investigations have conducted follow-up assessments of 12 months or more, with none reported beyond 18 months. However, research examining the natural course of tic disorders (Baker et al., 1983; Surwillo et al., 1978) has emphasized the characteristic "waxing and waning" of tics, particularly in Tourette's disorder, commonly due to varying levels of client stress. As a result, follow-up assessment periods of from 12 to 24 months are strongly recommended in interventions with tic disorders (Mostofsky, 1981). Periodic booster treatments may also be of considerable utility following termination of formal intervention programs.

Conclusions

From the preceding review of research on behavioral interventions with tic disorders of children and adolescents, it is apparent that studies incorporating well-controlled single-subject or group designs, reliable and valid dependent measures, and follow-up data of sufficient length have been conducted rather infrequently. As a result, definitive conclusions cannot be drawn regarding the relative efficacy of various behavioral treatment approaches for treating tics.

The findings of investigations by Azrin and his colleagues (1977, 1980) and Finney et al. (1983) do provide tentative support, however, for the utility of habit reversal treatments in reducing transient and/or chronic tic disorders. Since the habit reversal package involves components of several therapeutic approaches such as self-monitoring, incompatible response training, and social reinforcement, it would appear to be the most comprehensive and promising treatment method available at this time. Nevertheless, its applicability to Tourette's disorder has as yet been untested.

Based on the empirical literature, any general conclusions, however tentative, regarding preferred behavioral treatments for Tourette's would be highly speculative. Relatively few studies have demonstrated clinically significant change with this disorder, and one of the few successful cases reported (Thomas et al., 1971) has confounded application of self-monitoring procedures with training in systematic desensitization and administration of haloperidol. Nonetheless, use of behavioral approaches to deal with stressful events that may exacerbate Tourette's disorder (e.g., Friedman, 1980) appears promising.

CASE DESCRIPTION

IDENTIFICATION

Kim was a 14-year-old girl referred for treatment of a persistent tic involving pronounced tightening in the muscles of the right side of her neck and a drawing back of the right side of her mouth. Her symptoms began at the end of the previous school year during final exams. Over the subsequent summer, her tics reportedly subsided, then increased in frequency when school began the following fall. Psychological evaluation was requested by her parents when her tics did not remit at the end of the school year.

Kim was a very attractive adolescent who obtained grades of A's and B's in school. She was described as popular with both male and female peers and presented no behavior problems. She also was involved in extracurricular activities such as the school band. Her pediatrician reported no medical problems.

ASSESSMENT

In the initial interview, an attempt was made to determine the environmental stimuli associated with Kim's tics. Kim reported that she noticed her tics increased in frequency during periods of stress or tension. In particular, she noticed tics in situations where she felt attention was drawn to her, such as when she was directing the band, playing a solo, and auditioning for majorette, and when she attended dances with other adolescents she did not know. Kim indicated that she often worried she might start to tic in these situations and that she often tried to inhibit tics by holding her neck and head very still and tense. However, she said this strategy often made her feel more anxious and had little effect on tic frequency.

Kim was observed from behind a one-way mirror for a 5-minute period during the initial interview. Although she was informed that she would be observed, she did not know when the observation began. A total of 38 tics were observed during this initial 5-minute observation. Kim's mother was instructed to monitor tic frequency unobtrusively at home daily at unannounced times. Baseline tic frequency at home ranged from 25 to 30 tics per 5-minute interval. Kim also self-monitored the frequency of tics during band practice (which she reported as a high tic frequency situation). She reported an average of 10 tics per 5-minute observation period.

CONCEPTUALIZATION

Although Kim was aware of and concerned about her tics in general, she seemed to be unaware of roughly two-thirds of her tic responses. In order to teach her to control her tics, it was assumed that it would therefore be necessary to first improve the accuracy of her perception of their occurrence.

Additionally, Kim's tic disorder was hypothesized to be related to stressful situations. In particular, she seemed to exhibit tics most often in situations that she perceived as evaluative (i.e., when peers or instructors were expected to judge her performance). It was hypothesized that the physiological arousal and negative self-statements Kim experienced in these situations were likely associated with the occurrence of tics. Therefore, relaxation training and cognitive restructuring were expected to help reduce her arousal and thereby reduce the likelihood of tics.

TREATMENT

Treatment consisted of a habit reversal program similar to that employed by Azrin, Nunn, and Frantz (1980). An outline of the treatment program is presented in Table 9.1. The first stage of treatment focused on heightening Kim's awareness of tic occurrence. While the therapist observed, Kim watched herself in a mirror and described the movements and sensations she experienced when the tic occurred spontaneously as well as when she tried to produce the tic voluntarily. Kim was instructed to continue to monitor tic occurrence be-

TABLE 9.1   Outline of Treatment

Session 1	Baseline assessment
Session 2	Awareness training
Session 3	Competing response instruction
Sessions 4–8	General stress management (weekly)
	Relaxation training
	Audiotaped relaxation practice
	Cognitive restructuring
	In-vivo home assignments
Sessions 9–11	Maintenance and generalization (monthly)
Follow-up	Phone call one month posttreatment

tween sessions and to record those situations and negative self-statements that were associated with tic emission.

In the next session, a physical therapist was consulted to assist in developing and teaching Kim an exercise that was incompatible with tic movements. This competing response consisted of pulling her shoulders downward, tilting her chin as if nodding, and pursing her lips. Kim practiced the competing response in the session until she was able to inhibit the tic with movements that were only slightly noticeable to an observer. Kim was instructed to practice this response, holding the position for 5 seconds, whenever she felt she might have a tic or immediately following a tic.

Following competing response training, Kim's frequency of tics in-session decreased by 55% to 17 tics per 5-minute period. Her mother reported average daily frequencies of 10 to 11 tics per 5 minute period at home, an average decrease of 63%.

The next five therapy sessions involved general stress management training. Kim was taught a 16-muscle-group tension-release progressive relaxation procedure. In subsequent sessions, muscle groups were collapsed, until Kim was able to use cue-controlled, entire body relaxation and deep breathing to calm herself.

Considerable attention also was paid to the negative self-statements Kim made in stressful situations. She tended to catastrophize and to attribute unrealistic attitudes to others. Kim was coached in more adaptive coping statements to use in such situations. In each session, potentially stressful events in the upcoming week were discussed, relaxation and cognitive coping strategies were rehearsed, and between-session practice exercises were assigned.

Over the course of these sessions, Kim reported an increasing number of instances in which she noticed herself thinking negatively but was able to deal actively with the situation. The procedures used in such circumstances involved Kim's relaxing and combating the negative self-statements with coping statements she had rehearsed previously. For example, Kim reported using the stress management strategies to help her stop worrying and to enable her to fall asleep the night before an exam.

During the stress management training phase, Kim's in-session tics decreased to 10 per 5-minute period (a 74% decrease from baseline). Her mother reported an average rate of 9.5 tics per 5-minute period at home during this phase of treatment.

Three final sessions were conducted at approximately monthly intervals to facilitate maintenance and generalization of Kim's stress management skills. Kim's mother continued to record daily tic frequency at home during this period. Therapy was terminated when both Kim and her mother reported they were satisfied with her progress.

During the maintenance and generalization phase of treatment, Kim's mother reported home tic frequencies of 7.0, 7.2, and 4.0 tics per 5-minute period. Such frequencies respresent decreases from baseline of 77%, 76%, and 85%, respectively. The magnitude of tic movements also decreased over this period. Kim's mouth movements were no longer visible, and her neck movements were only slightly noticeable, appearing more like slight shifts in shoulder position than actual muscle tensing. In the final treatment session, only 4 tics were observed per 5-minute period (a decrease of 84% from baseline).

FOLLOW-UP

At 1-month follow-up, Kim's mother reported tic frequencies of near zero at home during the previous week. These data were particularly encouraging since Kim was able to maintain a low tic frequency despite having completed final exams during that week.

Commentary

The awareness training and competing response training phases of treatment resulted in reductions of approximately 55 to 65% in Kim's tics. However, with the addition of stress management training, tics were reduced to near zero. Although this case was seen in clinical practice and was not designed to document empirically which aspect of treatment actually produced improvements, one can speculate about the contributions made by the stress management phase of treatment. For example, extended practice in self-monitoring tics, stressful events, and positive and negative self-statements might have further improved Kim's awareness of her tics, thus allowing her to practice the competing response more frequently. Alternatively, training in relaxation and cognitive restructuring may have decreased arousal in stressful situations, thereby decreasing the likelihood of a tic.

The results of this case study may be contrasted with those obtained with an 11-year-old boy who demonstrated rapid eye blinking, gross motor tics including intermittent facial grimacing, neck and shoulder jerking, and repetitive neck pinching. Assessment of this case revealed a history of declining academic performance, resulting in the child's recent failure in all academic subjects and subsequent expulsion from school for fighting, as well as significant attention, memory, and motor deficits. The child frequently fought with peers and demonstrated considerable anger and frustration when repeatedly presented with difficult academic tasks. Despite the absence of verbal tics, a pediatric neurologist diagnosed the child's symptoms as "probable early Tourette's Syndrome."

Since it was speculated that school and peer stresses were exacerbating this child's tic disorder, relaxation training was combined with study skills training and reinforcement for completing school work. Completion of school assignments soon approached 100%, the child reported that he enjoyed school, and no incidents of fighting or anger outbursts were reported by his teacher. However, the rate of eye blinking and gross motor tics still remained high and extremely variable until treatment sessions were devoted specifically to coaching the child in the use of relaxation to control tics.

After several relaxation sessions, gross motor tics decreased from an average of 12 per minute to 4 per minute in the clinic setting. Self-monitoring data indicated a 60% reduction in gross motor tics; however, no change in eye blinking was observed in clinic or nonclinic settings. Reductions in eye-blink responses, from a mean of 14 to 3 per minute, were observed only after the child was taught a competing response (i.e., 5 seconds of eye closing following five or more eye blinks in succession).

Two important issues in the treatment of tic disorders are highlighted by these cases. First, differences in observed treatment effectiveness illustrate the disparity in outcomes generally observed for Tourette's disorder as compared to transient and chronic tics. Although many cases of transient and chronic tic disorders have been virtually eliminated with behavioral treatments such as habit reversal, few instances of elimination of tics have been reported in cases of Tourette's disorder. Second, the importance of including both environmental intervention and habit reversal training in the treatment of tics is illustrated. Although school and other stressors may well have exacerbated the tic disorders described, clinically significant reductions in gross motor tic responses were not obtained until clients were trained in specific competing responses.

SUMMARY

Transient tic disorder, chronic tic disorder, and Tourette's syndrome are classified as disorders of childhood and adolescence due to the typical age of clients at onset. Although varying theories exist regarding the etiology of these disorders, behavioral methods involving the clinical interview, direct observation of target responses, and client self-report are commonly employed in the assessment of tics. The advantages of direct observation in terms of defining tic responses and identifying antecedent conditions and consequences are especially emphasized.

A variety of behavioral treatment procedures including massed practice, self-monitoring, incompatible response training, presentation or removal of reinforcement, and habit reversal approaches have been successfully employed in altering tic responses in individual case studies. Few investigations have examined the effectiveness of such procedures in multiple cases, however, and conclusions regarding the relative efficacy of various behavioral interventions are limited due to lack of adequate controls, measurement considerations, and the absence of follow-up assessments of sufficient duration. Nonetheless, as illustrated by the case material presented, the use of habit reversal procedures involving competing response training and training in specific stress management strategies does hold considerable promise for the treatment of many tic disorders.

REFERENCES

Agras, S., & Marshall, C. (1965). The application of negative practice to spasmodic torticollis. *American Journal of Psychiatry*, *122*, 579–582.

American Psychiatric Association. (1980). *Diagnostic and statistical manual for mental disorders*. (3rd ed.). Washington, DC: Author.

Azrin, N. H., & Nunn, R. G. (1973). Habit-reversal: A method of eliminating nervous habits and tics. *Behaviour Research and Therapy*, *11*, 619–628.

Azrin, N. H., Nunn, R. G., & Frantz, S. E. (1980). Habit reversal vs. negative practice: Treatment of nervous tics. *Behavior Therapy*, *11*, 169–178.

Baker, Jr., E. L., Platt, J. A., & Fine, H. J. (1983). Tic de Gilles de la Tourette: Survey of the literature, case study, and reinterpretation. *Clinical Psychology Review*, *3*, 157–178.

Bakwin, H., & Bakwin, R. M. (1972). *Behavior disorders in children*. Philadelphia: Saunders.

Baron, M. Shapiro, E., Shapiro, A. K., & Rainer, J. D. (1981). Genetic analysis of Tourette syndrome suggesting major gene affect. *American Journal of Human Genetics*, *33*, 767–775.

Bauer, A. M., Shea, T. M. (1984). Tourette syndrome: A review and educational implications. *Journal of Autism and Developmental Disorders*, *14*, 69–80.

Billings, A. (1978). Self-monitoring in the treatment of tics: A single-subject analysis. *Journal of Behavior Therapy and Experimental Psychiatry*, *9*, 339–342.

Bruun, R. D. (1984). Gilles de la Tourette's syndrome: An overview of clinical experience. *Journal of the American Academy of Child Psychiatry*, *23*, 126–133.

Chapel, J. L. (1965). Behavior modification techniques with children and adolescents. *Canadian Psychiatric Association Journal, 15*, 315–318.

Clark, D. F. (1966). Behavior therapy in Gilles de la Tourette syndrome. *British Journal of Psychiatry, 112*, 117–118.

Cohen, D. J., Detlor, J., Shaywitz, B. A., & Leckman, J. F. (1982). Interaction of biological and psychological factors in the natural history of Tourette Syndrome: A paradigm for childhood neuropsychiatric disorder. In A. J. Friedhoff and T. N. Chase (Eds.), *Gilles de la Tourette syndrome*. New York: Raven.

Corbett, J. A., Matthews, A. M., Connell, P. H., & Shapiro, D. A. (1969). Tics and Gilles de la Tourette syndrome: A follow-up study and critical review. *British Journal of Psychiatry, 115*, 1229–1241.

Costello, C. G. (1963). The essentials of behavior therapy. *Canadian Psychiatric Association Journal, 8*, 162–166.

Doleys, D. M., & Kurtz, P. S. (1974). A behavioral treatment for the Gilles de la Tourette syndrome. *Psychological Reports, 35*, 42–48.

Dunlap, K. (1932). *Habits: Their making and unmaking*. New York: Liveright.

Feldman, R. B., & Werry, J. S. (1966). An unsuccessful attempt to treat a ticquer by massed practice. *Behaviour Research and Therapy, 4*, 111–117.

Fenichel, O. (1945). *The psychoanalytic theory of neurosis*. New York: Norton Press.

Ferenczi, S. (1921). Psycho-analytical observations on tic. *International Journal of Psychoanalysis, 2*, 1–30.

Finney, J. W., Rapoff, M. A., Hall, C. L., & Christophersen, E. R. (1983). Replication and social validation of habit reversal treatment for tics. *Behavior Therapy, 14*, 116–126.

Friedman, S. (1980). Self-control in the treatment of Gilles de la Tourette syndrome: Case study with 18-month follow-up. *Journal of Consulting and Clinical Psychology, 48*, 400–402.

Glaze, D. G., Jankovic, J., & Frost, J. D. (1982). Sleep in Gilles de la Tourette syndrome: Disorder of arousal. *Neurology, 32*, 153.

Golden, G. S. (1977). Tourette syndrome. *American Journal of Diseases of Children, 131*, 531–534.

Golden, G. S. (1982). Movement disorders in children: Tourette syndrome. *Developmental and Behavioral Pediatrics, 3*, 209–216.

Haynes, S. N., & Jensen, B. J. (1979). The interview as a behavioral assessment instrument. *Behavioral Assessment, 1*, 97–106.

Hollandsworth, J. G., & Bausinger, L. (1978). Unsuccessful use of massed practice in the treatment of Gilles de la Tourette's syndrome. *Psychological Reports, 43*, 671–677.

Hull, C. L. (1943). *Principles of behavior*. New York: Appleton-Century.

Hutzell, R. R., Platsek, D., & Logue, P. E. (1974). Control of symptoms of Gilles de la Tourette's syndrome by self-monitoring. *Journal of Behavior Therapy and Experimental Psychiatry, 5*, 71–76.

Kazdin, A. E. (1977). Assessing the clinical or applied importance of behavior change through social validation. *Behavior Modification, 1,* 427-452.

King, A. C., & Ollendick, T. H. (1984). Gilles de la Tourette disorder: A review. *Journal of Clinical Child Psychology, 13,* 2-9.

Lahey, B. B., McNees, M. P., & McNees, M. C. (1973). Control of an obscene "verbal tic" through timeout in an elementary school classroom. *Journal of Applied Behavior Analysis, 6,* 101-104.

Lucas, A. R. (1970). Gilles de la Tourette's disease: An overview. *New York Medical Journal, 70,* 2197-2200.

Mahler, M. S., & Luke, J. A. (1946). Outcome of the tic syndrome. *Journal of Nervous and Mental Disorders, 103,* 433-445.

Mash, E. J., & Terdal, L. G. (1981). Behavioral assessment of childhood disturbance. In E. J. Mash & L. G. Terdal (Eds.), *Behavioral assessment of childhood disorders.* New York: Guilford.

Morphew, J., & Sim, M. (1969). Gilles de la Tourette's syndrome: A clinical and psychopathological study. *British Journal of Medical Psychology, 42,* 293-301.

Mostofsky, D. I. (1981). Recurrent paroxysmal disorders of central nervous system. In S. M. Turner, K. L. Calhoun, & H. E. Adams (Eds.), *Handbook of clinical behavior therapy.* New York: Wiley.

Nicassio, F. J., Liberman, R. P., Patterson, R. L., Ramirez, E., & Sanders, N. (1972). The treatment of tics by negative practice. *Journal of Behavior Therapy and Experimental Psychiatry, 3,* 281-287.

Ollendick, T. H. (1981). Self-monitoring and self-administered overcorrection: The modification of nervous tics in children. *Behavior Modification, 5,* 75-84.

Ollendick, T. H., & Cerny, J. A. (1981). *Clinical behavior therapy with children.* New York: Plenum.

Poth, R., & Barnett, D. W. (1983). Reduction of a behavioral tic with a preschooler using relaxation and self-control techniques across setttings. *School Psychology Review, 12,* 472-476

Rafi, A. A. (1962). Learning theory and the treatment of tics. *Journal of Psychosomatic Research, 6,* 71-76.

Sand, P. L., & Carlson, C. (1973). Failure to establish control over tics in the Gilles de la Tourette syndrome with behaviour therapy techniques. *British Journal of Psychiatry, 122,* 665-670.

Sanders, D. G. (1973). Familial occurrence of Gilles de la Tourette syndrome. *Archives of General Psychiatry, 28,* 326-328.

Schulman, M. (1974). Control of tics by maternal reinforcement. *Journal of Behavior Therapy and Experimental Psychiatry, 5,* 95-96.

Shapiro, A. K., & Shapiro, E. (1982). An update on Tourette syndrome. *American Journal of Psychotherapy, 26,* 379-390.

Shapiro, A. K., Shapiro, E. S., Bruun, R. D., & Sweet, R. D. (1978). *Gilles de la Tourette syndrome.* New York: Raven.

Skinner, B. F. (1938). *The behavior of organisms.* Englewood Cliffs, N.J.: Prentice Hall.

Skinner, A. K., Shapiro, E., & Wayne, H. (1972). Birth, developmental and family histories and demographic information in Tourette's syndrome. *Journal of Nervous and Mental Disorders, 155,* 335–344.

Stevens, J. R., & Blachley, R. (1966). Successful treatment of the maladie des tics. *American Journal of Disease in Children, 112,* 541–545.

St. James-Roberts, N., & Powell, G. E. (1979). A case-study comparing the effects of relaxation and massed practice upon tic frequency. *Behaviour Research and Therapy, 17,* 401–403.

Surwillo, W. W., Shafii, M., & Barrett, C. L. (1978). Gilles de la Tourette syndrome: A 20-month study of the effects of stressful life events and haloperidol on symptom frequency. *Journal of Nervous and Mental Disease, 166,* 812–816.

Thomas, E. J., Abrams, K. S., & Johnson, J. B. (1971). Self-monitoring and reciprocal inhibition in the modification of multiple tics of Gilles de la Tourette's syndrome. *Journal of Behavior Therapy and Experimental Psychiatry, 2,* 159–171.

Turner, S. M., Hersen, M., & Alford, H. (1974). Effects of massed practice and meprobamate on spasmodic torticollis: An experimental analysis. *Behaviour Research and Therapy, 12,* 259–260.

Valente, M. B., & Valente, S. M. (1983). Tics in children and adolescents. *Pediatric Nursing, 9,* 323–326.

Varni, J. W., Boyd, E. F., & Cataldo, M. F. (1978). Self-monitoring, external reinforcement, and timeout procedures in the control of high rate tic behaviors in a hyperactive child. *Journal of Behavior Therapy and Experimental Psychiatry, 9,* 353–358.

Wolf, M. M. (1978). Social validity: The case for subjective measurement or how behavior analysis is finding its heart. *Journal of Applied Behavior Analysis, 11,* 203–214.

Yates, A. J. (1958). The application of learning theory to the treatment of tics. *Journal of Abnormal and Social Psychology, 56,* 175–182.

Yates, A. J. (1970). *Behavior therapy.* New York: Wiley.

CHAPTER 10

Stuttering

THOMAS M. DiLORENZO AND JOHNNY L. MATSON

Language ability is a skill that emerges in infancy and rapidly develops through childhood. By the age of 5, the typical child has 2000 words in his or her vocabulary. Therefore, it is not surprising that complications or problems in language ability would arise during this developmental period or that these difficulties would come to the attention of professionals at this time (Ollendick & Matson, 1983).

This chapter deals specifically with the speech disorder called stuttering. A great deal of information has been published in this century regarding stuttering. Actually, the literature on stuttering dates back to Hippocrates (Lanyon & Goldsworthy, 1982), but much of the scientific rigor necessary to draw reasonable conclusions has been inadequate (Webster, 1974). "Although the literature contains a wide array of etiological theories, basic research, and suggestions for treatment, the nature of the disorder is still not understood, and the treatment procedures have not been proved to be effective" (Lanyon & Goldsworthy, 1982, p. 814). Nevertheless, stuttering can be a particularly disabling problem, not only because communication is severely impaired, but also because it can lead to poor social relations due to isolation and teasing from peers. In addition, academic problems can occur from an avoidance of speaking in class.

At first glance, the reader may assume that individuals with a stuttering problem should seek help from a speech therapist. That approach may be the first important step. However, Rousey (1978) noted that the incidence of speech disorders among individuals who are experiencing psychological distress can be as high as 90%, a figure that is at least 9 times greater than the incidence of psychological distress in the general population. Moreover, a reduction in the number of speech disturbances is noted with the concomitant improvement in psychological functioning (Rousey, 1978).

An emphasis on psychological factors related to stuttering usually involves examining such factors as stress and disturbed interpersonal relationships

(Burns & Brady, 1980). A simple psychological overview of stuttering is provided by Burns and Brady (1980), who state that:

> the disorder called stuttering may be viewed as a system in which several components continually interact: an abnormal speech pattern (dysfluency), anxiety or tension in a variety of interpersonal interactions, and a series of beliefs or expectations that stuttering and intrepersonal failure will in fact occur whenever certain stressful situations are encountered. (p. 675)

Stuttering is clearly a multifaceted problem. There is not sufficient space in this chapter to cover the varied etiological theories of stuttering. Such an effort would per force include not only genetic or innate predispositional theories, biochemical, or physiological theories, and theories related to difficulties in phonatory processes, but also other psychological theories including a psychodynamic approach. Rather, this chapter will provide information on how stuttering has been defined as well as techniques used to assess and treat this disorder from a behavioral perspective.

DESCRIPTION OF THE DISORDER

Definition

Stuttering has been defined in a number of ways. Wingate (1964), in an article entitled "A Standard Definition of Stuttering," defined it as a "disruption in the fluency of verbal expression, which is characterized by involuntary, audible or silent, repetitions or prolongations in the utterance of short speech elements" (p. 488). Ollendick and Matson (1983) defined it operationally as "speech disruption or dysfluency that occurs when a person is speaking" (p. 238). Finally, the third edition of the *Diagnostic and Statistical Manual of Mental Disorders* (DSM-III; American Psychiatric Association, 1980) provides the following definition:

> The essential features are frequent repetitions or prolongations of sounds, syllables, or words, or frequent, unusual hesitations and pauses that disrupt the rhythmic flow of speech. The extent of the disturbance varies from situation to situation and is most severe when there is special pressure to communicate. (p. 78)

DSM-III provides some additional descriptive information on stuttering. "Stammering" is considered to be a synonym for stuttering. Also, speech may be either very rapid or slow. Further, a person may exhibit inappropriate inflection or may lack variation in pitch.

Associated Features

Among stutterers, the stuttering does not necessarily occur in all situations. Indeed, there may be periods when stuttering is absent completely, such as during oral reading, singing, or talking to inanimate objects or pets (American Psychiatric Association, 1980). In addition, DSM-III suggests that in moderate to severe cases, individuals may avoid particular words or situations in which stuttering is anticipated. Finally, a number of behaviors may be emitted concomitantly with stuttering, and the frequency and intensity of these collateral responses (e.g., eye blinks, tics, tremors of the lip or jaw, jerking of the head) may increase with greater severity of stuttering.

Incidence

Stuttering is more frequently a problem among young males, with the estimated sex ratio ranging from 3:1 to 8:1 (Bakwin & Bakwin, 1972; Jones, 1970). Although persistent stuttering is found in 1 to 2% of the population, transient stuttering appears in 4 to 5 of the population (Bakwin & Bakwin, 1972; Jones, 1970). Interestingly, nearly 50% of individuals with stuttering problems recover without treatment by age 12 and 80% do not stutter by the time they reach their late teens (American Psychiatric Association, 1980; Sheehan & Marlyn, 1966, 1967). In addition, parents with poor parenting skills and/or speech difficulties of their own are more likely to have children with speech difficulties. Other factors that correlate with the incidence of stuttering include inappropriate verbal stimulation by parents, illness, and negative parent-child interaction patterns (Irwin, 1969; Mysak & Gilbert, 1972).

Onset and Course

Problems with stuttering occur in childhood with two peaks of onset: between the ages of 2 to 3 ½ and 5 to 7 years (American Psychiatric Association, 1980). Young (1975) notes that there are essentially no onsets after age 9.

The progression of the problem is usually gradual and chronic. However, there may be periods of remission for up to several months, with exacerbations most frequently occurring when pressure is applied for the person to speak or communicate (American Psychiatric Association, 1980).

According to DSM-III, the disorder usually starts with a repetition of initial consonants, whole words at the beginning of phrases, or particularly long, complex words. As the disorder progresses, repetitions become more frequent, and stuttering occurs on the most important words or phrases. The child becomes aware of the speech difficulty, and in certain situations some words and sounds become more difficult for him or her to pronounce.

BEHAVIORAL ASSESSMENT

Before discussing specific procedures for behavioral assessment of stuttering, we will begin with an overview of behavioral assessment (or behavioral analysis) of any problem behavior.

The *sine qua non* of behavioral assessment is a functional analysis (sometimes referred to as a behavioral analysis). The importance of performing a functional analysis prior to initiating treatment cannot be overemphasized. A functional analysis is defined as a thorough assessment of maladaptive behavior and its interrelationship with variables that control its emission to determine cause-effect relationships (DiLorenzo, in press). These variables are located in a chain or series of behaviors, with the problematic behavior juxtaposed with antecedent and consequent events. The interactional sequence may be viewed in a molecular (e.g., antecedent–behavior–consequence) or in a molar (e.g., rate of response matches rate of reinforcement) sense.

This functional analysis would tie the assessment procedure directly to specific treatment approaches. Effective interventions rely on a comprehensive analysis of the functional relationships among behaviors in child–environment interactions. Without this process, treatments are too often adopted uncritically (Phillips & Ray, 1980).

In the interest of developing a treatment plan, several steps should be followed in the functional analysis:

1. The problem must be specified and the behavior of interest must be defined (each of these steps will be covered below as they relate to stuttering).
2. The controlling variables must be identified (Schreibman & Koegel, 1981).
3. Schreibman and Koegel (1981) suggest grouping behaviors according to common controlling variables. In this way, as with every functional analysis, treatment is automatically specified (Matson & DiLorenzo, 1984).
4. A procedure should be selected that would manipulate the controlling variables so as to effect the most significant behavior change (Schreibman & Koegel, 1981).

Throughout this process, data must be collected to determine whether treatment goals are being met (Mash & Terdal, 1981). Each of these four steps will be discussed as they relate to the assessment of stuttering.

In his behavioral analysis of stuttering, Brady (1968) viewed the disorder ''as consisting of two components which continuously interact: an abnormal speech pattern (dysfluency) and anxiety or tension in a variety of speaking situations'' (p. 844). Burns and Brady (1980) have added a third component: ''a series of beliefs or expectations that stuttering and interpersonal failure will in fact occur whenever certain stressful situations are encountered'' (p. 675). These three components roughly comprise the first two steps previously outlined.

In step 1 the behavior (i.e., stuttering or an abnormal speech pattern or dysfluency) must be defined concretely and operationally. Resick, Wendiggensen, Ames, and Meyer (1978) defined two specific types of dysfluencies: (1) repetition of all or part of a phrase, and (2) silent or vocal blocks prior to the onset of a word or syllable. Burns and Brady (1980) defined two additional dysfluencies: (3) prolongation of a sound, and (4) use of a filler (e.g., *ah, you know*). The investigators noted that these dysfluencies are assessed after having the client read for a 3-minute time period. Then, assessments (through observation) of the four dysfluencies will yield three parameters related to the problematic behavior: (1) total dysfluencies, (2) total words spoken (i.e., rate of speaking), and (3) percent dysfluency rate (i.e., ratio of total dysfluencies to the total words spoken). In this way, the therapist can maintain a record of the client's progress throughout treatment.

Step 2 (i.e., assessment of variables controlling stuttering) can be broken down into two parts. Brady (1968) noted ''that attention be focused on (1) the antecedent events (or situational requirements) which occasion stuttering in susceptible persons and (2) an examination of the consequences of stuttering which might illuminate reinforcing events important in its maintenance'' (p. 843). We will refer to these two components in a more general sense as situational and individual variables. This distinction may appear arbitrary at times, since the two variables unquestionably are interrelated. However, we feel that it is a helpful distinction to aid in conceptualization. We will begin with individual variables.

Ollendick and Matson (1983) note that from a behavioral perspective, stuttering is viewed as a learned behavior. One behavioral view of stuttering is that the problem is related to increased anxiety about speaking. From this perspective, stuttering is considered a complex set of cognitive, affective, and behavioral-motoric responses learned situationally by the speaker in an effort to avoid situations or to correct perceived self-deficiencies. Moreover, stutterers appear to hold certain distorted ideas, beliefs, or attitudes about speech and speaking in interpersonal situations. In one sense these distorted or irrational ideas serve as cues that set the occasion for anxiety and speech dysfluency. As anxiety level increases, so does prevalence and severity of stuttering. Burns and Brady (1980) address these issues by recommending an emotional assessment to ascertain maladaptive attitudes and feelings that have contributed to any behavioral difficulties.

Ollendick and Matson's (1983) second behavioral explanation for stuttering is that it is due primarily to poorly developed speech patterns. As such, this response class is nothing more than a negative habit (Dalali & Sheehan, 1974).

The second way in which variables that control stuttering can be viewed is through situational control. Burns and Brady (1980) state that for most clients,

> the dysfluencies occur only in social situations defined by the presence of one or more individuals who can hear and evaluate the stutterer's speech. For severe stutterers, the presence of any other individual may be a sufficient cause for difficulty; for others, periods of fluency may be interrupted by periods of dysfluency only in response to certain types of stimuli. Such stimuli may include members of the opposite sex, groups, telephones, authority figures, and so forth, as well as certain emotionally charged interactions (e.g., during angry encounters). (p. 674)

Zielinski and Williams (1979) also have shown changes in stuttering as a result of placing the stutterer in various types of assertive situations.

As discussed earlier, the two global varieties that control stuttering behavior are interrelated. Burns and Brady (1980) summed up the "stuttering cycle":

> The probability and severity of stuttering in response to such (emotionally charged) stimuli depend on the amount of tension and anxiety experienced by the individual as the moment of *speaking* approaches. The tension, frustration, and embarrassment experienced when the stuttering actually occurs tend to confirm the stutterer's belief that such situations will in fact be difficult, leading to an intensification of the link between the external stimulus and the conditioned emotional responses. In other words, the stutterer's prediction that he will stutter in certain situations tends to be confirmed over and over again in his everyday experience, resulting in a fixed belief that he is indeed bound to fail whenever such situations are encountered. Thus, the expectations and experiences interact in a self-confirming closed system. (p. 674)

Specific assessment techniques include self observations, ratings by observers (i.e., after the stutterer has supplied a sample reading assignment), ratings by significant others (e.g., a spouse or employer), role-plays, situation tests, and/or self-report instruments specific to stuttering (e.g., Stutterer's Self-Rating or Reactions to Speech Situations; Johnson, Darley, & Spriesterbach, 1963) or related to the stutterer's affect (e.g., Beck Depression Inventory; Beck, 1967).

Burns and Brady (1980) suggest a number of other areas that should be assessed, including the reason for referral, history of the problem and prior treatments, family history, medical history, and information on life adjustment, such as school, career, and interpersonal relationships. A final assessment technique may involve the assessment and construction of a hierarchy of feared situations.

Step 3 in conducting a thorough functional analysis is the grouping of behaviors according to common controlling variables. In addition to the four specific stuttering dysfluencies that have been defined, other behaviors that may occur concomitantly with stuttering (e.g., eye blinks, tics) also have been specified. These behaviors may or may not be controlled by the same variables.

As noted earlier, stuttering may be controlled by situation and/or individual variables. More specifically, stuttering may be (1) controlled by positive or negative reinforcement, (2) elicited by anxiety, (3) a function of poorly developed speech patterns, (4) due to rapid speech, (5) a result of overcompensation of slow speech, (6) controlled by certain beliefs or thoughts, (7) elicited by certain situations or people, and/or (8) due to anticipatory anxiety. Brady (1968) states that;

> indeed many clinicians have stressed that much of stuttering behavior, such as hesitations and blocks in speech and facial grimacing and tremors, is the direct result of efforts to control anticipated stuttering. Thus, the anticipatory anxiety elicited by speaking situations which have been difficult in the past leads to further stuttering in just these situations in a kind of vicious circle of anxiety and dysfluency. (p. 844)

Burns and Brady (1980) further assert that "the stutterer finds himself in a self-perpetuating cycle in which cognitive, emotional, and behavioral components continually interact in a closed system" (p. 718). These descriptions are certainly not an exhaustive view of the possible controlling factors. They are simply examples that indicate the potential complexity in assessing this disorder.

Treatment specification is the fourth and final step in the functional analysis. Notably, a procedure should be selected that would manipulate the controlling variables in the most efficacious way to change the behavior in a desirable direction. The following section details behavioral treatment strategies that have been used for stuttering.

BEHAVIORAL TREATMENT TECHNIQUES

A variety of techniques have been used to control or ameliorate stuttering: rhythmic speech, delayed auditory feedback (DAF), anxiety reduction, operant procedures, and several other lesser researched methods. Some techniques apply procedures designed specifically to diminish stuttering and are therefore linquistic in orientation (Lanyon & Goldsworthy, 1982). Others fall under the rubric of behavior therapy techniques and are aimed at ameliorating psycho·logical distress.

Linguistic Methods

The first set of procedures to be described is geared toward targeting and modifying speech patterns.

Rhythmic Speech

A stutterer will become fluent if an attempt is made to speak in a rhythmic manner. This phenomenon has been demonstrated by having the client pace one syllable to each beat of a miniaturized or desk metronome. The metronome sets the pace by manipulating the specific beat desired (Adams & Hotchkiss, 1973; Brady, 1969; Greenberg, 1970; Meyer & Mair, 1963; Umberger & Silverman, 1981). This technique is called Metronome Conditioned Speech Retraining (MCSR: (Brady, 1971). Brady (1971) demonstrated that the metronome "is not used passively as a prosthesis but is used to facilitate the acquisition of more fluent speech patterns" (p. 130). He used a desk metronome first and then progressed to a portable miniaturized apparatus (worn behind the ear like a hearing aid) and then to no metronome at all. Brady (1971) and others (Herscovitch & LeBow, 1973) have had some subjects end treatment with pacing their speech to imaginal or private beats. This area of research has received much attention in the literature. However, as Lanyon and Goldsworthy (1982) point out, even though some changes have been reported, the quality of speech is not ideal. Further, complete fluency is rarely achieved.

Delayed Auditory Feedback (DAF)

In DAF, stutterers hear their own speech milliseconds after it is emitted. This strategy creates an artificial fluency effect, thus prolonging speech. However, as Perkins (1973a) points out, there is more to normal speech than simple fluency. Therefore, DAF generally is employed as an initial step in shaping normal speech. According to Lanyon and Goldsworthy (1982), the popularity of DAF has diminished greatly since the 1960s. This is attributable in part to more recent investigative efforts showing that the type of prolonged speech promoted through DAF could be produced with equal effectiveness by simple instructions.

Behavior Therapy

A different approach to treatment of stuttering is to emphasize the amelioration of emotional disorders hypothesized to be causing the problem. As previously mentioned, behaviorally based methods frequently target anxiety. In addition, basic reinforcement or punishment methods are commonly aimed at problematic nuances in speech.

Anxiety Reduction

The emotional problem most frequently associated with stuttering is anxiety (Moleski & Tosi, 1976). Consequently, if anxiety is addressed therapeutically, the person's speech is likely to improve. This hypothesis is considered viable since constant failure in normal speech can result in anxiety. Procedures used typically involve systematic desensitization (Adams, 1972; Boucheau & Jeffry, 1973; Tyre, Stephen, Maisto, & Companik, 1973; Yonovitz, Shepard, & Garrett, 1977), cognitive therapy (Burns & Brady, 1980), an assertion training (Burns & Brady, 1980; Dalali & Sheehan, 1974).

The connection between anxiety and stuttering is still unknown. Lanyon and Goldsworthy (1982) indicate that anxiety may be the effect rather than the cause of stuttering. Further, the postulate that anxiety and stuttering may be effects of more basic difficulties.

Operant Procedures

Operant approaches have been used to treat stuttering for almost 30 years (see Flanagan, Goldiamond, & Azrin, 1958; Goldiamond, 1965). Because several procedures are often incorporated into a treatment program, it is difficult to classify the program to its specific approach. Some strategies that have been employed are positive reinforcement (Ryan, 1971), contingency management (Burns & Brady, 1980), shaping (Perkins, 1973a), token economies (Howie & Woods, 1982; Ingham & Andrews, 1973; Manning, Trutna, & Shaw, 1976), time-out (Adams & Popelka, 1971; Haroldson, Martin, & Starr, 1968; James, 1981), extinction (Shames & Egolf, 1976), response cost (Halvorson, 1971), and self-management techniques (Perkins, 1973b; Ryan & Van Kirk, 1974).

Ryan (1971) and Ryan and Van Kirk (1974) developed an operant model for treating stuttering that consists of establishing: (1) fluency, (2) transfer, and (3) maintenance. Basically, specific procedures are used to develop fluency, which is transferred to more difficult situations. Efforts are then made to maintain gains over time. Lanyon and Goldsworthy (1982) commented that Ryan's work contributed

significantly to the area by establishing a framework . . . within which nearly all therapeutic approaches to stuttering are now conceptualized, and by contributing a wealth of technology that is now utilized in more complex attempts to bring about the many types of behavior changes that are needed in treating this disorder. (p. 819)

Other Procedures

A number of other methods have been utilized to treat stuttering. However, they are relatively new, with little empirical support at this time. Some of these procedures include biofeedback (Lanyon, 1977; Moore, 1978), systematic slowed speech (Resick et al., 1978), the air flow technique (Schwartz, 1976; Weiner, 1978), and the regulated breathing method (Azrin & Nunn, 1974; Cote & Ladouceur, 1982).

Each strategy has demonstrated some success. In addition, some have been used as adjuncts or additions to other treatment packages. Others have been administered either alone or in conjunction with another treatment procedure.

The case presentation that follows describes one particular type of treatment with a hypothetical stutterer. Given that psychological issues are likely to be considered by the practicing mental health professional dealing with this disorder, our presentation will involve a case where psychological/emotional variables are of importance.

CASE PRESENTATION

IDENTIFICATION

Tommy was an 11-year-old who had been referred to the local mental health center for diagnosis and treatment of his stuttering. Tommy's speech had developed normally until age 8 when he started to experience difficulty. Initially, he had a problem only with words beginning with the letter *t*. Gradually, words beginning with *sh* also became a problem, and the difficulty continued and spread to other words. His stuttering consisted of the repetition of the first syllable of the word. This included two to three repetitions on the first syllable. Over time, this repetition increased in severity.

Tommy began stuttering at school, primarily when he was asked to recite. According to Tommy and his teacher, stuttering was precipitated primarily by anxiety. As Tommy had additional failure experiences, his anxiety and overall emotional instability associated with these speaking experiences rapidly escalated to the point that he had extreme difficulty speaking in public. This situation was exacerbated even further by the fear associated with the multiple failure experiences. A number of the children in his class began to tease him about these anxiety situations. In attempting to respond to this criticism by others, he began to stutter in those situations as well. This problem continued to generalize until it occurred in numerous settings.

Tommy's parents were from a lower-middle-class family. He was the third of four children. His father was a car mechanic and his mother worked part-time babysitting for preschool children in the neighborhood. Tommy's parents were very concerned about the problem and the emotional pain Tommy was experiencing and they feared the problem might continue. The situation led them to seek help at the local mental health center.

CONCEPTUALIZATION OF THE CASE

The case is conceptualized as a learning problem, a more detailed explanation of which has been presented elsewhere (see Brady, 1968). As stated previously, three components are recognized as continuously interacting: (1) an abnormal speech pattern, (2) anxiety and/or tension in a variety of speaking situations, and (3) a series of beliefs or expectations of stuttering and failure. To treat the problem effectively, antecedent events leading to the stuttering must be identified. These conditions will have made the disorder more pronounced and will have been instrumental in its maintenance. Also, these frequent failures lead to increased anxiety and a very low self-image (e.g., "I am inferior," "The other kids are not going to like me"). The goals of treatment then should be to pinpoint problem situations as well as the extent and type of anxiety. Treatment should focus on reinforcement of appropriate responses and increase the number, duration, and intensity of success experiences.

ASSESSMENT

Assessment of stuttering should be conducted primarily through behavioral interview. This procedure can be augmented by direct observations and/or parent reports. Several specific questions need to be addressed. These include: (1) When was the problem initially identified? (2) How long has the problem been occurring? (3) Under what conditions is it most likely to occur? (4) Why is the client seeking help at this particular time? (5) Have previous treatments been attempted and if so, when, for how long, and what did they consist of? (6) How does the child perceive others' reactions to the problem? and (7) Are there relatives with stuttering problems?

In addition to these questions, the therapist may wish to obtain further data on the specific conditions and on the type and intensity of the stuttering. Finally, reinforcers should be selected and pleasurable experiences noted.

TREATMENT

While several approaches to treatment are possible, the program to be described here includes positive reinforcement and systematic desensitization combined with a plan for generalization and maintenance.

After interviewing Tommy, it was evident that his difficulty was primarily due to learning. In effect, his bad experiences taught him to be anxious and apprehensive. This in turn resulted in a greater stuttering problem. In the first phase of treatment Tommy was taught to relax using the Jacobson relaxation procedure. Next, a hierarchy of 20 scenes depicting a range of anxiety-producing situations was constructed. After learning the relaxation procedure, Tommy received systematic desensitization, gradually, working up to more anxiety-producing situations. Between sessions, the child was asked to practice his response to anxiety-producing situations at home alone in his room while keeping a positive attitude and imagining success in these situations.

The next phase of therapy involved *in vivo* training beginning with low-anxiety and progressing toward high-anxiety scenarios. With the permission of Tommy and his parents, the therapist went to school and explained the treatment being employed, pointing out that considerable success had already been achieved. It was felt that, through practice in identifying anxiety and recognizing when dysfluencies were likely to occur, treatment could be more effectively carried out in this naturalistic setting. Strategies might include, but would not be confined to, rehearsing a relaxing visual image prior to speaking, practicing speaking with encouragement and reinforcement, pacing speech, and a contingency management procedure. By decreasing anticipatory anxiety, the strategies would thereby enhance the probability of success. Another strategy might be the identification of events that lead to more severe stuttering while speaking. Thus, slowing speech or trying to make it more rhythmical might prove very beneficial. Finally, some form of cognitive therapy would be helpful in combating negative beliefs and expectations. Continued self-monitoring and reinforcement by parents and teachers were expected to maintain these positive gains.

SUMMARY

This chapter was designed to provide information on the assessment and treatment of stuttering from a behavioral perspective. The disorder was described and defined both in operational terms and using DSM-III criteria. Assessment of the problem behavior was discussed thoroughly in terms of performing a functional analysis. This strategy provides a thorough assessment of the maladaptive behavior and its interrelationship with variables that control its emission.

The functional analysis ties the assessment procedure directly to specific intervention implications. A variety of treatment procedures and strategies were discussed that have been used successfully in previous research. Finally, a case description was provided to detail how research findings would apply to a specific case.

REFERENCES

Adams, M. R. (1972). The use of reciprocal inhibition procedures in the treatment of stuttering. *Journal of Communication Disorders, 5,* 59–66.

Adams, M. R., & Hotchkiss, J. (1973). Some reactions and responses of stutterers to a miniaturized metronome and metronome-conditioning therapy: Three case studies. *Behavior Therapy, 4,* 565–569.

Adams, M. R., & Popelka, G. (1971). The influence of "time-out" on stutterers and their dysfluency. *Behavior Therapy, 2,* 334–339.

American Psychiatric Association. (1980). *Diagnostic and statistical manual of mental disorders* (3rd ed.), Washington, DC: Author.

Azrin, N. H., & Nunn, R. G. (1974). A rapid method of eliminating stuttering by a regulated breathing approach. *Behaviour Research and Therapy, 12,* 279–286.

Bakwin, H., & Bakwin, R. M. (1972). *Behavior disorders in children* (6th ed.). Philadelphia: Saunders.

Beck, A. T. (1967). *Depression: Causes and treatment.* Philadelphia: University of Pennsylvania Press.

Boucheau, L. D., & Jeffry, C. D. (1973). Stuttering treated by desensitization. *Journal of Behavior Therapy and Experimental Psychiatry, 4,* 209–212.

Brady, J. P. (1968). A behavioral approach to the treatment of stuttering. *American Journal of Psychiatry, 125,* 843–848.

Brady, J. P. (1969). Studies on the metronome effect on stuttering. *Behaviour Research and Therapy, 7,* 197–204.

Brady, J. P. (1971). Metronome-conditioning speech retraining for stuttering. *Behavior Therapy, 2,* 129–150.

Burns, D. & Brady, J. P. (1980). The treatment of stuttering. In A. Goldstein & E. B. Foa (Eds.), *Handbook of behavioral interventions* (pp. 673–722). New York: Wiley.

Cote, C., & Ladouceur, R. (1982). Effects of social aids and the regulated breathing method in the treatment of stutterers. *Journal of Consulting and Clinical Psychology, 50,* 450.

Dalali, I. D., & Sheehan, J. G. (1974). Stuttering and assertion training. *Journal of Communication Disorders, 7,* 97–111.

DiLorenzo, T. M. (in press). Methods of assessment I: Standardized tests. In C. L. Frame & J. L. Matson (Eds.), *Handbook of assessment in childhood psychopathology: Applied issues in differential diagnosis and treatment evaluation.* New York: Plenum.

Flanagan, B., Goldiamond, I., & Azrin, N. H. (1958). Operant stuttering: The control of stuttering behavior through response-contingent consequences. *Journal of the Experimental Analysis of Behavior, 1,* 173–177.

Goldiamond, I. (1965). Stuttering and fluency as manipulatable operant response classes. In L. Krasner & L. P. Ullmann (Eds.), *Research in behavior modification:*

New developments and implications (pp. 106–156). New York: Holt, Rinehart and Winston.

Greenberg, J. B. (1970). The effect of a metronome on the speech of young stutterers. *Behavior Therapy, 1,* 240–244.

Halvorson, J. A. (1971). The effects on stuttering frequency of pairing punishment (response cost) with reinforcement. *Journal of Speech and Hearing Research, 14,* 356–364.

Haroldson, S. K., Martin, R. R., & Starr, C. D. (1968). Time-out as a punishment for stuttering. *Journal of Speech and Hearing Research, 11,* 560–566.

Herscovitch, A., & LeBow, M. D. (1973). Imaginal pacing in the treatment of stuttering. *Journal of Behavior Therapy and Experimental Psychiatry, 4,* 357–360.

Howie, P. M., & Woods, C. L. (1982). Token reinforcement during the instatement and shaping of fluency in the treatment of stuttering. *Journal of Applied Behavior Analysis, 15,* 55–64.

Ingham, R. J., & Andrews, G. (1973). An analysis of a token economy in stuttering therapy. *Journal of Applied Behaviour Analysis, 6,* 219–229.

Irwin, O. C. (1969). Infant speech effect of systematic reading of stories. *Journal of Speech and Hearing Research, 3,* 187–190.

James, J. J. (1981). Behavioral self-control of stuttering using time-out from speaking. *Journal of Applied Behavior Analysis, 14,* 25–37.

Johnson, W., Darley, F. L., & Spriesterbach, D. C. (1963). *Diagnostic methods in speech pathology.* New York: Harper & Row.

Jones, H. G. (1970). Stuttering. In G. G. Costello (Ed.), *Symptoms of psychopathology: A handbook.* New York: Wiley.

Lanyon, R. I. (1977). Effect of biofeedback-based relaxation on stuttering during reading and spontaneous speech. *Journal of Consulting and Clinical Psychology, 45,* 860–866.

Lanyon, R. I., & Goldsworthy, R. I. (1982). Habit disorders. In A. S. Bellack, M. Hersen, & A. E. Kazdin (Eds.), *International handbook of behavior modification and therapy* (pp. 813–851). New York: Plenum.

Manning, W. H., Trutna, P. A., & Shaw, C. K. (1976). Verbal versus tangible reward for children who stutter. *Journal of Speech and Hearing Disorders, 41,* 52–62.

Mash, E. J., & Terdal, L. G. (1981). Behavioral assessment of childhood disturbance. In E. J. Mash & L. G. Terdal (Eds.), *Behavioral assessment of childhood disorders* (pp. 3–76). New York: Guilford.

Matson, J. L., & DiLorenzo, T. M. (1984). *Punishment and its alternatives: A new perspective for behavior modification.* New York: Springer.

Meyer, V., & Mair, J. M. M. (1963). A new technique to control stammering: A preliminary report. *Behaviour Research and Therapy, 1,* 251–254.

Moleski, R., & Tosi, D. J. (1976). Comparative psychotherapy: Rational-emotive therapy versus systematic desensitization in the treatment of stuttering. *Journal of Consulting and Clinical Psychology, 44,* 309–311.

Moore, W. H., Jr. (1978). Some effects of progressively lowering electromyographic levels with feedback procedures on the frequency of stuttered verbal behaviors. *Journal of Fluency Disorders, 3,* 127–138.

Mysak, E. D., & Gilbert, G. M. (1972). Child speech pathology. In B. B. Wolman (Ed.), *Manual of child psychopathology.* New York: McGraw-Hill.

Ollendick, T. H., & Matson, J. L. (1983). Treatment of tics, stuttering and elective mutism in children. In T. H. Ollendick & M. Hersen (Eds.), *Handbook of child psychopathology* (pp. 227–252). New York: Plenum.

Perkins, W. H. (1973a). Replacement of stuttering with normal speech: I. Rationale. *Journal of Speech and Hearing Disorders, 38,* 283–294.

Perkins, W. H. (1973b). Replacement of stuttering with normal speech: II. Clinical procedures. *Journal of Speech and Hearing Disorders, 38,* 295–303.

Phillips, J. S., & Ray, R. S. (1980). Behavioral approaches to childhood disorders. *Behavior Modification, 4,* 3–34.

Resick, P. A., Wendiggensen, P., Ames, S., & Meyer, V. (1978). Systematic slowed speech: A new treatment for stuttering. *Behaviour Research and Therapy, 16,* 161–167.

Rousey, C. L. (1978). Speech disorders. In B. B. Wolman, J. Egan, & A. O. Ross (Eds.), *Handbook of treatment of mental disorders in childhood and adolescents* (pp. 185–201). Englewood Cliffs, NJ: Prentice-Hall.

Ryan, B. P. (1971). Operant procedures applied to stuttering therapy for children. *Journal of Speech and Hearing Disorders, 36,* 264–280.

Ryan, B. P., & Van Kirk, B. (1974). The establishment, transfer, and maintenance of fluent speech in 50 stutterers using delayed auditory feedback and operant procedures. *Journal of Speech and Hearing Disorders, 39,* 3–10.

Schreibman, L., & Koegel, R. L. (1981). A guideline for planning behavior modification programs for autistic children. In S. M. Turner, K. S. Calhoun, & H. E. Adams (Eds.), *Handbook of clinical behavior therapy* (pp. 500–526). New York: Wiley.

Schwartz, M. (1976). *Stuttering solved.* New York: McGraw-Hill.

Shames, G. H., & Egolf, D. B. (1976). *Operant conditioning and the management of stuttering.* Englewood Cliffs, NJ: Prentice-Hall.

Sheehan, J. G., & Marlyn, M. M. (1966). Spontaneous recovery from stuttering. *Journal of Speech and Hearing Research, 9,* 121–135.

Sheehan, J. G., & Marlyn, M. M. (1967). Methodology in studies of recovery from stuttering. *Journal of Speech and Hearing Research, 10,* 396–400.

Tyre, T., Stephen, M., Maisto, A., & Companik, P. (1973). The use of systematic desensitization in the treatment of chronic stuttering behavior. *Journal of Speech and Hearing Disorders, 38,* 514–519.

Umberger, F. G., & Silverman, F. H. (1981). Stutterers' initial reaction to the use of a miniature electronic metronome outside of the clinical setting. *Behavior Therapist, 4,* 2.

Webster, R. L. (1974). A behavioral analysis of stuttering: Treatment and theory. In K. S. Calhoun, H. E. Adams, & K. M. Mitchell (Eds.), *Innovative treatment methods in psychopathology.* New York: Wiley.

Weiner, A. E. (1978). Vocal control therapy for stutterers: A trial program. *Journal of Fluency Disorders, 3,* 115–126.

Wingate, M. E. (1964). A standard definition of stuttering. *Journal of Speech and Hearing Disorders, 29,* 484–489.

Yonovitz, A., Shepard, W. T., & Garrett, S. (1977). Hierarchical stimulation: Two case studies of stuttering modification using systematic desensitization. *Journal of Fluency Disorders, 2,* 21–28.

Young, M. A. (1975). Onset, prevalence, and recovery from stuttering. *Journal of Speech and Hearing Disorders, 40,* 49–58.

Zielinski, J. J., & Williams, L. J. (1979). Situational determinants of stuttering in assertive contexts: A case study. *Behavior Therapist, 2,* 13.

CHAPTER 11

Psychophysiological Disorders

DONALD A. WILLIAMSON, SANDRA J. McKENZIE, ANTHONY J. GORECZNY,
AND MICHAEL FAULSTICH

Psychophysiological disorders can generally be described as physical problems that are strongly influenced by psychological factors such as stress, emotions, or behavior. Disorders commonly categorized as psychophysiological are headaches, hypertension, asthma, Raynaud's syndrome, peptic ulcers, irritable bowel syndrome, and atopic dermatitis. The most common types of psychophysiological disorders observed in children are headaches (both tension and migraine), recurrent abdominal pain, bronchial asthma, and atopic dermatitis. The sections that follow discuss the behavioral assessment and treatment of each of these disorders. A case description is also provided to illustrate the application of these assessment and treatment approaches to a specific case.

HEADACHE

Description

The most common types of headache observed in children are migraine and tension headaches. Migraine headaches, which are diagnosed in approximately 5% of the child population (Bille, 1967; Brown, 1977), have the primary symptom features of unilateral (one-sided) pain that is very intense and is usually described as throbbing or pulsating. Nausea and vomiting are also commonly associated with the headache and, in children, vomiting may present a medical problem that is at least as serious as the head pain. Prensky and Sommer (1979) have suggested specific diagnostic criteria for childhood migraine, which are shown in Table 11.1. Prodromal symptoms occur in only about 20% of childhood migraine cases and sometimes occur in the absence of headache. Common prodromal symptoms are: blind spots or flashing lights in the visual field and numbness in certain areas of the skin.

One problem in assessing the headache symptomatology of childhood mi-

279

TABLE 11.1 Diagnostic Criteria for Childhood Migraine[a]

Child must report at least 3 of the 6 symptoms:
1. Headaches are predominantly one-sided.
2. Headaches are usually accompanied by nausea or vomiting.
3. Headaches are relieved by rest.
4. There is a positive family history for migraine headache.
5. Pain is described as throbbing or pulsating.
6. Visual, sensory, or motor prodromal symptoms precede headache.

Note: From "Diagnosis and Treatment of Migraine Children, by A. L. Prensky and D. Sommer, 1979, Neurology, 29, p. 507.

graine is that children generally report very vague descriptions of their pain and parents are usually able to provide information only about the behavioral manifestations of pain (e.g., vomiting, crying, social withdrawal, etc.). Therefore, the diagnosis of childhood migraine is often difficult, especially in young children.

Tension headache in children has not been studied as extensively as migraine headache. Common symptom features of tension headache are bilateral pain across the forehead or around the entire head. The pain is generally described as constant (i.e., not throbbing or pounding). Nausea and vomiting are generally not associated with tension headache. Relief can often be gained by taking aspirin and other over-the-counter medications (Litchfield, 1972).

Behavioral Assessment

The first step in assessing childhood migraine is to establish a diagnosis. It is essential that the child first be evaluated by a neurologist (preferably a pediatric neurologist) to rule out other medical causes of the headache and to obtain a medical diagnosis of the problem. To facilitate the diagnostic process, Labbé, Williamson, and Southard (1985) have reported the use of a questionnaire of headache symptoms that has been adapted for child headache patients and their parents. In evaluating the correspondence between child and parental reports of the child's headache symptoms, Labbé et al. (1985) found that for most of the objective symptoms (e.g., long duration of headache, medication intake, location of head pain, and antecedents of headache), there was very strong correspondence between child and parental reports. However, for more subjective symptoms (e.g., dizziness, sensitivity to loud noise, and quality of pain), correlations between child and parental symptom ratings were quite low. These data suggest that for objective, behaviorally referenced symptoms, parents may be a good source of data. However, for more subjective symptoms, the examiner must rely on the child's description. Using this type of questionnaire and a thorough diagnostic interview, the examiner may establish the symptom features of the childs' head pain so that a diagnosis of migraine, tension, or other headache can be established.

In addition to establishing a headache diagnosis, the examiner must also assess for the effects of environmental events on headache (i.e., antecedents and consequences). Common antecedents of childhood headache are environmental stress (e.g., headaches are often more problematic during the school year than during the summer and with overexertion and overheating). While the role of diet has been widely discussed as a possible cause of migraine in adults and children, controlled research has generally found foods to be relatively unimportant (Kohlenberg, 1982; Medina & Diamond, 1978), though selected cases may evidence signs of dietary influences. The most common approach for evaluating the role of environmental events on headache is a behavioral interview, which is designed to identify a consistent pattern of antecedent conditions, reporting of head pain, and positive or negative consequences. The positive consequences of reporting head pain cannot be ignored as a potential determinant of headache reports in children. For example, Ramsden, Friedman, and Williamson (1983) found that elimination of parental and teacher attention for reporting head pain and reinforcement of "well behavior" was a very powerful treatment program for a young child who had been diagnosed as having migraine headaches.

The self-monitoring procedures used for headaches in adults (see Williamson, Ruggiero, & Davis, 1985) have been successfully modified for use with children. Figure 11.1 illustrates the forms used by Labbé and Williamson (1984) for self-monitoring of headaches. Using this format, children (with the assistance of their parents) can record occurrence and intensity of head pain, events associated with the headache, and medication taken. During treatment children can record practice of relaxation exercises at home. In a test of the validity of this procedure, Labbé et al. (1985) found that self-monitored headache frequency and medication consumption significantly correlated with parental and child reports of headache frequency during an initial interview. Richardson, McGrath, and Cunningham (1983) also found that self-monitoring of headache by children is positively correlated with parental reports of headache in the same time period. Thus, there is substantial evidence in support of the validity of headache self-monitoring by children.

Treatment Methods

Behavioral approaches have received far more attention for treatment of childhood migraine than for the treatment of tension headache. The first report of a behavioral treatment for childhood migraine was reported by Diamond and Franklin (1975). They used autogenic feedback training (a combination of skin temperature biofeedback and autogenic training) to treat 32 childhood mig-

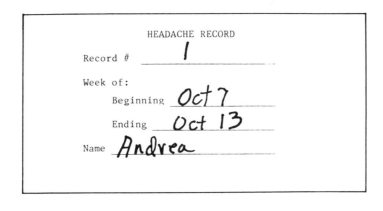

HEADACHE RECORD

Record # *1*

Week of:

Beginning *Oct 7*

Ending *Oct 13*

Name *Andrea*

RATING SCALE

0 = No Headache (HA)
1 = Very mild HA, aware of it only when
    attending to it
2 = Mild HA, could be ignored at times
3 = Moderate HA, pain is noticeably
    present
4 = Severe HA, difficult to concentrate,
    can do undemanding tasks
5 = Extremely intense HA, incapacitated

Date: _____

Rate your head pain at each of the 4 times shown below.
Record name & quantity of medication, what happened before
headache began, & whether you practiced your handwarming
skill.

TIME	RATING	MEDICATION	EVENTS BEFORE HA	PRACTICE
Breakfast	*0*			Session 1
Lunch	*2*	*Tylenol-1*	*At School*	10 min. *✓*
Dinner	*4*			Session 2
Bedtime	*1*			10 min. *✓*

Figure 11.1. An example of the self-monitoring records used for childhood headache.

raineurs, ranging in age from 9 to 18 years. They reported a reduction in headache frequency and severity in 26 of the 32 children. However, this single-group outcome study did not present objective data related to headache nor did it utilize any type of control group. Two studies utilizing multiple-baseline designs across subjects have also reported successful use of autogenic feedback training for childhood migraine. Andrasik, Blanchard, Edlund, and Rosenblum (1982) successfully treated two childhood migraineurs and found continued improvement at follow-up. Labbé and Williamson (1983) treated three cases (ages 9, 12, and 13 years) and found substantial reductions in headache 2 years following treatment. Labbé and Williamson (1984) followed this single-case experiment with a controlled group outcome study comparing autogenic feedback training to a waiting-list control group. The children in this study ranged from 7 to 16 years in age. The average age was 10.7 years. Autogenic feedback training was found to be very effective. A 75% reduction in pain at the end of treatment and at 1-month follow-up was found for the treatment group, while the control group showed no improvement. Even more impressive was the finding that 87% of the treated children were clinically improved following treatment. Although that degree of improvement declined at 6-month follow-up, 62% of the treated subjects were still clinically improved at 6 months. Andrasik et al. (1984) recently reported a replication of these very impressive findings and have shown that progressive muscle relaxation is equivalent in effectiveness to autogenic feedback training.

The only behavioral treatment study that has not utilized biofeedback or relaxation procedures is that of Ramsden, Friedman, and Williamson (1983). In this single-case experiment, contingency management procedures were used to reduce the frequency of headache reports in a 6-year-old girl. This child was determined to be a case of operant pain in which her reports of head pain were positively and negatively reinforced. Rearrangement of contingencies to reinforce "well behavior" and extinguish reporting head pain was very successful, resulting in the cessation of "headache" at 10-month follow-up.

Only one study has reported the use of behavioral approaches for the treatment of tension headache in children. Using EMG biofeedback, Andrasik, Blanchard, Edlund, and Attanasio, (1983) successfully treated an 11-year-old child with chronic tension headache. This child remained improved at 1-year follow-up.

Comment

In recent years, more controlled research concerning the treatment of childhood migraine has emerged. The controlled group outcome studies of Labbé and Williamson (1984) and Andrasik et al. (1984) have shown that autogenic feedback training and progressive muscle relaxation training are very effective treatment methods. In fact, these treatment methods appear to be even more effective for children than they are for adults. Treatment studies with adult migraineurs have generally found that between 40% and 70% of treated patients were clinically improved (Williamson, 1981). In both studies of childhood migraine, over 80% of treated patients were clinically improved. Thus, it appears that biofeedback and relaxation methods may be a very safe and effective treatment for childhood migraine. Treatment research concerning tension headache in children is very undeveloped. Therefore, much work remains before conclusions can be drawn regarding the efficacy of behavior therapy approaches for this disorder.

RECURRENT ABDOMINAL PAIN

Description

The symptom of abdominal pain is a common complaint of children seen by pediatricians and family practitioners. Frequent abdominal pain occurs in 10 to 15% of school-aged children (Apley, 1975; Apley & Nash, 1958). When the symptom recurs frequently over a prolonged time, it is generally referred to as recurrent abdominal pain (RAP) syndrome. The diagnosis of RAP usually results from the following signs: (1) an erratic history of recurrent abdominal pain; (2) additional or associated symptoms of facial pallor, headaches, dizziness, and pellet stools; (3) environmental stress that is associated with the onset or exacerbation of pain, and (4) negative laboratory and X-ray examinations (Green, 1967). Available data suggest that the likelihood of finding a disease process is less than 10% in children hospitalized for the complaint of abdominal pain (Apley, 1975) and even less likely in children seen in outpatient facilities (Liebman, 1978). Therefore, diagnosis of RAP is generally given in the absence of organic findings and is usually considered "psychogenic" in nature.

Peak age of onset of the disorder has been estimated at approximately 5 years of age (Apley, 1975). Although the syndrome is generally seen in preadolescence, its significance in the adolescent age range is uncertain due to inadequate data. Pediatricians frequently describe the disorder to parents as one that the child will "grow out of." However, available data concerning prognosis suggest that as many as one-third continue to experience recurrent abdominal pain episodes for many years (Apley, 1975; Christensen & Mortensen, 1975). According to Green (1967), approximately one-half of the children examined for complaints of abdominal pain will have had the problem for less than a year; the rest, for 1 to 5 years. The frequency of the complaints generally ranges from six or seven times a day to once a week or even once a month. In addition, onset of pain is often temporally related to observable environmental stressors, with the child having "well periods" in between episodes of RAP. Many authorities have based their treatment approaches on this stress conceptualization. Others, however, have conceptualized RAP as operant pain and have employed contingency management procedures to reduce pain reports by eliminating positive or negative reinforcement for complaints of pain.

Behavioral Assessment

Assessment of the child presenting with RAP is similar to assessment of other chronic and recurrent pain syndromes. The goals of assessment are to evaluate both symptoms of RAP and the functional implications of being a child with abdominal pain (Barr, 1983). An extensive physical examination to rule out organicity is imperative and should be conducted prior to initiating any type of behavioral treatment.

A clinical interview with both the child and the parents should focus initially on possible explanations of the abdominal pain. This interview serves to raise awareness of explanations other than organic disease. The child as well as the parents should be encouraged to look for associations and clues to help explain the pain episodes. Self-monitoring of the pain episodes and related environmental events often facilitates this process. Variables such as frequency of pain complaints, time of occurrence, duration and severity of complaints, predisposing factors (antecedents), and consequences of the pain complaints should be included in the self-monitoring (Barr & Feuerstein, 1983). Such data may be useful in detecting recurrent patterns and associations with other events. This type of functional analysis should also aid in the development of an effective treatment procedure. Unfortunately, no research related to the development of assessment procedures for RAP has been reported in the literature.

Treatment Measures

A review of the literature reveals a paucity of controlled outcome studies in the area of recurrent abdominal pain. In fact, most treatment approaches have centered around informal psychotherapy or patient counseling. Liebman (1978) reported helping 105 of 119 RAP children by advising parents to make specific changes in the child's environment. These changes were designed to create a less stressful atmosphere, making complaints of abdominal pain less likely. He also suggested that drug therapy may be countertherapeutic, in that it usually creates an unnecessary dependence on external agents to modify behavior. Green (1967) also suggested therapy based on a stress reduction conceptualization. Green provided family members with the opportunity to talk about their feelings and current problems in an attempt to reduce conflict within the family unit. He also suggested giving direct advice to the parents about changing their behavior (e.g., reducing excessive demands) in order to create a less stressful environment.

Two single-case studies utilizing specific behavior modification techniques have been conducted to date. Sank and Biglan (1974) treated a 10-year-old boy with a 2½-year history of RAP with operant procedures. Specifically, the child received a point for every half-day that the intensity rating was below baseline. Points could be redeemed for 5 cents each, activities chosen from a reinforcer menu, and specific parental attention. If the intensity rating was at or above baseline levels, the child was required to stay home from school. He had to stay in his bed and was allowed to look at school books as his only activity. His mother was instructed to withhold special attention. The parents and child were instructed to celebrate each milestone (e.g., 1 week of full school attendance). Once treatment was instituted, there was an immediate improvement in school attendance and a decrease in the intensity of pain and frequency of attacks. All pain episodes ceased after 7 weeks of treatment.

Miller and Kratochwill (1979) employed a time-out procedure to treat a 10-year-old girl's report of stomach pain complaints at home and school. Time-out consisted of removing the girl from adult attention and pleasurable activities contingent on verbal pain complaints. Implementation of treatment substantially reduced the frequency of pain complaints, which remained at zero levels at follow-up assessments 4, 6, and 8 weeks after the program was terminated.

Comment

Treatment studies of recurrent abdominal pain in children have been limited to informal psychotherapy techniques and single-case reports using behavior therapy techniques. Although the existing literature consists of successful interventions, there are no reports of controlled clinical treatment trials to date. Specific behavior modification techniques that have been shown to be effective in single cases are contingency management and time-out. What is now needed are controlled group outcome studies that could compare these behavioral approaches to control groups with other psychotherapeutic and medical treatment approaches.

ATOPIC DERMATITIS

Description

Atopic dermatitis (AD) is a chronic, puritic inflammation of the skin with possible symptom recurrence throughout the life span. It has been estimated that AD afflicts 7 to 24 individuals per 1000 (Johnson, 1977), accounting for

3 to 20% of all patients treated by dermatology clinics (Sulzberger, 1971). Other terms for AD include neurodermatitis, prurigo Besnier, and atopic eczema. Atopic dermatitis is often observed in individuals with a personal or familial history of so-called "atopic" or allergic manifestations such as asthma, allergic rhinitis, or hay fever (Gigli & Baer, 1979). This relationship to "atopic" disorders influenced the term of *atopic* dermatitis, but the affiliation has not been fully explained.

Sixty percent of AD patients have onset in the first year of life while 85% present symptoms before age 5 (Rajka, 1975). Therefore, the disease generally begins during infancy, with initial onset usually around the second or third months of life. The clinical features of infantile AD are characterized by erythematous and exudative lesions, commonly beginning on the cheek. These eruptions are markedly pruritic, and the infant may frequently rub against the affected area, possibly leading to secondary infection. There is a tendency towards symptom remission around 3 to 5 years of age. With increasing age in childhood, AD may recur; in other cases, initial onset may occur. This childhood AD is typified by a dry, thickening lichenification of the skin. In this childhood phase, sites of involvement usually include the wrists, neck, and elbows.

The etiology of AD is not well understood, although altered pharmacological and immunological responses have been identified (Butler, 1984; Hanifin, 1982). No curative therapy exists, but the palliative use of topical corticosteroids seems the most popular medical treatment, providing some patients with temporary relief (Baer & Gigli, 1979). In addition, psychological factors are believed to affect AD occurrences (Obermayer, 1970; Faulstich & Williamson, 1985). Research on behavioral assessment and treatment of this disorder is just beginning. The following sections describe existing research and provide suggestions for future directions.

Behavioral Assessment

Some research has suggested that psychological stress may be an initiating or exacerbating factor for AD. For example, on the State-Trait Anxiety Inventory, significantly higher state and trait anxiety ratings were found for AD patients compared to clinical and no-disease control groups (Garrie, Garrie, & Mote, 1974). Similarly, relative to a no-disease control group, AD patients were found to score significantly higher on the anxiety scale of the (SCL-90) and to respond with greater electromyogram (EMG) and heart rate increases during experimentally induced stress (Faulstich, Williamson, Duchmann, Conerly, & Brantley, 1985). Results of these studies suggest that anxiety or increased sympathetic arousal may play a role in AD manifestation. Accordingly, it has been speculated that emotional reactions in AD, such as anxiety, may lead to altered autonomic activity, which results in peripheral vascular changes and a lowering of itch thresholds (Beerman, 1962; Faulstich & Williamson, 1985). Consequently, an itch-scratch cycle would be easily initiated, allowing skin lesions to develop. It is possible that psychological factors could influence initiation of pathophysiological mechanisms related to occurrence of AD. Another hypothesis is that stress and anxiety may mediate the scratching events. Along these lines, AD patients have been found to develop conditioned scratch responses much sooner than no-disease controls (Jordan & Whitlock, 1974). Based on this research, the behavioral assessment of AD should center around the child's scratching behaviors and anxiety levels. Scratching of AD lesions is a major concern since it exacerbates the dermatological condition. Anxiety, on the other hand, could serve to trigger itching episodes and may be related to onset of underlying pathophysiological processes.

Initially, a history of the child's clinical course of AD should be obtained along with any records from the physician who provided the diagnosis. It should be noted that a confirmed diagnosis of AD, preferably from a dermatologist, should be obtained prior to any behavioral intervention.

Assessment of scratching and anxiety related to AD should logically follow the premises of a standard functional analysis, as employed for other problem behaviors. That is, attention should be focused on antecedents and consequences surrounding the child's symptom onset and exacerbations in general, as well as scratching behaviors in particular. Assessment should emphasize evaluation of stimuli associated with the itching of lesions (e.g., places and time of day scratching occurs, objects used for scratching, and environmental stressors that elicit scratching). Parents or guardians are a major source of such information, although interview data from older children can also be quite useful. In general, the goal of assessment for childhood AD should be to attain a clear symptom description, including an understanding of any associated environmental or psychological factors. Self-monitoring or parental monitoring of scratching may be helpful for determining the frequency of scratching and its environmental antecedents. These data may also be useful for evaluating treatment outcome.

Treatment Methods

Behavioral interventions for scratching of AD lesions should follow directly from assessment information and conclusions drawn from the functional analysis. However, because medical intervention has been the primary mode of therapy, there is a paucity of behavioral treatment studies on childhood AD. Two single-case studies have employed behavioral techniques to reduce scratching behaviors, since they serve to maintain and exacerbate AD (Allen & Harris, 1966; Bar & Kuypers, 1973). In both cases positive reinforcement was used along with extinction procedures. Specifically, both children were socially ignored while scratching and were reinforced with small presents given at various time intervals when no scratching occurred. In one case, scratching was eliminated after 6 weeks of treatment and remained absent at 4-month follow-up (Allen & Harris, 1966). The other study reported clear skin and elimination of scratching 13 weeks after treatment initiation; these efforts were maintained at 18-month follow-up (Bar & Kuypers, 1973). This contingency management approach attempts to eliminate the scratching of AD lesions in a manner similar to that used for reducing other childhood problem behaviors. From the limited data base, it can be concluded that behavioral strategies may have promise for assisting in the treatment of AD in children.

Although currently not empirically supported for childhood AD, relaxation training may be efficacious in cases where anxiety has been identified as a precipitant to disease onset and/or scratching behaviors. Research on adult AD, for instance, has found relaxation training via EMG biofeedback (Haynes, Wilson, Jaffee, & Britton, 1979) and progressive relaxation training (Ratliff & Stein, 1968) to yield significant treatment gains.

Comment

Atopic dermatitis is a common childhood dermatological problem with suspected psychological factors. Behavioral interventions such as contingency management and relaxation training are of potential benefit according to the limited available research. However, much more empirical investigation is needed to clarify the efficacy of these behavioral techniques and also to evaluate the precise effects of psychological variables on AD.

ASTHMA

Description

Bronchial asthma is a pulmonary disorder characterized by wheezing, coughing, and difficult breathing. The basic defect is hyperreactive airways (Curry & Lowell, 1948; Parker, Bilbo, & Reed, 1965). The airways respond to provocative stimuli with excessive constricting. Although many asthma attacks are brought on by allergic stimuli, several studies have shown that mere suggestion can elicit an attack (Godfrey, & Silverman, 1973; Luparello, Lyons, Bleecker, & McFadden, 1968; Phillip, Wilde, & Day, 1972; Strupp, Levenson, Manuck, Snell, Hinrichsen, & Boyd, 1974). Because of this psychological component of asthma, and because of the presumed association between asthma and anxiety, psychologists have attempted to find ways to help alleviate the symptoms of the disease.

Behavioral Assessment

Medical diagnosis of asthma is fairly straightforward (Burrows, 1979). Recalcitrant wheezing episodes, accompanied by dyspnea, are the primary characteristics. In children, the primary diagnostic distinction to be made is between asthma and the hyperventilation syndrome. It is imperative that medical evaluation precede psychological intervention.

Treatment outcome has been assessed mainly from changes in pulmonary functioning. One of the most frequently used measures is peak expiratory flow rate (PEFR), a measure of the maximum rate of air flow from the lungs during forced expiration. However, this measure is effort-dependent and therefore may not be indicative of true pulmonary functioning. Effort-independent measures do exist but have been rarely used. Although PEFR is generally easier to obtain than the effort-independent measures, the effort-independent measures are probably a better indicator of respiratory functioning and should be used more often. Other measures that have not been used as often as might be desirable are those of incapacitation caused by the disease (e.g, days missed from school, activity restriction).

Since emotional factors have been shown to play a role in asthma (Purcell, 1963; Tal & Miklich, 1976), and because of the relationship that exists between emotions and the autonomic nervous system (Black, 1970), it is reasonable to suggest that asthmatics may have abnormal autonomic nervous system reactivity. Although few studies have tested this hypothesis, what data exist indicate that this position may be tenable. Studies by Hahn (1966) and Hahn and Clark (1967) have shown that asthmatic boys do indeed have higher resting heart rates and finger temperatures than normal boys. Additionally, measurements of inspiration and expiration durations have shown that normal boys respond to stress (i.e., mental arithmetic task) with decreases in both inspiratory and expiratory duration, whereas asthmatic boys decreased inspiration duration only.

When assessing the impact of emotion on asthma attacks, it is important to establish in the interview whether stress or emotionality consistently precedes an attack. Another factor that must be assessed is whether or not there is an allergic component to the disorder (i.e., extrinsic versus intrinsic asthma). In extrinsic asthma, environmental allergens cause the attack. By contrast, in intrinsic asthma there is no identifiable allergen. This distinction may have applications both medically and psychologically. If there are specific allergens that cause a child's asthma attacks, then some form of hyposensitization or immunotherapy may be beneficial. However, if the asthma is intrinsic, the therapist must be aware of the possible involvement of emotional or conditioned factors or any reinforcement that the child might be receiving, such as avoiding school or responsibilities and receiving special attention when he or she is ill. Reinforcement contingencies are among the most important factors that need to be assessed because there is clear evidence that they can influence the frequency of asthma attacks (Gardner, 1968; Lazar & Jedliczka, 1979).

Treatment Approaches

Several different treatment approaches have been used in an attempt to alleviate some of the distress caused by asthma. Consistent with the hypothesis that anxiety can cause or exacerbate an asthma attack, most treatment procedures attempt to treat the anxiety component presumed to be associated with asthma. The two most common procedures are relaxation training and biofeedback training.

Relaxation training is used because it is assumed that as one becomes more anxious, breathing becomes more difficult and an asthmatic becomes more susceptible to an attack. Therefore, if one can reduce this anxiety, the asthmatic should be able to breath easier. Alexander, Cropp, and Chai (1979) trained subjects in relaxation and took pulmonary measures before and after a relaxation phase, using both effort-dependent and effort-independent measures. Small but significant increases were obtained on the effort-dependent measures. However, the effort-independent measures were unchanged after the relaxation phase. Thus, it appears likely that certain subject characteristics (e.g., motivation, expectancy) rather than true pulmonary functioning were the variables influenced by the relaxation treatment procedures in this study.

Several different biofeedback procedures have been used to help the asthmatic child. One method is EMG biofeedback for assist relaxation. Scherr, Crawford, Sergeant, and Scherr (1975) reported the successful use of EMG biofeedback in a summer camp setting. Although measures of pulmonary functioning were not improved, as indicated by differences between the treatment and control groups, the researchers reported that treatment was associated with a lower frequency of infirmary visits and a lower number of asthma attacks. However, they stressed the need for more rigorous control groups than they were able to employ.

In another study, Kotses, Glaus, Crawford, Edwards, and Scherr (1976) compared an EMG biofeedback-assisted relaxation group with a group receiving false feedback. They found that the EMG biofeedback group produced significantly greater improvement of PEFR than either the false-feedback group or a no-treatment control group. A later study showed that EMG biofeedback from the temporal area produced superior results as compared to feedback from the brachoradialis muscle (Kotses, Glaus, Bricel, Edwards, & Crawford, 1978).

An interesting use of biofeedback has been developed by Khan and his associates (Khan, 1977; Kahn, Staerk, & Bonk, 1974). They theorized that a child's asthma attacks have, over time, become conditioned to certain environmental stimuli. These stimuli are then able to trigger the attack. This theory is not new and has been postulated before (Franks & Leigh, 1959; Turnbull, 1962). Khan's approach to treatment is to attempt to countercondition the asthma attack by pairing increases in respiratory flow with social reinforcement (i.e., praise). The results of the initial study (Khan et al., 1974) indicated that the experimental group had significant reductions in the amount of medication taken, the number of emergency room visits, and the number of asthma attacks when contrasted to a no-treatment control group. However, attempts to replicate these findings have failed (Danker, Miklich, Pratt, & Creer, 1975; Khan, 1977).

Treatments based on operant theory have focused on removing positive consequences associated with exhibition of asthma symptoms. These consequences can include avoidance or escape from an aversive stimulus (e.g., school, interpersonal conflict) or attainment of special attention. Two studies have obtained positive results through use of behavior modification techniques to rearrange these contingencies (Gardner, 1968; Lazar & Jedliczka, 1979). However, both were case studies; therefore, before any definitive conclusions can be made, controlled group outcome studies are necessary.

Other techniques that have been used include systematic desensitization and hypnosis. Systematic desensitization has been used with moderate success in adult asthmatics (Yorkston, Eckert, McHugh, Philander, & Blumenthal, 1979; Yorkston, McHugh, Brady, Serber, & Sergeant, 1974). However, Miklich et al. (1977) had no success when this approach was tried with children. In fact, the control group actually rated its symptom frequency as more improved than the systematic desensitization group. Similarly, reports on hypnosis have not been encouraging. Although some investigators have achieved positive results (Aronoff, Aronoff, & Peck, 1975; Fry, Mason, & Pearson, 1964; Mun, 1969), confounded treatments, poorly controlled designs, and negative results (Smith & Burns, 1960) limit the conclusions that can be drawn.

Comment

Asthma is a pulmonary disorder characterized by wheezing and difficult breathing and is due to hyperreactive airways. Psychophysiological studies in children have shown that asthmatics may have abnormal autonomic nervous system reactions and that subgroups of asthmatics may also differ in this regard. However, further research is needed to confirm this observation. Assessment of an asthmatic child must take into account whether the asthma is intrinsic or extrinsic and the degree to which secondary gain is involved.

The behavioral treatment of asthma in children has produced mixed results. Although initially positive results were obtained with relaxation and biofeedback, more recent studies have not been as successful. Systematic desensitization and hypnosis have yielded inconsistent results; in addition, many of the studies were poorly controlled. Operant approaches have yielded positive results, but controlled group outcome studies are necessary before any firm conclusions can be reached.

As is evident, the results from the treatment studies have been disappointing. Even when statistically significant changes have been achieved, one must question their clinical relevance. Most studies have yielded changes in pulmonary functioning of between 2 and 5%, but changes of 15% are generally needed before there is any clinical significance. Similarly, the outcome measures that have been used must be questioned. More relevant than PEFR, which is not a stable measure, is the impact that treatment has on the individual's life. Studies are needed that assess changes in the amount of incapacitation caused by the asthmatic condition (e.g., frequency of emergency room visits, number of days hospitalized, days missed from school, the degree of activity restriction). Future studies should place more emphasis on these variables.

Although behavioral treatments of asthma have not been successful as the only procedure, it is possible that they may be beneficial as part of a comprehensive program. Asthma is a chronic medical problem; therefore, asthmatics need medical attention and supervision. Relaxation or biofeedback may be therapeutic when combined with proper medical care and certain ancillary services in a more comprehensive approach to treatment.

CASE ILLUSTRATION

PRESENTING PROBLEMS

Andrea, a 9½-year-old girl, was referred to the treatment program by her mother. Andrea's mother was participating in an adult treatment program for headaches at the time of the referral. Both Andrea and her mother were given a headache questionnaire and were interviewed for the diagnosis of migraine on referral. Andrea's personal physician also diagnosed the case as childhood migraine and ruled out any possible neurological basis for the head pain. Presence of the following symptoms, along with the results of the physical examination, warranted Andrea's diagnosis of migraine: (a) headaches were described as throbbing pain; (b) headaches were accompanied by nausea; (c) relief from head pain followed rest; and (d) a positive family history of migraine was noted.

Andreas headaches were described as severe and located across the forehead. Her mother reported that Andrea had experienced approximately four to eight headaches per month for the past 2 years. Each headache was reported to last about 4 hours, and Tylenol was frequently given when the head pain was severe.

ASSESSMENT PROCEDURES

A complete history and behavioral assessment of headache reports were included to screen for possible operant pain. No situational patterning of headache reports, in terms of time or situation, was noted. Andrea frequently experienced headaches while playing with friends and would often withdraw from the activity to rest. She also reported head pain while engaging in solitary activities. Although Andrea liked to go to school and obtained above-average grades, she would occasionally develop a headache at school that required her to go home to lie down. When Andrea reported a headache, she would go to her room and rest in a dimly lit environment. Aside from occasional checks by her mother to insure that she was ok, Andrea received little parental attention for reporting a headache. Self-monitoring of head pain did indicate, however, that Andrea frequently developed headaches and nausea when riding in the car for long periods of time.

During a 6-week baseline phase, Andrea was asked to fill out daily headache records (refer to Figure 11.1). She recorded the severity of her head pain, medications taken, and events preceding the headache four times per day. Andrea's self-monitoring data, as well as her initial diagnostic interview, indicated that she was not receiving positive reinforcement from others for reports of head pain, nor was she being negatively reinforced for avoiding unpleasant activities when she developed a headache. In addition, her self-monitoring data was consistent in terms of compliance and headache symptomatology. Therefore, Andrea's case was conceptualized as "true" childhood migraine without a functional component. She began biofeedback treatment immediately following collection of baseline data. Other behavioral treatment methods (e.g., contingency management) were not warranted.

TREATMENT

Andrea participated in 9 weeks of skin temperature biofeedback treatment. She was given 10 40-minute biofeedback sessions within this 9-week period. Each treatment session consisted of the following three phases: (a) 15 minutes in which she was given no instructions except to sit quietly (the last 10 minutes were utilized as baseline); (b) 15 minutes of skin temperature biofeedback; and (c) 5 minutes of self-control of skin temperature in the absence of feedback.

Operation of the skin temperature biofeedback system was explained to Andrea during a pretreatment laboratory session. She was told that learning to warm her hands was easy to do and would help alleviate headaches. Andrea was also given autogenic training instructions to teach her how to imagine her hands becoming warm as well as how to relax. She was instructed to practice the autogenic exercises and handwarming twice per day for approximately 10 minutes each time. Andrea was also instructed to begin monitoring hand-warming practice on her daily headache record (refer to Figure 11.1). After approximately 3 weeks of scheduled practice, Andrea was told to use the hand-warming procedure at the first sign of a headache. She was told that this procedure often helps people to stop their headache before the pain worsens. She was reminded to continue the use of the procedure on several occasions throughout the 9-week treatment period.

Self-monitoring of headache variables continued throughout treatment. Andrea's monitoring showed a decrease in her average headache index (defined as the average headache rating for the week) with the application of skin temperature biofeedback and autogenic training. Andrea's average headache index during baseline, treatment, and follow-up phases can be seen in Figure 11.2. During the final 3 or 4 weeks of treatment Andrea was headache-free.

FOLLOW-UP

At 1-month follow-up, Andrea's monitoring indicated that she had experienced only one headache (with an index of .14). No headaches were reported during the 4-week monitoring period 2 years following treatment. Interviews with Andrea and her mother indicated that she rarely experienced headaches following treatment.

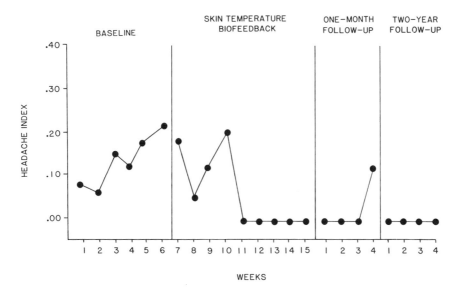

Figure 11.2. Headache activity for Andrea (case example) during baseline, treatment, and follow-up. Headache index is an average of headache ratings over a week of self-monitoring.

SUMMARY

Relative to the abundance of behavioral research concerning psychophysiological disorders in adults, research with children is just developing. Of the four psychophysiological disorders reviewed in this chapter, headache and asthma have received the most attention by behavioral researchers. It appears that biofeedback and relaxation therapies are very effective for childhood migraine. For tension headache, very little treatment research has been conducted. Earlier research concerning the treatment of asthma was quite positive, suggesting that biofeedback, relaxation, and desensitization might be quite effective. However, more recent studies question the clinical significance of the effects produced by these procedures. It is likely that these behavioral approaches may ultimately be found to be useful adjunctive therapies to traditional medical treatments for asthma. Only single-case treatment research has been reported for atopic dermatitis and abdominal pain. These studies have generally employed operant techniques to modify scratching in atopic dermatitis and pain behavior in recurrent abdominal pain syndrome. Clearly, much more extensive research is required before definitive conclusions can be drawn about the value of behavior therapy for these childhood disorders.

REFERENCES

Alexander, A. B., Cropp, G. J. A., & Chai, H. (1979). Effects of relaxation training on pulmonary mechanics in children with asthma. *Journal of Applied Behavior Analysis, 12,* 27–35.

Allen, K., & Harris, T. (1966). Elimination of a child's excessive scratching by training the mother in reinforcement procedures. *Behaviour Research and Therapy, 4,* 79–84.

Andrasik, F., Attanasio, V., Blanchard, E. B., Burke, E., Kapela, E., McCarrin, M., Blake, D. D., & Rosenblum, E. L. (1984, November). Behavioral treatment of pediatric migraine headache. In F. Andrasik (Chair), *Recent developments in the assessment and treatment of headache.* Symposium conducted at the meeting of the Association for Advancement of Behavior Therapy, Philadelphia.

Andrasik, F., Blanchard, E. B., Edlund, R., & Attanasio, V., (1983). EMG biofeedback treatment of a child with muscle contraction headache. *American Journal of Clinical Biofeedback, 6,* 96–102.

Andrasik, F., Blanchard, E. B., Edlund, S. R., & Rosenblum, E. L. (1982). Autogenic feedback in the treatment of two children with migraine headache. *Child and Family Behavior Therapy, 4,* 13–23.

Apley, J. (1975). *The child with abdominal pain.* London: Blackwell.

Apley, J., & Naish, N. (1958). Recurrent abdominal pains: A field survey of 1000 school-children. *Archives of Disease in Childhood, 33,* 165–170.

Aronoff, G. M., Aronoff, S., & Peck, L. W. (1975). Hypnotherapy in the treatment of bronchial asthma. *Annals of Allergy, 34,* 356–362.

Bar, H., & Kuypers, B. (1973). Behaviour therapy in dermatological practice. *British Journal of Dermatology, 88,* 591–598.

Barr, R. G. (1983). Recurrent abdominal pain. In M. D. Levine, W. B. Carey, A. C. Crocker, and R. T. Gross (Eds.), *Developmental-behavioral pediatrics.* (pp. 521–528). Philadelphia: Saunders.

Barr, R. G., & Feuerstein, M. (1983). Recurrent abdominal pain syndrome: How appropriate are our basic clinical assumptions? In P. J. McGrath & P. Firestone (Eds.), *Pediatric and adolescent behavioral medicine, 10,* New York: Springer.

Beerman, H. (1962). Aetiology and mechanisms in development of neurodermatitis. In J. Nodine & J. Mayer (Eds.), *Psychosomatic medicine.* London: Kimpton.

Bille, B. (1967). Juvenile headache: Its natural history in children. In A. Friedman & E. Harms (Eds.). *Headaches in children.* Springfield, IL: Thomas.

Black, P. (Ed.) (1970). *Physiological correlates of emotion.* New York: Academic.

Brown, J. K. (1977). Migraine and migraine equivalents in children. *Developmental Medicine and Child Neurology, 19,* 683–692.

Burrows, B. (1979). Diseases associated with airways obstruction. In P. B. Beeson, W. McDeurmott, & J. B. Wyngarnder (Eds.), *Cecil textbook of medicine.* Philadelphia: Saunders.

Butler, J. (1984). Disordered cyclic nucleotide metabolism—A basic defect in atopic dermatitis. *Australian Journal of Dermatology, 25,* 3–7.

Christensen, M. F., & Mortensen, O. (1975). Long term prognosis in children with recurrent abdominal pain. *Archives of Diseases in Childhood, 50,* 110–114.

Curry, J. J., & Lowell, F. C. (1948). Measurement of vital capacity in asthmatic subjects receiving histamine and acetyl-beta-methyl choline. A clinical study. *Journal of Allergy, 19,* 9–15.

Danker, P. S., Miklich, D. R., Pratt, C., & Creer, T. L. (1975). An unsuccessful attempt to instrumentally condition peak expiratory flow rates in asthmatic children. *Journal of Psychosomatic Research, 19,* 209–213.

Diamond, S., & Franklin, M. (1975). Autogenic training with biofeedback in the treatment of children with migraine. In W. Luthe & F. Antonelli (Eds.), *Therapy in psychosomatic medicine: Proceedings of the 3rd congress of the International College of Psychosomatic Medicine* (pp. 190–192). Rome.

Faulstich, M., & Williamson, D. A. (1985). An overview of atopic dermatitis: Toward biobehavioral integration. *Journal of Psychosomatic Research 29,* 1–8.

Faulstich, M., Williamson, D. A., Duchmann, E., Conerly, S., & Brantley, P. (1985). Psychophysiological analysis of atopic dermatitis. *Journal of Psychosomatic Research 29,* 415–417.

Franks, C. M., & Leigh, D. (1959). The theoretical and experimental application of a conditioning model to a consideration of bronchial asthma in men. *Journal of Psychosomatic Research, 4,* 88–98.

Fry, L., Mason, A. A., & Pearson, R. S. (1964). Effects of hypnosis on allergic skin responses in asthma and hay fever. *British Medical Journal, 5391,* 1145–1148.

Gardner, J. E. (1968). A blending of behavior therapy techniques in an approach to an asthmatic child. *Psychotherapy: Theory, Research, and Practice, 5,* 46–49.

Garrie, E., Garrie, S., & Mote, T. (1974). Anxiety and atopic dermatitis. *Journal of Consulting and Clinical Psychology, 42,* 742.

Gigli, I., & Baer, R. (1979). Atopic dermatitis. In T. Fitzpartick, A. Eisen, K. Wolff, I. Freedberg, & K. Austen, (Eds.), *Dermatology in general medicine,* (pp. 520–528). New York: McGraw-Hill.

Godfrey, S., & Silverman, M. (1973). Demonstration by placebo response in asthma by means of exercise testing. *Journal of Psychosomatic Research, 17,* 293–297.

Green, M. (1967). Diagnosis and treatment: Psychogenic recurrent abdominal pain. *Pediatrics, 40,* 84–89.

Hahn, W. W. (1966). Autonomic responses of asthmatic children. *Psychosomatic Medicine, 28,* 323–329.

Hahn, W. W., & Clark, J. A. (1967). Psychophysiological reactivity of asthmatic children. *Psychosomatic Medicine, 29,* 526–534.

Hanifin, J. (1982). Atopic dermatitis. *Journal of the American Academy of Dermatology, 6,* 1–13.

Haynes, S., Wilson, C., Jaffee, P., & Britton, B. (1979). Biofeedback treatment of atopic dermatitis: Controlled case studies of eight cases. *Biofeedback and Self Regulation, 4,* 195–209.

Johnson, M. (1977). Prevalence of dermatologic disease among persons 1–72 years of age: United States. *Advance Data from Vital and Health Statistics of the National Center for Health Statistics No. 4.*

Jordan, J., & Whitlock, J. (1974). Atopic dermatitis, anxiety, and conditional scratch responses. *Journal of Psychosomatic Research, 18,* 297.

Khan, A. U. (1977). Effectiveness of biofeedback and counterconditioning in the treatment of bronchial asthma. *Journal of Psychosomatic Research, 21,* 97–104.

Khan, A. U., Staerk, M., & Bonk, C. (1974). Role of counterconditioning in the treatment of asthma. *Journal of Psychosomatic Research, 18,* 89–92.

Kohlenberg, R. J. (1982). Tryamine sensitivity in dietary migraine: A critical review. *Headache, 22,* 30–34.

Kotses, H., Glaus, K. D., Bricel, S. K., Edwards, J. E., & Crawford, P. (1978). Operant muscular relaxation and peak expiratory flow rate in asthmatic children. *Journal of Psychosomatic Research, 22,* 17–23.

Kotses, H., Glaus, K. D., Crawford, P., Edwards, J. E., & Scherr, M. S. (1976). Operant reduction of frontalis EMG activity in the treatment of asthma in children. *Journal of Psychosomatic Research, 20,* 453–459.

Labbé, E. E., & Williamson, D. A. (1983). Temperature biofeedback in the treatment of children with migraine headaches. *Journal of Pediatric Psychology, 8,* 317–326.

Labbé, E. E., & Williamson, D. A. (1984). Treatment of childhood migraine using autogenic feedback training. *Journal of Consulting and Clinical Psychology, 52*(6), 968–976.

Labbé, E. E., Williamson, D. A., & Southard, D. R. (1985). Reliability of headache assessment for children with migraine headaches (Abstract). *Proceedings of the 6th annual convention of the Society of Behavioral Medicine,* p. 77.

Lazar, B. S., & Jedliczka, Z. T. (1979). Utilization of manipulative behavior in a retarded asthmatic child. *American Journal of Clinical Hypnosis, 21,* 287-292.

Liebman, W. M. (1978). Recurrent abdominal pain in children: A retrospective survey of 119 patients. *Clinical Pediatrics, 17,* 569-573.

Litchfield, H. R. (1972). Headache in children. *New York State Journal of Medicine, 72*(17), 2151-2153.

Luparello, T. J., Lyons, H. A., Bleecker, E. R., & McFadden, E. R. (1968). Influence of suggestion on airway reactivity in asthmatic subjects. *Psychosomatic Medicine, 30,* 819-825.

Medina, J. L., & Diamond, S. (1978). The role of diet in migraine. *Headache, 18,* 31-34.

Miklich, D. R., Renne, C. M., Creer, T. L., Alexander, A. B., Chai, H., Davis, M. H., Hoffman, A., & Danker-Brown, P. (1977). The clinical utility of behavior therapy as an adjunctive treatment for asthma. *Journal of Allergy and Clinical Immunology, 60,* 285-294.

Miller, A. J., & Kratochwill, T. R. (1979). Reduction of frequent stomachache complaints by time out. *Behavior Therapy, 10,* 211-218.

Mun, C. T. (1969). The value of hypnotherapy as an adjunct in the treatment of bronchial asthma. *Singapore Medical Journal, 10,* 182-186.

Obermayer, M. (1970). Psychocutaneous disorders. In S. Madden (Ed.), *Current dermatological management,* St. Louis: Mosby.

Parker, C. D., Bilbo, R. E., & Reed, C. E. (1965). Methacholine aerosol as a test for bronchial asthma. *Archives of Internal Medicine, 115,* 452-464.

Phillip, R. L., Wilde, G. J. S., and Day, J. H. (1972). Suggestion and relaxation in asthmatics. *Journal of Psychosomatic Research, 16,* 193-204.

Prensky, A. L., & Sommer, D. (1979). Diagnosis and treatment of migraine children. *Neurology, 29,* 506-510.

Purcell, K. (1963). Distinctions between subgroups of asthmatic children: Children's perceptions of events associated with asthma. *Pediatrics, 31,* 468-477.

Rajka, G. (1975). *Atopic dermatitis.* London: Saunders.

Ramsden, R., Friedman, B., & Williamson, D. A. (1983). Treatment of childhood headache reports with contingency management procedures. *Journal of Clinical Child Psychology, 12*(2), 202-206.

Ratliff, R., & Stein, N. (1968). Treatment of neurodermatitis by behavioral therapy: A case study. *Behaviour Research and Therapy, 6,* 397-399.

Richardson, G. M., McGrath, P. T., & Cunningham, S. T. (1983). Validity of the headache diary for children. *Headache, 23,* 184-187.

Sank, L. I., & Biglan, A. (1974). Operant treatment of a case of recurrent abdominal pain in a ten-year-old boy. *Behavior Therapy, 5,* 677-681.

Scherr, M. S., Crawford, P., Sergeant, C. B., & Scherr, C. A. (1975). Effect of biofeedback techniques on chronic asthma in a summer camp environment. *Annals of Allergy, 35,* 295–298.

Smith, J. M., & Burns, C. L. (1960). The treatment of asthmatic children by hypnotic suggestion. *British Journal of Diseases of the Chest, 54,* 78–81.

Strupp, H. H., Levenson, R. W., Manuck, S. B., Snell, J. D., Hinrichsen, J. J., & Boyd, S. (1974). Effects of suggestion on total respiratory resistance in mild asthmatics. *Journal of Psychosomatic Research, 18,* 337–346.

Sulzberger, M. (1971). Atopic dermatitis. In T. Fitzpoatrick (Ed.) *Dermatology in general medicine* (pp. 680–697). New York: McGraw-Hill.

Tal, A., & Miklich, D. R. (1976). Emotionally induced decreases in pulmonary flow rates in asthmatic children. *Psychosomatic Medicine, 38,* 190–200.

Turnbull, J. W. (1962). Asthma conceived as a learned response. *Journal of Psychosomatic Research, 6,* 59–70.

Yorkston, N. J., Eckert, E., McHugh, R. B., Philander, D. A., & Blumenthal, M. N. (1979). Bronchial asthma: Improved lung function after behavior modification. *Psychosomatics, 20,* 325–331.

Yorkston, N. J., McHugh, R. B., Brady, R., Serber, M., & Sergeant, H. G. S. (1974). Verbal desensitization in bronchial asthma. *Journal of Psychosomatic Research, 18,* 371–376.

Williamson, D. A. (1981). Behavioral treatment of migraine and muscle-contraction headaches: Outcome and theoretical explanations. In M. Hersen, R. Eisler, & P. Miller (Eds.), *Progress in Behavior Modification* (Vol. II).

Williamson, D. A., Ruggeiro, L., & Davis, C. J. (1985). Headache. In M. Hersen & A. S. Bellack (Eds.), *Handbook of Clinical Behavior Therapy with Adults* (pp. 417–441). New York: Plenum.

CHAPTER 12

Oppositional Behavior

ALAN M. GROSS AND JOHN T. WIXTED

The behavior of a young child is labeled "oppositional" if parents or teachers regard it as representing an unacceptable level of cooperation with their authority. Some of the most frequently cited oppositional behaviors include noncompliance with adult requests, rule-breaking behavior in the home or school, and resistive temper tantrums. Unfortunately, children who exhibit such behavior are variously referred to as oppositional, conduct disordered, or deviant (see Wahler, 1976; Wells, 1981). Although the term *deviancy* appears to have no clearly defined referent, the terms *oppositional behavior* and *conduct disorder* can be distinguished in that the former is characterized primarily by obstreperous disobedience, while the latter is characterized by physical aggression and violation of age-appropriate societal norms. In practice, a younger child is more likely to be labeled oppositional, though the disorder can occur in late childhood and adolescence as well (American Psychiatric Association, 1980).

Although the origin and development of oppositional behavior in children has received little empirical attention, it has been the subject of considerable theoretical speculation. Patterson (1976; Patterson, Cobb, & Ray, 1973) argues that oppositional behavior is a learned "coercive" technique by means of which the child exerts control over parental behavior. According to this account, disruptive behavior usually occurs in response to an aversive stimulus and is negatively reinforced by the subsequent removal of that stimulus. For example, in response to a request to take out the garbage (a parent-delivered aversive stimulus), the child may protest by throwing a furious temper tantrum, to which the parent may respond by withdrawing the command (reinforcing the tantrum). In this example the parent's capitulation is also reinforced by the termination of the child's negative behavior. This process of reciprocal reinforcement by the removal of aversive stimuli has been referred to as the "negative reinforcer trap" (Wahler, 1976).

The coercion hypothesis further maintains that parents may also learn to employ coercive control techniques. On some occasions, for example, the parent may react to the child's opposition with extreme hostility such that the child eventually complies with the parent's wishes. According to Patterson, extended interchanges between the parent and child can reach high levels of emotional turmoil before one participant surrenders, thereby reinforcing the coercive behavior of the other.

Wahler (1976) suggested that, in many cases, a child's oppositional behavior is maintained by the contingent application of positive social reinforcement in the form of parental attention. Such attention can come in a variety of forms, including verbal reprimands (a nominal punisher), reasoning with the child, or simply trying to "understand" the child's resistance by discussing the matter in great detail. In response to parental behavior of this kind, the child may behave in a cooperative manner, thereby reciprocally reinforcing the parental intervention. Wahler (1976) has referred to this process as the "positive reinforcer trap." In most cases, oppositional behavior is probably maintained by a combination of both positive and negative reinforcement (Gross, 1983).

The importance of treating families with oppositional children may extend beyond the immediate goal of establishing a cooperative and harmonious family atmosphere. A number of long-term follow-up studies have suggested that young children who exhibit deviant behavior at home or at school have a greater likelihood of encountering psychiatric disturbance in adolescence and adulthood (Robins, 1979). Wahler (1976) expressed the hope that by effectively modifying oppositional tendencies early in life, the chances of later psychiatric problems might be reduced.

ASSESSMENT

The assessment of oppositional behavior is an important element of every phase of a treatment program. Initially, the primary assessment goals include identifying the problem behaviors, their rates of occurrence, and the situational antecedents and consequences that maintain them. Such information is vital to the selection of target behaviors and to the design of an effective treatment program. In addition, assessment techniques are employed to provide on-going monitoring of treatment and to evaluate maintenance of treatment gains after the program is concluded. The most commonly used assessment procedures include the behavioral interview, behavioral questionnaires, and direct observation.

Behavioral Interview

Because the behavioral interview is usually the first direct contact between the therapist and the referring parents, the initial focus should be on obtaining demographic information about the child (e.g., age, sex, school) and information regarding any unusual medical or developmental issues. The bulk of the interview, however, should be devoted to gathering information about the problem behaviors exhibited by the child and the typical antecedent and consequent events that surround them. General information on these matters can be obtained by asking broad and open-ended questions about the nature of the presenting complaint (e.g., "What prompted you to seek help at this time?" "What problems have you been having with your child?"). In addition, parents can be questioned about how they have attempted to discipline the child when oppositional behaviors have occurred in the past. Such information will yield some insight into the controlling variables and also prepare the therapist for potential objections to treatments that, on the surface, resemble previously unsuccessful efforts to resolve the problem.

Once the presenting issues are broadly outlined, the therapist should initiate a much more detailed and exact inquiry into typical parent-child sequential interactions. Such information is best obtained through questions that focus on one aspect of the three-term contingency (occasioning stimulus, child response, and social reinforcer) at a time. For example: "Tell me exactly what your child does that you consider to be a problem?" "What is likely to be going on just before your child behaves like that?" "What do you do in response to such behavior?" An inquiry of this sort should be applied to each of the problem situations described by the parents. In addition, parents should be asked to provide an estimate of the frequency and duration of the behaviors in question. The behaviors initially targeted for treatment should be those that are of the shortest duration and that also appear to the therapist to be the most amenable to a behavioral intervention. Beginning a program with a quick success is likely to promote a successful outcome when more difficult and enduring behaviors are addressed.

In order to establish therapeutic goals more clearly, a portion of the initial interview should be directed toward evaluating parental expectations of their child's behavior. To this end, parents can be asked how they would like their child to behave in each of the situations where the child currently exhibits oppositional behavior. In some cases the preferred behavior may not be in the child's repertoire, requiring that the behavior be shaped. In other cases, however, the child may exhibit appropriate behavior in a variety of situations, but it has simply gone unnoticed by the parents. Information on these matters can be obtained by asking the parent to list some of their child's behavioral assets (e.g., "Can you think of any situations in which he usually does what he is told?" "When is she not a problem?"). In addition to providing some indication of the child's capabilities, an inquiry of this sort may help to ameliorate the parents' negative perceptions of their child. Finally, because the treatment intervention will involve parental application of contingent reinforcement, the parent should be queried about rewards that are likely to be particularly effective for their child. Preferred activities (e.g., watching television) are especially attractive reinforcers.

The interview with the parents should be closed with the therapist's providing a behavioral interpretation of the child's oppositional behavior. As part of this explanation, the therapist should emphasize that the parent behaviors that maintain the child's opposition are reciprocally maintained by the child's responses. This analysis will help to orient the parents to the type of intervention that will be recommended to alleviate the situation.

After meeting with the parents, the therapist usually conducts a brief interview with the child alone. This meeting gives the therapist an opportunity to orient the child to the treatment program as well as to obtain additional information regarding typical parental responses to the child's behavior. The interview can be initiated by asking why the child thinks the family has come to the clinic. It is important to explain to the child that he or she is not the core of the problem in isolation, but that the difficulties involve the entire family. In addition, the child should understand that his or her concerns will be given consideration throughout the treatment process. Although children under 5 years of age are unlikely to provide clinically significant information, older children can often provide valuable data for designing the treatment intervention.

Behavioral Questionnaires

In addition to simply asking parents open-ended questions about problem situations and behaviors, some therapists use standard behavioral questionnaires to gather assessment data. Although none is designed to measure oppositional behavior alone, a number of scales are available that assess a variety of global conduct problems in children (e.g., noncompliance, aggression). These scales include the Bipolar Adjective Checklist (Becker, 1960), the Walker Problem Identification Checklist (Walker, 1970), and the Behavior Problem Checklist (Peterson, 1961). With any of these forms, the parent is requested to estimate the rate of occurrence of a large number of problematic child behaviors.

While questionnaires are inexpensive and easy to employ, they are subject to situational bias (Forehand, Griest, & Wells, 1979) and frequently do not have strong reliability and validity data. Moreover, they do not provide the clinician with information concerning the antecedent and consequent conditions that control problem responses.

The major strength of parent questionnaires is in identifying problem areas that may be inadvertently overlooked. For this reason, Patterson, Reid, Jones, and Conger (1975) recommend that parents complete a behavior problem checklist prior to the initial interview. This information can then be used by the therapist to help determine the direction of the interview.

Observational Assessment

The essence of a behavioral assessment is the direct observation and quantification of both the child's problem behaviors and their presumed controlling consequences. In addition to these variables, however, some evidence suggests that several parental antecedents to oppositional behavior warrant careful evaluation. Three experiments have examined how parents of normal and clinic-referred children alter their behavior when simply instructed to make their child "look deviant" or "look cooperative." In each of these studies parents were successful in increasing deviant behavior in their children on the designated days. Johnson and Lobitz (1974), using a sample of normal families, reported that parents increased the rate at which they issued commands on "deviant" days relative to "cooperative" days. Lobitz and Johnson (1975) replicated this finding, but noted that for parents of clinic-referred children, the rate of negative parent behavior (e.g., criticisms) was a more important factor in producing deviant behavior in their children. Green, Forehand, and McMahon (1979) found that parents of clinic-referred children displayed more negative behavior and issued more vague commands (e.g., "Be careful") on "deviant" days in order to produce a higher rate of child noncompliance. Taken together, the above findings suggest that an observational assessment should include recordings of negative parental behavior, the types of commands used, and the rate at which the commands are delivered.

Ideally, observational assessment would be conducted in the child's natural environment by trained observers using one of several available coding systems (e.g., Forehand & McMahon, 1981; Patterson, 1976; Wahler, House, & Stambaugh, 1976). Any of these systems can be used as a framework for measuring targeted behaviors as well as recording patterns of interaction between the parent and child. The coding system described by Wahler et al. (1976), for example, employs 19 categories encompassing both child behaviors (e.g., compliance/oppositional, autistic, play, work, and social behaviors) and parental behaviors (e.g., rewards and criticisms). When an observer is present in the home, several restrictions on family activities are usually implemented. If possible, all family members should be present and should remain in two adjoining rooms for the entire observation period. Further, family members are instructed not to watch television, make outgoing telephone calls (incoming calls should be handled briefly), or have friends in the house. Aside from these restrictions, parents are encouraged to behave as naturally as possible and to try to ignore the observer. Parents are further assured that some feelings of awkwardness are normal at first, but that they will soon become more comfortable with the procedure.

Obviously, the use of trained observers is a time-consuming and expensive affair. Thus, while it is certainly the most desirable and objective assessment procedure, direct observation in the child's natural environment may not always be feasible. A common alternative is to observe and record the child's behavior in a clinic playroom setting (Hughes & Haynes, 1978). Typically, the playroom is equipped with a one-way mirror, tables and chairs, and age-appropriate toys. In order to expedite the acquisition of essential assessment information, parents are instructed to interact with their child in such a way that oppositional behaviors are likely to occur. For example, in their playroom sessions, Peed, Roberts, and Forehand (1977) instructed parents to alternate between child-determined and parent-determined play activities.

During playroom interactions, the therapist observes from behind the one-way mirror and records targeted child and parent behaviors. A common practice is to record the frequency of these behaviors over 30-second intervals, which permits the assessment data to be analyzed in terms of either responses per minute or proportion of intervals in which the behavior occurred. Forehand and his colleagues recommend that the duration of clinic observation periods be 10 minutes and that they be conducted during every clinic visit (Forehand & McMahon, 1981). The regular use of this procedure permits continuous monitoring of treatment progress and provides the therapist with objective information regarding the parent's mastery of behavioral techniques.

A second alternative to the use of trained observers in the home is to have one of the child's parents collect the observational data. Parents are instructed to record the frequencies of one or two of the behaviors reported as being the most problematic. To facilitate this process, data collection sheets that clearly indicate the important observational parameters can be provided. For example, the data sheets might contain columns for each oppositional behavior, the time at which the behavior occurred, and the parent behaviors immediately prior to and after the child response. One advantage of this assessment procedure is that it should heighten the parents' awareness of the antecedents and consequences that govern their child's behavior. An obvious disadvantage is that, when used in isolation, it eliminates a valuable source of objective information regarding interactional patterns between the parent and child.

Assessment of Untreated Behaviors

Some evidence suggests that the successful treatment of oppositional behavior in the home may result in increased oppositional behavior at school or vice versa (see Gross & Drabman, 1981, for a review). In most cases, however, the reported "contrast" effects were rather small; Breiner and Forehand (1981) even found some evidence for treatment generalization from home to school. Nevertheless, the clinician should be aware that for some children behavioral interventions in the home may have negative effects on behavior in other settings.

Another body of research has examined the covariation of oppositional behavior or noncompliance with other behaviors within the same setting. Wahler

(1975) recorded a variety of behaviors of two oppositional children over a 3-year period. For one subject, oppositional behavior was consistently inversely correlated with sustained toy play, suggesting that the modification of this behavior might provide an indirect means of controlling oppositional behavior. Indeed, Wahler and Fox (1980) showed that by reinforcing the solitary play activity of three children, oppositional behavior decreased, at least temporarily.

Finally, Russo, Cataldo, and Cushing (1981) examined the effect of compliance training on untreated deviant behaviors. They found that deviant behaviors consistently decreased when children were reinforced for compliance. Wells, Forehand, and Griest (1980) also found decreases in general deviant behavior when the child was treated for noncompliance.

The assessment procedures described should help to ensure the success of a parent training program for child oppositional behavior. The on-going evaluation of changes in oppositional and other behaviors, for example, will indicate which techniques are effective (and therefore worthy of retaining) and which are ineffective (warranting discontinuation). Careful attention to possible contrast effects will help in this evaluation. In addition, home observations, either by a trained observer or a parent, will indicate whether clinic treatment gains generalize to the home setting of their own accord or whether additional procedures are required to facilitate that process. Finally, when parents have participated in assessment activities, they can easily monitor maintenance of treatment gains following completion of the parent training program. Such information can help the parents and therapist decide whether subsequent booster sessions are necessary.

RANGE OF TECHNIQUES

The majority of programs designed to reduce oppositional behavior in children have employed direct training of parents in child management skills (e.g., Forehand, 1977; Patterson, 1976; Wahler, 1976). Typically, parents are taught to use a combination of contingent social reinforcement for appropriate behavior and either extinction (i.e., ignoring) or time-out from positive reinforcement for inappropriate behavior. The following section will describe the components of a parent training program for oppositional behavior. Subsequent sections will briefly review some adjunctive procedures and additional techniques that have been applied to oppositional behavior.

Parent Training

The purpose of a parent training program is to teach parents to modify their own behaviors in such a way as to decrease oppositional behavior and increase appropriate behavior of their child. In order to accomplish this task, careful attention to both parent-delivered antecedents and consequences of the child's behavior is required. The initial focus of treatment centers on teaching parents to reinforce acceptable behavior by means of contingent attention, and to steadfastly ignore unacceptable behavior. Frequently, this approach represents a complete reversal of the parents' typical style, which consists of constant attention to the least desirable behaviors (often in the form of verbal reprimands) and no attention to desirable behaviors. As such, the treatment intervention may require from the parents a degree of vigilance to which they are unaccustomed.

In order to train the parent in the use of selective attention, the therapist should employ extensive explanation, modeling, and behavior rehearsal in every session. Many parents will need clear illustrations of how to apply attention. The therapist should therefore demonstrate several examples, such as simple expressions of praise (e.g., "That's terrific!") or statements of approval that contain a description of the child's appropriate behavior (e.g., "I like it when you clean up your toys"). It is important for the therapist to explain that, in order to be effective, such reinforcement must be delivered immediately after the targeted behavior occurs (e.g., as soon as the child complies with a request). Further, inappropriate behavior, such as temper tantrums, must be ignored at all times. The parent should understand that even occasional attention can maintain deviant behavior at a high rate.

In addition to having parents rehearse these skills, the therapist should devote part of each session to allowing the parent to practice selective attention in a clinic playroom while the child engages in play activity. These sessions provide the therapist with an opportunity to gauge the parent's progress and to provide informed recommendations in order to correct any inadequacies. Forehand and his colleagues employ a bug-in-the-ear device in order to unobtrusively communicate with the parent during the playroom interaction sessions (Forehand, 1977). In this way, the therapist can direct and immediately correct the parent's behavior.

After the parent has achieved some degree of mastery with selective attention, the focus of training can be shifted to modifying parental antecedents to child opposition. Specifically, the parent is taught to avoid vague commands, which, based on research and clinical experience, result in a relatively high probability of noncompliance (Roberts, McMahon, Forehand, & Humphreys, 1978). Vague commands (e.g., "Be careful," or "Behave yourself") do not clearly indicate to the child what the desired behavior is. In contrast to such commands, the therapist instructs the parent in the use of clear commands and then models several examples. Such commands are specific (e.g., "Put the toys in the cupboard now"), issued one at a time, and are followed by a pause long enough to allow the child time to comply. Parent-child playroom interactions during this stage of training should be governed entirely by the parent (see Peed et al., 1977). In this way, commands delivered by the parent can be observed at a frequency high enough to permit accurate assessment. During this stage of training, parents should also be encouraged to issue commands at as low a rate as possible and to avoid criticisms directed toward their child.

Although the combined use of selective attention and specific commanding behavior may be sufficient to eliminate oppositional behavior, use of a punishment procedure is often required (Wahler, 1969). Thus, if necessary, the parent is taught to impose time-out for noncompliance and other inappropriate behaviors that are unlikely to diminish by being ignored (e.g., fighting with siblings). If the child does not comply with a command, for example, the parent is instructed to issue a warning that failure to comply will result in time-out (e.g., 3 minutes in a chair in a corner of the room). If the child complies with the command in response to the warning, the parent is instructed to provide a social reward. If the child still does not comply, the time-out contingency is imposed. When the child is released from time-out, the command is repeated, and the entire process repeats itself until the child complies. Because the initial use of time-out can be aversive for both the parent and the child, the technique is usually restricted to use in the clinic setting until some degree of proficiency is obtained.

Adjunctive Techniques

Although the treatment intervention described above is fairly comprehensive, several ancillary procedures have been found to enhance treatment success. McMahon, Forehand, and Griest (1981) showed that training parents in social learning principles (as opposed to only techniques) resulted in increased child compliance at the end of treatment as well as at a 2-month follow-up relative to a control group that received only a standard treatment package. These parents also perceived their children more positively and reported greater satisfaction with treatment. Similar findings have been reported by Gross, Magalnick, and Richardson (in press).

Wells, Griest, and Forehand (1980) added a self-control package to a parent training program in an effort to enhance temporal generalization. Essentially, the self-control technique involves having parents generate a list of activities they find rewarding and then treating themselves to one of those activities if they meet a particular behavioral criterion (e.g., four rewards per minute during a 15-minute homework session with the child). Regardless of whether or not the criterion was satisfied, parents were instructed to telephone the clinic and report self-collected data. Wells, Griest, and Forehand reported that at a 2-month follow-up, children of parents provided with self-control training were significantly more compliant than children of parents who received only the parent training program.

Other Techniques

Although parent training is without question the treatment of choice for oppositional behavior, several other techniques have been shown to be effective. As noted earlier, Wahler and Fox (1980) treated oppositional behavior in three children by reinforcing solitary play activity. This approach was based on the hypothesis (supported by an initial assessment) that solitary play and oppositional behavior form a functional cluster such that the direct manipulation of one behavior will result in the indirect modification of the other. Unfortunately, the decrease in oppositional behavior as solitary play increased was transient, and the imposition of a time-out contingency was required to reinstate treatment gains. Thus, although the concept of functional clusters is promising, a more prudent approach would be to treat noncompliance as an indirect intervention for oppositional behaviors in general (see Russo et al. 1981).

O'Brien, Riner, and Budd (1983) developed a child self-evaluation procedure for increasing compliance with parental instructions. In this single-case study, the procedure consisted of the mother's prompting the child as to whether or not he had complied with her instructions. If the child decided that he had complied, he procured a token reinforcer from a freely available dispenser. O'Brien et al. (1983) found that the self-control procedure was effective in increasing compliance, but only when presented following a maternal feedback condition in which, in addition to the prompts, the mother offered her own interpretation of whether or not the child had complied.

RESEARCH REVIEW

Effectiveness and Generalization

Forehand and King (1974) evaluated the effectiveness of a parent training program for child noncompliance. They treated eight children, ages 3 to 6 years, who were referred for fighting, disruption, and disobedience. The treatment program consisted of two phases, the first of which involved teaching reinforcing techniques and the second of which involved teaching the proper use of time-out for noncompliance. In all cases only the child's mother completed both phases of training. Clinic observations revealed that after an average of only six sessions, mothers increased their use of rewards contingent on compliance (i.e., rewards/complies) from 45 to 89%. Further, the average child compliance ratio (complies/command) increased from 43 to 81%. Forehand and King (1977) extended their earlier study by including comparisons with a nonclinic control group and by providing a 3-month follow-up evaluation. Eleven families with children referred for noncompliance and temper tan-

trums, and 11 normal families recruited by newspaper advertisement participated in the study. The child compliance ratio was lower for the clinic-referred
group at baseline (35% vs. 58%), but higher than the nonclinic group immediately following treatment (77%) and at the 3-month follow-up (84%).
Evaluations of similar treatment programs have also yielded positive findings
(Patterson, 1974; Patterson & Reid, 1973; Wahler, 1969).

Several other studies have examined the effectiveness and temporal generality of parent training programs in extra-laboratory situations. Peed et al.
(1977) assigned 12 families referred for child oppositional behavior to either
a parent training condition or to a waiting-list control condition. Three types
of data were collected for both groups prior to and immediately following
treatment: clinic observational data, home observational data, and parent verbal report measures that assessed parents' perceptions of their children. Prior
to treatment the two groups did not differ in any category scored by the
Forehand coding system in either setting. After completing the parent training
program, however, scores for the treatment group improved significantly along
almost every dimension in both the clinic and at home. Parents employed more
attends and rewards and issued fewer vague commands in both settings. The
ultimate indication of treatment success, child compliance, also improved significantly across settings. By contrast, scores for the waiting-list control group
remained unchanged over the waiting period.

Forehand et al. (1979) conducted a long-term follow-up analysis of a noncompliance treatment program for 11 families referred to a child behavior
management clinic. Observational data were collected by trained observers in
the home before and after parent training, and at 6- and 12-month follow-up
sessions. The results indicated that parental use of vague commands decreased
considerably following treatment and remained low at both follow-up evaluations. Parental use of attention contingent on compliance also increased significantly relative to baseline but returned to pretreatment levels by the first
follow-up observation. Nevertheless, child compliance remained significantly
higher than baseline even at the 1-year follow-up. Baum and Forehand (1981)
reported almost identical results in a follow-up assessment of 36 families conducted 1.5 to 4.5 years after treatment.

Strain, Steele, Ellis, and Timm (1982) conducted a very long-term follow-
up study of children treated for oppositional behavior via differential attention procedures 3 to 9 years earlier. Their findings showed that the classroom
behavior of former clients was indistinguishable from that of randomly selected class peers. Further, the behavior of teachers toward former clients and
their ratings of those clients on the Walker Problem Identification Checklist
also did not differentiate the two groups. These results are encouraging, given
the generally poor prognosis for severely deviant children. However, the data
must be viewed with caution since no follow-up data were reported for an
untreated sample of comparably behaviorally deviant children.

Parameters of Time Out

As noted earlier, the successful treatment of oppositional behavior often requires the use of a time-out contingency (e.g., Wahler & Fox, 1980). Indeed,
Roberts, Hatzenbuehler, and Bean (1981) offered evidence suggesting that the
time-out contingency may be the critical element of parent training programs.
Four groups of eight children each and their mothers participated in this laboratory study consisting of one baseline and one experimental session. In one
group, mothers were trained in attending and rewarding techniques only. In
a second group, mothers imposed time-out for noncompliance but did not
reward compliance in any manner. A third group of mothers was taught to
employ both methods, and a fourth group served as a waiting-list control.
Compared to the control group, attention alone was not effective in increasing
compliance, whereas time-out alone and time-out plus attention were both
very effective and did not differ from each other. These findings suggest that,
at least in the short term, the time-out contingency is of critical importance
in reducing noncompliance.

A number of studies have evaluated the effects of a variety of time-out
parameters, including duration, contingent versus noncontingent release, and
the effects of warned versus unwarned time-out. Hobbs, Forehand, and Murray (1978) employed a between-subjects design to evaluate the effects of three
time-out durations (10 seconds, 1 minute, and 4 minutes) on child noncompliance. Mothers were instructed to issue a series of 24 standard commands
to their children during a playroom interaction session. The commands were
issued at intervals of 20 seconds and consisted of instructing the child to move
various toys (e.g., "Put the football on the table"). The time-out contingency,
which consisted of having the child stand in the corner, was imposed each time
the child did not initiate compliance with the mother's command within 5
seconds. The results indicated that all three time-out durations were effective
in reducing noncompliance but that the 4 minute time-out was by far the most
effective. Further, when the time-out contingency was removed for two sessions, suppression of noncompliance was most effectively maintained for the
group that had received a 4-minute time-out.

Two studies have examined the effects of time-out release contingencies on
child noncompliance. Hobbs and Forehand (1975), using a nonclinic sample,
instructed mothers to issue a series of standard commands to the child at 30-
second intervals. Once again, time-out, which consisted of having the mother
gather up the toys and leave the playroom, was imposed for noncompliance.
For the contingent group, the child was released from time-out when the first
15 seconds elapsed in which he or she did not exhibit disruptive behavior. The
duration of time-out for the noncontingent group was yoked to that of the
contingent release group. Hobbs and Forehand found that disruptive behavior

during time-out was substantially less for the contingent release group, and overall compliance was greater. Based on these results, the authors strongly advocate the use of a time-out release contingency.

Bean and Roberts (1981) compared the effects of two types of time-out in 24 children, ages 2 to 6 years, referred for oppositional behavior. For half of the subjects, the mother imposed time-out contingent on noncompliance, but the child was free to terminate the punishment at any time. For the other half, time-out was imposed for 2 minutes and release was contingent on quietness during the last 15 seconds. The children were observed for one baseline and one experimental session. Both groups exhibited greater compliance during the experimental session, but only the parent-release group attained a level of compliance that was considered to be clinically significant.

Roberts (1982a) evaluated the effects of warned versus unwarned time-out on noncompliance in 24 children (ages 2 to 6 years) referred to a child management clinic. For one group, time-out was imposed without warning for noncompliance. A second group received a warning prior to the imposition, and a third group received warnings as well as praise for compliance. All three groups exhibited increased compliance relative to baseline during an experimental session, but the groups did not differ from each other. However, children who received warnings were placed in time-out far less often, which, from the parents' perspective, reduced the aversive nature of the intervention. The authors therefore recommend the use of warned time-out.

Children typically do not enjoy being placed in time-out and often exhibit their displeasure by throwing tantrums or attempting to leave the time-out setting before the time requirement has elapsed. Because of these tendencies, escape and release contingencies are typically imposed. Roberts (1982b) conducted a normative study on resistance to time-out so that therapists might be able to anticipate initial child reactions to it and to identify those children whose reactions are severe enough to warrant alternative measures. Thirty-two children (2 to 6 years) referred for oppositional behavior participated in the study. As in earlier studies, mothers were instructed to issue a series of standard commands in a playroom setting and to impose time-out (sitting in the corner for 2 minutes) for noncompliance. The escape contingency, which consisted of two spanks, was implemented if the child left the corner prematurely. The release contingency required 15 seconds of quietness prior to release. The average duration for the first time-out imposed was 5 minutes, 38 seconds, and the average number of attempted escapes was 3.4. Roberts recommends that resistance to time-out be considered excessive if measurements exceed one standard deviation above the mean, which, for the first time-out equals a duration of 10 minutes and 6 escapes. Roberts (1984) unsuccessfully attempted to reduce resistance by providing children with intensive training about the time-out contingency until they could correctly answer six questions designed to assess their understanding of it. Unfortunately, the pre-trained children resisted time-out as much as an untrained control group.

Despite evidence attesting to the importance of time-out contingencies, exclusive reliance on this technique would be inappropriate. A comprehensive treatment intervention is designed both to decrease the frequency of inappropriate behavior and to increase the frequency of appropriate behavior. While time-out may reduce noncompliance, the contingent application of positive reinforcement is the most efficient method of increasing the rate of other desirable behaviors. In addition, the child may display a variety of behavioral deficits, requiring the gradual shaping of the appropriate response. Again, such a process requires the skillful application of response-contingent rewards. Finally, when time-out is employed, a duration of 3 minutes and a 15-second quiet release contingency are recommended.

CASE ILLUSTRATION

The application of the parent training program for oppositional behavior described earlier is relatively straightforward and usually requires no more than 10 sessions. The following case study illustrates the various phases of a typical intervention procedure.

INITIAL INTERVIEW AND ASSESSMENT

Mark, a 6-year-old boy in the first grade, was referred to a behavior management clinic by his mother (Mrs. S.) for a variety of disruptive behaviors, including fighting with his younger brother (William, age 4) and obstreperous disobedience. During the intial interview, the therapist and Mrs. S. met alone while Mark played in an adjoining playroom. In order to obtain an overall picture of the problem situation, Mrs. S. was initially asked to provide globa information concerning her son's behavior. For example:

THERAPIST: What led you to come in to the clinic now?

MRS. S.: Well, I've just gotten so frustrated with Mark and I yell at him all the time. He never does what he is told. I've recently started to feel that he doesn't like me very much any more. I guess our relationship has just become intolerable.

THERAPIST: Has it always been like that?

MRS. S.: No, when he was younger he was always cooperative and affectionate. We used to get along so much better.

THERAPIST: When did it change?

MRS. S.:   I can tell you exactly when he changed. It was when his father started leaving town more often on business trips about a year ago. His behavior just went down hill after that, though he still does OK in school. Now he never listens to me and picks on his brother. I just can't handle him by myself.

The information that Mark was most disruptive when his mother was the sole disciplinarian suggested that Mrs. S. probably interacted with Mark in such a way as to maintain his oppositional behavior. Therefore, most of the remainder of the initial interview was directed toward specifying more precisely the problem behaviors and determining her typical reactions to them.

Although Mrs. S. seemed to feel that Mark's disobedience was pervasive, her response to a request for some recent examples of disobedience indicated that three home situations were particularly problematic. The first occurred in the morning just prior to leaving for school. Since William, the younger brother, often accompanied them in the car, Mrs. S. alternated allowing each child to sit in the front seat. When instructed to sit in the back seat, Mark very often reacted with anger and then pouted on the way to school. The second situation occurred immediately prior to dinner, at which time Mark was instructed to put away his toys and wash his hands. Mrs. S. reported that Mark rarely complied with this request without resistance of some sort. The last problem situation occurred when Mark was instructed to go upstairs, take a bath, and go to bed. Almost invariably he was very slow to comply with this request and occasionally succeeded in extending his bedtime by an hour or more.

Mrs. S. agreed that in addition to the boys' fighting, those three situations constituted most of the problem. In order to identify more clearly the variables that might be maintaining Mark's behavior, Mrs. S. was asked to provide more detailed accounts of the conditions that typically preceded and followed the behavior in each of the problem situations. For example:

THERAPIST: What usually leads up to the morning car seat confrontation?

MRS. S.:   Well, when it's his turn to sit in the back, I just tell him that today William gets to sit in the front. He never goes for this without some sort of fight. Most of the time he throws one of his screaming fits, which I just can't stand.

THERAPIST: What do you do when he throws a fit?

MRS. S.:   It depends on my mood. To be honest, I usually don't even push the issue any more, and I just let him sit in front. But sometimes I get really mad at him and I yell at him until he gets in the back. But then he pouts all the way to school, and I don't much like that either.

THERAPIST: What else have you tried?

MRS. S.:   Nothing really. I guess I have tried to explain how unfair he is being to William, but that never works either. He just doesn't care that he's being selfish.

The scene was much the same when Mark was instructed to put away his toys prior to dinner. Most of the time, he simply ignored the request, which infuriated Mrs. S. Her usual reactions included putting away the toys herself in order to avoid a battle or escalating the intensity of her demand that he put his toys away until he complied. Both reactions left her feeling bitter towards her son. At bedtime, the situation was quite different. In response to a request to go to bed, Mark usually engaged his mother in a conversation about his day and occasionally even asked about what she had done during the day while he was at school. Because Mrs. S. felt that these discussions were the only appropriate mother-son interactions in their lives, she was always very reluctant to terminate the discussion and send Mark to bed. On many occasions, she could recall encouraging Mark to initiate the bedtime conversations. Nevertheless, these nightly discussions were becoming longer and seemed to Mrs. S. to be somewhat manipulative since they served the purpose of extending bedtime.

In order to orient Mrs. S. to a behavioral approach, she was provided with a social learning interpretation of her child's difficulties. First, it was emphasized that Mark's behaviors did not reflect indomitable personality traits but that factors in the child's current environment, including her behavior toward him, determined his reactions. It was further emphasized that in no sense was this an indictment of her role as a parent, since many of her child's behaviors reciprocally determined her own reactions. Mark's resistance to sitting in the back seat of the car and her frequent withdrawal of the command to do so, for example, constituted a negative reinforcer trap. The temper tantrum was intermittently reinforced by getting to sit in the front seat and her "giving in" to this demand was reinforced by the termination of the tantrum. It was explained to Mrs. S. that such intermittent reinforcement can maintain negative behavior at a high rate. A similar conceptualization was provided for his refusal to pick up his toys prior to dinner. In addition, however, it was explained that her occasional "coercive" response to noncompliance (e.g., yelling) was also maintained by the removal of an aversive stimulus. Specifically, her yelling was reinforced by Mark's occasional compliance.

The bedtime situation was more easily conceptualized as a positive reinforcer trap. The mother's behavior of talking with Mark was positively reinforced by the child's self-disclosure and by the eventual peaceful end to the day. The child's behavior, in turn, was positively reinforced by parental attention and by getting to stay up later.

After presenting the behavioral conceptualization to Mrs. S., the purpose and procedures of observational assessment were discussed. The therapist explained that, prior to treatment, an initial baseline assessment was required in order to have some standard against which to measure treatment gains. For this purpose, Mrs. S. and her son were scheduled for two playroom observation sessions during which the therapist would record problem behaviors and the hypothesized controlling variables. For part of each session, Mrs. S. was instructed to permit Mark to play with whatever toy he desired. When the therapist tapped on the window, however, she was instructed to issue commands to Mark concerning such things as where to put a toy, what toy to play with, and what he was allowed to do with the toy. Finally, at the end of the playroom session, she was to instruct Mark to put away all of the toys. The therapist also explained the importance of evaluating treatment generalization to the home by means of observational assessment. Because no independent observer was available, however, Mrs. S. was selected to make the necessary observations. She was provided with data collection sheets with columns labeled "situation" (e.g., bedtime), "antecedents" (e.g., requested to go to bed), "child response," and "parent response." The therapist explained that additional assessment data would be collected during each of the following sessions while Mrs. S. and Mark interacted in the clinic playroom.

A brief interview with Mark alone followed the meeting with his mother. Mark realized that they had come in because he and his mother fought all of the time. The therapist explained to him that by working together, the whole family might be able to get along better. Mark expressed a willingness to cooperate with the treatment program. In addition, he was able to describe one of his responses that makes his mother mad; namely, refusing to put away his toys before dinner. His description of her typical response to this refusal was consistent with the picture provided by Mrs. S.

TREATMENT

The results of the assessment phase indicated that much of Mark's oppositional behavior was maintained by parent-delivered antecedents and consequences. Mrs. S. often did not wait for Mark to comply with a request, rarely responded to his appropriate behavior, and sometimes criticized him when he did not cooperate immediately. For his part, Mark rarely cooperated with his mother's commands unless they were repeated several times, and he became inappropriately angry when asked to put away the toys. The administration of the parent training program described earlier therefore seemed appropriate. During the first treatment session, the therapist explained that, initially, treatment would focus on teaching her how to become a more reinforcing agent to her child. Specifically, Mrs. S. was encouraged to increase attention to Mark's appropriate behavior and to decrease attention to his inappropriate behavior.

THERAPIST: It's very easy to ignore Mark when he's behaving the way you want him to and to attend to him when he misbehaves. You see, even when you yell at him, he has succeeded in obtaining your attention. If you can turn this around, I think that you'll begin to see a positive change in Mark's behavior.

MRS. S.:   How can I turn it around?

THERAPIST: Well, first we can work on how to attend to appropriate behavior. For example, when he's playing quietly, rather than just letting him alone you can say something like: "You're doing such a good job of playing by yourself!" You can also just describe some of the activities he happens to be engaged in, like: "That's a great house you're making with the tinker toys!"

MRS. S.:   I guess I really don't praise him as much as I should. I feel like I spend most of my time yelling at him.

THERAPIST: Just as it is important for you to attend to his appropriate behavior, it is important to ignore such behaviors as temper tantrums.

MRS. S.:   That doesn't sound very easy. He makes me so mad when he throws a fit.

THERAPIST: It probably won't be easy since you have become so accustomed to responding in a different way. But you will get better with practice.

Mrs. S. rehearsed attending behavior with the therapist until she became more proficient and comfortable with the technique. She then practiced attending to Mark in the clinic playroom while he simply played with the playroom toys. The session ended with the therapist's providing feedback on her performance and assigning a homework activity, which consisted of practicing attending behavior with Mark 10 or 15 minutes each day.

   The next several sessions followed the same format as the session described above, but greater emphasis was placed on playroom practice and therapist-supplied feedback. When Mrs. S. appeared to be attending to Mark's behavior reliably, she was taught to apply social reinforcers in such a way as to shape new behavior. It was emphasized that, in order to be effective, the rewards had to be delivered immediately following the child's behavior and, at least at first, every time the behavior occurs. Mrs. S. was asked to select one behavior that she would like to see her son exhibit more often. She decided that she would like Mark to talk about himself and his daily activities at times other than at bedtime. Since this intervention seemed to the therapist to stand a reasonable chance of success, a response by Mark of talking about a school activity between the time he arrived home from school and dinnertime was targeted for reward. At the same time, she was reminded that she should ignore such behavior if it occurred near bedtime. In addition, Mrs. S. was asked to expand her home data collection to include recordings of this behavior as well as the contingent reward she provided for it.

The daily behavioral records kept by Mrs. S. indicated that the differential attention procedure succeeded in increasing the frequency of the targeted behavior, and she was delighted by this result. She was encouraged to continue this procedure while the focus of therapy was shifted to the antecedents of noncompliance.

THERAPIST: When you try to get Mark to do something, such as sit in the back seat of the car, it's very important to phrase the question in the right way and to give him ample time to comply, even if you are expecting a fight. One type of command that is likely to lead to noncompliance is a command that doesn't tell him exactly what he is supposed to do, like: "Mark, be a good boy this morning." This is referred to as a vague command.

MRS. S.:   I think I see what you mean. It's like when I tell him to be nice to his brother.

THERAPIST: That's right. Mark will be much more likely to comply if he knows just what is expected of him. For example, you could tell him, "Mark, let William play with his tinker toys now," or "Mark, put your toys away." Can you think of a specific command?

MRS. S.:   Well, I could just say "Mark, you sit in the back seat this morning."

THERAPIST: Perfect. And don't forget to give him some time to comply, even if he's a little slow about it. Now why don't you practice this with Mark in the playroom?

In order to practice these skills, Mrs. S. was instructed to direct all playroom activities. She was further instructed to try to use specific commands exclusively and, for the time being, to ignore noncompliance. As before, the therapist provided feedback on her performance following practice playroom interactions.

Home observational records indicated that Mrs. S. was using specific commands reliably and that it was having some positive impact on Mark's dinnertime noncompliance. However, the degree of noncompliance was still unacceptably high, so the therapist introduced the time-out contingency. Essentially, Mrs. S. was taught to impose time-out for 3 minutes whenever Mark did not comply with both her initial request and a request coupled with a warning that failure to comply would result in punishment (e.g., "If you do not clean up your toys, you will have to sit in this chair"). While Mark was in time-out, she was instructed to ignore him unless he attempted to escape.

In that event, she was to warn him that any further attempts to escape would result in a spanking. In addition, a 15-second quiet release contingency was put into effect.

Because imposition of time-out in the playroom interactions proved to be a difficult process the first several times it was attempted, the therapist decided to wait until it was more successfully applied in the clinic before instructing Mrs. S. to practice it at home. During the next session, Mark accepted time-out punishment with much less resistance, and his mother appeared much more comfortable imposing it. Mrs. S. was therefore instructed to select a place at home that could be used for time-out. It was emphasized that the area selected must be devoid of reinforcing stimuli, which meant that Mark's bedroom was probably not an ideal location. Mrs. S. decided that a stool at the dining room table would be a good choice since there are no toys nearby, few people enter the room, and the television set cannot be seen.

The therapist emphasized to Mrs. S. that it was extremely important that she be prepared to follow through to compliance whenever she issued a command, both in the clinic and at home. Therefore, every time Mark did not comply with her command, she should impose time-out. Moreover, upon completion of time-out, she should repeat the command and impose the appropriate consequences (i.e., reward for compliance and time-out for noncompliance).

The final segment of training was continued until Mark exhibited an acceptably high level of compliance in the clinic setting. Mrs. S. reported that at home time-out had to be imposed almost every day for 2 weeks, but recently he had begun to comply on being warned of the time-out contingency. Usually, Mark completed time-out without attempting to escape and complied with the command on release.

TREATMENT EVALUATION

Home observations collected during the 3 weeks following the last session revealed that the parent training program had resulted in positive gains. Dinnertime difficulties had disappeared entirely, and Mark rarely offered any resistance to going to bed. It was interesting that Mrs. S. tended to attribute these changes to unknown forces rather than to the treatment techniques. Mark's fighting with William had decreased considerably, although it was still higher than Mrs. S. preferred. In addition, Mark still occasionally responded with a temper tantrum if he was not permitted to sit in the front seat of the car on the way to school. In response to the continued fighting behavior, it was suggested to Mrs. S. that she impose time-out for fighting. The morning tantrum behavior was more problematic since her records showed that tantrums were consistently ignored. It was suggested that the continued use of ignoring his tantrums would almost surely result in eventual success. Another positive change concerned the relationship between Mrs. S. and her son. De spite some continued problems, she reported that the two of them had not enjoyed each other's company so much in more than a year. Further, she fully intended to continue the daily attending period since both she and her son found it to be such a rewarding experience.

SUMMARY

Children who do not comply with adult requests, persistently break school or home rules, and exhibit resistive temper tantrums are considered to be oppositional. Since these behaviors are often maintained by parental reactions (e.g., withdrawal of a command in response to a tantrum), the most common treatment intervention is to train parents in the use of social learning techniques. The present chapter describes a comprehensive parent training program that teaches parents to use both social rewards for appropriate behavior and time-out from positive reinforcement for oppositional behavior. The training of parents in these procedures has been shown to result in increased child compliance and typically results in positive collateral changes, such as decreases in untreated oppositional behaviors. Long-term follow-up evaluations have indicated that positive effects of such treatment are very durable.

REFERENCES

American Psychiatric Association (1980). *Diagnostic and statistical manual of mental disorders* (3rd. ed.). Washington, DC: Author.

Baum, C. G., & Forehand, R. (1981). Long term follow-up assessment of parent training by use of multiple outcome measures. *Behavior Therapy, 12,* 643–652.

Bean, A. W., & Roberts, M. W. (1981). The effects of time-out release contingencies on changes in child noncompliance. *Journal of Abnormal Child Psychology, 9,* 95–105.

Becker, W. C. (1960). The relationship of factors in parental ratings of self and each other to the behavior of kindergarten children as rated by mothers, fathers, and teachers. *Journal of Consulting Psychology, 24,* 507–527.

Breiner, J. L., & Forehand, R. (1981). An assessment of the effects of parent training on clinic-referred children's school behavior. *Behavioral Assessment, 3,* 31–42.

Forehand, R. (1977). Child noncompliance to parental requests: Behavioral analysis and treatment. In M. Hersen, R. M. Eisler, & P. M. Miller (Eds.), *Progress in behavior modification* (Vol. 5, pp. 111–148). New York: Academic.

Forehand, R., Griest, D., & Wells, K. C. (1979). Parent behavioral training: An analysis of the relationship among multiple outcome measures. *Journal of Abnormal Child Psychology, 7,* 229–242.

Forehand, R., & King, H. E. (1974). Pre-school children's noncompliance: Effects of short-term therapy. *Journal of Community Psychology, 2,* 42–44.

Forehand, R., & King, H. E. (1977). Noncompliant children: Effects of parent training on behavior and attitude change. *Behavior Modification, 1,* 93–108.

Forehand, R. L., & McMahon, R. J. (1981). *Helping the noncompliant child: A clinicians' guide to parent training.* New York: Guilford.

Forehand, R., Sturgis, E. T., McMahon, R. J., Aguar, D., Green, K., Wells, K., & Breiner, J. (1979). Parent behavioral training to modify child noncompliance: Treatment generalization across time and from home to school. *Behavior Modification, 3,* 3–25.

Green, K. D., Forehand, R., & McMahon, R. J. (1979). Parental manipulation of compliance and noncompliance in normal and deviant children. *Behavior Modification, 3,* 245–256.

Gross, A. M. (1983). Conduct disorders. In M. Hersen (Ed.), *Outpatient behavior therapy: A clinical guide* (pp. 307–332). New York: Grune & Stratton.

Gross, A. M., & Drabman, R. S. (1981). Behavioral contrast and behavior therapy. *Behavior Therapy, 12,* 231–246.

Gross, A. M., Magalnick, L. J., & Richardson, P. (in press). Self-management training with families of insulin-dependent diabetic children: A long-term controlled investigation. *Child and Family Behavior Therapy.*

Hobbs, S. A., & Forehand, R. (1975). Differential effects of contingent and noncontingent release from time-out on noncompliance and disruptive behavior of children. *Journal of Behavior Therapy and Experimental Psychology, 6,* 256–257.

Hobbs, S. A., Forehand, R., & Murray, R. G. (1978). Effects of various durations of time-out on the noncompliant behavior of children. *Behavior Therapy, 9,* 652–656.

Hughes, M. M., & Haynes, S. N. (1978). Structured laboratory observation in the behavioral assessment of parent-child interactions: A methodological critique. *Behavior Therapy, 9,* 428–447.

Johnson, S. M., & Lobitz, G. K. (1974). Parental manipulation of child behavior in home observations. *Journal of Applied Behavior Analysis, 7,* 23–31.

Lobitz, G. K., & Johnson, S. M. (1975). Parental manipulation of the behavior of normal and deviant children. *Child Development, 46,* 719–726.

McMahon, R. J., Forehand, R., & Griest, D. L. (1981). Effects of knowledge of social learning principles on enhancing treatment outcome and generalization in a parent training program. *Journal of Consulting and Clinical Psychology, 49,* 526–532.

O'Brien, T. P., Riner, L. S., & Budd, K. S. (1983). The effects of a child's self-evaluation program on compliance with parental instructions in the home. *Journal of Applied Behavior Analysis, 16,* 69–79.

Patterson, G. R. (1974). Interventions for boys with conduct problems: Multiple settings, treatments, and criteria. *Journal of Consulting and Clinical Psychology, 45,* 471–481.

Patterson, G. R. (1976). The aggressive child: Victim and architect of a coercive system. In E. J. Mash, L. A. Hamerlynck, & L. C. Handy (Eds.), *Behavior modification and families* (pp. 267–316). New York: Brunner/Mazel.

Patterson, G. R., Cobb, J. A., & Ray, R. S. (1973). A social engineering technology for retraining the families of aggressive boys. In H. E. Adams & I. P. Unikel (Eds.), *Issues and trends in behavior therapy* (pp. 139–210). Springfield, IL: Research Press.

Patterson, G. R., & Reid, J. B. (1973). Intervention for families of aggressive boys: A replication study. *Behaviour Research and Therapy, 11,* 383–394.

Patterson, G. R., Reid, J. B., Jones, R. R., & Conger, R. E. (1975). *A social learning approach to family intervention: Families with aggressive children.* Eugene, OR: Castalia.

Peed, S., Roberts, M., & Forehand, R. (1977). Evaluation of the effectiveness of a standardized parent training program in altering the interactions of mothers and their noncompliant children. *Behavior Modification, 1,* 323–350.

Peterson, D. R. (1961). Behavior problems of middle childhood. *Journal of Consulting Psychology, 25,* 205–209.

Roberts, M. W. (1982a). The effects of warned versus unwarned time-out procedures on child noncompliance. *Child and Family Behavior Therapy, 4,* 37–53.

Roberts, M. W. (1982b). Resistance to time-out: Some normative data. *Behavioral Assessment, 4,* 237–246.

Roberts, M. W. (1984). An attempt to reduce time-out resistance in young children. *Behavior Therapy, 15,* 210–216.

Roberts, M. W., Hatzenbuehler, L. C., & Bean, A. W. (1981). The effects of differential attention and time-out on child noncompliance. *Behavior Therapy, 12,* 93–99.

Roberts, M. W., McMahon, R. J., Forehand, R., & Humphreys, L. (1978). The effect of parental instruction-giving on child compliance. *Behavior Therapy, 9,* 793–798.

Robins, L. N. (1979). Follow-up studies. In H. C. Quay & J. S. Werry (Eds.), *Psychopathological disorders of childhood* (pp. 414–450). New York: Wiley.

Russo, D. C., Cataldo, M. F., & Cushing, P. J. (1981). Compliance training and behavioral covariation in the treatment of multiple behavior problems. *Journal of Applied Behavior Analysis, 14,* 209–222.

Strain, P. S., Steele, P., Ellis, T., & Timm, M. A. (1982). Long-term effects of oppositional child treatment with mothers as therapists and therapists as trainers. *Journal of Applied Behavior Analysis, 15,* 163–169.

Wahler, R. G. (1969). Oppositional children: A quest for parental reinforcement control. *Journal of Applied Behavior Analysis, 2,* 159–170.

Wahler, R. G. (1975). Some structural aspects of deviant child behavior. *Journal of Applied Behavior Analysis, 8,* 27–42.

Wahler, R. G. (1976). Deviant child behavior within the family: Developmental speculations and behavior change strategies. In H. Leitenberg (Ed.), *Handbook of behavior modification and behavior therapy* (pp. 516–546). Englewoods Cliffs, NJ: Prentice-Hall.

Wahler, R. G., & Fox, J. J. (1980). Solitary toy play and time-out: A family treatment package for children with aggressive and oppositional behavior. *Journal of Applied Behavior Analysis, 13,* 23–39.

Wahler, R. G., House, A. E., & Stambaugh, E. E. (1976). *Ecological assessment of child problem behavior.* New York: Pergamon.

Walker, H. M. (1970). *The Walker Problem Identification Checklist.* Los Angeles: Psychological Services.

Wells, K. C. (1981). Assessment of children in outpatient settings. In M. Hersen & A. S. Bellack (Eds.), *Behavioral assessment: A practical handbook* (2nd ed., pp. 484–533). New York: Pergamon.

Wells, K. C., Forehand, R., & Griest, D. L. (1980). Generality of treatment effects from treated to untreated behaviors resulting from a parent training program. *Journal of Clinical Child Psychology, 9,* 217–219.

Wells, K. C., Griest, D. L., & Forehand, R. (1980). The use of a self-control package to enhance temporal generality of a parent training program. *Behaviour Research and Therapy, 18,* 347–358.

CHAPTER 13

Attention Deficit Disorder
with Hyperactivity

MARK D. RAPPORT

Attention deficit disorder with hyperactivity (ADD-H) is characterized by difficulties in sustaining attention, impulsivity, and excessive (non-goal-directed)
motor activity that are developmentally inappropriate for the child's age
(American Psychiatric Association, 1980). Historically, researchers and clinicians stressed the gross motor overactivity of the disorder (Chess, 1960). However, recent nosological advances have redirected this emphasis to diagnosti-
cally more relevant and pervasive behavior problems, such as deficits in impulse
control (Rapport, DuPaul, Stoner, Birmingham, & Masse, in press), attention
(Douglas, 1972; Goldberg & Konstantareas, 1981; Rapport, DuPaul, Stoner,
& Jones, in press), problem solving (Douglas, 1980), and rule-governed behavior (Barkley, 1981; 1982). Consequently, the latest edition of the *Diagnostic
and Statistical Manual of Mental Disorders* (DSM-III: American Psychiatric
Association, 1980) has replaced the labels *hyperactivity, minimal brain dysfunction,* and *hyperkinetic reaction of childhood* with *attention deficit disorder with hyperactivity.*

The core components of the disorder (i.e., inattention, impulsivity, hyperactivity) have been extensively documented in both laboratory and field settings using various observational and measurement techniques. The inattention component is typically characterized by a short attention span and an
inability to maintain and selectively attend to relevant stimuli (Busby &
Broughton, 1983; Douglas & Peters, 1979), especially in situations requiring
self-application (e.g., completing classroom academic assignments). Not un-
expectedly, a host of variables have been shown to differentially affect
ADD-H children's attentive behavior (see Rapport, 1983, for a review of crit-

The author wishes to express his grateful appreciation to Drs. G. J. DuPaul and G. Stoner for
their valuable comments on an earlier draft of this chapter.

ical treatment parameters). These variables include self-pacing (Whalen, Collins, Henker, Alkus, Adams, & Stapp, 1978; Whalen, Henker, Collins, Finck, & Dotemoto, 1979), immediate, negative feedback provided on a continuous basis (Rapport, Murphy, & Bailey, 1980; 1982), within-task stimulation (Radosh & Gittelman, 1981; Zentall, Zentall, & Booth, 1978), and the type of feedback delivery system employed (Cunningham & Knights, 1978; Firestone & Douglas, 1977; Freibergs & Douglas, 1969).

Problems with impulse control are typically evidenced by a failure to consider alternatives to or consequences of one's behavior (Douglas, 1972), deficient delay of gratification skills (Rapport, Tucker, DuPaul, Merlo, & Stoner, in press), an inability to delay responding under appropriate circumstances (Gordon, 1979; Rapport, DuPaul, Stoner, Birmingham, & Masse, in press), poor self-control (Hinshaw, Henker, & Whalen, 1984; Rosenbaum & Baker, 1984), dysregulation of behavior in accordance with situational demands (Routh, 1980), and deficiencies in learning rule-governed (vs. contingency-shaped) behavior (Barkley, 1981; 1982).

The traditionally cited and controversial hyperactivity component of the disorder has been deemphasized in recent years for several reasons. In general, objective and reliable measurements of motor activity in this population have yielded inconsistent results (see Barkley, 1977; Rapport, in press). In addition, overactivity *per se* is currently considered to be a less serious component of the disorder relative to inattention and impulsivity. Nevertheless, ADD-H children do exhibit higher than normal levels of motor activity, especially during structured school activities (Porrino, Rapoport, Behar, Sceery, Ismond, & Bunney, 1983).

Aside from the core components described above, ADD-H children frequently evidence a wide range of social-emotional problems. For example, they are frequently deficient in social skills (King & Young, 1982), less compliant to requests (Campbell, 1975), unusually sensitive to rewards (Douglas & Parry, 1983; Parry & Douglas, 1983), more talkative (Copeland, 1979), attention-seeking (Tallmadge & Barkley, 1983), easily frustrated (Freibergs & Douglas, 1969), and experience difficulties in peer (King & Young, 1981; Klein & Young, 1979) and parental (Tallmadge & Barkley, 1983) relationships. These difficulties tend to predominate at different stages of development (see Rapport, in press) and many continue well into adulthood (see Weiss & Hechtman, 1979). Thus, the popular belief that ADD-H children "outgrow" their problems is both inaccurate and empirically unsupported by long-term follow-up studies.

Not surprisingly, there has been an increased awareness and plethora of research investigations over the past decade regarding the diagnosis, course, and treatment of ADD-H. Among the reasons for this interest are the relatively high prevalence rate (3 to 5% of school-age children) of the disorder, the disproportionate number of ADD-H children referred to mental health/pediatric clinics for treatment (Safer & Allen, 1976), an increased risk for adult psychopathy (Wender, Reimherr, & Wood, 1981) and/or juvenile delinquency (Satterfield, Hoppe, & Schell, 1982), and the difficulties ADD-H children experience in educational settings (Rapport, in press). This last factor is perhaps the most serious due to its confounding nature (i.e., school failure usually precludes and contributes to the secondary difficulties ADD-H children experience) and impact on adult life.

The classroom behavior of ADD-H children is typically characterized by inattention, a failure to complete assignments on a consistent basis, motor restlessness, variability of mood, difficulty following directions and staying seated, disruptive behavior, and carelessness in completing academic work (Rapport, 1983). Consequently, these children make more failing grades, experience a disproportionately higher number of grade-level retentions (Cantwell & Satterfield, 1978), generally underachieve despite their intellectual abilities (Lambert & Sandoval, 1980), are frequently placed in special education classrooms, and encounter peer rejection (Milich, Landau, Kilby, & Whitten, 1982). Further complicating matters are the relatively recent findings that 50% (Lambert & Sandoval, 1980) to 80% (Safer & Allen, 1976) of ADD-H children experience some type of learning disability, while others present with severe forms of conduct disturbance (Loney, 1978).

This chapter is divided into five sections. The first section provides an overview of current behavioral assessment/diagnostic techniques used with ADD-H children. The importance of a thorough diagnostic evaluation will become readily apparent, as several childhood disorders share characteristics similar to those exhibited by ADD-H children. The second section selectively reviews a range of empirically based behavioral techniques that have been successfully used in classroom settings. Although psychostimulant treatment is not typically considered a behavioral technique in the strictest sense, owing to its widespread use and potential value, its application both alone and in combination with behavioral interventions will be discussed. A research review section provides an overview of recent developments in the field and an introduction to several variables that may influence treatment outcome. The fourth section highlights several clinical cases in which behavioral and psychostimulant treatments have been successfully applied with ADD-H children, with an overriding emphasis on classroom functioning. The last section summarizes our current knowledge of ADD-H and suggests future directions for therapeutic intervention.

DIAGNOSIS AND BEHAVIORAL ASSESSMENT

The diagnostic process used by mental health professionals has changed considerably over the past decade, owing to the laborious efforts of researchers across the country. As a result, professionals are no longer placed in the uncomfortable position of relying solely on clinical acumen or judgment. Standardized evaluative instruments such as behavioral rating scales, observational codes, and tests of academic/cognitive/intellectual abilities have become the *sine qua non* in behavioral assessment and, coupled with sound clinical judgment, facilitate the diagnostic and treatment process.

The diagnosis and assessment of attention deficit disorder with hyperactivity (ADD-H) is by no means an exception to these changes in the diagnostic process. The proliferation of research studies in this field, particularly those concerned with diagnostic/assessment issues, is overwhelming even to the most experienced research-practitioner. For example, a recent bibliography prepared by Natalie Reatig (1984) of the Pharmacologic and Somatic Treatments Research Branch of the National Institute of Mental Health lists over 300 publications that address the etiologic and diagnostic characteristics of ADD-H. Further, these references cover only the brief time span between 1976 and 1984.

The most significant change in the diagnosis of ADD-H is exemplified in the third edition of the *Diagnostic and Statistical Manual of Mental Disorders* (DSM-III; American Psychiatric Association, 1980). Inattention and impulsivity are considered the primary core components of the disorder; hyperactivity *per se* may or may not be present (see Table 13.1). This change in diagnostic emphasis may be attributed to at least two factors. The first stems from over a decade of laboratory-based research that conclusively shows that ADD-H children experience severe difficulties in sustaining attention and act more impulsively compared to "normal" children (see Douglas & Peters, 1979, for a review).

The second factor is based on long-term follow-up studies of ADD-H children, which show that difficulties in attention and impulsivity tend to persist into adulthood, despite a reduction in overactivity during adolescence (see Gittelman & Mannuzza; 1985; Weiss, 1985, for reviews). Several major researchers in the field have also proposed that more rigorous inclusion criteria be incorporated in the diagnostic process (Barkley, 1981) and also that ADD-H be designated as occurring "with or without" aggression (Loney, 1980) because of the poorer outcome associated with ADD-H with aggression.

The DSM-III criteria presented in Table 13.1 should not be exclusively relied on for diagnostic purposes, given the moderate correlations obtained in interobserver agreement during field trials (Rapoport & Ismond, 1984). Moreover, the diagnosis should not depend solely on a school-based psychological examination or on the child's behavior during the course of a pediatric examination. Indeed, as many as 80% of ADD-H children exhibit exemplary behavior and no sign of hyperactivity in office settings (Sleator & Ullmann, 1981). Fortunately, there are several assessment instruments specifically developed to aid the clinician in making the diagnosis. The most popular and reliable of these, as well as the most common rule-outs (i.e., disorders that

TABLE 13.1 Diagnostic Criteria for Attention Deficit Disorder with Hyperactivity[a]

The child displays, for his/her mental and chronological age, signs of developmentally inappropriate inattention, impulsivity, and hyperactivity. The signs must be reported by adults in the child's environment, such as parents and teachers. Because the symptoms are typically variable, they may not be observed directly by the clinician. When the reports of teachers and parents conflict, primary consideration should be given to the teacher reports because of greater familiarity with age-appropriate norms. Symptoms typically worsen in situations that require self-application, as in the classroom. Signs of the disorder may be absent when the child is in a new or a one-to-one situation.

The number of symptoms specified is for children between the ages of 8 and 10, the peak age for referral. In younger children, more severe forms of the symptoms and a greater number of symptoms are usually present. The opposite is true of older children.

A. *Inattention.* At least three of the following symptoms:
   1. Often fails to finish things he or she starts
   2. Often doesn't seem to listen
   3. Easily distracted
   4. Has difficulty concentrating on schoolwork or other tasks requiring sustained attention
   5. Has difficulty sticking to a play activity
B. *Impulsivity.* At least three of the following symptoms:
   1. Often acts before thinking
   2. Shifts excessively from one activity to another
   3. Has difficulty organizing work (not due to cognitive impairment)
   4. Needs a lot of supervision
   5. Frequently calls out in class
   6. Has difficulty awaiting turn in games or group situations
C. *Hyperactivity.* At least two of the following symptoms:
   1. Runs about or climbs on things excessively
   2. Has difficulty sitting still or fidgets excessively
   3. Has difficulty staying seated
   4. Moves about excessively during sleep
   5. Is always "on the go" or acts as if "driven by a motor"
D. Onset before the age of 7.
E. Duration of at least 6 months.
F. Not due to schizophrenia, affective disorder, or severe profound mental retardation.

[a]From the *Diagnostic and Statistical Manual of Mental Disorders,* 3rd ed., American Psychiatric Association, 1980.

present similarily to ADD-H) are listed in Table 13.2. In general, ADD-H children are rated two standard deviations or more above the mean for their age on the various screening scales. Also, their performance is typically within the abnormal range using standardized assessment instruments.

In addition to the diagnostic/assessment instruments described in Table 13.2, children being screened for ADD-H should be scheduled for a thorough pediatric examination and, in some cases, a neuropsychological workup to rule

TABLE 13.2 Diagnostic/Assessment Instruments for ADD-H and Rule-Outs[a]

Social/Classroom Behavior

Instruments Administered to Parents	Instruments Administered to Teachers
1. Home Situations Questionnaire. Assesses the occurrence and severity of the child's behavior at home (Barkley, 1981).	1. ADD-H: Comprehensive Teacher Rating Scale (ACTeRS). A recently developed rating scale for diagnosis and treatment monitoring (Ullmann, Sleator, & Sprague, 1984).
2. Werry-Weiss-Peters Activity Scale (WWPAS). Assesses the child's behavior in the familial and surrounding environment (Routh, Schroeder, & O'Tuama, 1974).	2. Abbreviated Conners Teacher Rating Scale (ACTRS). Useful in screening and assessing treatment outcome (Werry, Spraque, & Cohen, 1975).
3. SNAP Rating Scale. Incorporates the DSM-III diagnostic criteria in a rating scale format.	3. SNAP Rating Scale. Also for classroom use (Swanson, Nolan, & Pelham, 1981).
4. Personality Inventory for Children (PIC). Provides a comprehensive personality profile. Four scales distinguish ADD-H children from other clinical groups: adjustment, social skills, hyperactivity, delinquency (Lachar, 1982).	4. Teacher's Self-Control Rating Scale (TSCRS). Useful in assessing children's self-control and perceived competency (Humphrey, 1982).

Academic Behavior

Direct Classroom Observations	Classroom Assessment
1. Observational coding of percentage of time on-task, percentage of assignments completed, and percentage correct (Rapport et al., 1982).	1. Assess child's present curricula for appropriateness of content.
2. Classroom Observation Code. A recently developed coding system for differentiating ADD-H from normal children in classroom settings (Abikoff, Gittelman, & Klein, 1980).	2. Assess differences in child's performance in group vs. small-group instructional settings, appropriateness of classroom placement, and seating arrangement.

Clinical Assessment

1. Continuous Performance Test (CPT): Measures the child's ability to sustain attention (indicated by errors of omission) and inhibit impulsive responding (indicated by errors of commission). Clinicians may need to create their own test materials using slides of numeric or

alphabetic sequences (see Rapport, DuPaul, Stoner, & Jones, in press), or use the Gordon Diagnostic Test (GDS: Gordon, McClure, & Post, 1983).

2. Matching Familiar Figures Test (MFFT): A standardized test of children's cognitive tempo developed by Kagan, Rosman, Day, Albert, and Phillips (1964). ADD-H children tend to exhibit a "fast-inaccurate" tempo, characterized by a higher number of errors and shorter response latencies. Information regarding standardization, scoring, and developmental norms are available (Salkind, 1978).

3. Delay Test (GDS): A recently developed test of a child's ability to delay responding under appropriate circumstances. Complete information regarding standardization, scoring, and developmental norms as well as computerized administration are available (Gordon, McClure, & Post, 1983).

Rule-Outs

Childhood Disorders Similar to ADD-H[a]

---

1. *Anxiety Disorders:*
   a. Overanxious Disorder: generalized, persistent anxiety or worry (not related to separation).
   b. Separation Anxiety Disorder: excessive anxiety regarding separation from those to whom the child is attached.

2. *Adjustment Disorders:*
   a. Adjustment Disorder with Anxious Mood: A maladaptive reaction to an identifiable psychosocial stressor that occurs within 3 months of the onset of the stressor (predominant features include nervousness, worry, and jitteriness).
   b. Adjustment Disorder with Academic Inhibition: Predominant manisfestation is an inhibition in academic functioning in a child whose previous performance was adequate.

3. *Supplementary Conditions:*
   a. Parent-Child Problem: Problems not due to a mental disorder, such as child abuse.
   b. Family Circumstances: Problems not due to a mental disorder, such as sibling rivalry, recent change in residence and/or school placement.

4. *Disorders of Behavior:*
   a. Conduct Disorder: A repetitive, persistent pattern of conduct in which the basic rights of others or societal norms are violated. Four types: undersocialized, aggressive; undersocialized, nonaggressive; socialized, aggressive, socialized, nonaggressive.
   b. Oppositional Disorder: A pattern of disobedient, negativistic, and provocative opposition to authority figures without violating the basic rights of others or societal norms (e.g., violation of minor rules, temper tantrums, stubbornness).
   c. Childhood Antisocial Behavior: Involves isolated acts in contrast to repetitive pattern of antisocial behavior.

5. Tourette's Disorder: The essential features are recurrent, involuntary, repetitive, rapid, purposeless motor movements (tics), including vocal tics. The movements can be voluntarily surpressed and may vary in intensity, frequency, and location. First symptom may appear as a single tic (often an eye blink). Other initial symptoms often include tongue protrusion, squatting, sniffing, hopping, skipping, and throat clearing.

---

[a]Consult DSM-III (American Psychiatric Association, 1980) for specific diagnostic features of these disorders.

out potential medical problems and/or neurologic dysfunction. An electroencephalograph (EEG) evaluation is typically not indicated since abnormal EEGs are not specific to ADD-H, are equally common in "normal" and ADD-H children (Solanto, 1984), and tend to be of little prognostic value. In special cases, however, (e.g., ruling out seizure disorder), they should be routinely administered. The remainder of the diagnostic evaluation should include a thorough developmental history (Barkley, 1981), an educational assessment to rule out or include specific developmental disorders (e.g., reading, arithmetic), and a parent/child interview in cases where underachievement may be due to socioeconomic or cultural factors.

In conclusion, it should be apparent that assessing ADD-H is a multifaceted process that must proceed in a logical order and include multiple raters and ratings across settings. The ADD-H child will frequently meet more than one set of diagnostic criteria (e.g., ADD-H and specific developmental disorder) and diagnosis will be difficult owing to the child's "consistently inconsistent" behavior.

BEHAVIOR MODIFICATION STRATEGIES

The types of behavioral techniques used in treating ADD-H children fall into five broadly defined categories: contingency management, behavior therapy, cognitive behavior therapy, psychostimulant treatment, and various combinations of behavioral and psychostimulant treatments. In this section several of the more recent studies within these areas are reviewed, with emphasis on classroom interventions.

Contingency Management

Contingency management includes the more precise procedures incorporated in classroom management systems, as distinguished from behavioral techniques that rely on a general consultative or home-based delivery model (i.e., behavior therapy). Consequently, procedures that entail token delivery and immediate feedback (by means of checkmarks, electronic apparatuses, or praise) will be discussed.

Several studies have incorporated feedback delivery systems to effect attending behavior in ADD-H children. The majority have used contingent social reinforcement (Allen, Henke, Harris, Baer, & Reynolds, 1967; O'Leary, Pelham, Rosenbaum, & Price, 1976), specially constructed electronic apparatuses to provide positive (Alabiso, 1975; Patterson, 1964; Patterson, Whittier, & Wright, 1965; Quay, Sprague, Werry, & McQueen, 1967) or mild, corrective feedback (Rapport, Murphy, & Bailey, 1980; 1982), and token delivery for academic performance incompatible with disruptive behavior (Ayllon, Layman, & Kandel, 1975; Robinson, Newby, & Ganzell, 1981).

In general, each of the foregoing procedures has proven effective in increasing ADD-H children's attention in classroom settings. Thus, other factors must be considered in deciding which to use in a treatment protocol. For example, use of contingent social praise for sitting still, although effective, may be disruptive to the targeted child (or his or her neighbor), places an undue burden on the classroom teacher, and has the distinct disadvantage of falling under the "dead man rule." (Dr. Ogden Lindsley coined this phrase to describe interventions in which a nonliving person could meet the contingencies, for example, sitting quietly in a seat.) An alternative procedure frequently used in classroom settings is the incompatible response approach. Basically, this procedure targets an appropriate behavior (e.g., completing academic assignments) that is incompatible with the maladaptive response (e.g., disruptiveness) and provides direct or conditioned (i.e., tokens) reinforcement for its occurrence. The efficacy of this procedure has been convincingly demonstrated with both individual ADD-H children (Ayllon et al., 1975) and entire classrooms (Robinson et al., 1981).

A similar approach for increasing ADD-H children's attention and academic performance involves the response-cost paradigm (Rapport et al., 1982). In this strategy, the child is provided a card stand with numbers (arranged in a decreasing sequence) or an electronic apparatus. When the card stand is employed, the child is told that he or she can earn some maximum number of points (corresponding to the numbers on the card stand) for attending to and completing academic materials, and that these points may be traded in at a designated time for a previously agreed reinforcer (e.g., structured free time). The classroom teacher is provided with a similar card stand and requested to check visually on whether the child is meeting the contingencies (i.e., working on academic assignments) throughout the academic period. As long as the child remains on task, the teacher continues to go about his or her normal classroom activities, which is an advantage over alternative strategies that necessitate token delivery. When the child is off-task, the teacher flips down a card on the card stand, indicating to the child that he or she has been off-task. The child changes his or her cards to match the teacher's and loses a point from the accumulated total (i.e., off-task behavior has "cost" the child 1 minute of free time). The electronic version, although more expensive, is considerably easier to use. Here, the teacher simply pushes a button on her hand-held apparatus and a point is electronically deducted from the child's free-standing desk model. This method has the distinct advantage of providing the child with reinforcement on a programmable fixed-interval schedule (e.g., on a FI–1 schedule, the child's apparatus begins at zero and automatically increases the accumulated points showing by one per minute).

Behavior Therapy

The behavior therapy approach has been widely adopted by mental health professionals due to its relative ease of implementation and minimal time requirements. Typically, several target behaviors are identified in the classroom setting, the teacher provides some type of feedback for the occurrence of these responses (usually discrete ratings or checkmarks on a card), and a home-based management system is constructed such that parents provide reinforcement (on a daily or weekly basis) if a predetermined criterion has been met (e.g., a rating of 80% across behaviors or 4 out of 6 checkmarks). Despite the relative simplicity and previous reports of treatment gains using this strategy (Gittelman-Klein, Klein, Abikoff, Katz, Gloisten, & Kates, 1976; O'Leary et al., 1976; Pelham, 1977; Pelham, Schnedler, Bologna, & Contreras, 1980), home-based programs may be problematic for several reasons. First, there is limited control over parental compliance. Second, the typical delay between consequenting behavior and reinforcement is inherently undesirable given the inadequate delay skills of ADD-H children (Rapport, Tucker, DuPaul, Merlo, & Stoner, in press). Finally, parents are more likely to use material rewards that quickly lose their potency and generally distort a child's value system (e.g., that they should be paid to behave themselves in school).

Cognitive Behavior Therapy

Two of the most recent treatment strategies developed for ADD-H children are described as self-instructional (Meichenbaum & Goodman, 1971) or cognitive training programs (Douglas, Parry, Marton, & Garson, 1976). In using these programs, a therapist demonstrates appropriate planning and error correction strategies that incorporate a variety of cognitive, academic, or perceptual tasks. The child is taught to overtly, then covertly verbalize these "self-instructions" during task performance and is provided appropriate feedback and/or reinforcement. The program may also include a self-management component in which children are taught to evaluate their performance and provide themselves with overt or covert praise statements.

Over the past several years, the effectiveness of cognitive behavior therapy has been evaluated alone (Barkley, Copeland, & Sivage, 1980; Cameron & Robinson, 1980; Douglas et al., 1976; Egeland, 1974; Friedling & O'Leary, 1979) and in combination with behavioral (Kendall & Finch, 1976; 1979) or psychostimulant treatment (Cohen, Sullivan, Minde, Novak, & Helwig, 1981; Hinshaw et al., 1984). Thus far, results of these interventions have been equivocal, with the most salient problem being a lack of consistent generalization to real-life academic functioning (see reviews by Abikoff, 1979; Hobbs, Moguin, Tyroler, & Lahey, 1980). Interestingly, this lack of generalization addresses the basic assumptions of "self-control" paradigms; that is, can the child successfully complete the training steps after the role of the external agent is withdrawn? Unfortunately, the excess conceptual baggage implied in the term "self-control" obscures the underlying controlling variables in these treatments and should be discarded if this area is to advance. Consequently, the use of cognitive behavior therapy in treating ADD-H children should be curtailed until its effectiveness has been carefully demonstrated in controlled research.

Psychostimulant Treatment

Psychostimulant medication (primarily methylphenidate) is currently the most widely used treatment for ADD-H (Safer & Krager, 1983) due to its cost efficiency and demonstrated short-term effects on sustained attention (Rapport, DuPaul, Stoner, & Jones, in press; Sykes, Douglas, & Morgenstern, 1973), activity level (Porrino et al., 1983; Whalen & Henker, 1976), academic performance (Rapport et al., 1982; Rapport, Stoner, DuPaul, Birmingham, & Tucker, 1985), impulsivity (Brown & Sleator, 1979; Rapport, DuPaul, Stoner, Birmingham, & Masse, in press), and classroom deportment (Conners & Taylor, 1980).

Nevertheless, the use of psychostimulant treatment with ADD-H children is still regarded as controversial, due to its potential treatment emergent effects, frequent misuse, and failure to produce long-term benefits (Gadow, 1983). Several reasons have been offered to account for the lack of consistent results, with the most compelling ones being a failure to titrate the medication on an individual basis (i.e., a lack of treatment integrity) or to establish whether or not the child is a "favorable responder" to treatment (i.e., 15 to 25% of ADD-H children show little to no response to psychostimulant treatment), frequent misdiagnosis of the disorder, inadequate monitoring of treatment, and poor compliance with the treatment regimen. Several of these issues will be discussed in the section reviewing research and in the case description.

Behavioral and Psychostimulant Treatments Combined

The use of combined treatment protocols has become more popular in recent years owing to the severity, intractable nature, and multifaceted behavioral problems (e.g., poor social skills, aggression) associated with ADD-H. The most frequently used treatment combinations involve psychostimulant medication (usually methylphenidate) combined with contingency management (Rapport et al., 1980; Shafto & Sulzbacher, 1977), behavior therapy (Firestone, Kelly, Goodman, & Davey, 1981; Gittelman-Klein et al., 1976; Pelham et al., 1980), or cognitive therapy (Cohen et al., 1981; Hinshaw et al., 1984). In some cases the combination of treatments has proven superior to either treatment alone (Pelham et al., 1980; Shafto & Sulzbacher, 1977), while in others, the addition of behavioral (Firestone et al., 1981; Gittelman-Klein et al., 1976) or cognitive therapy components (Hinshaw et al., 1984) has not enhanced therapeutic outcome. The equivocal results obtained to date are largely due to ambiguous inclusion or diagnostic criteria (i.e., misdiagnosed ADD-H children), a lack of treatment integrity (e.g., using a single dose or failing to determine whether a child responds positively to medication and at what level, providing feedback and/or reinforcement after several hours vs. immediately), and the failure to incorporate multiple dependent measures (e.g., using only social ratings as an indication of improvement). The importance of identifying and including the critical components in a treatment protocol has been previously addressed (see Rapport, 1983) and will become evident in the following sections.

Comment

Several treatments, either alone or in combination, have proven effective in treating ADD-H children. It is doubtful, however, that any one treatment can be relied on to affect all ADD-H children positively (not to mention the differential effects each treatment may have on specific behavioral domains), and none of the treatments reviewed in this section have demonstrated long-term efficacy. Consequently, clinicians are still faced with deciding which treatment(s) to use in a particular case, and the decision will largely depend on the initial diagnostic evaluation (e.g., is the child's primary problem completing academic assignments or are there also problems with peer relationships and aggression?) and available resources (e.g., is the pediatrician and/or school psychologist willing to monitor carefully a trial of medication or initiate a streamlined behavioral program?).

A final word of caution is warranted. Due to the relatively high prevalence rate and severity of ADD-H and the misinformation provided by the media, a host of "other" treatments have been purported as quick "cures" for the disorder. Aside from the insignificantly few children (who were probably misdiagnosed in the first place) whose behavioral problems are lessened using these treatments, there is considerable evidence that megavitamins (Haslam, Dalby, & Rademaker, 1984), sugar ingestion (Wolraich, Milich, Stumbo, & Schultz, 1985), and strict dietary regimens (Conners, 1980; Mattes & Gittelman, 1981) play a minimal or nonexisting role in ADD-H.

RESEARCH REVIEW

Due to the large number of studies on treatment of ADD-H children over the past several years (see Reatig, 1984, for a comprehensive bibliography), this section will selectively review two areas of research that may be especially pertinent to clinicians: behavioral pharmacology and curricular interventions.

Behavioral Pharmacology

Dose-Response Relationships

The correspondence between the amount of drug and the magnitude of effect produced plays an important role in psychopharmacology and is an example of a dose-response relationship. These relationships are typically studied at several levels (e.g., molecular, cellular, organ system). However, their effects on *behavior* are especially meaningful to clinicians for therapeutic purposes.

Sprague and Sleator's seminal paper in 1975 served as an impetus for investigations examining the association between dose and ADD-H children's responsiveness to psychostimulant treatment. For example, three investigations initially demonstrated that both learning (Sprague & Sleater, 1975, 1977) and impulsivity (Brown & Sleator, 1979) are optimally affected at low (0.3 mg/kg) versus high doses (1.0 mg/kg) of methylphenidate. These data have been largely misinterpreted by clinicians and researchers alike as showing that 0.3 mg/kg is the ideal dose for ADD-H children receiving methylphenidate. For example, in the 1975 paper, careful examination of performance scores on a memory task over three experiments (p. 95) reveals that an identical number of children exhibited their optimal performance at 0.3 mg/kg and dosages exceeding 0.3 mg/kg (21.6% in both cases). Similarly, 35% of the children did not show their optimal response at the 0.3 mg/kg dose in the 1977 study.

Moreover, recent dose-response investigations have shown a linear relationship between increasing dose and ADD-H children's learning (Rapport, Stoner, DuPaul, Birmingham, & Tucker, 1985), attention (Rapport, DuPaul, Stoner, & Jones, in press), and impulsivity (Rapport, DuPaul, Stoner, Birmingham, & Masse, in press) in contrast to the quadratic (inverted U-shaped curve) relationships reported earlier. These findings were not unexpected. Sprague and Sleater (1976) initially hypothesized continued cognitive improvement beyond 0.3 mg/kg, which could not be tested by the interpolated curves drawn between placebo, 0.3 mg/kg, and 1.0 mg/kg in the 1977 and 1979 studies. Clearly, there is no single optimal dose for all ADD-H children. Perpetuation of this myth may result in a suboptimal treatment regimen for many of them.

Responder Status and Behavioral Specificity

The findings described above are incomplete, however, unless one considers the specific behavioral effects of treatment and whether or not a child demonstrates a "favorable response" to central nervous system (CNS) stimulants. For example, past estimates have shown that between 15 and 30% of ADD-H children exhibit no behavioral response or an adverse response to psychostimulants (Barkley, 1977; Kinsbourne & Swanson, 1979), which undoubtedly contributes to the poor long-term outcome associated with this treatment modality (Rapport, 1984). Moreover, even when children exhibit a positive response, it largely depends on the behavior assessed (i.e., behavioral specificity) and the child's unique reaction to dose, which cannot be adequately explained using a mg/kg calculation of children's body weight. An example of behavioral specificity is depicted in Figures 13.1 and 13.2. In this study (Rapport et al., 1982), the effects of systematically titrated dosages of methyphenidate were compared to a response-cost treatment over the course of an entire school year. Baseline levels of on-task behavior, academic performance (percentage of assignments completed), and teacher-rated improvement as assessed by the Abbreviated Conners Teacher Rating Scale (ATRS) were compared to individually titrated dosages of methyphenidate (lasting a total of 50 days) for two 20-minute academic periods (phonics and mathematics). Following return to baseline conditions, a response-cost procedure was implemented in multiple-baseline fashion for the two academic areas. After approximately 3 weeks of response-cost, the child was again administered methylphenidate for a 2-week period at the dose deemed most potent in the previous medication period (based on multiple dependent measures). Response-cost was reinstated in the last phase, completing the second reversal component of the design (ABACBC). Figures 13.1 and 13.2 show that both

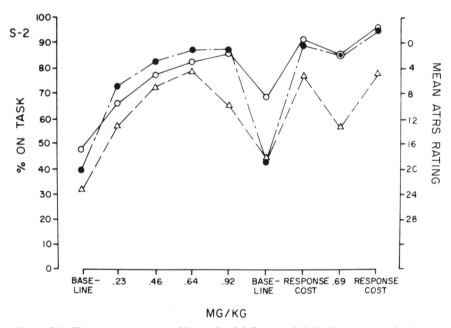

Figure 13.1. The mean percentage of intervals of daily on-task behavior across academic areas (closed circles = math; open circles = phonics) and experimental conditions. The right-hand ordinate represents teacher-rated social behavior (open triangle = ATRS teacher ratings) whereby the numbers become smaller as the child improves.

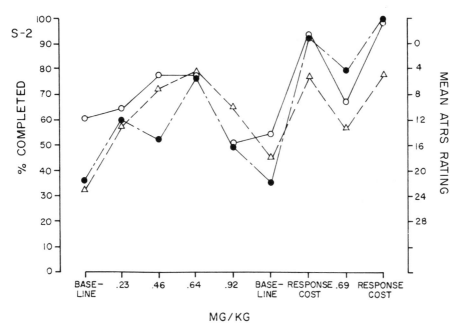

Figure 13.2. The mean percentage of daily problems completed across academic areas (closed circles = math; open circles = phonics) and experimental conditions. The right-hand ordinate represents teacher-rated social behavior (open triangle = ATRS teacher ratings) whereby the numbers become smaller as the child improves.

treatments had a dramatic impact on the child's classroom functioning. Of particular interest, however, was the child's reaction to the .92 mg/kg dose. If one were to base dosage recommendations on on-task behavior, for example, then .92 mg/kg would appear to be the ideal dose (see Figure 13.1). In examining the child's percent of academic assignments completed at this same dose (see Figure 13.2), a different picture emerges: a decrease in academic performance (i.e., behavioral toxicity). Consequently, behavioral assessment of drug responsiveness should always include multiple outcome measures to avoid placing a child in an "overfocused" state (Kinsbourne & Swanson, 1979).

Rate-Dependency

Past investigations in behavioral pharmacology have delineated several factors that may contribute to a drug's effect on an organism's behavior. For example, studies of CNS stimulant effects across a variety of animal species have consistently shown that the drug effect often depends on the rate of occurrence (the control rate) of a given behavior in a drug-free state (i.e., the behavioral effect of the drug is rate-dependent) (Dews, 1977; Dews & Wenger, 1977). In general, stimulants tend to increase relatively low rates of behavior but have limited effects on or decrease high rates of behavior. Moreover, there is an interaction between the drug-free rate of behavior and dose level. Lower doses tend to have the greatest enhancing effect on low rates of behavior, whereas higher doses tend to produce greater decrements in high rates of behavior.

When viewed in this manner, it becomes apparent that drugs typically labeled as "CNS stimulants" may exert a "depressantlike" effect on behavior, depending on the child's baseline rate (e.g., if higher doses were administered to a child exhibiting a high activity level, a decrease in behavior would be expected—hence, not a paradoxical effect). Preliminary evidence of rate-dependent effects on gross motor activity (Robbins & Sahakian, 1979), operant key-pressing (Rapport, DuPaul, & Smith, 1985), and classroom on-task (Rapport & DuPaul, 1985) behaviors of ADD-H children receiving methylphenidate have been reported thus far.

Law of Initial Value

Certain physiological variables have also been proposed as potential contributors to the description of a drug's behavioral effects. Similar to the rate-dependency phenomenon described above, Wilder's (1967) law of initial value proposes that the basal physiological response rate of an organism (e.g., heart rate) contributes to a drug's subsequent effect on that physiological response. The nature of this relationship is affected by both the dose administered and the time that has passed since drug ingestion. The potential implications of this principle for the pharmacological treatment of ADD-H children have been ignored thus far, yet they may play an important role in determining drug responsivity.

Conclusions and Future Directions

It appears that some combination of the drug-free frequencies of an ADD-H child's internal (physiological) and external (overt) behaviors may contribute to CNS stimulant responsivity. The concurrent assessment of these variables in combination with other contributing factors (e.g., responder status, dose, time after drug administration, behavioral domain being measured, idiosyncratic responsivity) may be required for a veridical description of the behavioral effects of pharmacological treatment.

Curricula Interventions

The various treatment approaches discussed in the preceding sections (behavioral, psychopharmacotherapy, combined treatments) are obviously beneficial to many ADD-H children. These same strategies, however, have been appropriately criticized for their limited scope and failure to produce substantial or lasting academic improvement (Gadow, 1983; Sprague, 1983). This is not surprising in that pills and most reinforcement paradigms were not intended to teach children new academic skills or make up for inadequate learning histories. Their goals were to enable the children to exhibit some control over their present behavior and day-to-day academic functioning. Nevertheless, the paucity of work in the area of curricula and educational remediation research is a curious state of affairs, given the disproportionate number of failing grades, grade-level retentions, high rate of learning disabilities, and lower educational achievement experienced by ADD-H children.

A few studies have shown that ADD-H children generally perform poorly under "other-paced" (vs. self-paced) teaching conditions (Whalen et al., 1978), when academic materials are laced with distractors such as colored borders (Radosh & Gittelman, 1981; Zentall et al., 1978), or if excessive noise is present (Whalen et al., 1979). Other investigations have demonstrated the benefits of using a prescriptive tutoring approach with ADD-H children, either alone (Rie, 1974) or in combination with psychostimulant treatment (Conrad, Dworkin, Shai, & Tobiessen, 1971; Gittelman, Klein, & Feingold, 1983). A concerted effort to develop alternative learning materials and remedial educational training techniques for these children has yet to be made, however. For example, there is a lack of research addressing some of the most fundamental questions inherent in skill acquisition and learning. Knowing that ADD-H children are easily frustrated, prefer stimulating events, have difficulty sustaining their attention, and act impulsively, why haven't we designed treatment protocols to take advantage of these deficiencies (e.g., computerized instruction, use of the Premack principle, short assignments with frequent changes in materials)? It is incumbent on professionals in this area to addresss such challenges.

CASE STUDIES

Identification and Diagnostic Criteria

Several individual cases demonstrate the relative efficacy of behavioral approaches or psychostimulant medication in treating ADD-H children in academic settings. Each of the families of these children presented with complaints of inattentiveness, impulsivity, and hyperactivity and were referred to the Children's Learning Clinic (CLC) of the University of Rhode Island by pediatricians and local school system personnel. Multiple criteria were used in designating a child as having an attention deficit disorder with hyperactivity (ADD-H) and included (a) an independent diagnosis by the child's pediatrician and CLC's directing clinical psychologist using DSM-III (American Psychiatric Association, 1980) criteria for attention deficit disorder with hyperactivity; (b) a maternal report of a developmental history consistent with ADD-H (Barkley, 1981); (c) a maternal rating of at least two standard deviations above the mean for the child's age on the Werry-Weiss-Peters Activity Scale (WWPAS: Routh, Schroeder, & O'Tuama, 1974); (d) a teacher rating on the Abbreviated Conners Teacher Rating Scale (ACTRS) above 15, the designated cut-off score for hyperactivity (Werry et al., 1975) (note: one child who was treated with methylphenidate obtained a baseline ACTRS score of 5 due to his lack of classroom disruptiveness and was included to illustrate the effects of medication on ADD without hyperactivity, but with documented learning disabilities); (e) performance on the Matching Familiar Figures Test (Kagan, Rosman, Day, Albert, & Phillips, 1964) characteristic of a "fast-inaccurate or impulsive" responder (i.e., faster than average responses and higher than average error rates for the child's age) (Salkind, 1978); (f) freedom from any gross neurological, sensory, or motor impairment; and (g) not currently taking medication. All children were of average or above average intelligence as assessed by the Peabody Picture Vocabulary Test–Revised, Form L (Dunn & Dunn, 1981), and were from families of low to middle socioeconomic class.

ASSESSMENT AND BEHAVIORAL TREATMENT

In the first two cases depicted, a multiple baseline design across academic periods was used to evaluate the effects of a response-cost treatment on the number of assignments completed and assignments completed correctly. Unobtrusive observations of children's classroom performance were conducted on a daily basis by trained graduate and undergraduate students during morning hours (from 9 a.m. to 11 a.m.).

Child 1. As evidenced in Figure 13.3 (pp. 344–345), the child completed an average of 55% of his daily writing and 40% of his phonics assignments, during baseline conditions. Despite the low rate of completion, the child's accuracy was suboptimal and moderately variable across days, with an average of 70% correct for writing and 61% correct for phonics. Response-cost treatment was instituted on day 7 for writing and day 10 for phonics. Results showed high and relatively stable rates of academic completion during these two periods. Interestingly, treatment positively affected the child's academic accuracy in completing these assignments despite an absence of contingencies for this variable. This finding was consistent throughout the 2-month school observation period. Thus, results did not appear to be due to a novelty effect.

Child 2. The second child (depicted in Figure 13.4, pp. 346–347) was similarly affected by the implementation of a response-cost treatment and exhibited increases in his academic completion rates from 60% for phonics and 38% for writing assignments during baseline conditions to near 98% for both. Relatively little (writing assignment) or no change (phonics assignment) was observed in this child's assignment accuracy as it was generally within acceptable limits prior to intervention. Treatment effects were persistent and relatively stable across days, again indicating a lack of novelty effect.

Weekly teacher ratings were obtained for the two treated children and matched classroom "normal-control" children using the ACTRS. Results shown in Figure 13.5 (p. 348) clearly demonstrate that response-cost not only affects academic behavior but teacher-rated social behavior as well, despite a lack of direct contingencies for the latter (i.e., a response-cost procedure that targets academic performance is generally considered an incompatible response approach and frequently circumvents the need to apply direct contingencies for prosocial behavior).

ASSESSMENT AND PSYCHOSTIMULANT TREATMENT

The four cases that follow were selected to demonstrate the importance of using multiple measures in assessing psychostimulant effects and determining optimal dosage response. A double-blind, placebo control, within-subject (crossover) experimental design was used in which all children received each of the five doses (following baseline measures) in one of 120 possible randomly assigned, counterbalanced sequences (i.e., the four children described herein were part of a larger, on-going dose-response study). Methylphenidate was prescribed by each child's pediatrician in the following doses: placebo, 5 mg, 10 mg, 15 mg, and 20 mg. Fixed doses (vs. mg/kg) were prescribed to reflect typical pediatric practice in the United States (*Physicians' Desk Reference,* 1985) and because optimal dose has not been shown to depend on a child's body weight (Rapport, Stoner, DuPaul, Birmingham, & Tucker, 1985; Rapport, DuPaul, Stoner, & Jones, in press). Mg/kg values are depicted in the figures for comparative purposes (see Figures 13.6, 13.7, 13.8, and 13.9). The methylphendiate and placebo were packaged in colored gelatin capsules by our university pharmacist to avoid detection of dose and taste. Capsules were then placed in individual daily dated envelopes to insure accurate dose administration. Used and unused envelopes were returned to the CLC on a weekly basis to control for medication compliance.

Clinic Measures. All four children were classified as favorable responders to methylphenidate using the Paired Associates Learning (PAL) test (i.e., a drug-induced facilitation in performance of 25% or more compared to baseline or placebo), in a manner similar to previous studies (Thurston, Sobol, Swanson, & Kinsbourne, 1979). The PAL test was administered once per week under double-blind conditions 90 minutes after oral ingestion for each dose level.

Classroom Measures. The classroom phase of the study involved 6 consecutive weeks of assessment and observation, which corresponded with the 6-week clinic testing period described above. Following baseline data collection (week 1), parents were given a week's worth of medication in predated en-

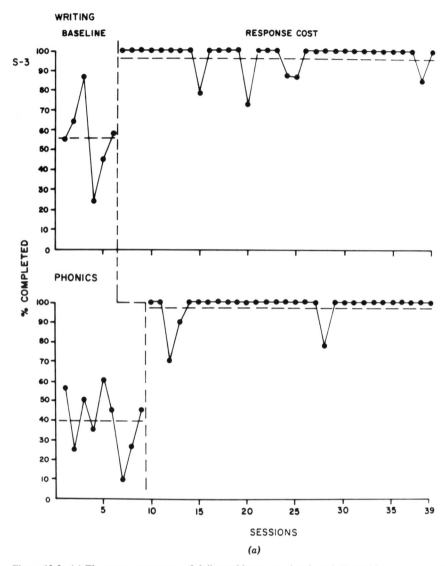

Figure 13.3. (a) The mean percentage of daily problems completed, and (b) problems completed correctly across academic areas (writing and phonics) and experimental conditions (baseline and response cost) for Child 1.

velopes at one dose (placebo, 5 mg, 10 mg, 15 mg, or 20 mg methylphenidate). This procedure continued until a child received each dose for 7 consecutive days. All weekly dosage changes occurred on Saturdays to control for potential rebound effects. Parents were instructed to give their child a medication

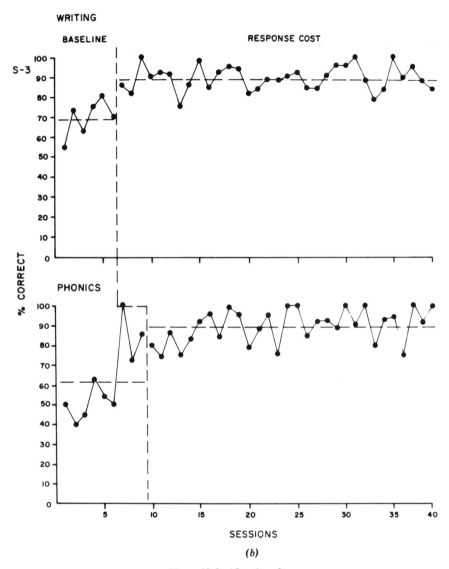

Figure 13.3. (*Continued*)

capsule each morning, ½ hour prior to breakfast, and to tell the child it was a vitamin supplement in order to control for expectancy (Rapport et al., 1982). Teacher ratings and classroom observations were completed during the morning hours due to the relatively short half-life of methylphendiate and to control for time after medication across dependent measures.

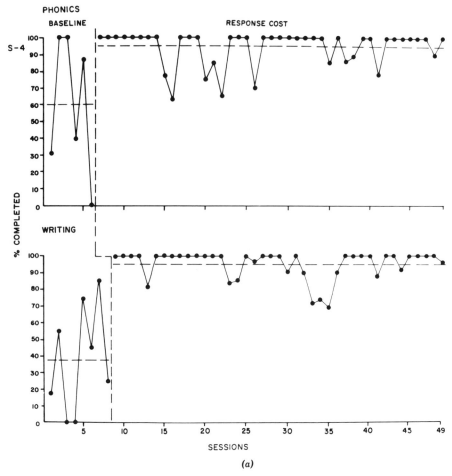

Figure 13.4. (*a*) The mean percentage of daily problems completed, and (*b*) problems completed correctly across academic areas (phonics and writing) and experimental conditions (baseline and response cost) for Child 2.

Classroom teachers completed the ACTRS each Friday throughout the experimental conditions, which reflected the children's behavior during the *morning* hours (until 11:30 a.m.) of that week. Teachers were blind as to when medication was administered and specific doses.

Children were observed in their regular classrooms for 20-minute intervals, 3 days per week across the 6-week evaluation period. Classroom observations began 1½ to 2 hours after the children's morning medication, during which time the class completed in-seat academic work assigned by the teacher. Chil-

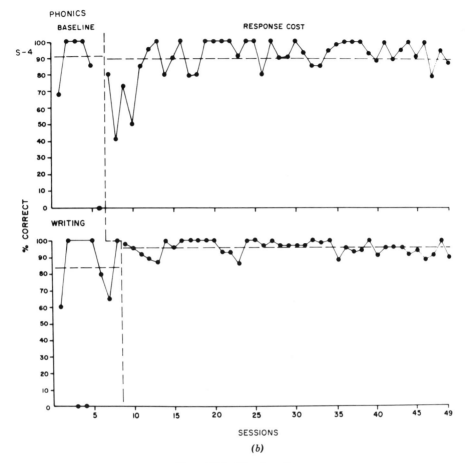

Figure 13.4. (*Continued*)

dren were unobtrusively observed by trained undergraduate and graduate students for 60 consecutive intervals during each observation period throughout the study. Each interval was divided into 15 seconds of observation followed by 5 seconds for recording. Observers were blind as to when medication was administered and specific doses. A child's behavior was categorized as either on-task or off-task in a manner identical to that used by Rapport et al. (1982).

Children's performance on regularly assigned academic work during the scheduled observation periods was used as a dependent variable in an effort to preserve ecological validity, yet still maintain adequate experimental control. Academic seatwork typically involved completing arithmetic problems or language arts assignments. Interobserver reliability checks of each child's on-

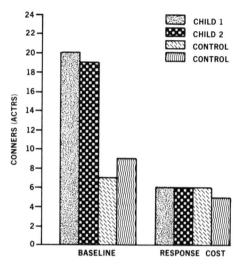

Figure 13.5. The mean weekly Abbreviated Conners Teacher Rating Scale (ACTRS) scores for Child 1 and 2, and two classroom control children across experimental conditions (baseline and response cost). Lower scores represent improvement in the child's behavior.

task behavior and assignment completion rates and accuracy were taken on at least 33% of the observation days and were uniformly high throughout the assessment.

Child 1 (R.H.). The effects of methylphenidate on this child's classroom functioning are depicted in Figure 13.6. Prior to intervention, R.H. was attending to his assignments (i.e., on-task) approximately 65% of the time allotted and completed 33% of the assigned materials on a weekly basis. His accuracy in completing these assignments was generally high throughout the evaluation. There was little or no change (except for the ACTRS ratings) when R.H. was administered 5 mg. However, a noticeable improvement was evidenced during the 10-mg week across the various dependent measures. Interestingly, R.H.'s on-task behavior and academic completion rate dropped precipitously during the 15 mg and 20 mg methylphenidate weeks, suggesting a possible overfocused state (i.e., behavioral toxicity). However, as the figure shows, the teacher rated his behavior as most improved at these latter two doses, which highlights the importance of using multiple measures in determining drug responsiveness.

Child 2 (P.G.). This child's initial baseline rate of responding was similar to the one previously described, with only 37% of his time on-task and 40% of his academic assignments completed, (see Figure 13.7). In contrast to R.H., little or no improvement in academic functioning was evinced until the 15 mg week, at which time a rather dramatic improvement was noticeable. Although the teacher rating (ACTRS) continued to improve through the 20 mg dose,

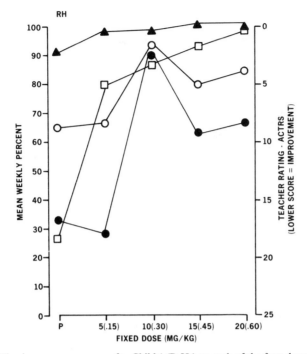

Figure 13.6. The dose-response curves for Child 1 (R.H.) on each of the four dependent measures are depicted across dose levels (mg/kg shown in parentheses) using the left-hand ordinate for percentages of on-task behavior (open circles), academic assignments completed (closed circles), and academic assignments completed correctly (closed triangles); right-hand ordinate for ACTRS weekly teacher ratings (open squares). P = placebo.

P.G.'s academic performance rapidly deteriorated at this same dose. Consequently, the recommendation to the pediatrician regarding on-going medication treatment was for 15 mg twice a day (in the morning and at noon). An alternative dosage schedule that can be used when a child performs optimally at 15 mg is to administer Ritalin-SR 20 mg plus 5 mg in the morning (equivalent to 15 mg in the a.m. and 10 mg at noon). Our experience in using this dosage schedule has been relatively successful for two reasons. First, there is a limited amount of research suggesting that when a larger dose is given in the morning, it tends to impact a smaller afternoon dose in a positive manner. Second, children typically spend their morning hours in school attending to and completing academic assignments that require greater concentration (e.g., reading and mathematics), whereas the afternoon is frequently spent engaged in less academically rigorous assignments. Consequently, careful consideration should be given to the child's daily curriculum schedule.

Child 3 (K.A.). The effects of methylphenidate on K.A.'s school perfor-

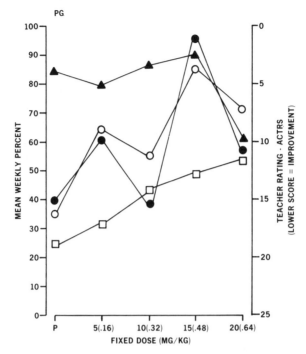

Figure 13.7. The dose-response curves for Child 2 (P.G.) on each of the four dependent measures are depicted across dose levels (mg/kg shown in brackets) using the left-hand ordinate for percentages of on-task behaviors (open circles), academic assignments completed (closed circles), and academic assignments completed correctly (closed triangles); right-hand ordinate for ACTRS weekly teacher ratings (open squares). P = placebo.

mance are depicted in Figure 13.8. In general, each of the dependent variables being monitored showed a linear dose-response effect (i.e., increases in performance with increasing dosage) until the 15 mg level was reached, at which time little or no further improvement was possible (i.e., ceiling effect). Although the teacher ratings (ACTRS) were within the normal range prior to intervention (ADD without hyperactivity), they continued to improve as a result of Ritalin treatment. The maintenance dose recommendation to the child's pediatrician was for Ritalin-SR 20 mg plus 5 mg in the morning (as described for Child 2).

Child 4 (G.E.). This last child's reaction to methylphenidate was somewhat unusual, if not remarkable, and is illustrated in Figure 13.9. G.E. showed little or no improvement in his academic performance until the 20 mg dose was administered (i.e., frequently described as a threshold effect). It is instructive to note that changes in percentage of assignments completed correctly and ACTRS ratings were observed at lower doses.

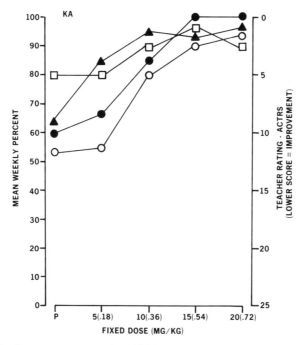

Figure 13.8. The dose-response curves for Child 3 (K.A.) on each of the four dependent measures are depicted across dose levels (mg/kg shown in brackets) using the left-hand ordinate for percentages of on-task behavior (open circles), academic assignments completed (closed circles), and academic assignments completed correctly (closed triangles); right-hand ordinate for ACTRS weekly teacher ratings (open squares). P = placebo.

Changes in any one or two dependent measures must be considered as only part of the overall assessment for several reasons. For example, G.E.'s accuracy in completing assignments was improved at the 10 mg dose, but he was only completing 50% of his assigned work. Moreover, we have observed other children whose accuracy was high prior to intervention (within the 90% range or above), but who were completing less than 10% of their assigned academic tasks on a daily basis. The primary reasons to incorporate this measure in a medication assessment are to insure that the child is (1) not placed in an over-focused state (e.g., one would typically see a high rate of on-task behavior, a concomitant drop in academic completion, and either no change or deterioration in accuracy rates), and (2) not completing assignments at the expense of accuracy (e.g., typically observed as high rates of on-task behavior and academic completion with corresponding decreases in accuracy). A final reason for not basing outcome decisions on one or two dependent measures involves the rating scales most frequently used in monitoring ADD-H childrens' reaction to medication. Despite their demonstrated cost-effectiveness and sen-

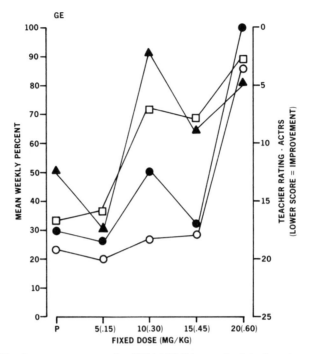

Figure 13.9. The dose-response curves for Child 4 (G.E.) on each of the four dependent measures are depicted across dose levels (mg/kg shown in brackets) using the left-hand ordinate for percentages of on-task behavior (open circles), academic assignments completed (closed circles), academic assignments completed correctly (closed triangles); right-hand ordinate for ACTRS weekly teacher ratings (open squares). P = placebo.

sitivity to medication-induced changes, all of them contain either no items or too few items relative to a child's academic performance. In fact, most items are related to social, impulsive, and attentive behaviors rather than academic performance. The recommended dose for G.E. was 20 mg twice daily, or two tablets of Ritalin-SR 20 mg in the morning.

SUMMARY

The use of behavioral, psychostimulant, or combined interventions are currently the *sine qua non* in treating ADD-H children. In considering the present state of the art, it is not possible to categorically assert that one treatment is superior to another, and attempts to do so are sophomoric, if not deceptive. For example, few alternative treatments, if any, can compare with a streamlined behavioral approach in positively affecting an ADD-H child's academic performance. Conversely, psychostimulant medication is more cost-effective and has the additional benefit of providing generalized effects throughout the day. The choice of which treatment(s) to use with a particular child will depend on a number of variables such as symptom severity, parental/child compliance, the teacher's/therapist's ability (or willingness) to carry out a treatment protocol, time constraints, setting characteristics, and therapeutic effectiveness. There are no easy answers to these questions, and each case must be considered as a unique treatment endeavor.

Attention deficit disorder with hyperactivity is currently viewed as one of the most serious developmental disorders of childhood for which there is no known "cure." Despite the abundance of research and professional dedication over the past two decades, there remains a significant gap in our understanding and ability to treat ADD-H children successfully. A thorough understanding of etiological mechanisms will remain, in all likelihood, somewhat a mystery until significant technological advances for pinpointing brain-behavior relationships are discovered. The design and implementation of practical treatment protocols must not await these discoveries, however, or millions of children will face a stressful and disfunctional adult life.

Although several attempts have been made in recent years to develop viable, behavioral treatment protocols for ADD-H children, psychostimulant medications continue to be the most widely used and successful treatments on a short-term basis. This is not entirely surprising, given the alternatives presently available. For example, how many teachers, parents, or caregivers would be willing to continually and systematically dispose positive reinforcement, ignore misbehavior, and "catch the child doing something right"? These basic learning principles, as they are currently employed, have never been particularly useful in treating ADD-H children on a long-term or widespread basis, owing to their impracticality, disregard for day-to-day exigencies, and empty promises of lasting behavioral diminution. (Note: they *are* useful in demonstrating short-term effects and methodological elegance for publication purposes, however.)

Consolidated endeavors in at least two areas are needed to facilitate the development of viable treatment protocols for ADD-H children. Because psychostimulant treatment is so frequently used with them (and thus, subject to both overuse and misuse), it is incumbent on professionals to (1) systematically delineate those cases that will benefit from this intervention (e.g., favorable responders vs. nonresponders or adverse responders), and (2) devise a method by which dosage can be titrated on an individual basis to maximize academic success. It is noteworthy that a recent study found that the strongest predictor of later pathology was academic failure during childhood (Dishion, Loeber, Stouthamer-Loeber, & Patterson, 1984). Concentrated efforts must also be undertaken to devise innovative curricular interventions for these children, as past attempts to reinforce them throughout their academic lives have not only failed but have clearly demonstrated that alternative learning approaches are required.

REFERENCES

Abikoff, H. (1979). Cognitive training interventions in children: Review of a new approach. *Journal of Learning Disabilities, 12,* 65–77.

Abikoff, H., Gittelman, R., & Klein, D. F. (1980). Classroom observation code for hyperactive children: A replication of validity. *Journal of Consulting and Clinical Psychology, 48,* 555–565.

Alabiso, F. (1975). Operant control of attention behavior: A treatment for hyperactivity. *Behavior Therapy, 6,* 39–42.

Allen, K. E., Henke, L. B., Harris, F. R., Baer, D. M., & Reynolds, N. J. (1967). Control of hyperactivity by social reinforcement of attending behavior. *Journal of Educational Psychology, 58,* 231–237.

American Psychiatric Association. (1980). *Diagnostic and Statistical Manual of Mental Disorders* (3rd ed.). Washington, DC: Author.

Ayllon, T., Layman, D., & Kandel, H. J. (1975). A behavioral-educational alternative to drug control of hyperactive children. *Journal of Applied Behavior Analysis, 8,* 137–146.

Barkley, R. (1977). A review of stimulant drug research with hyperactive children. *Journal of Child Psychology and Psychiatry, 18,* 137–165.

Barkley, R. A. (1981). *Hyperactive children: A handbook for diagnosis and treatment.* New York: Guilford.

Barkley, R. A. (1982). Specific guidelines for defining hyperactivity in children (Attention deficit disorder with hyperactivity). In B. Lahey & A. Kazdin (Eds.), *Advances in clinical child psychology* (Vol. 5). New York: Plenum.

Barkley, R. A., Copeland, A. P., & Sivage, C. (1980). A self-control classroom for hyperactive chidren. *Journal of Autism and Developmental Disorders, 10,* 75–89.

Brown, R. T., & Sleator, E. K. (1979). Methyphenidate in hyperkinetic children: Differences in dose effects on impulsive behavior. *Pediatrics, 64,* 408–411.

Busby, K. A., & Broughton, R. J. (1983). Waking ultradian rhythms of performance and motility in hyperkinetic and normal children. *Journal of Abnormal Child Psychology, 11,* 431–442.

Cameron, M. I., & Robinson, V. M. (1980). Effects of cognitive training on academic and on-task behavior of hyperactive children. *Journal of Abnormal Child Psychology, 8,* 405–419.

Campbell, S. (1975). Mother-child interaction: A comparison of hyperactive, learning disabled and normal boys. *American Journal of Orthopsychiatry, 45,* 51–57.

Cantwell, D. P., & Satterfield, J. H. (1978). The prevalence of academic underachievement in hyperactive children. *Journal of Pediatric Psychology, 3,* 168–171.

Chess, S. (1960). Diagnosis and treatment of the hyperactive child. *New York Journal of Medicine, 60,* 2379–2385.

Cohen, N. J., Sullivan, J., Minde, K., Novak, C., & Helwig, C. (1981). Evaluation of the relative effectiveness of methylphenidate and cognitive behavior modification in the treatment of kindergarten-aged hyperactive children. *Journal of Abnormal Child Psychology, 9,* 43–54.

Conners, C. K. (1980). *Food additives and hyperactive children.* New York: Plenum.

Conners, C. K., & Taylor, E. (1980). Pemoline, methylphenidate, and placebo in children with minimal brain dysfunction. *Archives of General Psychiatry, 37,* 922–930.

Conrad, W. G., Dworkin, E. S., Shai, A., & Tobiessen, J. E. (1971). Effects of amphetamine therapy and prescriptive tutoring on the behavior and achievement of lower class hyperactive children. *Journal of Learning Disabilities, 4,* 45–53.

Copeland, A. P. (1979). Types of private speech produced by hyperactive and nonhyperative boys. *Journal of Abnormal Child Psychology, 7,* 169–177.

Cunningham, S. J., & Knights, R. M. (1978). The performance of hyperactive and normal boys under differing reward and punishment schedules. *Journal of Pediatric Psychology, 3,* 195–201.

Dews, P. B. (1977). Rate-dependency hypothesis. *Science, 198,* 1182–1183.

Dews, P. B., & Wenger, G. R. (1977). Rate-dependency of the behavioral effects of amphetamine. In T. Thompson & P. B. Dews (Eds.), *Advances in behavioral pharmacology* (Vol. 1, pp. 167–227). New York: Academic.

Dishion, T. J., Loeber, R., Stouthamer-Loeber, M., & Patterson, G. R. (1984). Skill deficits and male adolescent delinquency. *Journal of Abnormal Child Psychology, 12,* 37–54.

Douglas, V. (1972). Stop, look, and listen: The problem of sustained attention and impulse control in hyperactive and normal children. *Canadian Journal of Behavioral Science* (pp. 149–168). Washington, DC: U.S. Office of Education.

Douglas, V. (1980). Treatment and training approaches to hyperactivity: Establishing internal or external control. In C. Whalen & B. Henker (Eds.), *Hyperactive children: The social ecology of identification and treatment.* New York: Academic.

Douglas, V. I., & Parry, P. A. (1983). Effects of reward on delayed reaction time task performance of hyperactive children. *Journal of Abnormal Child Psychology, 11,* 313–326.

Douglas, V. I., Parry, P., Marton, P., & Garson, C. (1976). Assessment of a cognitive training program for hyperactive children. *Journal of Abnormal Child Psychology, 4,* 389–410.

Douglas, V., & Peters, K. (1979). Toward a clearer definition of the attentional deficit in hyperactive children. In G. Hale & M. Lewis (Eds.), *Attention and the development of cognitive skills.* New York: Plenum.

Dunn, L. M., & Dunn, L. M. (1981). *Peabody Picture Vocabulary Test–Revised.* Circle Pines, MN: American Guidance Service.

Egeland, B. (1974). Training impulsive children in the use of more efficient scanning techniques. *Child Development, 45,* 165–171.

Firestone, P., & Douglas, V. I. (1977). The effects of verbal and material rewards and punishers on the performance of impulsive and reflective children. *Child Study Journal, 7,* 71–78.

Firestone, P., Kelley, M. J., Goodman, J. T., & Davey, J. (1981). Differential effects of parent training and stimulant medication with hyperactives. *American Academy of Child Psychiatry, 20,* 135–147.

Freibergs, V., & Douglas, V. I. (1969). Concept learning in hyperactive and normal children. *Journal of Abnormal Psychology, 74,* 388–395.

Friedling, C., & O'Leary, S. G. (1979). Teaching self-instruction to hyperactive children: A replication. *Journal of Applied Behavior Analysis, 12,* 211–219.

Gadow, K. D. (1983). Effects of stimulant drugs on academic performance in hyperactive and learning disabled children. *Journal of Learning Disabilities, 16,* 290–299.

Gittelman, R., Klein, D. F., & Feingold, I. (1983). Children with reading disorders–II. Effects of methylphenidate in combination with reading remediation. *Journal of Child Psychology and Psychiatry, 24,* 193–212.

Gittelman, R., & Mannuzza, S. (1985). Diagnosing ADD-H in adolescents. *Psychopharmacology Bulletin, 21,* 237–242.

Gittelman-Klein, R., Klein, D. F., Abikoff, H., Katz, S., Gloisten, A. C., & Kates, W. (1976). Relative efficacy of methylphendiate and behavior modification in hyperkinetic children: An interim report. *Journal of Abnormal Child Psychology, 4,* 361–379.

Goldberg, J. O., & Konstantareas, M. M. (1981). Vigilance in hyperactive and normal children on a self-paced operant task. *Journal of Child Psychology and Psychiatry, 22,* 55–63.

Gordon, M. (1979). The assessment of impulsivity and mediating behaviors in hyperactive and nonhyperactive boys. *Journal of Abnormal Child Psychology, 7,* 317–326.

Gordon, M., McClure, F. D., & Post, E. M. (1983). *Gordon Diagnostic System.* Golden, CO: Clinical Diagnostic.

Haslam, R. H., Dalby, J. T., & Rademaker, A. W. (1984). Effects of megavitamin therapy on children with attention deficit disorders. *Pediatrics, 74,* 103–111.

Hinshaw, S. P., Henker, B., & Whalen, C. K. (1984). Self-control in hyperactive boys in anger-inducing situations: Effects of cognitive-behavioral training and of methylphenidate. *Journal of Abnormal Child Psychology, 12,* 55–77.

Hobbs, S. A., Moguin, L. E., Tyroler, M., & Lahey, B. B. (1980). Cognitive behavior therapy with children: Has clinical utility been demonstrated? *Psychological Bulletin, 87,* 147–165.

Humphrey, L. L. (1982). Children's and teachers' perspectives on children's self-control: The development of two rating scales. *Journal of Consulting and Clinical Psychology, 50,* 624–633.

Kagan, J. Rosman, B. L., Day, D., Albert, J., & Phillips, W. (1964). Information processing in the child: Significance of analytic and reflective attitudes. *Psychological Monographs, 78,* (1, Whole No. 578).4

Kendall, P. C., & Finch, A. J. (1976). A cognitive-behavioral treatment for impulse control: A case study. *Journal of Consulting and Clinical Psychology, 44,* 852–857.

Kendall, P. C., & Finch, A. J. (1979). Analyses of changes in verbal behavior following a cognitive-behavioral treatment for impulsivity. *Journal of Abnormal Child Psychology, 7,* 455–463.

King, C. A., & Young, R. D. (1981). Peer popularity and peer communication patterns: Hyperactive versus active but normal boys. *Journal of Abnormal Child Psychology, 9,* 465–482.

King, C., & Young, R. D. (1982). Attentional deficits with and without hyperactivity: Teacher and peer perceptions. *Journal of Abnormal Child Psychology, 10,* 483–496.

Kinsbourne, M., & Swanson, J. M. (1979). Models of hyperactivity: Implications for diagnosis and treatment. In R. L. Trites (Ed.), *Hyperactivity in children: Etiology, measurement, and treatment implications* (pp. 1–20). Baltimore: University Park Press.

Klein, A. R., & Young, R. D. (1979). Hyperactive boys in their classroom: Assessment of teacher and peer perceptions, interactions, and classroom behaviors. *Journal of Abnormal Child Psychology, 7,* 425–442.

Lachar, D. (1982). *Personality Inventory for Children (PIC). Revised format manual supplement.* Los Angeles: Western Psychological Services.

Lambert, N., & Sandoval, J. (1980). The prevalence of learning disabilities in a sample of children considered hyperactive. *Journal of Abnormal Child Psychology, 8,* 33–50.

Loney, J. (1978). Childhood hyperactivity. In R. H. Woody (Ed.), *Encyclopedia of clinical assessment.* New York: Jossey-Bass.

Loney, J. (1980). Hyperkinesis comes of age: What do we know and where should we go? *American Journal of Orthopsychiatry, 50,* 28–42.

Mattes, J. A., & Gittelman, R. (1981). Effects of artificial food colorings in children with hyperactive symptoms. *Archives of General Psychiatry, 38,* 714–718.

Meichenbaum, D. H., & Goodman, J. (1971). Training impulsive children to talk to themselves: A means of developing self-control. *Journal of Abnormal Child Psychology, 77,* 115–126.

Milich, R., Landau, S., Kilby, G., & Whitten, P. (1982). Preschool peer perceptions of the behavior of hyperactive and aggressive children. *Journal of Abnormal Child Psychology, 10,* 497–510.

O'Leary, K. D., Pelham, W. E., Rosenbaum, A., & Price, G. H. (1976). Behavioral treatment of hyperkinetic children. *Clinical Pediatrics, 15,* 510–515.

Parry, P. A., & Douglas, V. I. (1983). Effects of reinforcement on concept identification in hyperactive children. *Journal of Abnormal Child Psychology, 11,* 327–340.

Patterson, G. R. (1964). An application of conditioning techniques to the control of the hyperactive child. In L. P. Ullmann & L. Krasner (Eds.), *Case studies in behavior modification.* New York: Holt, Rinehart & Winston.

Patterson, G. R., Whittier, J., & Wright, M. A. (1965). A behaviour modification technique for the hyperactive child. *Behaviour Research and Therapy, 2,* 217–226.

Pelham, W. E. (1977). Withdrawal of a stimulant drug and concurrent behavioral intervention in the treatment of a hyperactive child. *Behavior Therapy, 8,* 473–479.

Pelham, W. E., Schnedler, R. W., Bologna, N. C., & Contreras, A. J. (1980). Behavioral and stimulant treatment of hyperactive children: A therapy study with methylphenidate probes in a within-subject design. *Journal of Applied Behavior Analysis, 13,* 221–236.

Physicians' Desk Reference. (1985). Oradell, NJ: Litton Industries.

Porrino, L. J., Rapoport, J. L., Behar, D., Sceery, W., Ismond, D. R., & Bunney, W. E. (1983). A naturalistic assessment of the motor activity of hyperactive boys. *Archives of General Psychiatry, 40,* 681–687.

Quay, H. C., Sprague, R. L., Werry, J. S., & McQueen, M. (1967). Conditioning visual orientation of conduct problem children in the classroom. *Journal of Experimental Child Psychology, 5,* 512–517.

Radosh, A., & Gittelman, R. (1981). The effect of appealing distractors on the performance of hyperactive children. *Journal of Abnormal Child Psychology, 9,* 179–189.

Rapoport, J. L., & Ismond, D. R. (1984). *DSM-III training guide for diagnosis of childhood disorders.* New York: Brunner/Mazel.

Rapport, M. D. (1983). Attention deficit disorder with hyperactivity: Critical treatment parameters and their application in applied outcome research. In M. Hersen, R. Eisler, & P. Miller (Eds.), *Progress in Behavior Modification* (pp. 219–298). New York: Academic.

Rapport, M. D. (1984). Hyperactivity and stimulant treatment: Abusus non tollit usum. *Behavior Therapist, 7,* 133–134.

Rapport, M. D. (in press). Hyperactivity and attention deficit disorders. In V. B. Van Hasselt, P. S. Strain, & M. Hersen (Eds.), *Handbook of developmental and physical disabilities.* New York: Pergamon.

Rapport, M. D., & DuPaul, G. J. (in press). Methylphenidate: Rate-dependent effects on hyperactivity. *Psychopharmacology Bulletin.*

Rapport, M. D., DuPaul, G. J., & Smith, N. F. (1985). Rate-dependency and hyperactivity: Methylphenidate effects on operant responding. *Pharmacology, Biochemistry, and Behavior, 23,* 77–83.

Rapport, M. D., DuPaul, G. J., Stoner, G., & Jones, J. T. (in press). Comparing classroom and clinic measures of attention deficit disorder: Differential, idiosyncratic, and dose-response effects of methylphenidate. *Journal of Consulting and Clinical Psychology.*

Rapport, M. D., DuPaul, G. J., Stoner, G., Birmingham, B., & Masse, G. (1985). Attention deficit disorder with hyperactivity: Differential effects of methylphenidate on impulsivity. *Pediatrics. 76,* 938–943.

Rapport, M. D., Murphy, A., & Bailey, J. S. (1980). The effects of a response cost treatment tactic on hyperactive children. *Journal of School Psychology, 18,* 98–111.

Rapport, M. D., Murphy, A., & Bailey, J. S. (1982). Ritalin vs. response cost in the control of hyperactive children: A within subject comparison. *Journal of Applied Behavior Analysis, 15,* 205–216.

Rapport, M. D., Stoner, G., DuPaul, G. J., Birmingham, B. K., & Tucker, S. (1985). Methyphenidate in hyperactive children: Differential effects of dose on academic, learning, and social behavior. *Journal of Abnormal Child Psychology, 13,* 227–244.

Rapport, M. D., Tucker, S., DuPaul, G. J., Merlo, M., & Stoner, G. (in press). Hyperactivity and frustration: The influence of size and control over rewards in delaying gratification. *Journal of Abnormal Child Psychology.*

Reatig, N. (1984). Attention deficit disorder: A bibliography. *Psychopharmacology Bulletin, 20,* 693–718.

Rie, H. E. (1974). Therapeutic tutoring for underachieving children. *Professional Psychology, 5,* 70–75.

Robbins, T. W., & Sahakian, B. J. (1979). "Paradoxical" effects of psychomotor stimulant drugs in hyperactive children from the standpoint of behavioral pharmacology. *Neuropharmacology, 18,* 931–950.

Robinson, P. W., Newby, T. J., & Ganzell, J. L. (1981). A token system for a class of underachieving hyperactive children. *Journal of Applied Behavior Analysis, 14,* 307–315.

Rosenbaum, M., & Baker, E. (1984). Self-control behavior in hyperactive and non-hyperactive children. *Journal of Abnormal Child Psychology, 12,* 303–318.

Routh, D. K. (1980). Developmental and social aspects of hyperactivity. In C. K. Whalen, & B. Henker (Eds.), *Hyperactive children: The social ecology of identification and treatment.* New York: Academic.

Routh, D. K., Schroeder, C. S., & O'Tuama, L. (1974). Development of activity level in children. *Developmental Psychology, 10,* 163–168.

Safer, D., & Allen, R. (1976). *Hyperactive children: Diagnosis and management.* Baltimore: University Park Press.

Safer, D. J., & Krager, J. M. (1983). Trends in medication treatment of hyperactive school children. *Clinical Pediatrics, 22,* 500–504.

Salkind, N. J. (1978). *The development of norms for the Matching Familiar Figures Test.* Unpublished manuscript, University of Kansas.

Satterfield, J. H., Hoppe, C. M., & Schell, A. M. (1982). A prospective study of delinquency in 110 adolescent boys with attention deficit disorder and 88 normal adolescent boys. *American Journal of Psychiatry, 139,* 795–798.

Shafto, F., & Sulzbacher, S. (1977). Comparing treatment tactics with a hyperactive preschool child: Stimulant medication and programmed teacher intervention. *Journal of Applied Behavior Analysis, 10,* 13–20.

Sleator, E. K., & Ullmann, R. K. (1981). Can the physician diagnose hyperactivity in the office? *Pediatrics, 67,* 13–17.

Solanto, M. V. (1984). Neuropharmacological basis of stimulant drug action in attention deficit disorder with hyperactivity: A review and synthesis. *Psychological Bulletin, 95,* 387–409.

Sprague, R. L. (1983). Behavior modification and educational techniques. In M. Rutter (Ed.), *Developmental neuropsychiatry* (pp. 404–421). New York: Guilford.

Sprague, R. L., & Sleator, E. K. (1975). What is the proper dose of stimulant drugs in children? *International Journal of Mental Health, 4,* 75–104.

Sprague, R. L., & Sleator, E. K. (1976). Drugs and dosages: Implications for learning disabilities. In R. M. Knights, & D. J. Bakker (Eds.), *The neuropsychology of learning disorders* (pp. 351–366). Baltimore: University Park Press.

Sprague, R. L., & Sleator, E. K. (1977). Methylphenidate in hyperkinetic children: Differences in dose effects on learning and social behavior. *Science, 198,* 1274–1276.

Swanson, J., Nolan, W., & Pelham, W. (1981, August). *The SNAP rating scale for the diagnosis of the attention deficit disorder.* Paper presented at the meeting of the American Psychological Association, Los Angeles.

Sykes, D. H., Douglas, V. I., & Morgenstern, G. (1973). Sustained attention in hyperactive children. *Journal of Child Psychology and Psychiatry, 14,* 213–220.

Tallmadge, J., & Barkley, R. A. (1983). The interactions of hyperactive and normal boys with their fathers and mothers. *Journal of Abnormal Child Psychology, 11,* 565–580.

Thurston, C. M., Sobol, M. P., Swanson, J., & Kinsbourne, M. (1979). Effects of methylphenidate (Ritalin) on selective attention in hyperactive children. *Journal of Abnormal Child Psychology, 7,* 471–481.

Ullmann, R. K., Sleator, E. K., & Sprague, R. L. (1984). A new rating scale for diagnosis and monitoring of ADD children. *Psychopharmacology Bulletin, 20,* 160–164.

Weiss, G. (1985). Pharmacotherapy for ADD-H adolescents workshop: Followup studies on outcome of hyperactive children. *Psychopharmacology Bulletin, 21,* 169–177.

Weiss, G., & Hechtman, L. (1979). The hyperactive child syndrome. *Science, 205,* 1348–1354.

Wender, P. H., Reimherr, F. W., & Wood, D. R. (1981). Attention deficit disorder (minimal brain dysfunction) in adults: A replication study of diagnosis and drug treatment. *Archives of General Psychiatry, 38,* 449–456.

Werry, J., Sprague, R., & Cohen, M. (1975). Conners Teacher Rating Scale for use in drug studies with children—An empirical study. *Journal of Abnormal Child Psychology, 3,* 217–229.

Whalen, C. K., Collins, B. E., Henker, B., Alkus, S. R., Adams, D., & Stapp, J. (1978). Behavior observations of hyperactive children and methylphenidate (Ritalin) effects in systematically structured classroom environments: Now you see them, now you don't. *Journal of Pediatric Psychology, 3,* 177–187.

Whalen, C. K., & Henker, B. (1976). Psychostimulants and children: A review and analysis. *Psychological Bulletin, 83,* 1113–1130.

Whalen, C. K., Henker, B., Collins, B. E., Finck, D., & Dotemoto, S. (1979). A social ecology of hyperactive boys: Medication effects in structured classroom environments. *Journal of Applied Behavior Analysis, 12,* 65–81.

Wilder, J. (1967). *Stimulus and response: The law of initial value.* Bristol: Wright.

Wolraich, M., Milich, R., Stumbo, P., & Schultz, F. (1985). Effects of sucrose ingestion on the behavior of hyperactive boys. *Journal of Pediatrics, 106,* 675–682.

Zentall, S. S., Zentall, T. R., & Booth, M. E. (1978). Within-task stimulation: Effects on activity and spelling performance in hyperactive and normal children. *Journal of Educational Research, 71,* 223–230.

CHAPTER 14

Academic Problems

EDWARD S. SHAPIRO

A large portion of a child's life is spent within the school environment. During the critical school years children are expected to master a wide variety of academic skills. These include not only reading, writing, and arithmetic, but also content subjects such as science, social studies, cultural affairs, music, and art. It is not surprising that behavioral researchers have devoted extensive efforts toward the development of remediation programs to improve academic skills.

Historically, academic problems of children have always been of interest to behavioral investigators. For example, Staats, Minke, Finley, Wolf, and Brooks (1964) demonstrated in numerous studies that reading skills of children could be modified through contingent reinforcement programs. Hall, Lund, and Jackson (1968) showed that teacher attention could affect study behavior. Lovitt and Curtiss (1969) found that manipulation of points awarded for academic performance could improve performance on a wide variety of mathematics, reading, and language arts tasks.

Despite the success of early studies demonstrating that behavioral interventions can affect academic performance, most systematic attempts to determine the predictors of academic performance were conducted by traditional educational psychologists. During the late 1960s researchers examining the effects of teacher behavior on student performance concluded that what teachers did in classrooms seemed to have little impact on children's learning (Coleman, et al., 1966; Stephens, 1967). This conclusion was alarming and seriously questioned. Indeed, the influential reviews of Rosenshine and Furst (1973) and Dunkin and Biddle (1974) began to change the educational establishment.

At this time, the National Institute of Education began to fund research projects, such as Project Follow-Through, that examined in a systematic and effective way the critical variables within the classroom environment that are related to basic skills learning in elementary school children. This shift in emphasis resulted in a very fruitful and often replicated set of conclusions about improving and understanding the academic problems of children.

Although the research has emerged from two somewhat diverse sources, it appears to be converging on agreed-on parameters related to academic performance. At one pole has been the efforts of educational psychologists such as Rosenshine (1981), who have provided extensive reviews of studies examining variables that affect academic performance. Although much of his work is derived from the Beginning Teacher Evaluation Study (BTES: Denham & Lieberman, 1980), his conclusions across investigations are consistent.

Rosenshine (1979) identified two major factors that influence academic performance; (1) content mastered, and (2) academic engaged minutes. *Content mastered* is defined by a measure of the amount of material actually learned. It should not be surprising that the more material one masters, the more one learns. However, as Rosenshine (1979, 1981) notes, the implications of having to increase the rate at which a student progresses through curriculum materials are difficult to address.

Given the importance of mastering curriculum as a critical predictor of academic success, the amount of time a student actually spends engaged in academic activities is an extremely important variable. Berliner (1979), in data reported from the BTES study, compared the amount of allocated time (time assigned for instruction) and engaged time (time actually spent in academic tasks) in a second- and fifth-grade classroom. Although results showed wide variation across classrooms and grades, many second-grade classes were found to have under 100 hours of cumulative engaged time across an entire 150-day school year. Fredrick, Walberg, and Rasher (1979) examined engaged time and scores on the Iowa Tests of Basic Skills among 175 classrooms in Chicago and found engagement rates and achievement to be moderately correlated ($r = .54$). Additionally, Fredrick et al. (1979) found that 46.5% of time was lost due to listening, absence, and inattention.

Greenwood and his associates at the Juniper Garden's Children's Project in Kansas City have examined academic engaged time by focusing on opportunities to respond, which they defined as the interaction between teacher-formulated instructional stimuli and success in establishing the academic responding implied by the materials. Stanley and Greenwood (1981) developed the *Code for Instructional Structure and Student Academic Response* (CISSAR) to provide a detailed analysis of these variables. The measure contains 53 codes providing data on the activity, task, teacher position during instruction, structure of instruction, types of student academic responses (e.g., writing; reading aloud or reading silently; task management activities, which are prerequisites to academic responding), and competing responses. Data are collected through direct observation using time sampling procedures.

A number of studies have been conducted using the CISSAR (e.g., Hall, Delquadri, Greenwood, & Thurston, 1982; Stanley & Greenwood, 1983; Thurlow, Ysseldyke, Graden, & Algozzine, 1984; Ysseldyke, Thurlow, Meklenburg, Graden, & Algozzine, 1984). Investigators have consistently reported that the levels of academic engaged time of students in regular education having academic difficulties is alarmingly low. This has applied to classes for identified learning disabled students as well (Thurlow et al., 1983; Ysseldyke et al., 1984). Other studies using less complex methods of coding engagement rates have found similar results (Gettinger, 1984; Leach & Dolan, 1985; McConnell, Strain, Kerr, Stagg, Lenkner, & Lambert, 1984). In all studies direct relationships between engagement rates and academic performance have been observed.

Research on academic engaged time represents only one aspect of variables affecting academic performance. Equally impressive have been the efforts of researchers in applied behavior analysis in demonstrating the relationship of academic behavior and contingency management procedures. Explored most systematically in the Behavior Analysis Project Follow-Through studies (Bushell, 1978; Stallings, 1975), changes in academic behavior have been functionally related to antecedents and consequences surrounding performance. Likewise, use of the direct instruction model, which is related to and can enhance behavior analytic approaches to academic remediation, is also quite impressive in affecting academic performance (Gersten, 1985). Rosenshine and Berliner (1978) argue for the importance of direct instruction as the methodology for teaching, which can most directly increase engaged time. It is important to note, however, that Rosenshine and Berliner (1978) refer to direct instruction as a general instructional method incorporating a sequenced set of activities and settings designed to move students through a set of reading or mathematics materials. Specifically, direct instruction is viewed as teaching that is focused, has clear goals, contains sufficient and continuous academic engagement, provides extensive coverage of content, monitors student performance, asks questions at low cognitive levels that produce many correct responses, and offers immediate and frequent feedback to students.

In summary, the variables that appear to be most influential in affecting academic performance are related to time. Specifically, academic engaged time or opportunities to respond appear to be the most critical. Additionally, the amount of content covered and the instructional strategies used appear to predict successful performance. Finally, well-known contingency management strategies, such as contingent reinforcement, prompting, modeling, feedback, and stimulus presentation, are related to performance.

This chapter reviews recent research examining the modification of academic performance in children and adolescents. Given the extensive nature of the literature, the review is limited to those studies published from 1977 to the present. (For an excellent review of literature published prior to 1977, see Klein, 1978.)

In the next section, procedures designed to affect all types of academic behavior are presented. These strategies are considered to be applicable to any area of basic skills or content being taught. The following section reviews studies specifically designed to bring about change in reading, mathematics, spelling, and other language arts. The final section presents a case study examining interrelationships between reading responses.

GENERAL INTERVENTIONS FOR ACADEMIC PROBLEMS

Increasing Academic Engaged Time

Procedures that are capable of increasing academic engaged time must increase the opportunities to respond. Although this might be accomplished by increasing the time allocated for instruction, such increases are unlikely to be possible given the current structure of schools. Moreover, unless the response rates within the allocated time are increased, simply providing more time for instruction does not insure improvements in academic performance.

One procedure that has frequently been used to increase academic engaged time is peer tutoring. The logic underlying this procedure is that peer tutoring should result in significant increases in the frequency of academic responses. Instead of one teacher asking one question to 20 students and receiving one response, you have 10 students asking the same question of 10 students and receiving 10 responses all within the same time frame. In addition, in keeping with research on instructional methods, error correction is immediate and efficient, questions are at low cognitive levels, and the responses are given in the same modality as testing for mastery (e.g., writing of spelling words in practice instead of oral recitation).

Whorton et al. (in press) examined the effects of a classwide peer tutoring program on the academic response rates of children enrolled in a Chapter I reading program. Using a within-series reversal design, academic response rates were functionally related to the implementation of the tutoring program. In addition, collateral changes were shown on measures of oral reading rate as academic response rates increased. Greenwood, Dinwiddie, Terry, Wade, Stanley, Thibadeau, and Delquadri (1984) reported a series of three experiments that provide convincing evidence of the potential of peer tutoring for modifying academic response rates. The study involved 5 teachers and 128 students in grades 3 to 6. The four lowest students in each class were identified and targeted for intensive observation as interventions were employed with the entire class.

In the first experiment, data were obtained on academic response rates (CISSAR code), weekly scores on spelling and vocabulary, and scores on standardized achievement tests. Following baseline, students were exposed to either a teacher-mediated procedure or classwide tutoring. In the teacher-mediated condition, teachers were instructed to design a lesson for the content to be taught but not to use peer tutoring. It was suggested that teachers employ teacher-student discussion, media, readers, and paper/pencil tasks, in that order. Classwide peer tutoring was conducted by pairing students, having each student read the item to his or her partner, having the student write the response and correct it if incorrect, and awarding points for the correct response. These conditions were presented in a withdrawal design, counterbalancing the order of conditions across subjects.

Results of this study were as expected. Academic response rates significantly increased during peer tutoring. Likewise, gains in spelling and vocabulary were substantially higher with tutoring. Although results of this study were encouraging, Greenwood, Dinwiddie, Terry, Wade, Stanley, Thibadeau, and Delquadri (1984) reported that observations of teacher instruction using the CISSAR were possible only during the initial phase of the study.

In an attempt to address this issue, the second experiment of the series was conducted. Using a multiple baseline across content areas, student performance in spelling, vocabulary, and arithmetic was examined. In this study, a baseline procedure was compared to both the teacher-mediated and peer tutoring condition.

Results again confirmed the findings of previous studies. Academic responding was highest during peer tutoring. Gains in achievement were again evident during both procedures, although largest for peer tutoring. These gains were particularly evident for spelling and vocabulary.

Finally, in the third experiment, these investigators described an attempted replication of previous findings. Of interest was the unplanned deviation of the teacher from peer tutoring procedures. Results of the study replicated other findings, with declines in academic performance evident as the teacher deviated from the planned experimental condition.

This study along with others conducted at Juniper Gardens (Greenwood, Terry, Wade, Dinwiddie, Stanley, Thibadeau, & Delquadri, 1982, as cited in Greenwood, Delquadri, & Hall, 1984) provide strong and remarkably consistent evidence that peer tutoring can be an effective procedure for increasing academic response rates. Additionally, the procedure appears to result in significant improvements in academic performance. Other researchers have also found peer tutoring to have significant effects on academic performance in reading and mathematics (McKenzie & Budd, 1981; Redd, Ullmann, Stelle, & Roesch, 1979; Young, Hecimovic, & Salzberg, 1983). Some investigators have also explored parameters of peer tutoring such as the ability of tutoring procedures to be learned through observation of peer models (Stowitschek, Hecimovic, Stowitschek, & Shores, 1982) and the use of a home reinforcement contingency in addition to tutoring procedures (Trovoto & Bucher, 1980). The results of these studies all point to the potential implications of tutoring as a distinct mechanism for improving academic response rates.

Although the consistency of these results is highly encouraging, it is important to recognize that *all* studies examining peer tutoring also included a component of contingent reinforcement. The extent to which tutoring alone would have been effective has not been evaluated. Given the equally strong evidence supporting the use of contingent reinforcement in increasing academic responses, it is questionable whether tutoring alone would have the substantial effects it appears to have.

Performance Feedback

A simple procedure that has been found to be effective in modifying a variety of academic behaviors involves providing response-contingent feedback about performance. Van Houten and Lai Fatt (1981) examined the impact of public posting of weekly grades on biology tests with twelfth-grade high school students. Results of the first experiment found that the effects of public posting plus immediate feedback and praise increased accuracy from 55.7% to 73.2% correct across the 47 students in the study. In a replication of the study with 106 students, Van Houten and Lai Fatt (1981) showed that public posting alone with biweekly feedback increased student performance. These results were consistent with earlier studies examining the use of explicit timing and public posting in increasing mathematics and composition skills in regular elementary school students (Van Houten, Hill, & Parsons, 1975; Van Houten & Thompson, 1978).

Kastelen, Nickel, and McLaughlin (1984) found that use of public posting, immediate feedback, and praise improved the percent completion of tasks in reading among 16 eighth-grade students. Some generalization was evident on spelling and writing tasks.

These studies suggest that simply supplying students with immediate feedback and public recognition may be sufficient to alter academic behavior. Procedures such as these provide evidence that many interventions for academic problems are readily available for most classrooms. It is also important to note that these procedures were implemented with both elementary and secondary students in regular education classrooms.

Modeling, Self-Management, Contingency Contracting

Many of the procedures for modifying academic performance require the teacher to apply the specific contingency in effect. Although teachers are expected to exert instructional control in classrooms, it is equally important that students be capable of generating strategies and providing contingencies on their behavior without teacher control. The move toward self-management of child behavior has been prevalent in the behavioral literature (e.g., O'Leary & Dubey, 1979; Roberts & Dick, 1983; Shapiro, in press; Shapiro, Browder, & D'Huyvetters, 1984). Self-management procedures for academic performance have likewise been emerging.

Hendrickson, Roberts, and Shores (1978) describe the use of modeling in teaching sight vocabulary to learning disabled children. Although not conceptualized as a self-management procedure, use of modeling in learning academic skills can easily be applied in self-management formats, such as peer tutoring or observational learning. In a review article of modeling procedures, Hendrickson and Gable (1981) note that modeling can be performed as an antecedent or consequence to the modeled response. As an antecedent procedure—for example, in sight vocabulary training—the trainer presents a word by saying, "This word is . . . ," and then asking the child, "What is this word?" In contrast, contingent modeling involves presenting a word, saying "What is this word?" and modeling the correct response only if an error is made. Studies comparing the two procedures suggest that antecedent modeling may have a stronger effect with younger children than with older pupils. Hendrickson and Gable (1981) indicated that the strongest learning occurs when modeling is paired with contingent reinforcement of the desired response.

A more direct form of self-management involves goal setting. Although goal setting is only one component of self-management (Kanfer, 1977), it may provide an important mechanism for improving academic skills. In a series of studies, Kelley and Stokes (1982, 1984) found contingency contracts to be particularly effective in increasing basic academic skills among 16- to 21-year-old students enrolled in programs to obtain their general equivalency diplomas. In these studies students were paid contingently on a teacher/student negotiated contract for completion of academic assignments. Results of both studies found that the combination of contracting and money significantly improved performance over baseline in completion of academic tasks. In the final phase of the Kelley and Stokes (1984) study, students continued to set goals but were no longer paid for performance. Interestingly, during this phase performance decreased to levels lower than during contracting plus money but higher than baseline.

Gallant, Sargent, and Van Houten (1980) compared the effects of teacher-determined and self-determined access to a desirable science activity contingent on completion of reading and mathematics tasks with 95% accuracy within the allotted time with an 11-year-old boy. Results of the study found that the boy's academic performance remained very high after self-determined access was begun. It was impossible, however, to tell if the effects of self-determined access would have been equally as effective if implemented prior to its being teacher-determined.

In addition to goal setting and self-evaluating performance, an important component of self-management is self-monitoring. This behavior incorporates two components: self-observation of the response and self-recording. Pacquin (1978) examined the use of self-recording (he called it self-graphing) alone in improving performance on reading, arithmetic, and phonics lessons. After the student completed her assignments, the teacher simply told the student what her performance was on each task, and the student then plotted her scores. Results of the study showed that the number of correct problems substantially increased as the procedure was applied to reading and arithmetic. No generalization to phonics was observed.

In a more elaborate evaluation of a self-management program, Stevenson and Fantuzzo (1984) investigated the generalization effects of a multicomponent program to improve performance in mathematics with two fifth-grade pupils. The self-management program consisted of goal setting, self-monitoring, self-evaluation, and self-administered reinforcement. Data were obtained on both the targeted and nontarget subjects to assess cross-person generalization. Cross-setting generalization was assessed by collecting data at home and school, and cross-behavior generalization was assessed by examining performance on both math and disruptive behavior. Results showed that the target subject's behavior improved at home as the procedure was implemented at school. Likewise, cross-behavior generalization (decreases in disruptive behavior in school) were also evident. Similar decreases in disruptiveness at home were also observed. At follow-up, increases in mathematics performance at school and at home were maintained. Decreases in disruptive behavior, however, were not maintained. Some generalization of academic performance to the untreated boy was observed; however, withdrawal of the program for the treated child did not result in the reversal of effects for the untreated child, suggesting that the evidence for cross-subject generalization is somewhat questionable.

Comment

Taken together, the studies reviewed in this section provide strong evidence that behavioral procedures such as contingent reinforcement, goal setting, contracting, modeling, feedback, praise, and self-recording are all capable of changing academic performance. In addition, procedures specifically targeted at increasing academic engagement, such as peer tutoring, appear to be related to improvements in academic responding.

Although these procedures all seem to be effective, they have in common an underlying component of contingent reinforcement. Even peer tutoring, designed to affect academic performance indirectly, provided for earning points contingent on correct academic responding. Given the strong effects reinforcement has on behavior in general, inclusion of a reinforcement component is likely a critical variable for improving academic behavior. At present, few studies have effectively isolated the reinforcement components from other aspects of the procedures being employed. It is important that future efforts be devoted to examining the extent to which contingent reinforcement alone can be effective. Of particular interest is the degree to which reinforcement effects are enhanced by including other procedures such as contracting and goal setting. Studies that can provide answers to these questions are clearly needed.

While the procedures discussed in this section are applicable across types of academic skills, numerous studies have been conducted employing these or some variation of these procedures in changing specific academic skills. In the next section, academic performance in reading, math, spelling, and other language arts will be examined.

INTERVENTIONS FOR SPECIFIC ACADEMIC SKILLS

Reading

Historically, behavioral approaches to remediating reading difficulties in children and adolescents have had a well-established place in the literature (e.g., Staats & Butterfield, 1965; Staats, Finley, Minke, & Wolf, 1964; Staats, Minke, Finley, Wolf, & Brooks, 1964). These early efforts were primarily devoted to demonstrating that reading skills could be treated as operant responses and therefore modified using contingent reinforcement. Although these investigations may now appear to be trivial, it is important to recognize that research over the last 20 years has continued to support this position.

Research on improving reading skills has focused almost exclusively on oral reading rates (number of words per minute read correctly and incorrectly) as the dependent measures. Some investigations have also included measures of comprehension, such as the percentage of correctly answered questions from assigned reading passages. While these measures may seem simplistic, there is strong evidence that they provide clear indications of reading ability (e.g., Deno, Mirkin, & Chiang, 1982). Additionally, investigators have suggested that using a more molecular analysis to evaluate progress in reading is usually unnecessary (Lahey, McNees, & Brown, 1973).

Categorizing types of procedures used to remediate reading problems is very difficult. Almost all strategies incorporate some form of contingent reinforcement as a consequence for correct performance. However, some procedures do attempt to provide distinct intervention prior to the reading response. One such manipulation of antecedents has been the use of *previewing*. Essentially, this procedure requires the person to review the materials to be read before actually engaging in the targeted response. In a series of studies, Rose (1984a, 1984b) and Rose and Sherry (1984) have compared the use of silent previewing and listening in improving oral reading rates with learning disabled children, adolescents, and mildly mentally retarded children. Using an alternating treatments design, Rose found that in most cases both previewing procedures resulted in significantly higher rates of words correct per minute. Of the two strategies, listening appeared consistently better than silent previewing. Of importance, however, were Rose's finding that error rates may not improve. Taken together, Rose's studies suggest that listening as a previewing procedure may be a useful technique for increasing the rate of slow but accurate readers; however, it may not have any impact on reducing errors.

Another commonly used procedure for improving reading has been contingent reinforcement. Trice, Parker, and Furrow (1981) found that feedback and contingent reinforcement, using a written format for responses to reading materials, significantly improved the number of words written in replies to questions and the spelling accuracy of a 17-year-old learning disabled boy. Additionally, response generalization to reading accuracy was evident on a series of word recognition tests. Although the procedure used was novel, Trice et al. (1981) failed to examine reading levels in context, making the generalizability of the study to classroom reading somewhat questionable.

Other authors have explored issues of generalization in remediating reading skills in more detail. Jenkins, Barksdale, and Clinton (1978) examined reading comprehension and oral reading rates across behaviors, setting, and time. They also investigated the interrelationships among these measures. Using three reading-deficient 11-year-old children, Barksdale et al. (1978) had students write answers to comprehension questions after oral reading. Using a multiple baseline design with subsequent reversal phases, the children earned money for correctly answering comprehension questions within the remedial setting. Data were simultaneously collected in the regular classroom setting and on oral reading rate. In a later phase reinforcement was shifted to oral reading rate. Results of their study showed that contingent reinforcement improved the comprehension levels of all three boys. Similar improvement was observed in the regular classroom setting only when the procedure was implemented within that setting. Oral reading rates appeared unaffected by gains in comprehension and improved only when targeted.

Andersen and Redd (1980) also examined the impact of a specific instructional strategy on the generalization of oral reading levels. Four children deficient in reading skills were tutored by undergraduate college students using either a standard remedial teaching approach (physical and verbal prompts, social reinforcement) or generalization training—a systematic use of fading prompts, tutor assistance, and tutor presence. Employing a multielement design, Andersen and Redd (1980) found that all behaviors maintained their high levels of accuracy when generalization training was begun. Further, the standard procedure resulted in inconsistent performance across children.

In addition to the use of previewing and contingent reinforcement for improving reading skills, investigators have used such strategies as reading words contiguously with a tape recording (Freeman & McLaughlin, 1984), skipping and drilling of material contingent upon improved oral reading (Lovitt & Hansen, 1976), and the use of self- versus teacher-imposed schedules of setting criteria for oral reading rates to earn contingent reinforcement (Billingsley, 1977). All have proven successful as strategies for improving reading. Clearly, the numbers and types of procedures available for improving the reading of children and adolescents is extensive. Still, there have been few efforts devoted to the issue of response generalization. Almost all studies have focused on remediation outside the regular classroom environment. As such, the amount of transfer of these learned skills to reading in context is unknown. Studies are needed that examine whether deficient readers who improve reading in a basal reading series or with investigator-made materials show equal gains in reading content materials such as science or history books. This is a particularly important issue for adolescents, who often have difficulty in school due to their inability to read material in content subjects effectively. Studies that explore strategies for demonstrating how reading skills taught in the remedial setting can be generalized to regular education settings are also needed.

Mathematics

Extensive research has been conducted on the remediation of mathematics using behavioral interventions. Almost universally, dependent measures have consisted of the percentage of problems done correctly and/or a rate measure. In mathematics, the use of rate is especially important, since a child displaying highly accurate but slow performance may be viewed equally as deficient in skills as the child who has speedy but highly inaccurate performance (Hendrickson, Gable, & Stowitschek, 1985).

Procedures manipulating both antecedents and consequences have been used as interventions. Whitman and Johnson (1983) and Johnston, Whitman, and Johnson (1980) used a self-instruction training program to improve the addition and substraction regrouping skills of mildly mentally retarded children. Using both an individual and group training format, Whitman and Johnson (1983) and Johnston et al. (1980) found significant increases in the accuracy rates and number of problems correct across all children subsequent to self-instruction training. Interestingly, they also found that students consistently completed fewer problems. In essence, what was completed was done accurately, although they attempted fewer problems after training in self-instruction.

Albion and Salzberg (1982) also examined the use of self-instruction training in improving the mathematics performance of five 11- to 13-year old children. In addition to the self-instruction training, stars were given contingent on performance. Results of the study found that self-instruction improved the rate of correct problems for three of the five children. Unfortunately, inclusion of the contingent star makes it difficult to determine the exact effect of the self-instruction program.

Paine, Carnine, White, and Walters (1982) manipulated teacher presence and structure of the teaching strategy in improving the multiplication skills of three 8-year-old children. Using a reversal design, teacher-directed chalkboard instruction was compared to an individual worksheet, a contingency where children had to perform within a preset time, and a low-structured situation where the number of teacher prompts was faded. Generalization across types of multiplication problems was also assessed. Results showed that acquisition of the skills did not occur until the low-structure condition was applied. No improvement on the generalization measure was evident, but behavior did improve when the structured worksheet condition was implemented for the generalization response. Unfortunately, data obtained at follow-up showed inconsistent maintenance of the learned behaviors across subjects.

Lloyd, Saltzman, and Kauffman (1981) provided another procedure for improving the mathematics performance of four learning disabled children. Called "strategy training," the procedure teaches children general problem-solving rules rather than specific skills. Similar to self-instruction, strategy training assumes that children will then apply these skills once acquired. In their study Lloyd et al. (1981) began by first providing training in skills needed to solve multiplication and division problems (counting by 5s, 7s, etc.). After strategy training, children were then taught how to use their counting skills to learn sequences not taught. Results of their study strongly indicated that strategy training was effective and generalization for items similar to those trained was evident. Performance on those items most dissimilar to trained stimuli did not improve until training was begun specifically on those problems.

These studies suggest that the manipulation of antecedent conditions, such as providing a strategy for solving problems (self-instruction) or varying the environmental structure (teacher presence, chalkboard work), may significantly influence performance in math. Consistent with Cullinan, Lloyd, and Epstein's (1981) conclusion that the use of strategy training (teaching problem solving rather than specific skills) may be a useful method for increasing accuracy and generalization of mathematics skills, both self-instruction and problem solving appear promising for improving mathematics skills. Unfortunately, while some data on generalization are available, continued efforts to examine the parameters of generalizability of these procedures is needed.

As with reading studies, a significant number of mathematics studies have concentrated on the manipulation of consequences, particularly contingent reinforcement. Terry, Deck, Huelecki, and Santogrossi (1978) found that use of free time contingent on increased performance in the number of problems correct was highly effective in improving the mathematics performance of a fourth-grade learning disabled child. Similar procedures were found to be effective by Blankenship (1978), Johnson and McLaughlin (1982), Luiselli and Downing (1980), and McLaughlin (1981).

Spelling

Unlike reading and mathematics, procedures to improve spelling have incorporated multicomponent packages involving prompting, modeling, feedback, and rehearsal. In two single-case studies, Broden, Beasley, and Hall (1978) examined the effects of home tutoring on in-class spelling performance. Results of their studies showed that spelling scores significantly increased on Friday spelling tests when tutoring was employed.

Delquadri, Greenwood, Stretton, and Hall (1983) also investigated the effects of classwide peer tutoring on spelling of six low-achieving students in a regular third-grade classroom. Using a team game concept, students were awarded points for correct performance during tutoring. In addition, demonstration and feedback were employed when errors were made during tutoring sessions. Results of the study found significant reductions in the number of errors on Friday spelling tests when the peer tutoring and team game was in effect.

Gettinger (1985) examined the use of imitation to correct spelling errors as a means of increasing spelling performance. Using an alternating treatments design, Gettinger (1985) had students engage in one of four conditions. Following a no-instruction control, where students were told to study and practice, comparison was made between teacher- and student-directed study with or without cues regarding the incorrect portion of the word. In the teacher-directed condition, students were shown and told the correct spelling of the word. Cues consisted of having the part of the misspelled word circled. Results of the study found the highest performance on posttests occurred when student-directed study with cues was employed. All four conditions, however, were significantly better than the no-instruction control condition.

An interesting procedure used to improve spelling called "Add-A-Word" was developed by Pratt-Struthers, Struthers, and Williams (1983). The procedure involves having students copy a list of 10 words, cover each word and write it a second time, then check each word for correct spelling against the teacher's list. Misspelled words are repeated and remain on the list. If a word is spelled correctly on two consecutive days, the word is dropped from the list and replaced with a new word. Results of this study indicate that all nine of the learning disabled fifth- and 6th-grade students increased their percentage of correctly spelled words during a creative writing assignment using this procedure.

Although most procedures for academic remediation are based on positive procedures, as is typical in skill acquisition programs, use of a mild aversive technique has also been investigated for improving spelling performance. Foxx and Jones (1978) and Ollendick, Matson, Esveldt-Dawson, and Shapiro (1980) examined use of positive practice overcorrection in improving spelling. In the Foxx and Jones (1978) study, 29 students between fourth and eighth grade were assigned to one of four conditions. All students took a pretest on Wednesday and a graded spelling test on Friday. In the control condition, no other manipulation was employed. In the second condition students took only the Friday test followed by positive practice on Monday. The positive practice procedure involved having students write out for each misspelled word: (1) the correct spelling, (2) phonetic spelling, (3) part of speech, (4) dictionary definition, and (5) correct usage in five sentences. In the third condition, students took the pretest, did positive practice on those words, and then took the Friday test. Finally, in the fourth condition, students performed positive practice after both pretest and posttest conditions.

Results of their study found that all conditions in which positive practice was employed resulted in improved performance over the control condition. The condition in which positive practice was performed was, not surprisingly, the most effective in improving spelling performance. Similar findings were observed in the Ollendick et al. (1980) study in two single-case design experiments, where positive practice paired with a contingent reinforcement procedure also resulted in performance greater than traditional teaching procedures.

These studies suggest that spelling performance can be significantly improved using a variety of behavioral procedures. Included among these procedures is at least one, overcorrection, that may be construed as an aversive technique. Given the questionable acceptability of aversive procedures by teachers (Witt & Elliott, 1985), it is surprising that social validity data obtained from the students in these studies found that the students reported the procedures to be valuable. One possible explanation for this is that the technique used by Foxx and Jones (1978) and Ollendick et al. (1980) was not all that different from the "typical" instructional technique used by teachers.

Written Language

One final area where behavioral interventions have been successfully employed is in improving written language skills. Included among these skills are handwriting and composition, although some would also group spelling in this category (Kerr & Lambert, 1982).

Studies that have developed remediation programs for handwriting have concentrated primarily on manipulating antecedent conditions to the written response. Harris and Graham (1985) described an extensive self-management program using modeling, strategy training, practice, and feedback to improve the composition skills of two learning disabled 12-year-old boys. Results of the study found that use of selected words (action words, helper words, describing words) increased only after they were targeted by the training program. Other studies have also demonstrated that self-management procedures such as self-instruction and student-determined standards for performance can improve handwriting skills significantly.

Campbell and Willis (1979) investigated the use of a contingent reinforcement procedure for improving the creativity of the writing skills of 26 children in a regular fifth-grade classroom. Using well-defined responses described by Campbell and Willis (1979), based on Torrance's (1966) work in creativity, responses increased significantly over baseline when contingent reinforcement was applied. Unfortunately, no return to baseline was evident when the reinforcement procedure was eliminated, thus putting into question the controlling effects of the contingency.

CASE STUDY

This case study is of a boy who was part of a larger investigation of the interrelationship between different measures of reading performance.

SUBJECT

Bill, 10 years old, was enrolled in a diagnostic/tutorial program for learning disabled students within his home school. He was reading two grade levels below in overall reading as assessed on the Woodcock Reading Mastery test.

PROCEDURE

After placement into the appropriate reading level of the Laidlaw Reading Series, Bill was asked to read short passages (100–200 words) from the appropriate reader. Measures of oral reading rates (correct and incorrect words per minute) were collected. Bill then read another short passage (100 words) from the Barnell-Loft series and was asked 10 comprehension questions.

Following four days of baseline, Bill was given 30 minutes of instruction in comprehension skills using the Science Research Associates (SRA) reading laboratory series. Training consisted of teaching Bill to skim and keep the comprehension questions in mind while reading. After training, Bill was assessed with the Barnell-Loft materials and the reading passages from the Laidlaw series. Tokens exchangeable for desired back-up rewards were given if Bill's performance was at least two correct responses better than baseline.

After a reversal period, training was again instituted, but this time oral reading rates rather than comprehension were targeted. Contingent tokens were provided for increases of five words correct per minute above baseline and two errors less than the average of baseline.

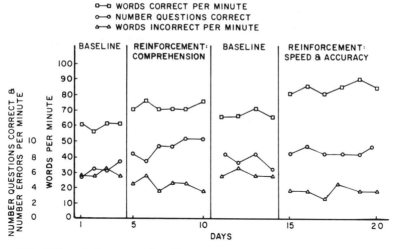

Figure 14.1. Collateral effects on oral reading rates and comprehension on a student in a reading program using contingent reinforcement.

RESULTS

Results of this program are shown in Figure 14.1. Applying a contingent reinforcement procedure for comprehension resulted in increases in comprehension levels and improvements in speed and accuracy. When reinforcement was shifted to oral reading, additional improvements in reading rates were noted. Comprehension, however, declined somewhat, although it remained above baseline levels.

This case study provides some indication of the potential interrelationship between and among measures of oral reading. It also demonstrates that contingent reinforcement can improve the academic behavior of a learning disabled youngster. While Bill's results are part of a larger study, his data are indicative of the overall effects found across nine students.

SUMMARY

Behavioral interventions clearly remain a useful and important means for increasing the academic skills of children and adolescents. Procedures based on the manipulation of antecedents, consequences, or a mixture of these have all been shown to affect reading, mathematics, spelling, and written language. Procedures designed to improve academic engaged time, such as peer tutoring, have also been found to have direct influences on academic behavior.

Despite the very positive outlook for the use of behavioral interventions to remediate academic skills, studies that can address the issues of generalization and maintenance of these procedures are needed. Few studies have provided adequate follow-up on students whose behavior was successfully improved using behavioral interventions. Moreover, the parameters of programming generalization are just now being explored. Continued efforts in this direction are required for behavioral interventions to be viewed as valuable tools in remediating academic difficulties.

Beyond issues of generalization and maintenance are those of acceptability of treatment. At present, studies examining the acceptability of treatment have concentrated on interventions for behavioral difficulties (e.g., Witt & Elliott, 1984). Questions may be raised about the acceptability of certain treatment programs for academic skills if the intervention is not consistent with the theoretical orientation of the teacher. Clearly, use of treatments that teachers do not consider acceptable are unlikely to succeed. In general, application of behavioral interventions for academic problems continues to be a fruitful area for research. It is clear that academic behavior can be viewed as any other operant response and can be changed as well. It is hoped that research will continue to determine the exact parameters of these interventions.

REFERENCES

Albion, F. M., & Salzberg, C. L. (1982). The effect of self-instructions on the rate of correct addition problems with mentally retarded children. *Education and Treatment of Children, 5,* 121-131.

Andersen, B. L., & Redd, W. H. (1980). Programming generalization through stimulus fading with children participating in a remedial reading program. *Education and Treatment of Children, 3,* 297-314.

Berliner, D. C. (1979). Tempus educare. In P. L. Peterson & H. J. Walberg, (Eds.), *Research on teaching* (pp. 120-135). Berkley, CA: McCuthchan.

Billingsley, F. F. (1977). The effects of self- and externally-imposed schedules of reinforcement on oral reading performance. *Journal of Learning Disabilities, 10,* 20-30.

Blankenship, C. S. (1978). Remediating systematic inversion errors in subtraction through the use of demonstration and feedback. *Learning Disability Quarterly, 1,* 12-22.

Broden, M., Beasley, A., & Hall, R. V. (1978). In-class spelling performance—Effects of home tutoring by a parent. *Behavior Modification, 2,* 511-530.

Bushell, D. (1978). An engineering approach to the elementary classroom: The behavior analysis follow-through project. In A. C. Catania & T. A. Brigham (Eds.), *Handbook of applied behavior analysis: Social and instructional processes* (pp. 525-561). New York: Wiley.

Campbell, J., & Willis, J. (1979). A behavioral program to teach creative writing in the regular classroom. *Education and Treatment of Children, 2,* 5–15.

Coleman, J., Campbell, E., Hobson, C., McPartland, J., Mood, A., Weinfield, F., & York, R. (1966) *Equality of educational opportunity.* Washington, DC: U.S. Office of Health, Education, and Welfare.

Cullinan, D., Lloyd, J., & Epstein, M. H. (1981). Strategy training: A structured approach to arithmetic instruction. *Exceptional Education Quarterly, 2,* 41–49.

Delquadri, J. C., Greenwood, C. R., Stretton, K., & Hall, R. V. (1983). The peer tutoring spelling game: A classroom procedure for increasing opportunity to respond and spelling performance. *Education and Treatment of Children, 6,* 225–239.

Denham, C., & Lieberman, (Eds.). (1980). *Time to learn.* Washington, D.C.: National Institute of Education.

Deno, S. L., Mirkin, P. K., & Chiang, B. (1982). Identifying valid measures of reading. *Exceptional Children, 49,* 36–45.

Dunkin, M., & Biddle, B. (1974). *The study of teaching.* New York: Holt, Rinehart & Winston.

Foxx, R. M., & Jones, J. R. (1978). A remediation program for increasing the spelling achievement of elementary and junior high school students. *Behavior Modification, 2,* 211–230.

Fredrick, W. C., Walberg, H. J., & Rasher, S. P. (1979). Time, teacher comments, and achievement in urban high schools. *Journal of Educational Research, 73,* 63–65.

Freeman, T. J., & McLaughlin, T. F. (1984). Effects of a taped-words treatment procedure on learning disabled students' sight-word oral reading. *Learning Disability Quarterly, 7,* 49–54.

Gallant, J., Sargeant, M., & Van Houten, R. (1980). Teacher-determined and self-determined access to science activities as a reinforcer for task completion in other curriculum areas. *Education and Treatment of Children, 3,* 101–111.

Gersten, R. (1985). Direct instruction with special education students: A review of evaluation research. *Journal of Special Education, 19,* 41–58.

Gettinger, M. (1984). Achievement as a function of time spent in learning and time needed for learning. *American Educational Research Journal, 21,* 617–628.

Gettinger, M. (1985). Effects of teacher-directed versus student-directed instruction and cues versus no cues for improving spelling performance. *Journal of Applied Behavior Analysis, 18,* 167–171.

Greenwood, C. R., Delquadri, J., & Hall, R. V. (1984). Opportunity to respond and student academic performance. In U. L. Heward, T. E. Heron, D. S. Hill, & J. Trap-Porter (Eds.), *Focus on behavior analysis in education* (pp. 58–88). Columbus, OH: Merrill.

Greenwood, C. R., Dinwiddie, G., Terry, B., Wade, L., Stanley, S. O., Thibadeau, S., & Delquadri, J. C. (1984). Teacher- versus peer-mediated instruction: An eco-behavioral analysis of achievement outcome. *Journal of Applied Behavior Analysis, 17,* 521–538.

Greenwood, C. R., Terry, B., Wade, L., Dinwiddie, G., Stanley, S. O., Thibadeau, S., & Delquadri, J. (1982). An ecobehavioral analysis of instruction: Contexts, student behavior, and achievement. Unpublished manuscript.

Hall, R. V., Delquadri, J., Greenwood, C. R., & Thurston, L. (1982). The importance of opportunity to respond in children's academic success. In E. B. Edgar, N. G. Haring, J. R. Jenkins, & C. G. Pious (Eds.), *Mentally handicapped children: Education and training* (pp. 107-140). Baltimore: University Park Press.

Hall, R. V., Lund, D. E., & Jackson, D. (1968). Effects of teacher attention on study behavior. *Journal of Applied Behavior Analysis, 1,* 1-12.

Harris, K. R., & Graham, S. (1985). Improving learning disabled student's composition skills: Self-control strategy training. *Learning Disability Quarterly, 8,* 27-36.

Hendrickson, J. M., & Gable, R. A. (1981). The use of modeling tactics to promote academic skill development of exceptional learners. *Journal of Special Education Technology, 4,* 20-29.

Hendrickson, J. M., Gable, R. A., & Stowitschek, C. E. (1985). Rate as a measure of academic success for mildly handicapped students. *Special Services in the Schools, 1,*(4), 1-15.

Hendrickson, J. M., Roberts, M., & Shores, R. E. (1978). Antecedent and contingent modeling to teach basic sight vocabulary to learning disabled children. *Journal of Learning Disabilities, 11,* 69-73.

Jenkins, J. R., Barksdale, A., & Clinton, L. (1978). Improving reading comprehension and oral reading: Generalization across behaviors, settings, and time. *Journal of Learning Disabilities, 11,* 5-12.

Johnston, M. B., Whitman, T. L., & Johnson, M. (1980). Teaching addition and subtraction to mentally retarded children: A self-instructional program. *Applied Research in Mental Retardation, 1,* 141-160.

Johnston, R. J., & McLaughlin, T. F. (1982). The effects of free time on assignment completion and accuracy in arithmetic: A case study. *Education and Treatment of Children, 5,* 33-40.

Kanfer, F. H. (1977). The many faces of self-control, or behavior modification changes its focus. In R. B. Stuart (Ed.), *Behavioral self-management: Strategies, techniques, and outcomes* (pp. 1-48). New York: Brunner/Mazel.

Kastelen, L., Nickel, M., & McLaughlin, T. F. (1984). A performance feedback system: Generalization of effects across tasks and time with eighth-grade English students. *Education and Treatment of Children, 7,* 141-155.

Kelley, M. L., & Stokes, T. F. (1982). Contingency contracting with disadvantaged youths: Improving classroom performance. *Journal of Applied Behavior Analysis, 15,* 447-454.

Kelley, M. L., & Stokes, T. F. (1984). Student-teacher contracting with goal setting for maintenance. *Behavior Modification, 8,* 223-244.

Kerr, M. M., & Lambert, D. L. (1982). Behavior modification of children's written language. In M. Hersen, R. Eisler, & R. M. Miller (Eds.), *Progress in behavior modification* (Vol. 13, pp. 79-108), New York: Academic.

Klein, R. D. (1979). Modifying academic performance in the grade school classroom. In M. Hersen, R. Eisler, & P. M. Miller (Eds.), *Progress in behavior modification* (Vol. 8, pp. 292-321), New York: Academic.

Kosiewicz, M., Hallahan, D.P., Lloyd, J., & Graves, A. W. (1982). Effects of self-instruction and self-correction procedures on handwriting performance. *Learning Disabilities Quarterly 5.* 71-79.

Lahey, B. B., McNees, M. D., & Brown, C. C. (1973). Modification of deficits in reading comprehension. *Journal of Applied Behavior Analysis, 6,* 475-480.

Leach, D. J., & Dolan, N. K. (1985). Helping teachers increase student academic engagement rates: The evaluation of a minimal feedback procedure. *Behavior Modification, 9,* 55-71.

Lloyd, J., Saltzman, N. J., & Kauffman, J. M. (1981). Predictable generalization in academic learning as a result of preskills and strategy training. *Learning Disabilities Quarterly, 4,* 203-216.

Lovitt, T. C., & Curtiss, K. A. (1969). Academic response rate as a function of teacher- and self-imposed contingencies. *Journal of Applied Behavior Analysis, 2,* 49-53.

Lovitt, T. C., & Hansen, C. C. (1976). The use of contingent skipping and drilling to improve oral reading and comprehension. *Journal of Learning Disabilities, 9,* 481-487.

Luiselli, J. K., & Downing, J. N. (1980). Improving a student's arithmetic performance using feedback and reinforcement procedures. *Education and Treatment of Children, 3,* 45-49.

McConnell, S. R., Strain, P. S., Kerr, M. M., Stagg, V., Lenkner, D. A., & Lambert, D. L. (1984). An empirical definition of elementary school adjustment: Selection of target behaviors for a comprehensive treatment program. *Behavior Modification, 8,* 451-473.

McKenzie, M. L., & Budd, K. S. (1981). A peer tutoring package to increase mathematics performance: Examination of generalized changes in classroom behavior. *Education and Treatment of Children, 4,* 1-15.

McLaughlin, T. F. (1981). The effects of a classroom token economy on math performance in an intermediate grade school class. *Education and Treatment of Children, 4,* 139-147.

O'Leary, S. G., & Dubey, D. R. (1979). Applications of self-control procedures by children: A review. *Journal of Applied Behavior Analysis, 12,* 449-465.

Ollendick, T. H., Matson, J. L., Esveldt-Dawson, K., & Shapiro, E. S. (1980). Increasing spelling achievement: An analysis of treatment procedures utilizing an alternating treatments design. *Journal of Applied Behavior Analysis, 13,* 645-654.

Pacquin, M. J. (1978). The effects of pupil self-graphing on academic performance. *Education and Treatment of Children, 1,* 5-16.

Paine, S. C., Carnine, D. W., White, W. A. T., & Walters, G. (1982). Effects of fading teacher presentation structure (covertization) on acquisition and maintenance of arithmetic problem-solving skills. *Education and Treatment of Children, 5,* 93-107.

Pratt-Struthers, J., Struthers, B., & Williams, R. L. (1983). The effects of the add-a-word spelling program on spelling accuracy during creative writing. *Education and Treatment of Children, 6,* 277–283.

Redd, W. H., Ullmann, R. K., Stelle, C., & Roesch, P. (1979). A classroom incentive program instituted by tutors after school. *Education and Treatment of Children, 2,* 169–176.

Roberts, R. N., & Dick, M. L. (1982). Self-control in the classroom: Theoretical issues and practical applications. In T. R. Kratochwill (Ed.), *Advances in School Psychology,* (Vol. II, pp. 275–314). Hillsdale, NJ: Erlbaum.

Rose, T. L. (1984a). Effects of previewing on the oral reading on mainstreamed behaviorally disordered students. *Behavior Disorders, 10,* 33–39.

Rose, T. L. (1984b). The effects of previewing on retarded learners' oral reading. *Education and Treatment of the Mentally Retarded, 19,* 49–52.

Rose, T. L., & Sherry, L. (1984). Relative effects of two previewing procedures on LD adolescents' oral reading performance. *Learning Disabilities Quarterly, 7,* 39–44.

Rosenshine, B. V. (1979). Content, time, and direct instruction. In P. L. Peterson & H. J. Walberg (Eds.), *Research on teaching* (pp. 28–56). Berkley, CA: McCutchan.

Rosenshine, B. V. (1981). Academic engaged time, content covered, and direct instruction. *Journal of Education, 3,* 38–66.

Rosenshine, B. V., & Berliner, D. C. (1978). Academic engaged time. *British Journal of Teacher Education, 4,* 3–16.

Rosenshine, B. V., & Furst, N. (1973). The use of direct observation to study teaching. In R. Travers (Ed.), *Second handbook of research on teaching.* Chicago: Rand McNally.

Shapiro, E. S. (in press). Behavior modification: Self-control and cognitive procedures. In R. P. Barrett (Ed.), *Treatment of severe behavior disorders: Contemporary approaches with the mentally retarded.* New York: Plenum.

Shapiro, E. S., Browder, D. M., & D'Huyvetters, K. K. (1984). Increasing academic productivity of severely multihandicapped children with self-management: Idiosyncratic effects. *Analysis and Intervention in Developmental Disabilities, 4,* 171–188.

Staats, A. W., & Butterfield, W. H. (1965). Treatment of nonreading in a culturally deprived juvenile delinquent: An application of reinforcement principles. *Child Development, 36,* 925–942.

Staats, A. W., Finley, J. R., Minke, K. A., & Wolf, M. M. (1964). Reinforcement variables in the control of unit reading responses. *Journal of the Experimental Analysis of Behavior, 7,* 139–149.

Staats, A. W., Minke, K. A., Finley, J. R., Wolf, M. M., & Brooks, L. O. A. (1964). Reinforcer system and experimental procedure for the laboratory study of reading acquisition. *Child Development, 35,* 209–231.

Stallings, J. (1975). Implementation and child effects of teaching practices in follow through classrooms. *Monographs of the Society for Research in Child Development, 40,* No. 7–8 (Serial No. 163).

Stanley, S. O., & Greenwood, C. R. (1981). *CISSAR: Code for instructional structure and student academic response: Observer's manual.* Kansas City, KS: Juniper Garden Children's Project, Bureau of Child Research, University of Kansas, Lawrence.

Stanley, S. O., & Greenwood, C. R. (1983). How much "opportunity to respond" does the minority disadvantaged student receive in school? *Exceptional Children, 49,* 370–373.

Stephens, J. (1967). *The process of schooling.* New York: Holt, Rinehart & Winston.

Stevenson, H. C. & Fantuzzo, J. W. (1984). Application of the "generalization map" to a self-control intervention with school-aged children. *Journal of Applied Behavior Analysis, 17,* 203–212.

Stowitschek, C. E., Hecimovic, A., Stowitschek, J. J., & Shores, R. E. (1982). Behaviorally disordered adolescents as peer tutors: Immediate and generative effects on instructional performance and spelling achievement. *Behavior Disorders, 7,* 136–147.

Terry, M. N., Deck, D., Huelecki, M. B., & Santogrossi, D. A. (1978). Increasing arithmetic output of a fourth-grade student. *Education and Treatment of Children, 1,* 25–29.

Thurlow, M. L., Ysseldyke, J. E., Graden, J., & Algozzine, B. (1984). Opportunity to learn for LD students receiving different levels of special education services. *Learning Disabilities Quarterly, 7,* 55–67.

Torrance, E. P. (1966). *Torrance test of creative thinking.* New York: Personnel.

Trice, A. D., Parker, F. C., & Furrow, F. (1981). Written conversations with feedback and contingent free time to increase reading and writing in a non-reading adolescent. *Education and Treatment of Children, 4,* 35–41.

Trovato, J., & Bucher, B. (1980). Peer tutoring with or without home-based reinforcement for reading remediation. *Journal of Applied Behavior Analysis, 13,* 129–141.

Van Houten, R., Hill, S., & Parsons, M. (1975). An analysis of a performance feedback system: The effects of timing and feedback, public posting, and praise upon academic performance and peer interaction. *Journal of Applied Behavior Analysis, 8,* 449–457.

Van Houten, R., & Lai Fatt, D. (1981). The effects of public posting on high school biology test performance. *Education and Treatment of Children, 4,* 217–226.

Van Houten, R., & Thompson, C. (1976). The effects of explicit timing on math performance. *Journal of Applied Behavior Analysis, 9,* 227–230.

Whitman, T., & Johnston, M. B. (1983). Teaching addition and subtraction with regrouping to educatable mentally retarded children: A group self-instructional training program. *Behavior Therapy, 14,* 127–143.

Whorton, D., Sasso, G., Elliott, M., Hughes, V., Critchlow, W., Terry, B., Stanley, S. O., Greenwood, C. R., & Delquadri, J. (in press). Teaching formats that maximize opportunity to learn: Parent and peer tutoring programs. *Education and Treatment of Children.*

Witt, J. C., & Elliott, S. N. (1985). Acceptability of classroom intervention strategies.

In T. R. Kratochwill (Ed.), *Advances in School Psychology* (Vol. IV, pp. 251–288). Hillsdale, NJ: Erlbaum.

Young, C., Hecimovic, A., & Salzberg, C. L. (1983). Tutor-tutee behavior of disadvantaged kindergarten children during peer tutoring. *Education and Treatment of Children, 6,* 123–135.

Ysseldyke, J. E., Thurlow, M. L., Mecklenburg, C., Graden, J., & Algozzine, B. (1984). Changes in academic engaged time as a function of assessment and special education intervention. *Special Services in the Schools, 1*(2), 31–44.

CHAPTER 15

Child Abuse

DAVID A. WOLFE

Child abuse has been a societal problem for many centuries. Past cultures openly or subtly condoned the physical abuse of children on the basis of moral, religious, and disciplinarian importance until the close of the nineteenth century (Radbill, 1968), when changes in attitudes led to major reforms in public treatment of children. However, the private maltreatment of children by family members remained largely unscrutinized by governmental policies until clinical reports and large-scale studies documented the extent and severity of this problem in the 1960s (Kempe, Silverman, Steele, Droegemueller, & Silver, 1962; Gill, 1970). In response to the need for services for abused children, the National Center for Child Abuse and Neglect was created under the Federal Child Abuse Prevention and Treatment Act in 1974, resulting in over $50 million being spent on research, demonstration, and evaluation activities over a six-year period (Besharov, 1982).

Perhaps as a reflection of these policy changes and the recent surge of concern about child abuse, the number of documented reports has risen dramatically (by 123%) since 1976. In 1982 the American Humane Association (1984) determined that almost 1 million children had been victims of parental abuse or neglect in the United States that year, leading to a national incidence rate of 20.08 per 1000 in the child population. Despite the increased concern about child abuse and the growing number of reports, however, in all likelihood the extent of the problem has not changed significantly in North American culture during the past generation (Russell & Trainor, 1984). Rather, increased attention to the issues of family violence by researchers and practitioners has resulted in dramatic changes in our understanding and approach to child abuse.

Preparation of this chapter was supported in part by Medical Research Council Grant MA-7807. The author gratefully acknowledges the assistance of Catherine Koverola, Betty Edwards, Ian Manion, and Darlene Elliot-Faust in developing the clinical procedures reported herein.

DESCRIPTION OF THE PROBLEM

The definition of acts that constitute "child abuse" continues to perplex lawmakers, researchers, and community residents. Many state laws were written primarily for the protection of the child rather than the prosecution or punishment of the perpetrator, which allows for more liberal interpretation than criminal codes. However, lack of uniformity and clarification in the statutes presents major problems for those involved in enforcement and rehabilitation. Many parents, for example, complain that they have been placed on the child abuse registry (operated by most states to record and monitor known child abusers) for conduct that was quite acceptable and common during their own childhood or in a different part of the country. Without the benefit of public awareness or information regarding community standards of parental conduct, such parents are surprised when they are accused of "abusing" their child, because their action was intended to discipline or "teach." Yet, these actions (i.e., resulting in injuries sustained by the child during the course of a disciplinary encounter) are most commonly documented as physical child abuse (Herrenkohl, Herrenkohl, & Egolf, 1983). The parent's "intent" or "malice" can seldom be ascertained; therefore, evidence of avoidable physical injury to the child remains a critical factor in defining an act as abusive.

The issues of detection and protection notwithstanding, a general definition of child abuse includes the presence of nonaccidental injuries as a result of acts of commission (physical assault) or omission (failure to protect) by caretakers (Giovannoni & Becerra, 1979; National Institute of Mental Health, 1977; Smith, 1984). For purposes of psychological assessment and treatment, this definition can be expanded to include a significant number of "at-risk" parenting practices that warrant professional attention. What is not immediately apparent from this definition, however, is the fact that the vast majority of child abuse cases involve additional factors that are weighed in determining whether or not to establish a given case as "abuse" as opposed to "overdiscipline" (Russell & Trainor, 1984). Somewhat surprisingly, abusive parents and abused children rarely fit a profile that easily matches the popular misconception of child abuse: that is, a severely disturbed, out-of-control parent who unleashes an unbridled attack on a defenseless child. In contrast, mounting research evidence seems to indicate that the majority of abusive parents do not have behavioral or psychological problems of such severity that they can be readily detected or distinguished from their nonabusive counterparts (Wolfe, 1985). As a result, the criteria that child protective service workers use to assess risk have been identified as a constellation of factors, including the age and functioning of the child, the cooperation and functioning of the primary caretaker, the intent of the perpetrator, and the severity of the present and/or past incidents (Meddin, 1985). Subsequent to the determination of risk, behavioral scientists and practitioners must be concerned with issues of parental competence and child development that determine the direction of services for this population.

As behavioral scientists have become more involved in research and treatment with abusive families over the past decade, a notable shift in paradigm has occurred. The individually focused "psychiatric model" of child abuse, which emphasizes adult psychopathology and intrapsychic explanations for extreme parental behavior, failed to result in meaningful distinctions between abusive and nonabusive parents (see Wolfe, 1985, for review). In parallel, the "social interactional model" (see Burgess, 1978; Parke & Collmer, 1975), which stresses relationships among individual, family, and social factors, found supporters among both applied and research professionals, leading to a rapid increase in empirical studies. This interactive model promoted an understanding of child abusive behavior in relation to eliciting and contextual stimuli that affect parental responses to the child and the parent's prior experiences and abilities. The major distinction between the two approaches to conceptualizing child abuse is the amount of significance that each places on the parent as the "cause" of abuse (Wolfe, 1985). This distinction emerges very clearly in the types of questions being addressed and the intervention approaches chosen by behavioral researchers. For example, the social interactional, or behavioral, model of child abuse places heavy emphasis on childrearing abilities of the parent, behavioral characteristics of the child that may contribute to stress and conflict, and numerous interrelated events (such as parental history, child development, and the nature of the aggressive act) that may culminate in an abusive episode (Belsky, 1980; Burgess, 1978). Accordingly, proponents of this conceptual model focus primarily on modifying maladaptive patterns of family interaction within the context of individual, family, and community circumstances.

A major implication of this model is that abusive behavior is seldom a function of any particular event or attribute (Wolfe, in press). In contrast, such behavior is viewed as the product of numerous, yet not necessarily unusual, factors that can build on each other in the absence of protective factors or buffers (Cicchetti & Rizley, 1981). Although determining the relative importance of these multiple factors can be very challenging with each family, noteworthy progress has been made toward understanding the functional relationship between adult aggression and situational factors (see Berkowitz, 1983; Patterson, 1982; Rule & Nesdale, 1976). Several of these findings are discussed below as they relate to clinical assessment and intervention with child abusive families.

The Abusive Parent

Major adult factors that have been associated with child abuse include the parent's prior childhood experiences and history, available social supports, characterological attributes and behaviors, and knowledge and perceptions of children. Stated briefly, studies addressing these concerns have supported the contention that the abusive parent often is the product of a multiproblem family. Histories of abusers' early childhood events are marked by traumatic or atypical experiences that may adversely affect interpersonal adjustment, such as family violence (e.g., Lewis, Pincus, & Glaser, 1979; Monane, Leichter, & Lewis, 1984) and extreme disadvantage (Gil, 1970). As an adult, the parent is often incapable of managing the degree of stress present and tends to avoid social contacts that may be perceived as additional sources of stress (Garbarino, 1976; Salzinger, Kaplan, & Artemyoff, 1983). Such limited social supports, furthermore, may serve to perpetuate inappropriate childrearing values and methods. Inadequate or inappropriate exposure to positive parental models, coupled with limited intellectual and problem-solving skills, serve to make childrearing a very difficult task.

On the other hand, despite a great deal of interest and precedent to describe child abusive behavior as the result of significant psychopathology (see Spinetta & Rigler, 1972), current evidence refutes this conclusion. When abusers have been compared to matched control subjects, a majority of studies has failed to detect symptoms of such frequency or magnitude as to be suggestive of psychiatric disorder (Wolfe, 1985). Instead of symptoms of major psychopathology, abusive parents have been found to report a number of physical and emotional symptoms indicative of health and coping problems (Conger, Burgess, and Barrett, 1979; Lahey, Conger, Atkeson, & Treiber, 1984; Mash, Johnston, & Kovitz, 1983). One feasible explanation for these findings postulates that the parent's psychological functioning (i.e., problem-solving, judgment, and self-control) is diminished as a result of chronic, unmanageable stressful events in their lives (Wolfe, 1985). Similarly, the notion of a preexisting deficit in knowledge of child development among abusive parents requires some clarification in the face of recent findings (e.g., Kravitz & Driscoll, 1983). Parental self-report data on general developmental norms and expectations of children have seldom differentiated abusive from nonabusive parents, leading to the suggestion that greater focus should be placed on observations or discussions of realistic child situations, as opposed to less salient questionnaires of child development and expectations (Wolfe, 1985).

In order to account for the high-intensity nature of abusive acts, behavioral researchers have considered two very important components of the abusive response that are not readily apparent when assessing more global adult attributes. These are the everyday family interactions and expressions of interest and concern for the child, and the parent's emotional and cognitive sensitivity to aversive events, which is suspected of mediating aggressive behavior (Vasta, 1982). Regarding family interactions, the considerable research investigating the style, frequency, and effectiveness of parent-child interactional behaviors in abusive families supports the overall conclusion that abusers are *less pos-*

itive but not necessarily more negative toward their children than nonabusers (e.g., Burgess & Conger, 1978; Lorber, Felton, & Reid, 1984; Reid, Taplin, & Lorber, 1981). When observing abusive families in the natural environment, researchers have reported that the parents interact with their children at a very low rate, seldom exhibiting positive or affectionate behaviors. When they do choose to interact with their child, abusers are more likely than nonabusers to rely on aversive control, which produces an imbalance in the proportion of negative to positive behavior (Wolfe, 1985).

Parental sensitivity to aversive events has also been demonstrated in recent laboratory and field investigations. The data support the hypothesis that abusive parents may develop an idiosyncratic arousal pattern that may be elicited by child and/or environmental stimuli (Frodi & Lamb, 1980; Wolfe, Fairbank, Kelly, & Bradlyn, 1983). Whereas aggressive behavior toward the child may be reinforced by its consequences (e.g., reduction in child aversiveness), a dual component learning-based model accounts for the high-intensity nature of abusive acts by incorporating the principles of respondent as well as operant conditioning (Vasta, 1982). In view of the mounting support for the understanding of aggressive behavior on the basis of learning principles (see Berkowitz, 1983; Averill, 1983; Patterson, 1982; Rule & Nesdale, 1976), child abusive behavior may be considered a special case of aggression that can be approached from the vantage point of established experimental and correlational research methods (Friedman, Sandler, Hernandez, & Wolfe, 1981). Conditioned arousal to the child's characteristics (such as negative bids for attention or facial expressions) coupled with acceptance of corporal punishment increases the propensity of a high-intensity aggressive response (Berkowitz, 1983; Vasta, 1982).

The Abused Child

Over the past decade research has documented many of the earlier assumptions of the relationship between child abuse and behavioral and emotional problems seen during childhood and adolescence (Cicchetti & Rizley, 1981; Friedrich & Boriskin, 1976; Frodi, 1981). Controlled studies of infant characteristics, parent-child interactions, and parent and teacher reports of abused children have favored the conclusion that these children evidence more developmental delays and behavior problems than their nonabused counterparts, yet no distinctive or global profile of the abused child has emerged (Elmer, 1977; Frodi, 1981; Wolfe & Mosk, 1983; Wolfe, in press).

From a developmental perspective, abused toddlers and preschool children emerge as being more difficult to manage and show more signs of delay than other nonclinic samples of children (Barahal, Waterman, & Martin, 1981; Friedrich, Einbender, & Lueke, 1983; Frodi & Smetana, 1984; George & Main, 1979; Hoffman-Plotkin & Twentyman, 1984). Whereas abused school-aged children are likely to be described by parents and teachers as being more difficult to manage and less socially mature than their nonabused counterparts (e.g., Herrenkohl, Herrenkohl, Toedter, & Yanushefski, 1984; Salzinger, Kaplan, Pelcovitz, Samit, & Kreiger, 1984), observational research with such families has produced equivocal findings regarding the extent and type of child behavior problems shown at home (Wolfe, 1985). The literature shows strong support for the position that during adolescence abused children are at increased risk of becoming involved in later delinquent and antisocial acts and are more likely to perform poorly in school (Lewis et al., 1979; McCord, 1983; Tarter, Hegedus, Winsten, & Alterman, 1984). However, the effects of powerful family and social factors on the child's development prohibit drawing any firm conclusions as to the impact of physical abuse per se. Disturbances in the abused child's social and behavioral development may be partially a function of the negative events that frequently accompany family discord and disadvantage in abusive families.

BEHAVIORAL ASSESSMENT

Unfortunately, a well-defined, standardized assessment and intervention strategy for child abuse does not currently exist. Abusive families are a very heterogeneous population that requires an ongoing, investigative approach in order to produce a functional understanding of the problem behavior. To arrive at a flexible and comprehensive approach to this problem will undoubtedly require innovative advances in conceptual and procedural thinking. The advantage of behavioral assessment and treatment in addressing the gap between available and ideal approaches to abuse lies in its emphasis on a functional analytic approach to each family unit. Detailed behavioral assessment is appropriate for determining the variability of parental behavior both within and between abusive families (Smith & Rachman, 1984). The use of continuous baseline recordings, direct as well as indirect (e.g., self-report) assessment methods, single-subject experimental designs, and well-defined target behaviors allows formulation of treatment goals for each family that take into account its unique resources and liabilities (Koverola, Manion, & Wolfe, 1985).

In developing an assessment strategy it is necessary to prepare for the extremely wide range of behavior that may be shown by abused children. It is not unusual to discover during a detailed family assessment that the abused child does not behave in a manner commensurate with the level of coercion or dysfunction present in the family. The child may, for example, exhibit very self-defeating behavior with no immediately obvious function, or may display no overt signs of maladjustment or discontentment. Similarly, some abused children are described by foster parents or teachers as seeming to "prefer" to be hit or mistreated by adults and are less responsive to positive methods.

Speculating on these reports, Green (1983) postulates that some abused children may suffer from a form of "posttraumatic stress disorder" in which their behavior may at times be erratic and maladaptive. Wahler and Dumas (1985) further propose that children in highly conflictual families may have adapted to the punitive atmosphere such that their behavior is more likely to produce a predictable outcome of anger and punishment. When abuse is discovered, the child has difficulty adapting to *nonabusive* treatment, since he or she has seldom experienced consistent, positive responses from caregivers. This cautionary preface to the following discussion of assessment methods is a reminder that the behavior of members of abusive families may be a function of historical or situational events that are often not readily apparent.

The assessment of abusive families is a multistage process that often begins with global, overriding concerns (such as the safety of the child and the major strengths and problem areas within the family) and narrows toward a more targeted focus (such as anger-control and child behavior problems). The following overview is intended to provide a basic, condensed framework for approaching the assessment and treatment of abusive families. The reader is encouraged to consult additional resources to establish a thorough familiarity with behavioral assessment of child abuse (e.g., Burgess, 1978; Friedman et al., 1981; Wolfe, in press).

Parental Assessment

Behavioral assessment of the abusive parent involves a range of procedures, including a semistructured interview, self-report questionnaires, and direct observations of parent-child interactions. Essentially, the interviewer must begin by screening for high-risk circumstances that elicit parental anger and possible physical aggression toward the child without creating an inquisitional, defensive atmosphere. It is useful to begin with a discussion of current child behavior and family issues that the parent perceives as problematic, followed by a standard psychological interview focusing on current and historical factors of significance (see Altemeier, O'Connor, Vietze, Sandler, & Sherrod, 1984; Wolfe, Kaufman, Aragona, & Sandler, 1981, for examples).

Although many "psychological risk factors," such as parental expectations, abilities, and needs, may be addressed by interview techniques, some very useful psychometric instruments have also been developed recently for assessing problems associated with the parental role. In particular, the Parenting Stress Index (PSI: Abidin, 1983) is a well-validated instrument that incorporates a wide range of variables linked to problems in the parent-child relationship. For the purpose of eliciting information regarding parental attitudes, knowledge, and expectations of children, perceptions of his or her own child, and areas of adult stress, the PSI provides a useful format for comparing a parent's sources of stress to normative data from clinical and nonclinical parental populations. Additionally, the Child Abuse Potential Inventory (Milner, 1980) has been specifically developed to screen abusive parents for major emotional and interpersonal problems, although its reliance on personality traits and psychopathology limit its degree of behavioral specificity (Wolfe, in press).

Once the parent has completed the interview and/or psychometric instruments to screen for major disturbances, a more detailed assessment of the parent's responses to childrearing demands may be initiated. A comprehensive assessment of the parent's daily and typical behavior with his or her child will enable a more complete understanding of the situationally defined anger and aggression that may precede abusive episodes. This requires an analysis of arousal patterns, fluctuations in mood and affect, and child management skills that occur during everyday interactions with the child.

The parent's perceived and observed sensitivity to annoyances in his or her environment is an important factor believed to mediate anger and aggression (Berkowitz, 1983). Because emotional reactivity is very difficult to observe under realistic conditions, however, this assessment issue has received little attention in the child abuse literature. In accordance with behavioral assessment procedures, parental emotional sensitivity can be determined from a multivariate approach that involves interview, self-monitoring, analogue, and physiological recordings of arousal during real or simulated episodes of child misbehavior. For example, parental feelings of anger, tension, and "loss of control" can often be elicited by providing the parent with distinctive cues or examples (see Koverola, Elliott-Faust, & Wolfe, 1984). The parent can then be instructed to self-monitor selected target behaviors in the natural environment or during structured interactions with his or her child in the clinic where the therapist can provide helpful self-control training and rehearsal. If the child is in the home with the parent, an anger diary (Wolfe, Kaufman, Aragona, & Sandler, 1981) can be completed daily to provide details of each incident in which the child elicits feelings of anger, frustration, or tension. Alternatively, physiological- and/or self-recordings of emotional reactivity to live or videotaped aversive child behavior can be obtained in the lab or clinic, although such recordings may be more applicable for research than for clinical purposes (Frodi & Lamb, 1980; Wolfe et al., 1983). Because questionnaires for assessing parental anger and arousal are limited, the above methods are valuable in providing the parent with situational cues that are specific enough to elicit recall or response. In this manner a functional relationship between parental aggression and specific aspects of child behavior can be established with a stronger focus on family assistance than on parental pathology.

Behavioral assessment of abusive families also includes a thorough analysis of the parent's current methods of controlling and teaching his or her child. Despite the limitations of direct observation, the consensus among child abuse researchers supports the validity and feasibility of this method for determining the amount of aversive and prosocial behavior exchanged in the home (Wolfe, 1985). Because abusive or highly aversive interactions cannot be observed, researchers have relied on the observation of other, more typical behaviors that are presumed to be related to aggression, such as threats, grabbing, and yelling (Burgess, 1978; Friedman et al., 1981). Parents are often asked to interact with their child in a fashion that elicits common childrearing problems, such as teaching a new task or completing a request, which allows for representative sampling of interactions over a reduced time period. Researchers have also expressed interest in the definition and recording of "qualitative" interactions, such as parental affect, responsivity, and social communication (Dowdney, Mrazek, Quinton, & Rutter, 1984). Standard observational systems developed for conduct-problem children often require considerable modification in order to be applicable to this population, and a highly suitable approach has not yet emerged.

Child Assessment

The task of assessing all areas of child development can become unmanageable, and therefore a problem-solving approach that focuses on developmental delays and behavior problems has been recommended (Friedman et al., 1981; Wolfe, in press). This approach centers around two major concerns: child features that stand out as problematic within the context of the child's family, and aspects of the child's development and adaptive behavior that may require assistance. Several sources of information about these concerns are available, including parental report, observations, and child self-report.

Child behavior problems that may exacerbate the risk of child abuse deserve careful consideration and multichannel assessment. Despite the possible bias of parental perceptions (e.g., Mash, Johnston, & Kovitz, 1983), two instruments stand out as valuable for obtaining a standardized measure of child behavior as reported by the child's primary caregiver. The Achenbach Child Behavior Checklist and Profile (Achenback & Edelbrock, 1982) and the Eyberg Child Behavior Inventory (Eyberg & Ross, 1978) provide comprehensive information on the parent's ratings of a child's problem behaviors, which may be a valuable starting point for assessment and intervention planning. These instruments may also be administered to other adults who know the child well (e.g., teachers, foster parents) to provide additional information regarding child behavior vis-à-vis situational variables. Subsequently, observations of child behavior may be conducted in the clinic or home to determine more precisely the nature of the problems that have been identified. Such observations serve a dual function: They enable the therapist to view the "typical" behavior of the child during interactions with one or both parents, and they also allow for an assessment of the child's range of appropriate and inappropriate behavior. For example, the therapist can focus on the child's "avoidant'' behaviors, such as dodging or flinching, which suggest that the child is fearful of the parent; also, the observer can document the manner in which the child approaches the parent and attempts to seek attention, since grabbing, pinching, tugging, and so on are common antecedents to physical punishment and abuse. Direct observations of child behavior can also be expanded to include peer interactions (George & Main, 1979), compliance tasks (Wolfe, Sandler, & Kaufman, 1981), and other highly salient child responses that may be linked to abuse in a particular family (e.g., self-injurious and self-stimulatory behavior; Green, 1978).

The child's adaptive behavior, such as language, self-care, and cognitive development, also deserves careful assessment planning, since these are common problems associated with abuse that may become major handicaps if left unattended (Frodi, 1981). Criterion-referenced instruments that survey the child's developmental progress and adaptive functioning, such as the Vineland Adaptive Behavior Scales–Revised (Sparrow, Balla, & Cicchetti, 1984), facilitate subsequent behavioral observations and remediation planning. In some cases of abuse, the parent may expect the child to perform at a level that is incongruent with the child's current abilities, and therefore a cross-check between parental perceptions and child performance is advisable. In association with developmental assessment, an individual interview with the preschool- or school-aged child can also assist in understanding the child's abilities, perceptions, and current fears and anxieties.

In sum, the assessment of low-frequency, private behaviors occurring between family members is a challenge that, at present, must be met by a comprehensive and individually tailored strategy. It has been argued herein that behavioral assessment procedures can be expanded and integrated with other approaches to yield complementary information that is valuable for intervention. Thus, a wide variety of methods, including parental report of problem situations and emotional reactivity, standardized tests, interviews, and direct observations, should be considered at the initiation of services to abusive families.

BEHAVIORAL INTERVENTION FOR CHILD ABUSE

In developing a practical and effective intervention strategy with abusive parents, behavioral researchers have focused primarily on aspects of the parents' childrearing and problem-solving abilities. Although child abuse is clearly the result of multiple factors, characteristics that may be amenable to treatment include knowledge of child development, child management skills, appropriate adult models and social supports, and stress management (Burgess, 1978; Friedman et al., 1981; Kelly, 1983; Wolfe, Kaufman, Aragona, & Sandler, 1981). There is little consensus on which characteristics should receive the highest priority (Helfer, 1982); therefore, it is advantageous to consider all methods that strengthen parental coping abilities.

The goals and objectives of a behavioral approach to treating abusive families are formulated on the theoretical assumption that child abuse is a learned behavior, accompanied by emotional and physical manifestations, that may be prevented if appropriate learning opportunities are available. Accordingly, treatment goals may be broadly stated as incorporating two critical concerns (Conger & Lahey, 1982): (1) helping to create the personal and social controls that inhibit violence towards family members, and (2) helping to cultivate social relationships and decrease environmental stress that interferes with the parental role. In view of these concerns, a range of behavioral procedures for assisting this population has evolved in recent years, including instruction and rehearsal in childrearing methods, cognitive restructuring and anger control, and adjunctive skills training to promote adult and child competence in dealing with their environment. A discussion of these approaches will be followed by a critique of the present state of knowledge.

Instruction and Rehearsal in Positive Child Management Techniques

Both instructional and direct training components have been employed with abusive parents, in accordance with behavioral parent training methods developed by Forehand and McMahon (1981), Patterson, Reid, Jones, and Conger (1975), Wahler (1976), and others. Parent-child interactions are typically recorded in the clinic or home, and target behaviors such as criticisms, threats, and physical punishment are selected for each family (Sandler, VanDercar, & Milhoan, 1978; Wolfe, Sandler, & Kaufman, 1981). The purpose of such training is straightforward: to provide parents with opportunities to observe how others handle child behavior problems in a noncoercive fashion, and to give them guided assistance in resolving the problems they experience with their child (Isaacs, 1982). Principles of positive and negative reinforcement, punishment, and extinction are taught to parents through concrete examples, and an active problem-solving approach is employed to encourage the parents to modify their methods of dealing with child behavior. Behavioral rehearsal with their own child, designed to facilitate performance of desired skills and generalization to new problems and situations, is a strong component of this training method. Such rehearsal may be followed by videotaped feedback to provide the parent with an interesting form of self-evaluation and correction (Wolfe & Manion, 1984).

The specific child management techniques emphasized in such training are aimed at appropriate ways to increase child compliance, to reduce child behavior problems, to improve parental attention and stimulation with the child, and to employ effective, nonviolent forms of punishment when necessary. These techniques are very similar to those developed for nonabusive parents;

however, they are delivered in a simplified format that parents may find easier to understand (and thus more acceptable). For example, abusive parents often have poor reading comprehension and limited tolerance for didactic presentations that resemble previous classroom struggles; therefore, their ability to understand principles of behavior change is often limited. This necessitates a training approach that guides them through the most significant aspects of child management at the expense of more in-depth knowledge and, possibly, generalization to new situations. With these restrictions and limitations in mind, it can be stated that child management training typically includes, at a minimum, instruction, modeling, rehearsal, and feedback in time-out procedure; reducing parental attention to inappropriate child behaviors; and teaching parents to state commands in a clear, firm voice and express positive responses to the child by using a variety of physical, verbal, and tangible reinforcers.

Anger- and Self-Control Training

In conjunction with parent training and related services, many abusive parents require assistance in learning new strategies to handle stressful events. For this reason anger management techniques have been applied with abusive populations to help them prepare for stressful encounters, apply more effective coping and resolution strategies, and deal with the possible consequences that follow from success or failure of the attempt (Denicola & Sandler, 1980; Nomellini & Katz, 1983). Although the approach to anger management reported in the literature is based largely on stress inoculation research (see Novaco, 1978), the utility of this method with abusive parents remains unclear at present. This is due perhaps to the difficulty of accurately determining whether the target behaviors (i.e., anger and aggression) have decreased following intervention since their measurement depends largely on parental report. Alternatively, this problem has been approached by using a modified *in vivo* desensitization procedure that begins by teaching the parent the use of relaxation and self-monitoring of anger and arousal, followed by direct interactions with the child during stressful situations such as noncompliance and conflict (Koverola et al., 1984). The therapist guides the parent in using the relaxation exercises and coping statements via a "bug-in-the-ear" transmitter device, and the parent indicates to the therapist the degree of stress and coping he or she is experiencing throughout the interaction. Unfortunately, the effectiveness of this latter method with abusive parents also remains unclear due to the lack of research on this issue. Nevertheless, self-monitoring, videotaped feedback, and direct intervention for stress and arousal during child interactions offer promising directions for this population.

Adjunctive Skills Training

The multifaceted nature of abuse has led to the emergence of a number of adjunctive treatment approaches to meet the demand for comprehensive services to this population. Clearly, the majority of abusive parents suffer not only from deficits in child management or self-control; many have also experienced failure or problems in reaching educational, occupational, or personal goals over a prolonged period. Child abuse, according to this reasoning, may be a possible outcome of parental inadequacy in dealing with very basic responsibilities, leading to frustration and emotional responding. To address these global needs, researchers have applied a wide range of behavioral counseling and training methods aimed at remediating the contributing causes of child abuse. Noteworthy among these adjunctive treatments are adaptations of programs developed with other clinical populations for training adults to develop more appropriate social interactions (Kelly, 1983), home safety (Tertinger, Greene, & Lutzker, 1984), marital adjustment (Campbell, O'Brien, Bickett, & Lutzker, 1983), social supports in the community (Garbarino & Stocking, 1980), and job skills and money management (Lutzker, Wesch, & Rice, 1984). These methods are considered "adjunctive" only in the sense that the primary treatment focus (i.e., the quality of the parent-child relationship) is often affected by related family and personal situations that require assistance. At present, such treatments have received less systematic evaluation than the previously mentioned training approaches, although the ongoing research by Lutzker and his colleagues (Project 12-Ways) offers an exemplary, comprehensive evaluation of the "ecobehavioral" approach to child abuse and neglect that is receiving considerable documentation (Lutzker et al., 1984).

Therapists using behavioral interventions with abusive families have also experimented with the application of adjunctive therapies to increase parental motivation and involvement in changing their behavior. Because abusive parents seldom seek assistance voluntarily, the therapist faces a difficult task in applying standard training techniques with this refractive population (Conger & Lahey, 1982). To increase parental compliance with the demands of learning unfamiliar methods of child management, behavioral contracting between parents, therapists, and social workers has been recommended (Doctor & Singer, 1978; Wolfe, Kaufman, Aragona, & Sandler, 1981). The use of contracts delineating treatment objectives (e.g., reduction in physical discipline) over a specified time period is aimed at reducing the parent's confusion and resentment of court and agency supervision. Because parents have input into the delineation of goals, time frame, and expectations, the contract approach appears to offer a more suitable form of incentive than the current practice of open-ended, nonspecific court requirements (e.g., "seek assistance in child-rearing"). Although some parents may still perceive the contract as coercive, their right to have their "penalty and retribution" clearly defined in behavioral terms is attractive to many parents, judges, social workers, and therapists (Wolfe, Kaufman, Aragona, & Sandler, 1981). In addition, behavioral practitioners have framed the treatment process in positive, attainable goals that may be more attractive to the parent. This is accompanied on occasion by tangible rewards, such as free passes to family activities (Wolfe & Sandler, 1981), or intangible consequences, such as termination of supervision or reduction in specific child problems (Wolfe, St. Lawrence, Graves, Brehony, Bradlyn, & Kelly, 1982), for attaining well-specified goals on a weekly or biweekly basis.

Research Evaluation of Behavioral Interventions

Empirical studies of treatment outcome with abusive families were quite uncommon until the mid to late 1970s, when behavioral researchers became more interested in this problem (Friedman et al., 1981). Prior to that time, a variety of intervention techniques had been used to prevent abusive episodes subsequent to child abuse reports, including traditional psychotherapy as well as methods aimed more specifically at the needs of this population, such as health visitors, crisis nurseries, and parent education (Kempe & Kempe, 1978). Unfortunately, the lack of experimental design and objective assessment led to pessimistic conclusions of treatment efficacy with this population (Berkeley Planning Associates, 1977). It was at this point that behavioral researchers began to apply some of the principles derived from previous experimental and applied research to the problem of child abuse, leading to clinical case studies and gradually improving in methodological sophistication (Conger & Lahey, 1982).

The earliest treatment outcome reports were essentially descriptive. They included home- or clinic-based training that focused on reinforcement, extinction, and time-out procedures (Tracy & Clark, 1974), supplemented by contracting (Polakow & Peabody, 1975), self-time-out (Mastria, Mastria, & Harkins, 1979), and/or programmed texts (Hughes, 1974). As reviewed by Isaacs (1982), these early clinical reports provided a useful foundation for future investigation of behavioral interventions with abusive populations, despite their lack of substantiation. In general, the authors of these studies reported that families responded favorably to structured methods for dealing with undesirable child behavior and parental aggression, and these efforts encouraged more controlled investigations.

An early treatment study to emerge from the University of South Florida Child Management Program studied the effects of several treatment components (reading and practice assignments, role-playing, and contingent reinforcement) in altering the negative interactions between parent and child in two abusive families (Sandler, VanDercar, & Milhoan, 1978). Using a single-subject design, they reported that the child management skills of both parents were successfully improved and changes in parent-child interactions were significantly altered, based on home observations. Wolfe and Sandler (1981) then investigated the effects of both parent training and contingency contracting on parent-child interactions in the home. This study also reported reduction in punitive forms of control, improvements in the child's difficult behavior, and maintenance of changes across the three families over a 12-month period. A third study was then conducted to expand the evaluation of the program to a group design involving more parents, more evaluation criteria, and more control of the treatment effectiveness. Wolfe, Sandler, and Kaufman (1981) assigned families to treatment and control conditions in order to compare a group receiving parent training with a control group that received only the standard services provided by the child welfare department. The authors reported that the combination of child management and anger control skills, delivered in a group format and through competency-based training in the home, resulted in improvements in parenting skills, parental report of child behavior problems, and caseworker report of family problems. Similar improvements were not found in the control group, who had been receiving biweekly supervision in the home. At a 1-year follow-up, child abuse had not been suspected or reported among those families who completed the training program.

Additional controlled-outcome studies have recently been published that, in the aggregate, support the efficacy of behavioral parent training with abusive families (Crimmons, Bradlyn, St. Lawrence, & Kelly, 1984; Crozier & Katz, 1979; Lorber, Reid, Kavanaugh, & Bank, 1984; Reid, Taplin, & Lorber, 1981; Wolfe et al., 1982). Moreover, two studies that focused more specifically on anger- and self-control found reductions in self-reported "anger-urges" and irritation (Denicola & Sandler, 1980; Nomellini & Katz, 1983). It appears that the addition of cognitive-behavioral training in conjunction with child management skills to help parents cope more effectively with problem situations is a promising strategy that deserves further investigation.

In an interesting extension of the small-N methodology, Szykula and Fleischman (1983) investigated reductions in out-of-home placements following behavioral intervention conducted within a social agency. Their results showed that social learning based intervention was effective in reducing, although not eliminating, out-of-home placements for abused children. Families who benefited most from the treatment were characterized as more stable, less troubled, but unable to manage the child in an authoritative yet nonabusive manner. These investigators reported that among multiproblemed families, where child abuse is just one of many serious problems, treatment was less successful. It is encouraging to note from this study that out-of-home placements dropped 85% following the program's inception, and no further abusive incidents were reported among the participants. Given the costs of out-of-home placements and the long-term negative impact on the child, such treatment can be considered cost-effective (Szykula & Fleischman, 1983).

The literature on behavioral interventions with abusive parents, therefore, suggests that specific skills training provides a viable intervention strategy for a significant proportion of abusive parents. However, this is a very heterogeneous population that requires flexible approaches to intervention in accordance with the needs of each family; thus, it cannot be stated at present to what degree this approach will prove to be of value. Furthermore, methodological weaknesses such as poor definitions of abuse, inadequate measures, lack of experimental control, and limited follow-up still exist (Isaacs, 1982). There is also debate as to whether behavioral intervention methods will surmount the criticisms that argue in favor of more prolonged, supportive interventions with this population (Gambrill, 1983; Kempe & Kempe, 1978; Resick & Sweet, 1979). In response to this concern, Smith and Rachman (1984) contend that behavioral techniques do make a contribution to the treatment of abusive parents, provided that: (1) the services are provided over an extended time period by the same person; (2) specific child management techniques are taught in a problem-solving format that helps families to manage their lives in a "normal" fashion; (3) treatment "failures" are carefully studied for clues about selection of families for treatment; and (4) the goals of the program are conceptualized more in terms of global quality of life for the child rather than parenting skills per se. Azar, Fantuzzo, and Twentyman (1984) further argue that behavioral researchers have understressed the importance of operational definitions of all relevant parameters of abuse (such as intensity, duration, and latency) and may have overlooked the contributions of research on attributions and aggressive behavior.

Despite these valid criticisms, the literature does reflect a responsive awareness of the unique needs of this population. Additional treatment strategies have emerged, based largely on the study of process variables during treatment, to reflect the multifaceted problems presented by abusive families, such as affect disorders (Conger, Lahey, & Smith, 1981), interpersonal problems and learning disabilities (Wolfe & Manion, 1984), and the myriad of daily living problems addressed by Project 12-Ways (Lutzker et al., 1984). Many arguments against the premature acceptance of these data exist, yet based on the first decade of behavioral research with abusive families, cautious optimism appears to be warranted (Wolfe, 1984).

CASE DESCRIPTION

This case description highlights several of the concerns discussed in the child abuse literature. Imaginal and *in vivo* desensitization in conjunction with behavioral parent training were used with an abusive mother who was experiencing multiple life stressors. Details of the case are presented in order to illustrate the assessment and treatment procedures used as well as the common problems often encountered when working with this population.*

IDENTIFICATION AND CONCEPTUALIZATION OF THE PROBLEM

The family was composed of the mother (Diane, aged 21) and her two male children (Curtis, aged 22 months, and Andy, aged 9 months). A public health nurse had been assigned to the family following the birth of Diane's second child because hospital staff expressed concerns that the mother seemed ill-prepared to handle another child in the home. During her visits to the home, the nurse observed that the older child clung to his mother very tightly and would scream very loudly whenever his mother attempted to put him down. On one occasion she had discovered that this same child had bruises on his arms and legs and scratches on his face. When questioned about these marks, Diane admitted that his crying at night and his demands for attention throughout the day had been too much for her, and she had struck him several times. Following several weeks of investigation and observation by child protective services, the social worker became convinced that Diane needed additional guidance in dealing with both children and referred the family to the Parent/ Child Early Education Program. Diane was not court-ordered to seek treatment, but involvement in a parenting program was a requirement of her supervision contract with the agency.

Diane's family history was replete with physical and emotional abuse and economic disadvantage. Her parents were both alcoholics with psychiatric histories, and Diane also had a long history of involvement with local medical and mental health professionals. She had been admitted to the psychiatric department of local hospitals on five occasions with diagnoses ranging from neurotic depression to hysterical personality disorder. Hospital records revealed numerous physical problems and complaints, and she had been described by various professionals as unmotivated and overly dependent on social agencies. At the time of referral Diane had received treatment for her personal problems that included psychotherapy, drug therapy, and surgery (for chronic pain). During her many hospital visits, the target child (Curtis) had been placed with emergency care shelters, relatives, and temporary foster homes on eight different occasions, with placement sometimes lasting for several weeks.

From the social history and presenting problems, it was clear that this parent was experiencing multiple stress factors that intefered with her parental capabilities. Curtis presented at the interview as a fussy, clinging, and very

*This case was reported in Koverola, C., Elliot-Faust, D., & Wolfe, D. A. (1984) *Journal of Clinical Child Psychology, 13*(2), 187–191. Excerpts and tables from this article are used by permission of the publisher.

demanding boy. He had severe temper tantrums for the duration of the intake interview. The infant, in contrast, was very passive and quiet, with observed delays in areas of sensory-motor and language development. An assessment strategy was therefore chosen to determine intervention priorities and to establish a functional relationship between situational events (involving the child's behavior and/or events outside of the family) and maternal behavior towards the child. The complex interaction between the parent's behavioral repertoire, cognitive and attitudinal factors, and physiological reactivity to child behavior formed a conceptual basis for the selection of assessment and intervention procedures.

BEHAVIORAL ASSESSMENT OF INDIVIDUAL AND SITUATIONAL VARIABLES

The intake interview was carefully structured to allow Diane to express her concerns about her children in a manner that would lead to constructive goals. The interview focused largely on current problems she was having with Curtis and how these problems seemed to relate to situational factors such as aversive contacts with family or community members. Diane was unable to pinpoint any persons or events that were particularly irritating to her, and she did not feel that her behavior toward Curtis was a function of any recognizable situation beyond his excessive bids for attention. On the other hand, her descriptions of daily problems and crises suggested that she was overburdened by the demands of childrearing. She related numerous situations that appeared to potentiate one another and led to increasing decrements in her parental role, such as a break-in to her home, physical threats from male companions, and financial pressures. At the close of the interview, it was suspected that the abusive incident was a function of several ongoing events that represented a level of environmental stress that exceeded her minimal coping abilities. The child was clearly at-risk of abuse or neglect unless considerable effort was made to reduce the degree of stress and to increase her parental competence.

The assessment strategy began with a global screening procedure to determine Diane's level of intrapersonal functioning, followed by more specific assessment of parent-child interactions and situationally based arousal to child behavior. In addition to the interview screening, the Child Abuse Potential Inventory and Beck Depression Inventory were administered to assess her adjustment in relation to historical and current events. The findings from these instruments concurred with her presenting complaints, revealing that she had had many negative childhood experiences and had distorted expectations of children, poor coping abilities, and a moderate level of depression. The causal ordering of these factors remained unclear, as did the functional relationship between them. However, on the basis of these results it was decided that Diane's level of functioning did not preclude her benefiting from intensive therapeutic efforts.

Diane also completed the Eyberg Child Behavior Inventory in reference to

Curtis, which produced a score falling well above the clinical range on this instrument. She endorsed items related to Curtis' screaming, noncompliance, sleep problems, clinging, poor eating habits, destructiveness, and aggressive behavior that amounted to a very high intensity of conflict during her interactions with her child. Curtis was assessed on the Denver Developmental Screening Test (Frankenburg & Dodds, 1968) by a nurse at the child protection agency and was also seen by a psychologist to evaluate his current level of sensory-motor development. The results confirmed that his language and social development were delayed or deviant (e.g., few attempts at verbal communication, little solitary play behavior, overanxious attachment to mother). Based on this initial assessment, Curtis was viewed as a very irritable and demanding toddler who was in need of appropriate stimulation in the home, positive methods of child management, and a stable family environment.

Parent-child interactions were assessed in the home and clinic to evaluate the rate of positive and negative exchanges between Diane and Curtis. Positive behavior included categories defined as praise and positive physical contact with the child, while negative behavior included criticism and negative physical contact directed toward the child. Child deviant behavior and compliance were also recorded during several 20-minute, unstructured observations. Home visits also revealed that the mother and her two children lived in a very impoverished environment that provided inadequate child stimulation and safety (assessed using the Home Observation and Measurement of the Environment Scale: Bradley & Caldwell, 1979).

Diane's behavioral, physiological, and self-reported responses to Curtis's aversive and nonaversive behavior were carefully assessed to determine her level of arousal during conflicts with her child. A multimodal assessment strategy was chosen in this particular case, due to the severity of her verbal report and behavioral history vis-à-vis anger and aggression toward Curtis. Diane's strongest complaint was Curtis's extremely aversive crying, which was recorded at a rate of .44 times per minute during home observations. She also complained of feelings of tension and loss of control whenever he cried incessantly. In order to assess Diane's reactivity to the aversive behavior of her child, videotaped segments from her clinic interactions with Curtis were edited into a stimulus tape consisting of three minutes of positive child behavior and three minutes of aversive child behavior. Her physiological responses of electromyogram (EMG, frontalis), galvanic skin response (GSR), and heart rate (HR) were recorded on a polygraph, and 11-point distress ratings (Subjective Units of Distress Scale, SUDS) were recorded during each minute of each scene. Four minutes of baseline preceded each presentation, and an experimental (ABAB) single-case study was conducted to determine changes from child-positive scenes (A) to child-aversive scenes (B).

Diane's responses of HR, EMG, GSR, and distress ratings are shown in Figure 15.1. Distress ratings revealed a close relationship to the scenes during both AB presentations, and correlational analyses indicated that her self-

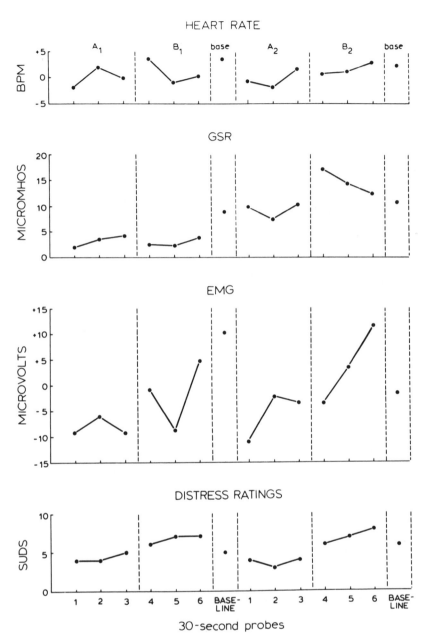

Figure 15.1. Subject's heart rate, galvanic skin response, electromyographic response, and distress ratings in response to her child's positive (A) and aversive (B) behavior (presented on videotape).

report of distress was significantly associated with changes in GSR and EMG recordings. As shown in Figure 15.1, changes in both EMG and GSR responses indicated arousal, which increased significantly during the second presentation of the child-aversive scene. Changes in HR did not reveal a pattern of arousal and did not correlate with self-report. These findings were useful in determining the topography of Diane's reactivity to her child, which is viewed as an indication of conditioned arousal that might serve as a moderator of aggressive behavior toward the child. Accordingly, it was decided to begin treatment with training in child management techniques, accompanied by a procedure that focuses on the awareness and control of cognitive, behavioral, and physiological arousal.

INTERVENTION WITH PARENT AND CHILD

An overview of the treatment procedures and interruptions is presented in Table 15.1. During the initial treatment phase Diane was taught child management skills that focused on increasing appropriate behaviors and decreasing her criticisms and harsh forms of punishment (see Wolfe, Kaufman, Aragona, & Sandler, 1981, for details of parent training procedures with abusive parents). The therapist modeled prosocial interactions with the child as the mother observed from behind a one-way mirror. The mother's interactions with Curtis were videotaped while she rehearsed the skills, and the tape was later shown to her so that she could receive feedback on her performance. Parent training continued in this manner, covering topics of positive reinforcement, commands, punishment, and stimulation of child speech and language.

As treatment was begun, however, other personal and situational factors interfered with parent training (Table 15.1, sessions 5–9). At this point, informal relaxation procedures were introduced to help the mother recognize tension and anger, and she practiced deep breathing and relaxation exercises in the clinic. These procedures were favorably received by Diane, who stated that she had never previously experienced feelings of self-control or relaxation to this extent. At the close of seven parent training sessions, Diane showed improvements in her use of targeted parenting skills; however, she reported that Curtis's behavior remained extremely aversive to her and that she was still afraid of losing control with him.

An imaginal desensitization procedure using physical, cognitive, and behavioral strategies was then implemented to teach the mother coping strategies for handling anger provocation. Three aversive scenes involving Curtis and based on existing problems reported by the mother were developed for this procedure: (1) Curtis making a mess of the kitchen, (2) temper tantrums, and (3) screaming at night. The critical aspect of each scene was carefully discussed with Diane in order to develop a realistic portrayal of the home situation that

TABLE 15.1   An Overview of Treatment Plans and Interruptions[a]

Weeks	Sessions	Treatment Plan	Major Concerns and Interruptions
1–2	1–2	Interview and assessment	Child behavior problems; change of residence
3–6	3–4	Parent-training	
7–9	5–9	Parent-training	Somatic complaints and personal problems; child-behavior problems; child hospitalized
10–12	10–14	Parent-training + informal relaxation	
13–14			Mother and children left residence unannounced
15–16	15–20	Anger control—imaginal desensitization	
17–18	21–22	Counselling only	House broken into; threats on children; children apprehended; mother hospitalized for suicidal ideation
19–20		Hospitalized (group and individual therapy)	
21–25	23–27	Anger control—In vivo desensitization	
26		Home Visit	
27		Children returned home	
29		Follow-up Visit	
30			Hospitalized for hernia operation; children in temporary foster care
37		Follow-up Visit	
38			Children in temporary foster care
43		Follow-up Visit	

[a]Clinical Issues in Behavioral Treatment of a Child Abusive Mother Experiencing Multiple Life Stressors, from C. Koverola, D. Elliot-Faust, & D. A. Wolfe (1984), *Journal of Clinical Child Psychology, 13,* p. 189, used by permission of the publisher.

triggered her arousal. She was then taught strategies for coping with arousal. These included behavioral and cognitive components: muscle relaxation, positive self-statements, and methods for handling the child or avoiding the stressor. The therapist taught Diane to relax and then gradually presented each scene to her. Diane was instructed to raise her finger when she began to experience distress, and the therapist would then present the coping imagery. Scene presentation was repeated until Diane could maintain herself at low distress (SUDS 0–4) for the entire scene.

After five sessions involving imaginal desensitization, increasing life stresses again resulted in an interruption of treatment and subsequent hospitalization. Upon her return, *in vivo* desensitization was begun in which Diane was instructed to rehearse coping skills while engaging in a difficult compliance task with Curtis. The therapist reviewed the coping strategies with Diane and modeled them while interacting with Curtis. Diane was then instructed to engage in the task and to indicate her distress by raising a finger. The therapist prompted the mother to relax and to initiate an adaptive response whenever she expressed a moderate degree of discomfort (usually in response to the child's crying, noncompliance, or grabbing at her clothing). This training continued over five sessions, during which time the children remained in a foster home and were brought to the clinic by foster parents.

TREATMENT EVALUATION AND FOLLOW-UP

Diane's children were returned to the home after being in foster care for 8 weeks. The family continued to receive adjunctive services from the social agency, including a support worker who visited the home weekly, foster daycare twice a week for the children, and involvement in a support group for young mothers. On completion of parent training and anger management training, Diane showed some improvements in her rate of criticism, although these changes remained unstable. Her mood and affect fluctuated considerably during therapist visits to the home, and she was placed on antianxiety drugs by her family physician.

Unfortunately, the first follow-up home visit indicated that Diane had not maintained the positive gains she had previously shown. The therapist remained in contact with her by telephone and through home visits, which indicated that her life-style pattern of crises continued to plague her parental functioning. The pattern of observational and clinical information indicated that Diane was becoming a more capable parent as long as the level of stress in her life remained manageable. There were no indications or suspicions of further child abuse or neglect; however, it was apparent that she was not providing the level of stimulation necessary to modify the behavior problems and developmental delay shown by the target child. For this reason the project team and agency decided to maintain a high level of supportive services for the family (e.g., homemaker services, group counseling, and social work visits) and to have the children remain with Diane. This strategy was successful in managing Diane's level of situational stress, allowing her more opportunity to be with her children without severe conflict or disruption. Because she had requested help in dealing with her children and strongly desired to keep them at home, this approach was viewed as more constructive than continuing to move the children to and from foster settings (permanent placement in foster care was not an option, since no incidents of abuse or neglect had been repeated).

Our case demonstrates a common concern in the delivery of services to abusive families. The parent's use of appropriate child management skills may be governed by his or her ability to focus attention and interest on the children and away from other coexisting problems. This appears to be a common problem among parents seen by social agencies (Wahler & Graves, 1983). The clinical importance of alternatively focusing on the child's behavior and the mother's emotional reactivity to stressful circumstances was suggested by the mother's self-report and follow-up visits in the home. Moreover, the effectiveness of establishing reasonable goals and flexible procedures, in alignment with additional community resources, is demonstrated by the events in this case. With such families, the therapist must strive to reduce the interference of multiple stress factors while simultaneously focusing on salient problems involving the child. The development and involvement of long-term support systems may also prove to be an essential component of treatment that has not been adequately addressed in the literature.

SUMMARY

The rapid expansion and sophistication of child abuse research over the past decade has advanced our understanding of the functional relationships among the vast number of etiological variables. This chapter has emphasized a conceptualization of child abusive behavior within the context of family and other situational variables rather than a more limiting view that focuses primarily on faults of the parent and/or child. Child abuse appears to have ramifications for the child's long-term adjustment as well as for the perpetuation of violence in the family. Increasing knowledge about child abuse has led to the identification of major antecedents to abuse, such as aversive child behavior and marital violence, and several mediating variables, such as the parent's emotional conditioning, social supports, and childrearing skills.

The nature of child abuse restricts the use of traditional behavioral and psychometric assessment procedures in significant ways. However, this problem has been approached by behavioral investigators who have defined other interactive behaviors in the family that can be observed and recorded for intervention purposes. In addition, a variety of expanded assessment procedures, including direct observation, parent self-report of problem situations and emotional reactivity, standardized tests, interviews, and self-monitoring techniques have evolved into usage with this population. This has led to behavioral interventions for child abuse that are tailored to the individual needs of each family, which is a very important consideration in view of the heterogeneity of this population. A range of behavioral procedures for assisting abusive families was presented, including instruction and rehearsal in child management, anger control, and adjunctive skills training to promote adult and child competence in dealing with their environment. These procedures were illustrated in a clinical case that highlighted some of the promising methods for assisting abusive families, as well as the unresolved problems that are often encountered when working with this population.

REFERENCES

Abidin, R. (1983). *Parenting Stress Index—Manual.* Charlottesville, VA: Pediatric Psychology.

Achenbach, T. M., & Edelbrock, C. S. (1983). *Manual for the Child Behavior Checklist and Child Behavior Profile.* Burlington, VT: Child Psychiatry, University of Vermont.

Altemeier, W. A., O'Connor, S., Vietze, P., Sandler, H., & Sherrod, K. (1984). Prediction of child abuse: A prospective study of feasibility. *Child Abuse and Neglect, 8,* 393–400.

American Humane Association. (1984). *Highlights of official child neglect and abuse reporting—1982.* Denver, CO: Author.

Averill, J. R. (1983). Studies on anger and aggression: Implications for theories of emotion. *American Psychologist, 38,* 1145–1160.

Azar, S. T., Fantuzzo, J. W., & Twentyman, C. T. (1984). An applied behavioral approach to child maltreatment: Back to basics. *Advances in Behaviour Research and Therapy, 6,* 3–11.

Barahal, R. M., Waterman, J., & Martin, H. P. (1981). The social cognitive development of abused children. *Journal of Consulting and Clinical Psychology, 49,* 508–516.

Belsky, J. (1980). Child maltreatment: An ecological integration. *American Psychologist, 35,* 320–335.

Berkeley Planning Associates (1978). *Evaluation of child abuse and neglect projects 1974–1977.* Berkeley Planning Association, Berkeley, CA.

Berkowitz, L. (1983). Aversively stimulated aggression: Some parallels and differences in research with animals and humans. *American Psychologist, 38,* 1135–1144.

Besharov, D. J. (1982). Toward better research on child abuse and neglect: Making definitional issues an explicit methodological concern. *Child Abuse & Neglect, 5,* 383–390.

Bradley, R. H., & Caldwell, B. M. (1979). Home observation for measurement of the environment: A revision of the preschool scale. *American Journal of Mental Deficiency, 84,* 235–244.

Burgess, R. L. (1978). Child abuse: A social interactional analysis. In B. B. Lahey & A. Kazdin (Eds.), *Advances in clinical child psychology* (Vol. 2, pp. 142–172). New York: Plenum.

Burgess, R. L., & Conger, R. (1978). Family interactions in abusive, neglectful, and normal families. *Child Development, 49,* 1163–1173.

Campbell, R., O'Brien, S., Bickett, A., & Lutzker, J. R. (1983). In-home parent training, treatment of migraine headaches, and marital counseling as an ecobehavioral approach to prevent child abuse. *Journal of Behavior Therapy and Experimental Psychiatry, 14,* 147–154.

Cicchetti, D., & Rizley, R. (1981). Developmental perspectives on the etiology, intergenerational transmission, and sequelae of child maltreatment. *New Directions for Child Development, 11,* 31–55.

Conger, R., Burgess, R., & Barrett, C. (1979). Child abuse related to life change and perceptions of illness: Some preliminary findings. *Family Coordinator, 28,* 73–78.

Conger, R. D., & Lahey, B. B. (1982). Behavioral intervention for child abuse. *Behavior Therapist, 5,* 49–53.

Conger, R. D., Lahey, B. B., & Smith, S. S. (1981). *An intervention program for child abuse: Modifying maternal depression and behavior.* Paper presented at the Family Violence Research Conference, University of New Hampshire, Durham.

Crimmons, D. B., Bradlyn, A. S., St. Lawrence, J., & Kelly, J. A. (1984). A training technique for improving the parent-child interaction skills of an abusive-neglectful mother. *Child Abuse & Neglect, 8,* 533–539.

Crozier, J., & Katz, R. C. (1979). Social learning treatment of child abuse. *Journal of Behavior Therapy and Experimental Psychiatry, 10,* 213–220.

Denicola, J., & Sandler, J. (1980). Training abusive parents in cognitive-behavioral techniques. *Behavior Therapy, 11,* 263–270.

Doctor, R. M., & Singer, E. M. (1978). Behavioral intervention strategies with child abusive parents: A home intervention program. *Child Abuse & Neglect, 2,* 57–68.

Dowdney, L., Mrazek, D., Quinton, D., & Rutter, M. (1984). Observation of parent-child interaction with two- to three-year-olds. *Journal of Child Psychology & Psychiatry, 25,* 379–407.

Elmer, E. (1977). A follow-up study of traumatized children. *Pediatrics, 59,* 273–279.

Eyberg, S., & Ross, A. (1978). Assessment of child behavior problems: The validation of a new inventory. *Journal of Clinical Child Psychology, 7,* 113–116.

Forehand, R., & McMahon, R. (1981). *Helping the noncompliant child: A clinician's guide to parent training.* New York: Guilford.

Frankenburg, W. K., & Dodds, J. B. (1968). *The Denver Developmental Screening Test-manual.* Boulder: University of Colorado Press.

Friedman, R., Sandler, J., Hernandez, M., & Wolfe, D. (1981). Child abuse. In E. Mash & L. Terdal (Eds.), *Behavioral assessment of childhood disorders* (pp. 221–225). New York: Guilford.

Friedrich, W. N., & Boriskin, J. A. (1976). The role of the child in abuse: A review of the literature. *American Journal of Orthopsychiatry, 46,* 580–590.

Friedrich, W. N. Einbender, A. J., & Luecke, W. J. (1983). Cognitive and behavioral characteristics of physically abused children. *Journal of Consulting and Clinical Psychology, 51,* 313–314.

Frodi, A. M. (1981). Contribution of infant characteristics to child abuse. *American Journal of Mental Deficiency, 85,* 341–349.

Frodi, A. M., & Lamb, M. E. (1980). Child abusers' responses to infant smiles and cries. *Child Development, 51,* 238–241.

Frodi, A., & Smetana, J. (1984). Abused, neglected, and nonmaltreated preschoolers' ability to discriminate emotions in others: The effects of IQ. *Child Abuse & Neglect, 8,* 459–465.

Gambrill, E. D. (1983). Behavioral interventions with child abuse and neglect. In M. Hersen (Ed.). *Progress in Behavior Modification,* (Vol. 15). New York: Academic Press. 1–56.

Garbarino, J. (1976). A preliminary study of some ecological correlates of child abuse: The impact of socioeconomic stress on mothers. *Child Development, 47,* 178–185.

Garbarino, J., & Stocking, S. H. (1980). *Protecting children from abuse and neglect.* San Francisco: Jossey-Bass.

George, C., & Main, M. (1979). Social interactions of young abused children: Approach, avoidance, and aggression. *Child Development, 50,* 306–318.

Gil, D. G. (1970). *Violence against children: Physical child abuse in the United States.* Cambridge, MA: Harvard University Press.

Giovannoni, J. M., & Becerra, R. M. (1979). *Defining child abuse.* New York: Free Press.

Green, A. H. (1978). Self-destructive behavior in battered children. *American Journal of Psychiatry, 135,* 579–582.

Green, A. H. (1983). Dimension of psychological trauma in abused children. *Journal of the American Academy of Child Psychiatry, 22,* 231–237.

Helfer, R. (1982). A review of the literature on the prevention of child abuse and neglect. *Child Abuse & Neglect, 6,* 251–261.

Herrenkohl, R. C., Herrenkohl, E. C., & Egolf, B. P. (1983). Circumstances surrounding the occurrence of child maltreatment. *Journal of Consulting and Clinical Psychology, 51,* 424–431.

Herrenkohl, E. C., Herrenkohl, R. C., Toedter, L., & Yanushefski, A. M. (1984). Parent-child interactions in abusive and non-abusive families. *Journal of the American Academy of Child Psychiatry, 23,* 641–648.

Hoffman-Plotkin, D., & Twentyman, C. T. (1984). A multimodal assessment of behavioral and cognitive deficits in abused and neglected preschoolers. *Child Development, 55,* 794–802.

Hughes, R. C. (1974). A clinic's parent performance training program for child abusers. *Hospital and Community Psychiatry, 25,* 779–782.

Isaacs, C. D. (1982). Treatment of child abuse: A review of the behavioral interventions. *Journal of Applied Behavior Analysis, 15,* 273–294.

Kelly, J. A. (1983). *Treating abusive families: Intervention based on skills training principles.* New York: Plenum.

Kempe, C. H., Silverman, F. N., Steele, B. F., Droegemueller, W., & Silver, H. K. (1962). The battered child syndrome. *Journal of the American Medical Association, 181,* 17–24.

Kempe, R. S., & Kempe, C. H. (1978). *Child abuse.* Cambridge, MA.: Harvard University Press.

Koverola, C., Elliot-Faust, D., & Wolfe, D. A. (1984). Clinical issues in the behavioral treatment of a child abusive mother experiencing multiple life stresses. *Journal of Clinical Child Psychology, 13,* 187–191.

Koverola, C., Manion, I., & Wolfe, D. A. (1985). A microanalysis of factors associated with child abusive families: Identifying individual treatment priorities. *Behaviour Research and Therapy, 23,* 499–506.

Kravitz, R. I., & Driscoll, J. M. (1983). Expectations for childhood development among child-abusing and non-abusing parents. *American Journal of Orthopsychiatry, 53,* 336–344.

Lahey, B. B., Conger, R. D., Atkeson, B. M., & Treiber, F. A. (1984). Parenting behavior and emotional status of physically abusive mothers. *Journal of Consulting and Clinical Psychology, 52,* 1062–1071.

Lewis, D. O., Pincus, J. H., & Glaser, G. H. (1979). Violent juvenile delinquents: psychiatric, neurological, psychological, and abuse factors. *Journal of the American Academy of Child Psychiatry, 18,* 307–319.

Lorber, R., Felton, D. K., & Reid, J. (1984). A social learning approach to the reduction of coercive processes in child abusive families: A molecular analysis. *Advances in Behavior Research and Therapy, 6,* 29–45.

Lorber, R., Reid, J., Kavanaugh, K., & Bank, L. (1984, November). *An analysis of prosocial interactions in child abusive families: The effects of a social learning based intervention.* Paper presented at the meeting of the Association for the Advancement of Behavior Therapy, Philadelphia.

Lutzker, J. R., Wesch, D., & Rice, J. M. (1984). A review of Project "12-Ways": An ecobehavioral approach to the treatment and prevention of child abuse and neglect. *Behaviour Research and Therapy, 6,* 63–73.

Mash, E. J., Johnston, C., & Kovitz, K. (1983). A comparison of the mother-child interactions of physically abused and non-abused children during play and task situations. *Journal of Clinical Child Psychology, 12,* 337–346.

Mastria, E. D., Mastria, M. A., & Harkins, J. C. (1979). Treatment of child abuse by behavioral intervention: A case report. *Child Welfare, 58,* 253–261.

McCord, J. (1983). A forty year perspective on effects of child abuse and neglect. *Child abuse and Neglect, 7,* 265–270.

Meddin, B. J. (1985). The assessment of risk in child abuse and neglect investigations. *Child Abuse and Neglect, 9,* 57–62.

Milner, J. S. (1980). *The Child Abuse Potential Inventory: Manual.* Webster, NC: Psytec Corp.

Monane, M., Leichter, D., & Lewis, D. O. (1984). Physical abuse in psychiatrically hospitalized children and adolescents. *Journal of the American Academy of Child Psychiatry, 23,* 653–658.

National Institute of Mental Health (1977). *Child abuse and neglect programs: Practice and theory.* Washington, DC: U.S. Government Printing Office.

Nomellini, S., & Katz, R. C. (1983). Effects of anger control training on abusive parents. *Cognitive Therapy and Research, 7,* 57–68.

Novaco, R. W. (1978). Anger and coping with stress. In J. Foreyt & D. Rathjen (Eds.), *Cognitive behavior therapy: Research and application* (pp. 135–173). New York: Plenum.

Parke, R. D., & Collmer, C. W. (1975). Child abuse: An interdisciplinary analysis. In E. M. Hetherington (Ed.), *Review of child development research* (Vol. 5). Chicago: University of Chicago Press.

Patterson, G. R. (1982). *Coercive family process.* Eugene, OR: Castallia.

Patterson, G. R., Reid, J., Jones, R. R., & Conger, R. E. (1975). *A social learning approach to family intervention, Vol. I: Families with aggressive children.* Champaign: Research Press.

Polakow, R. L., & Peabody, D. L. (1975). Behavioral treatment of child abuse. *International Journal of Offender Therapy and Comparative Criminology, 19,* 100–103.

Radbill, S. X. (1968). A history of child abuse and infanticide. In R. E. Helfer, & C. H. Kempe (Eds.), *The battered child* (pp. 3–17). Chicago: University of Chicago Press.

Reid, J. B., Taplin, P., & Lorber, R. (1981). A social interactional approach to the treatment of abusive families. In R. B. Stuart (Ed.), *Violent behavior: Social learning approaches to prediction, management, and treatment* (pp. 83–101). New York: Brunner/Mazel.

Resick, P. A., & Sweet, J. J. (1979). Child maltreatment intervention: Directions and issues. *Journal of Social Issues, 35,* 140–160.

Rule, B., & Nesdale, A. (1976). Emotional arousal and aggressive behavior. *Psychological Bulletin, 83,* 851–863.

Russell, A. B., & Trainor, C. M. (1984). *Trends in child abuse and neglect: A national perspective.* Denver, CO: American Humane.

Salzinger, S., Kaplan, S., & Artemyeff, C. (1983). Mothers' personal social networks and child maltreatment. *Journal of Abnormal Psychology, 92,* 68–76.

Salzinger, S., Kaplan, S., Pelcovitz, D., Samit, C., & Kreiger, R. (1984). Parent and teacher assessment of children's behavior in child maltreating families. *Journal of the American Academy of Child Psychiatry, 23,* 458–464.

Sandler, J., VanDercar, C., & Milhoan, M. (1978). Training child abusers in the use of positive reinforcement techniques. *Behaviour Research & Therapy, 16,* 169–175.

Smith, J. E. (1984). Non-accidental injury to children. I: A review of behavioural interventions. *Behaviour Research and Therapy, 22,* 331–347.

Smith, J. E., & Rachman, S. J. (1984). Non-accidental injury to children. II: A controlled evaluation of a behavioural management programme. *Behaviour Research and Therapy, 22,* 349–366.

Sparrow, S. S., Balla, D. A., & Cicchetti, D. V. (1984). *Vineland Adaptive Behavior Scales* (Revised). Circle Pines, MN: American Guidance Services.

Spinetta, J. J., & Rigler, D. (1972). The child abusing parent: A psychological review. *Psychological Bulletin, 77,* 296–304.

Szykula, S. A., & Fleischman, M. J. (1983). *Behavior therapy interventions with abusive mother-child dyads: Successes and failures.* Paper presented at the World Congress on Behavior Therapy, Washington, DC.

Tarter, R. E., Hegedus, A. E., Winsten, N. E., & Alterman, A. I. (1984). Neuropsychological, personality, and familial characteristics of physically abused delinquents. *Journal of the American Academy of Child Psychiatry, 23,* 668–674.

Tertinger, D., Greene, B., & Lutzker, J. (1984). Home safety: Development and validation of an ecobehavioral treatment program for abused and neglected children. *Journal of Applied Behavior Analysis, 17,* 159–174.

Tracy, J. J., & Clark, E. (1974). Treatment for child abusers. *Social Work, 19,* 338–342.

Vasta, R. (1982). Physical child abuse: A dual component analysis. *Developmental Review, 2,* 164–170.

Wahler, R. (1976). Deviant child behavior within the family: Developmental speculations and behavior change strategies. In E. Mash, L. Hamerlynck, & C. Handy (Eds.), *Behavior modification and families.* New York: Brunner/Mazel.

Wahler, R., & Dumas, J. (1985). *Maintenance factors in abusive mother-child interactions: The compliance and predictability hypotheses.* Manuscript submitted for publication.

Wahler, R. G., & Graves, M. G. (1983). Setting events in social networks: Ally or enemy in child behavior therapy? *Behavior Therapy, 14,* 19–36.

Wolfe, D. A. (1984). Treatment of abusive parents: A reply to the special issue. *Journal of Clinical Child Psychology, 13,* 192–194.

Wolfe, D. A. (1985). Child abusive parents: An empirical review and analysis. *Psychological Bulletin, 97,* 462–482.

Wolfe, D. A. (in press). Child abuse and neglect. In E. J. Mash & L. G. Terdal (Eds.), *Behavioral assessment of childhood disorders* (Vol. II). New York: Guilford.

Wolfe, D. A., Fairbank, J., Kelly, J. A., & Bradlyn. A. S. (1983). Child abusive parents' physiological responses to stressful and nonstressful behavior in children. *Behavioral Assessment, 5,* 363–371.

Wolfe, D. A., Kaufman, K., Aragona, J., & Sandler, J. (1981). *The child management program for abusive parents: Procedures for developing a child abuse intervention program.* Winter Park, FL: Anna.

Wolfe, D. A., & Manion, I. G. (1984). Impediments to child abuse prevention: Issues and directions. *Advances in Behaviour Research and Therapy, 6,* 47–62.

Wolfe, D. A., & Mosk, M. D. (1983). Behavioral comparisons of children from abusive and distressed families. *Journal of Consulting and Clinical Psychology, 51,* 702–708.

Wolfe, D. A., & Sandler, J. (1981). Training abusive parents in effective child management. *Behavior Modification, 5,* 320–335.

Wolfe, D. A., Sandler, J., & Kaufman, K. (1981). A competency-based parent training program for abusive parents. *Journal of Consulting and Clinical Psychology, 49,* 633–640.

Wolfe, D. A., St. Lawrence, J., Graves, K., Brehony, K., Bradlyn, A., & Kelly, J.A. (1982). Intensive behavioral parent training for a child abusive mother. *Behavior Therapy, 13,* 438–451.

PART THREE

Adolescent Disorders
and Problems

CHAPTER 16

Conduct Disorders

RONALD A. MANN

There is some disagreement among clinicians about the validity or importance of a number of diagnostic categories listed in the third edition of the *Diagnostic and Statistical Manual of Mental Disorders* (DSM-III: American Psychiatric Association, 1980). In general, problems of reliability are acute, particularly for the child and adolescent diagnostic categories (See Appendix F, DSM-III). Many of these categories include criteria and terms that have not been adequately defined in a manner that would allow clinicians or researchers to agree with high reliability. This includes some of the criteria for diagnoses of conduct disorders.

It is suggested that some diagnostic categories of the DSM-III could be more useful if the distinguishing diagnostic criteria were transposed into scientific definitions of behavior (see Mann, 1976). Such an approach would require objective descriptions of the specific behaviors that were problematic for a given individual. That is, the objectively defined behaviors would have to overlap sufficiently with the criteria of a specific diagnostic category to be relevant to both clinicians and researchers. Indeed, this would help clinicians and researchers, whatever their orientation, both to communicate better with one another and to evaluate their treatment effects more reliably.

Since the major emphasis of this chapter will be on an operant behavior therapeutic approach to conduct disorders, frequency of behavior will be a basic datum of evaluation. Initially, this requires defining and delineating an individual's behaviors in terms of excesses, deficits, and assets. Such an approach to conduct disorders could be accomplished in a manner that would allow objective behavioral definitions to overlap sufficiently with some of the current DSM-III criteria without contradicting them. Presumably, such definitions of behavior could be designed to facilitate assessment in terms of the frequency or duration of the behaviors in question. This type of measurement would lend itself to reliable assessment by clinicians, researchers, and laypersons.

If one relies on the assessment or evaluation of behavior in terms of frequency and/or duration, then "inappropriate behavior" can be conceptualized as behaviors that occur too frequently (i.e., behavioral excesses) or not frequently enough (i.e., behavioral deficits). Accordingly, behavioral excesses may be defined as any behaviors whose rates of occurrence and/or duration exceed socially defined standards of acceptability, desirability, or appropriateness within a given context (Mann, 1976). Of course, the converse is also valid. Behavioral deficits may be defined as behaviors whose rates of occurrence fall below the expected socially defined standards. These can include skills required in daily living, socialization, or task performance (Doke, 1976).

For the purpose of this chapter a conduct disorder is defined as a pattern of continuous repetitions of behaviors engaged in by children or adolescents and considered socially unacceptable by members of their family or by members of the community where that family resides. Thus, such unacceptable behaviors may occur within the home, the school, other environs of the community, or combinations of these. Examples of behaviors often identified with a diagnosis of conduct disorder include school truancies, persistent lying, stealing, substance abuse, tantrums, and refusal to do classwork or homework. Other examples include disobedience to authority figures, insulting remarks directed at peers or adults, and physical aggression. Typically, youngsters identified as having conduct disorders exhibit various combinations of these behaviors.

In general, the usual focus of attention with conduct disorders is directed primarily towards behavioral excesses. It is those behaviors that are most disturbing and disruptive to members of society. Such violations of conduct often draw the attention of various behavior-controlling agencies and institutions, such as law enforcement, school, and family. On the other hand, behavioral deficits, that is, those behaviors whose rates fall below the often required and socially expected standards, may also be associated with conduct disorders. Although subtle and less noticeable, they can pose serious problems. Thus, behavioral deficits should also be taken into account and often require treatment. Examples of these deficits include a low frequency of studying or doing homework, a deficit of social skills, a low frequency of peer-related participation, and failure to develop new interests or hobbies.

It should be noted that so-called conduct disorders can overlap or be associated with other serious problems such as depression, alcoholism, suicide attempts, a deficit of social skills, communication handicaps, and many types of criminal activities such as theft, burglary, or dealing in drugs.

In addition to the above, individuals engaging in conduct-disordered behaviors often have another important and complex problem that is not required in the usual definition of a conduct disorder: "low self-esteem." Problems such as low self-esteem frequently are associated with conduct disorders and may facilitate these disorders. Unfortunately, the term *low self-esteem* carries differing definitions depending on the orientation of the clinician.

From a behavioral perspective, individuals with low self-esteem may be defined as ones who frequently either make self-deprecating statements, do not or cannot identify and label many of their assets, talents, attributes, or interests, and often do not attempt to engage in new or novel endeavors commonly engaged in by other age-related peers. For example, refusal to join clubs, to engage in sports or hobbies, or to meet new friends can result in their having a deficit in interests, hobbies, and other means of adaptively obtaining gratification (i.e., reinforcement). Such deficits can further limit these individuals' ability to discuss or converse on a wide range of subjects. Thus, these individuals' deficits increase the probability of their becoming socially isolated from the broader spectrum of social intercourse engaged in by their peers. In effect, their choices of potential friends with common interests becomes or remains very restricted.

Often, individuals with "low self-esteem" maintain relationships with others who have talents or abilities that significant others identify as similar to or well below their own abilities and talents. Individuals with both low self-esteem and conduct disorders often associate with other individuals displaying similar repertoires of antisocial behaviors. Thus, their peer standards for "normal" or appropriate behaviors are both distorted and unfortunately mutually reinforced.

Individuals with low self-esteem often are passive, sometimes aggressive, and rarely assertive in their daily social interactions. Thus, an increase in both self-esteem and assertive skills often becomes a goals of therapy for youngsters with conduct disorders.

Finally, conduct disorders very frequently include combinations of problems associated with school such as truancies, tardiness, noncompliance with school and homework requirements, noncompliance with demands of authority figures, and disruption in the classroom.

BEHAVIORAL ASSESSMENT

When youngsters are having problems, parents are typically the ones to initiate assessment and treatment. Thus, an initial evaluation meeting is scheduled with the identified patient's parents, without the patient present. Prior to the initial phase of evaluating the youngster's presenting complaints, the parents are probed and evaluated for other problems that may be affecting intrafamily functioning. Specifically, the parents are assessed for personal and interpersonal problems, such as marital discord, alcohol or drug problems, depression, and stress reactions deriving from their own social environment or workplace. If there are problems, these issues and those involving their personal viewpoints on childrearing generally continue to emerge as therapy progresses. These types of problems may interfere with the parents' learning and applying new parental skills (Griest & Wells, 1983).

During the initial phase of evaluation, a history of the child's current problems is taken. The parents then are asked to identify and list the child's problem behaviors, deficits, assets, and potential reinforcers (i.e., frequently engaged-in activities, hobbies, allowance, etc.). These are delineated using behaviorally objective terms. For example, if the parents use terms such as "poor attitude," "is always angry," or "is insulting," the therapist helps them objectively describe the specific behaviors that cued use of those terms. Thus, their social definitions of behavior are transposed into scientific definitions (teaching the parents to describe behaviors in objective terms is also part of the therapeutic process during treatment). The parents are also asked to identify and specify the conditions under which those problems occur.

Later in the session, the patient is seen alone. First, the patient is probed to evaluate the existence of any personal problems outside of the home, such as peer rejection, loss of friends, and sometimes even pregnancies. The patient is also evaluated for child abuse in or out of the home. Second, the patient is asked if he or she agrees or disagrees with the identified problem behaviors, assets, deficits, and reinforcers specified by the parents. In addition, he or she is prompted to expand on those items. Finally, the patient is asked to identify those areas in which he or she feels the parents need to make changes in their behaviors and to identify and list their behavioral assets and deficits. At times, the patient will indicate the existence of parental problems such as alcoholism not previously revealed by the parents. The patient also is asked to identify the conditions under which both his or her problems and conflicts with parents occur.

Thus, two lists are generated: one from the parents and one from the patient. Both the patient and the parents are then seen together during the same session. With all parties participating, the lists are compared and initially used to help evaluate the factual issues of conflict between family members and to assess one another's recognition of the others' assets. Where relevant, issues involving siblings are included. At times, the therapist identifies maladaptive behaviors not recognized by the parents or youngster and proposes that they be included in the lists as treatment goals. Finally, and most important, the two lists will later help the therapist to design an individually tailored contingency contract that will sepcify treatment goals in terms of specific behaviors and their related consequences.

After basic agreement is established on major items of the lists, the patient and parents sign a consent for release of information from the patient's school. This allows the therapist to obtain copies of requested school records, including psychological testing results, attendance records (including truancies and excused absences), and cumulative grade reports. The presenting problems and history described by the parents (and confirmed by the patient) as well as the obtained school reports serve as a sort of baseline. That is, this information can be used later as a reference from which to make comparisons during and after treatment.

Where appropriate, the therapist can teach parents to record and collect frequency or duration data on important behaviors prior to, during, and after treatment interventions. For example, relatively easy behaviors to record would include frequency of teasing a sibling, frequency of insulting remarks or obscenities, duration of involvement with homework, completion of chores, and frequency of positive comments.

In addition, if there are school-related problems, arrangements can be made with a school psychologist, counselor, or teachers to have the patient bring home weekly progress reports (say every Friday). The reports would be signed by the patient's teachers and could specify his or her daily attendance for the week, daily record of homework completion in each class, class conduct, and cumulative grade average. Thus, the data from the weekly progress reports could be used to evaluate ongoing school performance during treatment. These data could also be used as a basis to determine some of the reinforcing and punishing consequences that could be specified in the contingency contract.

Finally, in order to continue assessment during treatment, each therapy session can be divided into a three-period format. During the first period, the parents are seen alone to assess the previous week's progress from their perspective (part of the session is also used for parent education). During the next period, the patient is seen alone and his or her viewpoint of progress is also evaluated. Then, during the final period of each session, evaluative discrepancies between parents and patient, if any, are resolved (this portion of each session is also used for other therapeutic purposes).

RANGE OF BEHAVIORAL TECHNIQUES APPLIED

Among most children and adolescents diagnosed as having a conduct disorder, there is an inconsistent or inappropriate use of consequences by parents. Frequently, the parents quarrel, disagree with one another with respect to parenting, and individually use different consequences with their children. At other times, the selection of a consequence is determined, in part, by the mood, level of stress or irritability, or state of a parent's emotions. Thus, rarely are specific consequences assigned to specific behaviors. Furthermore, positive consequences such as praise or compliments for adaptive or desirable behaviors often are lacking. This lack of praise often leads to problems of low self-esteem in the patient. Finally, in some affluent families another condition that can contribute to conduct disorders is "teenage retirement." *Teenage retirement* may be defined as any condition under which children or teenagers have all of their needs met regardless of their behavior (i.e., noncontingent rein-forcement). Thus, there may be no punishing consequences for inappropriate behaviors nor reinforcing consequences for desirable behaviors.

Many conduct disorders are associated with frequent and intense familial conflict. If allowed to continue with no intervention, these conflicts between conduct-disordered youngsters and their parents tend to progress to greater intensities. Typically, this is characterized both by increased arguing and yell-ing between one family member and another and by increased parental use of inconsistent punitive consequences.

The use of punitive consequences often can produce immediate short-term results or changes in a child's behavior, which, of course, serve to reinforce the parents' use of them. Further, since positive consequences take time and repetition to produce desired results, their use often is not reinforcing to par-ents. Thus, there sometimes is found in dysfunctional families a natural drift in the parents' behavior toward an increasing use of punitive consequences with an accompanying decrease in the use of reinforcing consequences. In brief, a vicious cycle becomes established. This may result in adolescents' engaging in various avoidance behaviors, such as isolating themselves in their rooms or spending minimal time in the home as positive reinforcers eventually cease to occur. If the singular use of aversive stimuli by parents continues to increase, it could result in the adolescent's running away from home both to avoid the aversive conflicts and to seek other sources of positive reinforcement.

Behavioral Family Therapy

There are a number of major assumptions that determine, in part, the range of behavioral techniques to be applied to conduct disorders: First, a conduct-disordered youngster is a problem of the family system and not simply a prob-lem of maladaptive or socially unacceptable behaviors exhibited by the iden-tified patient. This issue has been discussed extensively by behaviorists as well as family therapists of other orientations (Minuchin, 1974; Haley, 1976). Sec-ond, most of the behaviors of any individual in the family system are a func-tion of their presently occurring consequences. Additionally, the most impor-tant determinants of the identified patient's behavior are both the current consequences of his or her behavior and the significant role models to which he or she is frequently exposed (e.g., parents, siblings, peers, TV). Third, in order to effect desirable behavior changes in the identified patient, the parents' behavior must be the first and primary focus of change. It is they who have control over major relevant consequences within the home, and it is they who are the standards of "normality" in their function as role models. Thus, it is important for the therapist to discover and help provide reinforcing conse-quences for appropriate changes in parental behavior. This is a difficult task. Some of those consequences, it is hoped, can be provided by the promise and

realization of desired changes in their youngster's behavior. Fourth, peer-provided social consequences and modeling are powerful determinants of behavior and ones over which parents typically have little control. Thus, it is vitally
important to attempt to establish some positive reinforcing properties in the
parents. This can help to compete with peer-provided reinforcement. Finally,
the dysfunctional family systems that either generate, facilitate, or do not remediate conduct disorders almost always display inconsistent, unpredictable,
and/or inappropriate consequences.

In order to establish a consistent and predictable set of consequences for
the behavior of the identified patient, a number of treatment goals have to be
met. First, the parents must be taught the basic principles of reinforcement
and contingency management in a systematic manner. The instruction is, of
course, integrated into all subsequent therapy sessions and is a prerequisite to
being able to implement a contingency contract. Second, parents need to be
introduced to the concept and dangers of *parental traps*. Third, and most important, a contingency contract needs to be developed and implemented. Finally, ongoing weekly therapy sessions need to be conducted. These are used
to correct current or new problems, teach the patient and the parents to develop and implement new skills, and to evaluate the effectiveness of treatment
procedures.

Basic Principles

The parents are taught basic principles of reinforcement and punishment, with
their own reported experiences used as examples. In addition, the importance
of considering variables that facilitate the effectiveness of consequences are
presented using everyday illustrations. These include concepts such as the magnitude, duration, repetition, relevance, and immediacy of consequences. Further, parents are instructed in the use of extinction procedures. That is, they
are taught how to identify maladaptive behaviors that could be ignored, such
as argumentativeness or nagging. Further, they are carefully instructed on the
techniques and importance of shaping.

Another key concept taught to the parents is the importance of communicating their needs effectively. This involves teaching parents a number of
skills, including both how to appear calm and how to state their goals in a
clearly defined manner. For example, parents often make statements (angrily)
such as "I want you to be more responsible," or "I want your room clean."
Unfortunately, commonly used terms such as *responsible* and *clean room* often
have quite different meanings for teenager and parent. Thus, parents are taught
how to communicate their needs by describing and delineating behavioral goals
with statements such as, "I will consider your room clean when the dirty clothes
are placed in the hamper, the clean clothes hung up in the closet, the floors
vacuumed, the books placed in the bookshelves, and the dresser dusted."

Finally, and always emphasized to the parents (and the patient), is the importance of not taking any adaptive or desired behaviors for granted. That is, all family members are encouraged to praise and give recognition for a number of behaviors rarely or not previously attended to in one another. It is hoped that an increase in the use of social reinforcement by the family will help change a dysfunctional balance from one of negative comments, arguments, and criticism to one of increased positive interactions.

In summary, a parent education format is designed to help the parents make sound contingency management decisions, which ultimately will occur independent of the therapist.

Parental Traps

Parental traps are commonly engaged-in patterns of behavior that parents often use in response to the inappropriate behaviors of their children. These behavior patterns typically serve to reinforce, albeit inadvertently, the same inappropriate behaviors that the parents are attempting to eliminate. Other parental traps serve to extinguish or punish desirable behaviors when they occur.

The therapist presents many examples of parental traps to the parents, relying on previously taught basic principles of reinforcement and using examples often encountered from real life, including those derived from the parent's own experiences. An instance of one such trap is the parental use of persistent yelling, screaming, and arguing with their children. Arguing and yelling, typically as an immediate consequence, can serve to reinforce a child's argumentativeness; additionally, parents, when arguing between themselves or with their children, act as role models for this behavior.

Another common parental trap is the use of nagging and repetitive requests by parents. Such repetitions teach a child that consequences rarely occur when there is no compliance. Further, on those intermittent occasions when the parents do use consequences, it is typically only after they have used additional cues, such as yelling or threatening. Thus, if and when the child does comply, the parents are reinforced for a chain of maladaptive behaviors that include nagging, becoming agitated, yelling, and using threats to cue a change in their child's behavior. In addition, those parental displays of being extremely upset or angry may act to reinforce the child's delays and noncompliance, especially when he or she is angry at the parents. Commonly, when angry at their parents, youngsters will say or do things simply to aggravate, provoke, and elicit negative emotional responses in their parents. Such emotional responses are powerful reinforcers to the child at these times and are part of a cycle known in the trade as "pushing their parents buttons." It is pointed out to parents that it is they who teach their youngsters "where the buttons are."

The most common parental trap is the parent's use of long philosophic or insight-oriented discussions with their children immediately after they have engaged in some inappropriate behavior. This type of attention rarely occurs as a consequence of desirable behaviors such as doing chores or studying. Thus, "insight" can serve as one type of differential reinforcement for inappropriate behaviors, while desirable behaviors are taken for granted (i.e., ignored), which helps to extinguish them.

Numerous other examples of parental traps are explored and reviewed with the parents. It is hoped that eliminating such traps will help decrease conflict in the home and allow more adaptive family interactions to develop.

Contingency Contracting

The most important phase of treatment consists of designing and implementing an individually tailored contingency contract. A contingency contract is an explicit statement of contingencies; that is, it is a set of rules. From a behavioral perspective, a *rule* always specifies objectively those behaviors whose occurrence will produce specified consequences, in this case to be delivered by parents.

In order to be effective, such a contract requires a number of major considerations: First, it requires that the behaviors to be changed or maintained be specified in writing using clearly defined objective terms. Second, it requires that those behaviors occur in a measurable or observable manner. Third, it requires that the therapist or parent discover and gain systematic control over relevant consequences. Finally, it requires that the consequences be delivered at appropriate times.

An important function of the contract is that it helps the therapist gain stimulus control over the parent's behavior by specifying clearly the conditions under which they are required to present either reinforcing or punishing consequences. Thus, it facilitates a consistent and predictable set of consequences for the behavior of the patient. The consequences specified in the contract must always be based on the youngster's behavior and not on the parent's emotions.

Weekly Therapy Sessions

Each week the therapist meets first with the patient's parents. Weekly progress reports from school and the patient's progress in the home are reviewed. The therapist carefully scrutinizes use of contract contingencies and gives appropriate feedback and education to the parents as needed. Next, the patient is seen alone to ascertain from his or her point of view the progress that both patient and parents have made. The patient is also questioned about the accuracy of the parents' use of contract consequences. Finally, both patient and parents are seen together during the last part of each session to resolve discrepancies in contract implementation, if any, and to correct issues of conflict.

In addition, during these sessions both the patient and parents are prompted and encouraged, when appropriate, to display behaviors associated with affection, courtesy, and respect for one another. This includes the therapist's teaching them how and when to thank one another, how to use compliments and praise, and how to criticize one another in a constructive fashion. Equally important, a number of other relevant subjects and skills are commonly reviewed and taught to family members. Space does not permit their elaboration. Nevertheless, these subjects include the development of self-esteem, communication skills, assertion skills, and drug education. Naturally, the family is encouraged to use these skills out of the office and in the home. Finally, the therapist always serves as a role model, to illustrate the use of praise, compliments, and assertive skills.

RESEARCH REVIEW

Behavior modification procedures have been applied to child and adolescent behavior problems since the early 1960s (Schwitzgebel, 1964; Davidson & Seidman, 1974; Stumphauzer, 1976; Burchard, Harig, Miller, & Amour, 1976; Wahler, 1980; Wells & Forehand, 1981). Early research with delinquents in community settings demonstrated that operant procedures could be used effectively to recruit adolescent delinquents and maintain their attendance at traditional counseling and therapy sessions (Schwitzgebel, 1964). Later applications using token economies demonstrated effective treatment procedures for adolescent in home-style rehabilitation settings (Phillips, 1968; Phillips, Phillips, Fixsen, & Wolf, 1971; Liberman, Ferris, Salgado, & Salgado, 1975). Token economy procedures were also demonstrated to be effective with adolescents and young adults in hospital settings (Mann & Moss, 1973; 1976) and with children in home settings (Christophersen, Arnold, Hill, & Quilitch, 1972).

From the standpoint of cost effectiveness, the majority of conduct disorders will need to be treated in home settings with parents acting as major agents of change. Accordingly, this will require teaching parents contingency management techniques and other parenting skills. Behavioral training of parents has been clearly demonstrated to effect child behavior change (Forehand & Atkeson, 1977; Horne & Dyke, 1983). Nevertheless, generality and maintenance of parental changes in behavior needs to be better established and continues to be problematic (Sanders & James, 1983). To the extent that parents can be taught to use their newly established parenting skills and procedures in a consistent and durable fashion and under a number of differing conditions, adaptive behavior changes in their children will occur. Although effective parenting requires learning many different skills, a mechanism is needed for providing parents with clearly defined guidelines for administering consequences in a consistent fashion. It is suggested that such a mechanism is contingency contracting.

Over the past 15 years, contingency contracting has been discussed as a technique for use with child and adolescent behavior problems in the natural environment (Tharp & Wetzel, 1969; Stuart, 1971; Gelfand & Hartmann, 1975; DeRisi & Butz, 1975). Contingency contracting has been suggested for use in school settings with children (Homme, 1966; Homme, Csanyi, Gonzales, & Rechs, 1970; Cantrell, Cantrell, Huddleston, & Woolridge, 1969) and has also been demonstrated to be effective in those settings (Kelley & Stokes, 1982; 1984). In addition, contingency contracting has been used to treat addictive behaviors such as alcoholism (Miller, 1972; Miller, Hersen, & Eisler, 1974) and drug abuse (Boudin, 1972). Finally, contingency contracting has been shown to be effective with other difficult-to-change behaviors such as weight control (Mann, 1972, 1976).

The following case study employed a number of techniques to treat the behavior problems of a young adolescent male diagnosed as having a conduct disorder. However, the use of contingency contracting was considered to be the single most important aspect of the treatment.

CASE DESCRIPTION

Case Identification

The patient, Charles P., was a 14-year-old male. He was an only child. His mother had divorced his father when Charles was 12 years old and had remarried again 1 year later when he was 13. Charles lived with his mother and stepfather. His stepfather's two children, ages 19 and 21, were both married and thus not living in the home. Charles was under the regular care of a physician, and except for allergy problems he was in good physical health.

Presenting Complaints

An initial evaluation meeting was scheduled with Charles's mother and stepfather. Charles was not present. Charles and his parents had been referred by a school psychologist for treatment due to disruptive behavior in the classroom, truancies, and low school grades. Charles's mother also indicated that he had a history of increasing conflict with her and her present husband. She had stated that, "Whenever Charles does not get his own way, he becomes angry, argumentative, and often screams loud obscenities." Further, Charles was noncompliant with other parental requirements. He persistently refused to do chores or complete his homework assignments. In addition, Charles smoked cigarettes against his parent's wishes, took money from his mother without her permission, and often lied about these infractions even when caught. Charles's stepfather angrily stated that he was frequently "infuriated" over his stepson's insulting remarks and persistent lying, adding that he resented "his stubborn lack of any contributions to the home."

HISTORY

According to his mother, Charles had been "an A and B student" during most of elementary school. Prior to his parents' divorce, Charles had never been disruptive in class and reportedly got along well with most of his teachers. Furthermore, he had never been truant from any of his classes and was always on time to class.

His mother noted that during the 6 months before her divorce, "Charles had become more withdrawn and less involved with his peers." Furthermore, Charles's mother admitted that she and Charles's father had frequent arguments with one another in her son's presence. She added that before her divorce, the ongoing conflict and arguments with her husband had negated any positive interactions with Charles by either parent. In fact, it was during this stormy period that Charles increasingly began to watch more TV and do less homework. Accordingly, his grades began to decline noticeably. Shortly after the divorce, Charles's father had remarried and moved to another state with his new wife. Charles had almost no contact with his natural father except for an infrequent phone call or short letter. After his mother remarried, Charles began to express resentment towards his stepfather. In fact, his mother admitted that many times he had been punished for stating that he "hated" his stepfather.

During the assessment it was also discovered that in spite of his behavior problems, Charles was receiving many privileges without earning them. For example, he received a regular allowance of $5.00 per week and sometimes more if he wanted to go to a movie with a friend. In addition, his parents gave him $1.50 per day for lunch.

An initial evaluation meeting with Charles was conducted with his parents absent. Charles expressed "total" resentment of his stepfather. However, he did admit that he was doing poorly in school, adding quickly that his "teachers were bad" and that he "hated school any way." With respect to lying, Charles pointed out that telling the truth only resulted in receiving penalties. Charles indicated that his parents frequently criticized and rarely complimented him. In addition, he admitted that although he did yell at his parents, they often yelled at him when they were angry. These accusations were later confirmed by his parents.

Charles also indicated that he was angry with his mother for remarrying, and he resented her negative statements about his natural father. Further, he stated that his mother repeatedly told him that his father did not care about him. Finally, he expressed anger over being restricted to the home on a number of occasions for expressing his resentment towards his stepfather. It was clear that Charles had no difficulty expressing negative feelings such as anger and hatred. He refused to admit that his feelings were hurt or that he cared about either parent. When asked about his assets, Charles began to cry and apparently could not identify any.

TREATMENT

Charles' parents initially were seen alone as part of a standardized evaluation format. After a history of the current problems from the parent's perspective was taken, his parents were asked to identify and list his problem behaviors, deficits, assets, and potential reinforcers.

Later in the session, Charles was seen alone. He was asked to ascertain from his point of view if he agreed with the list of identified problem behaviors, assets, deficits, and reinforcers specified by his parents. He then was also asked to identify and list areas in which he felt his parents needed to make changes in their behaviors and to identify their assets and deficits.

Thus, two lists were generated, one from Charles and one from his parents. During a portion of the following session, Charles and his parents participated, the lists were used to help evaluate the issues of conflict between family members and to assess one another's recognition of the others' assets. Finally, basic agreement was established on major items of the lists. The agreed-upon lists were now used by the therapist to design an individually tailored contingency contract. Some of the items in the contract were open to negotiation, such as the amount of money Charles could earn as an allowance, which chores he would complete, and the times he was expected home during the week and on weekends. Other items obviously not open to negotiation included missing school, stealing, yelling insults, or smoking. It was made clear to Charles and his parents that these types of behaviors would have to result in punishing consequences.

The parents were instructed to make arrangements with the school psychologist to have Charles bring home weekly progress reports every Friday. The reports would be signed by Charles's teachers and specify his daily attendance for the week, provide a daily record of homework completion in each of his classes, and note conduct problems during the week, if any. This information would allow school performance requirements to be incorporated into his contingency contract. Thus, the data from the weekly progress reports were used to determine some of the reinforcing and punishing consequences that Charles would receive, as specified in that contingency contract. The data from the progress reports also helped in evaluating changes in Charles's academic performance and classroom conduct. During a review of the finished contract, it was made clear to Charles and his parents that most of the privileges that he had taken for granted would now have to be earned. This included the use of TV, radio, stereo, and telephone; receiving an allowance; using his bike to go to school; and going out with friends. It was also emphasized to his parents that the contract required them to present either reinforcing or punishing consequences based on Charles's behavior and not on their emotions.

The following is a copy of the completed contract administered by Charles's parents. It is a prototype of contracts that can generally be used with many children and adolescents diagnosed as having a conduct disorder:

It is understood that the full purpose and intent of this contract is that Charles P. be responsible for his own behavior. Thus, he agrees that his performance will determine any rewards or penalties, which are specified in the following clauses of this contractual agreement.

1. Charles's parents agree to pay Charles an allowance of $10.00 per week contingent on his completing the following chores to his parent's specifications: (A number of chores with objective criteria were listed. In addition, the times by which these chores had to be completed in order for Charles to be paid were specified.)

It is understood by Charles and his parents that neither credit will be advanced nor money loaned and allowance will be paid once per week after completion of chores.

2. Charles agrees to deposit with his parents a minimum of 50% of all money he earns both from his allowance and from any employment. It is understood that the deposited money may be used by Charles's parents for purposes of paying penalties if Charles violates contract rules.

3. It is understood that Charles may request for his own use a portion of the deposited money his parents are holding if two conditions are met: (a) Charles's behavior must have been appropriate for 4 consecutive weeks without violating any major clauses of this contract. (b) After withdrawal of the money, there must remain a balance equal to at least $15.00. In addition, after completing four consecutive weeks without major violations, Charles will receive his full allowance and full paycheck from any employment. On the other hand, should a major violation occur again, Charles will again be required to deposit with his parents 50% of all earned money for at least 4 consecutive weeks. Major violations include truancies, lying, stealing, and disruptive behavior in school.

4. Charles agrees to complete all homework assignments daily to his parent's approval prior to watching TV, listening to radio or stereo, using the phone, going out, or engaging in any pleasurable activities.

5. It is understood that Charles will bring home from school every Friday a weekly progress report. The report will specify daily attendance in all classes, homework assignments completed for the week, and class con-

duct, and it will be signed by teachers from each of his classes. Perfect attendance, all homework completed, and no reports of poor conduct will result in full weekend privileges. (Privileges were delineated. They included use of TV, use of phone, use of bike, where Charles could go and at what times he had to return home, etc.)

NOTE: Failure to bring home the weekly progress report for *any* reason will result in being restricted to the home without privileges for the entire weekend.

6. Charles agrees not to be truant from any of his classes. Any violation will result in immediate loss of all money deposited with Charles's parents and restriction to the house without privileges for one full week.

7. Charles's parents agree to reward Charles with $15.00 for every grade of A he receives, $10.00 for every B, and $2.50 for C grades. On the other hand, Charles agrees to pay his parents $10.00 for grades of D and $15.00 for F grades. In addition, Charles will be required to attend summer school in classes of which he has received failing grades.

8. Charles agrees not to lie to either parent. Any violation will result in a $5.00 fine and 2 days' restriction to the house without privileges.

9. Charles agrees not to direct obscenities or insulting remarks at family members. Any violation will result in the immediate loss of one-half hour of TV time and 50 cents for each obscenity or insulting remark.

10. Charles agrees not to steal. Stealing is defined as taking or "borrowing" anyone's property without his or her prior permission. Any violation will result in (a) payment of the money or value of the item taken, (b) restriction to the home without privileges for 3 days, and (c) a fine of $10.00.

11. It is understood that any reports of poor conduct from school will result in a restriction to the home and loss of privileges for 1 full weekend day.

12. Charles agrees not to smoke cigarettes. Any violation will result in a fine of $5.00 and loss of all privileges for 1 day.

13. Charles's parents agree that they will not punish him for expressing any of his feelings in an appropriate manner. This includes any statements describing his feelings such as "hating" or "disliking." In addition, neither parent will make any negative or derogatory comments about Charles's natural father.

14. Charles's parents agree that if Charles does not have any major violations of this contract for 6 consecutive weeks, they will celebrate by taking Charles and one friend to a movie and restaurant of his choice, all expenses paid.

I, Charles P. have read fully the above contract and understand and agree to the terms set forth in all of the clauses specifying various behavioral requirements and their consequences. Further, I understand that the conditions of this contract are binding on my parents as well as on myself. Finally, it is understood by all parties to this contract that should any revisions be considered necessary, such revisions shall be made only under the direct supervision of the therapist.

The contract was then signed by Charles, his parents, and the therapist as a witness. The contract was dated and copies presented to each family member. Charles was instructed to call the therapist at any time if he felt that his parents were not delivering consequences in the agreed-on manner.

COURSE OF TREATMENT

Charles and his parents were seen for therapy during 10 one-hour sessions. Subsequently, they were seen for two more follow-up sessions spaced 2 weeks apart. The first two sessions were used to obtain a history, evaluate objectively the family dynamics, and identify the family's behavior problems, assets, deficits, and reinforcers. The next two sessions were used for parent education with Charles's parents as well as to negotiate, develop, and complete the contingency contract. The remaining sessions were used to educate Charles and his parents, teach them new skills, correct current and new problems, and evaluate the effectiveness of treatment variables.

During the course of therapy, a number of important issues were addressed. Space does not permit even a partial account. For example, Charles's parents had, on a number of occasions, punished him for telling his stepfather that he hated him. As a result, the parents had been cautioned neither to criticize nor punish him for expressions of his feelings. Punishing consequences only served to diminish the expressions of certain feelings and cue further resentments towards his parents. Certainly, punishing a child for expressing negative feelings does not magically engender him to be more affectionate and loving. It was stressed to the parents that there never were inappropriate feelings, only inappropriate ways of expressing them. Further, it was made clear to Charles that angry or negative feelings did not give anyone license to engage in socially inappropriate behaviors such as making insulting remarks, having temper tantrums, or stealing. Accordingly, various means of expressing one's feelings were explored to help family members discriminate socially acceptable versus socially inappropriate expressions.

In addition to this issue, it was strongly suggested to the parents that they not make negative comments to Charles about his natural father. Certainly, he had a right to express his affection for his father without being belittled. Both parents were receptive, agreed with these arguments, and incorporated a clause of commitment into the final contingency contract at Charles's request. Finally, the parents were also taught other skills, such as helping Charles develop increased self-esteem.

It should be stressed that the contingency contract did not and could not address a number of other very important issues and other goals of therapy. The contract addressed only the major behavior problems that Charles had engaged in and remedied some of the ineffective consequences the parents had been using. For example, the contract could not require family members to demonstrate affection for one another nor could it require them to give praise, recognition, or constructive feedback to one another. All of these issues and others, such as helping Charles to develop self-esteem and assertion skills, needed to be dealt with in regular therapy sessions.

On the whole, parent education and the use of contingency contracting did pave the way for resolving major conflicts that had been plaguing the family. For example, Charles's parents had been taught to administer specified penalties dispassionately in a calm, matter-of-fact manner. On the other hand, all reinforcing consequences were to be presented paired with praise, compliments, and as much passion as honesty would allow. Finally, the contract did provide a mechanism that objectively specified the parent's behavioral expectations of Charles. In particular, it gave the parents a "sense of control" over the relevant consequences of Charles's behavior. But paradoxically, it also gave Charles a sense of control and predictability in his own life. For example, if a friend phoned Charles, say, on a Monday, and asked him if he could go to a movie on Saturday, Charles could easily respond with a yes. That is, the contract clearly specified to Charles those requirements that he needed to accomplish in order to have weekend privileges and to earn enough money to attend a movie. In other words, the contract was a guarantee to Charles that his needs would be realized if he met his specified responsibilities. Accordingly, Charles could earn reinforcing consequences, regardless of whether his parents were upset, irritable, or in a good mood. In summary, there now was more certainty and predictability in the family system.

During the course of therapy, Charles attended school with no truancies and began to complete his homework assignments in a reliable manner. He did come into contact with punishing contract consequences on a number of occasions prior to making more consistent changes in his behaviors. For example, after being disruptive in class on two occasions and also experiencing the specified consequences, Charles did conform to the contracted behavioral requirements. Major improvements in both his school performance and grades were later confirmed by the weekly progress reports that Charles was bringing home on Fridays.

In the home, both Charles and his parents reported that there was significantly less arguing, although it did not totally diminish. In addition, all members of the family indicated that there was both more affection shown and a sharp increase in positive comments towards one another.

Additionally, Charles pointed out that his parents were not as critical and nagged him less. Presumably, this was due in part to the fact that he was not required to do chores. His parents simply were instructed to refrain from nagging Charles and to give him an allowance only if his chores were completed at the specified times. Further, Charles was no longer taking money from his mother's purse without her permission. This was confirmed, unknown to Charles, by having his parents leave known amounts of money in the house in their absence. They would later verify if any money was missing. Finally, with respect to smoking, Charles was caught and penalized on four occasions during the course of therapy. However, Charles did accept the consequences without arguing and made no insulting remarks. Although Charles later stated that he was "going to stop smoking," there was no way of confirming this. In other words, this was one behavior specified in the contract that could not be monitored reliably. Nevertheless, the contract did indicate his parent's position on this matter and the consequences that would occur if Charles were caught smoking. Finally, as therapy continued, clinical observations of family members during the sessions indicated both a decline in the negative comments and an increase in the positive comments between one another.

SUMMARY

An important proposition of this chapter has been that most youngsters identified as having a conduct disorder engage in behaviors that are a function of current consequences and thus both their relationship with family members and their social environment is relevant. Accordingly, a behavioral family therapy approach is used in which, minimally, various behaviors of the patient as well as the parents are identified and targeted for change. In fact, a key element for success is that the parents initially make major changes in their behavior to effect changes in their offspring's behavior. It is they who have control over many relevant consequences of their child's behavior. Thus, the primary task of the therapist is to facilitate a change in the parents' behavior in a systematic fashion. This always includes parent education and directing the use of contingency management techniques. At times, it may include prescribing additional therapies that address specific problems of the parents, such as alcoholism, stress, or depression.

The use of parent and "patient" education, prompting and role modeling by the therapist, and teaching new skills such as communication and assertion are very important techniques for success. Still, it should be stressed that the use of contingency contracting to treat conduct disorders is considered to be the most salient aspect of treatment.

The effectiveness of contingency contracting is based on a number of assumptions. First, positive changes in the patient's behavior would, in fact, reinforce the parents to use the specified consequences of the contract systematically. Second, the consequences chosen for the patient's behavior are relevant. Third, the behaviors to be changed are observable. Finally, the consequences could be presented in a systematic fashion.

On the other hand, the results of these techniques can be attenuated or rendered ineffective by a number of other important variables. These can include personal problems of the parents, such as alcoholism, marital conflict, and stress. In addition, powerful peer influences also can interfere with treatment. Thus, if these "extra" problems are not treated, probabilities of success are often diminished.

Contrary to the success of the selected case presented above, the use of a behavioral family therapy approach has not always been effective. Some families have terminated treatment early for a variety of reasons. They have included those parents who essentially have expressed "a desire to drop their child off and go shopping while the therapist fixes the problems." At other times, parents have terminated treatment when some of the focus of behavior change has shifted to them after it becomes obvious that they have serious problems such as alcoholism. Nevertheless, in virtually all cases, treatment failure or a diminution of effectiveness has been correlated with the parents' not applying agreed-upon contingency contracting consequences in a consistent fashion.

REFERENCES

American Psychiatric Association. (1980). *Diagnostic and statistical manual of mental disorders* (3rd ed.). Washington, DC: Author.

Boudin, H. M. (1972). Contingency contracting as a therapeutic tool in the deceleration of amphetamine use. *Behavior Therapy, 3,* 604–608.

Burchard, J. D., Harig, P. T., Miller, R. B., & Amour, J. (1976). New strategies in community-based intervention. In E. Ribes-Inesta & A. Bandura (Eds.), *Analysis of delinquency and aggression,* Hillsdale, NJ: Erlbaum.

Cantrell, R. P., Cantrell, M. L., Huddleston, C. M., & Woolridge, R. L. (1969). Contingency contracting with school problems. *Journal of Applied Behavior Analysis, 2,* 215–220.

Christophersen, E. R., Arnold, C. M., Hill, D. W., & Quilitch, H. R. (1972). The home point system: Token reinforcement procedures by parents of children with behavior problems. *Journal of Applied Behavior Analysis, 5,* 485–497.

Davidson, W. S., & Seidman, E. (1974). Studies of behavior modification in juvenile delinquents: A review, methodological critique, and social perspective. *Psychological Bulletin, 81,* 998–1011.

DeRisi, W. J., & Butz, G. (1975). *Writing behavioral contracts.* Champaign, IL: Research.

Doke, L. A. (1976). Assessment of children's behavioral deficits. In M. Hersen &

A. S. Bellack (Eds.), *Behavioral assessment: A practical handbook*. New York: Pergamon.

Forehand, R., & Atkeson, B. M. (1977). Generality of treatment effects with parents as therapists: A review of assessment and implementation procedures. *Behavior Therapy, 8,* 575–593.

Gelfand, D. M., & Hartmann, D. P. (1975). *Child Behavior: Analysis and Therapy* (pp. 154–157). New York: Pergamon.

Griest, D. L., & Wells, K. C. (1983). Behavioral family therapy with conduct disorders in children. *Behavior Therapy, 14,* 37–53.

Haley, J. (1976). *Problem-solving therapy.* San Francisco: Jossey-Bass.

Homme, L. (1966). Human motivation and the environment. In N. Haring & R. Whelan (Eds.), *The learning environment: Relationship to behavior modification and implications for special education.* Lawrence: University of Kansas Press.

Homme, L., Csanyi, A. P., Gonzales, M. A., & Rechs, J. R. (1970). *How to use contingency contracting in the classroom.* Champaign, IL.: Research.

Horne, A. M., & Dyke, B. V. (1983). Treatment and maintenance of social learning family therapy. *Behavior Therapy, 14,* 606–613.

Kelley, M. L., & Stokes, F. S. (1982). Contingency contracting with disadvantaged youths: Improving classroom performance. *Journal of Applied Behavior Analysis, 15,* 447–454.

Kelley, M. L., & Stokes, F. S. (1984). Student-teacher contracting with goal setting for maintenance. *Behavior Modification, 8,* 223–244.

Liberman, R. P., Ferris, C., Salgado, P., & Salgado, J. (1975). Replication of Achievement Place model in California. *Journal of Applied Behavior Analysis, 8,* 287–300.

Mann, R. A. (1972). The behavior-therapeutic use of contingency contracting to control and adult behavior problem: Weight control. *Journal of Applied Behavior Analysis, 5,* 99–109.

Mann, R. A. (1976). The use of contingency contracting to facilitate durability of behavior change: Weight loss maintenance. *Addictive Behaviors, 1,* 245–249.

Mann, R. A., & Moss, G. R. (1973). The therapeutic use of a token economy to manage a young and assaultive inpatient population. *Journal of Nervous and Mental Disease, 157,* 1–9.

Mann, R. A., & Moss, G. R. (1976). The therapeutic use of a token reinforcement program with adolescent inpatients. Paper presented at the 28th annual meeting of the American Association of Psychiatric Services for Children, San Francisco.

Mann, R. A. (1976). Assessment of behavioral excesses in children. In M. Hersen & A. S. Bellack (Eds.), *Behavioral assessment: A practical handbook.* New York: Pergamon.

Miller, P. M. (1972). The use of behavioral contracting in the treatment of alcoholism: A case report. *Behavior Therapy, 3,* 593–596.

Miller, P. M., Hersen, M., & Eisler, R. M. (1974). Relative effectiveness of instructions, agreements, and reinforcement in behavioral contracts with alcoholics. *Journal of Abnormal Psychology, 5,* 548–553.

Minuchin, S. (1974). *Families and family therapy.* Cambridge, MA: Harvard University Press.

Phillips, E. L. (1968). Achievement Place: Token reinforcement procedures in a home-style rehabilitation setting for "pre-delinquent" boys. *Journal of Applied Behavior Analysis, 1,* 213–223.

Phillips, E. L., Phillips, E. A., Fixsen, D. L., & Wolf, M. M. (1971). Achievement Place: Modification of the behaviors of pre-delinquent boys within a token economy. *Journal of Applied Behavior Analysis, 4,* 45–59.

Sanders, M. R., & James, J. D. (1983). The modification of parent behavior: A review of generalization and maintenance. *Behavior Modification, 7,* 3–27.

Schwitzgebel, R. K. (1964). *Streetcorner research: An experimental approach to juvenile delinquency.* Cambridge, MA: Harvard University Press.

Stuart, R. B. (1971). Behavioral contracting within the families of delinquents. *Journal of Behavior Therapy and Experimental Psychiatry, 2,* 1–11.

Stumphauzer, J. (1976). Modification of delinquent behavior: Beginnings and current practices. *Adolescence, 11,* 13–28.

Tharp, R. G., & Wetzel, R. J. (1969). *Behavior modification in the natural environment.* New York: Academic.

Wahler, R. G. (1980). Behavior modification: Applications to childhood problems. In G. P. Sholevar, R. M. Benson, & B. J. Blinder (Eds.), *Emotional disorders in children and adolescents.* New York: Spectrum.

Wells, K. C., & Forehand, R. (1981). Childhood behavior problems in the home. In M. Hersen & A. S. Bellack (Eds.), *Behavioral assessment: A practical handbook.* New York: Pergamon.

CHAPTER 17

Substance Abuse

JOHN J. HORAN AND LAWRENCE K. STRAUS

We have chosen the words *substance abuse* in our chapter title rather than *drug abuse* because cigarettes and alcohol are rarely referred to as drugs, yet their adverse consequences to the individual and to society may be every bit as devastating as those attributable to the chronic consumption of illegal substances. Cigarette smoking alone represents an annual drain of $5 to $6 billion in health care expenses, plus an additional $12 to $18 billion due to declines in productivity, losses in wages, and increased absenteeism caused by smoking-related illness (Califano, 1979). The economic costs of alcoholism are also incredibly burdensome; moreover, this particular problem subjects us all to the additional personal threat of random vehicular violence. Alcohol-impaired driving ability is ultimately responsible for up to 25,000 traffic fatalities in the United States each year.

One's first puff of a cigarette can be terribly unpleasant, producing for example, feelings of dizziness and nausea. Why do many adolescents persist and eventually subject themselves to what is clearly the foremost preventable cause of death in America (Califano, 1979)? Alcohol is likewise an acquired taste. Why are there 3 million teenage problem-drinkers in this country (National Institute on Alcohol Abuse and Alcoholism, 1981), and what can be done about it? In our opinion the drug abuse field has been inappropriately preoccupied with the products used by "impolite" society; we hope to provide less arbitrary coverage.

Our chapter is divided into four major sections of somewhat uneven length. We open with a description of the substance abuse problem, noting definitional difficulties, epidemiological information, and various etiological factors. The second section focuses on assessment, and the third section covers various intervention modalities included in prevention programming and addictions-treatment categories. The final section illustrates the role of assertion training as a drug abuse prevention strategy and provides recommendations for comprehensive programming in applied settings.

DESCRIPTION OF THE PROBLEM

Definitional Difficulties

Some civil libertarians have argued that the drug abuse "problem" is largely one of our own making. By restricting the availability of a given substance we increase its market value, create an underground culture of users not amenable to help and suppliers not subject to taxation, and damage our law enforcement structure by draining its resources and exposing its personnel to overwhelmingly lucrative but corrupt alternatives. Rhetoric pertaining to freedom of choice—including that of self-destruction—is occasionally meshed with the libertarian perspective.

Although the civil libertarian case is not without merit, it is important to note that in a compassionate society the potential costs of self-abuse are not borne entirely by the abuser. Motorcycle helmet laws, for example, are frequently the targets of free-choice polemics, but in truth, the hundreds of thousands of dollars that may be required to rehabilitate the head trauma of a single cyclist are inevitably paid, not by the faulty decision maker, but by society at large. Likewise, the costs of drug abuse to our nation's economy are truly staggering.

Given the mores of current society, our own definition of abuse would be inextricably entwined with the frequency, quantity, and variety of adverse physical and social consequences of consumption experienced by the individual. Unfortunately, the experience of being arrested may be more hazardous on a number of dimensions than the actual act of consumption. In a society of our own making, we would prefer to define abuse strictly in terms of tissue damage and sustained psychological dysfunction. In so doing, it might surprise the reader to learn that maximum chronic use of alcohol may be more harmful than similar use of heroin (Irwin, 1973). On the other hand, the hazard potential of most drugs taken infrequently at a very low dosage level has not been clearly established. In view of these definitional difficulties, we do not distinguish between use and abuse. Rather we prefer to let readers define for themselves the boundary between these two concepts.

Epidemiological Findings

According to data gathered annually by L. D. Johnston and his associates during the past decade, overall drug use by adolescents can probably be said to have peaked in 1978. At that time experimentation with cigarettes, alcohol, and marijuana appeared to be the norm (Johnston, Bahman, & O'Malley, 1979). About 60% of all high school students had smoked at least one marijuana cigarette prior to graduation, and similar contact with alcohol and tobacco was almost universal. Conspicuous minorities of the high school population had also experimented with hallucinogens (14%), cocaine (13%), inhalants (12%), amphetamines (23%), and sedatives and tranquilizers (16%). (Percentages attached to the latter three drugs do not include medical prescription usage.) Experimental use of opiates was less common (10%), and only 1.6% of the sample had specifically tried heroin.

Further inspection of these 1978 data, however, underscores the importance of distinguishing between various levels of use. Although the percentages of students who have had one experience with a given drug may seem frightfully high, these numbers decline rather dramatically if a criterion of once or twice per month is applied. Figures for such usage are 2.6% for amphetamines and less than 1% for all other drugs except cigarettes, alcohol, and marijuana. Moreover, the percentages of students involved in higher levels of "chronic use" show continued substantial decrements.

Certainly these percentages, however small, amount to large numbers of drug-involved youth when extrapolated across the entire population. Nevertheless, the usage-distinction data temper the erroneous but popular impression that experimentation with drugs inevitably implies habit formation.

More recent epidemiological findings indicate some cause for optimism. A current survey by Johnston and his associates (University of Michigan, 1985) on the 1984 graduating class shows that overall substance abuse among adolescents has evidenced a gradual but consistent decrease since 1980. Daily and monthly use of marijuana, for example, have dropped, respectively, from 11% to 5% and 37% to 25% over the past few years. Cocaine is apparently the only substance exempt from this downward trend. Sharp increases in cocaine usage were evident between 1976 and 1979. Since 1979, however, consumption rates have remained relatively stable at 16% in one's lifetime, 12% annually, and 6% monthly.

This gradual decline in substance abuse by our nation's youth is hardly grounds for complacency. Large numbers of adolescents are currently involved with illegal drugs, and the percentages of those who abuse alcohol and/or cigarettes are serious indeed. For example, the Johnston data indicate that 5% of 1984 high school seniors drink daily and 39% acknowledge having five or more drinks on one occasion during the past two weeks (University of Michigan, 1985).

Moreover, the Surgeon General's Report (United States Public Health Service, 1979) provides especially troubling data on adolescent tobacco use: 4.9% of males aged 12 to 14, 18.1% of males aged 15 to 16, and 31% of males aged 16 to 17 smoked cigarettes at least weekly in 1974. Female rates for these age brackets were, respectively, 4.2%, 20.2%, and 25.9%. Two-thirds of the males and more than half of the females exceeded half a pack daily. These figures represent staggering increases since 1968 for young women in the 12 to 14 and 15 to 16 age categories (up 816% and 210%, respectively). Given that deaths from lung cancer in women now exceed those from breast cancer and are accelerating at nearly double the rate of increase for men (United States Department of Health and Human Services, 1984), the morally repugnant Virginia Slims advertisement fails to interpret what "You've come a long way, baby" really means. We in the substance abuse field have a long way to go. Johnston's 1983 data indicate that 21% of high school seniors continue to smoke cigarettes on a daily basis, with 13.8% exceeding the half-pack per day criterion (Johnston, O'Malley, & Bachman, 1984).

Etiological Factors

General Behavioral Variables

Of all the psychosocial correlates of drug use, perhaps the most convincing are the relationships between an individual's use of drugs and the drug-taking behavior of peers, older siblings, and parents. Reported correlations are conspicuous and convincing across all drug categories including smoking (Borland & Randolph, 1975; Levitt & Edwards, 1970; Wohlford, 1970), drinking (Kandel, Kessler, and Margulies, 1978), and the consumption of illegal substances (Kandel, 1974a, 1974b). These data lend themselves well to etiological hypotheses involving modeling and social reinforcement. Indeed, the power of these principles has been experimentally demonstrated on alcohol consumption (Dericco & Garlington, 1977) and in the formation of expressed drug attitudes (Shute, 1975; Stone & Shute, 1977).

There are, of course, potentially powerful modeling influences beyond the peer group and family. Commercial television, for example, is saturated with themes of "a pill for every ill," and the leaders of many prominent musical groups openly acknowledge their use of drugs. While modeling and social reinforcement undoubtedly play a role in the initiation of drug use, maintenance of a drug-taking habit is probably more complex. Several theoretical models exist. Pomerleau (1979), for example, offered a complex operant analysis in which cigarette smoking eventually provides a wide variety of positive and negative reinforcers independent from those that elicited exploration with the drug.

Other sources of reinforcement for the taking of drugs have been catalogued by Cahoon and Crosby (1972), Horan (1973), Miller (1973), and Miller and Barlow (1973). In addition to the positive physiological reinforcement (euphoria) resulting from drug use, positive social reinforcement may occur as well. Many readers will remember the status conferred on their adolescent peers who were able to master a cigarette inhalation without coughing. In the current youth culture, speaking from personal experience about the effects of other drugs may produce similar social benefits.

Positive reinforcement may act alone or in conjunction with negative reinforcement. In other words, one might use drugs because of the "reward" that follows or the "pain" that precedes such use, or both. As with positive reinforcement, the sources of negative reinforcement may be physiological or social. Examples of the former include chronic drug users' seeking to avoid or ward off the imminent discomforts of a withdrawal reaction by continued ingestion, and medically mismanaged "normal" individuals relying on pre- scription drugs to escape chronic pain. Similarly, one can find relief from nox- ious social situations, such as a miserable home, school, marital, or vocational life by taking drugs. The probabilities that a vicious circle will develop are high because continued use of drugs usually triggers a worsening of one's physical and social situation, which then may be followed by more and more relief-seeking (drug-taking) behavior—hence, the stereotypical alcoholic who drinks to forget the problems precipitated by previous drinking.

The Lichtenstein Model

Lichtenstein (1982) and his associates (Danaher & Lichtenstein, 1978; Lich- tenstein & Brown, 1980) have developed a four-stage "natural history" model of a smoker's career and suggested various factors responsible for each stage. First, *starting* to smoke is primarily determined by psychosocial factors, such as availability, curiosity, rebelliousness, and modeling influences. Second, *con- tinuing* the habit can be linked to the pharmacological effects of nicotine as well as to psychosocial and cognitive variables. Third, *stopping,* or at least the decision to quit, is determined by psychosocial factors, such as health, expense, aesthetics, and social support. Finally, *resuming* or relapsing can be brought about by the appearance of physiological withdrawal symptoms, al- cohol consumption, stress, social pressure, and what Marlatt has described as the "abstinence violation effect" (see next section).

The Marlatt Model

Marlatt and his associates (e.g., Marlatt, 1978; Marlatt & Donovan, 1981), have developed a cognitive-social learning model of the addiction process that accounts for acquisition, maintenance, and relapse of substance-abuse behav- ior. As with Lichtenstein's model, social factors such as availability, modeling, and peer pressure contribute to the initiation of drug use. Marlatt argues that a "predisposition" for continuing to use drugs, however, is linked to social skills deficits that produce a "perceived loss of control." The reinforcement (euphoria) derived from heroin, for example, then becomes a personally con- trollable alternative to reinforcement not attainable from complex social sit- uations, which instead spawn stress and frustration.

Maintenance of the habit occurs when the pharmacologically reinforcing properties of the drugs begin to supplant the social factors. Marlatt's concept of the "emotional paradox," however, extends our earlier discussion of general behavioral variables. At low doses alcohol, for example, leads to increased arousal subjectively labeled by the drinker as excitement, euphoria, energy, and power. As consumption increases over time, however, dysphoria sets in, but unfortunately this negative affective feedback occurs too late to exert any influence on subsequent drinking. Instead, the individual continues to drink under the mistaken belief that doing so will reduce the unpleasant feelings.

Marlatt's concept of an "abstinence violation effect" addresses the relapse problem. If a substance abuser after a prolonged period of voluntary abstinence has a subsequent drug experience, the likelihood of continued use (loss of control) increases because of two cognitive processes. The first, *cognitive dissonance,* occurs when beliefs ("I am an abstainer") and behavior ("I have consumed alcohol") are not consistent. The subsequent dissonance (guilt, depression, etc.) in itself may trigger drinking and will ultimately erode the initial belief concerning one's abstinence into something like "once a junkie, always a junkie" (see Ray, 1976). The second cognitive process, *personal attribution,* plays a corollary role in that the initial break with abstinence is perceived as being due to internal weakness and personal failure (rather than to situational factors). The subsequent dysphoria and loss of perceived self-efficacy rekindle beliefs about the drug as a means of coping and enhancing personal control.

ASSESSMENT

The third edition of the *Diagnostic and Statistical Manual of Mental Disorders* (DSM III: American Psychiatric Association, 1980) distinguishes between adult substance abuse and substance dependence, but does not make separate provisions for these problems when they occur in childhood or adolescence. *Substance abuse* is defined as a pattern of pathological use that causes an impairment in social or occupational functioning that lasts at least one month. *Substance dependence,* on the other hand, requires physiological involvement as evidenced by either tolerance or withdrawal symptoms. Thus, *dependence* means that increased doses are required to maintain the effect and that discontinuance of the drug produces unpleasant physical symptoms. Interestingly, tobacco is excluded from the abuse category; however, one can abuse and/or depend on all other drugs. Finally, DSM III describes the possible courses of the disorder as continuous, episodic, in remission, or unspecified.

Despite its widespread adoption, the DSM III is not particularly helpful for assessing the possible goals of various approaches to intervention. These goals can be classified along three dimensions, namely, *relevance, assessment mode,* and *success criteria.*

Relevance

The "bottom line" for professionals in the substance abuse field is drug abuse behavior. Has consumption frequency, quantity, and/or variety decreased as a result of our intervention? Several other variables are frequently mentioned in the literature, but their relevance falls along a wide-ranging continuum.

Some substance abuse intervention programs, for example, attempt to modify drug attitudes or drug knowledge in addition to drug behavior. The general rationale for doing so is presumably that both antidrug attitudes and increased knowledge about drugs will ultimately manifest themselves in lowered levels of substance-abuse behavior. Since attitude scales are typically more malleable than usage indices, they offer a potential consolation prize for the evaluator when no changes are registered in the actual behavioral data.

Similarly, gains in drug knowledge are relatively easy to effect. However, the relationship between drug knowledge and drug use is extremely complex. For example, the inhibiting effects of drug knowledge on drug use have yet to be clearly established. Moreover, some subsets of the knowledge variable either result from or covary with drug use (see Horan & Harrison, 1981).

Although the need to reduce actual drug abuse behavior in chronically addicted populations is obvious, there are a number of methodological difficulties involved with extrapolating that goal to projects seeking the prevention of future substance abuse. For instance, two junior high school classes exposed to experimental and control drug education programs will in all probability show no immediate differences on a behavioral use scale. In fact, eyeballing the data often will reveal that on a short-range basis, actual drug-taking behavior is negligible (if not nonexistent) among all subjects. Moreover, the interval between program completion and posttesting is inevitably so short that a majority of subjects could not be expected to even have access to many of the substances. In such cases, the project evaluator must wait several years after conducting the program, when the seducing influences of history and maturation have taken their toll, before collecting behavioral data capable of being analyzed in a meaningful manner.

In addition to the literature on assessing drug knowledge, attitudes, and behavior, there is a growing body of evidence that social-skill deficiencies play a causal role in the development of substance abuse, and that increasing one's interpersonal competence can contribute to the amelioration or prevention of a drug problem (e.g., Marlatt & Donovan, 1981; Van Hasselt, Hersen, & Milliones, 1978). Thus, measures of social skill appear highly appropriate to drug abuse assessment and program evaluation.

Unfortunately, many of the assessment devices that have been used in evaluation of drug abuse prevention projects are empirically irrelevant to the drug problem. The typical drug education program of the past decade, for example, is more likely to have been evaluated with a measure of self-acceptance than a survey of subsequent drug use. We believe that pursuits of popular human-istic goals ought to be supported on the basis of their own merits, rather than with redirected drug abuse prevention resources. Although such measures could certainly supplement a drug use assessment battery in order to examine pos-sible covariations, it's regrettable that many drug abuse prevention programs have abandoned their *raison d'être*.

Assessment Mode

In addition to the dimension of relevance, drug-abuse assessment variables can be examined from the standpoint of assessment mode. For example, data may be derived from self-report, other report, unobtrusive observations, and/or physiological monitoring. Although any drug-related outcome (including social-skills improvement) can be viewed through these channels, our primary concern here is with drug abuse behavior.

Self-reported drug use is the most common form of assessment, yet this data collection mode is inherently vulnerable to questions of validity. Might not subjects "fake good," for example, in order to avoid even the slightest possibility of eventual legal harrassment or criminal prosecution? Researchers who do not secure *à priori* legal guarantees may be subject to subpoena of their records or their knowledge of an individual's use of illegal drugs. Thus, respondent suspiciousness is adaptive, not paranoid!

Even when confidentiality is guaranteed by the experimenter, different self-report assessment procedures *per se* may exert systematic influence on out-come. In one study, only 18% of a group of interviewed subjects admitted to using or experimenting with drugs "harder" than marijuana and hashish, whereas 46% of an equivalent group acknowledged doing so on anonymous questionnaires (Horan, Wescott, Vetovich, & Swisher, 1974). Although inclu-sion of items such as, "How often have you taken curare?" (a little-known drug causing paralysis) can assist in identifying protocols of the "faking se-vere" variety (Horan, 1972; Swisher & Horan, 1973), self-report offers no way of determining how many individuals deny or minimize their drug-taking ac-tivity.

Attempting to confirm self-report data by questioning individuals residing with the subject ("other report"), can increase one's confidence in the data, or even provide an alternate measure. However, significant others are also quite capable of distorting the truth, and the validity of their answers depends on whether they have a pipeline to the subject's possibly very private con-sumption behavior.

Unobtrusive behavioral measures of the sort described by Webb, Campbell, Schwartz, and Sechrest (1966) would undoubtedly resolve some of the prob-lems with self-report. Present Orwellian speculation includes urinalysis via clandestine taps into institutional (or even residential) plumbing systems and the use of dogs trained in marijuana detection surreptitiously sniffing at experimental and control student lockers during the night. It goes without saying that such devices are at least costly and cumbersome and at most repugnant and illegal (see Flygare, 1979). At present, the art of unobtrusive drug behavior assessment remains impractical.

Chemical Verification of Self-Report: An Extended Digression

Chemical analyses of bodily products, such as breath, saliva, blood, or urine, are highly touted methods for verifying self-reported drug use. For example, smoking behavior can be objectively checked by noting the level of expired air carbon monoxide (CO) contained in a sample of a subject's breath (see Horan, Hackett, & Linberg, 1978; Lando, 1975). Nonsmokers rarely exceed a few parts per million (ppm) CO; smokers, on the other hand, typically range from 20 to 80 ppm CO, depending on the severity of their habit. Smoking behavior can also be detected by noting the level of thiocyanate in the blood (Brockway, 1978) or nicotine in the urine (Paxton & Bernacca, 1979).

Similarly, alcohol consumption is readily discernible from analysis of a subject's breath, blood, or urine. Indeed, when prosecuting drunk drivers, law enforcement personnel frequently rely on legal definitions of intoxication expressed in terms of blood alcohol concentration (Miller, Hersen, Eisler, & Watts, 1974). Finally, urine tests exist for detecting morphine, barbiturates, amphetamines, and other drugs. In fact, the Food and Drug Administration requires such testing on a regular basis for addicts enrolled in methadone maintenance programs (Edwards, 1972; Goldstein & Brown, 1969; Trellis, Smith, Alston, & Siassi, 1975).

The limitations of chemical assays for drug use have not received widespread publicity. In the first place, they are not foolproof. We know of one enterprising subject, for example, who wore a rubber bulb filled with his nondrug-involved roommate's urine in the pit of his arm. During assessment periods, he simply squeezed the bulb and forced the fluid through a pliable tube (concealed beneath his shirt-sleeve) into the test receptacle.

Other limitations may be much more serious. One problem emerges when the half-life of the substance being monitored is relatively brief. For example, in the test for verifying a smoker's self-report described above, the amount of CO in a smoker's breath actually reflects the quantity of carboxyhemoglobin (COHb) in the smoker's blood. COHb has a half-life of about five hours. This means that if a heavy smoker registering 80 ppm CO abstains for five hours, the reading will drop to 40 ppm, and then to 20 ppm after another five hours, and so forth. A smoker abstaining for a day or even less might not be detected with this technique. Ironically, the existence of a long half-life poses its own set of problems. Thiocyanate, for example, has a half-life of 14 days, which means that traces may be present nearly a month after subjects validly report that they stopped smoking.

Each chemical assay procedure has its own set of limitations. Some tests can easily be confounded by dietary habits of subjects or by their legitimate use of patent or prescribed medication. No test is fully reliable, even when conducted by closely supervised, highly competent personnel. However, unacceptably low reliability is only one of a host of problems that can occur when the researcher-therapist relies on commercial laboratories to conduct analyses (see Trellis et al., 1975). Researchers who choose not to delegate control face equipment costs that can run quite high. For example, an Ecolyzer (Energetics Science, Inc., Hawthorne, New York), which measures only CO, currently costs $1045. The capital costs of gas-liquid chromatography (glc) equipment often used in urinary analyses ranges from $4000 to $6000 (Paxton & Bernacca, 1979). Technical skill requirements also vary. The Ecolyzer mandates little more than literacy; glc equipment, on the other hand, demands a fair degree of laboratory savvy.

The obtrusiveness of chemical assays poses two sets of problems. First, subject resistance fluctuates with the nature of the bodily product being assayed. Breath and saliva tests routinely pose no problem. Urine specimen requests are occasionally refused. Many subjects, however, will balk at having blood samples drawn, especially if such monitoring is required on a regular basis. Second, the generalization potential of treatment programs evaluated with chemical assays is difficult to determine. The pretest is undoubtedly a highly reactive event. Therefore, complex Solomon-type experimental designs may be required to adequately sort out treatment effects from those attributable to testing-treatment interface (Campbell & Stanley, 1966).

In spite of the fact that the foregoing commentary might be construed as pessimistic, we strongly believe that chemical collaboration of self-report data is of utmost importance in the context of research on addictions treatment. Apart from the utility of biological assays in their own right, their use undoubtedly increases the accuracy of self-report measures. Most work with adolescents, however, is school-based and prevention-oriented. Although chemical assays can be routinely utilized in medical, military, or penal settings, their application to school populations, for example, may elicit objections grounded on the Constitution and Bill of Rights. Thus, except for a few recent endeavors targeting smoking behavior, no drug education program to our knowledge has ever been evaluated with chemically verified self-report data.*

*The School Board in East Rutherford, New Jersey, has just adopted a policy requiring high school students to undergo urine tests for drugs, which, if positive, may result in their being barred from classes and their names being turned over to police. This "assessment" endeavor is apparently not coupled with any other intervention effort, and its legality will likely be tested in the courts.

Success Criteria

The final assessment dimension is the definition of program success, which presumably ought to be the mirror image of what constitutes a clinical problem. Decreased consumption frequency (evidenced by self-report and/or lowered quantities of targeted biological compounds) is a consensually validated objective.

In the case of cigarette smoking, we would further argue that abstinence provides the most meaningful test of treatment efficacy. Complete elimination of the habit is the goal sought by most smokers undergoing treatment. This is a wise choice since those who simply reduce their consumption level eventually return to baseline (Lichtenstein & Danaher, 1976). Moreover, abstinence represents the ultimate reduction of health hazard. For research purposes, abstinence data generate the most confidence. In the first place, subjects can discriminate whether they are smoking or not with greater accuracy than rate estimation allows. Similarly, a person in the environment nominated by the subject to confirm the self-report can more readily do so with abstinence rather than with rate-reduction criteria. Finally, with biological assays, abstinence is easier to verify than lowered consumption level.

Perfect abstinence (i.e., zero consumption over time) is readily understood. However, researchers do not treat "blemished" abstinence (e.g., a single consumption episode in a follow-up period) with consistency. Moreover, given the previously discussed difficulties of distinguishing "use" from "abuse," and the epidemiological normalcy of experimentation with some substances, it is difficult to argue that perfect abstinence from all other drugs is either desirable and/or attainable. The concept of "controlled drinking," for example, has frequently been defended as a viable outcome in the treatment of alcoholism (Lloyd & Salzberg, 1975; Lovibond & Caddy, 1970; Pattison, Sobell, & Sobell, 1977), albeit not without controversy (Miller & Caddy, 1977).

INTERVENTION

Practitioners in the drug abuse field typically funtion in one of three roles: (1) prevention, (2) crisis intervention, or (3) treatment of the addicted. These three enterprises are also known respectively as primary, secondary, and tertiary prevention (see Swisher, 1979), although given that substance abuse is already occurring in the latter two cases, use of the term *prevention* is probably a misnomer.

The majority of drug abuse work with adolescents falls within the strictly defined *prevention* category. Drug education and drug abuse prevention are essentially interchangeable descriptors for intervention activities directed toward general audiences who are not (yet) using drugs. The emphasis is on avoidance of future abuse rather than on reduction of present consumption levels.

Crisis intervention usually occupies a very short period between that point in time when prevention has failed and treatment begins. Crisis intervention includes specific activities, such as "telephone hotline" work with highly anxious callers and emergency room management of barbiturate comas. This subset of the drug abuse field is outside the scope of our chapter.

Most of the *addictions treatment* literature involves adults, or at least older adolescents. Although the problem of youthful addiction may seem ubiquitous, published accounts of specific treatment programs are rare. There may also be conceptual difficulties with extrapolating the logic and data implications of adult treatment downward to the youthful addict.

Prevention Programming

There is an enormous body of literature written in the name of drug education (see Blum, 1976; Evans, D'Augelli, & Branca, 1976; Goodstadt, 1974; Ostman, 1976; Shain, Riddell, & Kelty, 1977). Horan and Harrison's (1981) review, however, indicated that only 26 published references were to intervention endeavors that included drug-related outcome measures. Further, only a third of the studies cited met the main requirement of true experimentation, namely random assignment to experimental conditions. Moreover, some projects were apparently conducted in the absence of a coherent theoretical base. Most were not replicable due to the undefined or undefinable nature of the independent variable. Also, data analysis errors seemed to be the norm rather than the exception. Schaps, DiBartolo, Moskowitz, and Churgin (1981) were able to locate 75 citable projects (of which 69% were unpublished) and expressed similar dismay about the lack of design quality in this literature.

Drug abuse prevention programs are typically directed at fostering one or more of the following objectives: (1) increasing knowledge about drugs, (2) promoting healthy attitudes about drugs, and (3) decreasing potential drug abuse behavior in the general population (Horan, Shute, Swisher, & Westcott, 1973; Warner, Swisher, & Horan, 1973). Unfortunately, serious conceptual and methodological problems are inherent in these goals (Horan, 1974; Horan & Harrison, 1981). For example, there is a lack of professional consensus on just what constitutes a "healthy" drug attitude. Moreover, "prevention" by definition implies a reduced probability of future substance abuse. Yet, only 4 of the 26 projects in the Horan and Harrison (1981) review included any sort of follow-up evaluation effort.

Information-based programming is the most common prevention modality. Its logic can ultimately be traced to classical decision theory (see Bauman, 1980; Broadhurst, 1976; Bross, 1953; Horan, 1979; Mausner, 1973). However, such linkage is rarely articulated. According to this perspective, our choice between two or more alternatives (e.g., the taking of or abstaining from drugs) depends on the utilities inherent in each alternative and their probabilities of occurrence. Essentially, we act to maximize subjectively expected utility (SEU); that is, we pick the alternative with the greatest likely payoff.

The logic of information-based programming is thus fairly clear: If we provide our youth with an awareness of the dangerous consequences of drug use (negative utilities) and indicate to them that these consequences are indeed highly probable, the drug avoidance option is virtually assured. No rational human being would select an alternative with a comparably low SEU value!

Unfortunately, drug educators, however well-intentioned, often distort the facts about drugs to such an extent that the potential user is apt to find more correct information about drugs in the drug culture than in the classroom. Most accompanying instructional materials (e.g., films, posters, pamphlets) likewise attempt to miseducate (see Globetti, 1975; National Coordinating Council on Drug Education, 1972). Consequently, consumer skepticism may now be a highly reactive obstacle to drug education program evaluation.

From an empirical standpoint, Horan and Harrison's (1981) review indicated that compared to no-treatment control groups, information-based drug education curricula can raise drug knowledge levels (as measured by achievement tests keyed to the particular program). Such findings are not especially noteworthy, however, given that we might expect parallel outcomes from any high school course in geometry or civics. Information-based programming is not likely to alter attitudes or drug use behavior meaningfully until its implementation corresponds to the decision-theory framework on which it ought to be based (e.g., the information needs to be perceived as accurate and relevant to the consumption decision). Data confirming that possibility remain to be collected.

Two additional approaches to prevention were also reviewed by Horan and Harrison (1981), namely, induced cognitive dissonance and behavioral group counseling. The former derives from extrapolations of Festinger's (1957) work by Rokeach (1971), who showed that decreases in racial prejudice could be brought about by pointing out the inconsistency between certain values claimed by subjects and the holding of a bigoted attitude. Behavioral group counseling evolved from the work of Krumboltz and his colleagues (see Krumboltz & Baker, 1973), who found that modeling and verbal reinforcement procedures could foster vocational information seeking. Drug educators presumed that similar procedures could foster the development of attitudes and behaviors incompatible with the taking of drugs. Unfortunately, the implementation of these techniques can be unwieldy (e.g., student models may model the wrong behavior), and the empirical stature of both approaches is equivocal at best.

The exhaustive review by Schaps, Di Bartolo, Moskowitz, and Churgin (1981) categorizes the literature into 10 intervention strategies: information, persuasion, affective-skill, affective-experiential, counseling, tutoring/teaching, peer group, family, program development, and alternatives. These investigators note that several of the strategies are relatively unused, while many others were deployed in various combinations. Only 10 studies met their minimal criteria for design quality and service delivery intensity, and of these only two showed an impact on drug use. Given that the Schaps et al. compilation began with 75 published and unpublished documents that contained 127 evaluated programs, the fact that two should emerge as promising is not surprising and indeed might be expected by chance alone. Unfortunately, their review does not provide a reference list, thus precluding closer inspection of the data base.

Against this pessimistic backdrop, there is emerging evidence in support of social skills approaches to prevention (see Botvin, 1983; McAlister, 1983; Pentz, 1983). Later in this chapter we provide a case example of assertion training as a drug abuse prevention strategy.

Addictions Treatment

Given that exploratory use of cigarettes and alcohol is virtually universal, the foregoing paragraphs on prevention are still relevant. Even though consumption behavior has occurred, there is no real evidence of a clinical problem, and interventions more intensive than, say, providing information and modeling social skills may not be cost beneficial. We would *cautiously* extend this suggestion to include trial episodes of marijuana and some other illegal substances as well. Despite the potentially devastating penal consequences, such behavior does not in and of itself imply psychopathology. Moreover, exploratory forays with several illegal substances occur at sufficient population percentages to be considered within the bounds of statistically normal behavior.

Chronic use of drugs, however, is another matter. Addictions treatment requires a far more extensive scope and budget than is needed for drug education. The classic comprehensive approach to addictions treatment (e.g., Miller & Eisler, 1977) includes three generic objectives: (1) decrease the immediate reinforcing properties of drugs through, for example, aversion therapies and medications such as methadone, (2) teach alternative behaviors (e.g., assertiveness), and (3) rearrange the environment so that reinforcement occurs for being "off" drugs. Marlatt's model (e.g., Marlatt & Donovan, 1981) also implies the need for problem-solving skills and cognitive restructuring. The latter is employed to challenge erroneous beliefs about the effects of drugs.

Other theoretical perspectives on addictions treatment are family systems therapy (e.g., Bry, 1983; Reilly, 1984; Rueger & Liberman, 1984), Pentecostal Protestantism (United States Department of Health and Human Services, 1980), and self-help derivatives of Alcoholics Anonymous. Although behavioral principles are rarely if ever articulated in this literature, they are nevertheless easily discernable:

A behavioral analysis shows that these groups provide a potently reinforcing group atmosphere which does not tolerate drug or alcohol abuse. New, more adaptive patterns of behavior are encouraged and reinforced through group approval and increased status within the group. Drinking buddies and addicted friends are replaced with more appropriate role models exhibiting complete abstinence. The fact that the "helping agents" were once abusers of drugs or alcohol and therefore represent successful coping models may foster imitation of their behavior and enhance their reinforcing value (Miller & Eisler, 1977, p. 392).

Regardless of its theoretical basis, most of the addictions treatment literature involves adults or at least older adolescents. Although the problem of youthful addiction may seem ubiquitous, except for occasional reports on individual cases, published accounts of specific treatment programs are rare. Those that are published frequently suffer from methodological inadequacies. The Teen Challenge program, for example, reports striking differences between graduates of their facilities and comparison groups on substance abuse indices (United States Department of Health and Human Services, 1980). However, since their program requires that participants be heterosexual, free of emotional disturbance, willing to give up TV, radio, and recordings, and become "born-again" Christians, and since the comparison groups consisted of drop-outs of their program, their data are difficult to interpret. Conventional cannons of evaluation, for example, require that drop-outs and success stories be combined and contrasted against alternative or control treatments initially formed by random assignment of subjects.

On the other hand, there is a growing body of treatment literature specific to cigarette addiction that has been subjected to reasonably rigorous empirical scrutiny. A synopsis and illustration of the rapid smoking technique and its alternatives follows. Unfortunately, most of the supporting data have been derived from adult or older adolescent populations; extrapolations downward may be tenuous.

Rapid Smoking

The single most effective treatment technique to appear in the literature over the past decade is an aversion-conditioning strategy known as rapid smoking. This technique was first described by Lublin (1969), although Lichtenstein and his associates are credited with most of the procedural refinement and validation (Lichtenstein, Harris, Berchler, Wahl, & Schmahl, 1973; Schmahl, Lichtenstein, & Harris, 1972). Rapid smoking essentially consists of having cigarette users take a normal inhalation every 6 seconds until they are no longer able to do so. Each trial usually lasts about 5 minutes, during which time an average of four or five cigarettes are smoked. Two or three trials punctuated by 5-minute rest periods are given in each of 8 to 12 treatment sessions. Subjects are instructed not to smoke between sessions, and initial sessions are scheduled daily. Early studies found that rapid smoking alone produced 60% abstinence rates (verified by independent informants) 6 months after treatment. However, multiple-year follow-ups of these investigations have shown some disappointing relapse (Lichtenstein & Rodrigues, 1977). Current research efforts have also produced less impressive results. Danaher's (1977) exhaustive review points out that many failures to replicate may be due to changes in standard treatment format.

The principal drawback to the rapid smoking procedure is medical risk. Rapid smoking is specifically designed to induce physiological discomfort. It does so through bodily absorption of greatly increased quantities of tobacco smoke, which contains particularly reactive ingredients like nicotine and carbon monoxide. Since larger doses of these compounds can severely strain one's cardiovascular system, the rapid smoking procedure is unsuitable for individuals with coronary or pulmonary diseases. Although the technique is probably safe for normal smokers, the question of which screening criteria are adequate for routine clinical practice has not been satisfactorily answered. Consultation with a cardiologist is highly recommended (see Linberg, Horan, Hodgson, & Buskirk, 1982).

Risk-Free Alternatives to Rapid Smoking

Normal-paced aversive smoking (NPAS: Danaher & Lichtenstein, 1978) and focused smoking (Hackett & Horan, 1978, 1979) are promising risk-free alternatives to the rapid smoking procedure. Although both approaches were independently conceived and developed, they continue to evolve in the same direction. NPAS was distilled from an attention-placebo treatment involving Bantron (a nicotine chewing gum). Focused smoking initially resembled an *in vivo* form of covert sensitization (i.e., horror images pertaining to the potential consequences of smoking experienced during the act of smoking). However, over the course of several unpublished pilot investigations, realistic images and experiences began to be emphasized. Both NPAS and focused smoking are now sufficiently alike to permit the following common description.

The general rationale and context are similar to rapid smoking. Subjects sit facing a blank wall and smoke at their normal rate while being cued by the experimenter to focus on the discomforts of smoking. These include, for example, a bad taste in the mouth, a burning in the throat, and feelings of light-headedness and nausea. As treatment progresses, other negative sensations reported by the subjects are incorporated, such as shakiness, sweating, dull headaches, difficulty in breathing, and an uncomfortable, heavy, tired feeling. Reminders to concentrate only on the effects of smoking are repeatedly provided. Hackett and Horan (1978, 1979) found that the procedure is comparable to rapid smoking in terms of reported discomfort and treatment success (verified abstinence 40 to 60% after 6 months). In addition, the medical risks associated with rapid smoking are avoided.

CASE DESCRIPTION

Assertion training is an extremely popular and thoroughly documented vehicle for enabling individuals to do "what they really want" in particular social situations (e.g., Alberti, 1977; Galassi, Galassi, & Litz, 1974; Heimberg, Montgomery, Madsen, & Heimberg, 1977; McFall & Marston, 1970). As a drug abuse prevention strategy, assertion training rests on the assumption that many youths who would otherwise opt to abstain from taking drugs reluctantly imbibe because they lack the interpersonal skills necessary to extricate themselves from social situations where drug use is imminent.

In terms of classical decision theory, the probable role of peer approval as a utility (or disapproval as a negative utility) occurring from drug abstinence or consumption is difficult to overstate, but SEUs other than those pertaining to the likelihood of peer approval-disapproval are also relevant to drug decisions. For example, the potential user may additionally estimate (however crudely) the probabilities of euphoric and adverse physiological consequences. Thus, the role of assertion training as a drug abuse prevention strategy is limited to simply increasing the possibility of free choice. Following such intervention, youths could still decide to take drugs (on the basis of other SEUs). But in so doing, they would not be capitulating to peer pressure since they would have the competence necessary to finesse themselves away from the drug consumption option without losing face.

In order to evaluate the efficacy of this approach, Horan and Williams (1982) randomly assigned 72 nonassertive junior high students to either assertion training (in which one-third of the training stimuli involved drug-use peer pressure), placebo discussions focused on similar topics, or no treatment at all. Experimental and placebo treatments were delivered in the context of five small-group counseling sessions of 45 minutes duration over a 2-week period. Each treatment group was composed of three same-sex subjects plus the counselor.

The assertion training treatment was based on the intervention model of Galassi, Galassi, and Litz (1974), 10 general assertiveness (nondrug) training stimuli borrowed from McFall and Marston (1970), and five additional training situations involving peer pressure to use drugs. Sessions began with the counselor's instructing about assertiveness and live modeling of an assertive response to a particular training stimulus. Subjects rotated twice in the roles of speaker, listener, and responder for each stimulus. The counselor provided feedback plus additional instruction and modeling when appropriate after each subject's role-played response. Three training stimuli (one involving drugs) were used in each counseling session. Typical examples are as follows:

General assertiveness training stimulus: Picture yourself just getting out of class on any old weekday morning. Hmm. You're a little hungry and some candy or some milk would taste good right about now, so you walk over to the machines and put your money in. You press the button . . . and . . . out it comes. You open it up. Mmm. Whatever it is you just bought, it sure tastes good. It's a good break, right after class. Oh, oh. Here comes your mooching friend again. This person is always borrowing money from you. He's getting closer now, and as he gets closer your relaxation sort of changes to irritation. Oh, here he comes. Moocher: "Hey, I don't have any money and I'm hungry. How 'bout loaning me 50 cents for a candy bar?"

Drug-specific assertiveness training stimulus: You are out for the evening with a group of close friends. While eating some food at a drive-in restaurant, you notice a friend you have not seen for awhile and invite him or her over to talk. During the conversation your friend says: "I just got back from the greatest vacation. I was up in the mountains with some friends of my older brother. We really had a wild time! Hey! You should have been there. I got a chance to try a lot of different drugs that some of the other kids had. I've got some stuff at home. My family isn't home. Come on over and I'll give you some. You all will have the greatest time! Are you coming?"

The results of this study were very promising. At posttest, compared to control subjects, the experimental students showed highly significant gains on behavioral and psychometric measures of assertiveness as well as decreased willingness to use alcohol and marijuana. At 3-year follow-up, these students continued to display higher levels of assertiveness and less actual drug use.

The role of assertion training as a drug abuse prevention strategy is limited to that of fostering the competence to say no in peer pressure situations focused on drug use. More fully developed social skills programs are currently being designed and evaluated with promising preliminary results (see Botvin, 1983; McAlister, 1983; Pentz, 1983).

Although social skills are critical to adaptive decisions about drugs, other competencies also seem relevant. Thus, to maximize benefit in applied settings, we would opt for a comprehensive programming approach. At the core of such a program we would envision an instructional unit conforming to the implications of classical decision theory. Namely, accurate information regarding the utilities of drug use and abstinence along with their probabilities of occurrence should be readily available (including synopses of dissenting opinions). The misinformation contained in most drug prevention endeavors is educationally and ethically abhorrent.

But classical decision theory is woefully inadequate to the task. For example, it assumes that all alternatives are known and that all utilities are rational. Consequently, when developing their curricula, drug educators should pay close attention to the expanding problem-solving and decision-making literatures, which include strategies to help students (a) define their choice problems, (b) enlarge their response repertoires, (c) identify pertinent information, and (d) implement their desired alternative (Horan, 1979; Moskowitz, 1983).

SUMMARY

Cigarettes and alcohol are often inappropriately excluded from discussions of drug abuse. The concepts of use and abuse are difficult to differentiate. We prefer to view the latter in terms of tissue damage and sustained psychological dysfunction. Behavioral variables and comprehensive models by Lichtenstein and Marlatt provide insights into the etiology of substance abuse, including, for example, the need to differentiate initiation from maintenance. Epidemiological work supports this distinction and further indicates that although the problem of substance abuse probably peaked in 1978, large numbers of our nation's youths are involved with drugs. Assessment devices and treatment goals can be generally classified along the dimensions of relevance (e.g., consumption behavior, social skills), mode (e.g., self-report, biochemical assays), and criteria for success. Interventions are similarly classified in terms of prevention, crisis management, and addictions treatment. Social skills training, particularly the enhancement of assertiveness, has proved to be an effective prevention mode. Addictions treatment, however, is quite complex. For cigarette addiction, rapid smoking and its less hazardous alternatives are appropriate for adult smokers. However, extrapolations downward to adolescence may be tenuous. Recommended prevention activity reflects a comprehensive programming perspective that includes, for example, accurate drug information, expanded social skills enhancement, and problem-solving training.

REFERENCES

Alberti, R. (1977). *Assertiveness: Innovations, applications, issues.* San Luis Obispo, CA: Impact.

American Psychiatric Association. (1980). *Diagnostic and statistical manual of mental disorders* (3rd ed.). Washington, DC: Author.

Bauman, K. E. (1980). *Predicting adolescent drug use: The utility structure and marijuana.* New York: Praeger.

Blum, R. H. (1976). *Drug education: Results and recommendations.* Lexington, MA: Brooks.

Borland, B. L., & Randolph, J. P. (1975). Relative effects of low socio-economic status, parental smoking and poor scholastic performance on smoking among high school students. *Social Science and Medicine, 9,* 27–30.

Botvin, G. J. (1983). Prevention of adolescent substance abuse through the development of personal and social competence. In T. J. Glynn, C. G. Leukefeld, & J. P. Ludford (Eds.), *Preventing adolescent drug abuse: Intervention strategies.* (National Institute on Drug Abuse Research Monograph 47, pp. 115–140). Washington, DC: U.S. Government Printing Office.

Broadhurst, A. (1976). Applications of the psychology of decisions. In M. P. Feldman & A. Broadhurst (Eds.), *Theoretical and experimental bases of the behavior therapies.* Chichester: Wiley.

Brockway, B. S. (1978). Chemical validation of self-reported smoking rates. *Behavior Therapy, 9,* 685–686.

Bross, I. D. J. (1953). *Design for decision: An introduction to statistical decision-making.* New York: Macmillan.

Bry, B. H. (1983). Empirical foundations of family-based approaches to adolescent substance abuse. In T. J. Glynn, C. G. Luekefeld, & J. P. Ludford (Eds.), *Preventing adolescent drug abuse: Intervention strategies.* (National Institute on Drug Abuse Research Monograph Series 47, pp. 154–171). Washington, DC: U.S. Government Printing Office.

Cahoon, D. D., & Crosby, C. C. (1972). A learning approach to chronic drug use: Sources of reinforcement. *Behavior Therapy, 3,* 64–71.

Califano, J. A. (1979). The secretary's foreword. In U.S. Public Health Service, *Smoking and health: A report of the Surgeon General.* (Department of Health, Education, and Welfare, U.S. Public Health Service Publication No. 79-50066). Washington, DC: U.S. Government Printing Office.

Campbell, D. T., & Stanley, J. C. (1966). *Experimental and quasi-experimental designs for research.* Chicago: Rand McNally.

Danaher, B. G. (1977). Research on rapid smoking: Interim summary, and recommendations. *Addictive Behaviors, 2,* 151–166.

Danaher, B. G., & Lichtenstein, E. (1978). *How to become an ex-smoker.* Englewood Cliffs, NJ: Prentice-Hall.

Dericco, D. A., & Garlington, W. K. (1977). The effect of modeling and disclosure of experimenter's intent on drinking rate of college students. *Addictive Behaviors, 2,* 135–139.

Edwards, C. C. (1972). Conditions for investigational use of methadone for maintenance programs for narcotic addicts. *Federal Register, 35,* 9014–9015.

Evans, K., D'Augelli, J., & Branca, M. (1976). *Decisions are possible.* University Park: Addictions Prevention Laboratory, Pennsylvania State University.

Festinger, L. (1957). *A theory of cognitive dissonance.* Evanston, IL: Row, Peterson.

Flygare, T. J. (1979). Detecting drugs in school: The legality of scent dogs and strip searches. *Phi Delta Kappan, 61,* 280–281.

Galassi, J. P., Galassi, M. D., & Litz, M. C. (1974). Assertion training in groups using video feedback. *Journal of Counseling Psychology, 21,* 5, 390–394.

Globetti, G. (1975). An appraisal of drug education programs. In R. J. Gibbins, Y. Israel. H. Kalant, R. E. Popham, W. Schmidt, & R. G. Smart (Eds.), *Research advances in alcohol and drug problems.* New York: Wiley.

Goldstein, A., & Brown, B. W. (1969). Urine testing schedules in methadone maintenance treatment of heroin addiction. *Journal of the American Medical Association, 214,* 311–315.

Goodstadt, M. S. (Ed.). (1974). *Research on methods and programs of drug education.* Toronto: Alcoholism and Drug Addiction Research Foundation.

Hackett, G., & Horan, J. J. (1978). Focused smoking: An unequivocably safe alternative to the rapid smoking procedure. *Journal of Drug Education, 8,* 261–266.

Hackett, G., & Horan, J. J. (1979). Partial component analysis of a comprehensive smoking program. *Addictive Behaviors, 4,* 259–262.

Heimberg, D. G., Montgomery, D., Madsen, C. H., & Heimberg, J. S. (1977). Assertion training: A review of the literature. *Behavior Therapy, 8,* 953–971.

Horan, J. J. (1973). Preventing drug abuse through behavior change technology. *Journal of the Student Personnel Association for Teacher Education (SPATE), 11,* 145–152.

Horan, J. J. (1974). Outcome difficulties in drug education. *Review of Educational Research, 44,* 203–211.

Horan, J. J. (1979). *Counseling for effective decision making. A cognitive behavioral perspective.* North Scituate, MA: Duxbury.

Horan, J. J., Hackett, G., & Linberg, S. (1978). Factors to consider when using expired air carbon monoxide smoking assessment. *Addictive Behaviors, 3,* 25–28.

Horan, J. J., & Harrison, R. P. (1981). Drug abuse by children and adolescents: Perspectives on incidence, etiology, assessment, and prevention programming. In B. B. Lahey & A. E. Kazdin (Eds.), *Advances in clinical child psychology* (Vol. 4). New York: Plenum.

Horan. J. J., Shute, R. E., Swisher, J. D., & Westcott, T. B. (1973). A training model for drug abuse prevention: Content and evaluation. *Journal of Drug Education, 3,* 121–126.

Horan, J. J., Westcott, T. B., Vetovich, C., & Swisher, J. D. (1974). Drug usage: An experimental comparison of three assessment conditions. *Psychological Reports, 35,* 211–215.

Horan, J. J., & Williams, J. M. (1982). Longitudinal study of assertion training as a drug abuse prevention strategy. *American Educational Research Journal, 19*(3), 341–351.

Irwin, S. (1973). Personal communication accompanied by published materials.

Johnston, L. D., Bachman, J. G., & O'Malley, P. M. (1979). *Drugs and the class of '78: Behaviors, attitudes, and recent national trends* (Department of Health, Education and Welfare, U.S. Public Health Service Publication No. ADM 79–877). Washington, DC: U.S. Government Printing Office.

Johnston, L. D., O'Malley, P. M., & Bachman, J. G. (1984). *Highlights from Drugs and American high school students 1975–1983.* Rockville, MD: National Institute on Drug Abuse.

Kandel, D. B. (1974a). Inter- and intra-generational influences on adolescent marihuana use. *Journal of Social Issues, 30,* 107–135.

Kandel, D. B. (1974b). Interpersonal influences on adolescent illegal drug use. In E. Josephson & E. E. Carroll (Eds.), *Drug use: Epidemiological and sociological approaches.* Washington, DC: Hemisphere.

Kandel, D. B., Kessler, R. C., & Margulies, R. Z. (1978). Antecedents of adolescent initiation into stages of drug use: A developmental analysis. In D. B. Kandel (Ed.), *Longitudinal research on drug use: Empirical findings and methodological issues.* Washington, DC: Hemisphere.

Krumboltz, J. D., & Baker, R. D. (1973). Behavioral counseling for vocational decisions. In H. Borow (Ed.), *Career guidance for a new age.* Boston: Houghton Mifflin.

Lando, H. A. (1975). An objective check upon self-reported smoking levels. *Behavior Therapy, 6,* 547–549.

Levitt, E. E., & Edwards, J. A. (1970). A multivariate study of correlative factors in youthful cigarette smoking. *Developmental Psychology, 2,* 5–11.

Lichtenstein, E. (1982). The smoking problem: A behavioral perspective. *Journal of Consulting and Clinical Psychology, 50,* 6, 804–819.

Lichtenstein, E., & Brown, R. A. (1980). Smoking cessation methods: Review and recommendations. In W. R. Miller (Ed.), *The addictive behaviors* (pp. 169–206). Oxford: Pergamon.

Lichtenstein, E., & Danaher, B. G. (1976). Modification of smoking behavior: A critical analysis of theory, research, and practice. In M. Hersen, M. Eisler, & P. M. Miller (Eds.), *Progress in behavior modification* (Vol. 3, pp. 79–132). New York: Academic Press.

Lichtenstein, E., Harris, D. E., Birchler, G. P., Wahl, J. M., & Schmahl, D. P. (1973). Comparison of rapid smoking, warm smoky air, and attention placebo in the modification of smoking behavior. *Journal of Consulting and Clinical Psychology, 40,* 92–98.

Lichtenstein, E., & Rodrigues, M. P. (1977). Long term effects of rapid smoking treatment for dependent cigarette smokers. *Addictive Behaviors, 2,* 109–112.

Linberg, S. E., Horan, J. J., Hodgson, J. E., & Buskirk, E. R. (1982). Some physiological consequences of the rapid smoking treatment for cigarette addiction. *Archives of Environmental Health, 37,* 88–92.

Lloyd, R. W., & Salzberg, H. C. (1975). Controlled social drinking: An alternative to abstinence as a treatment goal for some alcohol abusers. *Psychological Bulletin, 82,* 815–842.

Lovibond, S. H., & Caddy, G. R. (1970). Discriminated aversive control in the moderation of alcoholics' drinking behavior. *Behavior Therapy, 1,* 437–444.

Lublin, I. (1969). Principles governing the choice of unconditioned stimuli in aversive conditioning. In R. D. Kubin & S. M. Franks (Eds.), *Advances in behavior therapy 1968.* New York: Wiley.

Marlatt, G. A. (1978). Craving for alcohol, loss of control, and relapse: A cognitive-behavioral analysis. In P. E. Nathan, G. A. Marlatt, & T. Loberg (Eds.), *Alcoholism: New directions in behavioral research and treatment.* New York: Plenum.

Marlatt, G. A., & Donovan, D. M. (1981). Alcoholism and drug dependence: Cognitive social-learning factors in addictive behaviors. In W. E. Craighead, A. E. Kazdin, & M. J. Mahoney (Eds.), *Behavior modification: Principles, issues, and applications* (2nd ed., pp. 264–285). Boston: Houghton Mifflin.

Mausner, B. (1973). An ecological view of cigarette smoking. *Journal of Abnormal Psychology, 81,* 115–126.

McAlister, A. L. (1983). Social-psychological approaches. In T. J. Glynn, C. G. Leukefeld, & J. P. Ludford (Eds.), *Preventing adolescent drug abuse: Intervention strategies.* (National Institute on Drug Abuse Research Monograph 47, pp. 36–50). Washington, DC: U.S. Government Printing Office.

McFall, R. M. & Marston, A. R. (1970). An experimental investigation of behavioral rehearsal in assertion training. *Journal of Abnormal Psychology, 76,* 295–303.

Miller, P. M. (1973). Behavioral treatment of drug addiction: A review. *International Journal of the Addictions, 8,* 511–519.

Miller, P. M., & Barlow, D. H. (1973). Behavioral approaches to the treatment of alcoholism. *Journal of Nervous and Mental Disease, 157,* 10–20.

Miller, P. M., & Eisler, R. M. (1977). Assertive behavior in alcoholics: A descriptive analysis. *Behavior Therapy, 8,* 10–20.

Miller, P. M., Hersen, M., Eisler, R. M., & Watts, J. G. (1974). Contingent reinforcement of lowered blood/alcohol levels in an outpatient chronic alcoholic. *Behaviour Research and Therapy, 12,* 261–263.

Miller, W. R., & Caddy, G. R. (1977). Abstinence and controlled drinking in the treatment of problem drinkers. *Journal of Studies on Alcoholism, 38,* 986–1003.

Moskowitz, J. M. (1983). Preventing adolescent substance abuse through drug education. In T. J. Glynn, C. G. Leukefeld, & J. P. Ludford (Eds.), *Preventing adolescent drug abuse: Intervention strategies.* (National Institute on Drug Abuse Research Monograph Series 47, pp. 233–249). Washington, DC: U.S. Government Printing Office.

National Coordinating Council on Drug Education. (1972). *Drug abuse films.* Washington, DC: Drug Abuse Council.

National Institute on Alcohol Abuse and Alcoholism. (1981). *Fifth special report to the U.S. Congress on alcohol and health.* (Department of Health and Human Services Publication No. ADM 81-1080). Washington, DC: U.S. Government Printing Office.

Ostman, R. E. (1976). *Communication research and drug education.* Beverly Hills, CA: Sage.

Pattison, E. M., Sobell, M. B., & Sobell, L. C. (1977). *Emerging concepts of alcohol dependence.* New York: Springer.

Paxton, R., & Bernacca, G. (1979). Urinary nicotine concentration as a function of time since last cigarette: Implications for detecting faking in smoking clinics. *Behavior Therapy, 10,* 523–528.

Pentz, M. A. (1983). Prevention of adolescent substance abuse through social skill development. In T. J. Glynn, C. G. Leukefeld, & J. P. Ludford (Eds.), *Preventing adolescent drug abuse: Intervention strategies.* (National Institute on Drug Abuse

Research Monograph Series 47, pp. 195–232). Washington, DC: U.S. Government Printing Office.

Pomerleau, O. F. (1979). Why people smoke: Current psychological models. In P. Davidson (Ed.), *Behavioral medicine: Changing health styles.* New York: Brunner/Mazel.

Ray, M. B. (1976). The cycle of abstinence and relapse among heroin addicts. In R. H. Coombs, L. J. Fry, & P. G. Lewis (Eds.), *Socialization in drug abuse.* Cambridge, MA: Schenkman.

Reilly, D. M. (1984). Family therapy with adolescent drug abusers and their families: Defying gravity and achieving escape velocity. *Journal of Drug Issues, 14,* 2, 381–391.

Reuger, D. R., & Liberman, R. P. (1984). Behavioral family therapy for delinquent and substance-abusing adolescents. *Journal of Drug Issues, 14*(2), 403–418.

Rokeach, M. (1971). Long range experimental modification of values, attitudes, and behaviors. *American Psychologist, 26,* 453–459.

Schaps, E., DiBartolo, R., Moskowitz, J., & Churgin, S. (1981). A review of 127 drug abuse prevention program evaluations. *Journal of Drug Issues, 1,* 14–44.

Schmahl, D. P., Lichtenstein, E., & Harris, W. E. (1972). Successful treatment of habitual smokers with warm, smoky air and rapid smoking. *Journal of Consulting and Clinical Psychology, 38,* 105–111.

Shain, M., Riddell, W., & Kelty, H. L. (1977). *Influence, choice, and drugs.* Lexington, MA: Heath.

Shute, R. (1975). Impact of peer pressure on the verbally expressed drug attitudes of male college students. *American Journal of Drug and Alcohol Abuse, 2,* 231–243.

Stone, C. I., & Shute, R. (1977). Persuader sex differences and peer pressure effects on attitudes toward drug abuse. *American Journal of Drug and Alcohol Abuse, 4,* 55–64.

Swisher, J. D. (1979). Diagnosis and treatment of substance abuse. In K. W. Hylbert & K. W. Hylbert, Jr. (Eds.), *Medical information for human service workers.* State College, PA: Counselor Education Press.

Swisher, J. D., & Horan, J. J. (1973). The Pennsylvania State University Evaluation Scales. Chapter in L. A. Abrams, E. Garfield, and J. D. Swisher (Eds.), *Accountability in drug education: A model for evaluation.* Washington, D.C.: Drug Abuse Council, pp. 87–99.

Trellis, E. S., Smith, F. F., Alston, D. C., & Siassi, I. (1975). The pitfalls of urine survellience: The role of research in evaluation and remedy. *Addictive Behaviors, 1,* 83–88.

United States Department of Health and Human Services. (1980). *An evaluation of the teen challenge treatment program.* (National Institute on Drug Abuse Services Report). Washington, DC: U.S. Government Printing Office.

United States Department of Health and Human Services. (1984). *The health consequences of smoking: Chronic obstructive lung disease. A report of the Surgeon General.* Rockville, MD: USDHHS Public Health Service, Office on Smoking and Health.

United States Public Health Service. (1979). *Smoking and health: A report of the Surgeon General* (Department of Health, Education, and Welfare, U.S. Public Health Service Publication No. 70-50066). Washington, DC: U.S. Government Printing Office.

University of Michigan. (January 4, 1985). Drug study press release. News and Information Services, University of Michigan.

Van Hasselt, V. B., Hersen, M., & Milliones, J. (1978). Social skills training for alcoholics and drug addicts: A review. *Addictive Behaviors, 3,* 221–233.

Warner, R. W., Swisher, J. D., & Horan, J. J. (1973). Drug abuse prevention: A behavioral approach. *National Association of Secondary School Principals Bulletin, 57,* 49–54.

Webb, E. J., Campbell, D. T., Schwartz, R. D., & Sechrest, L. (1966). *Unobtrusive measures: Non-reactive research in the social sciences.* Chicago: Rand McNally.

Wohlford, P. (1970). Initiation of cigarette smoking: Is it related to parental behavior? *Journal of Consulting and Clinical Psychology, 34,* 148–151.

CHAPTER 18

Anorexia and Bulimia

FRANCIS C. HARRIS AND CAROLYN F. PHELPS

Anorexia nervosa and bulimia appear to be well on their way to becoming the "disorders of the eighties." In an era when "you can never be too thin," eating disorders and attention to them appear to be flourishing. The topics have been addressed in TV movies (*Best Little Girl in the World,* 1981), television shows with medical themes (e.g., *Trapper John, M.D.*), various "talkshows," and even soap operas. Women's magazines have featured articles such as *Cosmopolitan*'s "I suffered from Binge-Purge Syndrome" (November 1985), and well-known people (e.g., Jane Fonda, Cherry Boone) have "gone public" about their personal battles with anorexia or bulimia. The more entrepreneurial even have published memoirs complete with before-and-after pictures (O'Neill, 1982). Such widespread attention seems to have brought a certain degree of prestige and glamour to these disorders. The impact of this popular attention appears to be mixed. Some of our patients have reported learning "tricks" from these sources, while others have been prompted to recognize the need for professional help.

On the more scholarly level, at least nine books on eating disorders have been published within the last 5 years (Boskind-White & White, 1983; Emmett, 1985; Garfinkel & Garner, 1982; Garner & Garfinkel, 1985; Goodstein, 1983; Hawkins, Fremouw & Clement, 1984; Neuman & Halvorson, 1983; Sours, 1980; Wilson, 1983). Although various approaches to the conceptualization and treatment of anorexia and bulimia are represented in these volumes, all emphasize the seriousness and persistence of the disorders. The present chapter will present (1) a brief description of anorexia and bulimia, (2) a review of behavioral assessment and treatment strategies, and (3) a case history of a bulimia outpatient.

DEFINITION AND INCIDENCE OF ANOREXIA NERVOSA

The *Diagnostic and Statistical Manual of Mental Disorders,* third edition (DSM-III: American Psychiatric Association, 1980) has set the following diagnostic criteria for anorexia nervosa:

1. Loss of 25% of original body weight (from a normal weight)
2. Distorted body image
3. Intense fear of becoming obese
4. Refusal to maintain a normal body weight
5. No known physical illness that could account for the disorder (p. 67)

This disorder most often occurs in adolescent females; however, many authors have noted it in older patients (Garfinkel, 1974; Garfinkel & Garner, 1982; Hsu, 1983). Despite the syndrome's name, *anorexia,* and its "image" as an appetitive disorder, loss of appetite is *not* common among anorectics (Hsu, 1983). Instead, patients appear to *deny* that they experience hunger, even when emaciated.

A distinct set of psychological correlates of anorexia nervosa have been observed by numerous investigators (Bemis, 1978; Bruch, 1973; 1985; Crisp, Hsu, Harding, & Hartshorn, 1980; Garfinkel & Garner, 1982; Morgan & Russell, 1975). The anorectic often is described as withdrawn, isolated, introverted, stubborn, selfish, manipulative, and perfectionistic. She often denies the existence of any problems, especially those involving food or weight. In addition, avoidance of public eating, idiosyncratic and monotonous diets, preoccupation with food and weight, binge eating, vomiting, laxative abuse, hyperactivity, lying, and stealing are behaviors exhibited by many anorectics.

Despite the striking resemblance among these patients, there is strong evidence that anorexia nervosa is a heterogeneous syndrome. Two specific subtypes have been identified: *restricting anorectics* who control weight by food refusal and excessive exercise, and *bulimic anorectics* whose weight loss is a function of vomiting and/or laxative abuse (Beumont, 1977; Beumont, George, & Smart, 1976; Casper, Eckert, Halmi, Goldberg, & Davis, 1980; Garfinkel & Garner, 1982). Additionally, bulimic anorectics have been described as socially and psychologically more disturbed than restricting anorectics.

Epidemiological reports estimating the prevalence of anorexia nervosa have been fraught with methodological problems, inadequate archival records, and the use of inconsistent diagnostic criteria, which have made it difficult to measure precisely the number of new cases identified each year. Nonetheless, recent data support an increasing prevalence of anorexia, particularly in the last decade (Duddle, 1973; Jones, Fox, Babigan, & Hutton, 1980). Although public and professional awareness probably accounts for some of this reported increase, it is likely that other social and psychological factors also have contributed to the rise in the incidence of anorexia nervosa. Conservative estimates suggest 1 in every 250 females develops the disorder (American Psychiatric Association, 1980).

DEFINITION AND INCIDENCE OF BULIMIA

The alternation of binge eating with various behaviors designed to minimize the likelihood of weight gain, although first noted in anorectics (Casper, 1983), also has been observed in normal-weight women. This syndrome has been referred to as bulimia (American Psychiatric Association, 1980), bulimarexia (Boskind-White & White, 1983), bulimia nervosa (Russell, 1979), binge-purge syndrome (Hawkins, Fremouw, & Clement, 1984), and dietary chaos syndrome (Palmer, 1979). Unfortunately, these terms have often been used interchangeably, despite the fact that no two of them refer to the same symptom cluster. For example, "bulimia nervosa" has been used by some to denote a pattern of binge eating and purging in normal-weight women who may have had a history of anorexia (Hamilton, Gelwick, & Meade, 1984; Russell, 1979). DSM-III described the cardinal features of bulimia as:

1. Recurrent episodes of binge eating (rapid consumption of a large amount of food in a discrete period of time, usually less than two hours)
2. At least three of the following:
   a. Consumption of high calorie, easily ingested food during a binge
   b. Inconspicuous eating during a binge
   c. Termination of such eating episodes by abdominal pain, sleep, social interruption, or self-induced vomiting
   d. Repeated attempts to lose weight by severely restrictive diets, self-induced vomiting, or use of cathartics or diuretics
   e. Frequent weight fluctuations greater than 10 pounds due to alternating binges and fasts
3. Awareness that the eating pattern is abnormal and fear of not being able to stop voluntarily
4. Depressed mood and self-deprecating thoughts following binges
5. The bulimic episodes are not due to anorexia nervosa or any known physical disorder. (American Psychiatric Association, 1980, pp. 70–71)

DSM-III does not distinguish: (1) overweight binge eaters from normal-weight binge purgers, and (2) bulimic patients with and without a history of anorexia nervosa. It is possible, however, that these factors are important in terms of etiology, psychological and behavioral correlates of the disorder, response to treatment, and course of the disorder. While Hamilton and his colleagues (Hamilton et al., 1984) suggest that the DSM-III definition should be used as the standard because it is the most encompassing, we contend that this definition is too broad. Specifically, it obscures important differences between restricting anorectics and bulimic anorectics.

Bulimics appear to differ from anorectics on a number of behavioral and psychosocial variables. They exhibit more drug and alcohol dependency, suicidal ideation, affective reactivity, lability, impulsiveness, anxiety, depression, and sexual and social sophistication (Beumont, 1977; Beumont et al., 1976; Casper et al., 1980; Crisp et al., 1980; Hamilton et al., 1984; Russell, 1979). Onset of the disorder typically occurs in late adolescence through young adulthood, with 16- to 24-year-old women at greatest risk (Bruch, 1973; Hamilton et al., 1984). Four recent epidemiological studies have estimated the prevalence of bulimia at 7.7 to 13% (Crowther, Post, & Zaynor, 1985; Fairburn & Cooper, 1982; Halmi, Falk, & Schwartz, 1982; Hamilton et al., 1984). Various populations were sampled in these investigations including respondents to a woman's magazine survey, college students, and high school students. The highest prevalence estimates were obtained in a sample of college students (Halmi et al., 1982; Hamilton et al., 1984).

BEHAVIORAL ASSESSMENT OF EATING DISORDERS

Typical clinical assessment procedures used with anorectics and bulimics have focused primarily on the core features of the eating disorder, neglecting behavioral correlates that may be crucial to the design of an effective treatment program. A broad-based method of assessing eating-disordered patients would include a thorough clinical interview, use of valid and reliable instruments to evaluate eating attitudes and eating behaviors, and the evaluation of the behavioral correlates of eating disorders.

Outlines of clinical interviews designed to provide detailed information regarding the patient's presenting problem and psychosocial functioning have been presented elsewhere (Garfinkel & Garner, 1982; Garner & Garfinkel, 1985; Harris et al., 1983). In addition to eliciting information about eating and weight-control behavior, the interviews should collect information regarding (1) thoughts about eating and weight, (2) events preceding food refusal/binge-purge episodes, (3) attempts to alter the eating disorder (self-help and help from others), (4) medical status, (5) special relationships with family members and peers, (6) activities, (7) academic performance, (8) drug and alcohol use, and (9) motivation to change.

Several instruments have been developed to assess eating attitudes and eating behaviors among anorectic and bulimic patients. Unfortunately, the psychometric properties of many of these instruments are unknown. Instruments in which reliability and validity have been demonstrated include the Eating Attitudes Test (EAT: Garner & Garfinkel, 1979), the Eating Disorder Inventory (EDI: Garner, Olmstead, & Polivy, 1983), and the Binge Scale (BS: Hawkins & Clement, 1980). These inventories have been used as diagnostic tools and treatment outcome measures. We have provided detailed information regarding the psychometric properties of these instruments elsewhere (Harris & Phelps, in press). Each instrument is presented in a forced choice, self-report format. The EDI and the EAT are used primarily in the identification of anorectic patients. Although the EDI was developed to assess psychological and behavioral correlates of both anorexia *and* bulimia, important aspects of bulimia such as mood lability and impulsivity were omitted. Thus, until further validation studies are conducted using bulimic subjects, the EDI probably should be used only to differentiate restricting anorectics from bulimic anorectics. There appears to be a positive relationship between the BS and the EAT (Hawkins & Clement, 1984; Phelps, 1984). Unfortunately, neither instrument provides empirically derived scores that differentiate bulimics from other groups. However, we have found it useful to use a total BS score of 0 to 5 to identify "noneating-disordered" subjects (Phelps, 1984). These cutoff scores are based on the mean total BS score for normal-weight women, where a score of 14 is two standard deviations above the mean.

In addition to the assessment of specific eating attitudes and eating behaviors, the evaluation of depression appears to be a useful component of a comprehensive assessment program. A number of depressive features such as dysphoric affect, incidence of depression in immediate family members, abnormal cortisol functioning, and appetite and sleep disturbances have been observed in eating-disordered patients. On this basis, some have speculated that anorexia and bulimia are merely variants of affective disorder (Cantwell, Sturzenberger, Borroughs, Salkin, & Green, 1977; Hudson, Laffer, & Pope, 1982). However, evidence supporting this hypothesis has been inconsistent. Nonetheless, many of the depressive features associated with eating disorders do abate when normal weight and normal eating behavior is restored. Consequently, the Beck Depression Inventory (Beck, Ward, Mendelson, Mock, & Erbaugh, 1961) has been an efficient and valid method of assessing depression in eating-disordered patients.

Finally, our clinical experience suggests the importance of assessing psychosocial correlates of anorexia and bulimia. Specifically, the assessment of *interpersonal competence* appears necessary since diverse approaches to the conceptualization and treatment of eating disorders all indicate (1) food refusal and binge-purging are related to interpersonal stress, and (2) eating-disordered patients often use food refusal and binge-purging when an appropriate interpersonal response would be more effective. In an effort to approach systematically the assessment of interpersonal problem-solving skills in eating-disordered patients, we recently developed a 28-item self-report instrument. The instrument consists of problematic interpersonal situations typically encountered by eating-disordered patients. Respondents are asked to (1) list all *possible* responses in a given situation, (2) identify the "best" response, and (3) predict their own "most likely" response in that situation. Although information can be obtained regarding specific components of problem-solv-

ing skills (i.e., response generation, response evaluation, and response imple
mentation), preliminary data suggest deficits in eating-disordered patients
problem-solving skills are restricted to response implementation. That is, the}
have less difficulty in identifying an appropriate response than they do in im·
plementing that response. Preliminary analyses of the instrument's reliability
and validity are encouraging.

BEHAVIORAL TREATMENT OF EATING DISORDERS

A wide range of behavioral interventions, including operant conditioning, systematic desensitization, social skills training, and response prevention/expo-
sure, have been used in the treatment of eating disorders. Typically, these interventions focused on one or two particular features of the disorder (e.g.,
weight loss, fear of weight gain, or poor interpersonal interactions).

At least 30 investigations have used operant conditioning procedures aimed
at rapid weight restoration to treat anorexia (Agras, Barlow, Chapin, Abel, &
Leitenberg, 1974; Azzerad & Stafford, 1969; Bachrach, Erwin, & Mohr, 1965;
Bhanji & Thompson, 1974; Bianco, 1972; Blinder, Freeman, & Stunkard, 1970;
Blue, 1979; Brady & Rieger, 1972; Eckert, Goldberg, Halmi, Casper, & Davis,
1979; Elkin, Hersen, Eisler, & Williams, 1973; Fichter & Kessler, 1980; Garfinkel, Kline, & Stancer, 1973; Garfinkel, Molodofsky, & Garner, 1977; Geller,
1975; Halmi, Powers & Cunningham, 1975; Hauserman & Lavin, 1977; Leitenberg, Agras, & Thomson, 1968; Lobb & Schaefer, 1972; McGlynn, 1980;
Neumann & Gaoni, 1975; Parker, Blazer, & Wyrick, 1977; Pertschuk, 1977;
Pertschuk, Edwards, & Pommerleau, 1978; Poole & Sanson, 1978; Rosen,
1980; Rosman, Minuchin, Liebman, & Baker, 1976; Stumphauser, 1969; Vander-
eyecken & Pieters, 1978; Werry & Bull, 1975; Wulliemier, 1978). Typically, a
patient would be allotted material rewards or social privileges, such as time
out of her room, television access, or visitors based on her daily weight or
food consumption. Weight gain ($n = 25$) was used more frequently than caloric intake ($n = 7$) as a criterion for reinforcement, probably because changes
in weight are observed more easily and are less likely to be manipulated by
the patient. Since treatment always occurred in an inpatient setting where en·
vironmental manipulation was easily achieved, it was not surprising that all
of the investigations reported rapid short-term weight gains. Unfortunately,
only 5 of the 32 investigations used appropriate control procedures such that
treatment effects could be attributed to the behavioral intervention implemented (Eckert et al., 1979; Garfinkel et al., 1977; Pertschuk, 1977; Vander-
eyecken & Pieters, 1978; Wulliemier, 1978). Moreover, very little attention was
paid to the evaluation of adaptive functioning either during hospitalization or
following the patient's discharge. When follow-up contacts occurred, they
consisted chiefly of unsubstantiated reports from the patient or her relatives

and rarely assessed psychosocial functioning. In 9 of 14 investigations that did assess psychosocial functioning, no improvements or a deterioration in adaptive functioning was observed (Agras & Werne, 1978; Blinder et al., 1970; Brady & Rieger, 1972; Fichter & Kessler, 1980; Garfinkel et al., 1977; Halmi et al., 1975; Pertschuk, 1977; Rosman et al., 1976). Based on these results several investigators concluded that behavioral interventions aimed solely at weight restoration were not effective (Bianco, 1972; Blinder et al., 1970; Garfinkel et al., 1977; Geller, 1975; Hauserman & Lavin, 1977).

Systematic desensitization has been used in several cases to address the patients' marked fear of obesity (Hallsten, 1965; Lang, 1965; Ollendick, 1979; Schnurer, Rubin, & Roy, 1973). Desensitization hierarchies consisted of anxiety-producing situations associated with weight gain or eating. Patients constructed their own hierarchies, which included items such as travel away from home, being the center of attention (Lang, 1965), eating at home (Hallsten, 1965), changes in appearance associated with weight gain (Ollendick, 1979; Schnurer et al., 1973), food (Schnurer et al., 1973), and criticism (Lang, 1965; Ollendick, 1979). Results indicated that systematic desensitization, much like operant conditioning procedures, generally was effective only in short-term weight restoration. The exception was Ollendick's (1979) program, which combined systematic desensitization with cognitive restructuring to produce more durable effects. These findings suggest that a broad-based behavioral approach to treatment would be more effective than a "single-intervention" strategy.

Pillay and Crisp (1981) were the first investigators to address directly and attempt to improve interpersonal competence in eating-disordered patients. They developed a social skills training program to treat the social isolation and anxiety exhibited by many of their patients after they attained a normal weight. Anorectics receiving social skills training plus the "established therapy program" were compared to anorectics who received only the established treatment. Although social skills training initially appeared to be more effective than the established treatment alone, these differences were not maintained at a 1-year follow-up assessment. In fact, the standard group appeared to be more competent interpersonally than the group that received social skills training. While Pillay and Crisp (1981) concluded that social skills training was inferior to the standard treatment in promoting change both in weight and in psychosocial adjustment, the apparent inadequacy of the social skills program itself may account for these results. Specifically, social skills training consisted of practicing tasks such as responding to a word association test and to contrived, trivial, interpersonal situations. Therefore, it is possible that their program did not teach the necessary social skills that would have resulted in increased personal effectiveness. A more appropriate social skills program probably would (1) delineate the specific stressful situations or problematic responses that have some relationship to the patient's maladaptive eating behavior, and (2) teach alternative, effective interpersonal responses to those situations.

Far fewer accounts exist regarding the application of behavioral interventions in the treatment of bulimia (Leitenberg, Gross, Peterson, & Rosen, 1984; Linden, 1980; Rosen & Leitenberg, 1982). Linden (1980) used a multifaceted intervention that incorporated response delay, stimulus control, and assertiveness training and reported marked improvement in a bulimic patient's eating behavior. Interestingly, there was no evaluation of interpersonal competence, although the intervention was designed to alter interpersonal behavior.

Exposure plus response prevention treatment has been used in two separate investigations (Rosen, 1980; Rosen & Leitenberg, 1982). Results of these investigations indicated that all six treated patients exhibited improvements in eating behavior, eating attitudes, self-esteem, depression, and mood lability. During phase one of the two-phase program, patients were instructed to eat preselected food until they experienced a strong urge to vomit. Exposure was limited to three categories of food: large meals, junk food, and snacks. In an attempt to maximize the likelihood of generalization, sessions involving large meals and junk food were conducted in restaurants. When the patient experienced an urge to vomit, she was instructed to focus her attention on her anxiety level. Response prevention continued until the urge to vomit passed. In phase one, the patient was not instructed to decrease binge eating or vomiting between sessions. During phase two, exposure sessions continued and the patient was encouraged to avoid binging and vomiting throughout the week. Unfortunately, no long-term follow-up data were available.

Currently, behavioral conceptualizations of anorexia and bulimia use a negative reinforcement paradigm to explain the development and maintenance of eating-disorder behavior (Harris et al., 1983; Harris & Phelps, 1985; Leitenberg et al., 1984; Rosen & Leitenberg, 1982). According to this model, urges to eat result in a fear of gaining weight and concurrent feelings of anxiety. Food refusal and/or purging become strengthened since they decrease the likelihood of weight gain and minimize subjective feelings of anxiety. As this pattern continues, maladaptive eating behaviors generalize and are used to alleviate anxiety arising from sources other than a fear of weight gain (e.g., interpersonal conflict, academic performance). Then food refusal and/or binge-purging are further strengthened in a positive reinforcement paradigm where the patient perceives some secondary benefit from engaging in the behavior. These benefits might be attention for weight loss or an increased ability to manipulate others in a variety of ways (Harris et al., 1983; Harris & Phelps, 1985).

The remainder of this chapter is devoted to the presentation of the case of a bulimic patient who was successfully treated as an outpatient according to the assessment and treatment model presented above. Specifically, this case illustrates the importance of a thorough assessment and the use of the obtained information in the planning and evaluation of treatment. The approach uses behavioral strategies designed to (1) produce relatively rapid improvements in the acute aspects of the eating disorder, and (2) promote long-term maintenance and generalization of treatment effects.

CASE HISTORY

Linda was a 19-year-old, white, single student who sought treatment for bulimia at a university counseling center. At the time of her initial presentation she was a freshman, living in an off-campus apartment with several female roommates.

Linda described a pattern of eating that alternated between binge-purging and rigorous dieting. She estimated binge-vomiting three times daily and reported feelings of depression, self-disgust, and self-hatred following a binge-purge episode. A typical binge consisted of three sandwiches, 1/2 gallon of ice cream, and 1/2 pound of cookies. In addition to vomiting after every binge, Linda also admitted to vomiting when she consumed small amounts of "forbidden foods" (e.g., one cookie or one ice cream cone), or when she "just felt fat." Linda denied using laxatives, diuretics, diet pills, or excessive exercise to control her weight. She also denied the recreational use of alcohol or drugs. At the initial evaluation she was 68 inches tall and weighed 123 pounds (94% of ideal weight; Cooper, 1982). She appeared to have a limited social support network and very infrequent social activities.

Linda reported a 1½-year history of bulimia, dating the onset of her binge-vomiting to the summer preceding her senior year in high school. Prior to that time, she had lost 25 pounds through dieting and vigorous exercise. Finding it difficult to maintain her restrictive dietary habits, she began vomiting after meals. In fact, vomiting as a means of weight control was recommended to her by a friend who Linda described as "anorectic." Initially, she restricted her binge-purging to once a week. However, within 1 month the frequency increased to five times per week. Specific environmental stressors coinciding with the onset of the bulimia included her father's alcohol dependency, her parents' marital conflict, and anxiety regarding college plans. The frequency of her binge-purge episodes increased to once per day after she entered college. She described feeling lonely and estranged from her friends and family during this time and was afraid that her parents might divorce. Additionally, she reported feeling very anxious about her school performance. Her binge-vomiting increased to three times per day by the end of her first semester at college. She pinpointed a stressful visit with her family and a poor grade report from the previous school term as factors precipitating this increase.

Prior to seeking professional help, Linda's efforts to control the bulimia consisted of failed promises to "never do it again," and confiding in her mother and sisters about her problem. Not surprisingly, neither method was effective in reducing her binge-purge episodes. Resolutions to "never do it again" always followed a binge-purge episode and resulted in a severe restriction of dietary intake, an effort that only served to facilitate another episode. Likewise, the patient's mother and sisters offered no alternatives and were described as "not knowing what to do." In fact, Linda stated that her family's reaction only increased her feelings of disappointment, frustration, and despair. Nonetheless, she did not seek professional help until she began experiencing problems in concentration that severely affected her ability to study. Specifically, the patient described being preoccupied with thoughts about food or weight such that she was unable to focus her attention on school work.

Linda was the second of four children raised in a middle-class, Catholic family. Her 48-year-old father had been unemployed for 3 years since he quit his job as a banker to write a book. She described her father as a "very intelligent, lazy, alcoholic" who began drinking heavily when his attempts to write were unsuccessful. Her father's drinking coupled with his failed career ventures had resulted in financial problems for the family. Linda noted that she was afraid of developing her "father's problem," stating, "We both run away from things that bother us by overindulging." Her mother was 45 years old and had worked as a nurse for the previous 8 years. Linda described her mother as a loving, compassionate, hard-working woman who had been "depressed" since her husband started drinking heavily. In fact, Linda's mother frequently relied on her for emotional support. Linda always had a very close relationship with her mother and could "tell her everything." Linda has one older brother and two younger sisters (ages 21, 17, and 16, respectively). She maintained close, satisfying relationships with each of them. When the family was together their attention was focused either on the father's alcoholism or mother's depression. While her younger siblings were openly rebellious and disapproving of their father's drinking and mother's apathetic, helpless stance, Linda's efforts were aimed at maintaining the family unit. She also reported that her paternal grandmother and paternal grandfather died of complications related to chronic alcohol abuse. Her family history did not appear to be significant for any other psychiatric disorder. A thorough physical examination prior to the initiation of treatment revealed no significant medical problems.

Linda described herself as having been a superior student throughout grade school and high school. She had been very active in sports since the age of 7, and noted that she was a "perfectionist." She reported having a few close friends during her childhood years and played mostly with her siblings. Finally, she described having minimal experiences in heterosocial relationships.

The EAT, BS, Diet-Phelps Interpersonal Problem Solving Inventory (Diet-PIPSI) (Phelps, 1984), and Beck Depression Inventory (BDI) were administered. Her pretreatment scores on these instruments are presented in Table 18.1. She scored well within the eating-disordered range on both the EAT and

TABLE 18.1 Pretreatment and Posttreatment Assessment of a Bulimic Patient

	Pre	Post
EAT[a]	48	16
Binge Scale[a]	21	6
BDI[b]	19	5
Diet-PIPSI[c]	40	84

[a]Correlated positively with eating-disorder severity.
[b]Correlated positively with depression severity.
[c]Correlated positively with problem-solving competence.

BS. Her BDI score suggested moderate depression. However, data gathered from clinical interviews suggested that her dysphoric affect was secondary to the bulimic behavior. Finally, her Diet-PIPSI responses indicated that she had difficulty handling interpersonal conflict. Although she was able to generate an array of appropriate, likely-to-be-effective solutions to interpersonal problems, the ones she indicated she would be most likely to use were not likely to be effective. In fact, she often reported that she would binge-vomit when faced with a stressful interpersonal situation.

The evaluation indicated that the patient was experiencing difficulty (1) adjusting to college and an independent life-style; (2) redefining her relationships with her family, particularly her parents; and (3) handling various types of interpersonal conflict effectively. A formulation of her problem was presented to Linda in which it was hypothesized that she engaged in bulimic behavior to alleviate anxiety arising from a variety of sources. Though initially the bulimia may have been restricted to decreasing her fears of gaining weight, eventually she "learned" to use the binge-purging to relieve tension related to family, peer, and school problems. Finally, she also learned that engaging in the bulimia resulted in certain benefits. Linda agreed strongly with this conceptualization and reported never having viewed her problem in such a fashion.

Following the assessment and discussion of the conceptualization and formulation of the problem, a treatment plan was presented that focused on the modification and management of maladaptive eating behavior and interpersonal problem-solving training. Linda was seen in treatment for 23 sessions over 16 weeks. Due to the severity of her bulimia, Linda participated in therapy twice per week for the first 7 weeks of treatment. At the start of treatment Linda was instructed to generate a list of pros and cons for continuing her binge-purging. The purpose of this task was threefold: First, it illustrated the specific benefits that she obtained from engaging in bulimic behavior. Second, it demonstrated the need for developing alternative behaviors. That is, contrary to the patient's beliefs, simply "quitting" would not be sufficient in staving off binge-purge episodes on a long-term basis. Finally, the "cons" provided her with a concrete reminder of why the bulimia was worth "giving up."

Linda pinpointed six advantages provided by her bulimia. It provided (1) an easy method of weight control that allowed her to eat "anything and everything," (2) relief from tension, depression, and boredom, (3) an excuse for doing poorly in school, (4) increased attention from family members, (5) a reason to avoid social situations, and (6) an outlet for expressing anger. Conversely, health concerns, restricted lifestyle, poor interpersonal relationships, and a failure to resolve problems were disadvantages to continuing to binge-purge. Once the list of disadvantages was generated, Linda was instructed to refer to it when she experienced the urge to binge or vomit. To identify current eating patterns, including urges and actual binge-purge episodes, Linda was taught to record (1) the type and quantity of food eaten, (2) the time of day when the food was eaten, (3) others present when food was eaten, (4) subjective feelings while eating, (5) urges to binge and actual binges, and (6) urges to vomit and actual vomiting. Additionally, she was instructed to record the events preceding an urge or actual binge-purge episode. These exhaustive assessment procedures were followed during the first week of treatment. Through this task it was revealed that Linda experienced the impulse to binge-purge approximately 20 times per week. Binge-purge episodes occurred 17 times during the week. Notably, she was able to refrain from binge-purging on one of the seven days. Urges and actual episodes of bulimic behavior occurred in response to stressful interactions with family members and peers and anxiety regarding her school performance. The following are three examples of events that preceded Linda's binge-purge episodes:

> This was a very bad day. There is just too much work and not enough time. I didn't do well on two tests—at least not what I expected, not what I should have done. The whole thing just makes me so nervous 'cause I know I need good grades to get into med school. I was so worried and just kept on thinking, "What if I don't do well, then what?" that I stuffed my face to get my mind off things. I couldn't stand the thought of all that food in my stomach so I threw it up. This is disgusting.

> My mom called right when I was studying for a test. Dad's drinking a lot and he still doesn't have a job. She's talking about leaving him and moving up here with me. Sometimes I just want to hang up. I don't know what to do. It also made me kind of mad 'cause my mom *knew* I had a test and it seems like she always calls me before tests and tells me bad stuff and then I can't study. The other thing that she said is that I could go to

school down there. I was so uptight inside that I just started going through the refrigerator. I ate until I was sick. Sometimes I hate being me.

I was upset because my roommate borrowed my sweater without asking. So I ate the rest of the cheesecake that her mother had brought over (3/4 of the cake) and then I threw it up. I can always buy her a new one.

Data from the week of close self-monitoring also indicated that she was eating poorly during her binge-free periods. Specifically, she would restrict herself to a 500-calorie diet of fruits and vegetables to compensate for her binge-purge episodes. Unfortunately, this strategy only increased the likelihood of a binge-purge episode. Thus, to regulate Linda's eating pattern and to ensure a nutritionally adequate diet, an exchange system (Stuart & Davis, 1972) was implemented. This system stressed the importance of eating foods from each of the four basic food groups and *eating frequently but moderately throughout the day*. We have found the exchange system to be particularly useful in modifying patients' faulty dietary assumptions (e.g., "I can't eat certain foods, even in small amounts without gaining weight"), which often inhibit the restoration of normal eating behavior. Linda was started on a 2000 calorie meal plan, with the understanding that this would be modified based on changes in her weight. Initially, Linda was reluctant to be weighed and protested vociferously before each weigh-in. However, her protests diminished as she observed that she was able to eat normally, without vomiting, and still maintain her weight. Finally, Linda was instructed to generate a list of alternative behaviors that she could implement when she experienced the impulse to binge or vomit. The list was restricted to those behaviors that were reinforcing for her and incompatible with binge-eating or purging. Thus "watch TV" was deleted from the list since it would be possible for her to binge while she was watching TV. Activities that she found especially helpful in decreasing the likelihood that she would binge or vomit were running, taking a shower, "talking to herself," and talking to a friend.

Each session began with a review of every binge-purge episode since the previous meeting. Differences were delineated between events that precipitated an impulse that the patient subsequently controlled and events that precipitated actual binge-purge episodes. After four sessions in which treatment efforts were aimed primarily towards altering maladaptive eating behavior, the patient's binge-purge frequency decreased 71% to five times per week.

Initially, the most easily controlled urges involved events that were related to academic performance anxiety. In contrast, Linda continued to binge-purge in response to stressful interpersonal events with family and friends. To improve her interpersonal conflict resolution skills, Linda was instructed to (1) define problems in behaviorally specific terms, (2) "brainstorm" possible solutions to a particular problem, (3) evaluate each of the potential solutions according to its likely short-term/long-term consequences and personal/social

TABLE 18.2   Frequency of Binge-Vomit Episodes and Urges

Weeks in Treatment	Binge-Vomit Episodes	Binge-Vomit Urges
1	17	20
2	15	21
3	20	18
4	15	18
5	5	15
6	6	10
7	3	10
8	3	7
9	3	10
10	1	7
11	1	4
12	1	5
13	0	4
14	0	3
15	0	4
16	0	3

Weeks After Treatment	Binge-Vomit Episodes	Binge-Vomit Urges[a]
1	6	—
2	5	—
3	0	—
4	0	—
5	0	—
6	0	—

[a]The patient did not record urges during the follow-up period.

consequences, (4) select and implement a solution, and (5) evaluate the likely effectiveness of the selected solution. Through the use of behavioral rehearsal and role-playing, Linda acquired the skills to handle conflict with family members and peers. She noted a decrease in her impulses to binge-purge when she was able to be assertive in those situations. To counteract self-statements that were likely to inhibit effective conflict resolution (e.g., "What if they get mad? She probably won't talk to me again if I say something about it"), Linda was instructed to substitute positive self-statements (e.g., "Even though this makes me nervous, I always feel better afterwards") that would facilitate assertive behavior. She was able to use this process to set limits with family members and resolve conflicts with her roommates. Additionally, she was able to implement thought substitution techniques to counteract her impulses to avoid socializing. As her ability to handle interpersonal conflict improved and as she began socializing more with her peers, Linda's actual binge-purge episodes decreased to once per week. Nonetheless, she still experienced the urge to binge four to seven times per week (see Table 18.2).

The twelfth week marked the onset of the termination phase of therapy. This phase's onset was hastened by the approaching "end of the semester." During this time, treatment was directed towards reviewing previously learned strategies effective in ameliorating the patient's bulimic behavior and troubleshooting problems Linda expected to encounter when she returned home for the summer. During the thirteenth session Linda reported that she had not binged or vomited for 1 week. Moreover, for the remaining 3 weeks of treatment she denied engaging in any binge-purge episodes.

Linda's posttreatment scores on the Eating Attitudes Test, Binge Scale, Beck Depression Inventory, and Diet-PIPSI were within the normal range (see Table 18.1). A follow-up phone contact 6 weeks after the final session indicated that Linda and her family had entered therapy. She also stated that she had found a summer job and was socializing with newly made friends. Although she admitted that her family life was still stressful, Linda noted, "It doesn't bother me like it used to." Insightfully, she added, "My father's drinking is his problem, like the bulimia was mine. Others can help but only he can change it." A final follow-up contact 20 weeks after treatment revealed she had bingedpurged approximately once per month during the preceding 4 months. At this writing she has returned to school and made arrangements for "booster" sessions.

SUMMARY

Anorexia nervosa and bulimia appear to be related but distinct psychopathological disorders. Although a disturbance in eating behavior and attitudes towards eating, food, and weight dominate the clinical picture, a number of psychosocial sequelae also appear to be important in the development and maintenance of these disorders. The necessity of a comprehensive assessment was emphasized. Such an assessment should include:

1. A thorough clinical interview
2. The use of instruments with demonstrated reliability and validity in the evaluation of eating-disordered patients
3. An evaluation of interpersonal competence

Behavioral approaches to the treatment of anorexia and bulimia also were reviewed. Interventions including operant conditioning, systematic desensitization, social skills training, and response prevention all seem to be successful in obtaining short-term improvements in weight and/or eating behavior. It appears that inclusion of interpersonal problem-solving training may produce more durable treatment effects. A case study illustrating some of the aforementioned techniques was presented.

REFERENCES

Agras, S., Barlow, D. H., Chapin, H. N., Abel, G., & Leitenberg, H. (1974). Behavior modification of anorexia nervosa. *Archives of General Psychiatry, 30,* 279–286.

Agras, S., & Werne, J. (1978). Behavior therapy in anorexia nervosa, a data-based approach to the question. In J. P. Brady & H. K. H. Brodie (Eds.), *Controversy in psychiatry.* Philadelphia: Saunders.

American Psychiatric Association. (1980). *Diagnostic and statistical manual of mental disorders* (3rd ed.). Washington, DC: Author.

Azzerad, J., & Stafford, R. L. (1969). Restoration of eating behaviour in anorexia nervosa through operant conditioning and environmental manipulation. *Behaviour Research and Therapy, 7,* 165–171.

Bachrach, A. J., Erwin, W. S., & Mohr, J. P. (1965). The control of eating behavior in an anorectic by operant conditioning techniques. In L. P. Ullmann & L. Krasner (Eds.), *Case studies in behavior modification.* New York: Holt, Rinehart & Winston.

Beck, A. T., Ward, C. H., Mendelson, M., Mock, J., & Erbaugh, J. (1961). An inventory for measuring depression. *Archives of General Psychiatry, 4,* 561–571.

Bemis, K. M. (1978). Current approaches to the etiology and treatment of anorexia nervosa. *Psychological Bulletin, 85,* 593–617.

Beumont, P. J. V. (1977). Former categorization of patients with anorexia nervosa. *Australian and New England Journal of Psychiatry, 11,* 223–226.

Beumont, P. J. V., George, G. C. W., & Smart, D. E. (1976). "Dieters" and "vomiters and purgers" in anorexia nervosa. *Psychological Medicine, 6,* 617–622.

Bhanji, S., & Thompson, J. (1974). Operant conditioning in the treatment of anorexia nervosa: A review and retrospective study of eleven cases. *British Journal of Psychiatry, 124,* 166–172.

Bianco, F. J. (1972). Rapid treatment of two cases of anorexia nervosa. *Journal of Behavior Therapy and Experimental Psychiatry, 3,* 223–224.

Blinder, B. J., Freeman, D. M. A., & Stunkard, A. J. (1970). Behavior therapy of anorexia nervosa: Effectiveness of activity as a reinforcer of weight gain. *American Journal of Psychiatry, 126,* 72–82.

Blue, R. (1979). Use of punishment in the treatment of anorexia nervosa. *Psychological Reports, 44,* 743–746.

Boskind-White, M., & White, W. C., Jr. (1983). *Bulimarexia.* New York: Norton.

Brady, J. P., & Rieger, W. (1972). Behavioral treatment of anorexia nervosa. In

T. Thompson & W. S. Dockens, III (Eds.), *Proceedings of the International Symposium on Behavior Modification.* New York: Appleton-Century-Crofts.

Bruch, H. (1973). *Eating disorders: Obesity, anorexia nervosa and the person within.* New York: Basic.

Bruch, H. (1985). Four decades of eating disorders. In D. M. Garner & P. F. Garfinkel (Eds.), *Handbook of psychotherapy for anorexia nervosa and bulimia.* New York: Guilford.

Cantwell, D. P., Sturzenberger, S., Burroughs, J., Salkin, B., & Green, J. K. (1977). Anorexia nervosa: An affective disorder? *Archives of General Psychiatry, 34,* 1087–1093.

Casper, R. C. (1983). On the emergence of bulimia nervosa as a syndrome: A historical view. *International Journal of Eating Disorders, 2,* 3–16.

Casper, R. C., Eckert, E. D., Halmi, K. A., Goldberg, S. C., & Davis, J. M. (1980). Bulimia. Its incidence and clinical importance in patients with anorexia nervosa. *Archives of General Psychiatry, 37,* 1030–1034.

Cooper, K. H. (1982). *The aerobic program for total well-being.* New York: Bantam.

Crisp, A. H., Hsu, L. K. G., Harding, J., & Hartshorn, J. (1980). Clinical features of anorexia nervosa. *Journal of Psychosomatic Research, 24,* 179–191.

Crowther, J. H., Post, G., & Zaynor, L. (1985). The prevalence of bulimia and binge eating in adolescent girls. *International Journal of Eating Disorders, 4*(1), 29–42.

Duddle, M. (1973). An increase of anorexia nervosa in a university population. *British Journal of Psychiatry, 123,* 711.

Eckert, E. D., Goldberg, S. C., Halmi, K. A., Casper, R. C., & Davis, J. M. (1979). Behavior therapy in anorexia nervosa. *British Journal of Psychiatry, 134,* 55–59.

Elkin, T. E., Hersen, M., Eisler, R. M., & Williams, J. G. (1973). Modification of caloric intake in anorexia nervosa: An experimental analysis. *Psychological Reports, 32,* 75–78.

Emmett, S. W. (1985). *Theory and treatment of anorexia nervosa and bulimia: Biomedical, sociocultural, and psychological perspectives.* New York: Brunner/Mazel.

Fairburn, C. G., & Cooper, P. J. (1982). Self-induced vomiting and bulimia nervosa: An undetected problem. *British Medical Journal, 284,* 1153–1155.

Fichter, M. M., & Kessler, W. (1980). Behavioral treatment of an anorectic male: Experimental analysis of generalization. *Behavioral Analysis of Medicine, 4,* 152–168.

Garfinkel, P. E. (1974). Perception of hunger and satiety in anorexia nervosa. *Psychological Medicine, 4,* 309–315.

Garfinkel, P. E., & Garner, D. M. (1982). *Anorexia nervosa: A multidimensional perspective.* New York: Brunner/Mazel.

Garfinkel, P. E., Kline, S. A., & Stancer, H. C. (1973). Treatment of anorexia nervosa using operant conditioning techniques. *Journal of Nervous and Mental Disease, 157*(6), 428–433.

Garfinkel, P. E., Moldofsky, H., & Garner, D. M. (1977). The outcome of anorexia nervosa: Significance of clinical features, body image, and behavior modification. In R. A. Vigersky (Ed.), *Anorexia nervosa*. New York: Raven.

Garner, D. M., & Garfinkel, P. E. (1979). The eating attitudes test: An index of the symptoms of anorexia nervosa. *Psychological Medicine, 9,* 273–279.

Garner, D. M., & Garfinkel, P. F. (1985). *Handbook of psychotherapy for anorexia nervosa and bulimia.* New York: Guilford.

Garner, D. M., Olmstead, M. P., & Polivy, J. (1983). Development and validation of a multidimensional eating disorder inventory for anorexia nervosa and bulimia. *International Journal of Eating Disorders, 2,* 15–34.

Geller, J. L. (1975). Treatment of anorexia nervosa by the integration of behavior therapy and psychotherapy. *Psychotherapy and Psychosomatics, 26,* 167–177.

Goodstein, R. K. (1983). *Eating and weight disorders: Advances in treatment and research.* New York: Springer.

Hallsten, E. A. (1965). Adolescent anorexia treated by desensitization. *Behaviour Research and Therapy, 3,* 87–91.

Halmi, K. A., Falk, J. R., & Schwartz, E. (1982). Binge eating and vomiting: A survey of a college population. *Psychological Medicine, 11,* 697–706.

Halmi, K. A., Powers, P., & Cunningham, S. (1975). Treatment of anorexia nervosa with behavioral modification. *Archives of General Psychiatry, 32,* 93–96.

Hamilton, M. K., Gelwick, B. P., & Meade, C. J. (1984). The definition and prevalence of bulimia. In R. C. Hawkins, W. J. Fremouw, & P. F. Clement (Eds.), *The binge-purge syndrome.* New York: Springer.

Harris, F. C., Hsu, L. K. G., & Phelps, C. F. (1983). Problems in adolescence: Assessment and treatment of bulimia nervosa. In M. Hersen (Ed.), *Outpatient behavior therapy: A clinical guide.* New York: Grune & Stratton.

Harris, F. C., & Phelps, C. F. (1985). Anorexia nervosa. In M. Hersen & A. S. Bellack (Eds.), *Handbook of clinical behavior therapy with adults.* New York: Plenum.

Harris, F. C., & Phelps, C. F. (in press). Eating disorders. In L. Michelson & M. Ascher (Eds.), *Cognitive-behavioral treatment of anxiety disorders.* New York: Guilford.

Hauserman, N., & Lavin, P. (1977). Post-hospitalization continuation treatment of anorexia nervosa. *Journal of Behavior Therapy and Experimental Psychiatry, 8,* 309–313.

Hawkins, R. C., & Clement, P. F. (1980). Development and construct validation of a self-report measure of binge-eating tendencies. *Addictive Behaviors, 5,* 219–226.

Hawkins, R. C., & Clement, P. F. (1984). Binge eating. Measurement problems and a conceptual model. In R. C. Hawkins, W. J. Fremouw, & P. F. Clement (Eds.), *The binge-purge cycle.* New York: Springer.

Hawkins, R. C., Fremouw, W. J., & Clement, P. F. (1984). *The binge-purge syndrome: Diagnosis, treatment, and research.* New York: Springer.

Hsu, L. K. G. (1983). The etiology of anorexia nervosa. *Psychological Medicine, 13,* 231–238.

Hudson, J. I., Laffer, P. S., & Pope, H. G., Jr. (1982). Bulimia related to affective disorder by family history and response to the dexamethasone suppression test. *American Journal of Psychiatry, 139,* 685–687.

Jones, D. F., Fox, M. M., Babigan, H. M., & Hutton, H. E. (1980). Epidemiology of anorexia nervosa in Monroe County, New York: 1960–1976. *Psychosomatic Medicine, 42,* 551–568.

Lang, P. J. (1965). Behavior therapy with a case of anorexia nervosa. In L. P. Ullmann & L. K. Krasner (Eds.), *Case studies in behavior modification.* New York: Holt, Rinehart & Winston.

Leitenberg, H., Agras, W. S., & Thomson, L. E. (1968). Sequential analysis of the effect of selective positive reinforcement in modifying anorexia nervosa. *Behaviour Research and Therapy, 6,* 211–218.

Leitenberg, H., Gross, J., Peterson, J., & Rosen, J. C. (1984). Analyses of an anxiety model and the process of change during exposure plus response prevention treatment of bulimia nervosa. *Behavior Therapy, 15,* 3–20.

Linden, W. (1980). Multi-component behavior therapy in a case of compulsive binge-eating followed by vomiting. *Journal of Behavior Therapy and Experimental Psychiatry, 11,* 297–300.

Lobb, L. G., & Schaefer, H. H. (1972). Successful treatment of anorexia nervosa through isolation. *Psychological Reports, 30,* 245–246.

McGlynn, F. D. (1980). Successful treatment of anorexia nervosa with self-monitoring and long distance praise. *Journal of Behavior Therapy and Experimental Psychiatry, 11,* 283–286.

Morgan, H. G., & Russell, G. F. M. (1975). Values of family background and clinical features as predictors of long term outcome in anorexia nervosa: Four year follow-up of 41 patients. *Psychological Medicine, 5,* 355–371.

Neuman, P. A., & Halvorson, P. A. (1983). *Anorexia nervosa and bulimia: A handbook for counselors and therapists.* New York: Van Nostrand Reinhold.

Neumann, M., & Gaoni, B. (1975). Preferred food as the reinforcing agent in a case of anorexia nervosa. *Journal of Behavior Therapy and Experimental Psychiatry, 6,* 331–333.

Ollendick, T. H. (1979). Behavioral treatment of anorexia nervosa: A five year study. *Behavior Modification, 3,* 124–135.

O'Neill, C. B. (1982). *Starving for attention.* New York: Continuum.

Palmer, R. L. (1979). The dietary chaos syndrome: A useful new term? *British Journal of Medical Psychology, 52,* 187–190.

Parker, J. B., Jr., Blazer, D., & Wyrick, L. (1977). Anorexia nervosa: A combined therapeutic approach. *South Medical Journal, 70,* 448–452.

Pertschuk, M. J. (1977). Behavior therapy: Extended follow-up. In R. A. Vigersky (Ed.), *Anorexia nervosa.* New York: Raven.

Pertschuk, M. M., Edwards, N., & Pomerleau, O. F. (1978). A multiple-baseline approach to behavioral intervention in anorexia nervosa. *Behavior Therapy, 9,* 368–376.

Phelps, C. F. (1984). *Assessment of interpersonal competence in an eating disordered population: Development and evaluation of an instrument.* Unpublished master's thesis, University of Pittsburgh.

Pillay, M., & Crisp, A. H. (1981). The impact of social skills training within an established inpatient treatment program for anorexia nervosa. *British Journal of Psychiatry, 139,* 533–539.

Poole, A. D., & Sanson, R. W. (1978). A behavioral program for the management of anorexia nervosa. *Australian and New England Journal of Psychiatry, 12,* 49–53.

Rosen, J. C., & Leitenberg, H. (1982). Bulimia nervosa: Treatment with exposure and response prevention. *Behavior Therapy, 13,* 117–124.

Rosen, L. W. (1980). Modification of secretive or ritualized eating behavior in anorexia nervosa. *Journal of Behavior Therapy and Experimental Psychiatry, 11,* 101–104.

Rosman, B. L., Minuchin, S., Liebman, R., & Baker, L. (1976). Input and outcome of family therapy in anorexia nervosa. In J. L. Claghorn (Ed.), *Successful Psychotherapy.* New York: Brunner/Mazel.

Russell, G. F. M. (1979). Bulimia nervosa: An ominous variant of anorexia nervosa. *Psychological Medicine, 9,* 429–448.

Schnurer, A. T., Rubin, R. R., & Roy, A. (1973). Systematic desensitization of anorexia nervosa as a weight phobia. *Journal of Behavior Therapy and Experimental Psychiatry, 4,* 149–153.

Sours, J. A. (1980). *Starving to death in a sea of objects.* New York: Aronson.

Stuart, R. B., & B. Davis. (1972). *Slim chance in a fat world: Behavioral Control of Obesity.* Chicago: Research Press.

Stumphauser, J. S. (1969). Application of reinforcement contingencies with a 23 year old anorectic patient. *Psychological Reports, 24,* 109–110.

Vandereyeken, W., & Pieters, G. (1978). Short-term weight restoration in anorexia nervosa through operant conditioning. *Scandinavian Journal of Behavior Therapy, 7*(4), 221–236.

Werry, K. S., & Bull, D. (1975). Anorexia nervosa: A case study using behavior therapy. *Journal of the American Academy of Child Psychiatry, 14,* 567–568.

Wilson, C. P. (1983). *Fear of being fat: The treatment of anorexia nervosa and bulimia.* New York: Aronson.

Wulliemier, F. (1978). Anorexia nervosa: Gauging treatment effectiveness. *Psychosomatics, 19,* 497–499.

CHAPTER 19

Obesity

JOHN P. FOREYT AND JENNIFER H. COUSINS

Obesity is a widespread and serious problem in children and adolescents. It is estimated that 10 to 15% of young children and 15 to 30% of adolescents are obese (Colley, 1974; Garn & Clark, 1976; Hathaway & Sargent, 1962).

Obese children are at greater risk for a number of health problems as well as for difficulties in psychological and social adjustment. Childhood obesity has been associated with cardiovascular risk factors, including hypertension (Court, Hill, Dunlap, & Boulton, 1974; Londe, Bourgoignie, Robson, & Goldring, 1971) and elevated serum cholesterol and triglycerides (Clark, Merrow, Morse & Keyser, 1970; Lauer, Conner, Leaverton, Reiter, & Clark, 1975). In addition, there is some evidence that childhood obesity makes an independent contribution to risk for cardiovascular disease (Kannel & Dawber, 1972; Miller & Shekelle, 1976). Overweight in children also has been shown to contribute to the occurrence of orthopedic difficulties (Mayer, 1970), hyperinsulinism (Drash, 1973), and impaired physical work capacity (Boulton, 1981).

The health problems associated with early-onset obesity do not appear to be confined to the childhood years. The majority of obese children become obese adolescents, and most obese adolescents become obese adults (Abraham, Collins, & Nordsieck, 1971; Johnston & Mack, 1978; Weil, 1977; Zack, Harlan, Leaverton, & Coroni-Huntley, 1979). If overweight continues through adolescence, the odds against the child's becoming a normal weight adult are 28 to 1 (Stunkard & Burt, 1967). Presence of obesity in adulthood has been repeatedly found to be related to premature mortality (Stewart & Brooks, 1983). Thus, health risks that accompany obesity in adulthood are likely to be the legacy of the obese child.

While physical problems associated with childhood obesity may not appear

---

Preparation of this chapter was supported in part by Grant Number 1 RO1 HL33954-01 from the National Heart, Lung, and Blood Institute, National Institutes of Health, Bethesda, Maryland.

until adulthood, psychological and social problems generally appear during development. Contemporary American cultural values equate attractiveness, competence, and even intelligence with thinness. Although most if not all of the obese suffer from the consequences of such attitudes, children and adolescents are particularly vulnerable (Dwyer & Mayer, 1975).

In a survey of children's attitudes toward others, Lerner (1973) found that children indicated a desire to maintain greater personal distance from their overweight peers than from those of normal weight. Staffieri (1967, 1972) showed 6- to 10-year-old boys and 7- to 11-year-old girls silhouettes that were identical to each other except in body shape (thin, muscular, fat) and asked them to evaluate these drawings using a list of 39 adjectives. Even those who resembled the drawing described endomorphs negatively, disproportionately applying to them such adjectives as stupid, lazy, mean, and ugly. Nor are these prejudicial attitudes limited to children. Similar attitudes toward obese youngsters have been observed among adults, even among health professionals (Goodman, Richardson, Dornbusch, & Hastorf, 1963; Lerner, 1969; Morgavan, 1976).

The social and psychological problems associated with childhood obesity do not lessen during adolescence; if anything, they appear to intensify. As with obese children, obese adolescents are often negatively viewed by their peers (Lerner & Korn, 1972; Worsley, 1981), by adults (Henry & Gillies, 1978), and perhaps even by college admission boards (Canning & Mayer, 1966).

The pressure to conform to the socially determined standard of appearance intensifies during adolescence, particularly among females (Allon, 1980). Deviation from the "norm" of appearance is cause for concern and self-consciousness at some time for all adolescents, regardless of whether or not they are overweight. But for obese teenagers, these concerns may lead from feelings of unacceptability to more serious problems, such as self-condemnation and body-image distortions (Monello & Mayer, 1963). These problems in turn may lead to the development of eating disorders such as anorexia and bulimia (Cahnman, 1968; Dwyer, 1973; Miller, Coffman, & Linke, 1980).

ASSESSMENT

Assessment is an important component in the behavioral treatment of obesity. Before beginning treatment, baseline information is collected, and it provides the basis for treatment, including the goals, approach, length, and limitations of treatment (Foreyt & Goodrick, in press). During treatment, assessment continues to play a vital role in determining program adherence and progress toward treatment goals.

Assessing the Problem

Physical Measures

Obesity is an excess of body fat. Assessing obesity involves two steps: (1) measuring or estimating body fat, and (2) making a judgment regarding the extent to which body fat is excessive. Several methods for the measurement of body fat are summarized in the following paragraphs. Determining the extent to which body fat is excessive involves consideration of its effect on the present and future health status of the child and on the child's social and psychological functioning. Judging the extent to which a particular child's weight and body fat interfere with his or her physical and psychosocial health must be based on a thorough assessment of each of these aspects of the child's overall functioning (Foreyt & Goodrick, in press).

Several methods exist for the measurement of body fat. *Densiometry* is an approximation of the percentage of fat calculated from the amount of water displaced when the child is totally immersed in water. Although densiometry is the most direct measure of body fat, it is also the most expensive and least convenient method, and it is not free of questionable assumptions (Weil, 1977).

Skinfold measurement is the most commonly used indirect technique for approximating body fat. Several investigators (e.g., Franzini & Grimes, 1976; Grimes & Franzini, 1977; Weil, 1977) believe that skinfold measurement is the method of choice for assessing body fat because the most common alternatives, such as height/weight tables, are less related to the concept of obesity as excess body fat. Others (e.g., Bray, 1976; Johnson & Stalonas, 1977) disagree because of the difficulty in achieving adequate reliability and validity with skinfold measurements. Measurement error can be decreased by marking the skin to identify the site more clearly (Bray, 1976), and standards for measuring triceps and subscapular skinfolds have been published (Tanner & Whitehouse, 1975). There are no normed conversion tables that approximate percentage of body fat from children's skinfold, so the skinfold thickness itself is typically used. Triceps skinfold percentiles are available for boys and girls aged 6 to 17 years (Lauer et al., 1975). Obesity standards (defined as one standard deviation above the mean) are also available for children aged 5 to 18 (Seltzer & Mayer, 1965). These data are based on measurements of Caucasian children, so caution should be exercised in applying them to children of other ethnic or racial backgrounds.

Body weight is also frequently used as an indirect measure of body fat. However, because body weight is dependent on numerous factors other than body fat, particularly height, age, sex, body build, and composition (percentage fat), it should not be assumed that the overfat are always overweight nor that the reverse is always true. In spite of this qualification, several measures of body weight have proven useful in assessing obesity. The most commonly used measures are absolute weight, relative height, percentage over-weight, and the body mass index.

Absolute weight is useful because it is easily determined and readily under-stood. The degree of excess weight for height that is usually assumed to cor-respond to obesity in adults and sometimes children is 20% (Rowe, 1980); however, the validity of this figure for children and adolescents is question-able. Garn, Clark, and Guire (1975) investigated whether the overfat (85th percentile for triceps skinfold) were also the overweight (20% overweight) in a large sample of children and adults (aged 2 to 70 years). Although the two measures were generally in agreement for adults, they were not for children or adolescents. Many nonobese teenagers tended to be more than 20% over-weight, and many obese children, in contrast, tended to be less than 20% overweight. These results suggest that absolute weight and percentage over-weight should not be used singly in the assessment of juvenile obesity.

Relative weight is the percentage of the median weight for the child's age, sex, and height (Lauer et al., 1975; Wheeler & Hess, 1976). Normative data are available (see Foreyt & Goodrick, 1981). A disadvantage to using relative weight is that it does not take body build into account, so a normal child with a large frame may have a relative weight indicating obesity. Under 7 years of age, relative weights tend to underestimate fatness; at adolescence, these weights may overestimate fatness (Weil, 1977). *Percentage overweight,* cal-culated as (initial absolute weight/goal weight) × 100, is useful in treatment programs because it incorporates into the measure both initial absolute weight and goal weight. Goal weight is set as the median weight for children of the same age, sex, and height. The *body mass index* (weight/height^2) is also fre-quently advised because it relates most closely to measures of body fat (Bray, 1976; Michielutte, Diseker, Corbett, Schey, & Ureda, 1984).

Because no measure is capable of assessing obesity without error, research-ers and practitioners are encouraged to collect several measures of weight and body fat, including absolute weight, percentage overweight, the body mass index, and triceps and subscapular skinfolds (Brownell, 1983; Foreyt & Good-rick, in press; Foreyt & Kondo, 1983).

A medical history and examination are also advised in order to rule out underlying physical causes of obesity. The medical history and a conversation with the child's physician also can provide vital information concerning the child's experience with obesity, such as the age of onset and previous weight-loss efforts.

Physical assessment of the child would not be complete without a similar, though much less intensive, assessment of the parents (Foreyt & Kondo, 1983). In particular, a determination should be made of the existence and extent of overweight in both parents. If overweight is present in both, then it may be suspected that the child has a physical and an environmentally derived ten-dency toward the condition. In this case the child and the parents need to understand the presence of the familial tendency and the difficulty of the task before them.

Psychosocial Assessment

Part of the initial assessment should be used to examine the psychological status of the child. Especially important is a determination of the child's self-esteem, personal capabilities, physical image, and social attractiveness. As described earlier, overweight children are the recipients of substantial prejudice in our society. It can be expected that most overweight children reflect such treatment in psychological symptomatology (Israel & Stolmaker, 1980). Many obese children and adolescents assume that weight loss will solve all of their problems, when in fact an improved physique does *not* automatically result in improved self-concept or social skills (Giotto, 1980). Problems in psychological functioning and unrealistic expectations regarding the effects of weight loss should be identified and addressed during treatment.

In conjunction with a psychological assessment, the child's social life and interactions should be examined. Parental reports concerning the child's behavior at school, in the home, and with friends should be collected as part of this assessment. An outline of questions that can serve as the foundation for an exploration of the child's social life are available elsewhere (Foreyt & Kondo, 1983).

A final area of assessment is the family of the child. The practitioner needs to gain a reasonable understanding of the family's overall functioning. This may range from the relatively simple task of assessing the kinds and quantities of foods served in the household to the more complex task of uncovering the overt and covert messages that the parents give their children regarding their overweight. With respect to the latter point, it is important to determine whether it is the child or the parent who is most desirous of weight loss. If interviews reveal that the primary motivation for seeking treatment comes from the parents, the practitioner may structure a portion of the treatment to explore this matter.

It is also important to assess the extent to which the family can be expected to support the child's treatment. Depending in part on their own experience with overweight, family members may differ in the extent to which they view the child's overweight as a problem in need of treatment, their role in supporting treatment, and their expectations regarding the effects of treatment.

BEHAVIORAL METHODOLOGIES

The goal of behavioral treatment for overweight is to change the child's eating behaviors and physical activity patterns to ones that are more adaptive. Behavioral treatment programs are designed to assist the child in developing more adaptive approaches to food and exercise by teaching self-control methodologies that are intended to become an important part of the child's life. Four methodologies are used most frequently in behavioral approaches: (1) self-monitoring, (2) stimulus control, (3) eating management, and (4) contingency contracting. A brief description of each technique follows and may also be found elsewhere (e.g., DeBakey, Gotto, Scott, & Foreyt, 1984).

Self-Monitoring

Self-monitoring is an important aspect of most treatment programs. The child, if old enough, is asked to record the quantity and nature of food eaten, the time of ingestion, who shared the meal, where eating occurred, and the mood or feeling accompanying the event. Such information may be used as a diagnostic tool, allowing the therapist, working with the child and/or parents, to analyze the record to determine the presence of inappropriate eating patterns and related causative factors. Self-monitoring may also be used in the same manner to document aerobic activity and sedentary behavior and to identify situational factors controlling exercise. With this information a treatment plan can be tailored to the child's problematic eating and activity patterns.

During treatment, self-monitoring serves the important function of helping to assess behavioral change. That is, at any time during treatment, the child's eating behaviors may be compared with those of the pretreatment (baseline) period to determine the extent of improvement. Most preadolescents and adolescents are able to monitor and record their own behaviors. For very young children, recordings by the parents based on their own observations, as well as the children's reports, are suggested (Foreyt & Kondo, 1983).

Stimulus Control

Stimulus control is the modification of factors that appear to serve as cues leading to inappropriate eating. These cues vary considerably by individual. However, the following are common sources of difficulty: (1) handling food frequently; (2) having high-calorie snacks in the household; (3) having food located throughout the house; and (4) eating while watching television, doing homework, or reading.

The particular stimuli causing difficulty may be determined through the child's personal assessment of the problem as well as through an examination of eating records. Following this examination, alterations in the child's environment or life patterns are suggested so that the influence of the troublesome stimuli are effectively negated. This technique is exemplified by the child who finds that certain high-calorie foods in the home are the source of much of his or her difficulty. The resolution of this problem can take one of two directions: the child can (1) ask the parents to refrain from purchasing the foods, or (2) help them place the foods in places or containers that reduce their availability and, it is hoped, their power of temptation. By taking either of the above actions, the child controls the stimuli that lead to inappropriate eating.

Eating Management

Eating management techniques are applied to modify the act of eating. For some children, eating occurs so rapidly that there is insufficient time for satiation to reach cognitive awareness (Keane, Geller, & Scheirer, 1981). Treatment involves introducing techniques to slow the child's usual rate of eating, such as chewing slowly and thoroughly, laying down one's fork or spoon frequently, and taking an extended pause during the meal. An added advantage of this technique is that children often find that their enjoyment of food is increased. Some even find that the enhanced pleasure diminishes their desire to overeat.

Contingency Management

In many behavioral treatment programs, performance of appropriate behaviors is rewarded and inappropriate behaviors are either punished or are systematically not reinforced. Operant conditioning forms the basis for contingency management. Research on operant conditioning suggests that behaviors that receive consequent rewards are likely to strengthen, whereas those that are not reinforced or are punished are likely to extinguish. Contingency contracting is applied to treatment programs to enhance the probability of desired eating or exercise behaviors while reducing the probability of less desirable behaviors. The consequences of performing or not performing the behaviors may be administered by the child, family, friends, or therapist.

An example of contingency management is a contract made between a child and parent so that failure to complete a daily eating record will be punished by the addition of one household chore the following day. Or the child and therapist may determine that sitting in front of the television after school and in the evenings is a recurring and difficult problem. The child may decide to reward himself or herself for each week in which daily viewing does not exceed a specified amount of time.

Contingency contracts should focus on increasing adaptive and decreasing maladaptive *behaviors* associated with weight loss rather than on weight loss itself. Rewarding or punishing children contingent on achieving particular weight-loss goals may motivate them to use physically abusive techniques (e.g., laxatives, diuretics, self-induced vomiting), or short-term fasting to achieve "success."

Cognitive-Behavioral Methodologies

The earliest behaviorally oriented programs typically presented a standard package of the above techniques for all children, but more recent reviews of this research suggest that this may not be the most effective approach (Brownell, 1979; Coates & Thoresen, 1981). As indicated earlier, the ultimate goal of the behavioral approach to the treatment of obesity is to replace the child's maladaptive eating and activity habits with adaptive approaches to food and exercise that will be incorporated into the child's lifestyle. The view of cognitive behavior therapists is that the source of many of these maladaptive behaviors are maladaptive cognitions. Within this perspective, the role of the therapist is to alter the child's cognitions to ones that are more adaptive (Brownell & Stunkard, 1980; Coates and Thoresen, 1978; Foreyt & Goodrick, 1981; Foreyt & Kondo, 1983).

In treating overweight children, three areas of maladaptive cognitions should be considered: those related to (1) food and eating, (2) self-image and self-esteem, and (3) social interactions. Alone and in interaction these problems tend to exacerbate the presenting problem of obesity. Thus, a comprehensive approach to the treatment of childhood obesity requires multiple interventions using a variety of cognitive and behavioral strategies.

The success of the particular cognitive strategy used with a child depends on the child's level of cognitive development (Cole & Kazdin, 1980). Since research on the appropriateness of the various cognitive interventions at different stages of cognitive development is just beginning, the therapist must rely on judgment and experimentation in applying these techniques to a particular child.

A recent review of this approach with children (Kendall, 1981) suggests several promising strategies. Modeling (e.g., Bandura, 1971) combined with a variation of self-instructional training (Meichenbaum, 1977) is one approach that has been used successfully to modify eating pace and to sensitize children to internal sensations associated with eating, such as hunger and fullness (Foreyt & Kondo, 1983). Cognitive methodologies have also been used to treat problems of self-esteem and social interaction. For example, children with low self-esteem may be asked to list their positive qualities and practice self-statements that acknowledge their capabilities, talents, and worth. Other techniques that are applicable to the treatment of obesity in children and adolescents are role-playing (Fagan, Long, & Stevens, 1975), problem solving (Mahoney & Mahoney, 1976), covert modeling (Cautela, 1971), cognitive restructuring (Ellis, 1962), and imagery (Homme, 1965).

REVIEW OF RECENT RESEARCH

Early behavioral interventions for weight loss in children typically involved the application of a standard set of techniques derived from research with adults. Although the results of these approaches compared favorably to the poor results and potential dangers of traditional approaches (e.g., diets, fasting, hormones, and anorectic drugs), their success has been modest at best (Brownell & Stunkard, 1980; Coates & Thoresen, 1978; Israel & Stolmaker, 1980). As indicated in the previous section, an important innovation in the behavioral treatment of juvenile obesity is the use of cognitive-behavior modification. Its use should be a major part of behavioral treatment (Foreyt, Goodrick, & Gotto, 1981).

In addition to cognitive interventions, a reading of the recent research on behavioral treatment reveals a number of other innovative approaches currently being explored with children and adolescents. It is especially encouraging to note the increasing number of studies in which various treatment procedures are being combined and used in conjunction with behavioral strategies. Two trends are of particular note: (1) the inclusion of exercise and physical activity interventions; and (2) the use of social support, in the family and in other settings, in weight loss programs with children and adolescents.

Exercise and Physical Activity

It is a widely held belief that most obesity is caused by an imbalance between energy intake and energy expenditure. Until recently, however, most behavioral treatment programs for children placed considerably more emphasis on reducing caloric inputs than on increasing caloric expenditures (Foreyt & Goodrick, 1981). This focus appears to be changing. Reviews of recent research on the behavioral treatment of childhood obesity have recommended that greater emphasis be placed on energy output both in the assessment and treatment of childhood obesity (Coates & Thoresen, 1980; Foreyt & Goodrick, 1981; Foreyt & Kondo, 1983; Israel & Stolmaker, 1980).

The precise role that exercise plays in the etiology of obesity in children is not fully understood (Brownell, 1982). Studies with children are divided almost evenly into those that show obese children to be less active than nonobese, and those that find no differences. Carrera (1967) found that only 4% of obese children were overeaters. Most were characterized by below-normal activity levels. Some studies have supported this observation (Corbin & Pletcher, 1968; Mayer, 1975; Rose & Mayer, 1968), whereas others have found no differences in activity (Brownell & Stunkard, 1980; Wilkinson, Parkin, Pearlson, Strang, & Sykes, 1977).

The different findings may result in part from differences in the way observations are made and energy output is defined (Brownell & Stunkard, 1980). For example, Waxman and Stunkard (1980) observed boys aged 6 to 13 in the home and at school. They found that overweight children were about as active as the nonoverweight at school but were less active at home and at play. However, when measures of activity were converted to caloric expenditure (by measuring oxygen consumption), the obese boys, by virtue of their heavier weights, expended *more* calories through exercise than did thin boys.

Commenting on this research, Brownell (1982) has suggested that inactivity may be as much a consequence as a cause of obesity in children. Obesity in children has been linked consistently to low fitness levels (Epstein, Koeske, Zidansek, & Wing, 1983). Poor fitness may result both from inactivity and from the work "overload" caused by excess body weight. Simulating obesity by adding external weights to a thin person can produce the kind of impaired fitness performance found for obese individuals (Epstein et al., 1983; Hanson, 1973).

The addition of an exercise component to behavioral weight loss programs appears to have several beneficial effects. Exercise is thought to enhance weight loss by increasing calorie expenditure (Christakis, Sajeckie, Hillman, Miller, Blumenthal, & Archer, 1966; Epstein & Wing, 1980; Jokl, 1969) and via its effects on basal metabolism and appetite suppression (Mayer, 1968). Exercise also appears to increase the loss of fat while minimizing the loss of lean tissue (McArdle, Katch, & Katch, 1981; Moody, Wilmore, Girandola, & Royce, 1972). Exercise in children and adolescents has also been found to have a positive influence on health factors such as blood pressure (Brownell, Kelman, & Stunkard, 1983) and on psychosocial functioning (Foreyt & Goodrick, 1981).

Assessment of baseline caloric output is most frequently accomplished through a daily activity record. The child alone, or with the aid of the parents, may monitor brief daily routines and/or more prolonged activities (LeBow, 1984). Periods of inactivity may also be monitored.

Exercise programs for children may take several forms. Regular aerobic exercise is necessary for demonstrating appreciable effects on body fat and fitness level (Foreyt & Goodrick, 1981). However, as many overweight children are in poor physical condition, it is usually best if they begin by gradually increasing the amount of exercise required by everyday activities (Brownell & Stunkard, 1980; Foreyt & Kondo, 1983). This may be done by targeting a number of daily routines for modification. For example, if they live within a reasonable distance of school, they might walk or ride a bike instead of taking a bus or riding in a car. Or they might be encouraged to assist with the daily household chores, such as running errands, mowing the grass, or vacuuming the carpet.

Although the long-term goal of an exercise modification program should be regular aerobic exercise, participation in nonaerobic games has been found to be helpful for increasing baseline activity levels in children. Epstein, Wing,

Koeske, Ossip, and Beck (1982) compared the effectiveness of two types of exercise programs on weight loss in children 8 to 12 years of age. The programmed aerobic exercise component required one group of children to perform a structured aerobic exercise each day, while the lifestyle alternative program allowed the other group to choose from a wide variety of games and activities. Results showed similar weight loss in the two groups during the 8-week treatment, with the aerobics group achieving the better fitness measures. However, during maintenance and at follow-up, subjects in the lifestyle group continued to lose weight and improve their fitness scores while those in the aerobic group deteriorated. Using a low-intensity calisthenics group to control for nonspecific aspects of participating in an exercise program, the researchers (Epstein, Wing, Koeske, & Valoski, 1985) replicated their finding that life-style exercise was superior to programmed aerobic exercise for weight control in obese children.

These findings suggest that inclusion of a variety of activities that children can incorporate into their lives may improve the likelihood that exercise will continue after treatment. Increasing activity levels in a slow but progressive fashion allows children to develop skills and attitudes necessary for regular participation in and enjoyment of more rigorous exercise.

The Role of Parents

Epidemiological research indicates that a child's probability of being obese is 80% if both parents are obese and 40% if one parent is obese (Garn & Clark, 1976). While both generic and environmental variables undoubtedly contribute to this association (Stunkard, 1980), environmental variables may be assumed to contribute significantly, as husbands and wives in the same study correlated at the .30 level. Garn and Clark suggested that the mechanisms by which the family environment contributes to childhood obesity primarily involve "similarities in caloric intake, caloric expenditures, and attitudes toward food and eating" (1976, p. 454).

Recent research supports this interpretation (Baranowski & Nader, 1985b). Waxman and Stunkard (1980) found that mothers gave larger food portions to their obese children than to their nonobese children. Observations in the homes of families with both obese and nonobese children indicated that parents encouraged their obese offspring to eat more frequently and gave them more food prompts than they gave to their normal-weight children (Klesges, Coates, Brown, Sturgeon-Tillish, Moldenhauer, Holzer, Woolfrey, & Vollmer, 1983; Klesges, Malott, Boschee, & Weber, in press). Similarly, parents encouraged less physical activity in obese children than in their nonobese siblings (Klesges, Coates, Moldenhauer, Holzer, Gustavson, & Barnes, in press; Klesges, Malott, Boschee, & Weber, in press).

Parents also serve as models for child behavior. Griffiths and Payne (1976) found that the energy expended on physical activity by children of obese parents was only half that expended by children of nonobese parents. This finding was independent of the child's own body weight.

If parental behavior is related to development and maintenance of the child's overweight, it is reasonable to expect that parental involvement in treatment would enhance weight loss. However, results of studies on the role of the family in the treatment of childhood obesity suggest that this role is more complex than initially assumed (Foreyt & Kondo, in press).

Early behavioral studies (e.g., Aragona, Cassady, & Drabman, 1975; Kingsley & Shapiro, 1977; Wheeler & Hess, 1976) included parents in the treatment program by teaching them to implement changes in the diet and exercise habits of their children. Following Kingsley and Shapiro's finding of an unintended effect of weight loss in mothers included in children's treatment, more recent studies have included parents in the weight loss process itself.

Epstein et al. (1980) found strong associations between child and parent weight change. In a later study, Epstein et al. (1981) assigned preadolescents to one of three groups (parent/child target, child target, or nonspecific target). At the end of the 8-month treatment, children in the three groups did not significantly differ in percent overweight change, but parents in the parent/ child group lost significantly more weight during treatment. Weight losses for parents and children correlated positively at the end of treatment but not at the 13-month follow-up. The authors suggest that parental modeling may be important during treatment, but that long-term results are more the result of parental reinforcement and acquired child self-regulation.

In order to compare the relative effects of parental modeling and parental reinforcement, Israel et al. (1984) allowed parents of 8- to 12-year-olds to choose one of two conditions of involvement in their child's weight loss program: a weight loss condition and a helper condition. Parents in the weight loss condition contracted to lose weight by following a program parallel to their child's. Parents in the helper condition focused on improving their supportive skills, monitoring and contracting for rewards based on the performance of helping behaviors. The two conditions were equally successful in producing weight loss in subjects during treatment and at 1-year follow-up, and both were superior to a waiting-list control. The age of the children and the type of parental involvement appeared to related. The weight loss condition appeared to be more helpful to younger subjects, whereas the helper role appeared to improve weight loss in the older subjects.

Studies with adolescents also indicate potentially beneficial effects of parental involvement. Coates and Thoresen (1981) compared three single-subject interventions, two of which involved family participation in behavioral strategies. The two experimental participants demonstrated significant weight loss while the control subject gained. However, it was not clear whether family involvement or behavioral techniques were responsible for the weight loss.

Using similar behavioral techniques, Coates, Killen, and Slinkard (1982) found no differences in weight loss between two groups, one with parent participation and one without parent participation group.

Brownell et al. (1983) compared three types of parent-child involvement on adolescent weight loss. In one group parents and children were trained together, in another parents and children were trained separately, and in a third children were trained alone. Parents and children in the separate training group achieved the greatest posttreatment weight loss and maintained this weight loss at 1-year follow-up. Brownell et al. suggest that one of the reasons for the superior performance of the group in which parent and child received separate training involved the developmental process in adolescence of separating from the parent and establishing an independent identity. By meeting separately, the adolescents were allowed sufficient freedom from their parents, yet they also were provided with parents who were informed and involved in resolving the weight problem.

These studies suggest that the role of the family in weight loss in children and adolescents is complex and multidetermined. Of obvious importance is the child's age. For young children parental involvement is almost always necessary, for these children have neither the cognitive nor the physical resources to implement an eating and exercise modification program. In contrast, parental involvement may be perceived as intrusive by the older adolescent attempting to exert more control over his or her weight and eating and exercise behavior.

The quality of family functioning is an important factor in determining the type and extent to which the family should be involved in treatment. It is unreasonable to expect that all families, or all family members, will have such resources as time, skill, and motivation needed to give consistent and effective support to the obese child's struggle to change his or her behavior. Supportive strategies, furthermore, may vary across families and relationships. A behavior considered supportive in one relationship may not be interpreted as supportive in another.

At present, the existing research simply does not allow us to predict what type and how much family involvement will bring about the greatest behavior change, but it does indicate that the family has a powerful effect on the development, maintenance, and modification of children's eating and exercise habits (Foreyt & Kondo, in press). The type and extent of family involvement is best determined by the therapist after a thorough assessment of the child's relationship to other family members, the particular resources of each family member, and the goals of treatment.

For example, if maladaptive cognitions are contributing to the child's obesity, it is important to modify family members' contributions to those beliefs and attitudes. It may be almost impossible to effect long-lasting modifications in children's poor eating habits and activity patterns if other family members are resistant to such changes. On a more positive note, family support may be instrumental in achieving long-term treatment goals otherwise unattainable. For example, participation as a family in such activities as biking, walking, and swimming may promote changes in the child's attitudes toward exercise. Incorporating exercise into family life may encourage children to increase their activity levels by fostering the attitude that exercise is a natural part of life rather than a special chore they must undertake due to their problem.

Treatment in Other Settings

Implementation of behavioral programs for weight loss in the schools also emphasizes the importance of social factors in the treatment of obesity (Brownell, 1983). Children and adolescents have achieved significant weight losses through participation in school programs that have combined nutrition education, exercise, behavior modification, peer counselors, and psychological support (Botvin, Cantlon, Carter, & Williams, 1979; Brownell & Kaye, 1982; Foster, Wadden, & Brownell, 1985; Lansky & Brownell, 1982; Zakus, Chin, Cooper, Makovsky, & Merrill, 1981).

One advantage of treating obesity in the schools is that a large number of children can be reached at a minimal cost to the family. Another advantage is that many children can be treated before their obesity becomes severe. The problem may be better approached in an educational setting than in a medical setting (Seltzer & Mayer, 1970). School-based programs have also been designed to facilitate the involvement and support of family and peers outside of the school (Brownell & Kaye, 1982).

Lansky and Brownell (1982) found that different children may need different approaches. They found that very obese adolescents achieved greater weight loss when given structured, systematic assignments and concrete incentives in a behavioral program and did poorly in an exercise and nutrition instructional program lacking these elements. These elements may be less important to the moderately overweight students. The long-term effectiveness of school-based programs has not yet been addressed.

Summer camps are another setting in which programs to change eating and exercise behavior have been implemented (Brandt, Maschhoff, & Chandler, 1980; Southam, Kirkley, Murchison, & Berkowitz, 1984). The advantages of a camp setting for weight loss are that it provides an opportunity for intensive treatment and a supportive environment in which to practice changes in eating, exercise, and social behavior.

A program developed for use in either a 4-week or an 8-week day camp conducted by Southam et al. (1984) included four components: behavior modification, aerobic exercise, sports skills instruction, and an eating laboratory. In addition, parents were met with weekly to encourage a support system outside the program environment. At posttest, treatment improvements were noted in weight, percent overweight, and skinfold, with greater changes observed for the 8-week than the 4-week group.

Of equal note, attrition was 0% and daily attendance was high. The authors speculated that this was related to high level of satisfaction with the program reported by campers and parents and that it contributed to treatment effects. Further work is needed to investigate those aspects of treatment (e.g., the setting itself, the length of the sessions, the support of peers and family, or components of the program itself) that were most related to treatment outcome.

CASE DESCRIPTION

IDENTIFICATION

Ellen is an 18-year-old college freshman. She lives by herself in an apartment near the college she is attending. She called stating that she was sick and tired of her obesity and wanted to lose weight "once and for all." During the first interview Ellen said that she had always had a weight problem. She said that sometimes she cares about her weight and at others times she doesn't. The most she has ever weighed was 237 pounds, about six months earlier. She is 5 feet, 10 inches tall, weighed 225 pounds at her visit, and stated that she would like to weigh 170 pounds.

Both parents are obese. Her father weighs approximately 260 pounds, her mother about 210 pounds. A 19-year-old brother weighs 230 pounds. The family lives in Arizona.

Ellen was a heavy child who first became aware of her obesity when she was 9 years old in the third grade. Some of the boys in school made fun of her, she recalled. She has tried dieting on and off throughout her adolescence and her most recent diet helped her lose about 12 pounds.

Ellen has no major physical problems and was not taking any prescribed medications. She reported that her family has always enjoyed eating and that throughout her childhood she was served large, hearty meals. She was not particularly active during either elementary or high school but in the past year has been going to a health club where she uses a stationary bicycle and Nautilus equipment.

She watches little TV and is an avid reader. She enjoys her college classes and is a B student. She has a job working as a waitress in a local restaurant. She works five evenings a week from 5 P.M. until 11 P.M.

She dates, although she stated that, "Whenever someone shows any interest I always get involved emotionally." She feels that more males would ask her out if she lost weight.

CONCEPTUALIZATION

Ellen's case is particularly difficult because of the strong familial obesity. Both parents and her brother have been and currently are extremely obese. Ellen's long history of obesity also suggests that prognosis should be guarded. Her previous attempts at losing weight have resulted in losses of relatively small amounts with no maintenance. Regain was almost always immediate. No exercise history was seen until her recent enrollment in a local health club.

ASSESSMENT

Using the corrected Fogarty table (Robinett-Weiss, 1984), Ellen's recommended weight should be approximately 151 pounds. Her own goal is 170 pounds. We took skinfold measures of Ellen and estimated her percentage body fat to be about 33%.

We asked Ellen to keep a detailed food record of everything she ate and drank for one week. We then ran this baseline information on our computerized nutrient data base. Table 19.1 summarizes our baseline findings. Ellen was clearly obtaining a much higher percentage of her calories from fat (51%) than recommended.

TREATMENT

Ellen's treatment involved two phases. She was first referred to one of our eight-session, behaviorally oriented group classes in which she received training in our low-fat diet, an exercise program, and behavioral principles for

TABLE 19.1 Baseline Analysis of Seven-Day Food Diary Compared to Goal Values

2176 Average calories/day. Goal: 1600 calories/day.

Protein	61.0 gm	14% of calories	Goal: Approx 20% of calories
Carbohydrate	159.2 gm	35% of calories	Goal: Approx 50% of calories
Fat	102.9 gm	51% of calories	Goal: 30% of calories or less
Polyunsaturated	25.7 gm	15% of calories	Goal: Approx 10% of calories
Monounsaturated	25.9 gm	15% of calories	Goal: Approx 10% of calories
Saturated	34.5 gm	20% of calories	Goal: 10% of calories or less

P/S Ratio: 0.7   Goal: 1.0 or greater.
Cholesterol: 366 mg   Goal: No more than 300 mg.

Calcium	1127.2 mg	141% RDA		Thiamin	0.868 mg	79% RDA
Phosphorus	1112.4 mg	139% RDA		Niacin	8.717 mg	62% RDA
Vitamin A	3493 IU	87% RDA		Iron	6.511 mg	36% RDA
Riboflavin	1.612 mg	124% RDA		Vitamin C	114.6 mg	191% RDA
Sodium	3545 mg	107% RDA		Potassium	2372 mg	72% RDA

managing changes in lifestyle. In the behavioral training Ellen received instruction in learning how to use a food record and daily weight chart, limiting at-home eating to one place, slowing down consumption of food, rewarding herself for behavioral changes, controlling food consumption, eating cues, and indiscriminate eating, and managing eating away from home. The details of the diet-exercise-behavioral modification program can be found in *The Living Heart Diet* (DeBakey et al., 1984), which we use as a guide and text for all our patients. Following the eight group sessions, Ellen was referred to our monthly classes for further group social support, specific behavioral instruction in how to continue losing weight, and strategies for maintaining lost weight.

In addition to Ellen's behaviorally oriented group classes, she was also seen concurrently in individual treatment for help with her poor self-esteem and to look at the underlying reasons for psychological barriers to losing weight.

She has now been seen weekly in individual treatment for over a year. As part of her treatment Ellen was asked to keep an ongoing diary of her thoughts and feelings with respect to her weight. A recent entry nicely summarizes the therapeutic concerns we dealt with over the past year. The entry was taken verbatim from her diary, with only the names changed:

So much emotional upheaval in the past month it's a wonder I haven't done away with myself. It all culminated on Tuesday when Jim called me and asked me how I was. I totally dumped on him everything that had been happening and upsetting me. Wednesday was my tenth day in a row of work. I was pissed because Al still works at the restaurant and is so totally inept. I was suffering from low self-esteem, major stomach problems, no school motivation, etc. etc. etc. I told him I either needed to go away or lock myself up in the house alone for the weekend to get things in my head straight. He said I sounded like I shouldn't be alone, so I asked if I could stay with him—he said OK. I didn't know where else to go or turn. Dr. Foreyt was out of town and mom and dad were working the weekend. Nana couldn't relate at all. Ron would just want to go out—Beth can't relate— maybe she could but I just didn't feel like being with her. And the gang at home is sick to death of these crying jags and me being out of control, that's why I decided to see Jim. I didn't have to explain anything to him because he already knows it all—work, love life, health, self-esteem, etc. I felt like wouldn't have to explain anything to him.

Before I left to see Jim I talked with Mr. Dudley [employer] about the Al problem—he understood my concerns and listened. I guess that was the most important—he's aware and I've done what I feel is right about telling him everything Al does or doesn't do and how it affects the rest of the staff. We will see how it goes.

Jim and I talked and there is a lot he doesn't understand about what

I've been carrying around with me so long about being a fat person in what I see as a thin society. My major problems are not even problems. I have manifested them and I've let them rule my life and my outlook on life so much and so intensely. It's almost like a tumor that needed to be removed.

Every mind problem concern I have I have an excuse for and it all relates to either being fat or thin.

1. It does matter to me what people say and think about my size. I guess the whole low self-esteem thing began when I was little and other kids made fun of me for being fat—which basically I feel has continued until about a year ago. OK, fine, that is other people's rudeness and lack of sensitivity about someone's problem. Because of these assholes I have always had to try harder at everything to prove I wasn't just a fat blob—there was a person living, breathing, caring inside that has to be dealt with. This book had a very thick cover but once you get past the title page there's an amazing person under there. All that is from outside stimuli—Fuck it, I have to let it go.

2. The reverse of the outside stimuli is now that I feel I need it desperately to confirm what I have accomplished. I have listened to the old assholes about being fat for so long that that is basically the only way I can see myself. I should be able to look in the mirror or at a picture and say, Ellen, you are getting thin—fuck it and go on with your life. Instead I still see fat in the mirror—stomach, thighs, arms—and I can see thin in a picture, but just blow it off because I don't see it in the mirror.

The only explanation I can come up with for this one is being used to the negative reinforcement—I still need feedback, at a very crucial time—positive reinforcement. But just as I fell into the trap from about age 5–? of letting others' images of a fat me be my own self-image. I have now let myself get to the point of only accepting others' concept of my new getting-thin person and don't allow myself to think thin. There are times when I get what I need—either trying a smaller sized outfit, having a total stranger compliment me or a friend tell me I'm looking nice that day—I get high on those compliments and I can be fueled on them for a day or so and then I'm back to square one—who is this person in the picture?

Again, outside stimuli ruling my life. I call myself a woman of the 80s but when it comes to taking charge about the way I feel about myself, I am totally irresponsible and count on others.

3. I am scared. All my life I have wanted to be thin (because of outside stimuli) and I am finally so fucking close it isn't funny. I know the day I weigh 170 there won't be fireworks and a prince on a white horse. It will be a personal landmark celebrated by close friends who can pat me on the back and say good job—you finally did it (more fucking outside stimuli) but is the number that magic number of weighing 170—is that what will snap and finally make me realize, OK, asshole, you've done it—throw away

all the fat excuses, crutches, and ways of thinking—you are no longer fat and pray to God you never will be again. I guess the closer I get and the more confused/emotional I get about the whole thing and realize the number isn't going to make my mind snap into line and make me happy with my accomplishment.

The whole self-esteem thing seems as difficult if not more so than the actual weight loss. To lose weight you eat the right foods and exercise—the weight falls off—but to change how you feel about yourself is a whole different ball of wax. How do you change approximately 18 years of thinking about yourself one way when you are really no longer that person? In computer terms—I have changed the hardware and the software is no longer compatible. I don't know where to begin to write my new software program. And there I go again—it's not where do I go—it's what do I tell myself. How do I convince myself—do I write 500 times a day I am thin, worthwhile, nice, organized, good worker, pleasant personality, pretty, smart, logical mind, good advice giver? I know all these things about myself, but they are shadows of the tower of this whole fucking weight thing. I need a bulldozer to knock over that tower. Where does the bulldozer come from—from inside? But where is it buried, where are the good feelings, the easiness with myself, the self-confidence that I do look nice and desirable? Where is it buried? What mountain is it under and why can't I seem to move that mountain?

4. Sex and Men—Always have equated the two with self-worth. If I can go to bed with a guy I must be attractive and I'm OK. But for the past 4 months I don't get that "charge" feeling after being with someone. It's almost like my mind realizes—Hey Ellen, you don't need to fuck a guy and please him for you to feel good about yourself. You know you're good in bed and can please a man—maybe you should be a little more choosey and you'd be happier the morning after.

A large part of my feeling good about myself is that I can get a cute guy into bed—well big fucking deal—when it's over most don't call back and then I just slump back to the poor little old me situation. It's only a temporary high on myself, which usually can turn out to be a major bummer. It is only a temporary self-esteem lifter and I have to realize that—not put all my eggs in one basket.

5. I really fucked up on school for the first week. Economics is OK—our teacher was on vacation the first week—the sub lectured straight from the book and I have a friend's notes. I missed school Tuesday and Wednesday. Tuesday I couldn't physically move from my couch, Wednesday late at work and talking to Mr. Dudley. So I feel behind although I have the poly sci notes from Jennifer. It's all covered. I had planned on catching up on my reading during my get your head together trip—looked at the books a little, I really don't feel guilty because I needed the rest but I feel like Monday

is a new day, new week, new start, hopefully beginning a new attitude of talking to myself and reassuring myself that:

1.   Yes, I am an important and worthwhile human being.
2.   Yes, I am getting thin.
3.   Yes, I am smart.
4.   Yes, I am fun to be with.
5.   Yes, I am the most organized, neat person I know.
6.   Yes, I do my job better than Al.
7.   Yes, I can go to school and work full time and still function.
8.   Yes, I can give myself enough reassurance that I am/can all of the above so I don't have to drain my friends of everything they have to offer in support just so I can feel better for a little while.
9.   OK. where's the shovel, I'm going to start digging myself out.

FOLLOW-UP AND BOOSTER TREATMENT

Ellen continues to be seen in monthly social support group classes and in weekly individual therapy sessions. She weighs 182 pounds and continues to lose weight. Although the losses are now slow, they are consistent and Ellen expects to reach her goal of 170 pounds over the next 4 months. Her goal appears to be more realistic than the 151-pound goal dictated by the weight tables, and it is the one that we see as realistic. Because of the social support group and the individual therapy, Ellen may be able to better maintain her losses than in the past.

SUMMARY

Behavior therapy is a relatively recent approach in the treatment of obesity in children and adolescents. Results of the relatively few studies conducted in this field suggest few conclusions and many questions. Whereas behavioral programs appear to be more successful than previous approaches, results have been modest at best. Few subjects achieve goal weight, and findings are not always consistent regarding the effectiveness of various strategies. With only a slight risk of oversimplification, the best we can conclude at this point is that some techniques work for some children some of the time.

Several issues need to be addressed if the situation is to improve. In particular, the work on childhood obesity would benefit from an infusion of developmental and family theory. Developmental theory has been almost entirely absent from most research on the treatment of childhood obesity, a problem that has characterized much of child clinical work in general (Gelfand, 1985).

The behavioral techniques used in programs with children were originally developed for use with adults, and considerable modifications are necessary for their application to children. These modifications have not always been made. Studies that have addressed developmental issues have typically done so in a *post hoc* fashion. A more productive approach would be to use the developmental literature to generate and test hypotheses regarding the effects of social and cognitive development on treatment issues such as compliance, comprehension of instructions, parental involvement, self-regulation, and outcome.

The inclusion of the family in weight loss programs for children shows great promise. However, it also raises many issues that are only now beginning to be addressed in the behavioral weight loss literature. The most serious problem inherent in family-based weight loss programs is the lack of a theoretical framework to guide research and treatment (Baranowski & Nader, 1985a). There are profound differences in assumptions, methods, and goals that historically have separated behavioral and family systems perspectives. As a result, existing marital and family therapy orientations have been neglected as a source of theoretical and practical ideas for health behavior change programs in families. A second problem in this area is that the "role of the family" typically translates as the "role of the mother." A recent review of this literature was unable to document a single controlled study in which entire families served as the focus for behavioral treatment (Foreyt & Kondo, in press). Few of the studies reviewed considered the possible role of intrafamilial interactions as a factor in the etiology and maintenance of treatment.

Other challenges await the researcher and practitioner. Attrition has been a consistently difficult problem in weight loss programs, yet recent reports indicate that a good fit between treatment and subject can dramatically reduce the number of dropouts (e.g., Southam et al., 1984). Recent findings suggest that the more individualized the treatment, the greater the likelihood of success. On a related note, the degree of choice or control that subjects perceive themselves to have appears to have significantly positive effects on both immediate and long-term treatment outcomes. The difference between short-term and long-term strategies are just beginning to be explored.

Obesity is a serious physical and psychological health hazard for children. Weight loss is a difficult and, for many, an unsuccessful endeavor. If we are to improve our modest treatment results to date, attention should be increasingly directed to these issues.

REFERENCES

Abraham, S., Collins, G., & Nordsieck, M. (1971). Relationship of childhood weight status to morbidity in adults. *Public Health Reports, 86,* 273–284.

Allon, N. (1980). Sociological aspects of overweight youth. In P. J. Collipp (Ed.), *Childhood obesity* (2nd ed.). Littleton, MA: PSG.

Aragona, J., Cassaday, J., & Drabman, R. (1975). Treating overweight children through parental training and contingency contracting. *Journal of Applied Behavior Analysis, 8,* 269–278.

Bandura, A. (1971). Psychotherapy based on modeling principles. In A. E. Bergin & S. L. Garfield (Eds.), *Handbook on psychotherapy and behavior change: An empirical analysis.* New York: Wiley.

Baranowski, T. & Nader, P. R. (1985a). Family health behavior. In D. Turk & R. Kerns (Eds.), *Health, illness and families.* New York: Wiley.

Baranowski, T., & Nader, P. (1985b). Family involvement in health behavior change programs. In D. Turk & R. Kerns (Eds.), *Health, illness and families.* New York: Wiley.

Botvin, G. J., Cantlon, A., Carter, B. J., & Williams, C. L. (1979). Reducing adolescent obesity through a school health program. *Journal of Pediatrics, 95,* 1060–1062.

Boulton, J. (1981). Nutrition in childhood and its relationships to early somatic growth, body fat, blood pressure, & physical fitness. *Acta Paediatrica Scandinavia,* suppl. *284,* 80–85.

Brandt, G., Maschhoff, T., & Chandler, N. S. (1980). A residential camp experience as an approach to adolescent weight management. *Adolescence, 15,* 807–822.

Bray, G. A. (1976). *The obese patient.* Philadelphia: Saunders.

Brownell, K. D. (1979, May 24). Personal communication. Cited in T. J. Coates & C. E. Thoresen, (1981). Behavior and weight changes in three obese adolescents. *Behavior Therapy, 12,* 383–399.

Brownell, K. D. (1981). Assessment of eating disorders. In D. H. Barlow (Ed.), *Assessment of adult disorders* (pp. 329–404). New York: Guildford.

Brownell, K. D. (1982). Obesity: Understanding and treating a serious, prevalent, and refractory disorder. *Journal of Consulting and Clinical Psychology, 50,* 820–840.

Brownell, K. D. (1983). New developments in the treatment of obese children and adolescents. *Psychiatric Annals, 13,* 878–883.

Brownell, K. D., & Kaye, F. S. (1982). A school-based behavioral modification, nutrition education and physical activity program for obese children. *American Journal of Clinical Nutrition, 35,* 277–283.

Brownell, K. D., Kelman, J. H., & Stunkard, A. J. (1983). Treatment of obese children with and without their mothers: Changes in weight and blood pressure. *Pediatrics, 71,* 515–523.

Brownell, K. D., & Stunkard, A. J. (1980). Behavioral treatment for obese children and adolescents. In A. J. Stunkard (Ed.), *Obesity* (pp. 415–437). Philadelphia: Saunders.

Cahnman, W. J. (1968). The stigma of obesity. *Sociological Quarterly, 9,* 283–299.

Canning, H., & Mayer, J. (1966). Obesity: Its possible effect on college acceptance. *New England Journal of Medicine, 275,* 1172–1174.

Carrera, F. (1967). Obesity in adolescence. *Psychosomatics, 8,* 342–349.

Cautela, J. R. (1971). Covert conditioning. In A. Jacobs & L. B. Sachs (Eds.), *The psychology of private events: Perspectives on covert response systems.* New York: Academic.

Christakis, G. Sajeckie, S., Hillman, R. W., Miller, E., Blumenthal, S., & Archer, M. (1966). Effect of a combined nutrition education and physical fitness program on the weight status of obese high school boys. *Federation Proceedings, 25,* 15–19.

Clark, R. P., Merrow, S. B., Morse, E. H., & Keyser, D. E. (1970). Interrelationships between plasma lipids, physical measurements, and body fatness of adolescents in Burlington, Vermont. *American Journal of Clinical Nutrition, 23,* 754–763.

Coates, T. J., Killen, J. D., & Slinkard, L. E. (1982). Parent participation in a treatment program for overweight adolescents. *International Journal of Eating Disorders, 1,* 37–48.

Coates, T. J., & Thoresen, C. E. (1978). Treating obesity in children and adolescents: A public health problem. *American Journal of Public Health, 68,* 143–151.

Coates, T. J., & Thoresen, C. E. (1981). Behavior and weight change in three obese adolescents. *Behavior Therapy, 12,* 383–399.

Cole, P. M., & Kazdin, A. E. (1980). Critical issues in self instruction training with children. *Child Behavior Therapy, 2,* 1–21.

Colley, J. R. T. (1974). Obesity in school children. *British Journal of Preventative and Social Medicine, 28,* 221–225.

Corbin, C. B., & Pletcher, P. (1968). Diet and physical activity patterns of obese and nonobese elementary school children. *Research Quarterly, 39,* 922–928.

Court, J. F., Hill, G. J., Dunlap, M., & Boulton, T. J. C. (1974). Hypertension in childhood obesity. *Australian Pediatric Journal, 10,* 296–300.

DeBakey, M. E., Gotto, A. M., Scott, L. W., & Foreyt, J. P. (1984). *The Living Heart Diet.* New York: Raven.

Drash, A. (1973). Relationship between diabetes mellitus and obesity in the child. *Metabolism, 22,* 337–344.

Dwyer, J. (1973). Psychosexual aspects of weight control and dieting behavior in adolescence. *Medical Aspects of Human Sexuality, 7,* 82–114.

Dwyer, J., & Mayer, J. (1975). The dismal condition: Problems faced by obese adolescent girls in American society. In G. R. Bray (Ed.), *Obesity in perspective* (Vol. 2, Part 2, pp. 103–110). (DHEW Publication No. 75-708, National Institutes of Health). Washington, DC: U.S. Government Printing Office.

Edwards, K. A. (1976). An index for assessing weight change in children: Weight/ height ratios. *Journal of Applied Behavior Analysis, 11,* 421–429.

Ellis, A. (1962). *Reason and emotion in psychotherapy.* Secaucus, NJ: Stuart.

Epstein, L. H., Koeske, R., Zidansek, J., & Wing, R. R. (1983). Effects of weight loss on fitness in obese children. *American Journal of Diseases in Children, 137,* 654–657.

Epstein, L. H., & Wing, R. R. (1980). Aerobic exercise and weight. *Addictive Behaviors, 5,* 371–388.

Epstein, L. H., Wing, R. R., Koeske, R., Ossip, D., & Beck, S. (1982). A comparison of lifestyle changes and programmed aerobic exercise on weight and fitness changes in obese children. *Behavior Therapy, 13,* 651-665.

Epstein, L. H., Wing, R. R., Koeske, R., & Valoski, A. (1985). A comparison of lifestyle exercise, aerobic exercise, and calisthenics on weight loss in obese children. *Behavior Therapy, 16,* 345-356.

Fagan, S. A., Long, N. J., & Stevens, D. J. (1975). *Teaching children self control: Preventing emotional and learning problems in the elementary school.* Columbus, OH: Merrill.

Foreyt, J. P., & Goodrick, G. K. (1981). Childhood obesity. In E. J. Mash & L. G. Terdal (Eds.), *Behavioral assessment of childhood disorders* (pp. 573-599). New York: Guilford.

Foreyt, J. P., & Goodrick, G. K. (in press). Child obesity. In E. J. Mash & L. G. Terdal (Eds.), *Behavioral assessment of childhood disorders* (2nd ed.). New York: Guilford.

Foreyt, J. P., Goodrick, G. K., & Gotto, A. M. (1981). Limitations of behavioral treatment of obesity: Review and analysis. *Journal of Behavioral Medicine, 4,* 159-174.

Foreyt, J. P., & Kondo, A. T. (1983). Cognitive-behavioral treatment of childhood and adolescent obesity. In A. Ellis & M. E. Bernard (Eds.), *Rational-emotive approaches to the problems of childhood* (pp. 271-309). New York: Plenum.

Foreyt, J. P., & Kondo, A. T. (in press). The family in weight loss: A behavioral perspective. In J. Storlie & H. Jordan (Eds.), *Innovation in obesity program development.* New York: SP Medical and Scientific Books.

Foster, G. D., Wadden, T. A., & Brownell, K. D. (1985). Peer-led program for the treatment and prevention of obesity in the schools. *Journal of Consulting and Clinical Psychology, 53,* 538-540.

Franzini, L. R., & Grimes, W. B. (1976). Skinfold measures as the criterion of change in weight control studies. *Behavior Therapy, 7,* 256-260.

Garn, S. M., & Clark, D. C. (1976). Trends in fatness and the origins of obesity. *Pediatrics, 57,* 443-456.

Garn, S. M., Clark, D. C., & Guire, K. E. (1975). Growth, body composition, and development of obese and lean children. In M. Winick (Ed.), *Childhood obesity* (pp. 23-46). New York: Wiley.

Gelfand, D., & Peterson, L. (1985). *Child development and psychopathology.* Beverly Hills, CA: Sage.

Giotto, M. I. (1980). The effect of peer support upon ideal weight attainment and the self-concept of adolescent girls involved in a multidimensional physical education program. *Dissertation Abstracts International, 40,* 4413A-4414A.

Goodman, N., Richardson, S. A., Dornbusch, S. M., & Hastorf, A. H. (1963). Variant reactions to physical disabilities. *American Sociological Review, 28,* 429-435.

Griffiths, M., & Payne, P. R. (1976). Energy expenditure in small children of obese and nonobese patients. *Nature, 260,* 698-700.

Grimes, W. B., & Franzini, L. R. (1977). Skinfold measurement techniques for estimating percentage body fat. *Journal of Behavior Therapy and Experimental Psychiatry, 8,* 65–69.

Hanson, J. S. (1973). Exercise responses following production of experimental obesity. *Journal of Applied Physiology, 35,* 587–591.

Hathaway, M. L., & Sargent, D. W. (1962). Overweight in children. *Journal of the American Dietetic Association, 40,* 511–515.

Hendry, L. B., & Gillies, P. (1978). Body type, body esteem, school, and leisure: A study of overweight, average, and underweight adolescents. *Journal of Youth and Adolescence, 7,* 181–195.

Homme, L. E. (1965). Perspectives in psychology: XXIV. Control of coverants, the operants of the mind. *Psychological Record, 15,* 501–511.

Israel, A. C., & Stolmaker, L. (1980). Behavioral treatment of obesity in children and adolescents. In M. Hersen, R. M. Eisler, & P. M. Miller (Eds.), *Progress in behavior modification* (Vol. 10, pp. 82–109). New York: Academic.

Israel, A. C., Stolmaker, L., Sharp, J. P., Silverman, W. K., & Simon, L. G. (1984). An evaluation of two methods of parental involvement in treating obese children. *Behavior Therapy, 15,* 266–272.

Johnson, W. G., & Stalonas, P. (1977). Measuring skinfold thickness—A cautionary note. *Addictive Behaviors, 2,* 105–107.

Johnston, F. E., & Mack, R.W. (1978). Obesity, stature, and one year relative weight of 15-year-old youths. *Human Biology, 52,* 35–41.

Jokl, E. (1969). *Exercise, nutrition, and body composition.* Springfield, IL: Thomas.

Kannel, W. B., & Dawber, T. R. (1972). Atherosclerosis: A pediatric problem. *Journal of Pediatrics, 80,* 544–554.

Keane, T. M., Geller, S. E., & Scheirer, C. J. (1981). A parametric investigation of eating styles in obese and nonobese children. *Behavior Therapy, 12,* 280–286.

Kendall, P. C. (1981). Cognitive behavioral interventions with children. In B. Lahey & A. Kazdin (Eds.), *Advances in clinical child psychology.* New York: Plenum.

Kingsley, R. G., & Shapiro, J. (1977). A comparison of three behavioral programs for the control of obesity in children. *Behavior Therapy, 8,* 30–36.

Klesges, R. C., Coates, T. J., Brown, G., Sturgeon-Tillisch, J., Moldenhauer-Klesges, L. M., Holzer, B., Woolfrey, J., & Vollmer, J. (1983). Parental influences on children's eating behavior and relative weight. *Journal of Applied Behavior Analysis, 16,* 371–378.

Klesges, R. C., Coates, T. J., Moldenhauer, L. M., Holzer, B., Gustavson, J., & Barnes, J. (1984). The FATS: An observational system for assessing physical activity in children and associated parent behavior. *Behavioral Assessment, 6,* 333–345.

Klesges, R. C., Malott, J. M., Boschee, P. F., & Weber, J. M. (in press). Parental influences on children's food intake, physical activity and relative weight: An extension and replication. *Journal of Behavioral Medicine.*

Lansky, D., & Brownell, K. D. (1982). Comparison of school-based treatments for adolescent obesity. *Journal of School Health, 52,* 384–387.

Lauer, R. M. Conner, W. E., Leaverton, P. E., Reiter, M. A., & Clark, W. R. (1975).

Coronary heart disease risk factors in school children: The Muscatine study. *Journal of Pediatrics, 86,* 697-706.

LeBow, M. D. (1984). *Child obesity: A new frontier of behavior therapy.* New York: Springer.

Lerner, R. M. (1969). Some female sterotypes of male body-build-behavior relations. *Perceptual and Motor Skills, 28,* 363-366.

Lerner, R. M. (1973). The development of personal space schemata toward body build. *Journal of Psychology, 84,* 229-235.

Lerner, R. M., & Korn, S. J. (1972). The development of body-build sterotypes in males. *Child Development, 43,* 908-920.

Londe, S., Bourgoignie, J. J., Robson, A. M., & Goldring, D. (1971). Hypertension in apparently normal children. *Journal of Pediatrics, 78,* 569-577.

Mahoney, M. J., & Mahoney, K. (1976). *Permanent weight control: A total solution to the dieter's dilemma.* New York: Norton.

Mayer, J. (1968). *Overweight: Causes, cost, and control.* Englewood Cliffs, NJ: Prentice-Hall.

Mayer, J. (1970). Some aspects of the problem of regulating food intake and obesity. *International Psychiatry Clinics, 7,* 255-334.

Mayer, J. (1975). Obesity during childhood. In M. Winick (Ed.), *Childhood obesity* (pp. 73-80). New York: Wiley.

McArdle, W. D., Katch, F. I., & Katch, V. L. (1981). *Exercise physiology: Energy, nutrition, and human performance.* Philadelphia: Lea & Febiger.

Meichenbaum, D. (1977). *Cognitive behavior modification.* New York: Plenum.

Michielutte, R., Diseker, R. A., Corbett, W. T., Schey, H. M., & Ureda J. R. (1984). The relationship between weight-height indices and the triceps skinfold measure among children 5 to 12. *American Journal of Public Health, 74,* 604-606.

Miller, T. M., Coffman, J. G., & Linke, R. A. (1980). Survey on body image, weight, and diet of college students. *Journal of the American Dietetic Association, 77,* 561-566.

Miller, R. A., & Shekelle, R. B. (1976). Blood pressure in tenth-grade students. *Circulation, 54,* 993-1000.

Monello, L. F., & Mayer, J. (1963). Obese adolescent girls: An unrecognized "minority" group. *American Journal of Clinical Nutrition, 13,* 35-39.

Moody, D. L., Wilmore, J. H., Girandola, R. N., & Royce, J. P. (1972). The effects of a jogging program on the body composition of normal and obese high school girls. *Medicine and Science in Sports, 4,* 210-213.

Morgaven, C. B. (1976). Effects of degree of children's obesity and compliant vs. non-compliant behavior on adults' evaluation and reinforcement of the children. *Dissertation Abstracts International, 37,* 1919B.

Robinett-Weiss, N. G. (1984). Fogarty table corrected. *Journal of the American Dietetic Association, 84,* 1502.

Rose, H. E., & Mayer, J. (1968). Activity, caloric intake, fat storage, and energy balanch of infants. *Pediatrics, 41,* 18-29.

Rowe, N. R. (1980). Childhood obesity: Growth charts versus calipers. *Pediatric Nursing, 6,* 24–27.

Seltzer, C. C., & Mayer, J. (1965). A simple criterion of obesity. *Postgraduate Medicine, 38*(2), A101–107.

Southam, M. A., Kirkley, B. G., Murchison, A., & Berkowitz, R. I. (1984). A summer day camp approach to adolescent weight loss. *Adolescence, 19,* 855–868.

Staffieri, J. R. (1967). A study of social sterotype of body image in children. *Journal of Personality and Social Psychology, 7,* 101–104.

Staffieri, J. R. (1972). Body build and behavior expectancies in young females. *Developmental Psychology, 6,* 125–127.

Stewart, A. L., & Brooks, R. H. (1983). Effects of being overweight. *American Journal of Public Health, 73,* 78–82.

Stuart, R. B., & Davis, B. (1972). *Slim chance in a fat world.* Champagne, IL: Research Press.

Stunkard, A. J. (Ed.). (1980). *Obesity.* Philadelphia: Saunders.

Stunkard, A. J., & Burt, V. (1967). Obesity and body image: II. Age of onset in the body image. *American Journal of Psychiatry, 123,* 1443–1447.

Tanner, J. M., & Whitehouse, R. H. (1975). Revised standards for triceps and subscapular skinfolds in British children. *Archives of Diseases in Children, 50,* 142–145.

Waxman, M., & Stunkard, A. J. (1980). Calorie intake and expenditure in obese boys. *Journal of Pediatrics, 96,* 187–193.

Weil, W. B., Jr. (1977). Current controversies in childhood obesity. *Journal of Pediatrics, 91,* 175–187.

Wheeler, M. E., & Hess, K. W. (1976). Treatment of juvenile obesity by successive approximation control of eating. *Journal of Behavior Therapy and Experimental Psychiatry, 7,* 235–241.

Wilkinson, P., Parkin, J., Pearlson, G., Strang, H., & Sykes, P. (1977). Energy intake and physical activity in obese children. *British Medical Journal, 1,* 756.

Worsley, A. (1981). Teenagers' perceptions of fat and slim people. *International Journal of Obesity, 5,* 15–24.

Zack, P. M., Harlan, W. R., Leaverton, P. E., & Coroni-Huntley, J. (1979). A longitudinal study of body-fatness in childhood and adolescence. *Journal of Pediatrics, 95,* 126–130.

Zakus, G., Chin, M. L., Cooper, H., Makovsky, E., & Merrill, C. (1981). Treating adolescent obesity: A pilot project in a school. *Journal of School Health, 51,* 663–666.

CHAPTER 20

Social Isolation

KAREN A. CHRISTOFF AND ROBERT J. MYATT

Everyone, at one time or another, has elected to withdraw from social contact and spend time alone. Social isolation, like most behaviors, is normal and can even be beneficial in moderation. It becomes a problem worthy of intervention only when it continues for too long or occurs too often. When social isolation is excessive and occurs in response to a wide variety of situations and settings, it takes on a trait-like appearance and is often labeled "shyness." During adolescence, such isolation may be more problematic than in other life stages since many of the developmental tasks at this age involve acquiring effective social behaviors.

Most developmental psychologists define the primary task of adolescence as establishing a unique identity, or a "sense of self." The adolescent must interact with others (watch, listen to, and talk with them) as part of the process of establishing a unique set of personal thoughts, values, and goals. Specific skills and behaviors that seem to be important to establishing a sense of self include making and conversing with same-aged friends, participating in extracurricular activities, establishing oneself as part of a "peer group," beginning to date, and learning to make choices regarding religion, exclusive relationships, sexuality, birth control, continuing education, and careers (Douvan & Adelson, 1966; Havighurst, 1972). Since most of these skills require social involvement, the isolated adolescent will necessarily find them difficult to develop.

In addition to potential difficulties in mastering requisite developmental tasks, withdrawn adolescents are also likely to experience negative or undesirable affective states. Adolescents who are socially isolated tend to be self-conscious, shy, lonely, lacking in social and communication skills, suspicious, distrustful, selfish, somewhat paranoid, and unable to take social risks (Brennan, 1982; Weiss, 1973; Zimbardo, 1977). Ishiyama (1984) found that shy adolescents endorse significantly more questionnaire items tapping loneliness, lack of academic success, problems developing friendships, concentration difficulties, speech problems, and feelings of self-consciousness. A report by the

512

National Institute of Mental Health (1984) describes withdrawn adolescents as low in self-esteem (manifested in feeling worthless, unattractive, unpopular, and stupid), feeling powerless, passive in structuring leisure-time activities, shy, fearful of risk-taking, selfish, and lacking interest in others.

These negative affective states, coupled with a perceived inability to ameliorate them in socially acceptable ways, would seem to increase the risk for developing antisocial behavior patterns. Alcohol and drug abuse, for example, are obvious risks for these adolescents.

At the extreme end of what could be conceptualized as a continuum of social isolation is suicide, the ultimate social self-exclusion. Davis (1983) estimates that there were approximately 4000 self-inflicted deaths and 200,000 suicide attempts among adolescents in 1982. Adolescent suicide has risen dramatically in the last decade and is now the second leading cause of death in teenagers, second only to automobile accidents. Social isolation and withdrawal are critical factors in adolescent suicide (Davis, 1983). In fact, social isolation and withdrawal are considered to be the primary prodromal symptoms of suicide potential in adolescents. Adolescents who attempt suicide and those who succeed are almost uniformly described as having been alienated from their family, virtually friendless, and involved in only the most minimal social interactions.

While there are only sparse data to predict future problems for socially isolated adolescents, there is adequate information concerning withdrawn children. Presumably, the same predictions would hold, at least for those children whose isolation continues into adolescence. Evidence from follow-up studies of children (Cowen, Pederson, Babigan, Izzo, & Trost, 1973; Mednick & Schulsinger, 1969; Roff, Sells, & Golden, 1972), retrospective investigations of disturbed adults (Bower, Shellhammer, & Daily, 1960; Roff, 1961), and concurrent research regarding psychosocial characteristics of disturbed children (King & Young, 1981; Rolf, 1972) demonstrate that children with peer adjustment problems are at risk for mental health problems. Social isolation in children has been associated with subsequent depression (Lewinsohn, 1974), juvenile delinquency (Freedman, Rosenthal, Donahoe, Schlundt, & McFall, 1978), dropping out of school (Ullman, 1957), bad conduct discharges from the military (Roff, 1961), and mental disorder (Cowen et al., 1973). All of these associated difficulties suggest the need for some sort of remediation, if not preventive training programs, for socially isolated children and adolescents.

Social isolation seems, not surprisingly, to be negatively correlated with both popularity with peers and social competence. However, these correlational relationships have often led to causal inferences that may or may not be valid. According to Carp (1981), social competence requires a sense of control and mastery over the environment. However, it seems equally valid to argue that feelings of control and mastery require environmental and social competencies. While the two are highly correlated, it is not at all clear that one causes the other in all cases. What is apparent, however, is that social withdrawal and isolation serve to remove adolescents from the social context within which most children develop *both* social and environmental competencies and feelings of mastery.

Hartup (1983) points out that social participation and peer acceptance are also positively related. While again, direction of causality cannot be determined on the basis of available data, it seems likely that a reciprocal process occurs whereby sociability leads to peer acceptance, which in turn encourages further sociability. This process could lead to a "vicious cycle" when an adolescent either lacks social competence or is not accepted for some other reason. In this case attempts at social participation might elicit punishment, which would reduce the likelihood of future attempts at social interactions. Increased withdrawal and isolation would then lead to decreased opportunities to learn competent and appropriate social behaviors.

Thus, regardless of etiology, it makes sense to consider social isolation in adolescents to be a social competence problem that is likely treatable or preventable through the use of either social skills or anxiety-reduction training programs. It should also be viewed as a difficulty that, left untreated, is likely to lead to more serious social and psychological problems in the future.

BEHAVIORAL ASSESSMENT

Assessing social competence and identifying socially isolated individuals and target behaviors for remediation are challenging endeavors. As Schinke and Gilchrist (1984) note, the goal of behavioral assessment is to "find ways of making the best possible inferences on the basis of incomplete information about what's going on during adolescents' social interactions" (p. 28). While there is a multiplicity of assessment tools available to gather information about adolescents, the investigator must consider each device's particular strengths and shortcomings.

There are four main classes of assessment tools for assessing social participation: sociometric ratings, self-ratings, ratings by teachers and other adults, and ratings of performance in specific situations (Dodge & Murphy, 1984). Gresham (1981) has found that behavioral observations, sociometrics, and teacher ratings have been the methods most often used in assessing social competence, and he recommends using all three types of measures to secure a comprehensive picture of the child's social behavior. Others have suggested the inclusion of self-report measures as a useful adjunct to these three classes of methods. In the following sections each of these types of assessment devices will be discussed.

Sociometric Ratings

Sociometric ratings are the most commonly employed tools for assessing social participation in school-aged populations (Bradley & Newhouse, 1975; Connolly, 1983; Dunphy, 1972; Ford, 1982; Foster & Ritchey, 1979). In one form, the *roster-and-rating* method, adolescents are presented with a list of their peers and asked to rate each one on some variation of one or both of these dimensions: "How much do you like to work with this person?" and, "How much do you like to play with this person?" The rating scale usually consists of five points (1 = "I don't like to;" 5 = "I like to a lot"). A *best friend* peer nomination inventory may also be administered, either to supplement the roster-and-rating measure, or by itself. In this procedure adolescents are asked to name a specified number of their best friends. Selection for intervention can be based on few or no best friend nominations and/or low mean ratings.

The peer roster-and-rating scale and the peer nomination measure appears to assess different dimensions of sociometric status (Gresham, 1981). The peer rating scale assesses general intergroup acceptance while the peer nomination scale is useful in assessing actual friendships (Schofield & Whitley, 1983).

While these instruments provide relevant and useful data regarding adolescents' acceptance by their peers, they often are expensive and difficult to obtain. Parents and adolescents themselves may be reluctant to consent to the approach because of concerns about how data will be used. Eliminating those adolescents who have not consented to the procedure may bias the data obtained. Another problem with these measures is their extreme stability over time and corresponding insensitivity to short-term changes. Consequently, they are less useful as outcome measures of treatment effectiveness. Posttreatment ratings tend to reflect the entire history students have with each other rather than changes that have occurred as a function of a relatively short-term intervention. Despite their limitations, data obtained with these procedures are valuable. They may be useful for identifying target children for training and popular children for comparison, as well as for assessing efficacy of interventions.

Self-Ratings

Many measures have been utilized to allow adolescents to evaluate their own social competence and social participation. These include the Social Experience Inventory (Brodsky, 1976), the Adolescent Problems Inventory (API: Freedman et al., 1978), the Self-Esteem Scale (Rosenberg, 1965), the Discomfort Scale of the Psychological Screening Inventory (Lanyon, 1974), the Assertiveness Schedule (Hartman, 1979; Rathus, 1973), Rotter's Internal-External Locus of Control Scale (Adams, 1983), the Social Problems Check List (Jackson & Marzillier, 1982), a modified version of the Rathus Assertiveness

Schedule (McCullagh, 1982; Michelson, Andrasik, Vucelic, & Coleman, 1981), the Ohio Social Acceptance Scale (Tyne & Flynn, 1981), the Jesness Inventory (Jesness, 1972; Kunce & Hemphill, 1983), the Nowicki-Strickland Locus of Control Scale (Nowicki & Strickland, 1983), the Spielberger A-State for Children (Ollendick & Hersen, 1979; Spielberger, 1973), the Children's Assertive Behavior Scale (Michelson et al., 1981), the Conflict Resolution Inventory (McFall & Lillesand, 1971), and the Social Behavior Inventory (Galejs & Stockdale, 1978; 1982).

All of the instruments mentioned provide a forum for adolescents to rate and describe how they respond to particular situations; how they feel about themselves, others, and their social interactions; and whether or not they believe that an intervention is warranted or desirable. Further, they tap different aspects of social behavior. It is highly recommended that decisions regarding intervention for social isolation include some measure of the feelings and attitudes of the adolescents who might be included. Standardized measures such as those listed are not necessarily required. Simply asking adolescents whether or not they believe they have problems making friends or getting involved socially with their peers and if they would like some help learning how to do these things better will suffice.

Ratings by Teachers and Other Adults

Several teacher/adult rating scales have been employed in the literature, including Burk's Behavior Rating Scale (Burke, Broad, Byford, & Sims, 1983), the Behavior Problem Checklist (BPC: Quay, 1977), the Devereux Elementary School Behavior Rating Scale (DESB: Proger, Mann, Green, Bayuk, & Burger, 1975; Spivak & Spotts, 1965), Kohn's Social Competence Scale (Kohn & Rosman, 1972), the Positive Social Behavior Scale (Greenwood, Walker, Todd, & Hops, 1979), the Walker Problem Behavior Checklist (Begin, 1983; Walker, 1976), the Iowa Social Competency Scale (Galejs & Stockdale, 1982; Pease, Clark, & Crase, 1979), and the Social Behavior Rating Scale (Csapo, 1983). In addition, information from the Adaptive Behavior Checklist (ABCL) has been utilized with low-functioning individuals as a measure of social adaptation (Allen, Loeffler, Levine, & Aker, 1976). Although many of these instruments have been implemented mainly with younger children, they are potentially useful with adolescents as well. However, research evaluating their utility with older children has yet to be conducted.

Since teacher ratings of children's peer relationship difficulties predict social adjustment problems 9 to 15 years later (Janes & Hesselbrock, 1978), teacher ratings are an important component of the assessment package. If teachers are willing to cooperate, these ratings are relatively easy to obtain and have the advantage of allowing for comparative ratings of a large number of adolescents. Because parents see their children in different situations than do teachers, parent ratings also have been used as an adjunct. Any adult who regularly interacts with the adolescent can be a useful source of data.

Ratings of Performance in Specific Situations

Van Hasselt, Hersen, and Bellack (1981) have examined the usefulness of role-play tests for assessment of social competence. They found that role-play performance did not correlate highly with naturalistic observations, sociometric ratings, or teacher ratings. Further, these investigators concluded that the reliability of role-play measures in most instances is questionable. Similarly, Kazdin, Matson, and Esveldt-Dawson (1984) also found a low correspondence between role-play performance and other social competence criteria.

While we have found the foregoing to be generally true for structured role-plays of specific situations, we nevertheless find it useful to ask adolescents to show us how they talk with their friends in a relatively unstructured context. We typically audiotape brief conversations of two adolescents who have been instructed to "pretend you have just met this person and want to get to know her or him better." Tapes are then rated for performance of specific components of conversational skill, such as asking questions, making self-disclosing statements, talking about relevant and interesting topics, and using speech acknowledgers (e.g., "uhmmmm" or "OK"). These demonstrations have proven helpful in selecting targets for intervention and for assessing the impact of training.

Naturalistic observations of behavior are also frequently used to assess social competence. Adolescents are usually observed while participating in a variety of situations conducive to peer interactions (e.g., recess, gym period, lunch) and rated for occurrence or nonoccurrence of certain categories of behavior, such as initiating social interactions, positive social behavior, and negative social behavior. For example, Michelson and DiLorenzo (1981) revised and adopted existing direct behavior observation scales to form a new observation tool consisting of response codes such as Solitary Independent Play, Adaptive Peer Interaction, and Maladaptive Peer Interaction.

While these methods certainly provide useful information, the data obtained must be interpreted with some caution and sensitivity. Asher, Markell, and Hymel (1981) point out that many current studies have placed an emphasis on the total rate of peer interaction and have neglected to ascertain the quality and skillfulness of these interactions. In a similar vein, Strain and Shores (1977), in their research on social reciprocity, have stated that observational techniques must be sensitive to "who gives what to whom, when, and with what effect." Gresham (1981) posits that behavioral observations tap a separate dimension of social competence that is different from popularity or peer acceptance. Foster and Ritchey (1979) concur and propose that sociometric measures be utilized to identify socially competent and incompetent *children,* while behavioral observations be principally employed to specify *behaviors* related to social competence.

General Assessment Issues

Relatively low correlations have been found among various assessment procedures. Green, Forehand, Beck, and Vosk (1980) examined the relationship between four measures of social competence: (1) sociometrics, (2) behavioral observations, (3) teacher ratings, and (4) self-report ratings. They found that sociometric ratings, behavioral observations, and teacher ratings correlated well with each other but that self-ratings did not relate well to any of the other indices. La Greca (1981) used the Pupil Evaluation Inventory (PEI: Pekarik, Prinz, Liebert, Weintraub, & Neale, 1976) and discovered that teacher ratings of likability were the best predictors of peer acceptance for males, while teacher ratings of withdrawn behavior were the best predictors for females. Ledingham, Younger, Schwartzman, and Bergeron (1982) reported only minimal agreement among teacher, peer, and self ratings on the PEI. Adams, Schvaneveldt, Jenson, and Jones (1982), also found no significant relationship between adolescents' self-report and teacher ratings. Tyne and Flynn (1981), using the Ohio Social Acceptance Scale as a peer evaluation tool, found little association between peer and teacher ratings in assessing individuals experiencing social competence difficulties.

Because the disparate procedures employed seem to measure different aspects of social behavior, a "shotgun" approach to behavioral assessment, utilizing as many assessment tools as possible, is espoused by many investigators (e.g., Foster & Ritchey, 1979; McFall, 1982; Schinke & Lewayne, 1984). Others, such as Gottman (1977), contend that data showing that different measures generally do not tap the same dimensions of social behavior should lead us away from attempts to assess social competence as a unitary construct. At present, the best approach to assessing social competence and isolation would seem to be the same as for any behavioral excess or deficit: Design your assessment to isolate specific behavioral problems and the situational context within which they occur for the particular individuals being assessed. The wider the range of areas tapped by the assessment procedures, the more likely a comprehensive picture of strengths and deficits will emerge. We suggest conducting as comprehensive an assessment as possible given time, cost, and other resource constraints. The more specific and thorough the assessment, the easier it becomes to design of an appropriate treatment program.

RESEARCH ON BEHAVIORAL TECHNIQUES

Most researchers agree that some form of intervention is necessary for withdrawn adolescents and that it should be carried out as early in the adolescent's development as possible. However, there is no consensus regarding the most efficacious treatment approach. Nevertheless, the majority of strategies are behavioral and include skills training or anxiety reduction techniques.

If social isolation is viewed as a behavioral deficit, one or both of these two classes of intervention should prove beneficial. Skills training would have value with individuals who have never learned or have forgotten the requisite behaviors for effective social interaction, or who are in need of additional practice to establish them firmly in their repertoire. Anxiety reduction approaches would be useful for persons who have the skills to behave appropriately in social situations, but withdraw because these situations produce anxiety. Both of these interventions will be discussed in the following sections. In addition, recent interventions with socially isolated children and adolescents that have utilized peers as counselors will be described.

Skills Training

Social skills training to remediate social isolation has received considerable attention over the past several years and has been successfully implemented for withdrawn individuals with a wide variety of presenting problems. Populations receiving these interventions include young adolescents (Bierman & Furman, 1984; Christoff et al., 1985; Pease, 1979), asymptomatic adolescents (Hartman, 1979), unassertive adolescents (Rhodes, Redd, & Berggren, 1979), socially inept adolescents (Lindsay, Symons, & Sweet, 1979), socially rejected children (Csapo, 1983), extremely shy adolescents (Franco, Christoff, Crimmins, & Kelly, 1983), autistic adolescents (Gaylord-Ross, Haring, Breen, & Pitts-Conway, 1984), disruptive adolescents (Filipczak, Archer, & Friedman, 1980), juvenile delinquents (Ollendick & Hersen, 1979), depressed youths (Schloss, Schloss, & Harris, 1984), children referred to school-based mental health programs (de Apodaca & Cowen, 1982; McKenna & Gaffney, 1982), psychiatric patients (Christoff & Kelly, 1985; Kazdin, Esveldt-Dawson, & Matson, 1983), and hearing and visually impaired adolescents (Schloss, Selinger, Goldsmith, & Morrow, 1983; Van Hasselt, 1983).

Skills training strategies typically consist of some combination of coaching or instructions, modeling, behavior rehearsal, performance feedback, and positive reinforcement (Hops, 1983; Kelly, 1982). These techniques can be applied to modifying a range of social skills. Programs employed with withdrawn adolescents generally focus on developing skills in the areas of assertiveness, conversation, and interpersonal problem solving.

Assertiveness Training

Assertiveness, broadly defined, represents the polar opposite of social withdrawal and isolation. Consequently, many clinicians and researchers have treated withdrawal and social isolation by providing assertion training. Targets for intervention with withdrawn adolescents have included expressing personal thoughts, feelings, and ideas; making requests of others (particularly requests of others to join the trainee in some social activity); and refusing unreasonable requests.

Many reports of successful assertion training programs are available. For example, Rhodes et al. (1979) used instruction, modeling, rehearsal, and feedback to teach a shy adolescent to speak loudly, initiate requests for new behaviors, and make eye contact. McCullagh (1982) trained socially isolated adolescent males to express opinions, needs, and positive and negative feelings with audiotaped and videotaped feedback plus exercises in resolving specific assertiveness problems. Csapo (1983) used individual and group reinforcement to train socially rejected students to ask questions, give directions, praise and encourage others, and control their own negative social behaviors.

Conversational Skills Training

Conversational skills interventions with socially withdrawn adolescents are based on the premise that social involvement requires the ability to communicate verbally. Typical treatment targets are asking questions; speaking in a loud, clear, and firm voice; providing speech acknowledgers (e.g., "uhmmmm," "OK," "I see,") smiling and nodding one's head while another is speaking, and talking about relevant and interesting topics.

Minkin et al. (1976) trained adolescents to ask questions, provide positive feedback to others, and spend more time talking. Schloss et al. (1984) employed modeling, rehearsal, feedback, and contingent reinforcement to teach depressed youths to make appropriate statements, greetings, and goodbyes. These investigators found skills improvements and concomitant increases in acceptance by peers and self-perceptions of social efficacy. Bierman and Furman (1984) combined conversational skills training with a peer group experience for preadolescents. They concluded that while conversational skills training facilitated skill acquisition, the peer group experience led to increased self-perceptions of social efficacy and greater peer acceptance.

Interpersonal Problem-Solving Skills Training

Training in means-end problem solving was originally proposed in a series of studies by Platt, Spivack, and Shure. Based on observed deficits in psychiatric patients (Platt & Spivack, 1972), young children (Spivack & Shure, 1973), preadolescents (Shure & Spivack, 1972), and adolescents (Platt, Spivack, Altman, Altman, & Peizer, 1974), these researchers contend that positive mental health can be defined as the ability to solve problems effectively in life situations. Given that the "problem" to be solved by shy and withdrawn adolescents is how to become more socially active, most interventions for this population focus on developing strategies for increasing social participation. Component steps in the problem-solving process that are typically addressed consist of recognizing and defining the problem, selecting and clearly stating the goal, generating alternative solutions or means for reaching the goal, considering the probable consequences of each possible solution, comparing each alternative to the others, selecting the "best" solution, implementing the chosen solution, and evaluating the outcome of this action.

Higgins and Thies (1981) propose that there is a strong positive relationship between problem-solving ability and social status. In addition, they believe that efficient cognitive means-ends thinking is necessary for adequate social functioning to occur. Thus, training in interpersonal cognitive problem-solving skills should help adolescents develop the ability to engage in means-end thinking, which should increase their skill in dealing with everyday interpersonal problems. Asher (1983) suggests that adolescents behave in socially incompetent ways because they are unaware of the effects that their behaviors have on others in the environment, and that they need training to monitor their behavior and the responses of others in the environment. Kafer (1982) posited that unpopular and withdrawn adolescents utilize different interpersonal strategies from those of their more popular peers. If unpopular adolescents have the same goals as their popular peers but simply select less effective means to attain them, problem-solving training would be beneficial. Specifically, it would encourage exploration of alternative strategies for reaching a goal and anticipation of the consequences of each possible alternative.

Rickel, Eshelman, and Loigman (1983) found that social problem-solving training led to increased ability to generate alternative solutions to interpersonal problems, but did not lead to concurrent behavioral changes. They concluded that cognitive intervention alone is insufficient to generate positive behavior change. Rickel et al. (1983) suggest that cognitive intervention be combined an approach designed to improve behavioral skills. Christoff et al. (in press) combined social problem-solving training with conversational skills training in an attempt to develop cognitive efficiency in mean-ends thinking along with behavioral competence in conducting conversations. (This intervention will be discussed in detail in the case description section of this chapter.)

Anxiety Reduction and Cognitive Approaches

The treatment strategies described above were designed to train behaviors observed to be deficient or absent from the repertoire. Another general group of interventions were developed to alter some mediating condition that is postulated to interfere with performance when the withdrawn adolescent has the skills but does not use them. Some of these interventions, such as rational emotive therapy (RET: Ellis & Harper, 1975) target irrational cognitions that interfere with performance. Others utilize approaches such as flooding or systematic desensitization to reduce anxiety that suppresses social participation in some withdrawn individuals.

RET

Brodt and Zimbardo (1981) state that individuals who label themselves as "shy" adopt a series of cognitions that are both caused by and result in withdrawn behavior. According to these theorists, presence in an anxiety-producing social situation from which one withdraws evokes physiological arousal. This arousal state, by virtue of repeated pairings over time with withdrawal, eventually elicits a dispositional label of "shyness" or "social incompetence" to explain the arousal. Brodt and Zimbardo (1981) found that disrupting the labeling process by providing an alternative explanation for the arousal was sufficient to lead to decreased withdrawal and increased participation. More traditional rational emotive therapy is also effective for remediating adolescent withdrawal (Voelm, 1984). Successful intervention via this method, however, requires careful assessment of the maladaptive cognitions that serve to control withdrawal.

Anxiety Reduction Techniques

Given Wolpe's (1958) notion that training an incompatible behavior such as relaxation or an assertive response can inhibit anxiety, almost all interventions for social isolation can be construed as anxiety reducing. There have been few reports in the literature of attempts to rehabilitate social isolates using behavioral interventions such as flooding and systematic desensitization, which are more traditionally used for other anxiety-based disorders. Theoretically, these should be beneficial for those who withdraw from social situations because the situations induce high levels of anxiety. While Kandel, Ayllon, and Rosenbaum (1977) found both flooding and systematic exposure to be effective in treating extreme social withdrawal, there are apparently no other reports of the use of these methods.

Peer Counseling

Several investigators have trained peers to set up situations that elicit positive social behaviors from withdrawn classmates. Slavin (1975) used an instructional technique called "Teams-Games-Tournament," which provided for continued peer interactions in nonthreatening situations. Varenhorst (1974) established the Palo Alto Peer Counseling Program for junior and senior high school students to facilitate students' helping each other handle the transition from childhood to adulthood. Approaches using peers as trainers seem to have much promise. They are appealing in that they make use of resources that are readily available in the natural environment.

Peer counseling programs appear to promote generalization of training effects by moving the intervention into natural settings. However, care needs to be taken in their design and implementation. Attention must be paid to selection, training, supervision, and evaluation of the peer counselors. Further, the needs of the counselees must be carefully identified.

General Treatment Issues

Most interventions for socially isolated adolescents are carried out in schools. This is logical, given that teachers and others associated with school systems are usually the first to target the problem. Also, most adolescents spend the majority of their waking hours in school. All of the interventions described in this section seem to be effective; however, they all require that the withdrawn adolescent attend school. In extreme cases of isolation, adolescents may refuse to do so. If an adolescent has an isolation problem so severe that there are virtually no social contacts outside the family, more aggressive treatment will probably be necessary. The environment must be structured to provide reinforcers for venturing into settings where there is some potential for social interaction with peers (and where the interventions described previously can be implemented).

Many investigators believe that school systems have a responsibility to take an active role in cultivating the social and emotional development of their students. In addition, they contend that social skills training programs should be routinely implemented not only to remediate existing problems, but also as preventive measures. Given the premise that the ability to relate effectively to others is essential to success at school and on the job, as well as to good mental health in general, some form of social skills program in the school appears desirable. The program could be broad-based, such as the "life skills counseling" program proposed by Schinke and Lewayne (1984), which is designed to provide training in areas of social behavior contributing to peer interactions. It is suggested that training programs include such targets as dress and grooming, greeting others, joining ongoing activities, extending invitations, giving and receiving compliments and criticism, and making apologies. For a relatively minor investment of time, money, and effort, a great deal of value can be derived for students and for the school itself since there is evidence that such interventions are successful in preventing future maladjustment and more severe psychological and behavioral problems (Filipczak et al., 1980; Hartman, 1979). However, routine screening for social isolation could be construed as an invasion of privacy. While the ethical implications of such programs are beyond the scope of this chapter, those who propose, plan, and implement training interventions must be sensitive to the rights of potential adolescent clients.

CASE DESCRIPTION

We have found a group format to be most facilitative of social interactions. Therefore, we have conducted all of our training interventions with socially withdrawn children and adolescents in small groups. The particular group to be discussed here was formed at the request of the guidance counselor at a rural junior high school in Mississippi. This counselor had been working with several students whom she described as "painfully shy" and experiencing difficulty becoming emeshed in social networks at school.

IDENTIFICATION

Students considered for inclusion in the group were all seventh and eighth graders at the junior high school. Project coordinators met with the principal and all seventh- and eighth-grade teachers to explain the project and to solicit referrals. School personnel were told that we were interested in providing training for adolescents who were socially isolated, had few or no friends, seemed to spend most of their time alone, did not attend extracurricular events, and appeared to the school staff to be "loners." Teachers and the guidance counselor were asked to nominate students for whom they believed the training would be useful. Students independently nominated by two or more staff members were considered for training. Although we usually use roster-and-rating sociometric scores as an additional criterion for group inclusion, staff at this particular school was opposed to use of these measures, and we were unable to collect them.

Parents of nominated adolescents were informed of the availability of a shyness/friendship-making training program to be conducted at the school during regular school hours. Each adolescent whose parents provided consent was interviewed and given an explanation of the program. Adolescents were selected if both they and their parents desired the program.

Six students (four females and two males) who met all criteria were included in the final training program. One male and one female were eighth graders, and the remaining four students were in the seventh grade. Two of the females were black; the remaining four adolescents were Caucasian. Participants ranged in age from 12 to 14 ($\overline{X}$ = 12.8 years).

CONCEPTUALIZATION OF THE PROBLEM

Adolescents were referred to the group because adults in their environment observed that they spent most of their time alone while on the school grounds, participated in few extracurricular activities, and generally seemed to be deficient in skills necessary for making and keeping friends. Such students often seem to pass successfully through the grades in school systems and are often unnoticed because they do not cause problems or call attention to themselves. Although these students usually do reasonably well academically, their social development lags behind due to limited social interactions with peers.

Adolescence, particularly early adolescence, is a time when relationships are based more on social and conversational skills than on the physical play of childhood. Most social-developmental tasks of this period, such as making friends of the same and opposite gender, being included in social activities with peers, participating in extracurricular activities, beginning to date, and identifying oneself as a part of a peer group, require the use of effective social and conversational skills. Since most of these tasks are encountered for the first time during this period, shy and withdrawn adolescents can find them extremely difficult to master. Withdrawal from social situations limits the number of occasions the shy adolescent has to observe others engaging in these behaviors and to practice them.

We consider the etiology of withdrawal relatively unimportant. Whether social isolation and withdrawal is construed to reflect either a lack of the requisite skills or a supression of these skills due to social anxiety, skills training should be useful. If the adolescent does not behave adroitly because of skills deficits, skills training is the obvious treatment of choice. If withdrawal is due to anxiety, repeated exposure to these skills and guided practice in a relatively nonthreatening setting should diminish anxiety. Therefore, our choice of treatment for shy children and adolescents consists of training in conversational skills and in interpersonal problem-solving skills, with an emphasis on solving the "problem" of becoming more socially active and involved.

ASSESSMENT

Problem-solving skill. Problem-solving abilities of the six adolescents were assessed using a procedure similar to the means-end problem-solving (MEPS) approach proposed by Platt and Spivack (1977). This strategy requires students to write the middle portion of stories for which they are given a beginning and an end. Stories involved problems related to making friends and initiating social interaction. A sample story follows:

> Your church is sponsoring a field trip for the youth group. You know a kid in your school who does not go to church and you think that this field trip would be a good chance to get this person involved. The story ends with your going on the field trip with this person. Tell what happened between finding out about the field trip and going on the trip with this other person.

All students responded to the same four stories on seven different occasions: four different times during the 5 weeks prior to training, once following each of the two treatment phases, and again at follow-up. In addition, after each of the eight training sessions, all students wrote two similar stories that were selected at random from a pool of 16 stories. These additional stories were selected so that no student completed any story more than once, and no two students completed the same story at any given training session. Stories were rated on the number of steps the student described that were directed toward the stated outcome. Further, each story was given a rating on a 7-point scale (1 = "very poor," 7 = "very good") for effectiveness of steps taken in reaching the goal.

Conversational skill. During each assessment session and following each training session, group members were randomly assigned to pairs. They were asked to talk with each other for 5 minutes while being audiotaped and to "get to know each other better." These recorded conversations were subsequently rated for number of conversational questions and appropriate conversational statements (self-disclosures, positive opinion statements, and expressions of fact and comments) made by each conversant. Each conversation also was rated for overall quality on a 9-point scale.

Additional self-report measures. During seven assessment sessions (four prior to treatment, one following each of the two training phases, and one at follow up) each student completed additional measures, including a conversation diary and the Self-Esteem Scale (SES: Rosenberg, 1965). The conversation diary measures the number of self-reported conversations during the prior 24-hour period. The SES yields scores ranging from 10 to 40, with higher scores indicating greater self-esteem.

Social validation measures. Before training began and following program completion, students were rated by their teachers, parents, and themselves on six dimensions. These dimensions were rated on 5-point scales and included academic performance, social adjustment, conversational ability, number of friends, ease of interacting with others, and range of activities and interests. Pre-to-post change scores were computed for the mean rating on each dimension for all students.

TREATMENT

Group training sessions in problem solving and conversational skills were conducted sequentially across time in multiple baseline fashion. Intervention consisted of eight 40-minute training sessions conducted at the school during a free period for participants. Sessions were held twice weekly for 4 weeks and were led by two clinical psychology interns. Specific classes of skills taught were based on problem areas reported by trainees, their teachers, and their parents.

The first four training sessions focused on acquisition of problem-solving skills. Students were trained in component steps of problem solving. These included recognizing a situation as a problem, stating the nature of the problem, generating as many solutions as possible, predicting the probable positive and negative outcomes of each solution listed, determining the "best" solution, and developing a specific plan for implementing the selected solution. Students were then given practice in applying these steps to problems they suggested during group sessions or problems suggested by leaders. Each of the four sessions targeted a different type of social interaction problem: The first session was directed toward problems of initiating an interaction with one other person. The second dealt with problems of participating in class and getting involved with group activities. The third session concerned dealing with negative peer pressure, such as when a friend wants the student to do something the student does not want to do, or when others tease or "pick on" the student. The final session dealt with problems of making requests of adults.

The final four sessions consisted of training in conversational skills. Each session entailed a discussion of skills to be covered that day, followed by the leaders' modeling of skills and the students' practicing them with each other. Group leaders gave students corrective feedback and encouraged them to provide feedback to each other. These four sessions were devoted to four different sets of conversational skills. The first of these training sessions was directed toward listening skills, such as asking relevant questions, looking at the other person when speaking, smiling, nodding the head to show interest, talking about topics in which the other person has expressed an interest, and asking follow-up questions. The second session covered skills involved in talking about oneself: making positive self-disclosing statements regarding activities, interests, or hobbies and minimizing complaints and negative self-statements. The third session focused on initiating conversations. The group generated a list of conversational topics and appropriate greetings, then practiced using these with each other. They discussed ways to recognize opportunities for initiating conversation and ways to tell how their initiations were being received. The final session dealt with making requests of others. During this session students practiced planning a social activity, selecting a person who was likely to agree to participate and determining the appropriate occasion to ask the person, actually asking the person, and discussing specifics of the plan.

RESULTS

Results showed meaningful changes in some aspects of the students' behavior. Improvement was noted in the students' ability to generate steps relevant to a range of everday social problems and in their ability to generate solutions that were rated as likely to be effective and successful. Students also demonstrated enhanced skill in conversing with peers. Further, they reported that they were talking with others in their natural environments more often following training. Specific changes in assessment measures are detailed below. The interested reader is referred to Christoff et al. (1985) for further information.

While the intervention was relatively brief and inexpensive to conduct, it seems likely that longer or more intensive treatment would lead to even greater levels of improvement. We believe that school systems should be encouraged to provide similar skills training programs to remediate deficiancies in social performance as well as prevent the development of more severe social and psychological maladjustment problems.

Problem-solving skills. Students improved significantly at both posttest and follow-up in their ability to solve problems, as measured by the number of relevant steps they were able to generate per story and by the mean effectiveness rating given to stories they wrote. They were able to generate a mean of only 1.8 relevant steps per story prior to training, 3.9 per story following training in problem-solving skills, and 5.5 per story at 6-month follow-up. Mean effectiveness ratings improved from 2.9 at baseline to 4.7 following training to 5.0 at follow-up.

Conversational skills. Conversational abilities also increased as assessed by performance in audiotaped conversations. Number of questions asked per 5-minute conversation rose from 6.8 prior to conversational skills training to 8.4 following training but fell slightly, to 7.7, at follow-up. Number of appropriate statements per conversation went from 15.1 at baseline to 21.2 following conversational skills training to 19.5 at follow-up. Similarly, ratings of quality of conversations increased from 3.3 at baseline to 5.7 following training to 6.3 at follow up.

Additional self-report measures. There was also an overall increase in total number of conversations per day. Prior to training, students reported a mean of only 14.7 conversations each day. Following problem-solving training they reported a mean of 16.8; following conversational skills training, a mean of 22.8; and at follow-up, a mean of 25.3.

Self-esteem scale scores did not change significantly across treatment phases. They ranged from 28.2 at baseline to 29 following problem-solving training to 30 following conversational skills training to 30.8 at follow-up.

Social validation measures. Change scores on all six dimensions were in the positive direction. However, significant changes were found on only one of these dimensions: ability to carry on a conversation. The other five dimensions (academic performance, social adjustment, number of friends, ease interacting with others, and range of activities and interests) yielded nonsignificant positive changes.

SUMMARY

Adolescent social isolation is a complex behavioral syndrome in need of further research and treatment consideration. The behavioral pattern appears to predict serious social and behavioral maladjustment but responds well to school-based skills training programs.

Much of the literature on social isolation has centered on young children, which is logical from a primary prevention standpoint. However, many adolescents who were not provided with preventive interventions during their childhood are presently in need of remedial programs. Certainly wide-spread prevention programs in preschools or the early grades of elementary schools would be ideal. Eliminating the isolation pattern before it becomes a problem is the best possible goal and one that seems attainable. Programs such as the Primary Mental Health Project of Emory Cowen and his colleagues (cf. Weissberg, Cowen, Lotyczewski, & Gesten, 1983) have done much to convince us of the utility and feasibility of preventive approaches.

Some might argue that we need to establish a more standardized assessment methodology and treatment approach for this population. While this may be applicable to prevention programs, we believe standardization is an unnecessary and unattainable goal for programs to be used with adolescents who have already developed problematic behavior patterns. Since deficits associated with withdrawal and isolation are idiosyncratic to individuals, treatment programs should be designed to meet the specific needs of the target trainee or group of trainees. In this regard we agree with Gordon Paul's contention that the design of effective training programs requires consideration of *"what* treatment, by *whom,* is most effective for *this* individual with *that* specific problem, and under *which* set of circumstances" (Paul, 1967, p. 111).

REFERENCES

Adams, G. R. (1983). Social competence during adolescence: Social sensitivity, locus of control, empathy, and peer popularity. *Journal of Youth and Adolescence, 12,* 203–211.

Adams, G. R., Schvaneveldt, J. D., Jenson, G. D., & Jones, R. M. (1982). Sociometric research with adolescents: In search of a self-report alternative with evidence of psychometric validity. *Adolescence, 17,* 905–909.

Allen, R. M., Loeffler, F. J., Levine, M. N., & Aker, L. N. (1976). Social adaptation assessment as a tool for prescriptive remediation. *Mental Retardation, 14,* 36–37.

Asher, S. R. (1983). Social competence and peer status: Recent advances and future directions. *Child Development, 54,* 1427–1434.

Asher, S. R., Markell, R. A., & Hymel, S. (1981). Identifying children at risk in peer relations: A critique of the rate-of-interaction approach to assessment. *Child Development, 52,* 1239–1245.

Begin, G. (1983). Convergent validity of four instruments for teachers assessing social competence of kindergarten children. *Perceptual and Motor Skills, 57,* 1007–1012.

Bierman, K. L., & Furman, W. (1984). The effects of social skills training and peer involvement on the social adjustment of preadolescents. *Child Development, 55,* 151–162.

Bower, E. M., Shellhammer, T. A., & Daily, J. M. (1960). School characteristics of male adolescents who later became schizophrenic. *American Journal of Orthopsychiatry, 30,* 712–729.

Bradley, F. D., & Newhouse, R. C. (1975). Sociometric choice and self perceptions of upper elementary school children. *Psychology in the Schools, 12,* 219–222.

Brennan, T. (1982). Loneliness at adolescence. In L. A. Peplau & D. Perlman (Eds.), *Loneliness: A sourcebook of current theory, research and therapy.* New York: Wiley.

Brodsky, H. S. (1976). The assessment of social competence in adolescents. *Dissertation Abstracts International, 36,* 4144B–4145B.

Brodt, S. E., & Zimbardo, P. G. (1981). Modifying shyness-related social behavior through symptom misattribution. *Journal of Personality and Social Psychology, 41,* 437–449.

Burke, J., Broad, J., Byford, S. R., & Sims, P. (1983). Use of Burks' Behavior Rating Scale with a referred population. *Psychological Reports, 53,* 491–496.

Carp, J. M. (1981). Youth's need for social competence and power: The Community Building Model. *Adolescence, 16,* 935–951.

Christoff, K. A., & Kelly, J. A. (1985). Social skills training with psychiatric patients. In M. Milan & L. L'Abate (Eds.), *Handbook of social skills training and research.* (pp. 361–387). New York: Wiley.

Christoff, K. A., Scott, W. D., Kelley, M. L., Schlundt, D., Baer, G., & Kelly, J. A. (1985). Social skills and social problem-solving training for shy young adolescents. *Behavior Therapy, 16,* 468–477.

Connolly, J. A. (1983). A review of sociometric procedures in the assessment of social competencies in children. *Applied Research in Mental Retardation, 4,* 315–327.

Cowen, E. L., Pederson, A., Babigan, H., Izzo, L. D., & Trost, E. A. (1973). Long term follow up of early detected vulnerable children. *Journal of Consulting and Clinical Psychology, 41,* 438–446.

Csapo, M. (1983). Effects of social learning training with socially rejected children. *Behavioral Disorders, 8,* 199–208.

Davis, P. A. (1983). *Suicidal Adolescents.* Springfield, IL: Thomas.

de Apodaca, R. F., & Cowen, E. L. (1982). A comparative study of the self-esteem, sociometric status, and insight of referred and non-referred school children. *Psychology in the Schools, 19,* 395–401.

Dodge, K. A., & Murphy, R. R. (1984). The assessment of social competence in adolescents. *Advances in Child Behavioral Analysis & Therapy, 3,* 61–96.

Douvan, E., & Adelson, J. (1966). *The adolescent experience.* New York: Wiley.

Dunphy, D. C. (1972). The social structure of urban adolescent groups. *Sociometry, 26,* 230–246.

Ellis, A., & Harper, R. A. (1975). *A new guide to rational living.* Englewood Cliffs, NJ: Prentice-Hall.

Filipczak, J., Archer, M., & Friedman, R. M. (1980). In-school social skills training: Use with disruptive adolescents. *Behavior Modification, 4,* 243–263.

Ford, M. L. (1982). Social cognition and social competence in adolescence. *Developmental Psychology, 18,* 323–340.

Foster, S. E., & Ritchey, W. L. (1979). Issues in the assessment of social competence in children. *Journal of Applied Behavior Analysis, 12,* 625–638.

Franco, D. P., Christoff, K. A., Crimmins, D. B., & Kelly, J. A. (1983). Social skills training for an extremely shy young adolescent: An empirical case study. *Behavior Therapy, 14,* 568–575.

Freedman, B. J., Rosenthal, L., Donahoe, C. P., Schlundt, D. G., & McFall, R. M. (1978). A social-behavioral analysis of skill deficits in delinquent and nondelinquent adolescent boys. *Journal of Consulting and Clinical Psychology, 46,* 1448–1462.

Galejs, I., & Stockdale, D. F. (1978). *Social Behavior Inventory.* Iowa State University Research Foundation.

Galejs, I., & Stockdale, D. F. (1982). Social competence, school behaviors, and co-operative-competitive preferences: Assessments by parents, teachers, and school-age children. *Journal of Genetic Psychology, 141,* 243–252.

Gaylord-Ross, R. J., Haring, T. G., Breen, C., & Pitts-Conway, V. (1984). The training and generalization of social interaction skills with autistic youth. *Journal of Applied Behavior Analysis, 17,* 229–247.

Gottman, J. M. (1977). Toward a definition of social isolation in children. *Child Development, 48,* 513–517.

Green, K. D., Forehand, R. L., Beck, S. J., & Vosk, B. (1980). An assessment of the relationship among measures of children's social competence and children's academic achievement. *Child Development, 51,* 1149–1156.

Greenwood, C. R., Walker, H. M., Todd, N. M., & Hops, H. (1979). Selecting a cost-effective screening measure for the assessment of preschool social withdrawal. *Journal of Applied Behavior Analysis, 12,* 639–652.

Gresham, F. M. (1981). Validity of social skills measures for assessing social competence in low-status children: A multivariate investigation. *Developmental Psychology, 17,* 390–398.

Hartman, L. M. (1979). The preventive reduction of psychological risk in asymptomatic adolescents. *American Journal of Orthopsychiatry, 49,* 121–135.

Hartup, W. (1983). Peer relations. In P. H. Mussen (Ed.), *Handbook of Child Psychology* (Vol. 4, pp. 103–196). New York: Wiley.

Havighurst, R. J. (1972). *Developmental tasks and education.* New York: McKay.

Higgins, J. P., & Thies, A. P. (1981). Problem solving and social position among emotionally disturbed boys. *American Journal of Orthopsychiatry, 51,* 356–358.

Hops, H. (1983). Children's social competence and skill: Current research practices and future directions. *Behavior Therapy, 14,* 3–18.

Ishiyama, F. I. (1984). Shyness: Anxious social sensitivity and self-isolating tendency. *Adolescence, 19,* 903–911.

Jackson, M. F., & Marzillier, J. S. (1982). The Youth Club Project: A community based intervention for shy adolescents. *Behavioral Psychotherapy, 10,* 87–100.

Janes, C. L., & Hesselbrock, V. M. (1978). Problem children's adult adjustment predicted from teacher's ratings. *American Journal of Orthopsychiatry, 48,* 300–309.

Jesness, C. F. (1972). *Manual for the Jesness Inventory.* Palo Alto, CA: Consulting Psychologist Press, Inc.

Kafer, N. F. (1982). Interpersonal strategies of unpopular children: Some implications for social skills training. *Psychology in the Schools, 19,* 255–259.

Kandel, H. J., Ayllon, T., & Rosenbaum, M. S. (1977). Flooding or systematic exposure in the treatment of extreme social withdrawal in children. *Journal of Behavior Therapy and Experimental Psychiatry, 8,* 75–81.

Kazdin, A. E., Esveldt-Dawson, K., & Matson, J. L. (1983). The effects of instructional set on social skills performance among psychiatric inpatient children. *Behavior Therapy, 14,* 413–423.

Kazdin, A. E., Matson, J. L., & Esveldt-Dawson, K. (1984). The relationship of role-play assessment of children's social skills to multiple measures of social competence. *Behaviour Research and Therapy, 22,* 129–139.

Kelly, J. A. (1982). *Social skills training: A practical guide for interventions.* New York: Springer.

King, C. A., & Young, R. D. (1981). Peer popularity and peer communication patterns: Hyperactive versus active but normal boys. *Journal of Abnormal Child Psychology, 9,* 465–482.

Kohn, M., & Rosman, B. L. (1972). A social competence scale and symptom checklist for the preschool child: Factor dimensions, their cross instrument generality and longitudinal persistance. *Developmental Psychology, 6,* 430–444.

Kunce, J. T., & Hemphill, H. (1983). Delinquency and Jesness Inventory Scores. *Journal of Personality Assessment, 47,* 632–634.

LaGreca, A. M. (1981). Peer acceptance: The correspondence between children's sociometric scores and teachers' ratings of peer interactions. *Journal of Abnormal Child Psychology, 9,* 167–178.

Lanyon, R. (1974). Technology of personality assessment: The Psychological Screening Inventory. In B. Mahar (Ed.), *Progress in experimental personality research* (Vol. 7). New York: Academic Press.

Ledingham, J. E., Younger, A., Schwartzman, A., & Bergeron, G. (1982). Agreement among teacher, peer, and self-ratings of children's aggression, withdrawal, and likability. *Journal of Abnormal Child Psychology, 10,* 363–372.

Lewinsohn, P. M. (1974). Clinical and theoretical aspects of depression. In K. S. Calhoun, H. E. Adams, K. H. Mitchell (Eds.), *Innovative treatment methods in psychopathology.* New York: Wiley.

Lindsay, W. R., Symons, R. S., & Sweet, T. (1979). A programme for teaching social skills to socially inept adolescents: Description and evaluation. *Journal of Adolescence, 2,* 215–218.

McCullagh, J. G. (1982). Assertion training for boys in junior high school. *Social Work in Education, 5,* 41–51.

McFall, R. M. (1982). A review and reformulation of the concept of social skills. *Behavioral Assessment, 4,* 1–33.

McFall, R. M., & Lillesand, D. (1971). Behavior rehearsal with modeling and coaching in assertion training. *Journal of Abnormal Psychology, 77,* 313–323.

McKenna, J. G., & Gaffney, L. R. (1982). An evaluation of group therapy for adolescents using social skills training. *Current Psychological Research, 2,* 151–159.

Mednick, A. A., & Schulsinger, F. (1969). Factors related to breakdown in children at high risk for schizophrenia. In M. Roff & D. F. Ricks (Eds.), *Life history studies in psychopathology.* Minneapolis: University of Minnesota Press.

Michelson, L., Andrasik, F., Vucelic, I., & Coleman, D. (1981). Temporal stability and internal reliability of measures of children's social skill. *Psychological Reports, 48,* 678.

Michelson, L., & DiLorenzo, T. M. (1981). Behavioral assessment of peer interaction and social functioning in institutional and structured settings. *Journal of Clinical Psychology, 37,* 499–504.

Minkin, N., Braukmann, C. J., Minkin, B. L., Timbers, G. D., Timbers, B. J., Fixsen, D. L., Phillips, E. L., & Wolf, M. M. (1976). The social validation and training of conversational skills. *Journal of Applied Behavior Analysis, 9,* 127–139.

National Institute of Mental Health. (1984). *Adolescence and depression* (DHHS Publication No. ADM 84-1337). Washington, DC: U.S. Government Printing Office.

Nowicki, S., & Strickland, B. R. (1973). A locus of control scale for children. *Journal of Consulting and Clinical Psychology, 40,* 148–154.

Ollendick, T. H., & Hersen, M. (1979). Social skills training for juvenile delinquents. *Behaviour Research and Therapy, 17,* 547–554.

Paul, G. L. (1967). Strategies of outcome research in psychotherapy. *Journal of Consulting Psychology, 31,* 109–118.

Pease, D., Clark, B. G., & Crase, S. J. (1979). *Iowa Social Competency Scale: School-age and preschool manual.* Iowa State Research Foundation.

Pease, J. J. (1979). A social skills training group for early adolescents. *Journal of Adolescence, 2,* 229–238.

Pekarik, E. G., Prinz, R. J., Liebert, D. E., Weintraub, S., & Neale, J. M. (1976). The Pupil Evaluation Inventory: A sociometric technique for assessing children's social behavior. *Journal of Abnormal Child Psychology, 4,* 83–97.

Platt, J. J., & Spivack, G. (1972). Problem-solving thinking of psychiatric patients. *Journal of Consulting and Clinical Psychology, 39,* 148–151.

Platt, J. J., & Spivack, G. (1977). *Measures of interpersonal cognitive problem-solving.* Unpublished manuscript, Hahnemann Medical College and Hospital, Department of Mental Health Sciences, Philadelphia, PA.

Platt, J. J., Spivack, G., Altman, N., Altman, D., & Pelzer, S. B. (1974). Adolescent problem-solving thinking. *Journal of Consulting and Clinical Psychology, 43,* 787–793.

Proger, B. B., Mann, L., Green, P. A., Bayuk, R. J., Jr., & Burger, R. M. (1975). Discriminators of clinically defined emotional maladjustment: Predictive validity of the Behavior Problem Checklist and Devereux scales. *Journal of Abnormal Child Psychology, 3,* 71–82.

Quay, H. C. (1977). Measuring dimensions of deviant behavior: The Behavior Problem Checklist. *Journal of Abnormal Child Psychology, 5,* 277–287.

Rathus, S. A. (1973). A 30-item schedule for assessing assertive behavior. *Behavior Therapy, 4,* 398–406.

Rhodes, W. A., Redd, W. H., & Berggren, L. (1979). Social skills training for an unassertive adolescent. *Journal of Clinical Child Psychology, 8,* 18–21.

Rickel, A. U., Esehelman, A. K., & Loigman, G. A. (1983). Social problem solving training: A follow-up study of cognitive and behavioral effects. *Journal of Abnormal Child Psychology, 11,* 15–28.

Roff, M. (1961). Childhood social interaction and young adult bad conduct. *Journal of Abnormal and Social Psychology, 63,* 333–337.

Roff, M., Sells, S. B., & Golden, M. (1972). *Social adjustment and personality development in children.* Minneapolis: University of Minnesota Press.

Rolf, J. E. (1972). The social and academic competence of children vulnerable to schizophrenia and other behavior pathologies. *Journal of Abnormal Psychology, 80,* 225–242.

Rosenberg, R. (1965). *Society and the adolescent self image.* Princeton, NJ: Princeton University Press.

Schinke, S. P., & Gilchrist, L. D. (1984). *Life skills counseling with adolescents.* Baltimore: University Park.

Schloss, P. J., Schloss, C. N., & Harris, L. (1984). A multiple baseline analysis of an interpersonal skills training program for depressed youth. *Behavioral Disorders, 9,* 182–188.

Schloss, P. J., Selinger, J., Goldsmith, L., & Morrow, L. (1983). Classroom based approaches to developing social competence among hearing-impaired youth. *American Annals of the Deaf, 128,* 842–850.

Schofield, J. W., & Whitley, B. E. (1983). Peer nomination vs. rating scale measurement of children's peer preferences. *Social Psychology Quarterly, 46,* 242–251.

Shure, M. B., & Spivack, G. (1972). Means-end thinking, adjustment and social class among elementary school-aged children. *Journal of Consulting and Clinical Psychology, 38,* 348–353.

Slavin, R. E. (1975). *Teams-games-tournaments: A student team approach to teaching adolescents with special emotional and behavioral needs.* (Report No. 206). Baltimore: John Hopkins University, Center for Social Organization of Schools.

Spielberger, C. D. (1973). *State-Trait Anxiety Inventory for Children.* Palo Alto, CA: Consulting Psychologist Press.

Spivack, B., & Shure, M. B. (1973). *Social adjustment of young children: A cognitive approach to solving real-life problems.* San Francisco: Jossey-Bass.

Spivack, G., & Spotts, J. (1965). The Devereaux Child Behavior Rating Scale: Symptom behaviors in latency age children. *American Journal of Mental Deficiency, 69,* 839–853.

Strain, P. S., & Shores, R. E. (1977). Social reciprocity: A review of research and educational implications. *Exceptional Children, 43,* 526–532.

Tyne, T. F., & Flynn, J. T. (1981). Teacher nominations and peer evaluations in the identification of socioemotional at-risk students. *Exceptional Children, 48,* 66–68.

Ullman, C. A. (1957). Teachers, peers, and tests as predictors of adjustment. *Journal of Educational Psychology, 48,* 257–267.

Van Hasselt, V. B. (1983). Social adaptation in the blind. *Clinical Psychology Review, 3,* 87–102.

Van Hasselt, V. B., Hersen, M., & Bellack, A. S. (1981). The validity of role play tests for assessing social skills in children. *Behavior Therapy, 12,* 202–216.

Varenhorst, B. B. (1974). Training adolescents as peer counselors. *Personnel & Guidance Journal, 53,* 271–275.

Voelm, C. D. (1984). The efficacy of teaching rational emotive education to acting-out and socially withdrawn adolescents. *Dissertation Abstracts International, 44,* 3947B–3948B.

Walker, H. M. (1976). *Problem Behavior Identification Checklist.* Los Angeles, CA: Western Psychological Services.

Weiss, R. S. (1973). *Loneliness: The experience of emotional and social isolation.* Cambridge, MA: MIT Press.

Weissberg, R. P., Cowen, E. L., Lotyczewski, B. S., & Gesten, E. L. (1983). The Primary Mental Health Project (PMHP): Seven consecutive years of program outcome research. *Journal of Consulting and Clinical Psychology, 51,* 100–107.

Wolpe, J. (1958). *Psychotherapy by reciprocal inhibition.* Stanford, CA: University Press.

Zimbardo, P. G. (1977). *Shyness.* New York: Jove.

Author Index

Subject Index

The Role of the Father in Child Development *edited by Michael E. Lamb*

Handbook of Behavioral Assessment *edited by Anthony R. Ciminero, Karen S. Calhoun, and Henry E. Adams*

Counseling and Psychotherapy: A Behavioral Approach *by E. Lakin Phillips*

Dimensions of Personality *edited by Harvey London and John E. Exner, Jr.*

The Mental Health Industry: A Cultural Phenomenon *by Peter A. Magaro, Robert Gripp, David McDowell, and Ivan W. Miller III*

Nonverbal Communication: The State of the Art *by Robert G. Harper, Arthur N. Wiens, and Joseph D. Matarazzo*

Alcoholism and Treatment *by David J. Armor, J. Michael Polich, and Harriet B. Stambul*

A Biodevelopmental Approach to Clinical Child Psychology: Cognitive Controls and Cognitive Control Theory *by Sebastiano Santostefano*

Handbook of Infant Development *edited by Joy D. Osofsky*

Understanding the Rape Victim: A Synthesis of Research Findings *by Sedelle Katz and Mary Ann Mazur*

Childhood Pathology and Later Adjustment: The Question of Prediction *by Loretta K. Cass and Carolyn B. Thomas*

Intelligent Testing with the WISC-R *by Alan S. Kaufman*

Adaptation in Schizophrenia: The Theory of Segmental Set *by David Shakow*

Psychotherapy: An Eclectic Approach *by Sol L. Garfield*

Handbook of Minimal Brain Dysfunctions *edited by Herbert E. Rie and Ellen D. Rie*

Handbook of Behavioral Interventions: A Clinical Guide *edited by Alan Goldstein and Edna B. Foa*

Art Psychotherapy *by Harriet Wadeson*

Handbook of Adolescent Psychology *edited by Joseph Adelson*

Psychotherapy Supervision: Theory, Research and Practice *edited by Allen K. Hess*

Psychology and Psychiatry in Courts and Corrections: Controversy and Change *by Ellsworth A. Fersch, Jr.*

Restricted Environmental Stimulation: Research and Clinical Applications *by Peter Suedfeld*

Personal Construct Psychology: Psychotherapy and Personality *edited by Alvin W. Landfield and Larry M. Leitner*

Mothers, Grandmothers, and Daughters: Personality and Child Care in Three-Generation Families *by Bertram J. Cohler and Henry U. Grunebaum*

Further Explorations in Personality *edited by A.I. Rabin, Joel Aronoff, Andrew M. Barclay, and Robert A. Zucker*

Hypnosis and Relaxation: Modern Verification of an Old Equation *by William E. Edmonston, Jr.*

Handbook of Clinical Behavior Therapy *edited by Samuel M. Turner, Karen S. Calhoun, and Henry E. Adams*

Handbook of Clinical Neuropsychology *edited by Susan B. Filskov and Thomas J. Boll*

The Course of Alcoholism: Four Years After Treatment *by J. Michael Polich, David J. Armor, and Harriet B. Braiker*

Handbook of Innovative Psychotherapies *edited by Raymond J. Corsini*

The Role of the Father in Child Development (Second Edition) *edited by Michael E. Lamb*

Behavioral Medicine: Clinical Applications *by Susan S. Pinkerton, Howard Hughes, and W.W. Wenrich*

Handbook for the Practice of Pediatric Psychology *edited by June M. Tuma*

Change Through Interaction: Social Psychological Processes of Counseling and Psychotherapy *by Stanley R. Strong and Charles D. Claiborn*

Drugs and Behavior (Second Edition) *by Fred Leavitt*

(*continued on back*)